POLICE OFFICER STRESS

Sources and Solutions

DENNIS J. STEVENS, Ph.D.
University of Southern Mississippi

PEARSON

Prentice
Hall

Upper Saddle River, New Jersey 07458

Library of Congress Cataloging-in-Publication Data

Stevens, Dennis J.
  Police officer stress : sources and solutions / Dennis J. Stevens.
    p. cm.
  Includes bibliographical references.
  ISBN 0-13-117881-4
  1. Police—Job stress.   2. Police—Mental health services.   3. Stress management.   I. Title.
  HV7936.J63S74 2008
  363.201'9—dc22   2006101521

Editor-in-Chief: Vernon R. Anthony
Senior Editor: Tim Peyton
Editorial Assistant: Jillian Allison
Marketing Manager: Adam Kloza
Managing Editor: Mary Carnis
Production Liaison: Ann Pulido
Production Editor: Patty Donovan
Production Management: Pine Tree Composition, Inc.
Manufacturing Buyer: Cathleen Petersen
Composition: Laserwords Private, Ltd.
Senior Design Coordinator: Miguel Ortiz
Cover Design: Anthony Gemmellaro
Cover Illustration: Mark Cardwell, CORBIS/Reuters

Pearson Education LTD.
Pearson Education Singapore, Pte. Ltd
Pearson Education, Canada, Ltd
Pearson Education-Japan
Pearson Education Australia PTY, Limited
Pearson Education North Asia Ltd
Pearson Educatión de Mexico, S.A. de C.V.
Pearson Education Malaysia, Pte. Ltd.

ISBN-13: 978-0-13-117881-6
ISBN-10:   0-13-117881-4

This work is dedicated to all those street cops who sat in my university classrooms over the past 16 years. I heard you.

Contents

Chapter 4   Police Organizations and Police Subculture   86

Chapter 5   Critical Incident Stressors, Debriefing, and Intervention   129

Chapter 9 Stress in Small-Town and Rural Policing 277

Chapter 10 Individual and Person-Centered Initiatives 304

Chapter 11   Options and Obstacles of Person-Centered Stress Providers   337

Chapter 12   Change, Professionalization, and Hiring Process   359

Preface

Police Officer Stress: Sources and Solutions is a timely examination of the sources of police officer stress and how to prevent it. Begging an answer from this work is the question: Does membership in a specific organization lead its members to extraordinary behavior—behavior members are less likely to exhibit if they were members of another organization? That is, is a stressed officer the product of the officer's fruition or did the officer have help? Asked another way, when the media reported Robert Davis, a 64-year-old retired teacher, was punched in the head and handcuffed by three of New Orleans' finest after Hurricane Katrina, although tragic, what dynamics contributed to the behavior of those officers? Were those officers simply stressed from the storm? Of course, stress doesn't excuse unlawful behavior and officers must be accountable for their performance. Nonetheless, it will become evident in the pages ahead that when inappropriate or corrupt behavior is powered by stress and individual or in-house remedies are utilized to change (or rehabilitate) an officer, those remedies must coincide with a change (or a restructure) of the police organization to be effective. Otherwise, a "cured" officer returns to the same organization or environment that contributed to an officer's downfall.

This work will argue that because officer stress is developed and reinforced by the police organization, one implication is that officer stress is actually a symptom of an antiquated organization that has performed well and now must be redesigned to meet the challenges of a new people—a new time. This work differs from previous works on stress because it explains the police organization's contributions associated with law enforcement officers and makes recommendations from a practical perspective. Equally important, it is a timely examination of officer stress as it reaches into the jaws of Hurricane Katrina through interviews with 24 Gulf (Mississippi coast and New Orleans) Coast officers and another 558 officers (New England, North Carolina, and Florida) who were surveyed for this textbook. These cops were asked about their jobs, their families, and the organizations that employ them. They were asked about burnout and stress, and how their jobs relate to the performance of keeping

America safe. The new information learned from this study relates to the problem-solving processes of public safety, which should move to the decision-making responsibilities of the personnel who implement, operate, and evaluate police initiatives and strategies—the street cop.

Police Officer Stress: Sources and Solutions explores occupational stress, on-the-job stress, critical incident stress, and stress produced from the police organizational structure wrapped in its bureaucratic hierarical mandates and old-fashioned leadership styles. In the final analysis, police initiatives and practices must meet the changing American landscape and that landscape is changing at a faster pace than it has in its entire history. What is happening is that well intentioned but uninformed policymakers design police policy and expect it to be practiced, when in fact a huge gap exists between policy and practice. This gap appears to escalate police officer stress levels and interferes with the delivery of quality police services, which in turn stifles the evolution of policing as a profession. The central theme of this work is that among the typical street cop, the risks of the streets are less traumatic than the police organizational dynamics. That it is almost more nerve-racking to deal with a police executive at noon than crazed villain at midnight.

It will become clear that stress control initiatives must be redefined to fit the profession of law enforcement as opposed to reemploying tired traditional methods that fit other occupations. Policing is different from other professions and far more important to the democratic process because policing is the buffer between anarchy and order.

Recent case studies, detection of street cop stress, and its remedies, which include individual treatment and in-house counseling, are also examined and this information should be more helpful to you than previous works because its centerpiece is today's reality, as opposed to yesterday's theory. By the end of the book, you will not become a Dr. Phil, but you will be a more informed student or criminal justice practitioner about the capabilities of street cops, the organizations that employ them, and the most efficient individual and organizational approaches to prevent police officer stress.

Dr. Dennis J. Stevens
Pass Christian, Mississippi

Acknowledgments

The author wishes to acknowledge the efforts of many individuals who contributed to this work. Willard M. Oliver, an associate professor of Criminal Justice in the College of Criminal Justice at Sam Houston State University and Cecil A. Meier, a retired fire fighter from Virginia, wrote Chapter 9 exclusively for this book. Their project was supported by a cooperative agreement (#97-DD-BX-0061) awarded by the Bureau of Justice Assistance, U.S. Department of Justice. Points of view or opinions contained within this document are those of the authors and do not necessarily represent the official position or policies of the U.S. Department of Justice or that of Dennis J. Stevens. Others who contributed at different levels include: Timothy Bakken, Professor of Law, U.S. Military Academy at West Point who reviewed Chapter 7; two successful former students, Sergeant Steven Dickenson, Palm Beach County Sheriff's Department, and Sergeant John Wiggins, Investigations and Internal Affairs and an instructor at North Carolina Justice Academy, helped distribute, collect, and retain questionnaires; Supervisor Peter Cartmell, Crime Analysis Unit, Fort Lauderdale Police Department, provided statistics; Wesley G. Skogan and David L. Carter for earlier contributions; municipal officers (and former students) in the Commonwealth of Massachusetts, which includes Boston, Officers Debra Blandin, Kenisha Stewart, Maria Gonzales, George Kelley, Sergeant Roy Chambers, Jennifer Costa, Detective Joseph Fiandaca; Salem Officer Christian Hanson, Paul Vansteenberg; Michael Marino; Nantucket Officer Nadya Marino, Detective Daniel O'Neill, Gang Unit, and Officer Kenisha Stewart. Others who contributed include Captain Robert Dunford (Superintendent of Uniforms, Boston); Former Commissioner of Boston Police Paul F. Evans; Chief Theron Bowman, Arlington Police Department; Sheriff Frank G. Cousins, Jr., Essex County, Massachusetts; Chief Harley Schinker, Long Beach, Mississippi; University of Southern Mississippi students: Lt. William Seal, Long Beach; Officers Vince Myrick and Shane Steele, Biloxi; and Special Agent Brandon Hendry, Mississippi Bureau of Narcotics. Also Salem State College students (who are destined for greatness) contributed many parts of this work, which includes questionnaire development, survey distribution, statistical computer formatting, interviews, and for some, presentations of their findings at the Academy of Criminal Justice Sciences annual conference in Las Vegas: Joseph Cafasso, Kristina D'Angelo, Chad LaBrie, Becky E. MacDonald, Robert Monk, Kyle O'Connor, Kathryn Tiezzi, Rachelle L. Tierney, and Kara Zanazzo; and finally, Massachusetts State Troopers Lisa Cisso and Jason Powers. Finally, a father has to acknowledge his children for their patience, caring, and inspiration during the development of major projects such as this: David, Mark, and Alyssa—all my love.

The author also wishes to thank the following reviewers: Terry Campbell, Kaplan University, Macomb, IL; Nicolas Irons, County College of Morris, Randolph, NJ; and Roger Pennel, Central Missouri State University, Warrensburg, MO.

About the Author

Dr. Dennis J. Stevens received a Ph.D. from Loyola University of Chicago in 1991. Currently, he is Associate Professor of Criminal Justice and Director of the Ph.D. program at the University of Southern Mississippi. Formerly, he worked for the Commonwealth of Massachusetts at the University of Massachusetts Boston and Salem State College. In addition to teaching traditional students, he has taught and counseled law enforcement and correctional officers at law academies such as the North Carolina Justice Academy and the Boston Police Academy and felons at maximum-custody penitentiaries such as Attica in New York, Eastern and NC Women's Institute in North Carolina, Stateville and Joliet near Chicago, CCI in Columbia South Carolina, and MCI Framingham (women) and Norfolk in Massachusetts. In addition to the current text, Stevens is the author of *Community Corrections: An Applied Approach*; *Applied Community Policing in the 21st Century*; *Case Studies in Applied Community Policing*; *Policing and Community Partnerships*; *Case Studies of Community Policing*; *Measuring Performance: A Guide to Evaluative Research*; *Perspective in Corrections*; and *Inside the Mind of the Serial Rapist*. He has also published almost 100 scholarly and popular literature articles on policing, corrections, and criminology. Dr. Stevens has been retained by state legislators, federal agencies, and foreign countries such as the Provincial Government of Canada to aid in specific criminal justice investigations including drug trafficking, sexual assault, and correctional systems including sex offender programs, classification systems, and education. Dr. Stevens has guided many sexually abused children in church-affiliated programs in New York, North Carolina, and South Carolina and has lead group crisis sessions among various police and correctional agencies. He is a former group facilitator for a national organization that specializes in court-ordered cases of sexual offenders. After Hurricane Katrina touched down the Mississippi Gulf coast, Dr. Stevens provided crisis intervention for police and continues to provide services on a limited basis.

Dr. Stevens would appreciate your comments and suggestions for the next editions of this book and can be reached at dennis.stevens@usm.edu.

Chapter 9 was written by Willard M. Oliver, Associate Professor of Criminal Justice in the College of Criminal Justice at Sam Houston State University and Cecil A. Meier, a retired firefighter from Virginia's Tide Water area and a volunteer with the American Red Cross.

1

Assumptions, Theme, and Flow

"It is totally reprehensible that the cops we expect to protect us, come to our aid, and respond to our needs when victimized should be allowed to have the worst fatigue and sleep conditions of any profession in our society." William C. Dement, M.D.[1]

Learning Objectives

Once you finish reading this chapter, you will be better prepared to:

- Identify the two underlying assumptions about this work.

- Characterize the discrepancies between crime control imagery and operational realities of police officers.

- Explain the characteristics of a profession and identify limitations associated with the profession of policing.

- Clarify the central theme of this work.

- Describe the rationale supporting the idea that the organization is a greater stressor than an officer's job or family.

- Describe two functions police officers tend to perform in their role as gatekeepers.

- Describe what is meant by the revolving door of justice and articulate its consequences upon police officer stress.

- Explain why a view of the "big picture" of policing and stress could be beneficial.

Authoritative intervention   Judicious   Posttraumatic Stress
Blaming the victim   Revolving door of justice Symbolic justice

INTRODUCTION

Many countries would have less anarchy and government corruption if the human rights of their populations were safeguarded through professional police initiatives.[2] This compelling argument is evidenced among Americans who enjoy a steady rise in their quality of life experiences, which includes influencing decision-making routines of police management linked to hiring standards, training curriculums, officer regulation enforcement, police discipline processes and investigations, deployment, service priorities, and limitations on the use of force.[3] Democratic policing includes the routine that police personnel must deliver services of public safety while guaranteeing individual human rights, especially due process mandates.[4] Influencing police decision-making processes is a signpost of democratic policing, as is police accountability.

Police are accountable to the communities they serve, the taxpayers who pay their bills, and the legal order governing their authority.[5] In this regard, Dr. William Dement asks, how can the police deliver quality services designed to control crime, reduce the fear of crime, enhance constituent quality of life experiences, defend the U.S. Constitution, and be accountable all at the same time, if they are stressed?

Complicating this issue, stressed officers avoid help because it would be construed among coworkers (and reinforced through the police subculture) that they are weak, untrustworthy, and unlikely to back up an officer in a critical altercation.[6] Also, the police organization blames the officer for his or her stressed situation, which in turn reduces the officer's chances of promotion (or recovery).[7] Therefore, despite attempt to avoid embarrassment, potential disciplinary action, or lawsuits, many officers resolve stressful feelings privately, even covertly.[8] For officers to admit that they feel suicidal or have domestic problems is close to admitting a loss of control.[9] "And being a law enforcement officer is all about control."[10]

TWO UNDERLYING ASSUMPTIONS

Two underlying assumptions about this work are:

1. The police cannot nor should they attempt to control crime alone. This idea includes the consequences arising from law enforcement endeavors, namely stress. In a democratic society, the public has a re-

sponsibility to govern themselves and when they don't, law enforcement can intrude upon their privacy. To that end, the public has an obligation to ensure its own well-being, which includes an evaluation of the organizational police structure and its impact upon the delivery of police services. Los Angeles Police Chief William Bratton[11] says it this way: "The role of police power in a democracy should be the expression of social consensus (agreement)."

2. Officers are not equal because each officer is affected differently by events and circumstances that produce stress. Officers should accept the responsibility and the consequences of their own conduct. However, the police organizational structure must also own up to its responsibility of providing a suitable environment where personnel can bring the agency closer to its mission in an admirable (and stress-free) fashion.

An analogy about stress might include building materials, which are often tested to discover breaking points: a steel bar, for instance, is subjected to increasing pressure to discover weaknesses or the stress point at which the bar will fracture or eventually break. Building materials have a different stress resistance, and therefore each officer reacts differently even when confronted by similar events and circumstances.

RATIONALE OF THIS WORK

When an officer arrests a suspect, how can the arrest be justified when both scholars and the court recognize that the law on the books is not "what law is"?[12] For that matter, it is generally agreed that police work is what the police say it is.[13] Said another way, there exists compelling evidence that police policy and crime control imagery are distinctively different than the operational realities of policing and police practice.[14] These differences or inconsistencies significantly influence an officer's compliance with policy and laws when delivering routine police services. For example, in some jurisdictions where a mandatory arrest policy is linked to all domestic violence calls, officers responding to calls do not always conduct an arrest even when the evidence (and policy) says they should.[15] Another example is found among officers conducting searches among drug suspects. Nearly two-thirds of the officers in a study conducted unconstitutional searches of drug suspects, and surprisingly, the courts challenged none of those searches.[16] Police performance tends to produce huge social costs when police performance does not match policy or when officers violate the due process rights of suspects. Furthermore, many officers view the justice system as too lenient and refer to it as a "revolving door" of justice (discussed later), which in turn diminishes the occupational status and social worth of officers regardless of how many people they helped or how many bad guys they arrested.[17] Additionally, the social costs often include a challenge of the legitimacy of law enforcement by the public, policymakers, and interest groups.

LEGITIMACY OF LAW ENFORCEMENT

Policy versus practice issues are widened depending on how the media reports the police effort and how the public responds to those reports. If you're in doubt, tune in to *Law and Order, CSI Miami, Without a Trace*, or any television show where law enforcement is featured or simply visit your local movie theater and watch any violent spectral depicting police action. Is the media changing an officer's reality? Similar to most criminal justice professors, students often proclaim that they want to be a crime scene investigator (CSI). I tell them to go to Hollywood and audition because real CSI specialists engage in different activities than those shown by the popular shows. Finally in this regard, I enjoy television, particularly cop shows. However, one concern is the amount of harm fostered by the entertainment media to both officers and the public. For example, when Tammy Klein began investigating crime scenes 8 years ago, it was virtually unheard of for a killer to use bleach to clean up blood.[18] "Today, the use of bleach, which destroys DNA, is not unusual in a planned homicide," says the senior criminalist from the Los Angeles County Sheriff's Department. Klein and other experts attribute such sophistication to television crime dramas like *CSI: Crime Scene Investigation*, which provide helpful tips on how to tamper with and in some cases destroy evidence. "They're actually educating these potential killers even more," said Captain Ray Peavy, also of the Los Angeles County Sheriff's Department and head of the homicide division. "Sometimes I believe it may even encourage them when they see how simple it is to get away with crime on television."

Centered in this thought, it could be argued that the self-image of an officer is usually developed somewhere between media portrayals and how the public views those portrayals. The public who encounter an officer on the street reinforce the media's perspective with an end result that challenges both the self-image an officer holds and the legitimacy of law enforcement as an institution.[19] Sam Walker reveals that the "sharp contrast between the crime-fighting imagery of the police and the peacekeeping reality of police activities was one of the first and most important findings of the flood of police research that began in the 1960s."[20]

As an officer better understands what style of performance is expected of him or her as a peacekeeper, the notion of violence seems entirely out of place or vice versa. The fact is that the expectations held by policymakers, interest groups, and the public are at the core of police legitimacy and that legitimacy provides the police with the power (and budget) to exercise crime-control tactics and police stress-control options. The public and government agencies, including the judiciary, frequently challenge the legitimacy of police authority, which has become a major problem in the 21st-century. To clarify this issue, if you are not a sworn officer, take a ride-along with an officer and count the number of individuals who challenge the authority of law enforcement, even during a routine interaction.[21] How well does an officer's self-image hold up to these legitimacy discrepancies and in what way do these discrepancies affect the performance of the officer? One answer could be that the police redefine a rationale about their experiences that is closer to media accounts than what their job actually is. What the "job" produces for most law enforcement officers other than the satisfaction of helping others and putting away the bad guy is that stress is an occupational hazard for law enforcement of all ranks. "The effects of stress—low morale, high turnover, absenteeism, and early death . . . exact a high cost from officers, their families, and their agencies."[22]

Nonetheless, another piece of the professional status puzzle is that police professionals do not control police policy, yet are given the responsibility of management and setting day-to-day directives to mirror policy.[23] Relevant to this discussion is the compelling argument that reveals that police policy, in a democratic society, rightfully belongs outside the control of those who perform a police function. For example, a study shows that policing is being reconstructed worldwide. Its distinguishing features are:[24] (a) the separation of those who authorize policing from those who do it and (b) the transference of both functions away from government.

To understand what is happening to policing, it is essential to distinguish the way in which policing is authorized from the way in which it is provided. Because police have a monopoly on the use of force and detainment power, if they developed the laws linked to use of force and detainment, what could happen? Who guards the guardians?[25] More on these thoughts in Chapters 3 and 4.

RATIONALE SUPPORTING PUBLIC POLICE

Socializing costs of reproducing labor spreads the expense of various community needs such as education, housing, health and welfare, and methods of social control (i.e., police, courts, and corrections). In a democratic society, socialization is accomplished by shifting these costs from individual and industrialists to governments through taxation. For instance, instead of a railroad company building schools for their personnel's children, sewage, water, and police protection, the workers themselves as well as businesses are taxed to provide the funds to accomplish these aims.[26] The other critical factor that helps to convince civic leaders that a strong municipal police department is superior to private police, local militia, and even the military relate to issues of legitimacy.[27] "For policing in a democratic society to be effective, it must be considered legitimate by the vast majority of the people."[28] Police must be seen as having the "right" to exercise force. Frankly, if a police agency does not have legitimacy, then it must operate by the use of brute force.[29] The public will perceive the police as professional and comply with their directives when the police utilize their legally mandated prerogative such as discretion and use of force as objectively as circumstances permit. That is, police agencies must be perceived as performing *judiciously* during public intrusions.[30]

> Judicious: Sensible and wise. Showing wisdom, good sense, or discretion, often with the underlying aim of avoiding trouble or waste.[31]

When police practice judiciously meets community standards, the community is generally satisfied and most community members attempt to comply with standards and the directives of the police. Simply put, the community will support the police when the community feels police mirror their own ideals. The greater the legitimacy of a police agency, the fewer the violators and the less coercion of force required by the agency toward social order.[32] How the police do their job or their style is far more important to their status than apprehending the bad guys.

These trends are hardly unique to the United States, as evidenced by a report in Great Britain that "an abrupt wake-up call was delivered to the entire [police] service in October 2003 when the BBC proved . . . a startling insight was given to the whole country as to who it is that dictates the nature of everyday policing."[33] The answer was not police commanders, as you have already anticipated. These realities can become clear to the typical officer early in his or her career and how an officer responds to these realities might determine the quality of police services provided by that officer.[34]

IMBALANCE

Another way to look at the policy versus practice issue is to say that an inconsistency or imbalance exists in the policing profession—an imbalance between mandates, regulations, and expectations of police behavior and the passion of officers to serve and protect. This disparity between dictates and ideals can produce more stress among officers than dealing with even some of the worst problems on America's mean streets. A word of caution: It is possible that the disparity between organizational policy and officer practices will well be the best model of a police organization. However, to make the point clear, a spouse of a former cop shares, "My husband came home more screwed up with department problems than with anything he ever encountered on the streets." The officer eventually resigned because of his inability to cope with departmental contingencies. Should the evidence in the chapters ahead support the theory of this book, then it could be argued with confidence that the passion of officers to serve and protect gives rise to a set of officer practices that are often in violation of organization policy.

In fact, a former big-city chief argues that within most police organizations, there exists a deep-seated cultural problem that corrupts an officer's decision to serve and protect.[35] The chief calls for a radical, top-down reform of the policing institution because of its inherent culture of racism, sexism, and homophobia that is pervasive in 21st-century police departments, resulting in misdirected law enforcement priorities that squander resources on victimless crimes while allowing cycles of violence to perpetuate through generations.[36] Is this view worth considering? In the final chapter of this book, this thought is addressed and confirmed, but for different reasons than those offered by the chief.

Nonetheless, legitimacy of police practice depends on the finesse demonstrated by an officer when he or she intrudes upon the daily life of constituents. It makes sense that the more professionalism demonstrated by officers, the more likely it is that the public accepts police intrusion as legitimate. But, the professionalism of police officers is seriously flawed.[37] When the flaw is unmasked, the self-image of most cops (and consequently quality police service) is affected in ways too numerous to describe.

One result is that policing is not a profession because occupational professionalism includes, among other qualities, autonomy. When outsiders mandate police policy, officers (and commanders) would seem to possess less autonomy and authority than other occupational groups.[38] This idea is discussed in more detail in Chapter 12, but for right now what you need to know is that moments to professionalize the police might mean to widen the little autonomy held by officers, which would amplify the potential of the police to act as moral entrepreneurs. Could it be argued that what is required "at present are not professional police but accountable police."[39] Accountability might mean different things to different observers; yet, more accountability might suggest less autonomy and more control over police performance. Alas, no one really wants smart or intellectual officers but cops who follow orders like blind insects (otherwise entry requirements and pay scales might be enhanced to match the importance of the job).

Imagine how much stress an officer experiences when he or she discovers the realities about policy and practice for themselves during the early months of their career. In Chapter 2, stress is defined and in Chapter 3, the consequences of workers in the general workplace, including law enforcement is discussed. As you read the next section, think about what drove the officers to do what they did and think about how you would officially respond to them (as a citizen, a police chief, or a town council member) to guard against similar future outcomes.

CONSEQUENCES OF STRESSED OFFICERS

Think about the consequences of stressed officers who have been trained to deliver violence. For instance:

- Wednesday, April 10, 2002: Policeman suspected in shooting spree that kills five. A veteran police officer went on a rampage in two New Jersey towns, killing five of his neighbors and wounding two people, police said. Authorities were searching early Wednesday for Edward Lutes, a Seaside Heights police officer for 15 years. Assistant Ocean County Prosecutor Gregory Sakowicz could not give a motive for the shootings when asked if Lutes might be going after other targets.[40]

- Joseph Gray, 41, a 15-year veteran with the New York Police Department, was convicted of manslaughter for an alcohol-fueled crash that killed a family of four. Gray received a 15-year prison sentence for instantly killing a pregnant woman, Maria Herrera, 24; her 4-year-old son, Andy; and her 16-year-old, sister Dilcia Pena. Gray pleaded innocent to four counts of manslaughter, including one charging him with killing Herrera's unborn child.[41]

- Captain Phil Peters had been on the job 16 years and was a captain in charge of the department's Special Response Team and Street Crimes Unit. His love for the job and the stress it caused had taken a toll on his marriage. He was separated from his wife and began a relationship with a female officer. It outraged the chief enough that he conducted a 9-month internal investigation, resulting in reassignment of the captain to nights and firing the female officer.[42]

- Christmas Day, 1997: police who said they mistook the keys he was carrying for a gun killed William J. Whitfield, an unarmed African American man in a New York supermarket. Although the officer who shot him was cleared of wrongdoing, it was revealed that the officer had been involved in eight prior shootings. The New York Police Department Police Commissioner subsequently set up a monitoring system for officers involved in three or more shootings.[43]

Stress or what can be called distress is part of every occupation, but it is inherent in most police activities, and when officers act upon their distress, as evidenced above, innocent people die.

The public pays a price for stressed officers but so do the officers. They are 30% more likely to experience health problems than other personnel, three times more likely to abuse their spouses, five times more likely to abuse alcohol, five times more likely to have somatization (multiple, recurrent), six times more likely to experience anxiety, 10 times more likely to be depressed, and oddly, officers are the least likely of most occupational group members to seek help.[44]

In addition, chronic, sustained, untreated stress can lead to a compromised immune system, illness, and even death. *Posttraumatic stress disorder* is a serious condition that requires immediate care. However, stress can also be positive, or eustress, which propels us toward positive activities such as competitive sports, going back to school, or driving us to excel at work. More will be discussed about distress and eustress in Chapter 2. Prevention, or at least the reduction of the negative impact of stress, proves crucial to the health of street cops and to the health of our communities and ultimately the nation. Thus the importance of this work lies in the fact that officer stress control should have a priority in police policy.

BLAMING THE VICTIM

When you perused the above brutal scenarios, what thought crossed your mind? Most often when police brutality rears its ugly head, one common thought is that an officer can't cope with the job and consequently that officer is blamed for his or her indiscretions. That is, if an officer were in better control, quality police services would be delivered and police corruption and brutality would appear less often. Blaming the victim is a common response: the unemployed are told that they are lazy and undisciplined, rape victims are thought to be equally guilty in their own attack, battered spouses are said to provoke the abuse received and then remain with their abusers, and incest victims are told they must have asked for it. Conversely, some successful people actually believe they were chosen by a divine power to be successful. An American myth is that the strong succeed because they are strong, and the weak fail because they're failures in the first place.

It is efficient to blame a victim because by doing so, uncertainty and social order can be resolved much quicker and with less pain. Of course, victims have a difficult time fighting back. For that reason, most stress programs are designed to alter the behavior of officers, or what can be called "person-centered programs." While helping officers resolve their stress is a worthwhile strategy, one indefensible limitation is that policymakers do little to resolve the organizational stressors that promote stressful policies. Another thought is that the actions of police officers can be easily associated with the nature of policing immoral and corrupt members in a free society, many of whom possess networks, wealth, and knowledge to turn the courts into tools that further their own criminal and unethical ambitions.[45]

CENTRAL THEME OF THIS WORK

In developing the central theme of this book—both the underlying assumptions discussed earlier and the thought that police officer stress has more than one stressor (origin or events)—the most serious stressor, it will be argued, is associated with the police organization.

Specifically, the central theme of this work will show that law enforcement organizational structure, including its internal and external influences, represent the principle stressors for officers because of the:

- Political climate in the United States. Police commanders develop policy and strategies less often than anticipated by the officers reporting to them and the public in their jurisdiction.
- Organizational command strategies consistent with a hierarchal bureaucratic structure, stifling the delivery of quality police services and influences public perception of police legitimacy.
- Paramilitary police models initiated in a response to the war on crime and drugs alienates the typical police officer.
- Initiatives developed to respond to terrorism, which includes local federal intervention, is a beehive of stress for most law enforcement officers and their commanders.
- Professionalism among police officers is inhibited by police organizational issues.
- To date, there is yet to be an earnest effort to aid police officers in preventing stress.

> The central theme of this work is that among police officers, the risks of the streets are less traumatic than the organizational factors they face, which includes policy developed by non-police professionals, top-down bureaucratic practices, and policy initiatives linked to strategies developed as a law enforcement response to the war on crime, drugs, and terrorism.

Politicians, organizational structures, and federal local intrusions are a greater source of obstructive stress for municipal and rural police officers, investigators, and administrators as opposed to responsibilities and practices of the job or the families of the law enforcement personnel. This thought is consistent with many experts who explored links between police organizational structures, professionalism (or lack of it), police reform, and recent changes in police performance.[46]

In a simplified version, official change tends to be a product of policy. Administrators and commanders "order" officers toward compliance. It is expected (by regulation) that officers carry out those orders. For some, that could mean that they are expected to carry out orders even when those orders might violate the law.[47] In the final analysis, the policy–practice gap produces an inconsistency that makes it appear that supervisors and street cops work in two different worlds. Another way to look at "orders versus practice" is to say somewhere between the directive of a policy and the passion of an officer to serve and protect, more stress is exerted by a law enforcement officer than his or her experiences on America's meanest streets.

If the evidence is confirmed in this book, then it can be argued with a great degree of confidence that because officer stress is developed and reinforced by the police organization, it could be said that officer stress is actually a symptom of an antiquated organization that has performed well and now must be resigned to meet the challenges of a new people and a new time.

Nonetheless, it needs to be articulated that most somatic or behavioral problems exhibited by police officers are not necessarily a result of organizational stress. Because some officers drink excessively, suffer heart conditions, develop ulcers, experience insomnia, and treat everybody including family members as if they were criminals, this does not automatically translate to his or her organization or job as being necessarily the culprit.[48] As is obvious by the many officers who consistently demonstrate professional behavior, just because the job is frustrating does not translate to a job that affects the officer adversely. The truth is officers differ in their reactions to events and circumstances. Most officers are resilient, resourceful, and have high levels of coping competence. Such individuals obviously deal effectively with untoward circumstances and many may even flourish under adversity.[49]

EVIDENCE BROUGHT TO THIS STUDY

To curb stress among law enforcement officers with a dual perspective in mind of resolving it and enhancing public safety, stress should be examined for what it is rather than what is said about it. The obvious must be made obvious.[50] We need to look beneath the official explanation on the origins of police stress and how officers respond to it. A behavior researcher at Stanford University says it this way: "America and the world have arrived at a moment of great challenge and opportunity. We know enough. It is time to act."[51]

One way to learn more about the consequences of policy versus practice can be found in data gathered for this textbook provided by 558 sworn officers from numerous police departments serving the public from New England to the Gulf of Mexico, including rural departments of Virginia.[52] In addition, 24 law enforcement officers serving the hardest-hit parts of the country by Hurricane Katrina contributed to this work. Officers were asked about their jobs, families, and departments. They provided data about everything from their sex life, to policing training, to deceitfulness. They were asked about the trustworthiness of their supervisors and the condition of the equipment they used to serve and protect. The findings are offered throughout this work to aid you in better understanding police officer stress and its origins. However, through past research and the findings of this study, the inconsistency between mandates or policy dictated by police commanders and the ideals and practices of street cops suggest that some officers work in a different world than do their commanders and policymakers.[53]

WHAT THIS BOOK IS ABOUT

This textbook contains 13 chapters, which describe occupational stress, police organizations and strategies, person-centered intervention, and departmental initiatives to curb stress. There are three parts: Part I highlights the realities of the justice community, police organizations, and stressors at both the critical-incident and general-work levels. Part II examines the war on crime, describes paramilitary models and terrorism, and their relationship to stress; and Part III offers individual and person-centered intervention, options of person-centered programs and obstacles, professionalism, and finally, organizational concerns.

Chapter 1 focuses on the assumptions and theme, and provides an introduction into the world of policing and the consequences of stress. Chapter 2 emphasizes a working definition of stress and its consequences. Chapter 3 offers an inside look at occupational stress in policing and other professions. Chapter 4 reveals how police organizational structures operate and their contributions as stressors. Chapter 5 specifically highlights critical-incident stressors, and Chapter 6 examines general-work stressors, which include family stressors and a description of female officer stressors that influence their jobs and their promotions within the department.

Part II examines the effects of the war on crime and drugs in Chapter 7, the military model and a comparison between cops and soldiers is highlighted in Chapter 8, terrorism and the federal approach to local intervention is detailed in Chapter 9, and rural policing is examined in Chapter 10.

Part III consists of a description of person-centered stress providers and obstacles of stress control in Chapter 11. Police professionalism is emphasized in Chapter 12, and organizational issues linked to stress are provided in Chapter 13. This study's methodology, a copy of the questionnaire, and data from the study conducted for this book are in the Appendix, along with other materials that can guide your understanding of this work. Once you have finished this book, you will be a more informed student or criminal justice practitioner about the capabilities of street cops, the organizations that employ them, and the most efficient individual and organizational approaches to prevent police officer stress.

EXPECTATIONS ABOUT YOU

It is believed you have an interest in advancing one of America's most valuable services—policing—and that you want police officers to perform at peak yet legal efficiency. One method to ensure peak efficiency is to go to the source of potential problems and offer ways to change the institution for the better. Another assumption is that you are a cadet or a student at a justice academy, a college, or an independent student of criminal justice. You might be on the job as a patrol officer, supervisor, commander, or a "wanna be" or you are widely versed in criminal justice studies and have participated in a number of academic and practitioner courses. It is hoped that you want to better understand police officer organizational policy and its implications. It is also expected that this textbook will be a guide to a safe environment for many police departments and the public they serve. How police organizations function in relation to the social networks that define and utilize their services is important to know for its own sake. Finally, the behavioral consequences of a stressed officer can be worth review, especially if you want to do something about it.

FUNCTION OF THE POLICE

Part of the rationale of an arrest, the primary function of the police, is to reduce crime and criminal victimization through detection and apprehension of suspects.[54] Police seek to achieve this goal by arresting and threatening to arrest those who violate criminal law. The police organize themselves to produce this result by:

1. Patrolling city streets hoping to detect and deter crime.
2. Responding to calls for service as quickly as time and circumstance permits.
3. Conducting investigations after crimes have been committed to identify criminal offenders and develop evidence toward a defendant's prosecution.

The police are gatekeepers of the justice community because all future criminal justice intervention begins with police intrusion into the public and private lives of others. However, officers in reality perform two functions: authoritative intervention and symbolic justice.[55]

Authoritative intervention is the primary function of most patrol and traffic officers and usually occurs after a violation has been committed or what can be a reactive response to crime. Few attempts or priorities are made to confront or correct the underlying conditions that have lead to the need for police intrusion.[56] The police continually "look back" at past events before moving into action.

Symbolic justice is the realm of detectives and service call (9-1-1) officers who react to violations. Its purpose is to show offenders and the public that law enforcement indeed exists. The success of law enforcement is dependent on "information supplied by the public, just as the mobilization of patrol officers is for authoritative intervention."[57] Few if any resources of law enforcement efforts are devoted to anticipation of criminal events and those that tend to be symbolic or paramilitary models (discussed in Chapter 5). For instance, traffic signals aid the flow of traffic and can be called preventive devices, yet many drivers ignore those signals, producing the victimization of others.

Then, too, ordinances and laws aid social order, yet many individuals ignore ordinances and laws as evidenced by the crime rates, no matter the consequences. As these thoughts in some form or another become part of the big picture to a typical street officer, he or she might come to view the job of public safety differently, especially once an officer realizes that criminal offenders, whom he or she along with their colleagues had arrested once before, are returned to the community.

THE BIG PICTURE

In the final analysis, the police represent and implement the government's right to use coercion and force to guarantee specified conduct (such as obeying the laws) from each person while at the same time act as defenders of human rights.[58] That is, the government must use organized coercion to prevent private coercion while guaranteeing the Constitutional rights of every individual encountered.[59] However, hidden resentment could well exist among officers when it is learned that suspects were returned to the community after their cases were rejected for insufficient evidence or even when those defendants had been convicted of a crime and placed on probation or what can be called the "revolving door" of justice. For the purposes of this work, the *revolving door of justice* refers to defendants charged with violent crimes that are returned to the community, whether by being freed, making bond, or being placed on probation after a guilty plea. An analogy might come from an educational perspective whereby a college instructor failed a student in several (major) courses, yet the student graduated college.

Law enforcement issues are more complex than educational issues, particularly when the consequences arising from the revolving door of justice are clarified. For instance, 19-year-old Keith Carter was arrested after a fierce gunfight with two Pittsburgh police officers in the summer of 2005.[60] Carter was freed on a $5,000 straight bond following a similar shooting incident involving one of the officers. Deputy Police Chief William Mullen says he was infuriated that Carter was freed after the earlier shooting on what he considered to be an inappropriately low bond. Carter has been charged earlier with reckless endangerment, possession of a weapon and firearms (machine gun) violations, and scheduled to appear at a hearing. "It's ridiculous," says the deputy chief, "not only do the bad guys have no regard for the lives of police officers, but apparently the people responsible for setting that low bond don't, either."[61]

When officers locate their job in the big picture, they do not see themselves as merely doing a job, but rather see themselves as part of a large team sharing similar experiences toward public safety.[70] Equally important, the promise of public safety is to find ways of resolving professional and personal issues arising from those experiences, such as delivering quality police services and de-

Revolving-Door Justice[62]

Nationally, for instance, at yearend 2003, among offenders on probation, almost one-half (49%) of them were convicted of felonies, 49% were convicted of a misdemeanor, and 2% were convicted for other infractions.[63] In what way would a felon's appearance on the free streets affect an officer who had taken a risk to apprehend the defendant only to be confronted with the individual once again?

In other cases, after an arrest, suspects are freed without going to court because of what some refer to as legal loopholes. That is, cases are dropped from prosecution after an arrest for one of three reasons.[64] First, some arrests are dismissed by police supervisors when they are convinced that the case lacks sufficient evidence. A noted expert adds that the police in California drop an estimated 11% of all arrests because of a lack of sufficient evidence.[65] Second, prosecutors reject or refuse to prosecute some cases because of a lack of sufficient evidence to win the conviction. Third, some cases are dismissed even after a prosecutor decides to proceed with a case by a judge or a grand jury because of insufficient evidence. A study in New York City and San Diego was conducted, which supports case rejections.[66] That is, of all the cases rejected by the prosecutors, 61% in New York City and 51% in San Diego were rejected because of insufficient evidence. Apprehending a suspect only to see the suspect returned to a free society could make reference to an officer's efficacy or integrity, which in turn increases the level of stress an officer experiences.[67]

Continuing along this path of discussion, 40% of all narcotics officers place themselves at risk to build a case only to see suspects freed or conditionally released back into the community.[68] Some say the institutional contradictions of law and order are at work when it comes to freed suspects.[69]

veloping efficient methods to curb the stressful experiences from the events such as the revolving door of justice (and encounters such as gunfights).[71] But what has been learned in the past 10 years, despite societal and organizational change, relates to two issues: 1. services provided officers with mental illness (or stress) have not improved,[72] and (2) the qualities that relate to a good officer candidate are often difficult to identify, as is reviewed in Chapter 13.[73]

What you need to know right now about quality candidates is that traits such as intelligence, common sense, dependability, and honesty appear more frequently than others in the police literature, but this issue is complicated by the difficulty in linking job tasks to personality characteristics, and the different ways officers respond to stress, which includes the realization of the revolving door of justice.

Law enforcement personnel across the nation work under similar conditions and directives, and many may even feel alienated (this does not suggest that alienated officers "act out" their alienation, producing conduct unbecoming of an officer) by the criminal justice system, the public, and policymakers.

Some agencies have more police conduct irregularities than other agencies.[74] Is it the officer or the agency that permits those irregularities to happen? Both answers could be supported with compelling evidence because policing is one profession in which an individual is expected to regularly confront potential danger, even death, and must make crucial decisions during pressured circumstances.[75] Other times, the routine of boredom can be overwhelming.

But when we look at police management, their challenge is to effectively recognize, relate, and assimilate global shifts in culture, technology, and information, says one police chief.[76] Bobby D. Moody, Chief of Police of Marietta, Georgia, reveals that changing community expectations, workforce values, technological power, governmental arrangements, policing philosophies, and ethical standards must be constructively managed by police managers in order to help officers deliver quality police services and to help officers maintain a professional approach to policing. Chief Moody, like many police chiefs, reveals that officers and police organizations must look beyond day-to-day routines and focus on the bigger picture in order to meet today's challenges of policing, which absolutely includes stress control.[77] But what about the big picture of stress among street cops?

Factually, an underlying perspective of police executives is more control of the police structure, which they believe promotes healthier departments and allegedly aids in personnel retention, professional development, and ultimately enhances quality of life experiences among the department's constituents. It is interesting to note that police departments are not always managed by law enforcement professionals but rather by state-level officials and town hall cronies who are often "wanna-be" cops and prefer to enhance votes rather than reduce victims, especially if those victims are cops. One typical response from town hall officials regarding help for officers to combat stress might be found in this response: "After all, we're in a war on crime, and casualities are expected"[78] (more on this topic in Chapter 7). Nonetheless, state-level officials, town hall politicians, and policymakers know that professional changes are expected in police organizations, yet keep police managers busied keeping their agencies afloat from the waves of budgetary cutbacks, homeland security issues fostered by federal agencies, and enhanced service mandates demanded by a litigious public rather than providing assistance to personnel who are drowning in a sea of blue stress.[79]

SUMMARY

Countries would have less anarchy and official corruption if the human rights of their populations were safeguarded through professional police services. In this regard, how can the typical police officer balance quality police services and be the defender of human rights when he or she is stressed and tired? It was suggested that stressed officers avoid help because it would be construed among coworkers that they are weak, untrustworthy, unlikely to back up an officer in a critical altercation, and the police organization blames the officer for his or her stressed situation, which in turn reduces the officer's chances of promotion (or recovery). For officers to admit that they feel suicidal or have domestic problems is close to admitting a loss of control.

Two underlying assumptions include the idea that the police cannot nor should they attempt to control crime alone because the public has a responsibility to govern themselves, and officers are not equal because they are affected differently by stress. Even when stressed officers are "cured" or rehabilitated, they continue employment at the same agency that had done little to alter the organizational structure or initiatives that produced their stress. The primary question of this work is that the risk of the streets are less traumatic than the police organization, its policy, and its paramilitary top-down principles supported by the political climate where commanders manage their agencies less often than anticipated, and specific police initiatives or strategies are serious stressors. Those initiatives include those developed to combat the war on crime and drugs, and finally, initiatives developed to respond to terrorism, including federal or local intrusion.

An imbalance exists in policing between mandates, regulations, and expectations of officer behavior and the passion of officers to serve and protect. The consequences of stressed officers are seen as police brutality and often, officers are blamed for their inability to cope with police work. Organizational factors that perpetuate stress should be better understood to promote appropriate change, which will encourage prevention and treatment prerogatives. Currently, police practice serves two functions and both support the notion that policing is reactive to crime: authoritative intervention of suspects rather than correcting the underlying conditions that have lead to the need for police intrusion, and symbolic justice demonstrates that law enforcement exists despite the fact that the community supplies most information leading to an arrest.

Most officers and commanders see the big picture of law enforcement particularly as it relates to the revolving door of justice. Seeing the big picture can help provide resolution toward contingencies, including the delivery of quality police services and individual and organizational stress control methods.

WHAT WOULD YOU DO IF YOU WERE IN CHARGE?

Deputy Chris Smithcom was a deputy sheriff at the Calcasieu Parish Sheriff's Office in Louisiana for 10 years. In late 1997 while working night patrol, he received a missing persons report involving a mother and daughter. He proceeded to the station to complete the paperwork rather than answer a disturbance call, which was close to his location. During the drive, the dispatcher advised that shots had been fired at that location and someone was down. A vehicle pursuit was in progress. Several police vehicles respond including

Smithcom. The pursuit lasted for 10 minutes and Smithcom and the subject engaged in a gunfight. Both were injured. After Smithcom was hospitalized, he learned that his closest friend had been killed at the original location along with the subject's wife. Smithcom was devastated because he felt that he should have backed up the call but wanted to start the paperwork on his missing person case. Smithcom was honored by his department for his heroics during the gunfight but he was miserable with grief and guilt. He couldn't face his dead officer's family and retreated into his own world of despair. He alienated family, friends, and the department. Smithcom says, "It has been a year and a half of hard work and forgiving and realizing that I didn't pull that trigger, the subject did. My department and fellow deputies never saw what I have become, or they didn't want to see."[80] It appears that Smithcom is demonstrating the police "code of silence," which implies to never show signs of weakness. What would you have done differently than Smithcom? If you were his supervisor, what would you do?

OFFICERS KILLED IN NEW YORK

Two detectives with the New York City Police Department were murdered in Staten Island at 8:00 P.M. on March 10, 2003, in an unprovoked attack. The detectives were working undercover and conducting an illegal firearm purchase from the inside of an unmarked vehicle. The incident began with the first detective, 36 years old with nearly 6 years' experience, driving the vehicle, his partner, 34 years old with nearly 7 years' service, in the front passenger seat, and two individuals in the backseat. The detectives were carrying money to purchase a gun from their passengers. When the detective who was driving parked the vehicle to conclude the purchase, one of the men in the rear seat allegedly produced a .44-caliber revolver and shot the detective's partner, killing him with a single bullet to the side of the head. Apparently, the individual then put the gun to the rear of the driver's head, demanded the money, and shot him once in the back of the head, killing him. The suspects then pulled the officers' bodies from the car, took the 9-mm semiautomatic handgun belonging to the detective who was the driver, and stole the vehicle. After losing contact with the detectives, backup officers following the operation began to search for them. They discovered the victim officers lying in the middle of the street. Police located a 17-year-old, who was allegedly a passenger in the car, the detective's service weapon, and the stolen money several blocks from the scene of the incident. The individual was arrested the next day. On March 12, the police arrested the 20-year-old alleged shooter. Four other individuals, ranging in age from 18 to 21, were arrested for their alleged involvement with the murders; they were believed to have planned the killings, provided the weapon used, or witnessed the disposal of the murder weapon. All six were charged with felony murder.[81] Anything you would have done differently if you were these officers?

DISCUSSION QUESTIONS

1. Identify two underlying assumptions about this work.
2. Characterize the discrepancies between crime control imagery and operational realities of police officers.
3. Explain the characteristics of the law enforcement profession and identify limitations associated with policing.
4. Clarify the central theme of this work. What kind of evidence do you think the author will gather to support the central themes of this book?
5. Describe the rationale supporting the idea that the organization is a greater stressor than an officer's job or family. In what way might you agree or disagree with the rationale of this work?
6. Describe the two functions police officers tend to perform in their role as gatekeepers of the justice community. In what way would you agree with the gatekeeper description of officers?
7. Explain why the "big picture" of policing and stress could be beneficial to the public and police officers.
8. Describe what is meant by the revolving door of justice and articulate its consequences upon police officer stress. Provide some examples that can support the revolving door of justice perspective. In what (legal) way could the revolving door of justice be remedied?

ENDNOTES

1. William C. Dement (2004, April 23). Stanford University Center of Excellence. For the diagnosis and treatment of sleep disorders. 4th Annual FOCUS conference on respiratory care and sleep medicine, Baltimore.
2. Chief Charles H. Ramsey (2002). Preparing the community for community policing: The next step in advancing community policing. In Dennis J. Stevens (Ed.), *Policing and community partnerships*, (pp. 29–44). Upper Saddle River, NJ: Prentice Hall.
3. A. P. Cardarelli, J. McDevitt, and K. Baum (1998). The rhetoric and reality of community policing in small and medium sized cities and towns. *An International Journal of Police Strategies and Management*, 21(3), 397–415.
4. Charles H. Logan (1993). Criminal justice performance measures for prisons. In Charles H. Logan (Ed.), *Performance measures for the criminal justice system* (pp. 19–60). Washington, DC: U.S. Department of Justice, Office of Justice Programs.
5. Jerome H. Skolnick (1999, August). *Ideas on American policing: On democratic policing.* Retrieved online May 13, 2004: http://www.policefoundation.org
6. John P. Crank (2004). *Understanding police culture*, 2nd edition. Cincinnati, OH: Anderson. pp. 276–278.
7. Katherine W. Ellison (2004). *Stress and the police officer*, 2nd edition. Springfield, IL: Charles C. Thomas. p. 62.

8. Patricia A. Kelly (2002). Stress: The cop killer. In John M. Madonna Jr. and Richard E. Kelly (Eds.) *Treating police stress: The work and the words of peer counselors* (pp. 33–54). Springfield, IL: Charles C. Thomas.

9. Sandra D. Terhune-Bickler (2004). Too close for comfort negotiating with fellow officers. *Federal Law Enforcement Bulletin*, 73(4). Retrieved online May 30, 2005: http://www.fbi.gov/publications/leb/2004/apr2004/april04leb.htm#page_2

10. Captain Robert Dunford (2003). Forum at University of Massachusetts Boston. Commander of Boston Law Academy and superintendent of uniform division, Boston Police Department.

11. William Bratton (1999, February 28). Dispelling New York's latest fear. *New York Times*, Section 4, p. 19.

12. Jon B. Gould and Stephen D. Mastrofski (2004). Suspect searches: Assessing police behavior under the U.S. Constitution. *Criminology and Public Policy*, 3(3), 315–362.

13. Cheryl Maxson, Karen Henningan, and David C. Sloane (2002, October 24). *Not just a popularity contest: Factors that influence public opinion of the police.* Washington, DC: U.S. Department of Justice, Office of Justice Programs. Retrieved online March 15, 2005: http://www.ncjrs.org/pdffiles1/nij/grants/197062.pdf

14. Sam Walker (2001). Broken windows and fractured history. In Roger G. Dunham and Geoffrey P. Alpert (Eds.), *Critical issues in policing: Contemporary readings*, 4th ed. (pp. 480–493). Prospect Heights, IL: Waveland Press.

15. Eve Buzawa and C. Buzawa (1996). *Domestic violence: The criminal justice response.* Thousand Oaks, CA: Sage. Also see Eve Buzawa, Gerald T. Hotaling, and Andrew Klein (2000, March). *Response to domestic violence in a pro-active court setting – final report.* Washington, DC: U.S. Department of Justice, Office of Justice Programs. Retrieved online March 15, 2005: http://www.ncjrs.org/pdffiles1/nij/grants/181427.pdf.

16. Jon B. Gould and Stephen D. Mastrofski (2004, July).

17. Jon B. Gould and Stephen D. Mastrofski (2004, July). p. 316.

18. Lexisnexis News. (2006, January 26). TV crime dramas aiding real life killers. Retrieved online March 3, 2006: http://yahoo.theherrens.com/index.php?tag=tammy

19. Sam Walker (2001). p. 486.

20. Sam Walker (2001). p. 486.

21. For instance, while writing this paragraph on April 23, 2005, a Salem police officer who was also a student of the writer was on an extra detail controlling traffic while a roadway was being repaired. A motorist refused to obey the officer's directions and decided to drive over the uniformed officer, sending him to the hospital in serious condition. It is unlikely the officer will be able to report to duty for a year or more. Unusual? In Chapter 3, the number of officers assaulted and killed will confirm the idea that many officers are disrespected on a daily basis.

22. National Institute of Justice (2004, February). *National Institute of Justice 2001.* Annual Report. NIJ 195076. Washington, DC: U.S. Department of Justice, Office of Justice Programs. Retrieved online May 20, 2005: http://www.ncjrs.org/txtfiles1/nij/195076.txt

23. Andrew Cohen (2003, March 3). *Justices get tough on crime.* CBSNews.com. Court Watch. Retrieved online March 15, 2005: http://www.cbsnews.com/stories/

2003/03/05/news/opinion/courtwatch/main542892.shtml Christopher S. Koper (2002, March). Federal legislation and gun markets: How much have recent reforms of the federal firearms licensing system reduced criminal gun suppliers. *Criminology and Public Opinion*, 1(2), 151–178.

Get tough on crime, public demands (2004, April 3). *The Miami Herald*. Retrieved online March 15, 2005: http://www.latinamericanstudies.org/argentina/tough.htm.

Tomislav V. Kovandzic, John J. Sloan III, and Lynne M. Vieraitis (2002, July). Unintended consequences of politically popular sentencing policy: The homicide promoting effects of "Three Strikes" in U.S. cities (1980–1998). *Criminology and Public Opinion*, 1(3), 478–498.

24. David H. Bayley and Clifford D. Shearing (2001, July). *The new structure of the police: Description, conceptualization, and research agenda*. Washington, DC: U.S. Department of Justice, Office of Justice Programs. NCJ 187083. Retrieved online May 25, 2005: http://www.ncjrs.org/pdffiles1/nij/187083.pdf

25. Ronald D. Hunter (1994). Who guards the guardians: Managerial misconduct in policing. In Thomas Barker and David L. Carter (Eds.), *Police deviance*, 3rd *ed.* (pp. 169–184). Cincinnati, OH: Anderson.

26. Steven Spitzer (1981). The political economy of policy. In David F. Greenberg (Ed.), *Corrections and punishment*. (pp. 239–264). Beverly Hills, CA: Sage.

27. David E. Barlow and Melissa Hickman Barlow (2004). p. 78.

28. David E. Barlow and Melissa Hickman Barlow (2004). p. 78.

29. Dennis J. Stevens (2003). *Applied community policing in the 21st century*. Boston: Allyn & Bacon. pp. 20–21. Also see Robert C. Trojanowicz and S. L. Dixon (1974). *Criminal justice and the community*. Englewood Cliffs, NJ: Prentice Hall. pp. 147–148.

30. Robert C. Trojanowicz and S.I. Dixon (1974). p. 147.

31. Dictionary.com. Retrieved online July 26, 2005: http://dictionary.reference.com/search?q=Judiciously

32. Dennis J. Stevens (2003). p. 21.

33. Damian Warburton (2004). Drawing the thin blue line: The reality of who controls the police. *Police Journal*, 77(2), 135–144.

34. John P. Crank (2004). *Understanding police culture*, 2nd ed. Cincinnati, OH: Anderson. pp. 325–327.

35. Norm Stamper (2005). *Breaking rank: A top cop's exposé of the dark side of American policing*. New York: Nation Books.

36. Norm Stamper (2005).

37. John P. Crank (2004). pp. 110–111.

38. John P. Crank (2004).

39. John Van Maanen (2004). The asshole. In Steven G. Brandal and David S. Barlow (Eds.), *The police in America* (pp. 197–215). Belmont, CA: Wadsworth.

40. CNN.Com News. Retrieved online February 6, 2005: http://www.cnn.com/

41. *U.S. News and World Report*. Retrieved online February 6, 2005: http://www.usatoday.com/news/digest.htm Also see Court tv.com for details. Retrieved online February 20, 2005: http://www.courttv.com/trials/gray_joseph/verdict_ctv.html

42. Captain Phil Peters (2001). Letter from a captain. Retrieved online February 20, 2005: http://www.tearsofacop.com/police/ct/captain.html

43. Amnesty International. Retrieved online March 26, 2004: http://www.amnestyusa.org/refugee/document.do?id=5F9BD29EB536DB05802569A50071 98E8

44. Robin Gershon (1999). Washington, DC: U.S. Department of Justice, National Institute of Justice, Public Health Implication of Law Enforcement Stress, video presentation, March 23.

45. Dennis J. Stevens (2003). pp. 214.

46. David L. Carter (2001). *The police and the community*. Upper Saddle River, NJ: Prentice Hall. Also see Hans Toch (2001). Stress in Policing. Washington, DC: American Psychological Association.

47. Victor E. Kappeler (2005). *Critical issues in police civil liability*, 3rd ed. Prospect Heights, IL: Waveland. See pages 1–4.

48. Hans Toch (2001). *Stress in policing*. Washington, DC: APA. pp. 8–9.

49. Hal Toch (2001). p. 9.

50. Peter L. Berger (1963). *Invitation to sociology: A humanistic perspective*. New York: Doubleday. p. 125.

51. William C. Dement (2004).

52. See Appendix II for the research design concerning this study.

53. Personal communication during an interview with a Miami-Dade law enforcement officer. March 15, 2005. Also see Dennis J. Stevens (2004). Origins of police officers' stress before and after 911. *Police Journal*, 77(2), 145–173. Dennis J. Stevens (2005). Police officer stress and occupational stressors: Before and after 911. In Heith Copes (Ed.), *Policing and stress* (pp. 1–15). Upper Saddle River, NJ: Prentice Hall. Dennis J. Stevens (1999). Stress and the American police officer. *Police Journal*, 72(3), 247–259. Dennis J. Stevens (1998). What do officers really think about their job? *The Journal*, 51(1), 60–62.

54. Geoffrey P. Alpert and Mark H. Moore (2001). Measuring policing performance in the new paradigm of policing. In Roger G. Dunham and Geoffrey P. Alpert (Eds.), *Critical issues in policing: Contemporary readers* (pp. 238–254). Prospect Heights, IL: Waveland Press.

55. David H. Bayley (1996). *Police for the future*. New York: Oxford University Press. p. 34.

56. David H. Bayley (1996).

57. David H. Bayley (1996). p. 34.

58. Roger G. Dunham and Geoffrey P. Alpert (Eds.) (2001). *Critical issues in policing: Contemporary readings*. Prospect Heights, IL: Waveland Press. p. 1.

59. William F. McDonald and Sergei Paromchik (1996). Transparency and the police: External research, policing and democracy. *Policing in Central and Eastern Europe*. Retrieved online March 15, 2005: http://www.ncjrs.org/policing/trans17 .htm

60. Cindi Lash (2005, June 7). Gunfight suspect was free on bond. *Pittsburgh Post-Gazette*. Retrieved online April 17, 2006: http://www.post-gazette.com/pg/ 05158/516885.stm

61. Cindi Lash (2005, June 7).

62. Developed by the author for this section.

63. Bureau of Justice Statistics (2005). *Probation and parole in the United States 2003.* Washington, DC: U.S. Department of Justice, Office of Justice Programs. Retrieved online March 13, 2005: http://www.ojp.usdoj.gov/bjs/pandp.htm

64. Samuel Walker (2001). *Sense and nonsense about crime and drugs: A policy guide,* 5th ed. Belmont, CA: Wadsworth. pp. 46–47.

65. Joan Petersilia (1983). *Racial disparities in the criminal justice system.* Santa Monica, CA: Rand. p. 21.

66. Samuel Walker (2001). pp. 46–47.

67. Hans Toch (2001). *Stress in Policing.* Washington, DC: APA. pp. 56–57.

68. Victor E. Kappeler, Mark Blumberg, and Gary W. Potter (1998). *The mythology of crime and criminal justice.* Prospect Heights, IL: Waveland Press.

69. Dennis J. Stevens (1999). Corruption among narcotic officers: A study of innocence and integrity. *Journal of Police and Criminal Psychology,* 14(2), 1–19.

70. Dennis J. Stevens (1999).

71. Victor E. Kappeler, Mark Blumberg, and Gary W. Potter (1998). Also see Dennis J. Stevens (1999).

72. P. A. Collins and A. C. C. Gibbs (2003). Stress in police officers: A study of the origins, prevalence and severity of stress-related symptoms within a county police force. *Occupational Medicine,* 53, 256–264.

73. Beth A. Sanders (2003). Maybe there's no such thing as a "good cop": Organizational challenges in selecting quality officers. *An International Journal of Police Strategies and Management,* 26(2), 313–328.

74. Geoffrey P. Alpert and Mark H. Moore (2001). Also see George L. Keeling and Catherine M. Coles (1996). *Fixing broken windows: Restoring order and reducing crime in our communities.* New York: Free Press. pp. 175, 216, 230–231.

75. George T. Patterson (2001). Reconceptualizing traumatic incidents experienced by law enforcement personnel. *The Australasian Journal of Disaster and Trauma Studies,* 1174–4707. Retrieved online March 7, 2005: http://www.massey.ac.nz/~trauma/issues/2001-2/patterson1.htm

76. Chief Bobby Moody is the past president of the International Association of Chiefs of Police (IACP). This statement came from recommendations Chief Moody offered at his first leadership conference. Bobby D. Moody (1999, May). *Police leadership in the twenty-first century achieving and sustaining executive success.* International Association of Chiefs of Police. Retrieved online May 13, 2004: http://www.theiacp.org/documents/pdfs/Publications/policeleadership%2Epdf

77. Chief Bobby Moody (1999). Chief Charles H. Ramsey (2002). Preparing the community for community policing: The next step in advancing community policing. In Dennis J. Stevens (Ed.), *Policing and community partnerships* (pp. 29–44). Upper Saddle River, NJ: Prentice Hall. Chief Francis D'Ambra (2002). Community partnerships in affluent communities: The phantom menaces. In Dennis J. Stevens (Ed.), *Policing and community partnerships* (pp. 17–28). Upper Saddle River, NJ: Prentice Hall.

78. This local politician in Fayetteville, North Carolina, wanted to remain anonymous. The statement cited was in response to a request by the chief of police of Fayetteville who had concerns about stress reduction programs for personnel of the Fayetteville Police Department. The author was present at this town hall meeting and noted the discussions between the chief and town hall officials.

79. Chief Bobby Moody (1999). Also see John M. Madonna, Jr. and Richard E. Kelly (2002). *Treating police stress: The work and the words of peer counselors*. Springfield, IL: Charles C. Thomas. pp. 8–12.

80. Deputy Chris Smithcom (2001). *My story*. Retrieved online February 20, 2005: http://www.tearsofacop.com/police/ct/shots.html

81. FBI (2005). *Law enforcement officers killed and assaulted 2003*. Retrieved online May 7, 2005: http://www.fbi.gov/ucr/killed/leoka03.pdf p. 50.

2

Stress Defined

What lies behind us and what lies before us are small matters compared to what lies within us. —Ralph Waldo Emerson

Learning Objectives

Once you have finished reading this chapter, you will be better prepared to:

- Characterize the relevance of external stressors and internal responses.
- Define stress.
- Describe the necessity of stress in everyday experiences.
- Explain the coping stress initiatives employed by many individuals.
- Describe the characteristics of eustress and its affects.
- Describe the sources of stress.
- Articulate reasons that stress is inherent in almost every activity associated with policing.
- Explain the rationale supporting a "fully functioning person."
- Identify the use of the Social Readjustment Rating Scale.
- Explain the influence of the police subculture upon getting help for stressed officers.
- Describe the priorities of most police agencies toward stress control.
- Define CYA initiatives and describe its importance among officers.

CYA
Distress
Emotional-focused
   strategies
Eustress

External stressors
Fully functioning person
Homeostasis
Internal responses
Mediators

Problem-focused strategies
Stimulus
Stressor
Social Readjustment
   Rating Scale

INTRODUCTION

Previously it was revealed that the police and the public have a mutual responsibility toward policing, and each officer responds differently to similar situations, although every officer is responsible for his or her own behavior, which includes coping with stress. However, police executives do not create police policy and the day-to-day routines of officers is distinctively different from that of policy, which promotes the task of redefining their own individual performance to match police mandates. Police policy and crime control imagery are distinctively different than the operational realities of policing and police practice, producing an imbalance or inconsistency that furthers officer stress levels. The implications are that law enforcement professionalism is flawed, and the police organization is the leading source of stress among officers, the central theme of this work. Finally, the promise of seeing the big picture reveals that commanders and officers can find organizational and individual resolutions toward stress control and at the same time enhance the quality of police services.

Chapter 2 describes external stressors and internal responses to those stressors or events. It provides a definition of stress, and explains the necessity of stress toward individual development because stress is linked to almost every human experience. Problem-focused and emotional-focused coping strategies are examined. Eustress (positive stress) and distress (negative stress) are equally taxing on an individual's well-being, and it is explained that stress is pervasive in every police activity. It explains that the sources of stress come from daily living experiences, personality types, and job-related sources, for example, the job and management of the organization. Since the author, among others, is optimistic about individuals becoming "fully functional persons," it is articulated that learning to deal with life's events would help toward that aim. The Social Readjustment Rating Scale is provided to aid in better understanding how events might lead to stress. However, it is noted in the chapter that police organizations do little to inoculate their personnel from stressful encounters and take few steps to remedy organizational initiatives responsible for stress. Also many officers feel best served by an initiative referred to as "cover your ass" (CYA) because of a lack of adequate support from state officials, town hall managers, policymakers, the public, and sometimes even police executives.

EXTERNAL STRESSORS AND INTERNAL RESPONSES

An important fact to know is how stress works: it includes *external stressors* (an event or circumstance or what psychologists call stimuli) and *internal reactions* (response). That is, for every action (stimuli) there is a reaction. The term *stressor* or stimuli serves as a "trigger" for a response (for occupational stressors, see Chapter 3).[1] Normally, stressors are located outside (external) of the individual and "are translated within the individual through a myriad of causal associations and manipulated by the individual through various coping mechanisms and personality propensities, and are manifested outwardly into various behavioral tendencies and physical reactions."[2] Every stressor produces a reaction and those reactions are often different from person to person. The factors that influence whether an external stressor will serve as a stressor (since not everyone might see an event as a stressful situation) and specific responses are often referred to as *mediators* or moderator variables (which serves as a conduit to other problems).[3] Both the trigger or stressor and the response or mediators are relevant factors in the production of stress. Stress builds from reactions since it is not really only external nor internal, but both at the same time.[4] There are coping initiatives that many officers employ when confronted by a stressor.

COPING STRATEGIES

Coping refers to an individual's efforts to modify, redefine, or to tolerate a stressor. Individuals including police officers cope with stressors in many ways, yet their efforts can be characterized as problem-focused or emotional-focused strategies.[5]

Problem-focused strategies are aimed at changing the stressor itself.[6] This process can include reality testing: assessing what is going on in the altercation or circumstance in oneself and being realistic about the options, resources, and limitations an officer might have to meet the challenge. Although most traditional writers on police stress report on the fight or flight options, years of experience among officers is telling of a third response, which can be called a freeze or ignore option. That is, sometimes officers fight, flee, freeze, or ignore the situation when confronted in an altercation. For example, an officer not getting along with his partner might request a change, or try to talk their difficulties out, or might, if this third perspective has any validity, the officer might ignore his partner during every interaction. Others might look for the benefits of his or her partner and concentrate on those benefits. That is, this officer is performing a problem-focused strategy to reduce a stressor's effect.

Emotional-focused strategies are attempts to manage the emotional effects of the stressor. This strategy can include "defense mechanisms" such as denial or projection of blame.[7] Simply explained, defense mechanisms are psychoanalytic or Freudian constructs created to help explain individual responses to anxiety. They have been borrowed from their original context to help explain police officer coping strategies. Defense mechanisms are supposedly "unconscious" responses that reveal that an officer is not consciously aware of the use of them. They are also individualized, suggesting that different officers use different sets of defense mechanisms. Finally, it is important to express that an emotional-focused coping strategy is part of normal behavior, suggesting that everybody uses them. However, defense mechanisms can become a problem because the body will respond with "a mind of its own" if serious stress or distress remains unchecked (more on this thought later in the chapter). Humor is often an emotional strategy used among officers, as well as cynicism (a cynic is an individual disposed to rail or find fault and shows a disposition to disbelieve in the sincerity or goodness of human motives and actions and a wont to express this by sneers and sarcasm).

Truth in the perception of control of an altercation or circumstance (rather than actual control) is an important dynamic in determining whether a stressor will result in harm or good. A better coping strategy might relate to knowing that you cannot control certain stressors (such as destruction from a hurricane or a hostage situation) of an actual situation, therefore it is advantageous to focus on the control of the way you experience it or think about it. For instance, in the chaotic wake of Hurricane Katrina in the summer of 2005, there were accusations of euthanasia or the mercy killings of patients by the doctors at Memorial Hospital in New Orleans.[8] It was believed that doctors were so overwhelmed by their stressful experiences of Katrina that they administered overdoses of morphine to make the lives of their patients more comfortable. Factually, perception of control where control is impossible can lead to frustration, a learned helplessness,[9] and the potential of the demise of others, as indicated above.[10] The individual who attempts to control an uncontrollable event tends to use a pessimistic explanatory style to evaluate situations in his or her life. There are advantages to both optimistic and pessimistic explanatory styles. Certain jobs call for an optimistic outlook, such as policing, mental health care, and education. Other jobs, such as accounting or quality control, call for a pessimistic outlook.

Part of a discussion of optimistic coping devices includes predictability—a crystal ball, if you will. Hiring capable young men and women who can be trained, retrained, evaluated, and reevaluated so that they know what to expect and what is expected in a stressful situation even if what happens is negative. That's a good starting point, but there's so much more because the warning signs are not always present and knowledge and technology are replaced by (hopefully) better knowledge and technology. Officers who employ positive coping strategies rather than pessimistic problem-focused strategies (which can include defensive mechanisms, denial, and projection, at an extreme) are more capable of delivering quality police services. Also optimistic coping skills help an officer to control stress primarily because they have learned firsthand in the lives of their coworkers and constituents that stress is accumulative—it keeps building off of itself until suddenly a cop or the coroner is called.

STRESS IS CUMULATIVE

Stress is cumulative in nature. The more a stressor is acted upon, the more stress levels increase. But what must also be emphasized is that work-related stress and family-related stress are inherently interconnected and an officer who is stressed cannot easily compartmentalize him- or herself and separate one from the other.[11] Pessimistic strategies do little toward good mental health or toward recovery. For example, an officer says, "When I check in at night, drivers still do road rage and others still beat the crap out of others. So I'm not going to get myself all worked up over nothing when I'm on the job."

Nonetheless, not every individual reacts to every stressor, nor do they react the same way as others. This thought is congruent with Herbert Benson and other medical specialists who study stress. Their findings are that a stressor and its outcome can produce more stress.[12] Think of it this way: the dynamics of the stressor and the response of the individual are both crucial factors in manufacturing more stress. The patrol officer who says he will look the other way when confronted by road rage and people who assault others could be opening himself to dereliction of duty offenses, civil suits, and the knowledge that maybe he could have saved someone on the road. Benson might tell us to look for that officer every night in the local hangout with a tear in his eye, as he wonders why bad things happen to him.

One interpretation of Benson's perspective is that an actual stressor itself does not necessarily cause health or other problems. What does cause problems are other factors such as (1) how events are interpreted, (2) whether behavior is changed because of an interpretation, and (3) initiatives used (or not used) to cope with stressful experiences.

Another implication is that no single method of treatment works on every individual because each person responds differently to similar stressors. Ralph Waldo Emerson resonates this thought: "What lies behind us and what lies before us are small matters compared to what lies within us." How we respond to a stressor can far outweigh the stressor's significance itself. This thought should reveal that the public views stressful events differently, too. It is difficult for a new police recruit to learn that an individual who has had little exposure to a life-threatening situation actually believes he or she is close to death even when they're not, but they respond as though they were close to death's gate, complicating the task of responding to their needs.

A stress expert reports that the environment includes the "social situation, a variety of individual variables such as personality, genetics, background, culture and the like.[13] We have then, a model that begins with events, filtered through the unique makeup and experiences of the individual, and expressed in a variety of outcomes."[14] Therefore, the terms stressor, stressful event, or trigger refer to what is called the *stimulus* or roots of the presumed cause of stress, and the term stress reaction or stress response describes the behavior or physical changes that occur. Finally in this regard, the general term is called stress, which typically describes the entire process. However, bear in mind that stress produces more stress and is cumulative, as previously mentioned.

DEFINITION OF STRESS

There are many ways to define stress. One source defines stress as a mental, emotional, or physical strain caused by anxiety or overwork (more on strain in Chapter 3). Stress also is[15]:

a. An applied force or system of forces that tends to strain or deform a body.
b. The internal resistance of a body to such an applied force or system of forces.
c. A mentally or emotionally disruptive or upsetting condition occurring in response to adverse external influences and capable of affecting physical health, usually characterized by increased heart rate, a rise in blood pressure, muscular tension, irritability, and depression.
d. A stimulus or circumstance causing such a condition.

Stress can escalate symptoms related to blood pressure or depression. Medical doctors utilize physiological issues related to stress whereas psychologists focus on its cognitive impact and sociologists link their descriptions with environmental concerns. Nonetheless, a reasonable definition of stress can be defined through this generic description:

> *Stress* can be described as the wear and tear our bodies and minds experience as we react to physical, psychological, and environmental changes in our daily lives.

Herbert Benson says that stress is the term used to define the body's automatic physiological reaction to circumstances that require behavioral adjustment.[16] Confronted by a threat—physical or emotional, real or imagined—the hypothalamus causes the sympathetic nervous system to release epinephrine and norepinephrine (also known as adrenaline and noradrenaline) and other related hormones.[17] When released into the body, these messengers propel us into a state of arousal (your metabolism, heart rate, blood pressure, breathing rate, and muscle tension all increase). This is known as the fight-or-flight response, as named by Walter B. Cannon of the Harvard Medical School at the turn of the last century. Therefore, "stress is a physical, chemical, or emotional factor that causes bodily or mental tension resulting from factors that tend to alter an existing equilibrium."[18] Stress takes us out of our comfort zone and forces us to change, adapt, freeze, or ignore a circumstance or event.

"Forces us" might be too strong a description but the biological concept of homeostasis helps put this idea into perspective. *Homeostasis* is the process that keeps all bodily functions, such as breathing and blood circulation, in balance.[19] The body (and our mind) automatically seeks a balance or comfort within our social and physical environment. To see homeostasis at work, run in place for a few minutes and then sit down. The running stresses your body, temporarily putting it out of balance. After you sit for a while, regardless of what you want to happen, physically your body returns to normal.

THE NECESSITY OF STRESS

In general terms, stress is the nonspecific "response of the body to any demand."[20] Just staying alive creates a demand on the body for life-maintaining energy and balance. We're hungry, we eat; we want money, we work; we're lonely, we meet people; we feel unsafe, we seek protection. This description reveals that stress is a fundamental part of being alive.[21] Therefore, stress can be described as any demand placed on an individual, especially change. The change (stimulus) in the weather, light to dark, dry to wet, close to open, happy to sad, truth to lies, intimacy to rejection solicits a response from each of us. Of course, responses vary depending on the individual, as a similar event or situation is experienced differently by each of us.[22] This is an important idea and we will often return to this perspective throughout this work. You should be getting the message that stress is all around us and it can be both detrimental and beneficial to ordinary development. That is, both good stress (eustress) and bad stress (distress) contribute to every person on this planet, almost every minute of their existence.

EUSTRESS AND DISTRESS

Robert M. Yerkes and John D. Dodson first described the relationship between stress and performance in 1908.[23] And Hans Selye notes that without stress, there could be no life.[24] Just as "distress" produces disease, it seems plausible that good stressors, or eustress, promote wellness.

Distress refers to the "bad" type of stress or opposite of eustress, and occurs when we have excessive adaptive demands placed upon us.[25] This occurs when the demands on us are so great that they lead to physical and mental damage with or without our contributions. Distress is damaging, excessive, or pathogenic (disease producing). Said another way, distress goes beyond a mental process as one might think, and produces both psychological and physiological products, and for that reason, coping, controlling, and preventing negative stressors should become a priority.

However, at appropriate levels, stress can increase both efficiency and performance. For example, before an athletic event, competitors involuntarily elicit the stress response. Before an examination, test-takers exhibit increased heart rate and blood pressure.[26] Then, too, in today's high-powered competitive environment, the stimulus of the stress response (fight, flight, or freeze) is essential to success. (Yes, sometimes freezing or doing nothing might be part of the solution; experienced officers learn that timing has a lot to do with outcomes during an altercation.) Stress is essential for the productivity and well-being of personnel, too. Workers in a variety of jobs experience positive stress or eustress, which can be derived from a job promotion, for instance. *Eustress* can be defined as a pleasant or curative stress. Often, eustress can provide an individual with a competitive edge in performance and as stress and/or anxiety increase, so do performance and efficiency. For instance, Officer David Murphy, from Newbury, Massachusetts, says that stress pushes him to work harder to achieve higher goals and provide quality police service.[27]

Yet this relationship does not continue indefinitely. When too many situations demand adjustment, stress exceeds a threshold. This stress overload contributes to diminishing performance, efficiency, and even health. This relationship is known as the Yerkes-Dodson Law and can be referred to as negative stress or distress, as Figure 2.1 reveals.

The "eu" or "dis" refer to the stressor (source of the stress) not the affect of the stressor. However, both can be equally taxing on an individual's body and mind. Once more, all stress is cumulative in nature and as such can snowball into serious problems, as previously mentioned—it's cumulative in nature. Stress produces more stress and alters the psychological and physiological well-being of an individual, which can include his or her intimate and working relationships, promotion potentials, and ability to deliver quality police services.

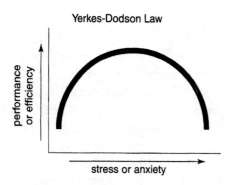

FIGURE 2.1
Adapted from Herbert Benson.[28]

SOURCES OF STRESS

It could be said that stress commonly arises from uncertainty, lack of control, pressure, and an unsafe or unprofessional social environment. Sources of stress are found in a person's daily living, personality, and job.[29]

Daily living or general sources of stress. Common stress agents of daily living are changing relationships, expectations of relationships unfulfilled, a lifestyle that is inconsistent with values (unfulfilled living arrangements), money problems (credit-card debt), loss of self-esteem (falling behind professionally), and fatigue or illness (poor diet, lack of sleep, or lack of exercise).

Personality as a source of stress. Psychologists often divide individuals into two types: type A personality, an aggressive, hyperactive "driver" who tends to be a workaholic; and type B personality, who has the opposite characteristics. The type A person is more likely to experience high stress levels more often than the type B person, probably because this individual gets into more activity.[30] There are two cardinal features of type A personality: "time urgency or time-impatience, and free-floating (all pervasive and ever-present) hostility."[31] For instance, Arthur talks fast, at the rate of 140 words per minute or more. His voice is grating, harsh, irritating, excessively loud, and just generally unpleasant. His posture is tense, with abrupt, jerky movement. Every few minutes, he raises his eyebrows in a tic-like fashion. Likewise, every few minutes, he raises or pulls back one or both shoulders in a tic-like fashion.[32] Also the free-floating hostility includes a constant apprehension of future disasters (which is not a symptom of an anxiety disorder or depressive disorder). Additionally, as we have already discussed, with coping strategies this individual tends to utilize a pessimistic explanatory style more often than an optimistic explanatory style like the type B personality, who tends to be more relaxed than a type A personality.

Personality type is a modified version of the Jenkins Activity Survey. This survey was originally formulated to detect behaviors that lead to heart attacks. Type A personality generally refers to hard workers who are often preoccupied with schedules and the speed of their performance. Type B personalities may be more creative, imaginative, and philosophical. The test consists of 30 multiple-choice items. Scores range from 35 to 380. Type A is associated with a high score whereas Type B is associated with a low score. (Click onto their website and take the survey, if you wish, at http://www.psych.uncc.edu/pagoolka/TypeA-B-intro.html)

Job-related sources of stress. While on the job, there are six possible sources of stress:

1. The job itself: for example, delivering police services.
2. The subculture of personnel, managers, and clients: police subculture
3. The managerial style or management: hierarchical top-down directives based on intimation rather than values. Autocratic managers

who seek no input from personnel, fail to keep personnel informed, and disregard objective processes.

4. The employing organization: for example, the Boston Police Department.

5. The policy or rules of the organization: for example, *Massachusetts Criminal Law and Motor Vehicle Handbook* and *The Boston Police Handbook for Personnel.*

6. The "lack of fit" of an individual with the police job or the organization: for example, a passive female who believes everyone has a redeeming quality might be less efficient as a sexual assault investigator for the Boston Police Department than an aggressive female who doesn't herself see anyone with redeeming qualities.

STRESS AND POLICE WORK

Contemporary police officers must function as counselors, social workers, psychologists, negotiators, and investigators, as well as traditional police officers, and then they have to go home to their families and friends.[33] What is known about stress is that it is inherent in almost every activity associated with police work, from training to a typical "Terry" stop. Job stress or a stressor such as making a high warrant arrest can have hidden consequences aside from making the arrest.[34] That is to say that "of all governmental functions, the policing function is arguably the most visible, the most immediate, the most intimately involved with the well-being of individuals and the health of communities."[35]

"Police stress is found wherever there are functioning police officers. In our [FBI Nationwide Law Enforcement Training Needs Assessment] surveys, the activity statement, 'handle personal stress,' has consistently been rated a top priority activity for all types and sizes of state and local law enforcement agencies," says James T. Reese, a unit chief of the FBI.[36]

In Chapter 3, there are 10 reasons provided why the work police officers perform is different from other occupations, but for now what is relevant to this discussion is that the noble profession of policing is constantly changing and new strategies of policing are at many stages of development from those in planning to implementation to those being fazed out. Many influences are brought to bear on police service and implementation efforts of new strategies.[37]

Many sources of stress contribute to police officer stress[38]: organizational influences such as conflict with regulations, poor supervisor support, career frustrations, the war on crime, and the hierarchal paramilitary organizational structure (Chapter 3, 4, and 7); critical incident stressors such as harming or killing of an innocent person or another police officer (Chapter

5); and general work stressors such as excessive paperwork, shift work, job overload, and public, media, and judicial criticism (Chapter 6).

As one police sergeant put it, "It's unrealistic for police officials to think that they can train us one way and expect us to perform another way. For instance, the amassing grace of police departments, community policing, is actually babysitting."[39] Another officer adds, "We're the agency of last-resort. Everybody with an ass-itch dials 9-1-1."[40] This thought is consistent with Boston Police Department records: of 625,000 emergency 9-1-1 calls, over two-thirds did not justify any police investigation in 2004.[41] Finally, in this regard, what we know about cops is that many veteran officers (including my dad) is that they typically have the idea that they should handle their problems of stress with laughter and fun at the local bar until eventually, they're drinking alone in their patrol cars and at home.[42]

STRESS AND CHANGE

Changes in the lives of individuals affect their behavior to some degree or another. That is, psychological, sociological, and economic changes in the lifestyles of most individuals shape their behavior. Some experts say that when those changes are favorable, the entire personality of an individual can be altered. For instance, Carl Rogers talks about a *fully functioning person*.[43] In part, his perspective implies that people have within themselves the resources for self-understanding in order to enhance self-concept, attitudes, and self-directed behavior.[44] Rogers holds that human nature is basically good and he sees the positives of people and is optimistic about them in the sense that most of us want to do our best. We have a natural drive toward self-actualization, which means achievement of our full potential. Yet, without stress, it is unlikely that any of us can effectively reach our full potential. How different is this from the sexual assault investigator mentioned previously? It's not. But an optimistic strategy, if employed at all, would be better suited for the officer him- or herself or the victim.

This assumption is an accentuated centerpiece consistent with the thoughts of this author and, equally important, is considered an objective or goal that most of us strive toward. But, should stressors dominate an individual's daily routines, it would seem that he or she might not have an opportunity to take advantage of eustress helping him or her move toward becoming fully functional. There are other contributors that will lend support to similar thoughts, yet utilizing Rogers's notion, let's look into ourselves. Isn't it true that many of us have experienced various levels of change or stress and when those events have happened, we just aren't ourselves and our behavior is different than when we weren't experiencing distress? Which changes in your life altered your behavior? And how many of those changes affected where you are now, as we speak, and will contribute to the decisions you make tomorrow? The Social Readjustment Rating Scale can guide us to better understand how stressors alter both present and future behavior.

SOCIAL READJUSTMENT RATING SCALE

The *Social Readjustment Rating Scale (SRRS)* was the first instrument of its kind to focus on identifying and quantifying stressful life events.[45] Although you might disagree with the variables and measurements used, its importance lays in the notion that each of the items produce different levels of stress that have the potential of accumulating as an individual experiences other life events. This device should be used as a guide. Numerous studies have demonstrated that people with high scores on a SRRS-type scale have more illnesses than those with low scores.

Here's how it works. The amount of life stress a person has experienced in a given period of time is measured by the total number of life change units (LCUs). These LCUs result from the addition of the values shown in the right column associated with the events that the person has experienced during the target time period.

The original creators of SRRS were able to correlate with some accuracy, they say, the number of stress points a person accumulated in any 2-year period. For example, death of a spouse results in 100 stress points, divorce results in 73 points, and so on (See table 2.1). As you can see, getting married is almost as stressful as getting fired from your job.

> The results show that more than 250 points within a 2-year period is likely to be followed by a life-threatening illness; 150 points by an illness that may be serious, but not life-threatening; with 20–50 points, recurrent bronchitis, cold sores, or other illnesses may result.

Disadvantages of a SRRS depends on the age of the person taking it and the standards of the day, which in itself suggests that Americans continually expect change. See how many items you might update or change the items listed. This scale does not include an individual's perception of life events. Each of us experience an event or stressor in a different way. For instance, some who have experienced divorce have a different perspective about its outcome. Divorce could represent a great relief such as given a second chance to start life over again, whereas others view it as the end of the world. This is to say that for every action there is a reaction and that reaction depends on the individual experiencing the event or stimuli (action) or stressor. What can be said is that stimuli produce a different response from different people, de-

TABLE 2.1 SOCIAL READJUSTMENT RATING SCALE[46]

Life Event	LCU	Life Event	LCU
1. Death of spouse	100	23. Son or daughter leaving or returning home	29
2. Divorce	73	24. Trouble with in-laws	29
3. Marital separation	65	25. Outstanding personal achievement	28
4. Jail term	63	26. Spouse begins or starts work	26
5. Death of a close family member	63	27. Begin or end school	26
6. Personal injury or major surgery	53	28. Change in living conditions	25
7. Marriage	50	29. Revision of personal habit	24
8. Fired from job	47	30. Conflict with employer	23
9. Marital or intimate-other reconciliation	45	31. Change in work hours or conditions	20
10. Retirement	45	32. Change in residence	20
11. Change in health of family member	44	33. Change in schools	20
12. Pregnancy	40	34. Change in recreation	19
13. Long-term sex difficulties or dysfunction	39	35. Change in religious activities	19
14. Gain of a new family member	39	36. Change in social activities	18
15. Business readjustments	39	37. Loan less than $50,000	17
16. Change in financial state or bills unable to pay	38	38. Change in sleeping habits	16
17. Death of a close friend	37	39. Change in number of family get-togethers	15
18. Change to different line of work	36	40. Change in eating habits	13
19. Change in number of arguments with spouse	35	41. Vacation	13
20. Mortgage over $50,000	31	42. Holidays	12
21. Foreclosure of mortgage	30	43. Minor violations of the law	11
22. Change in responsibility at work	29		

pending on the person as opposed to the event. For many, they experience both positive and negative aspects of this and other phenomena.

INOCULATING OFFICERS

Little is done to inoculate new police officers against the poisonous effects of negative stress.[47] Less is done to alter police models to curb stress. Complicating the issue, most police officers avoid stress guidance because it is often construed within the police subculture as an individual weakness suggesting that an officer is untrustworthy to back up other officers.[48]

It should be clear that policing, at least in the United States, is a "macho" culture, dominated by white heterosexual males or at least the dominant traits representing those individuals.[49] The perception of danger and a display of things such as courage, strength, and bravado are at the core of a reliable police officer's description. It is within this perception that comradely fosters a "we versus them" mentality in a traditional police subculture. Much of this thought lacks empirical support in the literature, a thought congruent with many researchers such as Hans Toch and Katherine W. Ellison[50]; however, among the ranks of most cops, a label of "weakness" dies hard and those with the label have difficulty in continuing working and personal relationships with other cops.[51] John Crank offers the following example: five federal officers confronted eight armed tax protesters in an incident in North Dakota.[52] After a gunfight two of the officers were killed and two more received incapacitating injuries. A supervisor subsequently helped one survivor receive individual professional assistance. The arrangement was done covertly because personnel policy limited agency assistance to adequate time off, which consists of 30 days of administrative leave at most. The fees for the counseling were charged to the officer's private insurance carrier to avoid detection. When it became known that the officer had been counseled during his recuperation period, he was tarnished and labeled as "weak." Those close to the agent drifted from him for fear of them accepting his weakness. The stigma of being "weak" haunted the officer until he retired, 4 years later. Crank says that "management's exposure of the officer's counseling obstructed the psychological recovery of the officer and contributed directly to his early retirement."[53]

Additionally, from the ranks of the Boston Police Department, two officers interviewed for this book told a similar story to the one above about "one of their own" who sought clinical help to deal with a gunfight that had occurred while the officer was off-duty.[54] At first, some on his shift respected his decision to seek help but then as the officer continued his visits, many officers pulled away from him on the street, in the locker room, and during inservice training, including shooting sessions. The officer felt isolated and was reassigned to a desk job because he couldn't get along with other cops. When the officers being interviewed were asked what should he have done to help himself after the gunfight, they responded, "He should'a braved it out, like the rest of us." One implication is that the police subculture is a powerful entity.

The police organization compounds stress control by blaming the officer for his or her condition, which in turn reduces the officer's chances of promotion, particularly when assigned a desk job during treatment.[55] Thus, even an attempt to deal with it has cumulative results toward assignments and future promotions.

BUSINESS AS USUAL

Scholars and police practitioners agree that the police organization takes few steps to remedy organizational initiatives responsible for stress among officers.[56] When policymakers, interest groups, and the public push for organizational change, it is to update strategy or make officers more accountable. They argue that police organizational change means to identify and implement protocols and strategies to increase police officer accountability.[57] For instance, to enhance the quality of police service, reduce police officer civil and criminal liability, and influence quality of life experiences of police constituents, improve the cultural competence of officers by hiring better quality candidates and more officers of color.[58] While some merit could be given to these recommendations, without changing the organizational structure that affects street cop uncertainty and stress, the only behavior that is likely to be changed is the intellectual level of lip service officers provide their superiors. For instance, when state police officers were polled about stress, findings show that 66% of the participants reported that the source of their stress was associated with issues about their commanders and less than one-third reported that their job was dangerous. The researcher's recommendation was to develop another study "implementing a stress reduction program that will fit the needs of Department of State Police personnel and be more likely to be used by them."[59] If someone were thinking appropriately, a study of the department would have been recommended as opposed to a study of personnel.

One researcher characterizes organizational ventures to focus on officers as the preoccupation with the symptoms of a problem rather than with the problem itself.[60] Another writer elegantly advises that organizational preoccupation with the officer and not the system represents "the pervasive presence of bullshit," and "the bullshit is as thick in medium-sized departments as it is in large ones."[61] Finally in this regard, Van Maanen, after an evaluation of officer versus commander scenarios, uses the terms "suspicion" and "betrayal."[62] But Van Maanen says that a single word can best describe the attitudes of street cops toward management. You guessed it—"bullshit." Most officers distance themselves from their commanders or management because it is felt that the liberal nature of their commanders would be the path to an officer's destruction.

How strange that most observers sing praises of the police organization and their commanders and forget the street cops who are ordered to change social disorder—"use the ways you've been taught and follow orders," as one commander states in confidence. It may be for this reason CYA (cover your ass) is a popular initiative among police officers. *CYA* can be defined as a behavioral response least likely to result in disciplinary action or managerial attention.[63] Some believe that it is influenced by cultural predispositions, although that hardly seems likely because the police subculture promotes its use, and at some law academies there are courses on CYA. But part of its perspective is to pace your work so as not to stand out from others. How does CYA work? "Do not trust bosses to look out for your interests," or "Always cover your ass."[64] Since officers accept this strategy, it reveals that a gap likely exists between policy and practice. Then, too, most commanders were street cops at one time because command is usually a matter of seniority. One way to explain the popularity of CYA initiatives is to say that officers see their administrators as being preoccupied with bureaucracy efficiency (controlling the street cops) as opposed to controlling the problem of crime. Make arrests, reduce response time, control crime—no matter the method. "The public wants to see us making arrests of gang members and they don't care how we do it," said a commander in Chicago. Of course, it is not necessarily the commander taking the suspect into custody, it's the street cop, and he or she is always subject to the stress of the job and litigation issues (more on this later) of the job—not the commander.

It's hard to understand why even the precepts are strongly practiced as they are nor can the public fully capture the full sentiment officers hold toward commanders or the regulations and rules that dictate police performance. For instance, in a study specifically conducted for this book, of 558 participants:

> Seventy-five percent of the officers polled from New England to the Gulf of Mexico report that they would rather be tried by 12 than carried by 6.

What is interesting about this finding is that other data from the same sample show that the reason these participants became a law enforcement officer was first because they wanted to help people and second, they wanted to put away bad guys. Using force against violators was not a priority among this sample, and probably among most officers across the country. This last finding is consistent with data provided by the Bureau of Justice Statistics, which shows that among the few officers who used force to take a suspect into custody, pepper spray was used most often.[65] However, it's curious why there is a consensus among the 558 officers polled that it is better to be tried by 12 than carried by 6.

In keeping with the above thoughts, it should be indicated that the officers polled for this study might respond differently if they were employed in

Police Use of Force: Collection of National Data

A pilot test of the Police–Public Contact Survey (administered as a supplement to the BJS National Crime Victimization Survey) gives results of 6,421 interviews (presenting an estimated 216 million people) with U.S. residents age 12 or older representative of the U.S. population as a whole.

- The survey reports that about 21% of the residents (presenting an estimated 44.6 million contacts) age 12 or older had at least one face-to-face encounter with a police officer in 1996.
- Of these, 14 said that they were hit, pushed, choked, threatened with a flashlight, restrained by a police dog, threatened with or actually sprayed with chemical or pepper spray, threatened with a gun, or that they experienced some use of force.

Source: Bureau of Justice Statistics[66]

the West or Midwest region of the United States. However, in my experience of studying many departments in those regions, the responses might vary, yet it is expected that many of the stressful experiences that affect officers in Boston are also experienced in Phoenix, but maybe at different degrees. That said, the historical experiences of each jurisdiction, resources, professional levels of management and policymakers, and the socioeconomic levels of the populations policed should bring to the table differences in individual police attitudes.

DEPARTMENTAL CHANGE

When police organizations change it usually means they identify and implement protocols and strategies to increase police officer accountability such as improve the cultural competence of officers by hiring better-quality candidates and more officers of color. While some merit could be given to these recommendations, without changing the organization that affects street cop uncertainty and stress, the only behavior that is likely to be changed is the intellectual level of lip service new officers provide their superiors, mainly because many supervisors tend to blame individual officers for any problems those officers experience such as dealing with crisis points.

DEALING WITH CRISIS POINTS

Most often there is a tendency to focus on stress treatment among individual officers or what can be referred to as a "person-centered" approach. While that approach might be effective, it does not address the underlying organizational problems that form the basis of much of the stress experienced by officers.[67] However, there is a combined responsibility for dealing with stress, especially once it gets to a crisis point resting with the police department and specific officer concerned.[68]

MILITARY AND EMERGENCY SERVICES

Experts on military and emergency occupations, which includes law enforcement officers, recognize five traumatic stress disorders[69]:

1. Acute stress disorder (posttraumatic stress, consisting of overwhelming fear and revulsion). Posttraumatic stress is discussed in Chapter 3.
2. Conversion reaction (hysteria, the development of physical symptoms such as blindness or paralysis in response to stress).
3. Counterdisaster syndrome (excessive excitement and inappropriate overinvolvement). This topic is discussed in more detail in Chapter 5.
4. Peacekeepers' acute stress syndrome (rage, delusion, and frustration in response to atrocities).

5. Stockholm syndrome (identification by the victim with the perpetrators of violence).

This is not to say that police officers experience each of these traumatic disorders. This information is presented to guide your thoughts about traumatic stress and to prepare you for further discussions on these topics.

SUMMARY

This chapter describes external stressors and internal responses to those stressors or events. Stress was described as the wear and tear of our body's physiological reaction to circumstances that require behavioral adjustment. Stress is the nonspecific response of the body and mind to any demand because stress is a natural and normal part of life and it is positively and negatively linked to almost every human experience. Problem-focused coping and emotional-focused coping initiatives, which includes employment of defense mechanisms, were explained. The perception of control of an altercation or circumstance (rather than actual control) is an important dynamic in determining whether a stressor will result in harm or good. Eustress (positive stress) and distress (negative stress) are equally taxing on an individual's well-being, and it is described as pervasive in almost every police activity. The sources of stress come from daily living experiences, personality types, and job-related sources, such as the job and management of the organization. Many observers of human behavior share an optimistic feeling about individuals and want those individuals to become "fully functional," which is mentioned in this chapter. One way to accomplish this goal is through the Social Readjustment Rating Scale, which can help toward a better understanding of how events might lead to stress. It is explained that police agencies generally treat the victim or the officer and rarely alter those stressors (such as police strategies) that produce stress. While some merit could be given to these recommendations, without changing the organization that affects street cop uncertainty and stress, the only behavior that is likely to be changed is the intellectual level of lip service officers provide their superiors. For these and other reasons, a CYA strategy exists among many officers, which includes the attitude that it is better to be tried by 12 than carried by 6. Therefore, there is a combined responsibility for dealing with stress, especially before it promotes a crisis point.

WHAT WOULD YOU DO IF YOU WERE IN CHARGE?

"I am tough, or so I thought! After all, I am a member of SWAT. But, I guess I am not as tough as I thought. I have seen a lot of death and suffering in my seemingly short 6½ years as a police officer. Not only the average run of the mill, routine simple death investigations, but I am also a member of our Crash Investigation Team (CIT); therefore, I get to see twisted, mangled bodies all of the time. I thought all the exposure I have had would somehow make me impervious to the effects of the scenes. But I guess I was wrong! Having responded to three hangings in 3 weeks, and another attempt to kill oneself by carbon monoxide asphyxiation, I guess I'm not as tough as I thought! The first hanging, no big deal. The second, a lot tougher. I don't know why. Maybe because it was an 82-year-old man. . . .I mean, come on, why did he need to go and do that? As if death wasn't lurking around an unforeseen corner anyway? That night was very tough to sleep. Not only could I not get the face of the latest victim in my death parade out of my mind, but it brought back all the rest!"[70]

OFFICER KILLED IN SOUTH CAROLINA

At 5:30 P.M., on August 17, 2003, a 24-year-old deputy with the Greenville County Sheriff's Office was shot and killed while investigating a suspicious person. When an individual alerted the deputy that a burglary suspect was in a nearby trailer park, the deputy, who had over 2 years' law enforcement experience, requested assistance. He then proceeded in his patrol vehicle to the noted location, where he spotted the suspect in the parking lot. According to witnesses, the deputy approached the suspect and began to handcuff his right wrist. After struggling with the deputy, the suspect broke free and fled; a foot chase ensued. When the two came to a fence, the deputy apparently tried to use pepper spray on the suspect and then drew his service weapon, a .40-caliber semiautomatic handgun. Authorities believe that the suspect overpowered the deputy, took the handgun, and fatally shot the deputy on the left side of his head with the service weapon. The suspect then fled on foot. The 19-year-old male, who was a known drug user and under the influence of narcotics at the time of the incident, committed suicide with the officer's service weapon when SWAT/Tracking Teams located him the following morning.[71] Anything you would have done differently if you were this officer?

DISCUSSION QUESTIONS

1. Characterize the relevance of external stressors and internal responses. Supply examples of both and show how these variables are related.
2. Describe the three primary sources of stress and explain in what way stress can be curbed in each.
3. Define stress.
4. Describe the necessity of stress in everyday experiences. In what way is stress pervasive in everyone's lives?
5. Explain the coping initiatives employed by many individuals when confronted by a stressor.
6. Describe the characteristics of eustress and its effects on individuals. In your own experiences provide several examples that show eustress at work.

7. Articulate reasons supporting the notion that stress is inherent in almost every activity associated with policing. In what way do you agree with this perspective?

8. Explain the rationale supporting a "fully functioning person." In what way might a police officer who is not fully functioning deliver police service differently from others that are fully functioning?

9. Identify the use of the Social Readjustment Rating Scale. What events in your life are on the scale and which stressful events that you have experienced are not present?

10. Explain the relevance of the police subculture upon individual stress guidance avoidance. What other important incidents among officers might be influenced by the police subculture, too?

11. Describe the priorities of most police agencies toward stress control. In what way do you agree or disagree with their priorities?

12. Define CYA initiatives and describe its importance among officers. In what way do you see this strategy as a positive stress coping device among officers and in what way do you see this strategy as dangerous among constituents?

ENDNOTES

1. Katherine W. Ellison (2004). *Stress and the police officer*, 2nd ed. Springfield, IL: Charles C. Thomas. p. 6.

2. Judy Van Wyk (2005). Hidden hazards of responding to domestic disputes. In Heith Copes (Ed.), *Policing and stress* (pp. 41–54). Upper Saddle River, NJ: Prentice Hall. p. 42.

3. A "mediator" is a variable that is part of events from the cause to the effect, or the stimulus to the response, possibly contributing to an overall effect and it could be in a large way or a small way. For example, in this case of stress and illness, we could say that a mediator in illness could be the diet you had as a child or your family background. A moderator is almost the opposite in effect—it's something that has an immediate effect on the outcome by changing the experience and its effects. Support in times of anxiety can have a great effect on the outcome. It can either decrease or increase the factors involved. There exists a complicated and complex link between stress and illness. Mediators and moderators can swap to each other, depending on the effects the variables have had. Health habits may be altered by stress, thus causing illness, helping to outline a relationship between stress and illness. Coursework.com. "Defining the link between stress and illness." Retrieved online April 24, 2005: http://www.coursework.info/i/10654.html.

4. Judy Van Wyk (2005).

5. Katherine W. Ellison (2004). pp. 30–31.

6. Katherine W. Ellison (2004). P. 30.

7. See Sigmund Freud. Retrieved online March 4, 2006: http://www.freudfile.org/search.html

Denial is the reality that causes anxiety is simply not perceived. For example, a mother may unconsciously refuse to see her son's true character because it is too anxiety-arousing. The use of denial may lead to abrupt intrusion of reality into one's life. The mother, for example, may receive the news that her son has been arrested for armed robbery. Projection of blame refers to blaming others for the problem.

8. CNNews (2005, August). *Katrina*. Retrieved online March 4, 2006: http://transcripts.cnn.com/TRANSCRIPTS/0512/21/acd.01.html

9. The theory of learned helplessness provides a model for explaining depression, a state characterized by a lack of affect and feeling. Depressed people become that way because they learned to be helpless. Depressed people learned that whatever they do, it's futile. During the course of their lives, depressed people apparently learned that they have no control. Learned helplessness explains a lot of things, but there are exceptions, such as people who do not get depressed even after many bad life experiences. The depressed person thinks about a bad event in a more pessimistic way than a nondepressed person. This thinking is referred to as an "explanatory style," borrowing ideas from attribution theory. For more information, see Martin Seligman (1992). *Helplessness: On depression, development, and death*. New York: W. H. Freeman, p. 250.

10. Katherine W. Ellison (2004). p. 31.

11. Hans Toch (2001). *Stress in policing*. Washington, DC: American Psychological Association. p. 61.

12. Herbert Benson with Miriam Z. Klipper (1976). *The relaxation response*. New York: William Morrow. pp. 14–17.

13. Katherine W. Ellison (2004). pp. 4–7.

14. Katherine W. Ellison (2004). p. 6.

15. Dictionary.com. Retrieved online April 23, 2005: http://dictionary.reference.com/search?q=stress

16. Herbert Benson and Eileen M. Stuart (1992). *Wellness book: The comprehensive guide to maintaining health and treating stress related illness*. New York: Fireside.

17. Herbert Benson (2005). *The Mind Body Medical Institute*. Retrieved online March 4, 2006: http://www.mbmi.org/pages/mbb_s1.asp

18. J. F. Volpe (2000, October). A guide to effective stress management. *Law and Order*, 48(10), pp. 183–188.

19. Wayne W. Bennett and Karen M. Hess (2004). *Management and supervision in law enforcement*. Belmont, CA: Wadsworth. p. 403.

20. Hans Selye (1979). Stress, cancer, and the mind. In J. Tache, H. Selye, and S.B. Day (Eds.), *Cancer, stress, and death* (pp. 11–27). New York: Plenum. Also see Hans Selye. (1974). *Stress without distress*. Philadelphia: Lippincott.

21. Brain J. Gorman. (2003). *Attitude therapy for stress disorders*. Retrieved online April 24, 2005: http://www.stressdoctor.com/index.htm

22. Hans Selye (1979).

23. Herbert Benson (2005). Retrieved online April 13, 2005: http://www.mbmi.org/pages/mbb_s2.asp

24. Hans Selye (1979).

25. Psychology Glossary. Retrieved online March 4, 2006: http://www.alleydog.com/

26. Herbert Benson (2005).

27. Officer David Murphy, Newbury, Massachusetts Police Department, as reported to assistant researcher Kerri Mahoney, April 26, 2005.

28. Herbert Benson (2005).

29. Wayne W. Bennett and Karen M. Hess (2004). p. 405.

30. For information on how to change a type A personality, see Carol F. Lankton (1998, November 11). *Transforming a type A personality.* Retrieved on-line May 3, 2005: http://goinside.com/98/11/typea1.html

31. Vijai P. Sharma (2004). *Characteristics of "Type A" personality.* Cleveland, TN: Mind Publications. Retrieved online May 3, 2005: http://www.mindpub.com/art207.htm

32. Vijai P. Sharma (2004).

33. James T. Reese (2001, January). 6 keys to stress-free living. *The Associate*, pp. 14–17.

34. Bruce A. Arrigo and Karyn Garsky (2001). Police suicide: A glimpse behind the badge. In Roger G. Dunham and Geoffrey P. Alpert (Eds.), *Critical issues in policing: Contemporary Readings, 4th ed.* (pp. 664–680), Prospect Heights, IL: Waveland Press.

35. Jeremy Travis (2003, September). Plenary address. Paper presented at the Conference on International Perspectives on Crime, Justice, and Public Order, Budapest, Hungary.

36. James T. Reese (1991, May). Behavioral Science Services Unit, FBI, testimony presented to the 102nd Congress, Washington, DC.

37. Richard Quinney (1970). *The social reality of crime.* Boston: Little, Brown.

38. For a larger list of specific stressors among police, see J. M. Brown and E. A. Campbell (1994). Sources of occupational stress in the police. *Work and Stress*, 4, 305–318.

39. Personal communication with a Boston police officer, March 2, 2005.

40. Personal communication with a Boston police officer, March 2, 2005.

41. Boston Police Department: 2004 annual report. City of Boston.

42. Lynn Atkinson-Tovar (2003, September). The impact of repeated exposure to trauma. *Law and Order*, 51(9), 118–120.

43. Carl R. Rogers (1980). *A way of being.* Boston: Houghton Mifflin. Rogers is the founder of the human potential movement in the United States and he expands his ideas on personal growth.

44. To clarify self-concept, Rogers referred to it as an image of what we really are and included in this perspective is an ideal self, which is what we want to become. When the self-concept and ideal self contain similar dimensions, that individual may experience less distress than an individual who has a great discrepancy between the two. An individual is left with improving their self-concept or by changing their ideal self. Some of us recognize that this perspective is linked to humanistic psychology and also associated with Abraham Maslow's and the self-actualized personality. If this concept interests you, read Carl Rodgers or Abraham H. Maslow (1970). *Motivation and personality.* New York: Harper and Row.

45. Thomas H. Holmes, and Richard H. Rabe (1967). The Social Readjustment Rating Scale. *Journal of Psychosomatic Research*, 11, 213, 218.

46. Developed by the author for this textbook. You might take issue with the point system developed for this chart but it is provided to help you better understand that many life events have different effects on individuals and it is unlikely that

everyone would agree with the point value or all of the items provided in each category. Use this scale as a guide. The differences between the scale shown and the traditional scale relates to (19) mortgage amounts from $10,000 to $400,000 and the rewording of some of the items.

47. Robin Gershon (1999, March 23). *Public health implication of law enforcement stress.* Washington, DC: U.S. Department of Justice, National Institute of Justice. Video presentation.

48. John P. Crank (2004). *Understanding police culture.* Cincinnati, OH: Anderson. p. 351.

49. Katherine W. Ellison (2004). p. 71.

50. Hans Toch (2001). *Stress in policing.* Washington, DC: American Psychological Association. Katherine W. Ellison (2004). p. 71.

51. John P. Crank (2004). *Understanding police culture.* Cincinnati, OH: Anderson. p. 351.

52. John P. Crank (2004). p. 351.

53. John P. Crank (2004). p. 351.

54. Personal communication between two Boston police officers and the author. Both officers were also students of the author at the University of Massachusetts Boston.

55. Hans Toch (2001). *Stress in policing.* Washington, DC: American Psychological Association.

56. Geoffrey P. Alpert and Mark H. Moore (2001). Measuring policing performance in the new paradigm of policing. In Roger G. Dunham and Geoffrey P. Alpert (Eds.), *Critical issues in policing: Contemporary readers,* 4th ed. (pp. 238–254). Prospect Heights, IL: Waveland Press. Francis D'Ambra (2002). Community partnerships in affluent communities: The phantom menaces. In Dennis J. Stevens (Ed.), *Policing and community partnerships* (pp. 17–29). Upper Saddle River, NJ: Prentice Hall. Hans Toch (2001). Samuel Walker and Charles M. Katz (2004). *The police in America: An introduction,* 5th ed. Boston: McGraw Hill College. pp. 341–345.

57. Donna Hale and T. Bricker (2005). Police organizational change: Strategies for effective police management in the 21st century. In Roslyn Muraskin and Albert R. Roberts (Eds.), *Visions for change: Crime and justice in the 21st century* (pp. 390–404). Upper Saddle River, NJ: Prentice Hall.

58. For an excellent discussion on necessary cultural change, see David E. Barlow and Melissa Hickman Barlow (2000). *Police in a multicultural society: An American story.* Prospect Heights, IL: Waveland Press. pp. 8–10.

59. Sue Hunter (2002). Department of Transportation. State of Wisconsin. Retrieved May 18, 2004: http://www.dot.wisconsin.gov/library/research/docs/briefs/01-07dspstress-b.pdf

60. Peter K. Manning (2001). Policing and reflection. In Roger G. Dunham and Geoffrey P. Albert (EDs.) *Critical issues in policing: Contemporary readings,* 4th ed. (pp. 149–158), Prospect Heights, IL: Waveland Press.

61. John Crank (2004). p. 311. Consistent with this thought, see Elizabeth Reuss-Ianni (1983). *Two cultures of policing: Street cops and management cops.* New Brunswick, NJ: Transaction Books. p. 16.

62. John Van Maanen (1978). Kinsmen in repose: Occupational perspective of patrolman. In Peter K. Manning and John Van Maanen (Eds.), *Policing: A view from the street* (pp. 115–128). Santa Monica, CA: Goodyear Publishing.

63. John P. Crank (2004). *Understand police culture.* Cincinnati, OH: Anderson. p. 322.

64. Elizabeth Reuss-Ianni (1983), p. 16. Also see John Crank (2004). pp. 52–54.

65. Bureau of Justice Statistics (2000). *Law enforcement statistics.* Washington, DC: U.S. Department of Justice. Office of Justice Programs. Retrieved online July 14, 2004: http://www.ojp.usdoj.gov/bjs/lawenf.htm

66. Bureau of Justice Statistics (2000). Law enforcement statistics.

67. Peter Finn (1997, August). Reducing stress: An organization centered approach. *FBI Law Enforcement Bulletin.* Retrieved online March 4, 2006: http://www.fbi.gov/publications/leb/1997/aug975.htm

68. A. Gore (2002). *Operation manual for human beings.* Retrieved online February 7, 2005: http://pacificcoast.net/~rustym/manual/omch4.html

69. Douglas Paton (2005). Critical incidents and police officer stress. In Heith Copes (Ed.), *Policing and stress* (pp. 25–40). Upper Saddle River, NJ: Prentice Hall. John H. Pearn. (2001). *The victor as victim: Stress syndromes of operational service.* Retrieved online May 24, 2005: http://www.defence.gov.au/dpe/dhs/infocentre/publications/journals/NoIDs/ADFHealthNov99/ADFHealthNov99_1_1_30-32.pdf. Also see *Diagnostic and statistical manual of mental disorders,* 4th ed. (1994). Washington, DC: American Psychological Association. pp. 431–433. Note: APA does not discuss counterdisaster syndrome.

70. *Not as tough as I thought.* Anonymous. Retrieved online February 20, 2005: http://www.tearsofacop.com/police/ct/notastough.html

71. FBI (2005). *Law enforcement officers killed and assaulted 2003.* Retrieved online May 7, 2005: http://www.fbi.gov/ucr/killed/leoka03.pdf p. 43.

3

Occupational Stressors and Consequences

Success is to be measured not so much by the position that one has reached in life as by the obstacles which he has overcome while trying to succeed. Booker T. Washington

Learning Objectives

Once you have finished reading this chapter, you will be better prepared to:

- Define job stress.
- Describe the nature of stress and identify the fuel that powers job stress.
- Explain why personnel aptitudes are imperfect predictors of job performance.
- Characterize the key components of job strain.
- Identify two individual responses that influence the impact that job stress can play upon an individual.
- Identify economic and individual primary costs of job stress.
- Describe the dictum about "definition of the situation" and how it applies to our daily routines.
- Identify 10 reasons why policing is different from other jobs.
- Characterize stress and burnout issues.

- Characterize posttraumatic stress and its consequence.

- Explain worker at-risk of assault issues.

- Characterize managerial at-risk of assault issues.

- Discuss the high at-risk job victimization concerns, including warning signs, and appropriate techniques to minimize violence.

- Identify officer work tasks when they are victimized.

- Describe workers at-risk of homicide issues.

KEY TERMS

Acute stress disorder | Job strain | Posttraumatic stress
Burnout | Job stress | disorder
Cynicism | Occupational stressors | Voluntary resignation
Definition of the situation | Police stress syndrome

INTRODUCTION

Previously, external stressors (stimuli) and internal responses were described as a common reaction. That is, for every action (stimuli) there is a reaction (stress). Stress is the nonspecific response of the body and mind to any demand. Stress is a natural and normal part of living. Stress can be positively and negatively linked to almost every human experience. Sources of stress come from daily living experiences, personality types, and job-related sources. Becoming a "fully functional person" requires stress control. It was explained that police agencies generally blame and treat the stressed officer and rarely alter organizational factors, which act as stressors among officers. Therefore, once an officer is "cured" he or she is returned to the same organization that produced and reinforced the stress in the first place. For these and other reasons, a CYA strategy exists among many officers, which includes the attitude that it is better to be tried by 12 than carried by 6. It was explained that when individuals, including police officers, see the big picture they can enhance their delivery of quality service and broaden effective resolutions to curb stress. By looking at the big picture, stressors in the organization can be identified as opposed to blaming the victim.

Chapter 3 is about occupational stressors and their consequences. It explains that job stress is a result of the interaction of the worker and the conditions at work. It reports that 80% of all workers experience job stress, and that 50% of all workers say they need help to cope with it. The nature of stress is compounded because employees work longer and harder, all the while being regulated by a host of policies and regulations, which seems to affect their work capacity or outputs. There is little consistency in the workplace between hard work and financial remuneration, and police manager incomes are inconsistent with incomes of managers in other occupations.

Overall, the fuel that powers occupational stress (stimuli) lays in the reality that most employees have little control over their work environment. Job strain is shown as originating from the combination of high demands, low control (over job policies), low social support, and acts as a catalyst to reduce acquired skills of employees, or a dumbing down of the personnel. Because each individual responds differently to stressors regardless of the source of those stressors, and because each individual has a different way to resolve or control the psychological and physiological stress experienced, the impact that job stress can play upon an individual is different.

Absenteeism and low productivity are two primary outcomes of organizational stress and family dysfunctions and illness, among other consequences, are individual outcomes of stress. It is explained that because our bodies contain their own pharmacy, it responds to stimuli in a programmatic way. Burnout leading to posttraumatic stress can be characterized as the tendency to cope with stress by a form of distancing, or what can be described as physical or psychological avoidance.[1] The incredible number of workers, managers, and police officers assaulted and killed at the workplace is discussed, characterizing police officers as victims more often than any other occupational group.

JOB STRESS

Job stress results from the "interaction of the worker and the conditions of work," advises the National Institute for Occupational Safety and Health (NIOSH).[2] Occupational stress can be defined as the harmful physical and emotional responses that occur when the requirements of the job do not match the capabilities, resources, needs, or expectations of the worker. Some highlights that impact occupational stress are offered by the "Attitudes in the American Workplace VI" Gallup Poll, sponsored by the Marlin Company[3] and other sources, which reveals:

- 80% of all workers experience stress on the job.
- 50% of all workers want to learn how to manage stress.
- 42% of all workers say their coworkers need help to overcome stress.
- 14% wanted to strike a coworker in the past year, but didn't.
- 25% wanted to scream or shout because of their job stress.
- 10% of all workers fear they could become violent at work.
- 9% are aware of an assault or violent act in their workplace against workers.
- 18% experienced a threat or verbal intimidation in the past year at work.
- 82% of top executives say violent work incidents have increased in the past year.[4]

- 60% of the managers studied say disgruntled employees have threatened them.[5]
- 26% of all police officers on duty have been victimized.[6]

It goes without saying that when an individual is on the job (even if that person legally carries a weapon) that the threat of a clear and present danger has an effect on performance.[7] The concept of job stress is often confused with challenge, but these concepts, while similar in some respects, are not the same. Challenge energizes us psychologically and physically, and it motivates us to learn new skills and master our jobs. When a challenge is met, we feel relaxed and satisfied. Challenge is an important ingredient for healthy and productive work efforts. The importance of challenge in our work life is probably what people are referring to when they say some stress is good for you.

   Finding ways of coping with stress, especially among police officers, aids in the well-being of the individual and provides quality service opportunities that can bring the agency closer to its mission of public safety. If, for instance, making a routine patrol stop a stressed officer's body language shows signs of stress and uncertainty, it is possible that those signs could be read by a suspect and used in some way to the advantage of the suspect. In fact, you can count on it. The literature is well supplied with studies that provide quantitative analysis supporting the need to reduce occupational stress, especially among high-risk occupations such as emergency first-responders, which includes law enforcement, firefighters, social workers, and medical technicians who experience job stain.[8]

THE NATURE OF STRESS

Employees today,[9] regardless of their employer, tend to work longer and harder, all the while being regulated by a lot of policies and regulations; however, their work effort is lower than expected. In addition, there exists little consistency between occupational descriptions, hard work, and financial remuneration.[10] Furthermore, the income of police managers is inconsistent with typical managerial incomes in other occupations.[11] Overall, the fuel propelling occupational stress, regardless of the sophistication or promises of an employer, lays in the reality that most employees have little control of their work environment primarily because of ongoing change due in part to market influences, legal dictates, and organizational anorexia caused by layoffs, downsizing, and "rightsizing."[12] Increased feelings of helplessness and an inability to balance work demands and life demands increase stress among personnel.[13] Work in America is challenging, and the following generalities can guide your thoughts about the nature of stress:

Americans Work Longer

The International Labor Organization[14] reports that Americans put in the equivalent of an extra 40-hour workweek in 2000 as compared to the previous 10-year period. Japan had the record until 1995, but Americans work almost a month more than the Japanese and 3 months more than Germans. Then, too, 3 million years' worth of days—that's how many vacation days American workers do not bother to take in a given year.[15] Even when American workers should vacation, they choose not too.

Americans Work Harder

In a 2001 survey, nearly 40% of American workers described their work environment as most like a real-life survivor program.[16] That is, many items utilized by personnel to perform routine tasks might be unsafe, inoperative, or simply unavailable.[17] First-responders (usually cops) to emergencies such as traffic accidents, armed robberies, and domestic conflicts produce a host of different concerns than other workers. However, despite unsafe, inoperative, and unavailable equipment at work, finding ways to assure that at the end of a shift a worker is homeward bound is of utmost concern to many employees, especially cops.

American Personnel are Regulated by a Lot of Policies and Regulations

Although a gap in the literature exists relative to this perspective, there are implications that may support this perspective, such as the huge number of malpractice suits against professionals, which, according to some sources, are out of control and require government intervention to aid distressed doctors and lawyers among others to stay alive,[18] the number of class action suits against products,[19] and the stifling number of civil rights and other claims against law enforcement officers.[20] For instance, the city of Chicago has paid almost $100 million over a 5-year period to complainants who were wrongfully treated by Chicago cops.[21] Additionally, turnover and training practices of most companies suggest that either many employees cannot or will not comply with organizational policy or many concerns have their own style of operation (policy and rules).[22] One example comes from the Commonwealth of Massachusetts, *Department of Corrections Handbook for Correctional Personnel*.[23] In 2004, it contained 941 pages. In Germany, a similar handbook for its correctional personnel contained 112 pages, and in France, 210 pages.[24] Then, too, the Los Angeles Police Department's Personnel Book totals 921 pages, not counting the additional 200 pages dedicated to its appendix.[25]

Americans Work up to 55% of Their Capacity

The typical employee works longer and harder than other workers in other industrialized nations and during previous periods in American history, the typical worker works up to about 45% of his or her capacity.[26] This finding is consistent with results from a study that shows 75% of employees surveyed took care of personal responsibilities while on the job and 36% from the sample say personal responsibilities are a daily routine for them.[27] Most often, it takes 2 hours a day to complete personal business while at work.

Why would Americans put in more time and work harder, yet output efforts do not meet their work capacity? One implication is that personnel know how to look busy when being observed, but it also could relate to a study conducted almost 80 years ago.

Elton Mayo's Hawthorne study grew out of preliminary experiments at the Hawthorne plant in Chicago from 1924 to 1927 on the effect of light on productivity.[28] However, implications arising from his study changed American management techniques forever. Elton Mayo came to the following conclusions:

- The aptitudes of individuals are imperfect predictors of job performance. Although they give some indication of the physical and mental potential of the individual, the amount produced is strongly influenced by social factors.
- Informal organization affects productivity. The Hawthorne researchers discovered a group life among the workers. The studies also showed that the relations that supervisors develop with workers tend to influence the manner in which the workers carry out directives.
- Work-group norms affect productivity. The Hawthorne researchers were not the first to recognize that work groups tend to arrive at norms of what is "a fair day's work." However, they provided the best systematic description and interpretation of this phenomenon.
- The workplace is a social system. The Hawthorne researchers came to view the workplace as a social system made up of interdependent parts. The worker is a person whose attitudes and effectiveness are conditioned by social demands from both inside and outside the work plant. Informal groups within the work plant exercise strong social controls over the work habits and attitudes of the individual worker.
- The need for recognition, security, and sense of belonging is more important in determining workers' morale and productivity than the physical conditions under which he works.

The major finding of Mayo's study was that almost regardless of the experimental manipulation, worker production seemed to continually improve, or appeared to improve. One reasonable conclusion is that the workers were happy to receive attention from the researchers who expressed an interest in them, or they knew how to fool their supervisors. Originally, the study was expected to last 1 year, but since the findings were inexplicable when the researchers tried to relate the workers' efficiency to manipulated physical conditions, the project was incrementally extended to 5 years.

Other explanations concerning low worker output has to do with inadequate or poor management, unproductive organizational structures (both factors are the focus of this textbook on police officer stress), and incentives,[29] which includes income (especially because today's dollar buys far less than it did 10 years ago or even last year[30]). The U.S. Department of Labor's Bureau of Labor Statistics (BLS) reports on, among other things, the hourly and annual wages for wage and salary workers in 22 major occupational groups and in 770 detailed occupations.[31]

Table 3.1 shows the estimated number, hourly mean wages, and annual mean wages for various occupations. The BLS lists many more occupational groups than these chosen to demonstrate the disparity in income.[33] For instance, a review of the wages among 12 manager occupations, represents an estimated 4 million employees, shows a mean hourly wage of $41.00, producing a yearly annual mean wage of $116,000. The four business and financial operations occupations, representing approximately 1.8 million employees, shows a mean hourly wage of $27.00, producing an estimated $53,500 annual income. The region of the country would influence individual hourly and annual incomes.

Overall, BLS reports that management and legal occupational groups were the highest paying of the 22 major occupational groups in 2003.[34] About 30% of the workers in these two occupational groups earned more than $44.00 per hour. The occupational group with the highest employment level in May 2003 was office and administrative support workers, followed by sales and related workers, production workers, and food preparation and serving workers. The occupational groups with the lowest average wages were food preparation and serving related; farming, fishing, and forestry; building and grounds cleaning and maintenance; and personal care and service. At least 40% of all workers in each of these groups earned less than $8.50 per hour.[35] Police officers earn more than postal workers and less than secondary school teachers. There are two issues, among others, that emerge from this representative income table:

1. There is little consistency linked to the idea that the harder someone works, the more income he or she could expect to earn. The assumption is that retail cashiers whose mean annual wage is estimated at $17,000 could work as hard and as long as a chief executive whose annual income is reported at $141,000.

2. Correctional, policing, and firefighters can look forward to less income as they approach first-line supervision positions than middle managers or managers in management occupations.

TABLE 3.1   NATIONAL EMPLOYMENT AND WAGE DATA BY OCCUPATION MAY 2003[32]

Occupation	Numbers Employed*	Hourly Mean Wages*	Annual Mean Wages*
Management Occupations			
Chief Executives	400,000	$68.00	$141,000
General & Operations Managers	1,900,000	43.00	89,000
Advertising and Promotion Managers	183,000	44.00	92,000
Marketing Managers	314,000	44.00	92,000
Sales Managers	58,000	36.00	92,000
Public Relations Managers	58,000	36.00	75,000
Administrative Services Managers	278,000	31.00	64,000
Computer and Information Systems Managers	266,000	46.00	95,000
Human Resources Managers	172,000	41.00	87,000
Industrial Production Managers	166,000	37.00	77,000
Purchasing Managers	91,000	34.00	71,000
Transportation, Storage, and Distribution	97,000	34.00	70,000
Business and Financial Operations Occupations			
Purchasing Agents and Buyers, Nonfarm	237,000	24.00	51,000
Claims Adjusters, Examiners, and Investigators	234,000	23.00	46,000
Management Analysis	424,000	35.00	74,000
Accountants and Auditors	924,000	27.00	43,000
Computer Programmers	432,000	31.00	65,000
Middle School Teachers	604,000	N/A	45,000
Secondary School Teachers	1,000,000	N/A	47,000
Registered Nurses	2,200,000	25.00	51,000
Janitors	2,000,000	10.00	20,000
Cashiers, Retail	3,500,000	8.00	17,000
First-Line Supervisors/Managers of Correctional Officers	34,000	23.00	48,000
First-Line Supervisors/Managers of Police and Detectives	102,000	30.00	63,000
First-Line Supervisors/Managers of Firefighters	59,000	29.00	59,000
Firefighters	273,000	18.00	38,000
Correctional Officers and Jailers	417,000	17.00	35,000
Detectives and Criminal Investigators	87,000	26.00	47,000
Police and Sheriff's Patrol Officers	610,000	22.00	45,000
Postal Service Mail Carriers	345,000	19.00	39,000
Electricians	584,000	21.00	44,000
Carpenters	852,000	18.00	37,000
Food Preparation and Serving Workers	2,000,000	7.00	15,000

*Wages rounded

As you review Table 3.1, you are looking at the larger picture of occupational incomes. One result arising from this process is that you are better prepared to make decisions about your job and the jobs of other individuals. For instance, seeing the annual pay scales of police officers across the nation can help.

2004 POLICE OFFICERS AVERAGE BASE PAY BY REGION[36]		
Region	**Min Base Pay**	**Max Base Pay**
West	$47,197	$66,214
Midwest	$38,208	$54,180
Northeast	$37,881	$56,558
South	$33,308	$51,753

The average median income of a police officer in the United States as of May 2005 was $44,153.[37] An academic instructor's mean annual pay is $74,926; a high school teacher $47,565; a Level I lawyer, $79,040; a Level II plumber, $43,350; a Level II carpenter, $42,698; a Level II electrician, $42,722; a judge magistrate, $129,663; and a court reporter, $44,873.

On average, officers attributed 35% of police overtime worked to off-duty court appearances; 20% to making late arrests or writing reports; 11% to taking extra shift assignments to fill in for someone who was sick, on vacation, or disabled; and 9% to covering special events such as crowd control, parades, and missing children.

OCCUPATIONAL STRESSORS

Job stress through job strain can have its way with the typical employee, placing an individual at risk of the numerous consequences of stress, which are described in more detail later in this chapter.

Occupational stressors are defined as a "large number of work-related environmental conditions (or exposures) thought to impact on the health and well-being of the worker."[38] *Job strain* includes a worker's psychological and physiological reaction to such exposure, and his or her negative health outcomes as a result of job stress.[39] Strain can be described as felt stress, since stress itself is not directly tangible.[40] However, there are, among others, at least two compelling matters that can have a neutralizing effect upon job stress: (1) each person responds differently to stressors regardless of the source of those stressors[41] and (2) each person has a different way to resolve or cope with the psychological and physiological stress experienced.[42]

Comparable stimuli (stressors) do not necessarily produce a comparable or similar response from those individuals experiencing it. Muscle cars, fast boats, and rap music produce different reactions among different individuals as can occupations associated with retail establishments, health and welfare agencies, and criminal justice occupations. Then, too, when relieving stress some individuals work out, others eat, and some engage in various hobbies. Unfortunately, some individuals relieve stress through self-destructive routines, which can include drugs and alcohol, use of unnecessary violence at work or during recreation, and unprofessional (and often illegal) techniques such as corporate or agency theft, delivering poor services, and denial of due-process rights of others. Others can be so overloaded or are high functioning that they do both, "Workout to relieve the stress but since it causes them pain, they self-medicate with (illegal) drugs taken from creeps on the streets every other day of the week to relieve the pain from the workouts."[43]

Stress is cumulative, as you already know, and works off other stressors regardless of its source. Since stressors are found in every aspect of work and the personal lives of most police officers, individual personalities and psychological characteristics interact and intervene in many ways with various stressors to compound both the outcomes of stress and the treatment of stress[44] (more detail in Chapter 11). In this regard, some experts argue that some stressors can actually buffer the likelihood of strain instead of increase it. However, one of the hardest tasks of this textbook is to make the obvious more obvious.[45] That is, seeing mangled bodies in vehicle accidents and arresting individuals who were once thought to be moral will have an effect upon delivering quality police services unless the effects of those experiences are managed by the officer and the department. Of course, many officers manage their own stress,[46] and in Chapter 5 there is a discussion about resilience, but for now what we need to know is that officers affected by stress smoke more, eat more, have more alcohol and drug problems, are less motivated, have more trouble with coworkers, are ill, and are involved in accidents more often than other officers. Then, too, they are more often on self-destructive paths that started voluntarily, but rapidly send them on a dangerous descent ending in personal demise that includes family dysfunctions, addictions with compulsive behavior, and even death.[47]

JOB STRAIN

In addition to the above definition of job strain, in a study, job strain was described as a combination of:[48] (1) high (job) demands, (2) little control (over job policies); and (3) little social support (from the public). It can be argued that the more experiences we have while on the job associated with these three variables, the more likely we are confronted by job strain, which acts as a catalyst to reduce acquired skills of employees (a dumbing-down effect).

Job strain produces the greatest risk to physical and mental health from stress, which occurs to most employees who face high psychological workload demands or pressures combined with little control or decision latitude in meeting work demands.[49] Demanding working conditions such as repetitive and changing shift work, assembly-line work, electronic monitoring or surveillance, involuntary overtime, piece-rate work, inflexible hours, arbitrary supervision, promotion, disciplinary and grievance processes, and deskilled work have been studied in many professions including policing.[50] Job demand realities are usually characterized by employees as work activities that are "very fast" or they might say they are "working very hard" and they do not have "enough time to get the job done." While these variables seem to be stressors, job strain is actually the push-and-pull products of these variables. You might say a double whammy: stress from the variables themselves and strain from the interaction levels of the three variables.

Little or no control or decision-making input at work can influence occupational behavior. For instance, there was consensus among police officers in one study who expressed thoughts that reveal that law enforcement does not control the streets they patrolled and they had little if any influence over street policy concerning tasks such as deployment, limits upon the use of force, or inservice training.[51] One result was that the officers did not nor would they work up to the standards expected of them while on duty and often took shortcuts when involved in altercations. Although the officers had not admitted that they participated in any inappropriate or corrupt behavior, there were indicators that they would if the opportunities were present.

Finally, another result of job strain is that it acts as a catalyst to reduce the acquired skills of employees and promotes passivity, a learned helplessness, and a lack of participation (at work, in the community, and in politics) among workers.[52] In the final analysis, job strain appears to have a "dumbing-down" effect upon police personnel.

An implication arising from job strain is compulsive behavior, which can include corruption, brutality, and recklessness. Imagine for a moment if this compulsive behavior were practiced by individuals trained to use violence such as police officers, football players, and military personnel. Appendix I, at the end of these chapters, is a job strain quiz that can help readers determine the level of strain he or she is experiencing on the job.

OUTCOMES OF OCCUPATIONAL STRESS

Job stress is costly, with a price tag for strikes in industry in the United States estimated at over $300 billion annually—more than 15 times the cost of all strikes combined (year ending 2001).[53] The cost of stress to business (and individuals) is staggering. In Canada, the annual cost to business is $16 billion, which is 14% of total net profits.[54]

The economic costs of job stress in general (absenteeism, lost productivity) are difficult to estimate but could be as high as several hundred billion dollars per year.[55] Most importantly, there is the potential for preventing much illness and death. More than 50 million Americans have high blood pressure, and, in 95% of cases, the cause is unknown. While estimates of the proportion of heart disease possibly due to "job strain" vary greatly between studies, up to 23% of heart disease could potentially be prevented (over 150,000 deaths prevented per year in the United States) if we reduced the level of "job strain."[56]

In addition, the individual cost is difficult to measure because so many lives, personal property, and relationships are lost in a maze of mishaps too numerous to measure. As Booker T. Washington suggests, success can be measured by the obstacles that had to be resolved. Yet not everything counted produces success and not every successful experience tells of the obstacles that had to be bridged. Because police officers through a police subculture cannot show any personal weakness among colleagues or adversaries including suspects, it is unlikely that all of their private battles are known or even counted, this researcher argues. But we can count occupational accidents and injuries, alcoholism, family dysfunctions, and personnel corruption, often influenced through job strain.

HOW JOB STRESS WORKS

Twenty-four centuries ago, the father of medicine, Hippocrates, believed that illness had a physical and a rational explanation.[57] Disease was not only pathos (suffering), but it was also ponos (toil), as the body fights to restore normalcy. Change can produce a physical response to some degree or another, with or without the knowledge or consent of an individual. Why?

> One reason for a physical change in our bodies when confronted by external or environmental change is that our bodies contain their own pharmacy. Bodies respond to stimuli in a programmed way.

For instance, when an individual "perceives" danger, the body responds in ways that prepare to cope with the threat. There are "major outpourings of powerful hormones creating dramatic alterations in bodily processes many of which we sense in the case of a pounding heart, sweating, trembling, fatigue, etc."[58]

What W.I. Thomas (1863–1947)[59] seems to have in mind when he made his famous dictum: "If people define situations as real, they are real in their consequences,"—fear itself is greater than the reality, or what he called the *definition of the situation.*[60]

Relative to policing, the fear of crime often has a greater impact on the population than the crime itself. For instance, when it is thought that the police can't or won't do their job, and the public is fearful of an assault from criminals, some buy guns and others lock themselves in their homes. Some researchers imply that the fear of crime is a greater challenge to social order than social disorder, says Wesley Skogan.[61]

Then, too, individuals can change socially constructed inner realities (their ideas, attitudes, or feelings) into socially observable outer realities (conduct). Whenever they think of themselves as traveling in a jet, they behave as if they are afraid even when there is little to fear. Does the individual believe he or she should fear the flight? His or her body thinks so, and responds fearfully when they think about airline travel. How could the fear of flying be minimized? Becoming aware of how the body responds to stimuli such as flying and perhaps making jets safer or at least making the perception of traveling in a jet more desirable through advertising: dealing with both the individual and the structural levels. But, think about the fear a stressed officer might imagine when apprehending a speeder on the highway, especially if the driver is a heinous offender of sorts. Can the offender detect the perceived fear of the officer? Will the offender use that fear against the officer? Might an assaulted cop be sprawled on the wet pavement because the officer's nonverbal clues gave him or her away? That is to say that a high percentile of officers were attacked and some were killed during routine traffic stops in 2005.[62]

Workers, Police, and Risk of Stress

The public generally accepts the unrealistic icons associated with policing implying that cops are the only individuals relentlessly confronted by danger and stress. But there are many occupations that are both dangerous and stressful, for example, imagine driving a taxi in Manhattan or working the third shift at a convenience store. Then, too, think about correctional officers who deal daily with offenders, their shift work, and their organizational command resembles that of most law enforcement organizations. While patrol officers occasionally confront serious offenders, depending on the assignment, correctional personnel confront offenders as part of their daily routine.

Other occupations engage in occupational trauma as part of their job descriptions. For instance, emergency room personnel treat and help injured people. Also, probation officers, parole officers, and counselors interact with violators with assorted backgrounds on a daily basis. Miners often die when trapped in mines and firefighters die in buildings. Police officers are exposed to domestic violence and assault of children, but so too are ambulance attendants, medical personnel, and social workers. Although bartenders and waitresses are on a different level as police officers, how often do they witness the traumatic episodes of others or confront danger themselves. As we review the experiences of mental health, social services, peer support personnel, and schoolteachers across the country, their experiences compare and often exceed law enforcement experiences, levels of risk, which include injury and homicide, and levels of burnout.

Nonetheless, one of the first observers to draw attention to the stress of policing was W. Clinton Terry,[63] who coined the term *police stress syndrome* to characterize police stress as special and not due to danger, insecurity, or job dissatisfaction like other job stress. Some writers refer to police stress as the "police paradox" because both the safe and unsafe aspects of policing can combine to produce the symptoms.[64] The work police officers perform is reported as distinctively different from other occupations. For instance, the Society for Police and Criminal Psychology[65] supports the position that there are 10 reasons why law enforcement officers face different stressors than other occupations.[66]

1. Police are seen as authority figures.
2. Police are isolated (badge, uniform, and gun separates them from others).
3. Police work in a quasimilitary structured institution.
4. Shift work.
5. Camaraderie can be a two-edged sword (us and them).
6. Police have a burst stress (they go from calm to high activity in one burst).
7. Police need to be in constant control.
8. Police work is fact-based world with everything compared to written law.
9. The world of police work is very negative, which can cause cynicism.
10. The children of officers have more difficulty adjusting.

Although officers are on constant alert, they face constant boredom, too. For instance, patrol, surveillance, and general "guard" duty has its dull moments. Then, too, there is paperwork. Negotiating with violators can be boring, too. Also, officers are not always aware of the outcomes of their "cases" and "the day-to-day stress of dealing with people and their problems . . . can traumatize officers and poison their spirits."[67] Finally, in this regard, what we know about cops is that veteran officers typically have the idea that they should handle their problems, especially stress, with silence or calling in sick.[68]

Stress and Job Absenteeism

Absenteeism due to job stress has escalated. According to a survey of 800,000 workers in over 300 companies, the number of employees calling in sick because of stress tripled from 1996 to 2000. An estimated 1 million workers are absent every day due to stress.[69] The European Agency for Safety and Health at Work reported that over half of the 550 million working days lost annually in the United States from absenteeism are stress related and that one in five of all last minute no-shows are due to job stress. Unanticipated absenteeism is estimated to cost American companies $602 per worker per year and the price tag for large employers could approach $3.5 million annually. A 3-year study conducted in 1997 by one large corporation found that 60% of employee absences could be traced to psychological problems that were due to job stress.[70] Concerning officers, one report shows that it is difficult to determine how many law enforcement officers have left policing as an occupation after a traumatic incident, but the number is probably very high. Nationwide, departments have experienced increasing levels of turnover among sworn officers.[71]

Stress and Worker Health

Stress has an "add-on" health hazard that has an energy of its own when left untreated. For example, the National Institute for Occupational Safety and Health (NIOSH) reports that stress is responsible for the following health hazards[72]:

- Asthma, allergies, hives
- Exhaustion, irritability, fatigue
- Anxiety, depression, phobias, panic attacks, behavior disorders, low self-esteem
- Arthritis, chest pains, headaches, ulcers, irritable bowel, nausea and vomiting, Crohn's disease

Stress and Job Insecurity

In 2003 more Americans lost more jobs than at any other time in the last two decades. The American Management Association (AMA) advised in 2003 that for the first time since the 1990–91 recession, more than half of major U.S. companies reported layoffs.[73] Fifty-eight percent of 1,631 surveyed firms said they eliminated jobs in the year ending June 30, 2001, the highest percentage in the AMA survey's 15-year history. Consequently workers are fearful of losing their jobs and the problem has worsened considerably since then. There were massive layoffs due to downsizing and bankruptcies including the collapse of over 200 dot.com companies. The unemployment rate continues to be unstable. One report released on September 10, 2001, reported that more than 1 million Americans lost their jobs that year, 83% higher than last year's total. That was a day before the World Trade Center disaster, which added to the problems of job stress and insecurity for many workers. Since then, Americans have witnessed the collapse of Enron and its tidal wave of repercussions on other companies and their employees. There are many fears that this may be just the tip of the iceberg as accounting irregularities of a similar nature may augur the downfall of other large organizations widely assumed to be on a solid financial footing. Their personnel may feel a little less secure than other personnel. Furthermore, due to liability and criminal concerns many more organizations are monitoring and practicing surveillance on their personnel, advises the AMA.[74] Therefore, learning to deal with stress in such a way that it does not trigger the silent health response is an important clue to living another day. This can be called a "lose–lose" situation. That is, a police officer either takes it upon him- or herself to end the life of a drug dealer using the rationale that the criminal justice system is not punishing known offenders appropriately, an act that can be referred to as street justice.[75]

Stress and Burnout

That said, "burnout" might be the best term used for the stressful careers of many officers in police service. It should be understood that the idea of burnout has captured the public's imagination to the extent that it has become fashionable.[76] In fact, it is in vogue to be a victim of something in the 21st century, and in vogue to deal with victimization through counseling. Malaise of every description is now attributed to its pernicious effect. We hear of burnout and its alleged effects among students, criminals, athletes, and executives, and why not police officers?

Burnout is the tendency to cope with stress by a form of distancing, at an extreme, or what can be described as physical or psychological avoidance.[77] Distancing can be a matter of degrees. A police officer can become cynical and develop negative thoughts about his clients. That is, dehumanize criminals even if they aren't convicted of a crime[78] (e.g., referring to violators as "scum-bags"). John Crank implies that burnout is part of an initiative referred to as cynicism.[79] *Cynicism* can refer to a response that tends to be sarcastic or mocking, scornful, or sneering. It is a doubting or contemptuousness of human nature or of the motives, goodness, or sincerity of others. A substance abuse counselor related the following: An officer who was an alcoholic said to me, "How can I quit drinking? My father was an alcoholic and a cop, and his father was an alcoholic. That don't mean my kid can't be a cop, now does it? That's all I want." Cynicism might be described as a cultural phenomenon, nuanced with frustration toward administrators and violators,[80] and could be another pervasive initiative employed by officers, similar to CYA initiatives as described in Chapter 2. For example, in an analysis of cynicism, it is in the early career of an officer that the officer learns through culturally transmitted behavior of veteran officers and police trainers how to deal with departmental "bullshit" and violators. Bottom line? Young officers want to emulate their mentors.[81] Cynicism does not burn out an officer, it is merely a sign of a burned-out officer who uses this device to an extreme and may also, at an extreme, withdraw from his or her job and family members.

Some officers withdraw from everything. That is, they withdraw from contact by hiding behind a desk completing reams of unnecessary paperwork or hiding behind clipboards or an officer utilizing a strategy that can be referred to as voluntary resignation. *Voluntary resignation* can be described as withdrawing or retreating from police work, while still employed as a sworn officer. For example, an officer withdraws from doing his or her job on the street or asks for a desk job. The officer might also withdraw from his or her personal life and loved ones, never wishing to discuss work or its process with a spouse.[82] Overall, this individual can be described as a person who has been transformed from the individual he or she once was to a different person altogether—a mechanical bureaucrat.[83] Burnout is more likely among officers who at an extreme employ distancing techniques. This is not to say that officers using cynicism or withdrawing are candidates as burnouts, but it does say that one of the visible signs of burnout might be in the extreme behavior described as cynicism and voluntary resignation.

Posttraumatic stress can be characterized as an extreme reaction to stress revolving around core symptoms experienced after a life-threatening event, which includes reexperiencing the trauma in the form of nightmares and intrusive thoughts and avoiding reminders of the event, among other reactions. Without appropriately identifying stress or curbing it, stress can produce, at an extreme, *acute stress disorder* (ASD) or *posttraumatic stress disorder* (PTSD) and is responsible for many more problems with transitory symptoms, such as intrusive thoughts, sleeping difficulties, changed eating patterns, and muted emotional responses.

Acute stress disorder can develop within 1 month after an individual experiences or sees an event that involved a threat or actual death, serious injury, or another kind of physical violation to the individual or others, and responded to this event with strong feelings of fear, helplessness, or horror.[84] This diagnosis was established to identify those individuals who would eventually develop posttraumatic stress disorder. ASD was brought to light as it became clear that for a short period, people might exhibit PTSD-like symptoms immediately after a trauma.

PTSD is defined by the *Diagnostic and Statistical Manual of Mental Disorders (DSM-IV)*[85] this way:

> The essential feature of Posttraumatic Stress Disorder is the development of characteristic symptoms following exposure to an extreme stressor involving direct personal experience of an event that involves actual or threatened death or serious injury, or other threat to one's physical integrity; or witnessing an event that involves death, injury, or a threat to the physical integrity of another person: or learning about unexpected or violent death, serious harm, or threat of death or injury experienced by a family member or other close associate. The person's response to the event must involve intense fear, helplessness, or horror. . . . persistent reexperiencing . . . persistent avoidance of stimuli associated . . . persistent symptoms of increase arousal . . . must cause clinically significant distress or impairment in social, occupational, or other important areas of functioning. (p. 424)

The American Psychiatric Association introduced PTSD as a diagnosable condition in 1980 and associated it with ASD. Most discussions of these extreme reactions to stress revolve around core symptoms experienced after a life-threatening event and include:

- Reexperiencing the trauma in the form of nightmares and intrusive thoughts;
- Avoiding reminders of the event; and
- Experiencing numbing to the point of not having loving feelings, increased arousal in the form of exaggerated startle response, hypervigilantism, and sleeping difficulties.

Recent research suggests that certain factors predict the likelihood of someone experiencing PTSD and its symptoms.[86] Most predictive of PTSD was a dissociative experience during or in the immediate aftermath of the traumatic event and high levels of emotion during or shortly after the traumatic event.[87] Other predictors of PTSD include individual prior trauma, psychological adjustment before the trauma, and a family history of mental illness. Prior exposure to a similar event probably is the most difficult to understand because it is counterintuitive.[88] In most other aspects of life, experience helps. Unfortunately, many law enforcement officers discover that repeated exposure to certain events can have serious detrimental effects. The frequency, duration, and intensity of stressors represent determining factors toward PTSD. It is almost as if repeat events reinforce the original traumatic event. Again, stress reactions vary among individuals because perceptions of situations differ and reactions are subjective.

These debilitating symptoms are not the worst things that can happen. Sadly, among law enforcement officers, job-related stress frequently contributes to the ultimate maladaptive response to stress: suicide.[89]

We might agree that if an officer is experiencing PTSD that that officer might not be our first choice to deliver quality police service until the condition is at least remedied or controlled. Furthermore, there is a significant association between anger and the presence of a circulatory disorder only in patients with PTSD.[90]

The literature shows that police officers have a high burnout rate, caused in part by a lack of coping with family problems, occupational stress, little status, and low public trust. They are also likely to be involved in a civil liability suit more than any other occupation.[91] Some argue that it is not one source but combinations of those contributors that matter.

However, some researchers argue that "critical incidents alone do not cause most law enforcement officers undue stress; neither do cumulative stressors, such as organizational and job factors, nor personal stressors, such as physical and psychological elements. Instead, the confluence of all of these different factors does."[92] For example, cumulative stress can contribute to high rates of gastrointestinal disorders, high blood pressure, and coronary heart disease in the law enforcement community. Nonetheless, workers engaged in the jobs are often assaulted and it could be argued with a great degree of confidence that knowing you will be victimized at work has a lot to do with how well you perform regardless of other stressor factors.

Workers At Risk of Assault

Approximately, 18,000 nonfatal violent crimes such as sexual and other assaults also occur each week while the victim is at work, or about a million a year.[93] The figures are probably higher since many attacks are never reported, but the estimates are that assault at the workplace is rapidly rising in the United States and worldwide.[94] Certain dangerous occupations like police officers and cab drivers understandably have higher rates of nonfatal assaults. Nevertheless, postal workers who work in a safe environment have experienced so many fatalities due to job stress that "going postal" has crept into our language. "Desk rage" and "phone rage" have become increasingly common terms.

Factors that place workers at risk for violence in general include interacting with the public, exchanging money, delivering services or goods, working late at night or during early morning hours, working alone, guarding valuables or property, and dealing with violent people or volatile situations.[95] BLS estimates that 5.7 million injuries to workers occurred in 1997 alone, while the National Institute for Occupational Safety and Health (NIOSH) estimates that about 3.6 million occupational injuries were serious enough to be treated in hospital emergency rooms in 1998.[96]

During the period from 1980 through 1995, at least 93,338 workers in the United States died as a result of trauma suffered on the job, or an average of about 16 deaths per day, says NIOSH.[97] The BLS identified 5,559 workplace deaths from acute traumatic injury in 2003.[98]

Assaults in workplaces resulting in days away from work are distributed almost equally between men (44%) and women (56%).[99] The majority of the nonfatal assaults reported occurred in the service (64%) and retail trade (21%) industries. Of those in the service industry, 27% occurred in nursing homes, 13% in social services, and 11% in hospitals (see Table 3.2). In retail trade, 6% occurred in grocery stores, and another 5% occurred in eating and drinking places. The source of injury in 45% of the cases was a health care patient, with another 31% described as *other person* and 6% as *coworker* or *former coworker.*

Most worker assaults occur in service settings such as nursing homes, social service agencies, and hospitals. U.S. residents suffered an annual average of 1.7 million violent workplace victimizations from 1993 through 1999, the BJS reported.[100] In addition to those nonfatal workplace crimes against people age 12 and older, there were about 900 workplace-related homicides

TABLE 3.2 VIOLENT ACTS RESULTING IN DAYS AWAY FROM WORK IN 1992, BY INDUSTRY

Industry (% of total)	Percentage of violent acts resulting in days away from work
Services	64
Nursing homes	27
Social services	13
Hospitals	11
Other services	13
Retail trades	21
Grocery stores	6
Eating and drinking places	5
Other retail	10
Transportation/communication public utilities	4
Finance/insurance/real estate	4
Other	4

per year during that period, according to the BJS study released in December. Workplace violence accounted for 18% of all violent crimes committed during the period studied. Of the occupations examined, police officers were victimized at the highest rate at 26%, whereas university professors and teachers had the lowest rate of victimization, below 1%.

Of selected occupations examined from 1993 to 1999, police officers were the most vulnerable to be victims of workplace violence, as well as correctional officers, taxicab drivers, private security workers, and bartenders.[101] Police officers were victims of a nonfatal violent crime while they were on duty between 1993 to 1999 at a rate of 261 per 1,000 officers. In 2000, 56,054 officers, or an average of almost 13 of every 100 officers, were assaulted while on the job.[102] A study conducted for the Bureau of Justice Statistics shows occupational risks.[103] U.S. residents suffered an annual average of 1.7 million violent workplace victimizations from 1993 through 1999.

Managers At Risk of Assault

There exists a gap in the literature concerning this topic, but the gap disappears when executives and public managers are asked about their experiences. Some 82% of top executives say the number of violent incidents at their workplaces has increased since 2002, according to a poll of 602 companies nationwide.[104] Nearly 6 out of 10 companies say disgruntled employees have threatened to assault or assassinate senior managers in 2004. Furthermore, those employees have made those threats in person or in an email. In fact, 17% of those companies reported that enraged and embittered personnel had deliberately downloaded computer viruses onto corporate computers, and 10% said workers had tampered with their products.

Paul Viollis, president of Risk Control Strategies, a New York security consulting firm, reports that most workplace violence is unavoidable.[105] And violence toward management is a national epidemic. It could get worse before it gets better because of downsizing, outsourcing, offshoring, pay cuts, and wage garnishments. This thought is consistent with the experiences of public managers who are attacked more frequently than expected, and their attackers tend to be benefit recipients provided for by the public agencies that employ those managers.[106]

High At-Risk Jobs

Of the occupations examined, police officers were victimized at the highest rate at 26%, whereas university professors and teachers had the lowest rate of victimization, below 1%, reports the Bureau of Justice Statistics.[107] Corrections officers were second from the top of the list of those most often victimized at work. Almost 16% of all corrections officers suffered some sort of victimization on the job. Victimization in the report includes nonfatal violence in the workplace including assault and theft from person, workstation, or vehicle.

Government employees had violent victimization rates that were almost triple the rate of people who work for private companies and almost four times as high as those who are self-employed (see Table 3.3 for details). The following are additional findings:

- The number of workplace homicides fell by 39% during the 7 years of the study.
- Caucasian workers reported workplace victimization at a rate 25% higher than blacks and almost 59% higher than those of other races.
- In about 60% of cases, offenders were the same race as their victims.
- About 1 in 8 victimized workers were injured.
- About 1 in 9 faced multiple offenders.
- About 40% of the victims had a prior relationship with the offender.
- Unarmed offenders committed about 75% of all workplace violence.
- More than 80% of workplace homicides were committed with firearms.

According to corrections experts, the following indicators have been associated with acts of workplace violence. These warning signs do not necessarily mean the individual actually will be violent, but they might show cause for concern:

TABLE 3.3   VIOLENCE VISITED UPON WORKERS[108]

Occupation	Rate per 1,000 workers
Law enforcement officers	260.8
Taxicab drivers	155.7
Bartenders	81.6
Mental health custodians	69.0
Special education teachers	68.4
Gas station attendants	68.3
Mental health professionals	68.2
Junior high school teachers	54.2
Convenience store workers	53.9
High school teachers	38.1
Nurses	21.9
Physicians	16.2
College teachers	1.6

- Sudden irrational beliefs and ideas
- Verbal, nonverbal, and written threats of intimidation
- Disregard for the safety of other employees
- Fascination with weapons
- Productivity and attendance problems
- Signs of alcohol and drug abuse
- Argumentative or altercations with others
- Chronic signs of depression
- Significant personal, family, or financial stress
- Quick to place blame
- Paranoia
- Feelings of being victimized

To deescalate potentially violent situations:

- Project calmness: move and speak slowly
- Be an empathetic listener
- Encourage the person to talk
- Acknowledge the person's feelings
- Indicate that you can see they are upset
- Maintain a relaxed, attentive posture and position yourself at a right angle to the person

Do not:

- Immediately reject the person's demands
- Make sudden movements that can be seen as threatening
- Challenge, threaten, or dare the individual
- Make false statements or promises
- Invade the individual's personal space

CIRCUMSTANCES OF OFFICER ASSAULTS

In 2002, the majority (31%; percents rounded) of officers assaulted were responding to disturbance calls, which include family quarrels, bar fights, persons with firearms, etc. Over 13% of the officers were assaulted while maintaining custody of prisoners, 11% were assaulted during traffic pursuits or stops, and 10% were investigating suspicious persons or circumstances. Over 16% of the officers assaulted were attempting other types of arrests. Officers assaulted by mentally deranged assailants and those investigating burglary, robbery, or civil disorder incidents accounted for 5% of officers assaulted. The smallest percentage of assaults on law enforcement officers—0.3—were ambush situations. Officers performing all other duties comprised 13% of the assaults (see Table 3.4).

Types of Assignments

Of those officers assaulted in 2002, 81% were assigned to vehicle patrols, of which 63% were assigned to one-officer patrols and 17% were assigned to two-officer patrols. Of the total number of officers assaulted, 6% were on detective or special assignment, and 14% were performing other duties. Fellow officers were at the scene assisting 70% of the assaulted officers.

In a review of Table 3.4, it appears that service calls to families seem to be as dangerous an encounter for officers as intervening in barroom brawls and both are more dangerous than interrupting a robber or pursuing a burglar. This untenable position concerning the safety of officers and the community can easily foster a stressed-out or threatened officer to employ excessive force to secure order in many altercations that could have been controlled through less violent means. Maybe those attackers have little respect for law and order and do as they please. Had Alexis de Tocqueville been accurate in his 1831 evaluation of the American democratic system that promotes individual rights even among its criminals?[110] Do too many rights lead individuals to criminal lifestyles? De Tocqueville advanced the idea that God makes humans unequal, democracy attempts to make them equal, which includes violators. You will have to sort out an answer for yourself, but these notions reveal that when some individuals have little regard for the rights of others, anything is possible including assaulting and murdering the very individuals who are sworn to defend the rights of others—cops.

TABLE 3.4   LAW ENFORCEMENT OFFICERS ASSAULTED
TYPE OF WEAPON BY CIRCUMSTANCE AT SCENE OF INCIDENT, PERCENT
DISTRIBUTION, 2000

Circumstances at Scene of Incident	Total	Percent	Firearm	Knife or Cutting Instrument	Other Dangerous Weapon	Personal Weapon
Total & Percent	56054	100%	1705	994	7559	45796
Disturbance calls: family quarrels, bar fights	17224	31%	541	469	1567	14647
Burglaries in progress/ pursuing burglary suspects	787	1%	37	25	157	568
Robberies in progress/ pursuing robbery suspects	516	.09%	105	7	114	290
Attempting other arrests	9239	17%	192	105	1058	7884
Civil disorder (mass disobedience, riots)	799	2%	9	8	264	518
Handling, transporting, custody of prisoners	6779	12%	28	34	509	6208
Investigating suspicious persons	5834	10%	220	117	754	4743
Ambush situations	189	.03%	54	3	57	75
Mentally deranged assailants	781	1%	31	60	109	581
Traffic pursuits /stops	6234	11%	201	52	1888	4093
All other	7672	14%	287	114	1082	6189

Source: FBI[109]

Clearance Rates of Assaulted Officers

Of the total number of assaults on law enforcement officers in 2002, 90% were cleared by arrest or exceptional means. By circumstance, the greatest number of clearances for assaults on law enforcement officers, 92%, was for disturbance calls (family quarrels, bar fights, persons with firearms, etc.). The circumstance with the lowest percentage of clearances, 73%, was for officers assaulted in ambush situations.[111]

WORKERS AT RISK OF HOMICIDE

The BLS identified 5,915 workplace deaths from acute traumatic injury in 2000.[112] On the average, 20 workers are murdered each week in the United States. The majority of these murders are robbery-related crimes.[113] During the 13-year period 1980–92, the greatest number of deaths occurred in the retail trade and service industries, whereas the highest rates per 100,000 workers occurred in retail trades, public administration, and transportation/communication/public utilities.

When occupations were analyzed for 1990–92 (see Table 3.5), the highest homicide rates were found for taxicab drivers/chauffeurs, sheriffs/bailiffs, police and detectives (public service), gas station/garage workers, and security guards. Compared with previously published data for the 7-year period 1983–89, these data indicate that rates increased more than two and a half times for sales counter clerks and nearly two times for motor vehicle and boat sales workers

The FBI reports[117]:

The data collected on the circumstances surrounding officers' deaths in 2003 revealed that 14 were killed during traffic stops or pursuits and 11 of the officers were slain in arrest situations. A further breakdown of the arrest situations showed that one officer was murdered during a robbery, one was killed during a burglary, one was slain while attempting a drug arrest, and eight officers died while attempting other types of arrests. Ten officers were murdered while investigating disturbance calls, five of whom were killed while investigating family quarrels and five while investigating bar fights or a person with a firearm, etc. Nine of the victim officers who were killed in 2003 were slain in ambush situations, three of whom died during unprovoked attacks and six officers were killed in entrapment or premeditated situations. Six officers were killed while investigating suspicious persons or circumstances, and two were killed while transporting or handling prisoners. During the 10-year period 1994 through 2003, 616 law enforcement officers were killed.

The FBI adds:

The year 2001 will always be remembered as the year terrorists turned commercial airliners into murder weapons and used them to kill 3,047 innocent people. Counted within that number are 72 local, state, and federal law enforcement officers, the most officers ever lost in a single day. Seventy officers were feloniously killed during 2001 in incidents not related to the events of September 11, and 78 officers died in duty-related accidents. Data submitted to the Uniform Crime Reporting Program indicate that 56,666 law officers were assaulted during the year and, of those, 16,202 received injuries.

TABLE 3.5   RANK ORDER OF WORKER HOMICIDE RATES

Rank (based on homicide rate per 100,000 workers)	Occupation
1.	Taxicab driver/chauffeur
2.	Sheriff/bailiff
3.	Police and detective—public service
4.	Gas station/garage
5.	Hotel clerk
6.	Security guard
7.	Stock handler/bagger
8.	Supervisor/proprietor, sales
9.	Supervisor, police and detective
10.	Barber
11.	Bartender
12.	Correctional institution officer
13.	Salesperson, motor vehicle and boat
14.	Salesperson, other commodities
15.	Sales counter clerk
16.	Firefighter

Source: NIOSH.[114]

*High-risk occupations have workplace homicide rates that are twice the average rate during one or both time periods.

†Data for New York City and Connecticut were not available for 1992.

and sales workers in other commodities (includes workers in jewelry, food, sporting goods, book, coin, and other retail stores). Certainly, the rank order will vary depending on national disasters such as the World Trade Center, but Table 3.5 is offered to demonstrate that many occupations can be high risk.

OFFICER KILLED IN 1792

On May 17, 1792, Deputy Sheriff Isaac Smith with the New York City Sheriff's Office investigated a disturbance at an inn owned by Levi Hunt, located in what is now the Bronx.[115] The victim deputy was shot with one of two flintlock pistols carried by John Ryer, an unruly drunk, who the officer was attempting to arrest. Although Ryer fled north to Canada, he was shortly located, arrested, and extradited to New York, where he was tried and hanged for the murder on October 2, 1793.

This scenario describes what is now believed to have been the first law enforcement officer feloniously killed in the line of duty in the United States. Present-day deaths of law enforcement officers number around 52 murders and 82 accidental deaths in 2003.[116]

SUMMARY

This chapter talked about occupational stressors including those found in policing. It defined job stress as a result of the interaction of the worker and the conditions of work. It explained that 80% of all workers experience stress at the workplace, and 50% say they need help to cope with it. The nature of stress is compounded because employees seem to work longer, harder, are regulated by a lot of policy and regulations, yet their work effort is below expectations. There exists little consistency in the workplace between hard work and financial remuneration, and police manager incomes are inconsistent with managerial incomes in other occupations. Overall, the fuel that powers occupational stress lays in the reality that most employees have little control of their work environment. Job strain was defined by the combination of high demands, low control (over job policies), low (job) social support, and it acts as a catalyst to reduce acquired skills of employees or a dumbing-down effect upon personnel. Because each individual responds differently to stressors regardless of the source of those stressors, and because each individual has a different way to resolve or control the psychological and physiological stress experienced, the effects of stress individually can be reduced or neutralized.

Absenteeism and low productivity are the primary organizational effects of stress and family dysfunctions and illness, among other consequences, are individual effects of stress. It was explained that because our bodies contain their own pharmacy, our bodies respond to stimuli a programmed way. Burnout leading to posttraumatic stress was characterized as the tendency to cope with stress by a form of distancing, or what can be described as physical or psychological avoidance. Posttraumatic stress was characterized as an extreme reaction to stress revolving around core symptoms experienced after a life-threatening event, which include reexperiencing the trauma in the form of nightmares and intrusive thoughts; avoiding reminders of the event; and experiencing numbing to the point of not having loving feelings, increased arousal in the form of exaggerated startle response, hypervigilantism, and sleeping difficulties. The huge number of workers, managers, and police officers assaulted and killed was detailed, characterizing police officers as victims more often than any other occupational group.

WHAT WOULD YOU DO IF YOU WERE IN CHARGE?

A 22-year-old man was hanging out with friends, sitting on top of a car in their neighborhood during the evening of November 14, 2001. Plainclothes officers from a Staten Island narcotics unit drove up in a van to the group and asked a few of them what they were doing and where they lived. The young man told an inquiring detective that he lived down the block. When the detective asked the man if he had anything on him, the man said, "No, not me, Jack." The officer responded by leaving the van and threatening the man, "If you call me Jack again, I'll wrap your lip around your head." The detective threw the man against the van's hood. The man admitted to grabbing hold of the detective's hand until another officer assisted the detective, who repeatedly forced the man's head against the hood of the vehicle. The detective then frisked the man and searched his pockets without finding any contraband. He took the man's wallet and prepared a stop and frisk report. Though he was not arrested or issued any summonses, the man filed a complaint the next day.[118] If you were the narcotics unit superior how would you deal with the complaint against your officers? Why?

OFFICER KILLED IN CALIFORNIA

A 33-year-old deputy sheriff with the Los Angeles County Sheriff's Department was shot and killed during a traffic stop near Irwindale at 10:40 A.M. on April 29, 2002. The 7-year veteran of law enforcement, who initiated the stop for unknown reasons, entered the vehicle's license plate number into his Mobile Digital Terminal. According to witnesses, the man, known to law enforcement as a drug dealer, exited his vehicle and began walking toward the patrol unit. The deputy exited his vehicle, stood behind his opened car door, and ordered the individual to stop. The suspect stopped near the back of his own vehicle. The deputy approached the suspect from behind and was patting him down when the suspect grabbed a 9-mm semiautomatic handgun from his waistband with his right hand, spun around, and fired a shot at the deputy. The deputy fell to the ground and the suspect fired four more shots at him before fleeing in his vehicle. The victim officer suffered two fatal injuries, a chest wound from a bullet that went through his left arm before entering through the armhole of his protective vest and a wound to the front of his head. The suspect, a male in his mid-20s who has an extensive criminal history including various drug and weapons charges, remains at large at the time of publication. Anything you would have done differently if you were this officer?[119]

DISCUSSION QUESTIONS

1. Define job stress and describe stress at your workplace or the workplace of someone you know.
2. Describe the nature of stress.
3. Characterize the fuel that powers job stress and explain in what way this perspective is (or is not) as powerful as the author implies.
4. Explain why the aptitudes of employees are imperfect predictors of job performance. In what way do you agree and disagree with this perspective?
5. Characterize the components of job strain. Of the four listed, which component might be the most important and why?
6. Identify two individual responses that influence the impact that job stress can play on an individual. Describe an experience where you were unaf-

fected by the event or circumstance yet a friend or family member reacted differently.

7. Identify the economic and individual primary costs of job stress.

8. Describe the dictum about "definition of the situation" and how it applies to stress. Can you recall any "unwarranted fear" that altered your behavior?

9. Identify 10 reasons why the job of policing is different from other jobs. Which of these reasons apply to other jobs too?

10. Characterize stress and burnout concerns.

11. Characterize posttraumatic stress and its consequences. What other jobs might involve posttraumatic stress?

12. Explain workers at risk of assault concerns and consequences.

13. Characterize managers at risk of assault issues. In what way could you see something like this happening?

14. Discuss the high at-risk job victimization concerns, including warning signs, and appropriate techniques to minimize violence. In what way do the warning signs, dos, and don'ts apply to other scenarios?

15. Characterize the circumstance at assault scenes when officers are attacked.

16. Describe the workers at risk of homicide issues.

ENDNOTES

1. Allen R. Cates (1999). *CopShock: Surviving posttraumatic stress disorder*. New York: Holbrook Street Press. pp. 101, 217, and 421.

2. National Institute for Occupational Safety and Health (NIOSH) (2002), p. 5. Retrieved online May 4, 2005: http://www.cdc.gov/niosh/stresswk.html

3. Attitudes *In The American Workplace VI Gallup Poll*. Work Life Statistics. Retrieved online May 7, 2005: http://64.233.161.104/search?q=cache:5T_37gq_qkAJ:www.e-dependentcare.net/images/Work-Life_Statistics.doc+Attitudes+In+The+American+Workplace+VI%22+Gallup+Poll+&hl=en&client=firefox-a. Also see, The Marlin Company (2005). Communications. Retrieved online May 7, 2005: http://www.themarlincompany.com/.

4. John Strahinich (2005, May 6). Memo to bosses: Be afraid. *Boston Herald*, pp. 22–23.

5. Paul Viollis (2005, April 11). Most workplace violence avoidable. *Business Insurance*. Retrieved online May 7, 2005: http://www.ncdsv.org/images/MostWorkplaceViolenceAvoidable.pdf

6. FBI (2005). *Enforcement Officers Killed and Assaulted 2003*. Retrieved online May 5, 2005: http://www.fbi.gov/ucr/killed/leoka03.pdf

7. Studs Terkel (1997). *Working: People talk about what they do all day and how they feel about what they do*. New York: W.W. Norton.

8. Brian Littlechild (2005, March 21). The nature and effects of violence against child-protection social workers: Providing effective support. *British Journal of Social Work*, 35(3): 387–401.

    Mark L. Dantzker (2004) Reflections on policing and stress. In Heith Copes (Ed.), *Policing and stress* (pp. 178–201). Upper Saddle River, NJ: Prentice Hall.

Suzanne McLaren (1997). Heart rate and blood pressure in male police officers and clerical workers on work and nonwork days. *Journal of Work and Stress*, 11(2), 160–174. Also see *Occupational Hazard Datasheets of Occupations*. Retrieved online May 5, 2005 at: http://www.ilo.org/public/english/protection/safework/cis/products/hdo/htm/firefightr.htm. For instance: Firefighters work under constantly changing and often unstable environments.

A burning building with occupants in need of rescue may lack its normal structural integrity and means of access such as stairs or elevators may be compromised by the fire. The work is also often strenuous and many situations require the use of specialized personal protective equipment. Firefighters may be called on to work in different emergency situations such as traffic accidents, industrial disasters, floods, earthquakes, civil riots, hazardous chemical or hazardous materials spills, aviation or maritime accidents. They may also be called on to perform rescue in different environments such as rescue from vehicles, rescue from heights, and rescue from underground.

As the nature of the environment may differ from one emergency call to the next, the firefighter is seldom aware of all of the risks in the environment where the work takes place.

Vehicles for emergency response may include fire trucks, rescue vehicles, boats, helicopters, and all-terrain vehicles for off-road access. The risks of transportation accidents are heightened during response to emergencies.

Firefighters face an increased risk of cardiovascular disease, post-incident psychological stress, and strain injury due to improper lifting techniques.

Source: Occupational Hazard Datasheets of Occupations. Retrieved online May 5, 2005 at: http://www.ilo.org/public/english/protection/safework/cis/products/hdo/htm/firefightr.htm

9. Work has not always been an honored virtue. From a historical perspective, the cultural norm of placing a positive moral value on doing a good job because work has intrinsic value for its own sake was a relatively recent development. Work, for much of ancient history, has been hard and degrading. Working hard—in the absence of compulsion—was not the norm for Hebrew, classical, or medieval cultures. For the Romans, as an example, work was to be done by slaves, and only two occupations were suitable for free men, agriculture and big business. A goal of these endeavors, as defined by the Roman culture, was to achieve an honorable retirement into rural peace as a country gentleman. Any pursuit of handicrafts or the hiring out of a person's arms was considered to be vulgar, dishonoring, and beneath the dignity of a Roman citizen. It was not until the Protestant Reformation that physical labor became culturally acceptable for all persons, even the wealthy. See Roger B. Hill (1996). *The history of work ethic.* Retrieved online April 30, 2005: http://www.coe.uga.edu/%7Erhill/workethic/hist.htm

10. U.S. Department of Labor Statistics (2004, April 30). *Occupational employment and wages: 2003.* Retrieved online May 1, 2005: http://www.bls.gov/news.release/archives/ocwage_04302004.pdf

11. U.S. Department of Labor Statistics (2004, April 30).

12. Ravi Tangri. (2003, March). *Calculating the costs of stress.* Retrieved June 1, 2004: http://www.teamchrysalis.com/Calculating_Stress.htm

13. Katharina Naswall, Magnus Sverke, and John Hellgren (2005). The moderating role of personality characteristics on the relationship between job and insecurity and strain. *Work and Stress*, 19(1), 37–49.

14. International Labor Organization. Washington, DC. Retrieved online May 9, 2005: http://www.us.ilo.org/ Also see U.S. Department of Labor Statistics (2004, April 30).

15. *Balancing life and practice* (2005, June 20). Harris Interactive, Expedia.com, and Universal Parks and Resorts (2005, June 21). Retrieved online June 21, 2005: http://www.lexisone.com/balancing/articles/060005h.html

16. U.S. Department of Labor Statistics (2004, April 30).

17. Kari Tapiola (2005, May 9). *The search for solutions.* Washington, DC. International Labor Organization. Retrieved online May 9, 2005: http://www.us.ilo.org/ontherecord/otr_tapiola_may03.cfm

18. John Wagner (2005, May 6). Malpractice funds delayed: Doctors, legislators frustrated by wait for promised subsidies. *Washington Post.* p. B06. Rob Moritz (2005, May 6) *Hearing in malpractice claim ordered.* Arkansas News Bureau. Retrieved online May 6, 2005: http://www.arkansasnews.com/archive/2005/05/06/News/321000.html. AP New Jersey (2005, May 4). *Court overturns malpractice verdict against Woodbridge firm.* Retrieved online May 6, 2005: http://www.newsday.com/news/local/wire/newjersey/ny-bc-nj—wilentz-malpracti0504may04,0,4545131.story?coll=ny-region-apnewjersey.

19. *Examiner editorial – still more reform needed in courts* (2005, May 1). *Washington Examiner.* Retrieved online May 6, 2005: http://www.dcexaminer.com/articles/2005/05/02/opinion/editorial/12edit02shakedowns.txt

20. "Suing the government is the second most popular indoor sport in America, and police are often the targets of lawsuits, with over 30,000 civil actions filed against them every year, between 4–8% of them resulting in an unfavorable verdict, where the average jury award is $2 million. This isn't even counting the hundreds of cases settled thru out-of-court settlements, which probably run in the hundreds of millions and involves about half of all cases filed. It may take up to 5 years to settle a police liability case." Source: Thomas O'Connor. Wesleyan College, Rocky Mount, NC. Retrieved online May 6, 2005: http://faculty.ncwc.edu/toconnor/205/205lect12.htm

Also see Rolando V. del Carmen and Jeffrey T. Walker (2003). *Briefs of leading cases in law enforcement.* Thousand Oaks, CA: Sage. Rolando V. del Carmen (1991). *Civil liabilities in American policing.* Englewood Cliffs, NJ: Prentice Hall.

21. The city of Chicago reports that the total payout in 2001 was $26.4 million. In 2002, it was $13.1 million, 2003 brought $11.2 million in settlements and 2004's figure rose to $27.2 million. Last year the figure was at $20.7 million. Overall, there were 864 cases totalling $98.6 million. That is, Chicago has spent nearly $100 million over a 5-year period to settle lawsuits against Chicago police officers, reports the NBC5 news. Retrieved online March 4, 2006: http://www.nbc5.com/news/7367923/detail.html?rss=chi&psp=news

22. Rodger W. Griffeth and Peter W. Horn (2004). *Innovative theory and empirical research on employee turnover.* Greenwich, CT: Information Age Publishing.

23. Commonwealth of Massachusetts, *Department of Corrections Handbook for Correctional Personnel.* Boston: Commonwealth of Massachusetts.

24. Personal communication with correctional personnel who attended a professional conference in July 2005.

25. Los Angeles Police Department. Retrieved online May 11, 2005: http://www.lapdonline.org/pdf_files/manual/Table_of_Contents.pdf

26. The option institute: Learning and training (2005). Retrieved online May 7, 2005: http://www.option.org/stress.html. However, workers working less than their capabilities is not a new incite, see Peter F. Drucker (1993). *The practice of management.* New York: Harper and Row, pp 302–305.

27. Welcome to triangle concierge (2001). Retrieved online May 7, 2005: http://www.triangleconcierge.com/statistics.htm

28. Teri Russell and Daiv Russell (2005, March 20). *The Hawthorne effect and modern motivation management.* Retrieved online May 1, 2005: http://www.envisionsoftware.com/articles/Hawthorne_Effect.html

29. Peter F. Drucker (1993). *The practice of management.* New York: Harper and Row, pp. 262–264, 314.

30. Consumer Price Index (2005, May). *Consumer Price Index: March 2005.* Washington, DC: Bureau of Labor Statistics. Retrieved online May 9, 2005: http://stats.bls.gov/news.release/cpi.nr0.htm

    The Consumer Price Index for All Urban Consumers (CPI-U) increased 0.8% in March, before seasonal adjustment, the Bureau of Labor Statistics of the U.S. Department of Labor reported today. The March level of 193.3 (1982–84=100) was 3.1% higher than in March 2004.

    The Consumer Price Index for Urban Wage Earners and Clerical Workers (CPI-W) increased 0.7% in March, prior to seasonal adjustment. The March level of 188.6 was 3.1% higher than in March 2004.

31. U.S. Department of Labor Statistics (2004, April 30). *Occupational employment and wages: 2003.* Retrieved online May 1, 2005: http://www.bls.gov/news.release/archives/ocwage_04302004.pdf

32. Adapted from the U.S. Department of Labor Statistics (2004, April 30). *Occupational employment and wages: 2003.* Retrieved online May 1, 2005: http://www.bls.gov/news.release/archives/ocwage_04302004.pdf

33. Bureau of Labor Statistics (2005). Retrieved online May 5, 2005: http://data.bls.gov/cgi-bin/surveymost?ce

34. Bureau of Labor Statistics (2005).

35. Another point of interest provided by the BLS is that from 1995 to 2005, professional and business services workers earned $12.38 to $17.85, an increase of $6.47; education earned an hourly rate of $11.71 to $16.52, an increase of $4.81; and transportation workers earned $13.05 to $16.38, or $3.33. Using these occupations as guides, it would appear that the small increases in hourly wages over a 10-year period of time had hardly kept up with a cost of living inflation during the same period, which is estimated between 2–2.5% per year, advises BLS.

36. *2004 police officers average base pay.* Adapted from *Police Labor Monthly.* Retrieved online May 20, 2005: http://www.sspba.org/career_survey.htm

37. Salary wizard. Retrieved online May 20, 2005: http://swz.salary.com/salarywizard/layoutscripts/swzl_compresult.asp?jobcode=LG12000003&jobtitle=Police+Patrol+Officer&pagenumber=2&isforcompanalyst=1&r=salswz_swzresbtn_psr&p=&geo=the+United+States&isgeometro=0&fterangecode=1&narrowcode=LG01&narrowdesc=Fire%2C+Law+Enforcement%2C+and+Security

38. J. J. Hurrell Jr., D. L. Nelson, and B. L. Simmons (1998). Measuring job stressors and strains: Where we have been, where we are, and where we need to go. *Journal of Occupational Health Psychology, 3*, 368–389.

39. J. J. Hurrell Jr., D. L. Nelson, and B. L. Simmons (1998).

40. Judy Van Wyk (2005). Hidden hazards of responding to domestic disputes. In Heith Copes (Ed.), *Policing and stress* (pp. 41–54). Upper Saddle River, NJ: Prentice Hall.

41. Katherine W. Ellison (2004). *Stress and the police officer.* 2nd ed. Springfield, IL: Charles C. Thomas. p. 6. Herbert Benson (2005). Retrieved online April 13, 2005: http://www.mbmi.org/pages/mbb_s2.asp. Hans Selye (1979). Stress, cancer, and the mind. In J. Tache, H. Selye, and S.B. Day (Eds.), *Cancer, stress, and death* (pp. 11–27). New York: Plenum. Also see Hans Selye. (1974). *Stress without distress*. Philadelphia: Lippincott.

42. Hans Toch (2001). *Police stress*. Washington, DC: American Psychological Association. Katherine W. Ellison (2004). *Stress and the police officer.* Springfield, IL: Charles C. Thomas. pp. 47–50.

43. Personal communication with patrol officer in Denver who wishes to remain anonymous. March 14, 2005.

44. J. J. Hurrell Jr., D. L. Nelson, and B. L. Simmons (1998). Also see Judy Van Wyk (2005), p. 43.

45. Peter L. Berger (1969). *An invitation to sociology: A humanistic perspective.* New York: Doubleday. One principle Berger assumes is that things, including events, are rarely what they seem. That is, sociology is a particular way of seeing the world. To see the basic principles of order and social control such as policing, for instance, and to look beneath the official explanation or rhetoric of how things work or supposedly work, can help in a better understanding of what things actually are rather than how individuals want to view those things or events. That is, debunking myth will help make the obvious, obvious, and the truth can be discovered. One truth is that many officers try to "cure" themselves because it is believed that officers are personally responsible for their weaknesses. Any display toward a weakness is unbecoming of a law enforcement officer, and he or she is not to be trusted by other officers including commanders. See John P. Crank (2004). *Understanding police culture.* Cincinnati, OH: Anderson. p. 351.

46. S. P. Glowinkowski and C. L. Cooper (1985). Current issues in organizational stress research. *Bulletin of the British Psychological Society*, 38, 212–216.

47. Barry Perrou (2004). Antecedent (pre-death) behaviors as indicators of imminent violence. In Vivian B. Lord (Ed.), *Suicide by cop: Inducing officers to shoot* (pp. 231–237). New York: Looseleaf Law Publications. Also see Hans Toch (2001). *Police stress.* Washington, DC: American Psychological Association.

48. Peter Schnall, Karen Belkic, Paul Landsbergis, and Dean Baker. (200). *The workplace and cardiovascular disease.* Beverly Farms, MA: Hanley and Belfus.

49. Robert A. Karasek and Tores Theorell (1990). *Healthy work.* New York: Basic Books. Peter Schnall (1998, May). A brief introduction to job strain. *Job Stress Network.* Retrieved online May 2, 2005: http://www.workhealth.org/strain/briefintro.html

49. Peter Schnall (1998, May).

50. Paul Landsbergis, Peter Schnall, Karen Belkic, Dean Baker, Joseph Schwartz, and Thomas Pickering. (2002). The workplace and cardiovascular disease: Relevance and potential role for occupational health psychology. In J. Quick and L. Tetrick (Eds.), *Handbook of Occupational Health Psychology.* Washington DC, American Psychological Association. Also see Dennis J. Stevens (2003). Applied

community policing. Boston: Allyn & Bacon. David L. Carter and Lewis A. Radelet (1999). *The police and the community*. Upper Saddle River, NJ: Prentice Hall. Mark L. Dantzker and M. A. Surrette (1996). The perceived levels of job satisfaction among police officers: A descriptive review. *Journal of Police and Criminal Psychology*, 11(2), 7–12.

51. Dennis J. Stevens (1999). Police officer stress. *Law and Order*, 77–81. And Dennis J. Stevens (2005). Police officer stress and occupational stressors. In Heith Copes, *Policing and strategies* (pp.1–24). Uppers Saddle River, NJ: Prentice Hall.

52. Peter Schnall (1998, May). Peter Schnall reports that hypertension and coronary heart disease are factors that contribute to the development of illnesses such as excessive caloric and fat intake leading to obesity, and elevated blood cholesterol, cigarette smoking, high blood pressure, and diabetes, all of which contribute to atherosclerosis. Atherosclerosis is a common arterial disease in which raised areas of degeneration and cholesterol deposits (plaques) form on the inner surfaces of the arteries. These tend to obstruct blood flow when the blood clots on the roughened plaques.

53. Reuters (2005). *Job stress taking larger toll on U.S.: More employees face illness, depression and violence*. MSNBC.News. Retrieved online May 9, 2005: http://www .msnbc.com/news/950045.asp?cp1=1

54. Clare Mellor. (2003, March 8). Job stress taking high toll. *The Mail-Star, The Chronicle Herald*. Retrieved June 1, 2004: http://www.teamchrysalis.com/ Articles/Stress_Toll.htm

55. Peter Schnall (1998, May).

56. R. A. Karasek and T. Theorell (1990). *Healthy work*. New York: Basic Books. p. 167.

57. Hippocrates's most important contributions were in the development of the medical profession and in a code of conduct for doctors. Even today, doctors entering the profession can still choose to swear on the Hippocratic oath. This oath was an attempt to place doctors on a higher footing than other healers and set them apart as specialists.

58. Alan Monat and Richard S. Lazarus (Eds.). (1991). *Stress and coping*. 3rd ed. New York: Columbia University Press.

59. W. I. Thomas (1923). *The unadjusted girl*. Boston: Little, Brown.

60. Thomas (1923) writes: . . . animals, and above all man, have the power of refusing to obey a stimulation that they followed at an earlier time. Response to the earlier stimulation may have had painful consequences and so the rule or habit in this situation is changed. We call this ability the power of inhibition, and it is dependent on the fact that the nervous system carries memories or records of past experiences. At this point the determination of action no longer comes exclusively from outside sources but is located within the organism itself.

    Preliminary to any self-determined act of behavior there is always a stage of examination and deliberation, which we may call *the definition of the situation*. And actually not only concrete acts are dependent on the definition of the situation, but gradually a whole life-policy and the personality of the individual himself follow from a series of such definitions. Source: W.I. Thomas. Retrieved online May 7, 2005: http://www2.fmg.uva.nl/sociosite/topics/texts/thomas.html

61. Wesley G. Skogan. (1990). *Disorder and decline: Crime and the spiral of decay in American cities*. New York: Free Press.

62. FBI.gov. Retrieved online April 25, 2005: http://www.fbi.gov/

63. Terry, W. Clinton. (1985). *Policing society*. New York: Wiley.

64. Francis T. Cullen, Bruce G. Link, Nancy Travis, and Terrance Lemming (1983). Paradox in policing: A note on perceptions of danger. *Journal of Police Science and Administration*, 11, 457–462.

65. Society of Police and Criminal Psychology. Retrieved online May 4, 2005: http://psychweb.cisat.jmu.edu/spcp/journal.htm

66. The Heavy Badge. Retrieved online May 4, 2005: http://www.heavybadge.com.

67. Joseph A. Harpold and Samuel Feemster (2002). Negative influences of police stress. *FBI Law Enforcement Bulletin*, pp. 1–7.

68. Lynn Atkinson-Tovar (2003, September). The impact of repeated exposure to trauma. *Law and Order*, 51(9), 118–120.

69. Reuters (2005). *Job stress taking larger toll on U.S.: More employees face illness, depression and violence.* MSNBC.News. Retrieved online May 9, 2005: http://www.msnbc.com/news/950045.asp?cp1=1

70. Reuters (2005).

71. W. Dwayne Orrick (2002). Calculating the cost of police turnover. *The Police Chief*, pp. 100–104.

72. National Institute for Occupational Safety and Health (NIOSH) (2002), p. 5. Retrieved online May 4, 2005: http://www.cdc.gov/niosh/stresswk.html

73. American Management Association. Retrieved online April 25, 2005: http://www.amanet.org/research/archives.htm

74. American Management Association. Retrieved online April 25, 2005: http://www.amanet.org/research/archives.htm

75. Carl B. Klockars (1999). Street justice: Some micro-moral reservations: Comments on Sykes. In Victor E. Kappeler (Ed.), *The police and society*, 2nd ed. (pp. 150–154). Prospect Heights, IL: Waveland Press.

76. L. Morrow (1981, September 18). The burnout of almost everyone. *Time*. p. 4.

77. Katherine W. Ellison (2004). *Stress and the police officer*, 2nd ed. Springfield, IL: Charles C. Thomas.

78. I. L. Densten (2001). Rethinking burnout. *Journal of Organizational Behavior*, 22(8), 833–847.

79. John P. Crank (2004). *Understanding police culture*. Cincinnati, OH: Anderson. p. 324.

80. John P. Crank (2004). p. 325.

81. John P. Crank (2004). p. 325.

82. J. P. Brodeur (1998). *How to recognize good policing: Problems and issues.* Thousand Oaks, CA: Sage.

83. C. Maslach (1976). Burned out. *Human Behavior*, 1, 16–22. I. L. Densten (2001).

84. Acute stress disorder. *Psychology Today*. Retrieved online May 9, 2005: http://cms.psychologytoday.com/conditions/acutestress.html

85. *Diagnostic and statistical manual of mental disorders (DSM IV)*, 4th ed. (1994). Washington, DC: American Psychiatric Association. p. 424.

86. Donald C. Sheehan and Vincent B. Van Hasselt (2003, September). Identifying law enforcement stress reactions early. *FBI Law Bulletin*, 72(9). Retrieved online July 21, 2004: http://www.fbi.gov/publications/leb/2003/sept2003/sept03leb.htm#page_13

87. E.J. Ozer, S.R. Best, T.L. Lipsey, and D.S. Weiss (2003). Predictors of post-traumatic stress disorder and symptoms in adults: A meta-analysis. *Psychological Bulletin*, 129(1), 52–73.

88. Nancy Jo Dunn, Elisia Yanasak, Jeanne Schillaci, Sofia Simotas, Lynn P. Rehm, Julianne Souchek, Terri Menke, Carol Ashton, and Joseph D. Hamilton (2004). Personality disorders in veterans with posttraumatic stress disorder and depression. *Journal of Traumatic Stress*, 17(1).

89. Donald C. Sheehan and Janet I. Warren (Eds.) (2002). *Suicide and law enforcement.* (pp. 205–209). Washington, DC: U.S. Department of Justice, Federal Bureau of Investigation.

90. Paige Ouimette, Ruth Cronkite, Annabel Prins, and Rudolf H. Moos (2004, August) Posttraumatic stress disorder, anger and hostility, and physical health status. *Journal of Nervous and Mental Disease*, 192(8), 563–566.

91. David L. Carter and Lewis A. Radelet (1999). *The police and the community.* Upper Saddle River, NJ: Prentice Hall. Mark L. Dantzker and M. A. Surrette (1996). The perceived levels of job satisfaction among police officers: A descriptive review. *Journal of Police and Criminal Psychology*, 11(2), 7–12.

92. Donald C. Sheehan and Vincent B. Van Hasselt (2003, September). Identifying law enforcement stress reactions early. *FBI Law Bulletin*, 72(9). Retrieved online July 21, 2004: http://www.fbi.gov/publications/leb/2003/sept2003/sept03leb .htm#page_13

93. Bureau of Labor Statistics (2005). Retrieved online May 4, 2005: http://data.bls.gov/cgi-bin/surveymost?ce

94. International Labour Organization (2005). *Number of work related accidents and illnesses continues to increase.* Retrieved online May 9, 2005: http://www.ilo.org/

95. Bureau of Labor Statistics (2005).

96. National Institute for Occupational Safety and Health. Retrieved online May 5, 2005: http://www.cdc.gov/niosh/homepage.html

97. National Institute for Occupational Safety and Health (NIOSH) (2001, October 1). Retrieved online May 6, 2005: http://www.cdc.gov/niosh/civinj.html

98. Census of Fatal Occupational Injuries (2004). Washington, DC: Department of Labor. Retrieved online May 6, 2005: http://stats.bls.gov/news.release/cfoi.nr0 .htm

99. Bureau of Labor Statistics (2004). Retrieved online May 4, 2005: http://data.bls .gov/cgi-bin/surveymost?ce

100. Bureau of Justice Statistics. Retrieved online May 5, 2005: http://www.njspba .com/corrections/bjs%20workplace%20violence.htm

101. Bureau of Justice Statistics (2005). *Workplace violence.* Washington, DC: U.S. Department of Justice, Office of Justice Programs. Retrieved online May 21, 2005: http://www.ojp.usdoj.gov/bjs/cvict_c.htm#findings

102. FBI (2003). Table 36. Retrieved online May 5, 2005: FBI (2003). *Law enforcement officers killed and assaulted, 2003.* Table 36. Retrieved online May 5, 2005: http://www.fbi.gov/ucr/killed/leoka03.pdf

103. Bureau of Justice Statistics (2004). *One of the top careers for workplace violence.* Washington, DC: U.S. Department of Justice. Office of Justice Programs. Retrieved online May 5, 2005: http://www.njspba.com/corrections/bjs%20 workplace%20violence.htm.

104. John Strahinich (2005, May 6). Memo to bosses: Be afraid. *Boston Herald*, pp. 22–23.

105. Paul Viollis (2005, April 11). Most workplace violence avoidable. *Business Insurance*. Retrieved online May 7, 2005: http://www.ncdsv.org/images/MostWorkplaceViolenceAvoidable.pdf

106. David Walker (2005, April 6). Paying the price: The knives are out for public managers. *The Guardian*. Retrieved online May 7, 2005: http://society.guardian.co.uk/comment/column/0,7882,1452717,00.html Also see Department of Health and Human Services (2000, March). *Workplace violence: Perceptions and experiences of local public assistance and child support enforcement staff and managers*. Retrieved online May 7, 2005: http://oig.hhs.gov/oei/reports/oei-06-98-00044.pdf

107. Bureau of Justice Statistics: One of the top careers for workplace violence study shows only police officers face higher risk. Retrieved online May 5, 2005: http://www.njspba.com/corrections/bjs%20workplace%20violence.htm

108. Bureau of Justice Statistics: One of the top careers for workplace violence study shows only police officers face higher risk.

109. FBI (2005). *Enforcement Officers Killed and Assaulted 2003*. Retrieved online May 5, 2005: http://www.fbi.gov/ucr/killed/leoka03.pdf

110. Richard D. Heffner. (1956). *Alexis de Tocqueville: Democracy in America*. New York: Mentor Books.

111. FBI (2005). *Clearance rates*, p. 79. Retrieved online May 6, 2005: http://www.fbi.gov/

112. National Institute for Occupational Safety and Health. Retrieved online May 4, 2005: http://www.cdc.gov/niosh/injury/

113. See government website: What are the hazards? http://www.cdc.gov/niosh/violphs.html

114. NIOSH.

115. FBI (2005). *Enforcement Officers Killed and Assaulted 2003*. Retrieved online May 5, 2005: http://www.fbi.gov/ucr/killed/leoka03.pdf

116. FBI (2005). *Enforcement Officers Killed and Assaulted 2003*.

117. FBI (2005). *Enforcement Officers Killed and Assaulted 2003*.

118. New York City. Civilian Complaint Review Board. Retrieved online February 7, 2005: http://www.nyc.gov/html/ccrb/home.html. Also, applying principles of search and seizure law to this particular case, the board determined that even if the detective saw the man put his hands in his waistband and take a step back, the detective was not entitled to forcibly stop and frisk the man for a weapon. Before an officer can frisk an individual, an officer must reasonably believe that the individual possesses a weapon (or has committed, is in the process of committing, or is about to commit a crime). In evaluating the evidence—particularly the information contained in the stop and frisk report—the board concluded that the detective threatened the man, threw him on the car, frisked him, and searched him because the detective took umbrage at being referred to as "Jack." On September 27, 2002, the board substantiated these allegations and recommended that the department file charges and specifications. In January 2003, the department issued the detective a level B command discipline.

119. FBI (2003). *Uniform Crime Reports*. Retrieved online April 25, 2005: www.fbi.gov

4

Police Organizations and Police Subculture

So much of what we call management consists in making it difficult for people to work. —Peter Drucker

Learning Objectives

Once you read this chapter, you should be better prepared to:

- Describe an organization and its rationale.
- Describe 10 typical components of most organizations.
- Explain the criticism of those components as they apply to law enforcement.
- Operationalize a hierarchy of command within a law enforcement organization.
- Operationalize a police bureaucracy and explain its rationale.
- Define management and explain its functions.
- Describe the internal organizational factors.
- Define leadership and identify excellent leadership qualities.
- Identify the external factors that affect organizations.
- Describe civil liability issues and their impact on law enforcement.

- Describe the police culture's function and explain what promotes its existence.

- Define a subculture and explain its relationship to police officers.

KEY TERMS

Bureaucracy	Hierarchy of command	Span of control
Civil liabilities	Leadership	Specialization
Cognitive dissonance	Organization	Vicarious liability
Division of labor	Police subculture	
Fragmentation	Rulification	

INTRODUCTION

Upon a closer look at stress, most of the stressors encountered by street cops are linked to the police organizational structure, which is the focus of this chapter. Be prepared to think about descriptions of the police organizational structure and their influences on police management and police leadership, which are often thought to be interchangeable variables but aren't, yet both contribute to police officer stress. The importance of better understanding police organizations and their structure is that they are "remarkably similar in terms of organizational structure and administrative style."[1]

THINKING ABOUT ORGANIZATIONS

When thinking about an organization, think about formal (rules, regulations, and policies) and informal (organizational culture or subculture of personnel) or official and unofficial parts of an organization, its management, and the leadership styles of its managers. Each of these elements will be discussed later in the chapter. Specifically, an *organization* is an artificial structure created to coordinate or control people or groups and resources to achieve a mission or goal.[2] Its rationale relates to four primary components: order, accountability, accomplishment, and predictability.[3] Being organized creates an appearance of order (since things have a place) and the focus upon personnel performing in a certain way and if they do not, they are accountable to official and unofficial directives of the organization. Finally in this regard, because performance is delegated to move along a certain path toward organizational objectives (organizations are goal directed), qualitative measures could be expected or a prediction about outputs or production. That is, an organized group, guided by a similar mission or goal, can accomplish more than an individual,[4] but there are always problems, we are informed by Peter Drucker, a management expert.

Think about working on a group project to better the community where you live but every plan and every action you and your neighbors devise is criticized or shot down by the town's most prominent business owner who resides outside the city boundaries. Although local political and business leaders encourage your group's participation, contribute numerous resources including funding and guidance to aid in the group's success, and reward group members for a job well done, you and the committee are faced with the reality that no matter how much expertise is utilized by each member or the level of sophistication of the program developed, everything can be altered and discredited by the business leader outside of town. Now think about cops.

COMPONENTS OF ORGANIZATIONS

Organizations in general such as educational and human service systems, corporations and trade associations, and criminal justice systems including law enforcement agencies evolve through design and a rational plan that can produce unexpected outcomes such as the emergence of a bureaucracy and personnel stress.[5] There are, among others, 10 components described below that are typical of most organizations, which includes a brief analysis of many of the organizational components associated with law enforcement organizations.[6]

- A clear purpose
- Precise communicated statements
- Structure
- Levels
- Division of labor
- Degrees of specialization
- Hierarchy of command
- Bureaucracy
- Management
- Clear career paths

A *clear purpose* refers to an organization's mission and goals. Generally, the purpose of an organization is the primary focus and driving force of that organization.[7] The glue bonding the organization together is its intention to reach specific goals. Organizations are goal driven. For instance, Chief Timothy Tompkins at the Brookings (North Dakota) Police Department[8] reports that the purpose of the BPD is that it is responsible for protecting and serving the citizens of the City of Brookings. This is accomplished through proactive and reactive law enforcement services. Proactive initiatives are accomplished through public visibility and community programs. The reactive initiative is to respond to emergency and non-emergency calls from the public, the chief advises.

Analysis of a clear purpose. The traditional philosophy among law enforcement across the nation relates to its control and arrest powers. That is, the old idealism is the civics-book picture of justice.[9] The predominate philosophy of law enforcement, and thus its clear purpose, is powered by what policymakers, interest groups, and the public see as diligent and hardworking police officials enforcing the law as it is written in the statutes. Lawbreakers should be arrested, according to this view.[10] One assumption linked to this philosophy is that social order can only be maintained through control of the criminal element. Officers never question whom specifically the criminal element represents.

The traditional police effort centers on crime control objectives and assumptions. The objectives and assumptions are actually shared philosophical beliefs held by policymakers, interest groups, and the public, and are part of the clear purpose that bonds law enforcement efforts, and consist of:[11]

1. Police action can prevent a crime from occurring;
2. Police intervention during the commission of a crime can influence the outcome; and
3. Police efforts after the crime has occurred can resolve the situation, ideally by solving the crime, arresting the perpetrator, and, in appropriate cases, restore stolen property.

Traditional police efforts rely on patrol as the first line of offense and defense, and special units, high-tech gadgets, sophisticated law analyses, and investigative follow-up to complement crime control efforts on the streets.[12]

Another belief about law and order is that it portrays a chaotic system where neither the law and order or justice prevails.[13] Cops are out of control and arrest anybody, especially members of racial or low socioeconomic groups, and employ whatever fashion suits them best—beating, shooting, or killing, the perspective goes. The purpose or intent of the police according to some critics is to guard the interests of the privileged and control lower class members, otherwise known as the dangerous class, through the process of an arrest even if the police have little or no evidence to conduct a probable cause arrest.[14] In this fashion, nothing succeeds like failure. That is, the police must fail to succeed because the only way to maintain order is through the rule of law.[15] The police "fail in the fight against crime while making it look as if serious crime and thus the real danger of society is the work of the poor," argues Reiman.[16] He calls it the "pyrrhic defeat theory," which is a military victory purchased at such a cost in troops and treasure that it amounts to a defeat. That is, the cops tend to control the lower classes more often than the affluent classes since one purpose of law enforcement is to enforce the law, but the reality, says Reiman, is that police enforce certain laws in certain jurisdictional matters such as the behavior of the lower classes. However, another way to explain pyrrhic defeat is to say that through the number of officers who are assaulted, murdered, and unable to cope with their stress, how great is the victory linked to crime control in America? Finally, how clear is the purpose of most law enforcement endeavors?

Precise communicated statements are usually written and available for personnel and others to read. These statements usually consist of the purpose and goals of the organization. They also include mission and objectives, work plans that include day-to-day operations, and values, which include the rules, regulations, and expectations that are interdependent and necessary to carry out the organizational purpose or mission (a mission statement reveals the values of an organization, too).

Analysis of precise communicated statements. In this regard, contemporary traditional police organizations can be described as utilizing rulification practices concerning precise and communicated statements. That is, *rulification* focuses on the relevance of rules and departmental regulations.[17] Policy, procedures, and directives are disseminated in a systematic process that duplicates efforts of disseminating information. Personnel can review written documents in order to better understand organizational mandates and take command in specific directives as opposed to arbitrary perspectives. For example, consider felony pursuits in police vehicles. If documents are available for officers to review before patrol, each would understand the standing orders of the department. Orders that might counter those written directives would be provided for in the documentation, which is often the case. Consequently, an officer would know what to do in each situation and would feel assured that he or she complies with agency directives. Ideally, officers would have read all the relevant materials, laws, and regulations and they would never change, and reading and carrying out regulations might be one in the same variable. However, in the final analysis, rulification lends itself to control of officer performance, which aids police accountability. Then, too, rulification can further intimidation methods of control of officers. Nonetheless, if truth be told, many officers have little time before a shift to review materials, others have less patience to read materials because they want to get to the streets or their assignment, but still, officers have little idea what activities or "mix" they might be thrown in while on the job. The importance of rulification is linked to police accountability, personnel control, and "doing the right thing" on the streets.[18] In particular, some officers think that "doing the right thing" is a means to avoiding civil liability or lawsuits (more on this point later) and sometimes it refers to delivering quality police services.[19] "But in any event, at the end of a shift, I'm going home," explains an officer. Said another way, regardless of the clear purpose and precise communicated rhetoric delivered by police organizations, one study, in addition to the sample polled in this book, shows that most officers surveyed accept the idea that it is better to be tried by 12 than carried by 6.[20]

Structure is best described to the extent of its *levels* of organizational authority (policymakers, managers, and rank-and-file officers). Early in this chapter, it was mentioned that there are remarkable similarities between police departments in terms of organizational structure and administrative style.[21] However, one observer argues that although most large police organizations perform the same tasks, a tremendous variation exists in how individual organizations are structured.[22] To account for this variation, a new theory was developed that attributes the formal structures of large municipal police agencies to the contexts in which they are embedded. This new theory finds that the relevant features of an organization's context are its size, age, technology, and environment.

Analysis of structure. While police agencies are clearly different in matters such as size, technology, and environmental attributes, a hierarchal structure with top-down directives is pervasive, implying that differences vary only in the sense of the degree of organizational components, yet the primary elements are present. For instance, generally in municipal police departments there is a chief of police, and below the chief's position are various other levels of personnel who hold a rank similar to the military (i.e., recruits, sergeants, captains, and majors, and so on). In smaller agencies, perhaps the rank of a major does not exist, but that does not mean that the authority of a major (as compared to an agency with a major's rank) is unavailable. In the typical traditional police structure, levels of authority are crucial to its method and rationale of operation.

Levels are represented by various ranks of authority: commanders, majors, captains, lieutenants, sergeants, and so on (authority is vested in the position or rank as opposed to the person occupying the position) within a division of labor. Upper-level ranks hold more authority than lower-level ranks. Most law enforcement organizations have levels of authority, the higher up the ladder, the more authority and power over subordinates are vested in that position. Figure 4.1 illustrates the various levels at a typical police department in the United States.

Analysis of levels. Levels do not necessarily mean that the person occupying a higher position than another has more experience, knowledge, or expertise, particularly in light of the hiring requirements of better-educated candidates who might represent specific ethnic and gender groups. Then, too, is promotion into a higher position always a matter of experience, knowledge, and expertise or are there other factors? The problem is that many officers are under the impression that delivering quality police service is not the only requirement that determines promotion.

A *division of labor* is represented by different occupational positions within the organization situated at various levels within the structure whereby personnel can have a degree of specialization.

Analysis of division of labor. In this regard, contemporary traditional law enforcement agencies can be described as utilizing levels as a *delegation of authority* that can maintain the integrity of a police agency by clearly defining tasks, responsibilities, and assignments linked to specific positions occupied

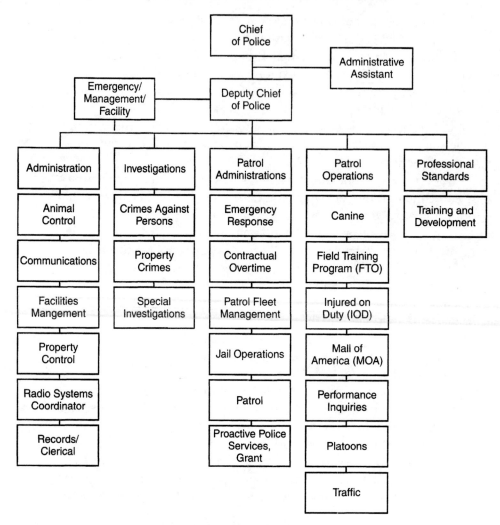

FIGURE 4.1
Typical police department organizational chart.

by personnel. Delegation of authority also provides police personnel with the authority, resources, and skills to complete those tasks, responsibilities, and assignments. That is, each officer knows what is expected from him or her and each is given documented (written directives or verbally at role call) power and the opportunity to enhance professional working skills or degrees of specialization through various means such as in-service training at a justice academy or advanced education at a university.

Degrees of specialization are comprised of skills, training, and certifications held among police personnel regardless of rank or organizational level such as patrol officers, investigators, tactical specialists, and training officers.

In this regard, contemporary traditional law enforcement that employ degrees of specialization within the organization also utilize a strategy known as a *span of control*. A *span of control* refers to a specific number of police person-nel that can be adequately supervised by any one individual.[23] Most often, the span of control refers to the ratio of sergeants to officers. As you expect, a spe-cific number is debated among scholars and practitioners alike. For instance, how many patrol officers should a sergeant supervise during the graveyard shift? Would that number be different than a Saturday evening shift?

Analysis of degrees of specialization. Sergeants often develop close relation-ships with some of their officers, which can affect decisions about deploy-ment, discipline, and the grievance process. These relationships can become a focal point in police subcultures.[24] Sergeants control the activities of the sta-tionhouse and often have more unofficial power over subordinates than top command because sergeants engage in every aspect of daily routines among street cops.[25] Consistent with this thought, in Luther Gulick's classic work on span of control, it was argued that span of control structures relationships be-tween leaders and subordinates in organizations.[26] In addition, Gulick viewed three key determinants of span of control: diversification of function, time, and space. Each of these determinants depends on the organization, the re-sources, and the expertise of management. Sometimes police management can miscalculate a situation and when they do, the results can be detrimental to constituents and street cops. For example, in the mid-1990s, the Los Ange-les County Sheriff's Department experienced a number of officer-involved shooting incidents among officers assigned to the Century Station.[27] An in-vestigation by Special Counsel Merrick Bobb—the department's form of citi-zen oversight—found that the source of the problem was not a few bad cops, but bad management.[28]

Bobb found that at times each sergeant was supervising 20–25 officers, "a ration that far exceeded the department's own standard of 8 to 1."[29]

Hierarchy of command or top-down authority and responsibility refers to personnel who legally and morally can issue orders to those who are legally and morally obliged to follow those orders.[30] A hierarchy of command also reveals that ultimate responsibility rests with the chief and each position down the hierarchy shares a relevant amount of responsibility.

Because of the quasi-military nature of law enforcement operations, the primary method of organization is by formation of rank.[31] The figure depicts the most commonly found rank structure. At the top are administrators, which include the chief, deputy chiefs or second/s in command, and majors, called "command-level" personnel. Captains and lieutenants are often called "middle-level" management, and sergeants and first-line leaders (officers who actually have contact with officers on an ongoing basis) are referred to as lower-level management. Officers are referred to as "line" personnel. Of course, a lot depends on the size of the department.

Lieutenants tend to be morale specialists who do not exercise regular supervision, but are called in when a street cop is having a problem. Their talents and leadership come into play when something unexpected happens.

Sergeants are generally first-level supervisors. They are either stationhouse oriented or street oriented, depending on how much they have abandoned the patrol officer's mentality. The sergeant rank is one of the most sought-after positions, and perhaps the hardest one to obtain if not gained by seniority alone.

Corporals tend to be field-training officers (FTOs) and they are rewarded for their length of service by breaking in rookies or are given other duties related to employee development.

Officers make up the rest of the department, with patrol officers being the "backbone" of the department. This is not normally a career rank, but it is worth considering the concept of Master Patrol Officer (MPO) when it is a professional career.[32] Therefore, most law enforcement organizations can be described as hierarchical, quasi-military bureaucracies. A hierarchy of command encourages bureaucracy.

Here's a little about the foundations of American police quasi-military organizational structure (there's more in Chapter 7). The police resemble the military in some ways: uniforms, military-style rank designations, command structure, authoritarian organizational style (with penalties for failing to obey orders), the carrying of weapons and the legal authority to use deadly force and physical force, and depriving an individual of his or her freedom.[33] This style of organization originated with Robert Peel's plan for the London Metropolitan Police in 1829 and was adopted by American police departments. But the police are different from the military because they manage a citizen population, they provide services to help citizens, they are constrained by laws protecting the rights of citizens, and they exercise discretion.

Analysis of hierarchy of command. In this regard, contemporary traditional law enforcement agencies have a *defined command* referring to the assignment of a specific person in charge of a specific task or tasks and in charge of specific employees. For instance, during a critical incident such as a gunfight, the ranking detective onsite is in command. In this manner, confusion about whose orders to follow will be less likely to produce confusion. Also, a traffic sergeant can be in charge of a specific traffic unit and can issue orders from his or her superiors to the patrol officers under his or her authority.

Official communication moves vertically within the organization, similar to a military structure. For instance, commands and policy directives emanate from the top and are sent downward through the chain of command. Information and reports on the activities of subordinates or problems are sent upward to the appropriate levels.[34] Supporters of a paramilitary command and its critics have debated the intrinsic worth of top-down hierarchy for some time. Supporters want to reinforce the paramilitary structure with greater resources for aggressive patrol strategies[35] while critics see paramilitary structures inconsistent with 21st century strategies such as decentralization and problem-oriented police strategies.[36] Advocates and management argue that

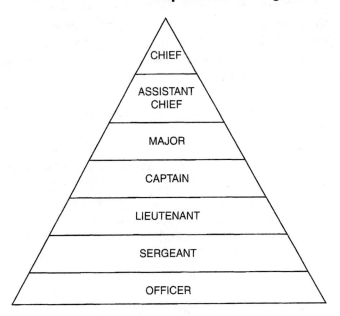

it provides more control, obedience, and loyalty to supervisors and the organization. Regardless of the outcomes of the debate on these issues, the reality is that most police organizations are operated through a hierarchy of command centered on two assumptions:

1. There is a relationship between the position and expertise (individuals in higher positions have more experience than those below).[37]
2. Hierarchy of command has greater predictive powers than other types of command strategies.

Bureaucracy refers to structured layers of the organization as originally defined by Max Weber.[38] First, something about the word "bureau" (French, borrowed into German) refers to a "desk." *Bureaucracy* is rule conducted from a desk or office (i.e., by the preparation and dispatch of written documents and, these days, to their electronic equivalent.)[39] In the office, records of communications are sent and received, files or archives are stored and then are consulted in preparing new ones. Weber argues that bureaucracy is a servant of government, and should be the government. It is a means by which government rules. It is objective and allegedly an impersonal or neutral servant of society, above politics, and Weber emphasizes that every bureaucracy has interests of its own and connections with other social strata (various groups) and other bureaucracies.

Analysis of bureaucracy. Formally and informally, bureaucracy is a means to an end in the traditional law enforcement agency. The hierarchical flow of "orders" can give way to an imbalance: the average officer has ideals and knows how best to perform the job, yet the organization must have its way. For example, the New York Police Department (NYPD) crime control model, or CompStat, is an innovation, and as such represents a sea of change in the NYPD and any other agency that initiates a similar strategy.[40] The effort that must be asserted to accommodate a CompStat initiative includes a significant change in the attitudes of patrol officers and a significant change in the way the department is managed. When personnel regardless of rank are uncertain or uncommitted about their "place" within an agency during significant agency changes, in what way could their behavior change? Then, too, some of the officers involved (their participation will be clarified in a later chapter) in this work can be typified by Officer Collins's remark: "There were changes made by the department that none of us knew until roll call and suddenly we were faced with a completely new procedure that was explained in less than a minute by the sergeant." Most often, officers first learn of new procedures, policies, and expectations seconds before engaging the public. But bureaucracies are resistant to change, and rapid change is certain in the American public and its organizations, especially policing (discussed later in the chapter). Therefore, police managers must embrace change and make it work for their department if the agency is to flourish.[41] Managers must develop new techniques to move street cops closer to the organizational objectives without pressuring the personnel who resist change.[42] However, there is a point when a resister has to come around, like it or not. Nonetheless, in the final analysis of bureaucracies, they are rigid, inflexible, and unable to adapt to external changes.[43]

Management can be described as occupational positions that legally administer policy of the organization and legally control its affairs or a particular sector of the organization.[44] Positions such as police commanders, chiefs, and supervisors control the degree to which rules and policies are formalized, and centralized—that is, the degree to which the decision-making capacity within an organization is concentrated in a single individual or small select group.[45] In total, you could say that police management includes personnel who possess the responsibility of creating, maintaining, protecting, and perpetuating its system. *Management* is the process of planning, organizing, and controlling resources in order to achieve public safety. Police management positions hold the authority of the organization.

Think about how managers use their leadership skills to move subordinates toward performance that they might not do otherwise, and how, because of the manipulation of skilled managers, their subordinates might even "passionately" pursue a vague and often redundant objective of the organization. One definition of power is the ability to exercise control over others to the extent of their compliance.[46]

Analysis of management. There is unofficially more to management than just the position in the organization. Managers represent the role models most often emulated by personnel. The behavior of a police manager should reflect professional behavior.[47] Honesty and integrity must exemplify their day-to-day routines.

Public servants typically have authority to make decisions over others and make decisions that influence the public good.[48] "Ethical mentoring and role modeling should be consistent, frequent, and visible" at all times if managers expect ethical behavior from their subordinates.[49] However, a "moral blindness" often exists in police organizations whereby fundamentally ethical people commit unethical blunders because they are blind to the implications of their conduct. Sometimes moral blindness could be the result of not knowing that an ethical dilemma exists, or it may arise from a variety of mental defense mechanisms. How often would managers and sergeants look the other way concerning unethical or outright corrupt behavior from colleagues and subordinates? Many view public service as enjoying a "double standard" rather than adhering to a "higher standard."[50] Some say that some politicians routinely get honorariums and "fees" from those over whom they make decisions, and police officers often follow the lead of their supervisors, routinely excusing themselves from some laws even while enforcing the laws.[51]

Knowing supervisors are the guardians of organizational directives toward fulfilling organizational objectives, most employees, regardless of the type of organization, are not asked to contribute to the development of those directives or objectives (don't forget the assumption that those at the top have more experience than others).[52] Consequently, personnel hostility toward organizational goals is a common reaction, especially when those dictates do not mirror their perspectives.[53] Supervisors often influence the career paths of younger officers.

Clear career paths refer to examining an officer's progress from recruitment to retirement.[54] "Good hires" are not enough unless the training and other organizational amenities are available. Then, too, poor management will take its toll on young officers and can hinder career success.

The hierarchical method of command (above) describes the vertical flow of orders down and the vertical rise of reports of patrol officers. Career paths in law enforcement are similar in that commanders and supervisors usually rise from the lower ranks. However, not all officers are eligible or want command positions.

Analysis of career paths. In the traditional police organization, clear career paths are obscure because bureaucracies are not conducive to career paths. Lateral movement is the exception rather than the rule, which means that those in field positions do not easily obtain desk jobs.[55] Upward mobility is also somewhat difficult, as it is easy to "lock in" to some "dead end" job. Obviously many officers do rise through the ranks, but their stories are different as to how they obtained higher command. Therefore, paths to supervisor jobs usually depend on who an officer knows more than on an officer's skills. Assignment to special units is usually done on a network-based decision. For example, a Boston police officer says that she applied several times for a special unit in the Boston PD only to be told that she did not have enough field experience. But the officer who did get the promotion to the juvenile unit was an officer with less experience, but the officer's father and the commander of the unit were friends.[56]

In summary, it appears that based on these 10 essential components associated with a police organization, can membership in an organization lead its members into extraordinary acts? Can police officers be "programmed" toward deviance as a result of their experiences with police organizational structure? Do officers assimilate into a normative organizational subculture? It would seem that an indecisive "yes" might fit each question. However, to imply that many street cops are routinely frustrated by the organizational system that employs them because they have little voice in the decisions might be ridiculous. Some cops don't want to be a part of the decision-making process and are content with being on patrol. But briefly examining typical internal factors within an organization could aid in producing an answer to the question of organizational impact upon its participants.

INTERNAL ORGANIZATIONAL FACTORS

Many internal organizational factors affect police practice. However, it should be acknowledged that most police agencies are operated through a bureaucratic organization and can include the following factors:

- Civil service rules and unions
- Measuring police performance
- Organizational size
- Fragmentation
- Resistance of new policy
- Leadership styles
- Leadership techniques

Although it has been explained that most police organizations are similar when organizational structures are compared, they are far different when it comes to *civil service rules and unions*. That is, some form of civil service that regulates personnel policy governs all but the smallest of agencies.[57] In addition, many large police agencies are legally bound by collective bargaining contracts with unions representing officers. In both cases, commanders do not have final authority over law enforcement personnel matters. Trying to dispose of a "bad apple," for instance, might cause a commander and other officers a great deal of anguish.

Measuring police performance refers to the criterion utilized by police organizations to determine if a department and its personnel are meeting the mission and objectives of the agency. For instance, there is day-to-day monitoring by the police of their operations to determine whether a department is doing well or not, which includes arrests, patrol stops and citations, racial data of arrests and stops, calls for service, response time, complaints against officers, and/or dollar amounts of confiscated contraband and property such as drugs, weapons, and cash.[58] These measuring practices are pervasive among police agencies and are used by a variety of social agencies, communities, and individuals to determine the level of police service provided to them.

The principal mechanism for determining police effectiveness has historically been counted and measured in numbers.[59] This practice can be described as bean counting. Ironically, police agencies have never provided a tangible product that lends itself to so easily being counted. That is, since police agencies deliver a service, and keeping their communities safe is a principle part of those duties, why do police agencies continue to place a heavy reliance on reports that count things? One reason might be that most people understand the results of those measurements easier than other results: monthly arrest data, case numbers, tickets issued, revenue generated, hours spent on foot patrol, and hours spent attending community meetings lend themselves to being easily quantified and measured. Perhaps the best example of nationwide standardization of categorizing reported crime is the Uniform Crime Report. Measuring perceptions, on the other hand, is relatively new to policing. Police agencies today are discovering the impact of new measurements, but that too represents a change in the way police agencies do business and their critics have other ideas. Agencies are recognizing that what they do and how well they do it is inherently subjective and personal to those who receive their services. Resident perceptions about quality-of-life issues such as fear of crime and police responsiveness are genuinely as important as crime numbers and, therefore, agencies might want to consider them as part of the equation. Management utilizes these counts to determine deployment and to deliver other services including recognition toward officers—rewarding cops for making more arrests than other cops!

The way police performance is measured might cloud the purpose of law enforcement and perhaps their personnel, too. Because the purpose of law enforcement is public safety, which includes acting as defenders of human rights and the U.S. Constitution,[60] what should be measured might be different than what is measured and rewarded.

Organizational size refers to the number of sworn officers employed at a particular law enforcement agency because size can influence how many different tasks each member of the agency performs.[61] The typical police department in the United States is comprised of approximately 45 sworn officers. Some additional data that might aid a student in a better understanding of police organizations is contained in the following:

- In state and local police agencies there were 708,022 full-time sworn personnel and 311,474 full-time civilian employees employed in 2000.[62]
- As of June 2000, local police departments had 565,915 full-time employees including about 441,000 sworn personnel. Sheriffs' offices had 293,823 full-time employees, including about 165,000 sworn personnel.[63]
- In most jurisdictions, there are approximately 23 sworn officers for every 10,000 residents.[64]

- Approximately 68% of most sworn officers respond to service calls, but in communities with a population of 25,000 or less the number of officers available reaches as high as 95% in communities of less than 2,500.[65]
- Approximately 81% of most sworn officers are patrol officers.
- Federal sworn officers total approximately 93,400 (as of June 2002).[66] The largest employers of Federal officers, accounting for 60% of the total, were:
  - Immigration and Naturalization Service (19,101)
  - Federal Bureau of Prisons (14,305)
  - U.S. Customs Service (11,634)
  - FBI (11,248)

What type of bureaucratic organizational structure best represents a police agency is difficult to say since there are so many different varieties of police structures that mark the estimated 18,000 agencies throughout the United States. Most local and state agencies are typical products of their local history, resources, and their constituents.[67] What is typical of most agency structure is that they are operated by local and state authority, while federal agencies have fewer agencies and less than 100,000 sworn officers in all their agencies combined. Size and authority are important factors that shape police practice, yet internal and external factors also shape police activity.

Fragmentation. Because of the large number of agencies, the variety of jurisdictions that operate those agencies, and resource differences and constituent needs and demands, police efforts are largely fragmented (each operates the way it sees fit). Experts would be hard pressed to argue a "best" police agency.[68] The sharing of information and investigative cooperation is practiced less often than expected. In fact, some officers say that competition exists between agencies, giving rise to more fragmentation. For example, state troopers see themselves as the ultimate police agency in a jurisdiction: better training, better equipment, and more resources.[69] During drug investigations, which might include personnel from both state and municipal enforcement units, there is a tendency for state officers to keep their information out of the hands of the locals. Then, too, municipal drug officers often keep their "drug leads" confidential from deputies employed by a sheriff for similar reasons.[70] It could be argued that competition exists between agencies to hire and retain sworn officers and some observers say that that competition is fierce.[71] Many cities, such as the New York City Police Department, go online and visit university campuses to recruit officers.

As a result, police departments can seem more like little countries, clans, and tribes as opposed to rational units, objective entities, or a service centered on professional management processes.[72] Although complex and conflicting perspectives among police agencies serve as constraints in an effort to serve and protect the public, consistent limitations through due process requirements guide police powers within a predictable framework. Because municipal departments answer to municipal patrons, that in and of itself reveals where loyalties of local departments remain.

Additionally, local loyalty between police and constituents is a product of the law that supports that relationship. That is, local police departments have a legal right to perform their duties in a legally prescribed manner couched in legislative enactments. That is, in every state there are state codes that indicate specific provisions for every aspect of policing in that state. For example, the Commonwealth of Massachusetts' Criminal Law 41:98 states[73]:

> The chief and other police officers of all cities and towns shall have all the powers and duties of constables except serving and executing civil process. They shall suppress and prevent all disturbances and disorder. They may carry within the commonwealth such weapons as the chief of police or the board or officer having control of the police in a city or town shall determine.

Resistance of New Policy

There is a tendency among police managers and officers alike to resist new police policy and policing directives.[74] Officers regardless of rank are not anxious to make organizational changes.[75] However, since policy is rarely developed at the police officer or even police middle manager levels, looking favorably upon policy and the changes it dictates adds fuel to the "we" and "them" split. This split between cops and everybody else is pervasive throughout most agencies and between most officers and top police managers.[76] Some refer to this split as a "siege mentality" in which the public is increasingly the "them." In part, strategies to control terrorism, the war on drugs, and the war on crime has widened the "we–them" split because the police turned to the federal government and the U.S. military for critical technical training, sophisticated weapons, and detailed intelligence on citizens. The public turned to enforcement of the law, particularly Posse Comitatus,[77] which is discussed in more detail in Chapter 8, and other forms of controlling police initiatives through police managers, especially police disciplinary determinations. The leadership qualities of police commanders and supervisors make a difference in how officers relate to changes.[78] It doesn't take a psychologist to know that poor leadership can compromise quality policing efforts in the sense of finding those breaking points among officers during times of change (or, for that matter, most of the time).

Leadership

The primary question seems to relate to police service models, which depend on the managerial skill levels of police supervisors or can be called leadership.[79] Are police managers professionally prepared to meet the organizational change expected of them to better serve their constituents and to manage police personnel? A worthy concern is that there is not, and probably never will be, one best way to lead, manage, and assist any organization including a police agency in the areas of strategy, policy, performance, productivity, human relations, or implementation.[80]

Unfortunately, police management as a distinct entity has developed less extensively when compared to other organizational management entities due to organizational variations from police department to police department and due in part to the variations of the diversity of the constituents they serve. There are universal characteristics that can be utilized by police supervisors to professionalize their management techniques.[81] One suggestion is that the quality of police leadership should automatically improve, not because of managerial training, professionalism, or public demand, but because the gap between private enterprise and public service will narrow in terms of administrative skills, technology, and fiscal responsibility.[82] Therefore, this chapter is an exploratory examination of the leadership characteristics of police managers since agencies must rely on those executives to plan, organize, and deliver quality police service from every employee, with the support of the community, to contribute to public safety and efficiently use every resource. Leadership characteristics, it could be argued, aid in bringing about appropriate police strategies without endangering public safety or compromising the integrity of the men and the women who work hard to provide a quality lifestyle for others through good police service. It can also be argued that police managers must process proficient leadership skills to deliver contemporary police service.[83] For instance, management's failure to reward its officers for excellent police performance can lead to cynicism, burnout, and reduced levels of effort by senior officers.[84]

Leadership Defined. Leadership is the process of directing and influencing the actions of others to bring a police agency closer to its objectives. Leadership is the style of a manager.[85] Leadership deals with people; management deals with things. You manage things and lead people.[86] This notion is consistent with writers who argue that leadership skills are typical of efficient management regardless of the service or product produced by an organization.[87] Leadership qualities are professional skills, characteristics, and/or a style of managing others.

Given the complexity of leadership in a police department, it appears that the situational or contingency approach might apply more often than a behavioral perspective largely because police management operates in an adversarial environment that tends to constrain police leadership more than advance it. Therefore, police leadership can be seen as a process that effectively accomplishes organizational objectives but depends on how a commander interacts with other domains of leadership outside the department and subordinates of the department.[88]

Leadership Techniques

Today's police executive must possess an extraordinary range of capacities.[89] Leadership characteristics among police supervisors are seen as crucial for commanders because they must work closely with individuals who provide police service (i.e., their own subordinates), and officers over whom they have little control (i.e., local, state, and federal personnel from other law enforcement agencies).[90] However, unlike their police sergeants, commanders have little direct influence over the daily lives of any of those officers.[91] They must also work closely with community members, business and social agency executives, and civic officials who can vigorously influence police service, yet these commanders seldom possess an outcome-decision in most of the enterprises those individuals represent.[92] Lastly, police managers are held accountable through courts and disciplinary committees with individuals whom police service affects, and again it appears that commanders have little influence in directing courts or committees to action. Nonetheless, it can be argued that should police managers lack specific leadership skills, tension among their officers could be very high. Thus, poor leadership style gives rise to stress among officers.

Police leadership styles have their critics, some of whom suggest that the authority of both top management and middle management are affected by a host of regulations and obstructions advanced by politicians, community leaders, and organizational leaders in both public and private sectors.[93] Also, surveys report that a large number of Americans hold a low opinion concerning decisions made by the police—even when a police agency engages in a justified critical response employing technical initiatives to further public safety, community members reject that deployment and imply the police are reckless.[94] Also almost 4 out of 10 Americans think that the police could not protect them from becoming a victim of a violent attack.[95] Yet the American public has a litigious nature and initiate civil suits against police departments and police personnel in record numbers, often influencing day-to-day service and protection decisions.[96] One assumption held by this researcher is that professional leadership skills can enhance public confidence toward the police and help bring the police closer to their organizational mission.

Taking direction from manager trainers, Jim Kouzes, president of Tom Peters Group/Learning Systems, says, "If people don't believe in the messenger, they won't believe in the message"—that is, it's *credibility*.[97] How does a police commander build credibility? Kouzes prescribes an acronym—DWWSWWD ("do what we say we will do"). But how?

There are a number of leadership skills required of modern police managers, many of which are congruent with corporate and private world perspectives.[98] When objectively engaged, these characteristics motivate police personnel to optimum performance, moves a department closer to its mission, reduces the fear of crime among constituents, and enhances community and personnel quality-of-life experiences.[99] The key points of police leadership are (in no particular order and including examples that hopefully are on target):

Organizational Change Police leaders must employ change as a continuum to fulfill modern police strategies.[100] For instance, try variations of community relation initiatives, until the initiative is working appropriately for personnel and community members alike. This necessitates change provisions and evaluation methods spelled out as part of a new initiative.

Planning and Organizing Competencies In order to initiate change, police executives must exercise the basic skills of managers, to plan and organize the department's competencies (or resources), which includes a chronological timeline for change to occur and the list of players involved in the change.[101] Failure to plan professionally (objectively) is commonplace among police executives.

Problem-Solving Competencies Although this perspective has been added to the original list, problem-solving abilities are vital to leadership styles in the 21st century. Problem-solving competencies contain three essential elements: defining public safety problems more precisely, analyzing each problem, and finding more effective solutions to each problem.[102] Knowing community problems, from the perspective of the community members—much like knowing the problems of the officers under their command—and resolving those problems goes a long way in winning respect and compliance. Evidence for problem-solving competencies comes from community relations initiatives that include a strategy known as SARA (scanning, analysis, response, and assessment). This model addresses crime in particular areas of a community. The SARA model helps police reduce the crime rate, as well as the fear of crime among citizens.[103]

Creative Ability Commanders must develop a mindset to see creative opportunities and different ways to deliver police services.[104] Rigid thinking is a thing of the past. Looking to officers and community members as partners and soliciting their thoughts about projects might be one way to add to the creative "pie."

Toughness Leaders should be decisive when making difficult choices or changes that must be made for the health of the department and the well-being of the community.[105] For example, when a program such as DARE isn't performing as well as another program that reaches out to youngsters, cancel it (after professional evaluation) and don't back down from criticism. Of course, if cancelled professionally, there wouldn't be much opposition to this change (see Creative Ability).

Subordinate Trust and Public Trust Empowering community policing officers and community members will enable them to mutually solve community problems and move the community closer to public safety.[106] But once empowerment is provided (preferably limited, and in writing), support the decisions made by them and their committees.

Delegation of Responsibility Fulfilling trust initiatives cannot be accomplished in a paramilitary hierarchy of command. For that reason, decentralization and delegation of responsibility are one of the options available to move the organization closer to its mission.[107] Once authority is provided to others, their motivational levels (assuming the communication skills of leaders are professional) can motivate officers toward change in an expeditious manner (see Subordinate Trust and Public Trust).

Decisions Making informed decisions about such things as deployment, technical and use of force response limits, and police disciplinary and promotional prerogatives requires input from many sources.[108] When the community and officers have input in the decision-making process, it is more likely that compliance will become commonplace among those individuals and the individuals they influence.

Taking Action Actuation/implementation competencies, which includes the idea that leaders need to take action as a facilitator as the appropriate managerial model versus the traditional authoritarian (previously discussed) of the traditional law enforcer.[109] Facilitating takes more time from the get-go, but in the long run saves grief and aggravation when changing initiatives and expecting compliance (see Organizational Change).

Communication Discovering what is being experienced by rank-and-file officers and by community members is one of the most important assets of top management. Change must be communicated to everyone in order to improve the quality of police service.[110] Professional leaders must communicate and listen all of the time. The more they talk, the less time for them to listen (see Decisions).

Sharing Command Evolutionary methods of sharing command is a way of doing police business that is both inevitable in a democratic society, and required to accommodate the changing demographics and expectations of American society.[111] Commanders are politicians in the sense of reaching out and sharing command with individuals affected by command.

Visionary Supervisors should be able to develop a mental picture of where the department is going and describe that vision to others so everyone is headed in a similar direction.[112] Drawing pictures for others fulfills the thought that a picture is worth a thousand words.

Integrity Leaders should exemplify the boundaries of moral, ethical, and legal behavior, which also produces an inner strength demonstrating integrity to personnel and constituents. A leader must hold the confidence of many difficult types of individuals, but each of them can relate to unprofessional behavior, even offenders.[113] To truly be effective, officers must operate collaboratively with internal and external stakeholders to work through and with others in a constantly changing environment.[114]

Commitment Leaders must demonstrate a commitment in today's climate of uncertainty to the individuals whom they serve, which includes both his or her constituents and personnel.[115] Police must become facilitators with an eye on quality police service toward enhancing quality of life experiences.[116]

One study examined the above leadership qualities among 97 police supervisors employed at 28 different police agencies across the United States.[117] All but three of the participants were responsible for an average of 60 officers, and those three were responsible for an average of 701 officers each. The findings were indecisive, but reveal that leadership characteristics of the police supervisors surveyed were typical of leadership characteristics of traditional police supervisors as opposed to leadership characteristics of supervisors required in the 21st century. One implication of these results is that most police managers operate from an "antiquated control, arrest, and command hierarchy with top-down dictates about deployment, tactical and use of force limits, and constituent conduct."[118] And what about the new variable added to the list? Since police executives tend to use other strategies than those listed above, it is expected that they are unlikely to employ a problem-solving strategy as often as they should.

If the overall findings from this study are typical of most police agency supervisors, then the traditional, incident-driven police organization (and policing as an institution) must alter policy, regulations, and expectations to fit within a contemporary framework of policing strategies for the 21st century. On the other hand, let's be real about the above demands. If a leader is capable of doing these key components, will his or her pay and status increase? Probably not! Should the commander move to private industry to be paid his or her worth? A few thoughts come to mind. First, the professional police leader must apply his or her skills to the city hall types who control the purse strings. Second, if that doesn't work, there are jurisdictions looking for professional police managers. Even in private industry, top executives move all the time for personal reasons. Third, the reality of a professional work ethic versus an unprofessional work ethic goes beyond income because delivering professional services is more rewarding than money, assuming a leader is interested in public safety and being a professional commander. Like my mom told me, "Anybody can make money. Respect—that's something else." Each of us has to decide what he or she expects from a job.

PROMOTION ASSESSMENT CENTERS AS A SCREENING AND DEVELOPMENT TOOL

Many police agencies utilize assessment centers, managed by outside consultants, as a promotional process. Typically an 8-hour interview comprised of job-related activities designed to assess a candidate's knowledge, skills, and abilities (KSAs) related to the promotional rank are emphasized. Multiple assessors observe and score candidates in simulations, mock-subordinate counseling sessions and community meetings (with role players), a timed in-basket, and writing exercises (such as a squad briefing on a new policy or a press release). Some agencies incorporate some form of an oral interview requiring the candidate to provide an overview of his or her readiness and accomplishments, although this is unrelated to the KSAs, and is the most subjective and least quantifiable aspect of a promotional process. Some oral panels have eliminated many very qualified candidates as potential supervisors because those candidates could not talk about themselves as well as others. The leadership competencies required of a candidate for law enforcement to be successful in managing a COP/POP project, as ranked by police managers and chiefs, consist of the items above, however managers and chiefs rank ordered these items[119]:

1. Communications and related interpersonal competencies
2. Problem-solving competencies
3. Motivational competencies
4. Planning and organizing competencies
5. Taking action: Actuation/implementation competencies

Ideally, these competencies could be identified early on and mentored as an officer progresses in rank and faces new challenges. The planning, organizing, problem-solving, and communicating skills involved are essential in effecting organizational change, and are measurable in an assessment center setting.

EXTERNAL FACTORS THAT SHAPE POLICE ORGANIZATIONS AND PRACTICE

In addition to examining components of organizational structures and their internal factors, four significant external factors shape organizational structures and ultimately police practice and stress, which include:

- Budget cuts
- Civil liabilities
- Policymakers, interest groups, and the public
- Rapid change

Budget cuts refer to the serious economic deterioration of local budgets to police organizations across the nation. Few municipalities and law enforcement jurisdictions have not been affected by budget cutbacks. These cuts have resulted in a hiring freeze of quality police candidates, the hiring of fewer and "marginal" candidates, and a freeze or reduction of payroll compensation for officers already in the field.[120] As a result, police agencies from Boston to Beaufort to San Francisco are not hiring the additional "quality" officers they need or the increase in compensation they deserve.[121] Less budget can be translated to fewer quality officers means fewer arrests, less preventive measures against constituent and police misconduct, and more stress for officers in the field. It can also mean the unavailability of replacement or upgrades of police equipment including weapons and some departments looking to hire part-time officers to control crime.[122]

President George W. Bush's budget cut in early 2005 of over $1 billion to law enforcement will have lasting effects upon officer performance until the end of the decade.[123] Chief Joseph Estey of the Hartford, Vermont, Police Department and president of the International Association of Chiefs of Police reports that:

> This administration talks about homeland security but then guts funding for the very programs that help secure our homeland. This budget cuts funding for critical law enforcement assistance programs by 90 percent, forcing many departments to continue using antiquated and inefficient communications equipment and others to lay off officers. In smaller communities like mine, some chiefs won't be able to hire desperately needed officers. The administration is asking police agencies to take on even greater responsibilities with less and less funding. Discretionary funds for departments to use for equipment and technology have been virtually eliminated at the local level over the years and, under this budget, it has been eliminated at the federal level. It just doesn't add up.[124]

Civil liabilities refer to lawsuits against enforcement officers, their organizations, and even their training centers (or *vicarious liability:* the legal responsibility one person has for the acts of another). Although civil liabilities has been discussed earlier in the chapter, there are probably five reasons why the public sue cops: (1) it is fashionable in the 21st century to sue officers and other public officials[125]; (2) it is fueled by the pursuit of a corruption-free government by means of exaggerated regulations, ambiguous judicial control, and misinformed intervention[126]; (3) a judicial trend toward allowing governmental liability has led to an explosion in the number of lawsuits[127]; (4) almost every aspect of police work can result in an incident that leads to civil litigation[128]; (5) the idea of being a "victim" in today's world is stylish. Being a victim creates attention and in this case, attention can be translated to making money.

There is also a potential for criminal liability under federal law for certain deprivations of constitutional rights. One estimate suggests that police are currently involved in more than 30,000 civil actions annually, and that the frequency of plaintiffs prevailing in their suits is on the rise.[129] One source suggests that during a 5-year period, at least 3,000 of approximately 600,000 U.S. police officers were officially sanctioned for misconduct ranging from theft to sexual assault, and many of those cases resulted in lawsuits.[130] However, there is also evidence saying something else. One study shows that justice professionals report that civil litigation is irrational and excessive.[131]

Nonetheless, the fear of being named a defendant in a suit seeking punitive damages is not unreasonable.[132] The possibility of litigation may cause an officer to question his or her abilities, second-guess decisions, and hesitate before taking appropriate police initiatives.[133] For some officers, the threat of litigation translates into looking the other way when new policy is mandated. Lip service to superiors, and in the field, its business as usual that protects a cop from potential lawsuits. Whether reality or conjecture, there is a popular conception that the American public possesses a litigious nature. Therefore, law enforcement practice a strategy referred to as "CYA" (explained later in this chapter).

Background of Civil Liability Issues

Suits filed against law enforcement officers alleging a constitutional violation are generally founded on Title 42 United States Code (U.S.C.), Section 1983, a statute that imposes civil liability on any person acting under state laws who deprives another person of his or her constitutional rights.[134] The constitutional protection claimed to have been violated is frequently either the Fourth Amendment (alleged unlawful arrest or search), the Fifth Amendment (alleged improperly obtained confession or deprivation of liberty or property without proper due process), the Sixth Amendment (violating the right to counsel), or the Eighth Amendment (incarceration of a plaintiff claiming to have been subjected to cruel and unusual punishment). The defenses available are technical in nature, including improper service and venue and lack of jurisdiction. In addition, the first argument to be made is that the plaintiff failed to state a claim against the police officer upon which relief can be granted. The second avenue is the qualified immunity defense, which shields the police officer from liability.[135]

Police officers acting illegally and outside their scope of authority may be liable under Section 1983 despite the requirement that they had to have been acting under "color of state law,"[136] which includes all conduct of a police officer when he or she is acting under statute, ordinance, regulation, custom, or usage of any law.[137] Then, too, it can be assumed that since officers are always on duty, they are always liable for their actions.

One way to interpret the statute is that any person who causes another person to be subjected to the deprivation of any rights, privileges, or immunities guaranteed by the Constitution may be liable even if that person is conducting police business. Most suits brought against police officers fall within Section 1983 of Title 42.

In recent years, the U.S. Supreme Court has demonstrated a tendency to narrow Section 1983 liability.[138] The Court tried to balance the needs of police personnel and criminal suspects by developing two types of immunity—absolute and qualified for police officials who are sued for alleged constitutional violations.[139] These developments have undoubtedly pleased police agencies that face the specter of civil liability while having to make quick decisions under difficult circumstances; however, limiting police officer exposure to Section 1983 claims is a double-edged sword. Over time, it may increase the incidence of unlawful police actions, and foster protectionism, police cover-ups, and divisiveness between the police and the community.[140] To the extent that civil remedies for constitutional violations are reduced, the rationale for retaining the exclusionary role remains. In many ways, civil liability threats heighten stress and corruption among police officers.

Civil Liability Concerns

It is curious that when liability suits rise, arrest rates decline. For instance, arrests have fallen sharply in New York City since four officers were indicted in the fatal shooting of Amadou Diallo.[141] According to figures released by the New York City Police Department, the number of people arrested in April 1999 fell to 30,134, from 35,813 in March, a 14% decline. Police officials attributed the decline in arrests to fewer crimes reported. They noted that complaints of crime were down 12% in the first 4 months of 1999 compared with the same period the preceding year. The April 1999 drop-off was considerably more pronounced than in previous months, but crime rates have been falling for years, even as the number of arrests has risen. This has some police officials searching for other explanations, including the possibility of fallout from the death of Diallo.[142] Clearly, criminal prosecution is far different from a civil liability suit, but a concern held by many officers is whether the department would back them in the event of a suit regardless of its nature. Certainly, high-profile cases can help shape public opinion, including among police officers. The president of the NYPD's Patrolmen's Benevolent Association, the city's largest police union, urged officers to use "maximum discretion" when citing people for minor offenses.[143] He said that the city's crackdown on minor violations, such as drinking alcohol in public, had harmed relations between the police and the public.

This is not to say that liability questions played a key role in arrest decisions since many factors influence them, but they certainly were part of the decision. For instance, the arrest rates in LA before and after Rodney King are common knowledge. Was crime down? Alternatively, maybe some would argue that there is a stronger predictor of probable cause arrests that relates to street justice. This thought is congruent with one observer who confirms that street justice exists to provide an order-maintenance strategy used by the police as a central function of policing at the local level.[144] Therefore, an arrest even when evidence is present would be less likely. Some officers justify street justice on moral grounds as part of their community-building and maintaining functions. This idea is also consistent with another observer who suggests that officers utilize street justice when they think the system is not administering appropriate justice or guidance to offenders.[145] If we accept this notion, then civil liability concerns may be less of an influence on arrests than street justice strategies. But after another citizen was killed by Cincinnati cops making the front page across the country, is it your perspective that street justice prevailed or the threat of liability impacts officer behavior so much that citizens commit crime even while officers helplessly observe it?

Nonetheless, as we look at the relationship between the threat of civil suits and arrest decisions, several implications link these two variables. For instance, it may be that liability concerns are doing exactly what they are supposed to do, which is to make police officers be concerned about their official actions with an eye on the law. This idea suggests that liability does provide a deterrent effect and protection for individuals in a democratic society. It might be safe to argue that arrests are down not necessarily because crime is down, because officers face more offenders than in the past, but largely because they are more likely to avoid an arrest than to make one, depending on the circumstances and the offender.

Policymakers, interest groups, and public opinion influence police policy more than police executives, which include police commanders. Police policy is usually developed outside the department by political factors within government fueled by the courts, interest groups, and public opinion.[146] The development of police policy is limited to policymakers, interest groups, and public sentiment, yet implementation is the job of police commanders, and compliance with policy is the job of police officers.[147] Depending on many factors such as the status of the commanders, the spirit of the policymakers, the agenda of interest groups, and the sentiment of the public, police executives are not free to design their organization or its strategies as they see fit.[148] For instance, a study conducted in the Fayetteville, North Carolina, Police Department, demonstrates how external constraints took precedence over professional police management:

> Fayetteville delivers an efficient method of problem-oriented policing as evidenced by surveys throughout the city. . . . One key component that works for Fayetteville is that all sworn officers have role in community problem-solving efforts. However, in this respect, opposition due in part to misinformed or

naive political figures tends to reinforce traditional ideals about policing, heightening resistance from some veteran officers. The push and pull of the political interests in Fayetteville might have more influence over police decisions than community members or its professional police management.[149]

After 14 years of service, town hall eventually replaced the chief of police of Fayetteville not because of the chief's professional agenda and experience but because of it. It is clear that political leaders with little knowledge of police strategies (or hidden agendas) have a great deal of input concerning the well-being of police departments including the unemployment of any officer (including chiefs) who might oppose political mandates or an abbreviated version of political incorrectness.[150]

Additional evidence of political subjectivity versus police professionalism comes from Camden, New Jersey, where the department failed at policing initiatives because of both unstable political and police leadership, incisive police history, pervasive officer resistance, ramped crime, and devastating poverty.[151] The Camden police department remains a paramilitary operation but it's the politicians making policy and evaluating police performance based on numeric results linked to arrests, calls, and stops. What it came down to for Camden is "too many chiefs of police, too many involved officials, too much poverty, too much crime, too much officer resistance, and too little professional leadership."[152] In fact, state government gave up on Camden when the sewers backed up and other city departments failed, and the third mayor of the city was indicted on corruption charges. The state of New Jersey stepped in and took control of Camden on July 17, 2000. It is the biggest city takeover in the United States since the Great Depression.

Law enforcement will always be subject to criticism as a department and its managers pursue both "crime control and due process because the public cannot agree on what goal or what balance of goals is appropriate."[153] What is true is that the face of crime, American society, and police strategies and policies are rapidly changing.[154]

Rapid change is a dynamic that affects most police organizations.[155] Change can be seen in the new approaches to crime control including community policing, compstat, and federal approaches associated with the U.S. Patriot Act, which in themselves represent a "sea" of change for law enforcement. There are also changes in the philosophical mandates of police agencies, and many of those changes challenge the way police organizations are managed.[156] For instance, one of the primary changes concerning police service is development, implementation, and maintenance of a community policing initiative. Police managers can no longer take comfort in the traditional response of a punishment-centered organizational bureaucracy accentuated through a reactive policy because in part of a due process revolution—the people in a democratic society want and will be heard even when many residents resist participation in community policing initiatives.[157]

The mass demonstrations linked to racial and gender civil rights issues of the 1960s and 1970s along with serious concerns of an unpopular war in Southeast Asia presented an untenable position to the American people and their leaders concerning political stability. Thirty years later, the war in Iraq and the response to terrorism on U.S. soil mustered a response from the American people revealing that they will use the political process to express their point of view. From the denial of due process in the name of social order, a clear message resonates from those who demand fairness: the seats of power are remedies to due process issues and power is centered squarely in community mobilization.[158] Unlike national elections that reflect an increase in voter apathy, local elections and campaigns produce many changes in the voting patterns of the American people. It is evident with the wave of the new political power base across the nation that lifestyles and personal choice, and ultimately police methods of safeguarding those lifestyles and choices, will change—prepared or not. For instance, due process safeguards applied to school busing and affirmative action often produced anger, uncertainty, and violence on all sides. While political and business leaders, including the current and former President of the United States, are involved in criminal and suspect activities, an immediate availability of illicit drugs, rise of juvenile violence, and breakdown of the traditional American family add to the despair and demand of the American people.

Police leaders have few prerogatives, but to give in to the demands of officials and the American people, they are compelled to give in to the rapid change of American lifestyles. They are encouraged to see it as a continuum in order to fulfill police obligations.[159] When police reject change, their resources dwindle and their status is reduced. In sum, maybe officers can be apprised of external factors through the educational process so that they can aid management in appropriate ways. One writer sums it up well[160]:

> To create change within an organization, such as creating a leadership development program, an agency must have a clear vision of the need for change, a base line from which to start, and a barometer by which to measure the results. To develop their employees into leaders, organizations must use the available tools to assess leadership potential and growth. In developing leaders, psychometric instruments such as the Leadership Skills Inventory (as discussed above) could be used to help develop leadership potential. Early feedback indicates that police agencies have not validated the relevance of early identification of leadership potential to actual future leaders.

ORGANIZATIONAL IMPACT ON OFFICERS: FINDING BALANCE

The 10 components of police organization and the internal and external organizational factors explained above support Chapter 1's proposition that an imbalance exists between police organizational structure and its policies on one side and the day-to-day routine of their personnel, which includes their attitudes and performance. In particular, a bureaucracy with its hierarchy of command implies that utility of the traditional model of police management is, at least from the viewpoint of typical law enforcement officers, in direct conflict with their job.[161] One expert reveals that the reason the traditional model has lasted so long is its ease with which supervision and the span of control can be routinized.[162] That imbalance exists whereby the typical police agency is command-friendly but antagonistic to the ideals and performance of the typical street cop.

Personnel who function within command-friendly but antagonistic environment devise ways to neutralize or resolve the antagonisms. They want balance. One way to explain the typical police officer's desire to strive for balance is something human beings often do, or what can be described as *cognitive dissonance*.[163] That is, an individual experiences a state of unpleasant tension when his or her attitude or behavior is inconsistent with organizational expectations, policy, or accepted knowledge. This gap, or what can be called dissonance, increases with:

- The importance of the subject or practice to the individual officer.
- How strongly the dissonant thoughts or behavior conflicts with expectations, policy, or accepted knowledge.
- The inability to rationalize and explain away the conflict.

Dissonance is often strong when we believe something about ourselves and then do something different or against that belief. Police officers understand that the job they perform and the organizations that employ them are incompatible. One indicator of this dissonance can be found in a typical thought offered by one officer interviewed for this book: "Damned if I do [follow policy or procedure during a stop or an arrest] and damned if I don't. It's a Catch 22. So I do what I think is best at the time, then CYA, and make sure I go home at the end of the shift." How often do we hear this type of a remark by a law enforcement officer?

An attempt at balance or a practical way to mask inconsistencies is often a priority for many cops. Some find balance at the gym, others take hobbies, some pray, others leave policing for other occupations, and others engage in unlawful and unethical conduct. This imbalance also promotes a police subculture that helps to justify the individual attitudes and performance of street cops, which remains at conflict with the expectations, policies, and established knowledge.

POLICE SUBCULTURE

It is easier to justify organizational expectations, policy, and established knowledge that is different from an individual's own attitudes and performance when encouraged by friends and coworkers, particularly if you share a lifestyle similar to that of your friends and coworkers.

A similar lifestyle could be defined as a culture because it consists of those shared assumptions that have an active, shaping influence on ideas, attitudes, and experience.[164] In this sense, culture is a signifying system that represents a "whole way of life of a social group or whole society."[165] To better understand this concept, culture is a learned lifestyle and a subculture suggests that many individuals share both the culture at large and many also share in a learned lifestyle from the workplace, school, church, and at play. Therefore, a culture and a subculture are man-made aspects of social organization, and its influence can operate invisibly at a deeper, almost mythic or subconscious level. Some authors write entire books on cultural and subcultural development, but what you need to know about a police subculture is that the occupation of policing develops its own way of doing business. For instance, it has its own terms and jargon that are used on a daily basis. Terms are used, for instance, to make verbal and radio communications easily understood and quick. Then, too, policing, as an occupation, has often been described as hours of boredom, followed by minutes of sheer terror. In any occupation where such extremes exist, it is necessary to have cultural characteristics that reinforce the collective and impersonal nature of the work.[166] In part, this working personality develops its own customs, laws, morality, and language or esoteric terms to communicate with each other and to control situations.[167]

Officers band together to make sense of their experiences and to protect themselves from the uncertainties of the job, which includes the organizational structure and their supervisors. A police subculture enables a wide variety of police activities on and off the job. It links together the experiences of officers in order to (1) make sense of those experiences, (2) provide justification to continue police work, and (3) help an officer balance the inconsistencies of the organization and the job.[168] Some refer to police culture as the thin blue line, but in essence, it is a shared lifestyle that also provides a support group for its members, which the police organization has little, if any control. One result of a subculture, whether it's a subculture of children, cops, or community members, is that peer pressure plays a significant role in influencing the performance of its participants. Also it is not a far reach to describe peer pressure as part of any cultural perspective because groups, depending on many variables, take on expectations and rules of their own. Members of the police culture (similar to most subcultures) encourage and justify attitudes and performance. Therefore, finding a balance between policy and practice can be justified by a police subculture.

Research confirms that well-entranced officers in a police subculture regard the police organization and their superiors as "bullshit."[169] Therefore it is safe to say that a police subculture aids officers toward finding a balance when dealing with (real or imagined) inconsistencies of the police organization. However, the police subculture also helps officers rationalize and justify their attitudes and behavior, on the job and at home, even when those attitudes and activities are corrupt and unlawful. At its extreme, a police subculture can widen the "us" (officers) and "them" (management and even citizen) gap. However, it could be speculated that if a police organization enhanced its professional standing and controlled its inconsistencies by reducing or controlling its bureaucratic foundations, that the influence of the police subculture would be doomed or at least weakened.

SUMMARY

One thing to know about organizations is that they are incredibly similar in terms of their structure and administrative style, regardless if they are in the private or public sector. An assumption is that most police departments share similar problems. A question asked relates to organizational membership influencing its members into extraordinary acts. Can officers be "programmed" toward corruption, frustration, and stress because of their organizational experience? Apparently, this chapter suggests that they can, and at the chapter's end, it is suggested that officers band together in a police subculture to protect themselves from the inconsistencies furthered by the police organization, but it is also revealed that a police subculture can help officers justify unlawful behavior.

An organization is defined as an artificial structure created to coordinate or control people or groups and resources to achieve a mission or goal. Its rationale relates to four primary components: order, accountability, accomplishment, and predictability. Its components are comprised of a clear purpose, precise communicated statements, structure, levels, division of labor, degrees of specialization, hierarchy of command, bureaucracy, management, and clear career paths. Internal organizational factors were described as civil service rules and unions, measuring police performance, organizational size, fragmentation, resistance of new policy, leadership styles, and leadership techniques. External factors affecting police organizations include budget cuts, civil liabilities, policymakers, interest groups, the public, and rapid change.

The 10 components and internal and external organizational factors support an earlier idea from Chapter 1 that an imbalance exists between the organizations that employ police officers and their day-to-day routines. In particular, a bureaucracy with its hierarchy of command implies that utility of the traditional model of police management is inappropriate. When personnel work under conditions that mirror an imbalance, there is a tendency to devise ways to neutralize or resolve inadequacies, which can include working out, substance abuse, and corruption. The stress of the police organization fosters a police subculture that can rationalize and justify even unlawful behavior.

By any measure, Prince George's County (near Washington, DC) police have shot and killed people at rates that exceed those of nearly any other large police force in the nation. Since 1990, they have shot 122 people, killing 47 of them. By one standard—the number of fatal shootings per officer—they killed more people than any major city or county police force from 1990 through 2000. Almost half of those shot were unarmed, and many had committed no crime. Unlike many departments, Prince George's top police officials concluded that every one of the shootings was justified. Examples of the shootings ruled justified pertains to an unarmed construction worker who was shot in the back after he was detained in a fast-food restaurant. An unarmed suspect died in a fusillade of 66 bullets as he tried to flee from police in a car. A homeless man was shot when police mistook his portable radio for a gun. And an unarmed man was killed after he pulled off the road to relieve himself. An investigation by *The Washington Post* found that during the past decade, Prince George's police miscalculated the threat they faced dozens of times— mistaking an object for a gun or a sudden movement for an act of aggression. Moreover, the police department defended shootings by issuing reports that were riddled with inconsistencies, contradictions, and half-truths.[170]

OFFICER KILLED IN TENNESSEE

On July 9, 2003, shortly after 9:30 A.M., a 43-year-old sergeant with the Mt. Juliet Police Department and a 49-year-old deputy with the Wilson County Sheriff's Department were killed while attempting to assist other law enforcement officers in pursuit of a subject driving a stolen vehicle. Earlier that morning, officers with the Tennessee Highway Patrol discontinued a high-speed chase near Knoxville when the subject, who was wanted for a felony, struck a pursuing unit with the stolen vehicle in order to escape. Responding to the new report, units from the Wilson County Sheriff's Department became involved in a second pursuit on an interstate near Mt. Juliet. The sergeant from the local police department, who had more than 13 years of law enforcement experience, and the deputy from the county agency, who had more than 15 years of experience, deployed a spike strip in order to stop the stolen vehicle. When the driver of the stolen car neared the spike strip, she swerved and struck both officers, who were standing by their patrol cars on the shoulder of the road, killing them instantly. The driver of the stolen vehicle, a 21-year-old woman who was on probation and had several prior arrests, including motor vehicle theft, criminal impersonation, and reckless driving and reckless endangerment, was under the influence of a controlled substance. She and a 33-year-old woman, who was also in the stolen vehicle, sustained injuries in the crash and were taken to a local hospital. The driver of the car was treated and released into the custody of law enforcement officers who transported her to a local jail. She was charged with two counts of pre-meditated first-degree murder and two counts of felony first-degree murder. The other woman remained in the hospital with a broken leg. Prosecutors did not charge the passenger of the vehicle with any crimes; she eventually provided information against the driver.[171]

DISCUSSION QUESTIONS

1. Describe a typical organization and explain its rationale.
2. Describe 10 typical components of most organizations.
3. Explain the criticism of those components as they apply to law enforcement. In what way is one of the 10 components most detrimental to law enforcement?
4. Operationalize a hierarchy of command within a law enforcement organization and explain its function and strengths.
5. Operationalize a police bureaucracy and explain its rationale and strengths.
6. Define management and explain its function.
7. Describe the internal organizational factors.
8. Define leadership and identify excellent leadership qualities.
9. Explain in what way management is different from leadership qualities.
10. Identify the external factors that impact organizations and describe their outcomes.
11. Describe the civil liability issues and their impact on law enforcement.
12. Define a subculture and explain its relationship to police officers. In what way do you agree with influences of a subculture upon officer behavior? Disagree?

ENDNOTES

1. Samuel Walker and Charles M. Katz (2005). *The police in America*, 5th ed. Boston: McGraw-Hill. p. 90.
2. Wayne W. Bennett and Karen M. Hess (2004). *Management and supervision in law enforcement*, 4th ed. Belmont, CA: Wadsworth. p. 2.
3. Samuel Walker and Charles Katz (2005). *The police in America*, 5th ed. Boston: McGraw-Hill. p. 233.
4. Wayne W. Bennett and Karen M. Hess (2004). p. 3.
5. Wayne W. Bennett and Karen M. Hess (2004). p. 11. Concerning bureaucracy, see Samuel Walker and Charles M. Katz (2005). p. 91.
6. Wayne W. Bennett and Karen M. Hess (2004). p. 11; David L. Carter and Louis A. Radelet (2001). *The police and the community*, 7th ed. Upper Saddle River, NJ: Prentice Hall. pp. 50–52; Peter Drucker (1999). *Management: Challenges for the 21st century*. New York: HarperCollins. Stan Stojkovic, David Kalinich, and John Klofas (2003). *Criminal justice organizations: Administration*

and management, 3rd ed. Belmont, CA: Wadsworth. pp. 6–7; Joycelyn M. Pollock (2001). Ethics and law enforcement. In Roger G. Dunham and Geoffrey P. Alpert (Eds.), *Critical issues in policing: Contemporary readings* (pp. 356–373). Prospect Heights, IL: Waveland. Robert Trojanowicz, Victor E. Kappeler, Larry K. Gains, and Bonnie Bucqueroux (1998). *Community policing: A contemporary perspective*, 2nd ed. Cincinnati, OH: Anderson. pp. 84–93.

7. Wayne W. Bennett and Karen M. Hess (2004). p. 11.

8. Brookings Police Department (2005). Retrieved online May 13, 2005: http://cityofbrookings.org/departments/police/polindex.php

9. Samuel Walker (2001). *Sense and nonsense about crime and drugs: A policy guide.* Belmont, CA: Thomson and Wadsworth. p. 27.

10. For a better read on this perspective, see Dennis J. Stevens (2006). *Applied community corrections.* Upper Saddle River, NJ: Prentice Hall. pp. 21–35. In part, this perspective is linked to a punishment philosophy held by the criminal justice community. Punishment is justified through just desserts or retribution, deterrence, and incapacitation actions conducted by the justice community in the name of social order. Criminals get what they deserve.

11. Robert Trojanowicz, Victor E. Kappeler, Larry K. Gains, and Bonnie Bucqueroux (1998). *Community policing: A contemporary perspective*, 2nd ed. Cincinnati, OH: Anderson. p. 87.

12. Robert Trojanowicz, Victor E. Kappeler, Larry K. Gains, and Bonnie Bucqueroux (1998). p. 87.

13. Samuel Walker (2001). p. 27.

14. Randall G. Shelden (2001). *Controlling the dangerous classes: A critical introduction to the history of criminal justice.* Boston: Allyn and Bacon. pp. 3–10.

15. Randall G. Shelden (2001). p. 8. Also see Jeffrey Reiman (1998). *The rich get richer and the poor get prison: Ideology, crime, and criminal justice.* Boston: Allyn and Bacon. pp. 4, 5, 59.

16. Jeffrey Reiman (1998). p. 5.

17. Max Weber (1946). *From Max Weber: Essays in sociology.* Translated by H. H. Gerth and C. Wright Mills. New York: Oxford University Press. Also see, for this interpretation, Gary Cordner and Gerald Williams (1998). Community policing and police agency accreditation. In Larry K. Gaines and Gary W. Cordner (Eds.), *Policing perspectives* (pp. 315–345). Los Angeles: Roxbury.

18. Roy R. Roberg, Jack Kuykendall, and Kenneth Novak (2002) *Police management*, 3rd ed. Los Angeles: Roxbury, pp. 265–278.

19. Personal communication with members of the Boston Police Department, May 2005.

20. Dennis J. Stevens (2006). Police apprehension of sexual offenders and sexual assault conviction levels: Why conviction levels are low in Boston. *Police Journal.* In press.

21. Samuel Walker and Charles M. Katz (2005). p. 90.

22. Edward R. Maguire (2003). *Organizational style in American police agencies.* New York: SUNY Press.

23. Geoffrey P. Alpert and Roger G. Dunham (1997). *Policing in urban America*, 3rd ed. Prospect Height, IL: Waveland. pp. 79–81. Samuel Walker and Charles M. Katz (2005). p. 478.

24. Samuel Walker and Charles M. Katz (2005). p. 478.

25. Wesley Skogan, Susan M. Hartnett, Jill DuBois, Jennifer T. Comey, Marianne Kaiser, Justine H. Lovig (1999). *On the beat*. New York: Westview. pp. 191–223.

26. Kenneth J. Meier and John Bohte (2003, January). Span of control and public organizations: Implementing Luther Gulick's research design. *The American Society for Public Administration*. Retrieved online May 15, 2005: http://unpan1 .un.org/intradoc/groups/public/documents/ASPA/UNPAN007281.html

27. Samuel Walker and Charles M. Katz (2005). p. 478

28. Samuel Walker and Charles M. Katz (2005). p. 478

29. For a closer look at these findings, see Special Counsel Merrick Bobb (1998). 9th Semiannual Report. Los Angeles: The Special Counsel. Police Assessment Resource Center. pp. 22–23. Retrieved online May 15, 2005: http://www.parc .info/. Also available at that website are updates of February 2005.

30. Stan Stojkovic, David Kalinich, and John Klofas (2003). *Criminal justice organizations: Administrative and management*, 3rd ed. Belmont, CA: Thomson and Wadsworth. pp. 24–25.

31. Thomas O'Connor (2005). North Carolina Wesleyan College. Retrieved online May 15, 2005: http://faculty.ncwc.edu/toconnor/205/205lect07.htm

32. For instance: Eligibility for Master Police Officer on the Hampton, Virginia, Police Department includes a 5% increase in pay and is given after at least 3 years of consecutive service as a Senior Police Officer. MPO elects must have received at least a "surpassed expectations" on their latest annual performance evaluation, and participated in at least two community events. They must have a minimum of three specialties such as K-9, field training instructor, firearms instructor, marine patrol, or school recourse officer, and three competencies such as radar certification, dive team, SWAT, or hostage negotiator. Retrieved online March 6, 2006: http://www.hampton.va.us/police/recruiting/career_paths.html

33. Sam Walker and Charles Katz (2005). p. 89.

34. Stan Stojkovic, David Kalinich, and John Klofas (2003). p. 24.

35. William Bratton (1996, February 12). New York crime rate down forty-five percent. *New York Times*.

36. Herman Goldstein (1990). *Problem-oriented policing*. New York: McGraw-Hill. Also see Dennis J. Stevens (2003). *Case studies in community policing in the 21st century*. Boston: Allyn Bacon.

37. Stan Stojkovic, David Kalinich, and John Klofas (2003). p. 4.

38. H. H. Gerth and C. Wright Mills (trans. and ed.), *From Max Weber* (New York, 1946).

39. Professor John Kilcullen supplied some of this information. Macquarie University, Australia. john.kilcullen@mq.edu.au

40. Phyllis Parshall McDonald (2002). *Managing police operations*. Belmont, CA: Wadsworth. p. 1.

41. Wayne W. Bennett and Karen M. Hess (2004). pp. 187–188.

42. Stan Stojkovic, David Kalinich, and John Klofas (2003). p. 364. For a look at resistance, see Jack R. Greene and William V. Pelfrey, Jr. (2001). Shifting the balance of power between police and community: Responsibility for crime control. In Roger G. Dunham and Geoffrey P. Alpert (Eds.), *Critical issues in policing: Contemporary readings* (pp. 435–465). Prospect Heights, IL: Waveland. p. 441.

43. Samuel Walker and Charles M. Katz (2005). p. 91.

44. Peter Drucker (1993). *Management: tasks, responsibilities, practices.* New York: HarperCollins.

45. Wayne W. Bennett and Karen M. Hess (2004). *Management and supervision in law enforcement,* 4th ed. Belmont, CA: Wadsworth. pp. 11–14.

46. Dictionary.com Retrieved online May 15, 2005: http://dictionary.reference .com/search?q=power

47. Rickey D. Lashley (1995). *The need for a noble character.* Westport, CT: Praeger.

48. Joycelyn M. Pollock (2001). Ethics and law enforcement. In Roger G. Dunham and Geoffrey P. Alpert (Eds.), *Critical issues in policing: Contemporary readings* (pp. 356–373). Prospect Heights, IL: Waveland. p. 441.

49. Achieving and maintaining high ethical standards (2002). p. 66.

50. Joycelyn M. Pollock (2001). p. 357.

51. Joycelyn M. Pollock (2001). p. 357. And, for example, Tom Delay and the GOP milking the system to live high on the hog. Tom DeLay saw a seat in Congress as a way to live large at someone else's expense. From the time he arrived in Washington after the 1984 elections, DeLay started working the system to line his own pockets. "I met Delay at the reception for freshmen members of Congress," recalls retired lobbyist Jackson Russ. "He walked up, looked at my name tag, introduced himself, and asked how he could get some honorariums." In 1984, honorariums were a quick way for members of Congress to line their own pockets. Special interest groups would invite the Congressman to a get-together with executives of their company or top members of the organization and then pay that Congressman directly for the appearance. Congress banned honorariums in 1989 but that gave DeLay 5 years to become one of the top earner of fees for appearances on the Hill, adding an average of $27,000 a year to his Congressional salary. "DeLay bugged everyone for honorariums," says Roy Abrahams, who lobbied Capitol Hill for oil interests from 1975 through 1990. "Others were subtle. He wasn't." Doug Thompson (2005, November 28). *CHB investigates.* Retrieved online March 6, 2006: http://www.capitolhillblue.com/ artman/publish/article_7709.shtml

52. A. P. Cardarelli, J. McDevitt, and K. Baum (1998). The rhetoric and reality of community policing in small and medium sized cities and towns. *Policing: An International Journal of Police Strategies and Management,* 21(3), 397–415.

53. Hans Toch (2001). *Stress in policing.* Washington, DC: APA.

54. Samuel Walker and Charles M. Katz (2005). p. 117.

55. Thomas O'Connor (2005). Police organization. Retrieved online May 16, 2005: http://faculty.ncwc.edu/toconnor/205/205lect07.htm

56. Personal communication with a Boston police officer who was also a student of this writer, February 2005.

57. Samuel Walker and Charles M. Katz (2005). p. 91.

58. Geoffrey P. Albert and Mark H. Moore (2001). Measuring police performance in the new paradigm of policing. In Roger G. Dunham and Geoffrey P. Albert (Eds.), *Critical issues in policing: Contemporary reading,* 4th ed. (pp. 238–255). Prospect Heights, IL: Waveland.

59. Geoffrey P. Albert and Mark H. Moore (2001). p. 239.

60. Chief Charles H. Ramsey (2002). Preparing the community for community policing: The next step in advancing community policing. In Dennis J. Stevens

(Ed.), *Policing and community partnerships* (pp. 29–44). Upper Saddle River, NJ: Prentice Hall.

61. David L. Carter and Louis A. Radelet (2001). p. 51.

62. Bureau of Justice Statistics (2005). *State and local law enforcement statistics.* Washington, DC: U.S. Department of Justice. Office of Justice Programs. Retrieved online May 10, 2005: http://www.ojp.usdoj.gov/bjs/sandlle.htm#personnel

63. Bureau of Justice Statistics (2005). *State and local law enforcement statistics.*

64. Bureau of Justice Statistics (2002). *Sourcebook of Criminal Justice Statistics. 2002.* State and local police and agencies. Table 1.21. http://www.albany.edu/sourcebook/1995/pdf/t121.pdf

65. Bureau of Justice Statistics (2002). *Sourcebook of criminal justice statistics* 2002. Table 1.32. p. 45. Albany, NY: U.S. Department of Justice, Office of Justice Programs. Retrieved online May 10, 2005: http://www.albany.edu/sourcebook/pdf/t132.pdf

66. Bureau of Justice Statistics (2005). *Federal law enforcement statistics.* Retrieved online May 10, 2005: http://www.ojp.usdoj.gov/bjs/fedle.htm

67. Edward R. Maguire. (2003). *Organizational structure in American police agencies: Context, complexity, and control.* Albany, NY: SUNY Press.

68. Peter Drucker (1999). *Management: Challenges for the 21st century.* New York: HarperCollins. p. 3. Drucker argues that the "basic assumptions about reality are the paradigms of a social science, such as management. They are usually held subconsciously by the scholars, the writers, the teachers, the practitioners in the field. Yet those assumptions largely determine what the discipline—scholars, writers, teachers, practitioners—assumes to be reality. The discipline's basic assumptions about reality determines what it focuses on." One interpretation of Drucker's thought is that each police agency has its own stable of scholars, writers, teachers, and practitioners who determine deployment practices, service call priorities, hiring and training and promotion procedures, use of force and fresh pursuit guidelines, grievance and discipline procedures, and police strategies or initiatives. That is, each police agency is like a small kingdom and with over 18,000 small kingdoms across the United States, it is a difficult challenge to get them to work together.

69. Personal communication with a state trooper in Massachusetts in May 2005.

70. Personal communication with officers in New York and North Carolina, June 2005.

71. Christopher S. Koper, Edward R. Maguire, Gretchen E. Moore, and David E. Huffer (2001). Hiring and retention issues in police agencies: Readings on the determinants of police strength, hiring and retention of officers, and the Federal COPS Program. *Urban Institute.* Retrieved online May 10, 2005: http://www.urban.org/urlprint.cfm?ID=7460.

72. Dennis J. Stevens (2003). *Applied community policing in the 21st century.* Boston: Allyn and Bacon. p. 22.

73. *Massachusetts Criminal Law and Motor Vehicle Handbook* (2003). New York: Gould Publishing. p. 38.

74. For a closer look at the causes of officer resistance, see T. J. Dicker (1998). Tension on the thin blue line: Police officer resistance to community oriented policing. *American Journal of Criminal Justice,* 23(1), 59–82. Dicker implies that supervisor trust, satisfaction with the amount of control of one's work environment, rank, organizational trust, and level of pride in the department play the largest role toward police officer resistance. Also see Robert Trojanowicz,

Victor E. Kappeler, Larry K. Gaines, and Bonnie Bucqueroux (1998). *Community policing: A contemporary perspective*, 2nd ed. Cincinnati, OH: Anderson. pp. 273.

75. John P. Crank (2004) *Understanding police culture*. Cincinnati, OH: Anderson. pp. 3–4. Crank indicates that organizational traditions are customary ways of doing things, and they take on commonsense value that cannot be changed easily or frivolously.

76. John Crank (2004), p. 119.

77. The Posse Comitatus Act of 1878. An act making appropriations for the support of the Army for the fiscal year ending June 30, 1879, and for other purposes. From and after the passage of this act it shall not be lawful to employ any part of the Army of the United States, as a posse comitatus, or otherwise. . . .

78. Daniel C. Ganster, Milan Pagon, and Michelle Duffy (1996). Organizational and interpersonal sources of stress in the Slovenian police force. *College of Police and Security Studies*. National Criminal Justice Reference Service. Retrieved online May 11, 2005: http://www.ncjrs.org/policing/org425.htm Also see John Van Maanen (2001). Making rank: Becoming an American police sergeant. In Roger G. Dunham and Geoffrey P. Alpert (Eds.), *Critical issues in policing: Contemporary readings*, 4th ed. (pp. 132–148). Prospect Heights, IL: Waveland Press.

79. For a detailed review of police management changes, see George L. Kelling and Catherine M. Coles (1996). Fixing broken windows. New York: Free Press, pp. 70–74, 109–114. Also see Roy R. Roberg, Jack Kuykendall, and Kenneth Novak (2002) *Police management*, 3rd ed. Los Angeles: Roxbury, pp. 3–5, 384–391. For a look at occupational change among police, see John Van Maanen (2001).

80. Dennis E. Nowicki, (1998). Mixed messages. In Geoffrey Alpert and Alex Piquero (Eds.), *Community policing* (pp. 265–274). Prospect Heights, IL: Waveland.

81. See Wayne W. Bennett and Karen M. Hess (2004); David L. Carter and Louis A. Radelet (1999); James G. Houston (1999). *Correctional management: Functions, skills, and systems*, 2nd ed. Chicago: Nelson Hall, p. 158; Carl Klockars (1985). *The idea of police*. Beverly Hills, CA: Sage; Peter K. Manning (1997). *Police work: The social organization of policing*. Prospect Heights, IL: Waveland Press. Dennis E. Nowicki (1998).

82. S. M. Cox (1990). Policing into the 21st century. *Police Studies*, 13(4), 168–177.

83. Dennis J. Stevens (2001). Community policing and managerial techniques: Total Quality Management techniques. *Police Journal*, 74(1), 26–41.

84. Samuel Walker and Charles M. Katz (2005). p. 117.

85. Wayne W. Bennett and Karen M. Hess (2004). pp. 38–40; Roy R. Roberg, Jack Kuykendall, and Kenneth Novak (2002) *Police management*, 3rd ed. Los Angeles: Roxbury, pp. 140–157. Peter Drucker (1993). *Management: tasks, responsibilities, practices*. New York: HarperCollins.

86. Stephen R. Covey (1992). *Principle centered leadership*. New York: Fireside. p. 34.

87. Norman M. Scarborough and Thomas W. Zimmerer (2006). *Effective small business management*. Upper Saddle River, NJ: Prentice Hall. pp. 740–782. Cox (1990); Roy R. Roberg, Jack Kuykendall, and Kenneth Novak (2002). pp. 143.

88. Stan Stojkovic, David Kalinich, and John Klofas (2003). H. L. Tosi, J. R. Rizzo, and S. J. Carroll (1986). *Managing organizational behaviour*. Marshfield, MA: Pitman.

89. Recommendations from the president's first leadership conference. May 1999. Police leadership in the 21st century achieving & sustaining executive success.

International Association of Chiefs of Police. Retrieved May 13, 2004: http://www.theiacp.org/documents/pdfs/Publications/policeleadership%2Epdf

90. Robert Trojanowicz and S. Dixon (1974). *Criminal justice and the community*. Englewood Cliffs, NJ: Prentice Hall. Also see Robert Trojanowicz, Victor E. Kappeler, Larry K. Gaines, and Bonnie Bucqueroux (1998). *Community policing: A contemporary perspective*, 2nd ed. Cincinnati, OH: Anderson. pp. 270–273.

91. Carl Klockars (1985); John Van Maanen (2001).

92. James Q. Wilson and George L. Kelling (1998). Making neighborhoods safe. In Geoffrey P. Alpert and Alex Piquero (Eds.), *Community policing: Contemporary readings* (pp. 35–44). Prospect Heights, IL: Waveland.

93. John Wiggins and Dennis J. Stevens (2000). The effects of police management. *The Journal: The Police Official Journal*, 6(2), 14–17.

94. S. Landry (1998, May). Police decry naming of Uhuru activist to panel. *St. Petersburg Times*. Bureau of Justice Statistics. (2005). *Sourcebook of criminal justice statistics: 2004*. Albany, NY: U.S. Department of Justice, Office of Justice Programs. Table 2.14. Retrieved online May 17, 2005: http://www.albany.edu/sourcebook/pdf/t214.pdf

95. Bureau of Justice Statistics (2004). *Sourcebook of criminal justice statistics: 2003*. Albany, NY: U.S. Department of Justice, Office of Justice Programs. Table 2.14. Retrieved online May 17, 2005: http://www.albany.edu/sourcebook/pdf/t214.pdf

96. Victor E. Kappeler (2001). *Critical issues in police civil liability*, 3rd ed. Prospect Heights, IL: Waveland. p. 5.

97. Jim Kouzes. President of Tom Peters Learning Challenge online. Retrieved online May 17, 2005: http://www.josseybass.com/WileyCDA/Section/id-10303.html

98. The magazine *Management Review* conducted a study to determine the attributes that leaders will need for the year 2000. However, see Dennis J. Stevens (2002) Community policing and police leadership. In Dennis J. Stevens, *Policing and community partnerships* (pp. 163–177). Upper Saddle River, NJ: Prentice Hall. Stevens added three: organizational change, sharing command, and police decisions. The purpose of these additions is in keeping with community policing strategies. Also see Norman M. Scarborough and Thomas W. Zimmerer (2006).

99. Dennis J. Stevens (2004). Police stress, before and after 9/11. In Heith Copes, *Police and strategies* (pp. 137–145). Upper Saddle River, NJ: Prentice Hall.

100. George L. Kelling and Catherine M. Coles (1996). pp. 70–71.

101. This particular trait was not included in the original list provided by Dennis J. Stevens (2004), and after additional research, this item was added, influenced by Rick Michelson (2006). Leadership issues: Managing change. IACP. Retrieved online March 15, 2006: http://www.hitechcj.com/chiefslist/id14.html

102. Lawrence Sherman and Heather Stang (1996). Policing domestic violence: The problem-solving paradigm. Retrieved online April 12, 2006: http://www.aic.gov.au/rjustice/rise/sherman-strang.html

103. Loreen Wolfer, Thomas E. Baker, and Ralph Zezza (1999). Problem-solving policing eliminating hot spots. *The FBI Law Enforcement Bulletin*. Retrieved online April 12, 2006: http://www.findarticles.com/p/articles/mi_m2194/is_11_68/ai_58177902

104. Dennis E. Nowicki (1998).

105. Bureau of Justice Assistance (1994, August). *Understanding community policing: A framework of action*. NCJ 148457. Washington, DC: U.S. Department of Justice.

Office of Justice Programs. Also see PERF (1996). *Themes and variations in community policing: Case studies in community policing.* Washington, DC: The Police Executive Research Forum.

106. Dennis J. Stevens (2003). p. 270.

107. David L. Carter and Louis A. Radelet (1999). p. 51.

108. A. P. Cardarelli, J. McDevitt, and K. Baum (1998). The rhetoric and reality of community policing in small and medium sized cities and towns. *Policing: An International Journal of Police Strategies and Management,* 21(3), 397–415.

109. Jill DuBois and Susan M. Hartnett. (2002). Making the community side of community policing work: What needs to be done. In Dennis J. Stevens, *Policing and community partnerships* (pp. 1–18). Upper Saddle River, NJ: Prentice Hall.

110. Robert Trojanowicz, Victor E. Kappeler, Larry K. Gaines, and Bonnie Bucqueroux (1998). *Community policing: A contemporary perspective,* 2nd ed. Cincinnati, OH: Anderson. pp. 270–273.

111. Robert Trojanowicz and David L. Carter (1988). *The philosophy and role of community policing.* East Lansing: National Neighborhood Foot Patrol Center, Michigan State University.

112. David L. Carter and Louis A. Radelet (1999). p. 52.

113. Wayne W. Bennett and Karen M. Hess (2004). pp. 280–288.

114. Rick Michelson (2006). Leadership issues: Managing change. IACP. Retrieved online March 15, 2006: http://www.hitechcj.com/chiefslist/id14.html

115. M. Moore (1998). The pursuit of integrity. *The Law Enforcement Journal* (Winter), 36–96.

116. Dennis J. Stevens (2003). pp. 280–281.

117. Dennis J. Stevens (2002) Community policing and police leadership. In Dennis J. Stevens, *Policing and community partnerships* (pp. 163–177). Upper Saddle River, NJ: Prentice Hall.

118. Dennis J. Stevens (2002). Civil liabilities and arrest decisions. In Jeffery T. Walker, *Policing and the law* (p. 53–71). Upper Saddle River, NJ: Prentice Hall.

119. Rick Michelson (2006).

120. Neil Trautman (2004). *Corruption to increase dramatically.* National Institute of Ethics. Retrieved online May 19, 2005: http://www.ethicsinstitute.com/corruptiontoincrease.htm

121. Beaufort facing $1 million in state cuts (2005, May 18). *Coastal Business Wire.* Retrieved online May 19, 2005: http://www.savannahbusiness.com/main.asp?FromHome=1&TypeID=1&ArticleID=3164&SectionID=50&SubSectionID=96. Adriel Hampton (2004, March 30). Daly: Stop babying the police budget. *The Independent. San Francisco Edition.* Retrieved online May 19, 2005: http://sfindependent.com/article/index.cfm/i/032504n_daly. Mayor says budget is tightest yet (2004, April 24). *Boston Globe.* p. 3B.

122. Hiroko Sato (2005, May 19). Dover budget shortage spurs ideas to cut back. Forster's Online: Dover, New Hampshire. Retrieved online May 19, 2005: http://www.fosters.com/apps/pbcs.dll/article?AID=/20050519/NEWS03/105190105

123. Interaction Association of Chiefs of Police (2005, February). Police chief's decry deep budget cuts that would make communities more vulnerable. Retrieved online May 23, 2005: http://www.theiacp.org/

124. Interaction Association of Chiefs of Police (2005, February).

125. Wayne W. Bennett and Karen M. Hess (2004). p. 187.

126. International Association of Chiefs of Police (1994). *Civil liability. Part 1: Basic principles of civil liability.* NCJ 50511 and *Part II,* NCJ 50512. Victor E. Kappeler (2001). *Critical issues in police civil liability,* 3rd ed. Prospect Heights, IL: Waveland.

127. Victor E. Kappeler (2001). p. 3.

128. International Association of Chiefs of Police (1994).

129. Victor E. Kappeler (2004). Also see, I. Silver (1996). *Police civil liability.* New York: Mathew Bender.

130. Neal Trautman (1997). *The cutting edge of police integrity.* Longwood, FL: National Institute of Ethics.

131. Frank Scogin and S. L. Brodsky (1991). Fear of litigation among law enforcement officers. *American Journal of Police,* 10, 41–44. See Eric G. Lambert, Daniel E. Hall, and Lois Ventura (2003). Litigation views among jail staff: An exploratory and descriptive study. *Criminal Justice Review,* 28(1), 70–87. There are few empirical studies related to the fear of litigation among police officers, but one interpretation from the findings of this study is that the longer personnel is on payroll, the more criminal justice personnel think about their retirement benefits and the less likely he or she will report illegal incidents that occur at this jail in Florida. However, most of the staff at the jail believed that the threat of civil litigation did not impact their performance. Finally in this regard, many of the jail keepers felt that they had not been trained well enough to protect themselves from civil liabilities.

132. Personal communication with former attorney of the Fayetteville, North Carolina, Police Department.

133. S. Stewart and B. Hart (1993). Reducing the cost of civil litigation: Use of force incidents. *Law and Order,* 41, 31. Also M. S. Vaughn (1996). Police civil liability and the First Amendment: Retaliation against citizens who criticize and challenge the police. *Crime and Delinquency,* 42, 50–75.

134. Title 42 U.S.C., Section 1983 (2005, February 25). Retrieved online May 18, 2005: http://www4.law.cornell.edu/uscode/html/uscode42/usc_sec_42_00001983––000-.html

135. J. Higginbotham (1985). Defending law enforcement officers against personal liability in Constitutional Tort Litigation. Part 1. *FBI Law Enforcement Bulletin,* 54, 24.

136. Roland V. del Carmen (1994). Civil and criminal liabilities of police officers. In Thomas Barker and David L. Carter (Eds.), *Police deviance,* 3rd ed. (pp. 409–429). Cincinnati, OH: Anderson.

137. For a more detailed discussion, see *Thomas v. Reagan,* USDC Cr. No. 84-3552. Retrieved online May 11, 2005: http://prop1.org/legal/843552/870415.htm

138. M. R. Smith (1995). Law enforcement liability under section 1983. *Criminal Law Bulletin,* 31, 128. NCJ 154219.

139. W. U. McCormick (1993). Civil liability and police prosecutor relations. *FBI Law Bulletin,* 62, 28.

140. Victor E. Kappeler (2004).

141. David Barstow (1999, May 6). After officers' indictment in Diallo case, arrests drop in New York City. *The New York Times,* p. 6.

142. Barstow (1999, May 6).

143. Barstow (1999, May 6).

144. Gary Sykes (1999). Street justice: A moral defense of order maintenance policing. In Victor E. Kappeler (Ed.), *The police and society: Touchstone readings*, 2nd ed. (pp. 134–150). Prospect Heights, IL: Waveland.

145. Carl B. Klockars (1999). Street justice: Some micro-moral reservations. Comments on Sykes. In Victor E. Kappeler (Ed.), *The police and society: Touchstone readings*, 2nd ed. (pp. 150–154). Prospect Heights, IL: Waveland.

146. There is a tendency to believe that chiefs, commissioners, and commanders, including sheriffs, actually make policy and most of the decisions in their respective agency. In studying over 65 various police agencies, it is clear that town managers or mayors, business entrepreneurs or politicians hand down directives to police managers. For a closer review, see Dennis J. Stevens. (2002). *Case studies in community policing.* Upper Saddle River, NJ: Prentice Hall. Also Dennis J. Stevens (2003). *Applied community policing.* Boston: Allyn and Bacon.

147. Edward R. Maguire (2003). *Organizational structure in American police agencies: Context, complexity, and control.* Albany: SUNY Press. p. 5.

148. Dennis J. Stevens (2001). *Case studies in community policing.* Upper Saddle River, NJ: Prentice Hall. pp. 3–14.

149. Dennis J. Stevens (2001). *Case studies in community policing.* Upper Saddle River, NJ: Prentice Hall. p. 201.

150. Samuel Walker and Charles M. Katz (2005). *The police in America.* Boston: McGraw-Hill. pp. 374–375.

151. Dennis J. Stevens (2001). pp. 228–245.

152. Dennis J. Stevens (2001). p. 285.

153. Stan Stojkovic, David Kalinich, and John Klofas (2003). *Criminal justice organizations*, 3rd ed. Belmont, CA: Wadsworth. p. 13.

154. Wayne W. Bennett and Karen M. Hess (2004). *Management and supervision in law enforcement*, 4th ed. Belmont, CA: Thompson Wadsworth. pp. 383, 516–518.

155. Wayne W. Bennett and Karen M. Hess (2004). pp. 516–519.

156. David H. Bayley (1994). *Police for the future.* New York: Oxford University Press. pp. 64–66, 155.

157. Wesley G. Skogan and Susan M. Hartnett (1997). *Community policing, Chicago style.* New York: Oxford. pp. 138–147.

158. Dennis J. Stevens (2003). p. 9

159. George L. Kelling and Catherine M. Coles (1996). p. 73.

160. Rick Michelson (2006). Leadership issues: Managing change. IACP. Retrieved online March 15, 2006: http://www.hitechcj.com/chiefslist/id14.html

161. Stan Stojkovic, David Kalinich, and John Klofas (2003). p. 196.

162. Goldstein (1990). p. 157.

163. Cognitive dissonance, a psychological term. Retrieved online May 19, 2005: http://changingminds.org/explanations/theories/cognitive_dissonance.htm Also see Leon Festinger (1957) *A theory of cognitive dissonance*, Stanford, CA: Stanford University Press. Festinger. Retrieved March 7, 2006: http://psychclassics.yorku.ca/Festinger/

164. Peter Brooker (2003). *A glossary of cultural theory*, 2nd ed. London: Arnold.

165. R. Williams (1981). *Culture.* London: Collins.

166. Stephen J. Harrison (2004). *Police organizational culture: Using ingrained values to build positive organizational improvement.* Retrieved online March 25, 2006: http://www.pamij.com/harrison.html

167. William A. Westley (1970). *Violence and the police: A sociological study of law, custom, and morality.* Cambridge, MA: MIT Press. Also John P. Crank (2004). pp. 25, 182.

168. John P. Crank (2004). *Understanding police culture,* 2nd ed. Cincinnati, OH: Anderson. p. 3. Also see Wayne W. Bennett and Karen M. Hess (2004). pp. 263–264.

169. Neil Trautman (2004).

170. Craig Whitlock and David S. Ellis. (2001, July 1). Officers killed with impunity. *Washington Post.* p. A01.

171. FBI (2005). *Law enforcement officers killed or assaulted 2003.* Retrieved online May 7, 2005: http://www.fbi.gov/ucr/killed/leoka03.pdf p. 44.

5

Critical Incident Stressors, Debriefing, and Intervention

It's not what happens to you that matters, but how you take it. —Hans Selye

Learning Objectives

Once reading this chapter, you should be better prepared to:

- Justify the assumption about critical incident reactions.
- Describe critical incident stressors.
- Explain the characteristics of critical incidents.
- Identify factors influencing the degree an officer can be affected by a critical incident.
- Explain the diagnostic criteria for acute stress disorder (ASD).
- Identify and rank-order the 14 critical incident stressors reported by police officers.
- Identify and rank-order the outcomes resulting from critical incidents.
- Describe the stress experiences offered by stress practitioners.
- Describe the basic principles of crisis intervention.
- Explain debriefing and its rationale.

- Describe the basic principles of a debriefing process.
- Articulate the justification and scope of critical incident stress management.
- Explain the criticism associated with crisis intervention and debriefing.
- Identify the advantages of critical incident participation among officers.
- Define and describe the issues of resilience among officers.
- Describe the merits of intuitive policing.
- Describe what is meant by a standard of care among law enforcement officers.

KEY TERMS

Acute stress disorder
Crisis
Crisis intervention
Critical incident

Debriefing
Intuitive policing
Primary victimization
Resilience

Secondary victimization
Standard of care

INTRODUCTION

This chapter explores critical incident stressors associated with police work. There is little doubt that family experiences[1] and public perceptions of the police[2] are responsible for officer frustration and stress. When 558 officers were asked how often they experienced job related discomfort, uncertainty, or stress on the job, 74 percent reported that they always or very often experienced those feelings (See Appendix). When the participants were asked how often they experienced stress from family members, less than 7 percent of the participants reported that their stressful experiences originated from family members. One implication arising from this latter finding is that either these officers did not take their day-to-day experiences home, or their problems at home were invisible to them, or they simply ignored their family members which in turn might be one reason law enforcement officers as an occupational group report extremely high divorce rates and family dysfunctions. Consistent with this thought are findings from a study of 244 veteran officers in the Tulsa, Oklahoma Police Department where over one-half of the officers were divorced, and those officers felt that being a police officer had had a negative effect on their marriages.[3] Then, too, the other one-half of the sample who were married reported that their occupation had a negative effect upon their marriages. In another study, when family members of police officers were asked the same question, spouses of participants reported that most of their stressful experiences were directly related to their spouse's occupation.[4]

One way to tease-out various police stressors is to divide stressors into two categories: critical incidents such as a gunfight, the focus of this chapter, and general work stressors, such as paperwork, the focus of Chapter 6.

AN ASSUMPTION ABOUT CRITICAL INCIDENT REACTIONS

Before we begin our journey through critical incident experiences, it is necessary to reveal that it is assumed that response to stress in the past magnifies the reactivity of present stress and stress in the future. That is, stress experiences are like bad credit reports, they never go away, and its influence on future credit checks even when an individual has met every deadline can snowball into a bad risk. Critical incident stressors work together, some even become pathways leading to other stressors and unexpected outcomes, and they are scratched upon the mind of the officer and never really go away. That is not to say that the experience of a critical incident will influence future behavior because each of us responds differently to stressors.

Keep in mind, however, what Hans Selye, the founder of stress reduction, said years ago about stress[5]: "It's not what happens to you that matters, but how you take it." One way to interpret Selye's thought is that officers can experience the same event at the same time, but each responds differently to the event and that response can come out at different times and in different ways.

Remember, not all stress and their stressors, including critical incidents, foster negative results. An event such as a felony pursuit on a highway or a routine arrest can be seen as very stressful to one officer, yet considered uneventful to another officer. Then, too, some officers enjoy the pursuit, the traffic stops, and might be very excited about participating in a gunfight. Police personnel (like other emergency responders such as firefighters, medical technicians, and correctional officers) are exposed to numerous situations that could be traumatic, but some individuals deal with it differently than others, and each can hold a different perspective about uncertainty, fear, and high-risk confrontations. For instance, a city cop would not consider patrolling alone with another officer's backup 30 minutes away unless he or she were assigned to an armored half-track.[6] Conversely, rural cops wouldn't want to walk down a New York City block in uniform unless the uniform were marked U.S. Postal Service. "There are differences, but each have their confronts and terrors."[7] Nonetheless, on to the task at hand of examining critical incident experiences among typical law enforcement officers.

CRITICAL INCIDENT STRESSORS

Critical Incidents Defined

Critical incidents are part of a typical law enforcement officer's job description, job training, and obligations. Critical incident involvement is expected and part of the work role of officers.[8] Therefore, critical incidents are both legal and moral mandates for sworn personnel.[9] Some law enforcement officers encounter a number of critical incidents during their career whereas others, even those in the same jurisdiction, experience few, if any at all.

A *critical incident* is any situation beyond the realm of a person's usual experience that overwhelms his or her sense of vulnerability and a lack of control over the situation.[10] A critical incident is not just an event such as a gunfight, but should include how an officer responds to the event or situation.

It is reported that most definitions of critical incidents should include a reference to an event in which an officer is subject to a sudden serious jeopardy such as a threat to his or her existence or well-being, or the well-being of another person.[11] Police officers, emergency first-responders, correctional personnel, and members of the military are vulnerable to critical incident stress. "Any situation faced by emergency service personnel that causes them to experience unusually strong emotional reactions which have the potential to interfere with their ability at the scene or later, generates unusually strong feelings in the emergency service workers."[12]

Conceptually, a critical incident refers to any high-risk officer–civilian encounter when an officer reasonably believes he or she might be legally justified in using deadly force, regardless of whether such force is used or averted.[13] Examples of such incidents can include apprehending emotionally disturbed offenders, organized domestic terrorists, hostage-takers, barricaded subjects, riot control, high-risk warrant service, and/or sniper incidents.[14] A simple definition of a critical incident can be a normal reaction to an abnormal event, and many critical incident events share specific characteristics.

A crisis response is often confused with a *critical incident* (crisis event). A critical incident is the stressor *event* that initiates the crisis response. More specifically, the critical incident may be thought of as the stressor that sets the stage for the emergence of the crisis response in those so adversely affected.[15] Those primary crisis responses (other responses are discussed later in the chapter) can be characterized when[16]:

1. Psychological homeostasis (the tendency of the body and the mind to naturally gravitate toward a state of equilibrium or balance)[17] is disrupted.
2. One's usual coping mechanisms (i.e., sports, hobbies, reading, quality time with your children, praying) have failed.
3. There is evidence of human distress or dysfunction (usually detected through compulsive behavior).[18]

Characteristics of Critical Incidents

Critical incidents that produce stress among law enforcement officers are "event" specific. There are specific characteristics that typifies an event as a critical incident. For example, a critical event can be characterized as[19]:

- Sudden and unexpected
- Disruptive to an officer's sense of control
- Disrupt beliefs, values, and basic assumptions about the world in which the officer lives and works and the people in it
- A damaging life threat
- An emotional trigger or physical loss

Not all of the items above need be present. The degree to which an officer will be affected by an incident depends on the following five factors, which are related to the incident itself, and the last three factors, which are related to things in existence prior to the incident[20]:

1. The actual event
2. Its intensity
3. Its duration
4. Its level of unexpectedness
5. *Primary victimization* (recipient of injury/violence)[21]
6. *Secondary victimization* (witnessing injury/violence)[22]
7. The mental health of an officer[23]
8. The previous experiences of an officer[24]

One thought might be to introduce officers to the psychological experiences of critical incidents during basic law enforcement training or during in-service training (in addition to tactical responses related to critical incidents). Often, after both primary and secondary victimization experiences, it is not uncommon for an officer to assume responsibility and to internalize feelings of guilt, which furthers his or her vulnerability toward traumatic stress reactions. Those reactions can be acute, occurring during the actual event, or they could be delayed reactions, occurring minutes, hours, months, or even years after the event. Delayed reactions can include a change in sleep patterns, disorientation, self-doubt, unresolved anger, irritability, fear, anxiety, agitation, flashbacks, and an increased use of drugs or alcohol.[25] The traumatic event can be persistently reexperienced in at least one or more of the following ways[26]:

- Recurrent images
- Thoughts
- Dreams
- Illusions
- Flashbacks
- Episodes
- A sense of reliving the experience

CONTRIBUTING FACTORS TO STRESS VULNERABILITY

Some officers are more receptive toward critical incident stress than others. Contributing factors that influence receptiveness or vulnerability (and *resilience:* an ability to recover from or adjust easily to misfortune or change) to critical incident stressors include personality, cognitive, group, and organizational factors.

Personality factors that contribute to vulnerability of critical incident stressors refers to most emergency care personnel who are trained to enhance certain personality characteristics, such as[27]:

1. Need to be in control
2. Obsessive/perfectionist tendencies
3. Compulsive/traditional values—wanting things to remain unchanged
4. High levels of internal motivation
5. Action-oriented
6. High need for stimulation and excitement (easily bored)
7. High need for immediate gratification
8. Tendency to take risks
9. Highly dedicated
10. Invested in the job due to months of training and preparation
11. View job as lifelong career
12. Identify strongly with their role as a police officer
13. High need to feel needed

You already know that these personality characteristics contribute to quality police performance and resilience of an officer. *Personal factors* that contribute to personal vulnerability (and resilience) also include three categories[28]:

1. Biological factors, which are genetically based predispositions (e.g., heightened autonomic and physiological reactivity) and changes in physiological reactivity because of prior traumatic exposure.[29]
2. Historical antecedents, which can include socioeconomic status and preexisting psychopathology.
3. Psychological vulnerability, which can be described as learned behavior (e.g., avoidance of threat situations, hypervigilance of threat-related cues), social skill deficits leading to problems obtaining and utilizing social support, inadequate problem-solving behavior, and drug and alcohol abuse. Vulnerability can be influenced by an officer's history of traumatic experiences.

Cognitive factors that contribute to vulnerability refer to the differences between routine police work, training, and the significance of the incident.[30] In cognitive models, if performance expectations required to control a disaster are beyond the reach of an officer mentally, then vulnerability toward stress levels are enhanced. This could also mean that an officer wasn't personally prepared to deal with the significance of the aftermath of events such as Hurricane Katrina, which destroyed everything in its path along the Mississippi coast and New Orleans.[31]

Group factors that contribute to vulnerability of stress suggest that officers usually work in teams to control most incidents, probably with the exception of first-responders.[32] Stress vulnerability is enhanced by inadequate coordination and possibly intergroup conflict between officers. With various officers in conflict with other officers, the sharing of information and proactive response management is less likely, adding to the uncertainty among officers.

Finally, *organizational factors* that affect vulnerability might include the level of trust and empowerment influences that tend to be found in hierarchical bureaucratic police organizations.[33] Developing managerial capacity as a resilience component would more likely be found in organizational structures where managers tend to be supportive of personnel and manage through values, for instance, as opposed to a discipline perspective as is so often found in typical police organizations.[34]

Critical Incidents and Crisis

Crisis is a term frequently used to describe a critical incident. Usually critical incident issues typically focus on macro-level events such as the death of a colleague, armed robbery, and terrorism attacks. While analysis at that level can contribute to a clear picture of critical incidents and could aid in determination of organizational risks, the identification of resource needs and tactical response strategies focusing on the macro-level provides a limited picture into the relationship between critical exposure and the experiences of the officer and his or her stress.[35] That is, the emphasis is on the event rather than an officer.

A critical incident can be thought of as any stressor event that has the potential to lead to a crisis response. More specifically, the critical incident may be thought of as the stimulus that sets the stage for the crisis response.[36]

Part of those responses can include perceptions of diminished future control, a strategy that is at the very heart of police initiatives. Recall from earlier chapters posttraumatic stress or acute stress disorder (ASD) and its consequences. The diagnostic criteria for ASD specifically includes[37]: (1) The person experienced, witnessed, or was confronted with an event or events that involved actual or threatened death or serious injury, or a threat to the physical integrity of self or others; and (2) The person's response involved intense fear, helplessness, or horror.

Can you envision an officer telling his or her partner, the sergeant, or other officers that he or she feels tremendous fear or a helplessness when patrolling the streets? The consensus of over a thousand Los Angeles law enforcement officers, many of whom experienced critical incidents, was that seeking crisis debriefing or seeking professional help after a critical incident was not an option for them.[38] When officers do respond to critical incident stress, almost regardless of its origins, the police subculture holds many of the myths that can lessen an officer's ability to appropriately address a critical incident experience. Those myths are typically found in the following statements made by officers about critical incident treatment[39]:

- "Real men can handle the heat!"
- "If you can't deal with it, find a new line of work."
- "Keep it to yourself."
- "If you can't deal with it, what's going to happen when I'm counting on your help on the streets?"

The reality is that police officers can experience deep emotional reactions to a critical incident. Attempts to deny these feelings can often cause law enforcement officers to mask their fear, suffer in silence, not seek help, and in some instances, disrupt their lives, the lives of their families, and the lives of their constituents. Suicide is always a possibility.[40]

REPORTS OF CRITICAL INCIDENT STRESSORS

In a recent study among 310 law enforcement officers after and 415 officers before September 11, 2001 (from many different police departments),[41] 14 critical incidents were rank-ordered as shown on Table 5.1.[42] Because of the

TABLE 5.1   RANK-ORDERED CRITICAL INCIDENT STRESSORS[43]

Critical Incident Stressors	After 9/11 N = 310 Mean Score	Before 9/11 N = 415 Mean Score
1. Harming or killing of an innocent person[44]	3.27	3.93
2. Harming or killing of another officer[45]	3.28	3.89
3. Line of duty deaths (another officer killed)[46]	3.02	3.71
4. Hate group/terrorists[47]	4.53	3.67
5. Riot control[48]	2.66	3.43
6. Barricaded subjects[49]	2.28	3.28
7. Hostage-takers[50]	2.66	2.96
8. Disturbed offenders[51]	2.29	2.91
9. High-risk offenders[52]	2.08	2.68
10. Sniper incidents[53]	2.61	2.20
11. Killing a criminal[54]	1.41	1.91
12. Hot pursuit[55]	1.50	1.81
13. Using excessive force[56]	1.54	1.68
14. Protecting VIPs[57]	1.29	1.52

nature of the study, along with each event or situation measured, endnotes provide the researcher/s who held a consistent thought with the participants regarding that particular incident or crisis as playing a serious role among officers. The mean scores shown reflect a numerical value from 1 to 5. That is, 725 officers were asked:

Following is a list of experiences that law enforcement officers like yourself experience some time in their careers. How often do these experiences create major stress for officers? What's your guess? 5 = always, 4 = very often, 3 = sometimes, 2 = seldom, and 1 = never. It would be expected that after 9/11 law enforcement officers would see hate group/terrorists as their greatest stressor because officers lacked control before, during, and after the attacks, and because of the enormous loss of 3,047 innocent lives, which includes 72 local, state, and federal law enforcement officers.[58] However, setting hate groups/terrorists aside, it becomes clear that the officers who participated in these studies rank-ordered specific events in a similar way. For instance, in the Before 9/11 group, the items are rank-ordered beginning with the first item (your harming or killing of an innocent person) through the last item (protecting VIPs). In the After 9/11 group response, the three items that apparently produce the greatest stress among similar participants are also the top three items in the Before 9/11 group. There is always concern about research design initiatives, therefore it is recommended that the critical incident stressors shown in Table 5.1 be considered a guide to better understand how some law enforcement officers rank-ordered critical incident events. Nonetheless, it should be mentioned that another study conducted before 9/11 at the Baltimore Police Department reports that two-thirds of the surveyed officers considered media reports of alleged police wrongdoing to be stressful to them. The same proportion said that what they view as lack of administrative support for officers in trouble was a major source of stress.[59] It could be speculated that police personnel in various jurisdictions have different perspectives about stress depending on the history or current situation a jurisdiction is experiencing at the time of the study, as is evident by the different responses between the before and after group concerning some critical incident stressors, which subsequently would affect stressor outcomes.

STRESSOR OUTCOMES RANK-ORDERED

Having a clue about outcomes associated with critical incident stressors can serve us well in getting a glimpse of the consequences.[60] The findings from Before and After 9/11 participants are not absolute and without methodological flaw, but represent a guide offered by the participants as to what they experienced. The participants were asked to "write in" their responses. Therefore, the results are the subjective thoughts of the participants. Also because the results should be accepted as a guide, only outcomes of the After 9/11 group are presented in Table 5.2. While each of the above behavioral

TABLE 5.2   RANK-ORDERED OF OUTCOMES

Sample A: After 911   N = 315

Reduced self-respect
Abusive toward their own children and/or lack of parental affection
Abusive partner relationships
Alcohol abuse
Isolation from family, friends, and coworkers
Embellished evidence
Separated/divorced and/or extramarital affairs
Compromised departmental policy/state laws
More stops, fewer arrests
Incomplete paperwork/patrols
Depression
Racism
Damaged equipment/personal property
Excessive force utilized

patterns are strongly associated with critical incident experiences, many of these 14 outcomes are related to all of the stressors to some degree or another. That is, it appears that many of the stressors tend to magnify and work off each other, often acting as a pathway or conduit leading to other outcomes. That is, stress is cumulative, as expressed previously.

Recall earlier in the chapter when an assumption was made about critical incident reactions. That is, it was assumed that response experiences of stress in the past magnify reactivity of stress in the future. Based on the data in Tables 5.1 and 5.2, it appears that that assumption is supported by the evidence.

It is unfortunate that reduced self-respect appears at the top of the 9/11 (it ranked 13th in the Before 9/11 group) officer list and only speculation can provide a window into how that happened. It could be implied that since terrorism and hate groups were on the minds of local officers that a lack of control over terrorist aggression led officers to believe that they cannot protect their constituents as promised. If this thought makes sense then it could be easy to add that the police feel as vulnerable to the collateral damage of terrorism as the population they were sworn to serve and protect.

OFFICERS AND CRITICAL INCIDENT EXPERIENCES

Although there are many accounts of critical incident experiences reported by law enforcement officers, three accounts follow to further your understanding.

One officer reveals, "It was one of the most difficult things I have ever encountered. I was the first one on the scene of a DOA. I thought there is no

way I could handle this. As I looked closer at the victim, I realized I had issued this kid a traffic citation earlier in the evening, and she cried about it,
afraid of what her dad would say. Oh my God, I thought I was seeing things. I
still see her face every so often when I work, when I sleep, when I'm playing
with my kids."[61] Another incident is revealed by a former officer with the
Chicago police department.

After a tour of duty with the U.S. Army in Iraq, 25-year-old Meryl Sloan
went to work for her hometown police department in Chicago.[62] After police
academy training, she went on gun runs ("seek and capture" of armed suspects) in Chicago's subway system with her training officer for 6 weeks. Meryl
wanted to "serve and protect" on the city's public transit systems, especially
the subway system with its rapidly moving trains screaming through tunnels
and under the Chicago River. She remembered her childhood experiences as
a passenger on those trains and wanted to make a difference for other children. She was everything a good urban cop should be: lean and muscular,
combat efficient, street-wise, and she had a cause.

Meryl familiarized herself with station platform arrangements, locations
of surveillance cameras, blue-light box phones at each station (emergency
communicators), the entrances and exits of each subway stop, the smell of
faulty railway equipment, and the faces of transit personnel. Officer Sloan was
prepared for her job, possessed a great deal of "intel" about the transit's operational procedures, and was anxious to stop playing "transit cop" and do the
real thing on her own.

Day One: Officer Sloan was informed of a complaint of a man who exposed himself on the subway platform. When she arrived, she saw the man
lying facedown on the cold station platform with his arms folded inward. Officer Sloan looked around the stopped subway train in front of her, glanced at
the driver of the train who was watching her through the dirty window of his
cabin, and smiled at the child standing at the opened door of the train pointing to the fallen man. Officer Sloan thought the incident would be over in
seconds, and that she would tell her dad, a retired Chicago cop, about her
first experience over breakfast. Sloan checked the security of her holstered
weapon, pushed on her angled weapon, snapped on protective hand covers,
and reached for the fallen man.

Now she saw blood flowing from him, heard a shot, and glanced up at
the train's driver, whose face was suddenly sliding down the cabin's window.
She immediately called for backup, and at the same time heard another shot
and felt a sharp pain in her leg. She thought she had a charley horse because
she had ran 2 miles through Chicago's Lincoln Park that morning. A gunman
stood at the opened doors of the train, it was the child whom she had smiled
at a few seconds ago. After all her experience, it had come to a gun-toting
child in the Chicago subways that would harm her. The last thing she remembered was watching the weapon lighting up, her face slamming into the

fallen man, the unsettling smell emanating from his sweaty body, and quietly whispering, "Shots fired, officer down. Officer down."

Officer Meryl Sloan recovered, left police work for customer service work with AT&T, and attended graduate school. Meryl felt that she took too much for granted before, during, and after the incident and should have better controlled the situation, but didn't. She says she was overconfident about her abilities and experiences. She had the knowledge, skill, and experience to do so. She thinks about the experience every so often and has difficulty in relating to children. She wonders if she could ever become intimate with someone and has issues with trust.

Another incident, offered by Officer Roger Dotson of the Toronto Police Department, recalls servicing a domestic violence call[63]:

When the officer arrived at the scene, the wife and daughter were crying. They had been assaulted by the daughter's father. He was upstairs in the dark shouting obscenities at the officer who was in the hallway in a well-lighted area. He asked the offender to come down so he could sit and talk about the problem. The officer heard a clicking sound and bolt action of a rifle and immediately shone his flashlight up the stairs as the offender lowered his 30-06 rifle at him.

The officer jumped back into the living room as the shooter fired a shot, but was nailed in the chest. Even though the officer was wounded, he tried talking the shooter into putting down the rifle. The officer called for an Emergency Task Force to assist him and an ambulance. The phone started to ring in the kitchen, down the hall from the officer. The shooter started to descend the staircase, carrying the rifle in front of him. The officer ordered him to stop and to put down the rifle. He reached the bottom of the stairs only 10 feet from where the officer was lying. With each step he took just added an overwhelming amount of pressure upon the officer and the officer started to justify everything about his life in his mind. His blood pressure was up, increased heart rate, etc. The shooter stopped and started to back up the stairs, when he reached the top he shouted at the officer, "Have you ever seen what a 30-06 can do to you?" as he lowered to fire another round at the officer. The officer fired once, hitting the shooter in the leg. To make a very long story short, after the shooter was finally arrested, the officer was told that the shooter had a loaded shotgun, two rifles, and many boxes of ammunition. To this day, the officer can still smell, taste, and feel the powder from the discharge. This event took place 35 years ago, says Officer Roger Dotson.

EXPERIENCES OF POLICE STRESS PRACTITIONERS

When stress counselors employed by the Massachusetts State Police, who also treat municipal officers from Boston and other jurisdictions, were asked about their difficult critical incident cases, information arose that merits attention.

One counselor's experience reveals that his most difficult case involved a police officer with an alcohol abuse problem.[64] The counselor said that he worked with this officer for 6 or 7 years of the officer's 15-year career on the force. They tried everything to turn around his abuse problem, including Alcoholics Anonymous and counseling. The officer was forced to resign. The counselor describes his experiences after arriving to the scene of a suicide:

> "When I got there, I didn't really know what to expect to see. I remember being taken upstairs by one of the detectives. I knew there was a suicide. Yet somewhere in my mind, I didn't really believe that it had taken place, and as I entered the apartment, we went through the apartment, came into the kitchen area, and observed this man who had taken his life with a revolver. I guess it is similar to going through a dream. I didn't really believe what I was seeing, and I went through the motions, and I spent a few minutes in the apartment. Later, I was involved with the family. It was a very unsettling situation. And I guess after that I always questioned myself as to what I could have done to have avoided this, the disaster that really took place. I questioned myself for quite a while. I guess that there was nothing [more] that I could've done. But, you know, we've seen some really bad ones make it back. So you always had a little thing in your mind of "Gee, what else could I have done, or what else could somebody have done to turn this gentleman's life around?"[65]

Another counselor adds that his experiences with death and dying cases among law enforcement officers were also the most difficult for him; however, he adds another dimension to our understanding of what constitutes a difficult critical incident case. The Massachusetts State Trooper employee whose job description is that of a stress counselor says that his stress has always been highest when having to fight with the administration to obtain resources to aid law enforcement officers in resolving their stress. "Knowing that help is both the moral and cost-effective things to do, and having to take energy away from treatment, to chisel away at some cement block, self-serving, egocentric, self-righteous thinking really raises my blood pressure. The analogy holds with policing in general . . . you don't mind fighting with the bad guys, you expect them to try to kill you . . . it pisses you off when you have to fight with the supposed good guys to get what you need to get the job done."[66] As you recall from Chapter 1, it was suggested that most often law enforcement agencies tend to blame police officers for their stressed conditions and one way to interpret the above message is that agencies tend not to cooperate with units designed to aid stressed officers while the police subculture adds its influence for officers to avoid treatment.

CRISIS INTERVENTION

Personal and organizational strategies to reduce and prevent stress among law enforcement officers will be discussed in Chapters 11, 12, and 13; however, crisis intervention and crisis debriefing (more details later in the chapter) is introduced in this section because most often intervention among officers is linked to a specific critical incident event. Many experts recommend that all officers engaged in every critical incident encounter be "debriefed" in order to head off future consequences.[67]

Crisis is a danger because it can overwhelm an individual to the extent that homicide and suicide may result.[68] Crisis is also an opportunity because the pain it induces impels the person to seek help. If an officer takes advantage of the opportunity, the intervention can help plant the seeds of self-growth and realization.

A brief overview of crisis intervention and debriefing would serve well toward a better understanding of the scope of critical incident stress.[69] *Crisis intervention* can be defined as the provision of emergency psychological care to officers to assist them in returning to an adaptive level of functioning and to prevent or mitigate the potential negative impact of psychological trauma.[70] This intervention can be long term and highly structured for officers who demonstrate stressed behavior, which includes alcoholism and other compulsive behavior that disrupts personal, family, and policing pursuits, or it can be a one-time process after a critical incident. Some jurisdictions mandate debriefing of all law enforcement personnel after a critical event.

BASIC PRINCIPLES OF CRISIS INTERVENTION

There are no single "best" models of crisis intervention, but there is common agreement on the general principles to be used to treat law enforcement officers.[71]

1. Immediate professional intervention after a crisis intervention can curb emotionally hazardous situations that place an officer at high risk for maladaptive coping or for becoming immobilized.
2. To stabilize an officer after a critical incident brings a semblance of order and routine. The goal is for the officer to function independently without guidance.
3. To facilitate understanding suggests restoring an officer to a pre-crisis level of functioning. This is accomplished by gathering the facts about what occurred, listening to the victim/s recount events, encouraging the expression of difficult emotions, and helping an officer better understand the impact of the critical event.
4. Focus on problem solving suggests actively assisting officers to use available resources to regain control. Assisting an officer in solving problems within the context of what the officer feels can enhance independent functioning.
5. Self-reliance is associated with active problem solving with a focus and objective on independent functioning. Officers should be assisted

in assessing the problems as the officers see them, in developing practical strategies to address those issues, and in fielding strategies to restore a more normal equilibrium.

6. Practitioners should guard against judgmental remarks or behavior (i.e., "Oh, that sounds serious") or nonverbal facial expressions denoting thoughts before, during, and after crisis intervention, especially if the practitioner is a nonsworn service provider or employed by another department within the jurisdiction.[72]

DEBRIEFING

Debriefing is a type of short-term psychological intervention used to help officers who experience temporary extreme emotions to recognize, correct, and cope with them as a result of a critical incident.[73] Debriefing comes from work with individuals in combat in the late 1940s who experienced a crisis reaction related to grief and depression. These individuals had no specific pathological diagnosis but simply exhibited severe emotional symptoms. Crisis intervention subsequently expanded in the 1960s to include individuals experiencing all types of traumatic life events.[74]

Using a peer model of debriefing, a group of officers who have experienced a specific traumatic incident are brought together to discuss their feelings and the event.[75] The leader may be a mental health professional or a trained peer who acts as a facilitator. Other times, debriefing can be accomplished individually whereby an officer would talk to a trained mental health professional or an appointed peer.

An idealized model recommended to accomplish debriefing consists of[76]:

1. An introductory phase, that outlines the purpose and supposed benefits of debriefing.

2. A fact phase, in which the participants tell what happened to them.

3. A thought phase, with participants relating their first thoughts about the critical incident.

4. A feeling phase, which requires participants to focus on the worst aspect of the incident and work through their emotional reactions to the incident.

5. An assessment phase, where participants note their physical, cognitive, emotional, and behavioral symptoms.

6. An educational phase, which provides information about the stress responses and ways to manage them.

7. The reentry phase, which summarizes and offers information about possible referrals.

Some studies have shown that debriefing is an effective, front-line intervention for law enforcement officers who have experienced critical incident stressors, especially the extreme stressors that can result in posttraumatic stress.[77] Support for the effectiveness of debriefing has been cited in several studies.[78]

BASIC PRINCIPLES OF DEBRIEFING

Group cohesion, catharsis (emotional release associated with the expression of unconscious conflicts), imitative behavior, and the sharing of information were traditional agents of change that represented the objectives of many practitioners.[79] Recently, debriefing practitioners tend to characterize three basic principles of the debriefing process: ventilation and abreaction, social support, and adaptive coping.

Ventilation and abreaction refers to an opportunity to vent or share any negative emotional feelings arising from a traumatic crisis, an important step toward recovery or resilience, whether engaged with a practitioner or merely discussing those feelings with a confidant.[80] Being able to share a painful traumatic experience permits an officer to share fear, understand the impact of the event, and begin the process of normal and independent functioning.

Social support networks provide officers with support, companionship, information, and instrumental assistance in returning to a state of mind prior to the incident.

Adaptive coping is the third agent of change, and includes both cognitive and behavioral skills with an emphasis on information gathering, cognitive appraisal, reasonable expectations of performance, and skill acquisition.

PRACTICAL DEBRIEFING GUIDELINES

There are some practical things that require mention, which have proved to be helpful toward aiding an officer. For example, it is recommended that the following guidelines, developed by the International Association of Chiefs of Police (ICAP)[81] in 1998, be adapted, along with additional comments.

It was the majority consensus of members of the IACP Police Psychological Services Section that debriefings become mandatory for all officers involved in a shooting incident. In the past, officers involved in on-duty shootings were often subjected to a harsh administrative/investigative/legal aftermath that compounded the stress of using deadly force. A "second injury" can be created by insensitively and impersonally dealing with an officer who has been involved in a critical incident. The guidelines are not meant to be a rigid protocol. These guidelines work best when applied in a case-by-case manner appropriate to each unique situation.

At the scene, show concern. Give physical and emotional first aid. Create a psychological break; it is advisable to get the officer away from the body and suspect(s) or remove the officer completely from the immediate scene.

Shielding the officer from media attention is essential. The officer should stay with a supportive peer or supervisor and return to the scene only if necessary.

Explain to the officer what will happen administratively during the next few hours and why. It is recommended that an administrator brief the officer again some time in the next 2 days regarding the entire process of investigation, media interaction, grand jury, review board, and any other potential concerns that might be encountered after a shooting.

If the firearm is taken as evidence, replace it immediately or when appropriate (telling the officer it will be replaced). Officers, especially when in uniform, may feel extremely vulnerable if they are left unarmed. Immediate replacement of a firearm also communicates support for the officer, rather than miscommunicating that an administrative action is being taken. If the firearm must be removed at the scene and cannot be replaced, it is desirable to assign an armed companion officer to stay with the involved officer.

If possible, the officer can benefit from some recovery time before detailed interviewing begins. This can range from a few hours to overnight, depending on the emotional state of the officer and the circumstances. Officers who have been afforded this opportunity to calm down are likely to provide a more coherent and accurate statement. Providing a secure setting, insulated from the press and curious officers, is desirable during the interview process.

Totally isolating the officer breeds feelings of resentment and alienation. The officer may benefit from being with a supportive friend or peer who has been through a similar experience. (To avoid legal complications, the shooting should not be discussed prior to the preliminary investigation.)

If the officer is not injured, either the officer or a department representative should contact the family with a telephone call first, perhaps followed up with a personal visit, and let them know what happened before other rumors and sources reach them. If the officer is injured, a department member known to the family should pick them up and drive them to the hospital. Offer to call friends, chaplains, etc., to make sure the family has support.

Personal concern and support for the officer involved in the shooting, communicated face-to-face from high-ranking administrators, goes a long way toward alleviating future emotional problems. The administrator does not have to comment on the situation, or make further statements regarding legal or departmental resolution, but can show concern and empathy for the officer during this stressful experience.

It is desirable to give the officer a few days of administrative leave to deal with the emotional impact. Make sure the officer understands this is an "administrative leave," not a "suspension with pay." It may well be in the best interests of the officer and the agency to keep the officer off the street until the criminal investigation, internal shooting review board, grand jury, coroner's inquest, and district attorney's statement have all been completed. This avoids placing the officer in potential legal and emotional double binds from being involved in another critical incident before the first one has been resolved, or being further involved with suspects or witnesses while working. Departments may wish to screen all emergency service personnel at the scene (including dispatchers) for their reactions and give administrative leave or the rest of the shift off, if necessary.

It is advisable that a confidential debriefing with a licensed mental health professional be scheduled for all involved personnel within 72 hours. While this can be a group session, it may not be legally or emotionally appropriate to include the officer(s) who did the shooting in a debriefing with others, as actually doing the shooting creates different issues. A one-on-one debriefing with a licensed mental health professional is recommended for the officer(s) who did the shooting prior to or in place of a group debriefing. Follow-up sessions for any personnel involved in the shooting may be appropriate.

Opportunities for family counseling and/or family group debriefings (spouse, children, significant others) should be made available. If the officer has a published home telephone number, it may be advisable to have a friend or telephone answering machine screen telephone calls, since there are sometimes threats to the officer and his or her family. When possible, an administrator should tell the rest of the department (or at least the supervisors and the rest of the officer's team) what happened so the officer does not get bombarded with questions and rumors are held in check. Screen for vicarious thrill seekers to protect the officers and the situation.

Expedite the completion of administrative and criminal investigations and advise the officer of the outcomes. Lengthy investigations can stimulate a secondary injury. Consider the officer's interest in preparing media releases. The option of talking to peers who have had a similar experience can be quite helpful to personnel at the scene. Peer counselors can also be an asset participating in group debriefings in conjunction with a mental health professional, and in providing follow-up support. Family members may also greatly benefit from the peer support of family members or other officers who have been involved in critical incidents. The formation and administrative backing of peer support teams for officers and family members will prove a wise investment during the stress of a critical incident.

It is advisable not to force a return to full duty before the officer indicates readiness. Allow a paced return, perhaps allowing the officer to "team" with a fellow officer, or work a shorter or different "beat" or shift. Prior to any event, attempt to train all officers, supervisors, and family members in critical incident reactions and what to expect personally, departmentally, and legally.

Shootings are complex events often involving officers; command staff; union representatives; internal affairs; peer support teams; district attorneys; investigators; city, town, or county counsel; personal attorneys; city, town, or county politicians; media; and others. It is recommended that potentially involved parties meet to establish locally acceptable procedures and protocols on handling these stressful, high-profile events to avoid conflict among the many different interests. It is recommended that they continue to communicate regularly to ensure smooth functioning and necessary adjustments.

CRITICAL INCIDENT STRESS MANAGEMENT

A relatively new term that has emerged in the crisis intervention literature within the last decade is critical incident stress management (CISM).[82] CISM is a comprehensive crisis intervention system consisting of multiple crisis intervention components that functionally span the entire temporal spectrum of a crisis. CISM interventions range from the pre-crisis phase through the acute crisis phase (can be debriefing, more later on this topic) into the post-crisis phase. CISM can be considered comprehensive in that it consists of interventions that may be applied to individuals, small functional groups, large groups, families, organizations, and even entire communities.

As a practical matter relative to law enforcement experiences, mandatory intervention or debriefing after a shooting or other life-threatening event, combined with realistic training to build an officer's decision-making skills under stress and positively exploit the adaptive stress reaction, remain the most effective and efficient approach to reducing the negative impact of the event on the officer and the agency.[83] Stress survival strategies, including controlled breathing, positive self-talk, and visualization or mental rehearsal, trained to a level of confidence and competence, may be critical to both improved performance under stress and increased resilience after a traumatic incident. CISM might represent the future model of crisis intervention.

CISM allows emergency mental health practitioners to tailor the intervention response to individual or organizational needs and is emerging as the international standard of care for police officers and other victims associated with disasters.[84]

In fact, variations of the CISM model have been adopted by numerous and diverse organizations in a wide variety of workplace settings including the Federal Aviation Administration (FAA), the United States Air Force, the United States Coast Guard, the U.S. Secret Service, the Federal Bureau of Investigations (FBI), the Bureau of Alcohol, Tobacco, and Firearms (ATF), the Airline Pilots Association (ALPA), the Swedish National Police, the Association of Icelandic Rescue Teams, the Australian Navy, and the Massachusetts Department of Mental Health.[85]

OFFICER'S GUIDE TO CRITICAL INCIDENT EXPERIENCES

There are many initiatives that guide officers through critical incident experiences. It should be acknowledged, however, that few survival techniques associated with critical incident experiences are taught to law enforcement recruits during basic law enforcement training.[86] In a review of many police academies, few if any techniques are taught during an inservice process.[87] The following initiatives can guide officers through critical incident experiences:[88]

1. Develop and use a tactical plan to adapt to the many circumstances encountered. The purpose of planning is to ensure that the officer can use proactive methods of command providing a tactical edge needed to avoid being overwhelmed.

2. Communication of coordinated actions with other officers. This thought includes both verbal and nonverbal communication. Without uninterrupted and clear communication, the best plan or strategy can fail.

3. Avoidance of independent action or separation of partners when in fresh pursuit. A subtle yet important fact is that when a criminal sees an officer, he or she runs. And less experienced officers take flight to the point of exhaustion. Torn uniforms, broken legs, dog bites, and blinding flashes of light from handguns fired point blank can often be avoided.

4. Gain and maintain familiarity with equipment.

5. Use proper tactics in response to diverse incidents.

6. Maintain effective physical condition and knowing one's own physical limits.

7. Keep a positive, dominant mental attitude ensuring the will to survive.

MACHO MACHO MAN

There is a tendency for law enforcement officers to compare and compete for performing the "toughest job."[89] Officers talk about shootings, gun battles, and high-speed chases. In police academies, there are stories on every aspect of combat among students and instructors.[90] These stories often take center stage and are focal points for coffee break discussions and stationhouse roll calls. These thoughts are consistent with experts who report on the Dirty Harry problem and advocates who argue that street justice has a moral defense concerning social order requirements.[91] In truth, and in spite of the media's portrayal of macho cops who deliver their own style of street justice, most officers will reach retirement without killing one person or for that fact, fire their weapon at a suspect.[92] The officers who do "fire their weapons will not reload, finish their shift, and have to have their memory jogged to remind them of the event."[93]

The vast majority of these gun battle confrontations happen within 10 feet or less, and the time span of actual shooting is usually less than 3 seconds, and up to 70% of those altercations occur in an environment of low, altered, or failing light.[94]

Furthermore, in a review of police gunfight statistics, real-world marksmanship performance among police officers varies from year to year, but the U.S. national average hit ratio is about 1 out of 6, or roughly 15%.[95] That is, for every six shots deliberately fired by officers during armed confrontations, only one of those six shots will hit its intended target. That means that 85% of the shots fired during these gunfights are hitting something other than the intended target, often causing expensive property damage, injury, and sometimes death. Then, too, a report from the FBI training section advises that the typical state, municipal, and local law enforcement officer draws his or her weapon three times in their entire career.

Critical incident experiences are not always linked to acts of violence or even involved in a gunfight. However, data for 2001 show that police used force 3.61 times during 10,000 service calls.[96] This translates to a rate of use of force of 0.0361%. Expressed another way, police did not use force 99.9639% of the time. The National Institute of Justice Research Report, published jointly with the Bureau of Justice Statistics, found that only 2.1% of 7,512 arrests involved the use of weapons by police.[97] Another study involved 1,585 adult custody arrests in Phoenix, Arizona. The findings were that force was used infrequently by the police and even less frequently by suspects. Suspects interviewed reported levels of police force similar to those obtained from officer self-reports.[98] It sounds as if police use of force and critical incidents are not as widespread as anticipated.

CRITICISM OF CRISIS INTERVENTION AND DEBRIEFING

Most of the evidence that supports critical incident intervention and in particular debriefing in general is actually sketchy and indecisive.[99] One expert implies that despite the good intentions of police agencies that mandate a peer or individual debriefing process after a critical incident, many of their efforts are overzealous psychological interventions.[100] It was implied that crisis incidents such as Columbine High and the World Trade Center paved the way for a "grief racket," which is in full swing.[101] Some researchers argue that responsibility dictates the need for urgent psychological support, but they acknowledge that the exposure to a traumatic stressor, while necessary, is not a sufficient condition for the development of posttraumatic stress disorder. Another source reports that debriefing and crisis intervention is popular because it is inexpensive and allows an officer to return to active duty. Then, too, should officers have future problems, the administration can say that it made an attempt to help its personnel and it aids an agency toward less exposure to a lawsuit.[102]

Other studies imply that crisis intervention cannot necessarily prevent serious long-term psychological disturbances and that debriefing could accentuate the stress response and exacerbate the traumatic stress response.[103]

Some studies have concluded that debriefing has little or no effect on subsequent psychological morbidity and can even exacerbate psychological morbidity over time.[104] There is a debate in progress as to the merits of debriefing but it certainly makes sense for officers to discuss critical incidents with others if for no other reason than to clarify facts and temper litigation potentials. Nonetheless, there are basic principles that apply toward crisis intervention regardless if the intervention is mandated or is a systematic process.

The ability to cope with stressful incidents is a personal journey that can depend on an officer's past experiences with trauma, appropriate development of coping strategies for stress, availability of support networks (e.g., family, friends, and colleagues), and recognition of the dangers of ignoring signs and symptoms of post-incident stress.

In an attempt to protect other officers from embarrassment, potential disciplinary action, or lawsuits, some members of law enforcement try to resolve stressful encounters privately, even covertly. For officers to admit that they feel suicidal or have domestic problems is close to admitting that they have lost control.[105] In a profession that expects its members to always be in control, law enforcement can be unforgiving or ill-prepared to handle an officer's admission of personal or interpersonal problems. This does not mean that officer-involved crisis incidents could be prevented if law enforcement culture became more accepting of vulnerabilities among its own personnel. Rather, it is important to acknowledge that these situations do occur and law enforcement personnel must remain mindful of how best to respond to that unexpected, dreaded phone call.[106]

ADVANTAGES OF CRITICAL INCIDENT EXPERIENCES

Traditional police organizations often put the cart before the horse as they attempt to solve personnel problems by blaming the victim and making stress a person-centered initiative rather than crafting strategies to fit the personnel problems.[107] In this regard, critical incident experiences have both negative and positive attributes. Critical incident experiences can bring officers closer to the mission of public safety. Also, critical incidents can produce positive experiences. For instance, an officer can experience distress from a child abuse case, but the same officer can gain a sense of accomplishment that he saved the life of a child.[108]

This thought is supported by a study of over 1,300 law enforcement officers who experienced critical incidents in Los Angeles. A majority of those officers reported that they found the critical incident interaction valuable.[109] The finding was consistent with an evaluation of both worker's compensation claims and stress disability retirements among the officers. On the positive side, increased attention to detail and tunnel vision, as well as overall heightened sensory awareness, helps officers attain a level of focused concentration that leads to a type of dissociation or disconnectedness that improves the officers' sense of control and ability to perform while experiencing fewer internal and external distractions. On a negative side, this restriction of the senses may result in an increased tendency to screen out other information that may later have proven valuable to officers.[110]

One characteristic of a critical incident as you may recall is linked to a sense of helplessness among officers. However, in one study an estimated 8% of the participants involved in a shooting incident felt completely helpless, as if the suspect definitely had the upper hand.[111] That is, 92% of the officers had not experienced feelings of helplessness. Relative to cognitive behavior of the officers, more than one-third indicated experiencing increased startle responses, concentration problems, and physical distress after the shooting incident, though the majority only identified the reaction as mild. Approximately 40% of respondents reported feelings of anger or rage after the incident, while 13% of those reactions rated as severe. On a positive note, officers appeared to be experiencing fewer and less significant legal concerns. Another variable, job satisfaction and style of law enforcement after the incident, over 80% of the officers reported no change in their policing style, 14% described themselves as more aggressive in their approach, possibly in response to their increased sense of vulnerability. This increase in aggressiveness could translate into higher levels of use of force if not addressed. The results of both the current and earlier study tend to support the concept of a high degree of resilience in peace officers after exposure to a life-threatening event.

Concerning coping activities, the three most popular means of coping with critical incidents include talking to peers, talking to family, and reviewing the incident in one's mind. Evidence shows that 90% of Americans are exposed to a traumatic stressor, yet there are natural and personal remedies that guide them away from traumatic responses.[112] Then, too, the resilience level of many officers is probably higher than expected.

RESILIENCE

Police officers and other emergency workers share many common characteristics that contribute to the resilience of officers through appropriate personality traits, cognitive skills, group or support networks, and organizational competence that redirect stress responses. In fact, there are advantages of critical incidents.

Resilience can be described as an ability to maintain relatively stable, healthy levels of psychological and physical functioning after an exposure to an isolated and potentially highly disruptive event, such as those described as critical incident experiences among police officers.[113] Resilient people do not necessarily possess "extraordinary strength" nor are they invulnerable.[114] One expert actually summarizes resilience research with the words "ordinary magic."[115] Resilience is generally a common phenomena when a person's "adaptational systems" are working well.[116]

Highly resilient personalities can be achieved through effective pre-employment selection strategies and intensive, frequent, and repetitive training techniques. But resilience is also supported (or hindered) by comradely, peer, and organizational support and preventive care strategies that identify early warning signs of distress and direct resources to help officers deal with highly traumatic events in a way that minimizes disruption to normal functioning.[117] One source reports that after exposure to a critical incident, resilient officers could still experience transient perturbations in normal functioning (such as several weeks of sporadic preoccupation or restless sleep), but they also exhibit a stable trajectory of healthy functioning across time.[118] Sometimes it may be difficult for police administrators to distinguish between resilient behavior and something called intuitive policing.

INTUITIVE POLICING

Experienced officers observe behaviors exhibited by criminals that send danger signals to officers that those officers react to, furthering the objectives of the police. If cops are shielded from critical incident experiences and training or are taught to repress their thoughts about those experiences, could officers place themselves at risk? It could be strongly argued that *intuitive policing* represents a decision-making process that officers use frequently, but find difficulty in explaining to those unfamiliar with the concept.[119] Another practitioner refers to this process as "blink."[120] Specifically, officers learn intuitive policing strategies through experience, responding to situations based on a few indicators as opposed to many indicators or even a body of knowledge. That is, there is a perspective that more knowledge leads to better responses. But intuitive policing strategies or rapid cognition is centered in "the power of thin slicing"—which says that as human beings we are capable of making sense of situations based on the thinnest slice of experience.[121] However, there are differences in the results of rapid cognition, which in some cases can be called racial profiling or negative or illegal rapid cognition.

Nonetheless, experienced officers observe actions and behaviors exhibited by criminals that send danger signals or indicators that they react to. Intuitive policing represents a decision-making process that law enforcement officers use frequently. The purpose of intuitive policing will become clear as you read through an account presented by federal agents, including a senior scientist and clinical forensic psychologist in the Behavioral Science Unit at the FBI Academy.

On a warm summer evening in a large American city, narcotics officers, working the 4:00 P.M. to midnight shift, began a "buy–bust" operation at an intersection known as an open-air drug market where approximately 50 to 60 persons, many presumably involved in narcotics trafficking, had congregated on the sidewalk. Five minutes earlier, two undercover officers had walked into the area and purchased illicit narcotic substances from several street dealers. The undercover officers then walked away from the intersection and broadcast the physical descriptions of the sellers to arrest teams, consisting of three unmarked vehicles containing three officers each, who began canvassing the vicinity to locate the suspects.

When the unmarked cars approached the street corner, the crowd immediately began dispersing. At this time, one officer observed a subject matching the description of one of the sellers provided by the undercover team and instructed the driver to stop. The doors of the unmarked police car swung open, and the crowd began to clear the area in a more-hurried fashion. As the officer who spotted the alleged dealer began yelling to the other officers to identify which of the suspects he intended to stop, another officer simultaneously exited the vehicle and pointed to a different individual approximately 30 feet farther down the sidewalk. The second officer began calling out to the others, as well as broadcasting on the radio, to "get the one in the red shirt; he's got a gun." The man in the red shirt started to run down the sidewalk after he observed plainclothes officers approaching from both sides with their weapons drawn. The male surrendered, and the officers removed a .357-caliber revolver from his waistband and placed him under arrest. The remaining members of the arrest team continued to canvass the area until they located, identified, and arrested the suspects who had made the illegal narcotics sales.

While the officers were in the stationhouse processing the prisoners and completing the necessary paperwork, the officer who originally identified the seller turned to the officer who spotted the gunman and asked, "How did you know he had a gun?" The officer who noticed the gunman hesitated for a moment and stated, "I'm not sure why; I just knew." He then finished processing his prisoner and sat down to prepare his statement of facts for presentation to the prosecutor's office. As he began to recall the details and circumstances of the incident, he had to make a conscious effort to remember the observations that led him to conclude that the suspect possessed a handgun. First, the officer recalled that when pulling up to the scene, he saw the suspect sitting on the curb. As the officers approached and the crowd began to scatter, the man stood up and adjusted his waistband. Next, the officer remembered that although the weather was extremely warm, the suspect had on a long-sleeved dress shirt with the shirttails hanging out. Finally, he recalled that immediately after the male stood up, he turned the right side of his body away from the officer and began to walk in another direction, grabbing the right side of his waistband as if securing some type of object. The combination of these factors led the officer to correctly believe that the individual in the red shirt was armed. The officer made these observations so rapidly that he experienced an "instantaneous recognition" of danger. However, he could not articulate these reasons to his fellow officers until after the incident was resolved.[122]

How often do police officers see suspects and immediately "know" that those suspects are armed or engaged in illicit narcotics possession? Often, officers are unable to articulate their accurate reactions that may represent building blocks to reasonable suspicion or probable cause indicators.[123] Equally important, why can officers not explain their reasons for reacting in such appropriate ways that actually saved their lives or prevented an offender from assaulting them? On the other hand, it does not take a rocket scientist to learn about danger signs through rapid assessment or rapid cognition about the circumstances that could lead to danger. One example might include defensive driving techniques, which keeps many of us out of the morgue.

Understanding our environment is something most of us learn from an early age and it really isn't a mystery if a person is vigilant about things around him or her. Nonetheless, examples of individuals "perceiving" the need to act without first becoming consciously aware of why they were acting have surfaced repeatedly in recent studies in the neural sciences. For example, in the case of a young man walking along a canal, when he came upon a woman staring into the water, he made some right decisions.[124] He recognized the look of fear on her face. But, before being consciously aware as to why, he found himself diving into the canal. Only when he entered the water did he realize that the woman had been staring at a child who was drowning. Thanks to his rapid cognitive process or initiative thinking, he saved the young child. How did the man know about the drowning child, you might ask? One answer is in the work of neuroscientist Joseph LeDoux.[125]

Three major, interrelated portions comprise the human brain: the brain stem, the cerebellum, and the cerebrum. LeDoux's research about the anatomy of the brain and its emotions seems to point to what law enforcement officers have experienced since the first peace officer—they become aware of danger signals and can act on them without first being consciously aware of these warnings.

LeDoux's work reveals that the most telling discovery about emotions of the last decade has been how the architecture of the brain gives the amygdala a privileged position as an emotional sentinel, which has an ability to, in essence, hijack the brain. Sensory signals from eye to ear travel first in the brain to the thalamus, and then—across a single synapse—to the amygdala; a second signal from the thalamus is routed to the neocortex—the thinking brain. This branching allows the amygdala to begin to respond before the neocortex, which mulls information through several levels of brain circuits before it fully perceives and finally initiates its more finely tailored response.

Essentially, people often perceive danger signals and can begin to initiate responses to them before becoming consciously aware of them. This preconscious recognition of danger and how humans can react appropriately to it have been explained by several authors.[126]

Law enforcement officers will find that their delivery of police services and public safety will prosper depending on their ability to recognize the danger signs in the sense of positive intuitive policing or rapid cognition, which has several implications for "realistic" law enforcement training and procedures.

REALISTIC TRAINING

Realistic academy training can present pragmatic and practical situations that approach the kinds of events officers will experience on the street. If the scenarios are realistic and simultaneously arouse the autonomic nervous system, officers begin to develop a bond between situations and circumstances that represent potential threat and subcortical awareness of the limbic system, their fight–flight mechanism of defense. Upon graduation, these new officers are assigned to veteran training officers on the street. Experienced, qualified training officers can reinforce these biopsychological responses learned at the academy by having the young officers verbalize what they felt following high-arousal incidents. New recruits, as well as seasoned officers, must make constant checks on their environment. They must continually and persistently conduct "reality checks" on themselves and recurrently and consciously say to themselves, "Look around; take note." They must constantly ask themselves, "What do I see? What do I hear? What do I smell? What do I feel?"

In-service training also should include scenarios where officers must recall as many details as possible, along with their own feelings and thoughts that occurred to them as the incident took place. These feelings and thoughts can later trigger important details of the incident that they will need for reports and testimony. Moreover, inservice training by specially trained mental health workers can further assist in helping officers relate their feelings to the circumstances occurring in the immediate environment.

Throughout the realistic and practical preparation at the academy, in-service training, and on-the-job experience, several important processes occur. The high-arousal, realistic training prepares officers to recognize the kinds of physiological reactions they can expect to experience during high-stress activities. This training also engages the neural wiring within the brain, already present in each officer, to react to certain threatening stimuli in the environment. By becoming accustomed to associating these feelings with their triggers and then verbalizing these feelings both at the academy and during on-the-job training, officers become better able to recognize the environmental cues triggering the impulses to act.

One concern is that if officers engaged in too few critical incidents on the training field and on the streets, how could they sharpen their skills as law enforcement officers? That is, there are advantages to critical incidents and a standard of care needs to be universally mandated in response to critical incidents.

STANDARD OF CARE

There is a need to develop an operational "standard of care" among law enforcement officers.[127] Traditional professions such as law and medicine, for example, have struck a balance between responsiveness and accountability that should be emulated by police work. Attempts to develop standards of care have been isolated or never undertaken in many departments. That is, police manuals rarely tell officers how to respond to crimes in progress. Officers' arrest discretion, especially but not limited in situations excluding domestic abuse, is not often subject to any official guidance. Many agencies provide officers with no meaningful guidance about how to handle encounters with mentally or emotionally disturbed persons and violent subjects without using more force than necessary.

Obviously, if officers are not prepared to deal with critical incidents when they occur and little is done to encourage treatment, the conduct of some officers might produce serious consequences. For example, the Christmas Day incident when an unarmed African American was shot to death in a New York supermarket by a police officer who had been involved in eight prior gunfights and never went through any type of therapy or group discussions on the subject. It is estimated that one in three officers involved in a shooting incident leave police work after a year of a critical incident regardless if they have a job waiting for them or not.[128] Other evidence, such as police suicide rates outnumbering police homicides, supports this thought.[129] It should be acknowledged that the evidence for the occurrence of critical incidents among police officers and others engaged in emergency intervention worldwide is compelling.[130] Emergencies are frequent, and no nation or group of individuals is exempt from these events. Equally clear is the intense human suffering, physical injury, and death, and accompanying psychological trauma and PTSD in the surviving victims of, or witnesses to, these critical incidents.

SUMMARY

This chapter is about critical incident experiences among police officers and intervention initiatives applied to officers who experienced these incidents. An assumption that guides this chapter is associated with the idea that response experiences of stress in the past magnifies the reactivity of present stress and stress in the future. A critical incident was described as any situation beyond the realm of a person's usual experience that overwhelms his or her sense of vulnerability and a lack of control over the situation. A critical incident is not just an event such as a gunfight, but includes how an officer responds to the event or situation. A critical incident is defined as the stressor event that initiates a crisis response and sets the stage for the emergence of the crisis response in those so adversely affected. Those responses were identified as psychological homeostasis, the failing of one's usual coping mechanisms, and evidence of human distress or dysfunction. The characteristics of most critical incidents include that they are sudden and unexpected; they disrupt an officer's sense of control, beliefs, and values; they represent a life threat; and they are an emotional trigger or physical loss. The degree to which an officer can be affected by a critical incident depends on the actual event and its intensity, duration, and level of unexpectedness, whether the officer was a primary or secondary victim, and the mental health and previous experience of the officer. The contributing factors to stress vulnerability include personality, cognitive, group, and organizational factors. The APA's diagnostic criteria for acute stress disorder specifically includes: the person experienced, witnessed, or was confronted with an event or events that involved actual or threatened death or serious injury, or a threat to the physical integrity of self or others, and the person's response involved intense fear, helplessness, or horror. There were 14 critical incident stressors identified by officers, of which the top three includes the harming or killing of an innocent person, the harming or killing of another officer, and line of duty deaths. There are several outcomes implied by the officers, which includes reduced self-esteem, abuse toward their own children, abusive partner relationships, and alcohol abuse. Stress practitioner experiences included alcoholism, suicide, and negotiating with the police administration for resources to aid stressed officers. There were several basic principles of crisis intervention offered but the top three include immediate professional intervention, to stabilize an officer after a critical incident, and moving the officer toward independent functioning. Debriefing is explained as a type of short-term psychological intervention used to help officers who experience temporary extreme emotions to recognize, correct, and cope with them as a result of a critical incident. Debriefing practitioners characterize three primary basic principles in the debriefing process: ventilation and abreaction, social support, and adaptive coping. Critical incident stress management has been justified by crisis or disasters around the world. It allows emergency mental health practitioners to tailor the intervention response to individual or organizational needs and is emerging as the international standard of care for police officers; and other victims associated with disasters. An officer's guide through critical incident experiences includes the development and use of a tactical plan to adapt to the many circumstances encountered; the communication of coordinated actions with other officers; and the avoidance of independent action or separation of partners during felony pursuits. Some of the criticism concerning crisis intervention is that crisis intervention cannot necessarily prevent serious long-term psychological disturbance, and that debriefing could accentuate the stress response and exacerbate the traumatic stress response. Some of the advantages derived from critical incident participation have to do with better-trained, experienced officers. The issue of resilience bowed its head throughout this chapter, suggesting that the same factors that contribute to the vulnerability of police officers to traumatic stress are the same factors that enhance resilience. Experienced officers observe behaviors exhibited by criminals that send danger signals to officers that those officers react to, furthering the objectives of the police. Intuitive policing represents a decision-making process that officers use frequently, but is a concept that is hard to explain to individuals unfamiliar with the concept. Officers learn intuitive policing strategies through experience—critical incident experiences. Finally, an operationalized standard of care was described as a meritorious initiative that should be developed among law enforcement organizations.

WHAT WOULD YOU DO IF YOU WERE IN CHARGE?

On January 27, 2000, an off-duty black police officer, son of the highest-ranking minority in the city police department, was shot and killed by two white police officers in Providence, Rhode Island. The incident occurred outside a local restaurant, where one of two women engaged in an altercation asked a Hispanic male friend to draw his weapon. The black off-duty officer, who was apparently attempting to assist the police officers who responded to the scene, was shot by white police officers under ambiguous circumstances.[131]

OFFICER KILLED IN PHOENIX, ARIZONA

On Tuesday, May 10, 2005, Officer David Uribe, a 22-year veteran of the Phoenix Police Department, was conducting a routine traffic stop in the area of 35th Avenue and Cactus. Officer Uribe ran a license plate through dispatch and when the plate returned stolen he turned his unit around to follow the vehicle with the stolen plate. Officer Uribe pulled over the maroon Monte Carlo and stepped out of his vehicle to approach the car to question the subjects. The two subjects, still inside the vehicle, opened fire on the officer, hitting him twice, once in the head and once in the neck. Officer Uribe never had a chance. The Monte Carlo left the scene and was dumped a few blocks away. Officer Uribe was left in the roadway to die. Neighbors heard the shots and saw the incident take place. Some ran to help the officer, one man pulling his own shirt off and wrapping it around the officer's head while another tried to plug the bullet holes with her fingers to slow the bleeding. The incident took place only a few blocks from the Cactus Park precinct in Phoenix. When other officers and EMT arrived, neighbors were found performing CPR on Officer Uribe. He was transported to John C. Lincoln hospital but later died.

The two subjects were picked up by a friend named David York who drove them to his home. The gun was disassembled and hidden in the attic.

The clothing of the subjects was burned. There were many eyewitnesses to the shooting and the identity of one of the subjects was learned. A massive manhunt took place and eventually the two subjects were found and taken into custody along with York. David Delahanty, 18, and Chris Wilson, 27, were charged with the murder of Officer Uribe. Delahanty was charged with first-degree murder and Wilson was charged with second-degree murder. David York, a former Arizona corrections officer, was also charged in the case for covering evidence and hiding Delahanty and Wilson.[132]

DISCUSSION QUESTIONS

1. Justify the assumption made by the author about critical incident reactions. In what way might that make sense to you?
2. Describe critical incident stressors.
3. Explain the characteristics of critical incidents. What other characteristics could be added?
4. Identify factors influencing the degree an officer can be affected by a critical incident. In what way might you disagree with some of these factors?
5. Explain the diagnostic criteria for acute stress disorder (ASD).
6. Identify and rank-order the 14 critical incident stressors reported by police officers. As you review the list, which stressors do you believe should have been rated higher or lower than those reported by the participants? Include a rationale for your thoughts.
7. Identify and rank-order the outcomes resulting from critical incidents. As you review the list, which outcomes do you believe should have been rated higher or lower than those reported by the participants? Include a rationale for your thoughts.
8. Describe the stress experiences offered by stress practitioners. In what way were you surprised by these practitioners' thoughts? What other common or serious experiences might stress practitioners have mentioned?
9. Describe the basic principles of crisis intervention.
10. Explain debriefing and its rationale. In what way does the rationale fit your thoughts about a debriefing process?
11. Describe the basic principles of a debriefing process. In what way do the principles make sense?
12. Articulate the justification and scope of critical incident stress management.
13. Explain the criticism associated with crisis intervention and debriefing. In what way might you disagree with the reports offered?
14. Identify the advantages of critical incident participation among officers. Add at least one advantage that you believe should have been included.

15. Define and describe the issues of resilience among officers. In what way can these resilience issues be seen in the general population?

16. Describe the merits of intuitive policing. Identify an experience that you have had or that you have heard about that supports intuitive policing or intuitive learning experiences.

17. Describe what is meant by a standard of care among law enforcement officers.

ENDNOTES

1. Katherine W. Ellison (2004). *Stress and the police officer.* Springfield, IL: Charles C. Thomas. p. 56.

2. Carole Barnes, Joseph Sheley, Valory Logsdon, and Sandra Sutherland (2004, February). In an urban sheriff's department: Contributions of work and family history, and job assignment. NCJRS 203978. Washington, DC: Office of Justice Program. Retrieved online May 20, 2005: http://www.ncjrs.org/pdffiles1/nij/grants/203978.pdf p. 14.

3. D. Gentz and D. Taylor (1994). Marital status and attitudes about divorce among veteran law enforcement officers. In J.T. Reese and E. Scrivner (Eds.), *Law enforcement families: Issues and answers.* Washington, DC: U.S. Government Printing Office.

4. On the job stress in policing: Reducing it, preventing it (2000). NCJ 180079. Retrieved online May 25, 2005: http://ncjrs.org/pdffiles1/jr000242d.pdf For more information on families of police officers, see policefamilies.com.

5. Hans Selye (1979). Stress, cancer, and the mind. In J. Tache, H. Selye, and S.B. Day (Eds.), *Cancer, stress, and death* (pp. 11–27). New York: Plenum. Also see Hans Selye. (1974). *Stress without distress.* Philadelphia: Lippincott.

6. Richard Kelly (2002). Psychological care of the police wounded. In John M. Madonna, Jr. and Richard E. Kelly (Eds.), *Treating police stress* (pp. 15–30). Springfield, IL: Charles C. Thomas.

7. Richard E. Kelly (2002). p. 7.

8. Michael S. McCampbell (2001) Field training for police officers. In Roger G. Dunham and Geoffrey P. Alpert (Eds.), *Critical issues in policing: Contemporary readings,* 4th ed. (pp. 107–116). Prospects Heights, IL: Waveland.

9. David H. Bayley and Egon Bittner (2001). Learning the skills of policing. In Roger G. Dunham and Geoffrey P. Alpert (Eds.), *Critical issues in policing: Contemporary readings,* 4th ed. (pp. 82–106), Prospects Heights, IL: Waveland. Michael S. McCampbell (2001) Field training for police officers. In Roger G. Dunham and Geoffrey P. Alpert (Eds.), *Critical issues in policing: Contemporary readings,* 4th ed. (pp. 107–116). Prospects Heights, IL: Waveland.

10. Roger Soloman (2004). *Police wives.org.* Retrieved online May 22, 2005: http://www.policewives.org/modules.php?name=News&new_topic=2

11. Han Toch (2001). *Stress in policing.* Washington, DC: American Psychological Association. p. 180.

12. J.T. Mitchell (1998). When disaster strikes: The critical incident debriefing process. *Journal of Emergency Medical Services,* 8, 36–39.

13. W.A. Geller (1985). Officer restraint in the use of deadly force: the next frontier in police shooting research. *Journal of Police Science and Administration*, 10(2), 151–177.

14. R.C. Davis (1998). *SWAT plots: A practical training manual for tactical units.* Washington DC: U.S. Government Printing Office.

15. George S. Everly, Jr. (2000). Five principles of crisis intervention: Reducing the risk of premature crisis intervention. Retrieved online June 1, 2005: http://www.icisf.org/articles/Acrobat%20Documents/TerrorismIncident/5princip.pdf

16. George S. Everly, Jr. (2000).

17. *The Psychological Dictionary.* Retrieved online June 2, 2005: http://allpsych.com/dictionary/h.html

18. This interpretation is based on the author's observations.

19. Daniel Goldfarb and Gary S. Aumiller (2005). Critical issues: Stress reductions. *The Heavy Badge.* Retrieved online May 28, 2005: http://www.heavybadge.com/cisd.htm

20. Roger J. Dodson (2000). *Critical incident stress.* NCJ-176330. Retrieved online May 23, 2005: http://www.ncjrs.org/txtfiles1/nij/176330.txt

21. M. MacLeod and Douglas Paton (1999). Police officers and violent crime. Social psychological perspectives on impact and recovery. In J.M. Violanti and Douglas Paton (Eds.), *Police Trauma: Psychological aftermath of civilian combat* (pp. 25–36). Springfield, IL: Charles C. Thomas.

22. M. MacLeod and Douglas Paton (1999).

23. Added by the author based on discussions with officers involved in critical incidents.

24. Added by the author based on discussions with officers involved in critical incidents.

25. Robin Gershon (1999). Washington, DC: U.S. Department of Justice, National Institute of Justice, Public Health Implication of Law Enforcement Stress, video presentation. March 23.

26. *Diagnostic and statistical manual of mental disorders*, 4th ed. (1994). Washington, DC: American Psychiatric Association. p. 432.

27. Daniel A. Goldfarb and Gary S. Aumiller (2005). *The heavy badge.* Retrieved online May 22, 2005: http://www.heavybadge.com/cisd.htm

28. J. R. Scotti, B.K. Beach, L.M. Northrop, C.A. Rode, and J.P. Forsyth (1995). The psychological impact of accident injury. In J.R. Freedy and S.E. Hobfoll (Eds.) *Traumatic stress: From theory to practice* (pp. 181–121). New York: Plenum.

29. Douglas Paton (2005). Critical incidents and police officer stress. In Heith Copes (Ed.), *Policing and stress* (pp. 25–40). Upper Saddle River, NJ: Prentice Hall.

30. Douglas Paton (2005).

31. In part, this component relates to cognitive psychology, which is a subfield of psychology associated with information processing and the role it plays in emotion, behavior, and physiology. *Psychology Dictionary.* Retrieved online June 2, 2005: http://allpsych.com/dictionary/c.html

32. Douglas Paton (2005).

33. Douglas Paton (2005).

34. A.P. Cardarelli, J. McDevitt, and K. Baum (1998). The rhetoric and reality of community policing in small and medium sized cities and towns. *An International Journal of Police Strategies & Management*, 21(3), 397–415.

35. Douglas Paton (2005). Critical incidents and police officer stress. In Heith Copes (Ed.), *Policing and stress.* (pp. 25–40). Upper Saddle River, NJ: Prentice Hall. p. 25.

36. Raymond B. Flannery, Jr. and George S. Everly, Jr. (2000). Crisis intervention: A review. *International Journal of Emergency Mental Health*, 2(2), 119–125. Retrieved online May 23, 2005: http://www.icisf.org/articles/Acrobat%20Documents/TerrorismIncident/CrsIntRev.pdf

37. *Diagnostic and statistical manual of mental disorders*, 4th ed. (1994). Washington, DC: American Psychiatric Association. p. 431.

38. Audrey L. Honig and Steven E. Sultan (2004, December). Reactions and resilience under fire: What an officer can expect. *The Police Chief*, 71(12). Retrieved online May 29, 2005: http://www.policechiefmagazine.org/magazine/index.cfm?fuseaction=display_arch&article_id=469&issue_id=122004

39. Daniel A. Goldfarb and Gary S. Aumiller (2005). *The heavy badge*. Retrieved online May 22, 2005: http://www.heavybadge.com/cisd.htm

40. Barry Perrou (2004). Crisis management training for law enforcement and first responders. In Vivian B. Lord (Ed.), *Suicide by cop: Inducing officers to shoot* (pp. 259–277). Flushing, NY: Looseleaf. p. 260.

41. The 415 officers were from several urban police departments and the 310 participants in the second study (similar questionnaire, distribution, collection, and analysis process) were primarily for one urban department (Boston). Age, years of experience, education, marital status, and rank were similar in groups. For more information on the research design, see Dennis J. Stevens (2004). Origins of police officers' stress before and after 9/11. *The Police Journal*, 77(2), 145–174. Dennis J. Stevens (2005). Police stress. In Heith Copes (Ed.), *Policing and stress* (pp. 1–14). Upper Saddle River, NJ: Prentice Hall.

42. Dennis J. Stevens (2004). Also Dennis J. Stevens (2005). For more information on critical incidents and some of these variables, see Wayne W. Bennett and Karen M. Hess (2004). *Management and supervision in law enforcement*, 4th ed. Upper Saddle River, NJ: Prentice Hall. pp. 412–414.

43. Dennis J. Stevens (2004). Origins of police officers' stress before and after 9/11. *The Police Journal*, 77(2), 145–174. Also see Dennis J. Stevens (2005). Police stress. In Heith Copes (Ed.), *Policing and stress* (pp. 1–14). Upper Saddle River, NJ: Prentice Hall.

44. Hans Toch (2001). *Stress in policing*. Washington, DC: American Psychological Association. Vivian B. Lord (2004). Suicide by cop: the issues. In Vivian B. Lord (Ed.), *Suicide by cop: Inducing officers to shoot* (pp. 3–9). Flashing, NY: Looseleaf. J.B. Stratton, D.A. Parker, and J.R. Snibb (1984). Post traumatic stress: Study of police officers involved in shootings. *Psychological Reports*, 55, 127–131.

45. Edward Conlon (2004). *Blue blood*. New York: Riverside Books. Robin Gershon, U.S. Department of Justice, National Institute of Justice, Public Health Implication of Law Enforcement Stress, video presentation, March 23, 1999. Douglas Paton and J. Violanti (Eds.) (1996). *Traumatic stress in critical occupations: Recognition, consequences, and treatment*. Springfield, IL: Charles C. Thomas.

46. John P. Crank (2004). *Understanding police culture*. Cincinnati, OH: Anderson. p. 341. Richard Kelly (2002). Psychological care of the police wounded. In John M. Madonna, Jr. and Richard E. Kelly (Eds.), *Treating police stress* (pp. 15–30). Springfield, IL: Charles C. Thomas. Robert Trojanowicz, Victor E. Kappeler, Larry K. Gaines, and Bonnie Bucqueroux (1998). *Community policing: A contemporary perspective*, 2nd ed. Cincinnati, OH: Anderson.

47. Edward Conlon (2004). R. M. Solomon (1996, October). Post shooting trauma. *The Police Chief*, 40–44.

48. Wayne Anderson, David Swenson, and Daniel Clay (1995). *Stress management for law enforcement officers.* Upper Saddle River, NJ: Prentice Hall.

49. Dennis J. Stevens (2005). Police stress. In Heith Copes (Ed.), *Policing and stress* (pp. 1–14). Upper Saddle River, NJ: Prentice Hall.

50. Philip Trapasso (2002). Traumatic incident reaction in law enforcement. In John M. Madonna, Jr. and Richard E. Kelly (Eds.), *Treating police stress* (pp. 55–61). Springfield, IL: Charles C. Thomas.

51. John Madonna (2002). The work done: The price paid. In John M. Madonna, Jr. and Richard Kelly (Eds.), *Treating police stress* (pp. 232–244). Springfield, IL: Charles C. Thomas.

52. George L. Kelling & Catherine M. Coles (1996). *Fixing broken windows.* New York: Free Press. Dennis J. Stevens. (1999, March). Police tactical units and community response. *Law and Order.* 47(3), 48–52.

53. Philip Trapasso. (2002). Traumatic incident reaction in law enforcement. In John M. Madonna, Jr. and Richard E. Kelly (Eds.), *Treating police stress* (pp. 55–61). Springfield, IL: Charles C. Thomas.

54. John Madonna (2002). The tough moments and the good ones. In John M. Madonna, Jr. and Richard E. Kelly (Eds.), *Treating police stress* (pp. 82–108). Springfield, IL: Charles C. Thomas.

55. Sam Walker and Charles Katz (2005). *The police in America: An introduction.* Upper Saddle River, NJ: Prentice Hall. pp. 216, 358, 371. Dennis J. Stevens. (2002). Civil liabilities and arrest decisions. In Jeffery T. Walker (Ed.), *Policing and the law* (pp. 53–70). Upper Saddle River, NJ: Prentice Hall.

56. Lawrence A. Greenfeld, Patrick A. Langan, and Steven K. Smith. (1998). Police use of force. National Institute of Justice, U.S. Department of Justice. NCJ-165040. Retrieved March 26, 2004. http://www.ojp.usdoj.gov/bjs/pub/ascii/puof.txt. Jerome Skolnick and James Fyfe (1993). *Above the law: Police and the excessive use of force.* New York: Free Press. Mark Blumberg (2001). Controlling police use of deadly force: Assessing two decades of progress. In Roger G. Dunham and Geoffrey P. Alpert (Eds.), *Critical issues in policing: Contemporary readings* (pp. 559–582). Prospect Heights, IL: Waveland.

57. Edward Conlon (2004). *Blue blood.* New York: Riverside Books.

58. FBI (2005). *Law enforcement officers killed and assaulted, 2001.* Washington, DC. U.S. Department of Justice, Office of Justice Programs. Retrieved online May 27, 2005: http://www.fbi.gov/ucr/killed/2001leoka.pdf

59. On the job stress in policing. Reducing it, preventing it (2000, January). *National Institute of Justice Journal.* Washington, DC: U.S. Department of Justice, Office of Justice Program. NCJ 180079. Retrieved online May 29, 2005: http://ncjrs.org/pdffiles1/jr000242d.pdf

60. Statistical analysis including cross-tabulation, correlation, and regression aided in determining relationships between variables.

61. Personal communication with the writer. Officer was a Quincy, Massachusetts, law enforcement officer and student of the writer.

62. Meryl Sloan is not her real name. Meryl wants to remain anonymous, but the facts are as accurate as she recalled them. She attended graduate school and was a student in a university course conducted by the author. Meryl volunteered bits of her story and the author developed it for this book.

63. Written by the author based on the accounts of Roger J. Dodson (2000). *Critical incident stress.* NCJ-176330. Retrieved online May 23, 2005: http://www.ncjrs .org/txtfiles1/nij/176330.txt

64. John Madonna (2002). The tough moments and the good ones. In John M. Madonna, Jr. and Richard E. Kelly (Eds.), *Treating police stress* (pp. 83–108). Springfield, IL: Charles C. Thomas.

65. John Madonna (2002). The tough moments and the good ones. In John M. Madonna, Jr. and Richard E. Kelly (Eds.), *Treating police stress* (pp. 83–108). Springfield, IL: Charles C. Thomas. p. 85.

66. John Madonna (2002). The tough moments and the good ones. In John M. Madonna, Jr. and Richard E. Kelly (Eds.), *Treating police stress* (pp. 83–108). Springfield, IL: Charles C. Thomas. p. 89. The counselor talking is Richard Kelly of the Massachusetts State Police, Stress Unit.

67. Douglas Paton, Leigh M. Smith, and Christine Stephens (1998) Work-related psychological trauma: A social psychological and organizational approach to understanding response and recovery. *The Australasian Journal of Disaster and Trauma Studies,* 1. Retrieved online May 29, 2005: http://www.massey.ac.nz/ ~trauma/issues/1998-1/paton1.htm

68. Richard K. James and Burl E. Gilliland (2005). *Crisis intervention strategies,* 4th ed. Belmont, CA: Wadsworth.

69. George S. Everly, Jr. Principles of crisis intervention: Reducing the risk of premature crisis intervention. *International Journal of Emergency Mental Health,* 2(1), 1–4. Retrieved online May 24, 2005: http://www.icisf.org/articles/Acrobat %20Documents/TerrorismIncident/5princip.pdf

70. George S. Everly, Jr. and James T. Mitchell (1999). *Critical incident stress management: A new era and standard of post-traumatic stress care in crisis intervention,* 2nd ed. Ellicott City, MD: Chevron.

71. S.R. Jenkins (1996). Social support and debriefing efficacy among emergency medical workers after a mass shooting incident. *Journal of Social Behavioral and Personality,* 11, 477–492. Also see R.C. Robinson, and J. T. Mitchell (1995). Getting some balance back into the debriefing debate. *Bulletin of the Australian Psychological Society,* 17, 5–10.

72. The author added this principle because many crisis practitioners are voluntary, often untrained participants trying to aid a law enforcement agency and need to know that refraining from verbal or nonverbal judgment expressions or utterances about a "client" story is one of the best ways to develop rapport and build trust.

73. Richard K. James and Burl E. Gilliland (2005). *Crisis intervention strategies,* 4th ed. Belmont, CA: Wadsworth.

74. Richard K. James and Burl E. Gilliland (2005). *Crisis intervention strategies,* 4th ed. Belmont, CA: Wadsworth.

75. Katherine W. Ellison (2004). p. 130.

76. Jeffrey T. Mitchell and George S. Everly (2001). *Critical incident stress debriefing: An operations manual for CISD, defusing and other group crisis intervention services.* Ellicott City, MD: Chevron.

77. George S. Everly, Jr., Robert B. Flannery, Jr., and James T. Mitchell (2000). Critical incident stress management: A review of literature. *Aggression and Violent Behavior: A Review Journal,* 5, 23–40. Katherine W. Ellison (2004). John M. Madonna, Jr. and Richard E. Kelly (2001). *Treating police stress.* Springfield, IL: Charles C. Thomas.

78. R. C. Robinson and J. T. Mitchell (1995, October) Getting some balance back into the debriefing debate. *The Bulletin of the Australian Psychological Society*, 5–10. A.Y. Shalev (1994). Debriefing following traumatic exposure. In R.J. Ursano, B.G. McCaughey, and C.S. Fullerton (Eds.), *Individual and community responses to trauma and disaster*. Cambridge, UK: Cambridge University Press.

79. George S. Everly, Jr. Principles of crisis intervention: Reducing the risk of premature crisis intervention. *International Journal of Emergency Mental Health*, 2(1), 1–4. Retrieved online May 24, 2005: http://www.icisf.org/articles/Acrobat%20Documents/TerrorismIncident/5princip.pdf

80. Raymond B. Flannery, Jr. and George S. Everly, Jr. (2000). Crisis intervention: A review. *International Journal of Emergency Mental Health*, 2(2), 119–125.

81. International Association of Chiefs of Police. Retrieved online June 26, 2004: http://www.theiacp.org/documents/index.cfm?fuseaction=document&document_type_id=1&document_id=167

82. Raymond B. Flannery, Jr. and George S. Everly, Jr. (2000). Crisis intervention: A review. *International Journal of Emergency Mental Health*, 2(2), 119–125.

83. Audrey L. Honig and Steven E. Sultan (2004, December). Reactions and resilience under fire: What an officer can expect. *The Police Chief*, 71(12). Retrieved online May 29, 2005: http://www.policechiefmagazine.org/magazine/index.cfm?fuseaction=display_arch&article_id=469&issue_id=122004

84. Jeffrey T. Mitchell and George S. Everly (1996). *Critical incident stress debriefing: An operations manual for the prevention of traumatic stress among emergency services and disaster workers*. Ellicott City, MD: Chevron.

85. George S. Everly, Jr. and James T. Mitchell (1999). *Critical incident stress management: A new era and standard of post-traumatic stress care in crisis intervention*, 2nd ed. Ellicott City, MD: Chevron.

86. National Institute of Justice (1997). *Critical criminal justice issues: Task force reports from the American Society of Criminology to Attorney General Janet Reno*. Also see John M. Violanti (2001). *Police psychological trauma*. Law Enforcement Wellness Association. Retrieved online May 24, 2005: http://www.cophealth.com/articles/articles_psychtrauma.html

87. The author checked with police academies in Boston, Chicago, Miami-Dade County, States of North Carolina and Florida, and Harris County, Texas. Although these academies might not be representative of all police academies, it would be expected that many academies would model their programs after these.

88. Lawrence N. Blum (2004). *Forge under pressure: How cops live and why they die*. New York: Lantern Books. pp. 19–21.

89. Richard Kelly (2002). Psychological care of the police wounded. In John M. Madonna, Jr. and Richard E. Kelly (Eds.), *Treating police stress*. (pp. 15–30). Springfield, IL: Charles C. Thomas.

90. Personal experiences of the author.

91. Carl B. Klockars (1999). The dirty Harry problem. In Victor E. Kappeler (Ed.), *The police and society*, 2nd ed. (pp. 368–387). Prospect Heights, IL: Waveland. Gary W. Sykes (1999). Street justice: A moral defense of order maintenance policing. In Victor E. Kappeler (Ed.) *The police and society*, 2nd ed. (pp. 134–149). Prospect Heights, IL: Waveland.

92. Richard Kelly (2002). p. 17. Also see Bill Lewinski (2002, May/June). Stress reactions: Related to lethal force encounters. *The Police Marksman*, 24–27.

93. Richard Kelly (2002). p. 17.

94. Dennis Tueller (2003, November 11). Why train on moving targets? Policeone.com. Retrieved online May 23, 2005: http://www.policeone.com/police-products/training/shooting-range/articles/72357/

95. Dennis Tueller (2003, November 11).

96. IACP releases research on police use of force (2002, January 22). Retrieved online May 23, 2005: http://www.theiacp.org/documents/index.cfm?fuseaction=document&document_type_id=7&document_id=180&subtype_id=

97. National Institute of Justice (1999, November). *Use of force by police: Overview of national and local data.* Washington, DC: U.S. Department of Justice, Office of Justice Programs. Retrieved online May 23, 2005: http://www.ncjrs.org/txtfiles1/nij/176330.txt

98. National Institute of Justice (1996). *Understanding the use of force by and against the police.* Washington, DC: U.S. Department of Justice, Office of Justice Programs. Retrieved online May 23, 2005: http://www.ncjrs.org/txtfiles/forcerib.txt

99. Katherine W. Ellison (2004). p. 130.

100. George S. Everly, Jr. (2000). Five principles of crisis intervention: Reducing the risk of premature crisis intervention. *International Journal of Emergency Mental Health*, 2(1), 1–4. Retrieved online June 1, 2005: http://www.icisf.org/articles/Acrobat%20Documents/TerrorismIncident/5princip.pdf

101. Jerome Groopman. The grief industry. *The New Yorker* (January 26, 2004), 31–37.

102. Katherine W. Ellison (2004). p. 130. Also see Victor E. Kappeler (2001). *Critical issues in police civil liability.* Prospect Heights, IL: Waveland. p. 200.

103. R.A. Bryant and A.G. Harvey (2000). *Acute stress disorder: A handbook of theory, assessment, and treatment.* Washington, DC: American Psychological Association.

104. J.A. Kenardy, R.A. Webster, T.J. Lewin, V. J. Carr, P.L. Hazell, and G.L. Carter (1996). Stress debriefing and patterns of recovery following a natural disaster. *Journal of Traumatic Stress*, 8, 37–50. Christine Stephens (2005). Workplace strategies for prevention of PTSD. In Heith Copes (Ed.), *Policing and stress* (pp. 140–157). Upper Saddle River, NJ: Prentice Hall.

105. Sandra D. Terhune-Bickler (2004). Too close for comfort negotiating with fellow officers. *Federal Law Enforcement Bulletin*, 73(4). Retrieved online May 30, 2005: http://www.fbi.gov/publications/leb/2004/apr2004/april04leb.htm#page_2

106. Sandra D. Terhune-Bickler (2004).

107. Lawrence W. Sherman (2001). Police in the laboratory of criminal justice. In Roger G. Dunham and Geoffrey P. Albert (Eds.), *Critical issues in policing: Contemporary reading*, 4th ed. (pp. 41–64). Prospect Heights, IL: Waveland Press.

108. Douglas Paton (2005). Critical incidents and police officer stress. In Heith Copes (Ed.), *Policing and stress* (pp. 25–40). Upper Saddle River, NJ: Prentice Hall.

109. Audrey L. Honig and Jocelyn E. Roland (1998, October). Shots fired: Officer involved. *The Police Chief*, 65. Audrey L. Honig and Steven E. Sultan (2004, December). Reactions and resilience under fire: What an officer can expect. *The Police Chief*, 71(12). Retrieved online May 29, 2005: http://www.policechiefmagazine.org/magazine/index.cfm?fuseaction=display_arch&article_id=469&issue_id=122004

110. Audrey L. Honig and Steven E. Sultan (2004, December).

111. Audrey L. Honig and Steven E. Sultan (2004, December).

112. George S. Everly, Jr. (2000).

113. George A. Bonanno (2004). Loss, trauma, and human resilience. *American Psychologist*, 59(1), 20–28.

114. Ann Kaiser Stearns (2005). *Resilience in the aftermath of adverse or traumatic events.* Washington, DC: American Psychological Association. Retrieved online May 29, 2005: http://www.apa.org/divisions/div31/CoOpArticles/Maryland/ Stearn%20Resilience%20in%20the%20Aftermath.pdf

115. Ann S. Masten (2001). Ordinary magic: Resilience processes in development. *American Psychologist, 56,* 227–238.

116. Ann S. Masten and J.L. Powell (2003). A resilience framework for research, policy, and practice. In S.S. Luthar (Ed.), *Resilience and vulnerabilities: Adaptation in the context of childhood adversities.* (pp. 1–25). New York: Cambridge University Press.

117. Audrey L. Honig and Steven E. Sultan (2004, December).

118. George A. Bonanno (2004).

119. Anthony J. Pinizzotto, Edward F. Davis, and Charles E. Miller III (2004). Intuitive policing: Emotional rational decision making in law enforcement. *FBI Law Enforcement Bulletin,* 73(2), 1–8. Retrieved online May 30, 2005: http://www.fbi .gov/publications/leb/2004/feb04leb.pdf

120. Gladwell (2006). Retrieved online March 8, 2006: http://www.gladwell.com/ tippingpoint/index.html

121. Malcolm Gladwell (2005). *Blink: The power of thinking without thinking.* New York: Little, Brown and Company. Gladwell is concerned with the smallest components of our everyday lives—with the content and origin of those instantaneous impressions and conclusions that bubble up whenever we meet a new person, or confront a complex situation, or have to make a decision under conditions of stress. He spends a lot of time in trying to explain fleeting moments.

122. Anthony J. Pinizzotto, Edward F. Davis, and Charles E. Miller III (2004).

123. Anthony J. Pinizzotto, Edward F. Davis, and Charles E. Miller III (2004).

124. Daniel Goleman (1995). *Emotional intelligence: Why it can matter more than IQ.* New York: Bantam.

125. Joseph LeDoux (1996). *The emotional brain: The mysterious underpinnings of emotional life.* New York: Touchstone.

126. Gavin DeBecker (1997). *The gift of fear: Survival signals that protect us from violence.* New York: Little, Brown and Company. pp. 6–7.

127. National Institute of Justice (1997). *Critical criminal justice issues: Task force reports from the American Society of Criminology to Attorney General Janet Reno.* NCJ 158837. Washington, DC: U.S. Department of Justice. Office of Justice Programs. Retrieved online May 22, 2005: http://www.ncjrs.org/pdffiles/158837.pdf p. 96.

128. Stratton, Parkers, and Snibbe (1984).

129. Douglas Paton & J. Violanti (Eds.) (1996).

130. Raymond B. Flannery, Jr. and George S. Everly, Jr. (2000). Crisis intervention: A review. *International Journal of Emergency Mental Health,* 2000, 2(2), 119–125. Retrieved online May 23, 2005: http://www.icisf.org/articles/ Acrobat%20Documents/TerrorismIncident/CrsIntRev.pdf

131. Case Profiles (2002). Excessive use of force. Fatal police shooting. Providence, Rhode Island. Retrieved online February 7, 2005: http://www.usdoj.gov/crs/ pubs/fy2000/FY2000_AnnualReport.htm#profiles_1

132. Policeone.com (2005, May 23). Officer down in Phoenix, Arizona. Retrieved May 23, 2005: http://www.policeone.com/policeone/frontend/parser.cfm?object=News &operation=officer_down_full&id=98992

6

General Work Stressors, Family Stressors, and Female Officers

Man creates problems. Government and bureaucrats magnify them 100 times.
—George Van Valkenburg

Learning Objectives

Once reading this chapter, you should be better prepared to:

- Characterize general work stressors among police officers.
- Identify the 14 general stressors described in the chapter.
- Describe each of the 14 general stressors.
- Characterize family problems concerning officer stress.
- Explain the reasons why the divorce rate is high among officers.
- Discuss police mortality and suicide issues.
- Characterize female officer stress.
- Explain the pressures female officers often face on the job.
- Clarify the advancements made by female officers.
- Explain why female officers resign from their jobs.

Conflict with regulations
Death notification
Disrespect of the courts

Domestic violence stops
Excessive paperwork
Lack of recognition

Police subculture
Poor supervisor support
Shift work

INTRODUCTION

This chapter describes general work stressors, family stressors, and provides information about female officers and their experiences. It's strange how George Van Valkenburg hit the problem on the head by implying law enforcement officers are in the business of serving and protecting society from society's own problems, and that stress produced through government bureaucrats magnifies those problems one-hundred times.

GENERAL WORK STRESSORS

General work stressors can be characterized as stressors that arise during the daily work routine of a police officer. What is known about most law enforcement officers in America is that some observers report that the prevalence of police fatigue can explain law enforcement accidents and other contingencies occurring to police officers.[1] As reported in Chapter 1, there is a tendency to blame the victim for his or her problems. Tired police officers can be reckless, and there are few regulations concerning the overtime police officers work. Where regulations and union and associational standards are in place concerning overtime or work outside the departments, it is unlikely that those standards are followed. In fact, police unions and associations such as the Fraternal Order of Police (FOP) generally fight to ensure that officers can work overtime. For instance, in the small community of Weston, Massachusetts, the median take-home pay for a Weston police officer in 2004 was $85,799, more than $25,000 a year greater than the median pay for firefighters and teachers in the town.[2] Weston reports that it paid its 27 unionized police officers 6,605 hours of overtime in 2004.

However, accounts of tragedies (there were no tragedies linked to Weston officers) associated with police fatigue are not new. The National Commission on Sleep Disorders Research heard testimony from officers who described terrible work schedules, high stress, and overwhelming fatigue.[3] It could be asked which came first, the terrible work schedules and stress or the overwhelming fatigue? This is not a chicken and egg story because there is only one answer. (Officers do deserve overtime hours, within reason.)

Nonetheless, concerning the job of officers, typically an average of 68% of all sworn personnel in local and state law enforcement agencies across the nation as outlined in their job description respond to emergency calls and provide many other forms of police service.[4] For instance, officers made 16.8 million traffic stops and almost 8.4 million arrests in 2002.[5] Nonetheless, the number of officers who respond to 9-1-1 calls depends on the size of the community and the size of the law enforcement agency. Then, too, 81% of most sworn officers are patrol officers, who, while on patrol, are first-responders at police service calls. The general work descriptions that follow pertain to the typical law enforcement officer who, as part of his or her job description, is deployed as a patrol officer and a first responder to most police service calls. Finally in this regard, when the 538 officers surveyed for this work were asked how often they experience stress working the streets, 6% of the responders said very often or always, 13% reported sometimes, 51% said seldom, and 30% said never. One way to understand their responses is to say that when law enforcement officers were engaged in typical police work, general work stressors affected their performance less often than critical incident stressors, as discussed in Chapter 5.

GENERAL WORK STRESSOR DESCRIPTIONS

Many professions have similar general work stressors as police officers, such as airline pilots, firefighters, and truck drivers. However, it appears that police officers generally lack an organizational standard of care as discussed in the preceding chapter (Chapter 5), and therefore, while stressors appear similar within other occupations, law enforcement officers tend to lack the standard of care that aids organizations better control of the effects of general work stressors. There are many other stressors in police work in addition to those stressors discussed in previous chapters, such as organizational stressors (Chapter 4) and critical incident stressors (Chapter 5). General work stressors (some seem to originate from the police organizational structure) can include conflict with regulations, domestic violence stops, losing control, child abuse calls, excessive paperwork, public disrespect, injuries of other officers, lack of recognition, poor supervisor support, disrespect of the courts, shift work, death notification, poor fringe benefits, and patrol vehicle accidents.

Conflict with regulations happens when officers experience frustration and anxiety because official goals and objectives are not clear and consistent with rank-and-file expectations or their understanding.[6] Goals and objectives of some police agencies are communicated unprofessionally to officers, resulting in an officer's attempt to redefine his or her understanding or extent of a goal and turn to his or her peers for rationalization and justification. Consequently, performance tends to mirror the redefinition as aided by peers usually through the police subculture rather than the organizational or supervisor's intended message. Sometimes conflicts with regulations can place an officer unintentionally at risk during a service call, especially if a supervisor or dispatcher neglected to communicate certain information that could signal a volatile circumstance. Additionally, redefining organizational objectives can give rise to street justice and corruption in the form of denial of due process rights of suspects. Street justice in reference to order maintenance policing is the detainment, search and seizure, and punishment of offenders by the police without judicial review.[7] Advocates of street justice justify its use in relation to reform and order. Studies of police discretion (as reinforced by the police subculture) reinforce the view that street decisions by officers to intervene, arrest, use force, or issue traffic citations are a function of "situational and organizational factors that reflect interpretations of community needs and expectations of police."[8] Street justice in this sense is seen as a response to community issues that crime be dealt with in an appropriate fashion. It comes down to street cops executing their own style of policing, which could elevate danger and reinforce a Dirty Harry problem typified through initiatives that deny the legal rights of suspects and use of excessive force before, during, and after an investigation.[9] It can also be said that the police subculture (as discussed in Chapters 1–3 and further in this chapter) discourages independent thinkers among officers and produces fewer officers who view their jobs exclusively in terms of public mandates and official dictums.[10] When peer pressure reinforces a dereliction of duty in the sense of making rules and acting as judge and executioner, it can lead to recklessness. For example, CRASH was the group of elite antigang units set up within the Los Angeles Police Department (LAPD) to tackle rising gang-related crime.[11] CRASH officers were required to get to know gang members and keep on top of their activities. Although CRASH was successful citywide in reducing gang crime, critics say officers harassed and abused suspects and falsified reports. This scandal lead to the release of over 100 convicted offenders and the eventual oversight of the LAPD by the U.S. Department of Justice.[12] Even before allegations surfaced, the LAPD was investigating suspicious activity among some officers in that unit. However, critics like Detective Russell Poole claim the department wasn't really concerned in getting to the bottom of what was happening. Poole claims crucial leads were ignored in the early stages of the investigation. Others say administrative decisions, taken after the scandal surfaced, discouraged officers with critical information from coming forward.[13]

Then, too, some law enforcement organizations develop ambiguous or conflicting regulations and policies that might have been originally designed as part of another strategy. Additionally, some agencies attempt to design rules for every situation, resulting in confused officers who have little time (or patience) to interpret numerous and ambiguous regulations. Also officer routine and expectations can be disrupted when agencies attempt to alter existing programs and strategies and other times agencies attempt to implement initiatives that are counter to officer belief systems or expectations such as community policing.[14] Finally, as one expert argues, "Police agencies have long been notorious for urging rank-and-file officers to do one thing, while rewarding them for doing something else."[15] CRASH officers should have been held accountable if their actions were unlawful, but had the administration provided unconflicting directives and professional management, which included awards for homicide (Officer David Mack gunned down an unarmed suspect), would the scandal have been as widespread?

Domestic violence stops as a general work stressor refer to officer experiences responding to domestic violence calls.[16] Domestic violence stops can begin with a 9-1-1 call, which can involve serious and continual altercations between family members.[17] Domestic violence disputes can include intimate partners, married and unmarried, but can concentrate on disputes that result in violence.[18] In a study consisting of almost 1,000 officers, one-half of the participants reported feelings of stress as a result of official intervention in a case of violence.[19] The "problem is that sometimes it's hard to tell which one of them was the rat and beat the other one up. They're [husband and wife] both beat up but it seems that I've been to that address five times in the last two months," says one officer.[20]

Of further concern, the dynamics or outcome of a domestic call can change regardless of victimization characteristics. That is, outcomes of police intervention in domestic cases (as well as other cases) has less to do with the aggressor and more to do with the dynamics or characteristics of the officers and the victim, which includes sexism, racism, accepted norms of partner violence, normative perceptions of family and privacy, and the media and publicity.[21]

In domestic violence cases sexism and accepted norms of partner violence can be illustrated in the account of Marlene Goodman, who entered the police academy at age 40 and worked her way up to become a Des Moines police detective specializing in domestic violence cases.[22] But Goodman was forced to quit after failing to report that she herself had been battered—by a fellow cop. When a domestic violence victim is also a police officer, careers are often in jeopardy. That's because law enforcement agencies not only have poor track records at reining in abusive officers, police officials blame the victim (discussed in Chapter 1) for an officer's problem. "There's this belief that police officers should be able to take care of themselves," said Penny Harrington, founder of the National Center on Women and Policing in Arlington, Virginia.[23] Typical roles and expectations are assumed by the domestic violence participants. When officers mirror behavior or practices that vary from those assumed roles and expectations held by the actors, conflict arises. It goes without saying that stereotypical assumptions tend to be culturally defined and centered in the lifestyles of the domestic participants. Domestic participants might, depending on their cultural nuances, see various domestic behavior, such as violence or "defending your man," as appropriate, adding to officer stress levels and challenging an officer's standards.

Normative perceptions of family and privacy are also cultural beliefs and often are so counter to an officer's perspective that many officers become frustrated. That is, there is a belief that articulates the connection between family violence and the idea that family is a private institution and therefore children and wives are property to be used in whatever way is deemed appropriate and beneficial by the "father."[24] Victims also believe in cultural nuances that reinforce and support their own victimization. For instance, a study concerning sexual assault in Boston reported that immigrants are told by their aggressors that the American culture is similar to the previous country of their origin and greater harm would come to them.[25] It is clear that breaking the cycle of family violence might be one of America's most challenging opportunities. However, when experienced officers face negative normative perceptions placing human rights at risk, stress levels intensify, particularly when some supervisors may hold exaggerated perspectives about reporting in the hierarchy of male dominance.

Media and publicity refers to police pressures as a result of bad press. The media is quick to point to police inadequacy when an officer fails to make an arrest, and of course, the media has much to say when police make too many arrests or stop too many citizens.[26] Unfavorable media attention of specific officers can lead to intensified stress for officers, especially if the attention is unnecessary.

Finally, it must be a disappointment for officers to see human beings beat and abuse each other. They grow up wanting to be a help to others, and suddenly realize that the best help in a domestic is to arrest an aggressor.

Losing control refers to the perceptions that an officer has little control if any over work conditions.[27] This happens when an officer makes a request for an assignment, specific equipment, shift, promotion, transfer, or partner and those requests are ignored. Also a loss of control is implied when officers obtain rewards because of who an officer knows within the department chain of command as opposed to police performance. Ambiguous directives and feedback about performance might also signal to an officer that he or she has a loss of control over the working relationship with their supervisors.

Another variable furthering a loss of control perspective relates to the methods employed to measure performance of law enforcement officers. Traditionally law enforcement productivity has been measured by factors such as arrests, stops, traffic citations, the value of recovered property, and the reduction of crashes and crime.[28] It appears that a typical patrol officer would have little control over any of these factors with perhaps the exception of crashes and that might depend on a number of other variables. The productivity of policing is often measured by the quantity of services provided by a department as a unit as opposed to individual accomplishments.[29] Also, in most law enforcement organizations, management operates within a hierarchical system (as explained in Chapter 4) that also measures antiquated levels of performance that tends to confuse the mission of policing with popular beliefs about policing.[30] In the final analysis, police officers are promoted to management through networks or friendly support as opposed to positive work ethics. Some departments are pulling away from a network process or a good-ole-boy system and oral boards, written exams, and evaluations are playing larger roles toward promotion. Yet, unpopular candidates with command have less chances of promotion than those who are favored.

Child abuse refers to police service calls whereby the victim is an abused or injured child.[31] For instance, "I was in an emergency room and I saw this other cop come rushing in, giving a baby mouth-to-mouth resuscitation. He was still trying to breathe life into the child who was dead, and this big cop just fell to his knees and started to cry, right there. I never forgot that."[32] Another officer talks about the stress from finding a young kid that committed suicide by hanging himself. Injured children as a result of auto accidents, circumstance, or criminal activity which includes sexual abuse or neglect creates a great deal of stress among most police officers especially because most officers became cops (according to the consensus of the 538 officers polled for this book) to help people and to make a difference. An abused child is beyond their individual assistance. The child is already harmed and the officer can only see to it that it ends, but they learn there is little they can do.

Excessive paperwork refers to the completing of forms that require information from arrests, stops, traffic citations, and other forms relating to policing.[33] One source recommends officers to "control the paper flood or it will control them."[34] The sheer volume of reports required of officers makes them both time consuming and difficult to absorb. Some officers feel as though they are clerks rather than professionals.[35] Although a "paper trail" is critical to some aspects of law enforcement, all too often forms are obsolete and redundant, and officers are called upon to do paperwork that could easily and efficiently be accomplished by clerical staff or officers could be aided with advanced technology, which is not forthcoming as often as expected.[36] Officers respond to a call and it is expected that only he or she can complete the paperwork. For instance, video techniques are available that could enhance police intervention, further public safety, and others could translate video into words, if necessary.

Public disrespect has to do with public trust[37] (also see Court Disrespect, below). If the public does not trust police officers, then one way to demonstrate those feelings is through the disrespect of police officers.[38] Evidence supporting a lack of trust of law enforcement has to do with a high percentage of unreported crimes, which was discussed in Chapter 2, less budget funding for police operations including equipment and training, and less police power through a rise in civil liabilities.[39] Officers feel that the public holds a negative perspective about them and the public's perspective is reinforced by the media.[40]

Practices of disrespect toward police officers, it can be argued, is found within cultural norms of various groups across the country. For instance, some youngsters learn at an early age that disrespecting police might add to their reputation. One urban officer said, "Kids are just running their mouths at ya because you're a cop and ya gotta learn not to take it personal otherwise you'd be arresting everybody living in the west-end." Then, too, early police disrespect can turn to subsequent violence. For example, it's been said that in the inner city, young children learn to play a game that is fairly simple: when law enforcement rolls by, juveniles do their best to "punk 'em out."[41] The tougher juveniles have fathers, brothers, and maybe even mothers in jail, and are usually willing to go the furthest. They spit at patrol cars, call the cops filthy names, and maybe even wave one-fingered salutes to officers. Some juveniles build reputations that last a lifetime. But by adulthood, mouthing off at cops can have grown-up consequences.

After decades of practicing disrespect, there are generations of inner-city guys who don't know when it's best to remain silent or provide straight answers to officers. That's a problem the local chapter of the American Civil Liberties Union heard again and again when interviewing people claiming to have been abused or disrespected by city police.[42] Hoping to plug the huge gap in communications between law enforcement and their constituents, the ACLU in 2000 joined forces with the National Council for Urban Peace & Justice and wrote a pamphlet titled "Rights, Responsibilities & Reality."

Most of us might agree that a stressed officer facing the youngsters described above might resort to violence more often than officers who are not disrespected.

How officers respond to perceived disrespect might have a lot to do with the end result of a street cop's job. For instance, a Swampscott, Massachusetts, patrol officer stood in the courtroom "attempting to swallow his rage and mash his mortification."[43] A youth the officer described as a virtual one-person crime wave just had his case dismissed by the judge. The street cop apprehended the youth breaking into a home. The homeowner was a witness to the arrest and came to court numerous times to testify but the case was delayed a number of times. On this day, the homeowner was told by her boss that she was risking her job if she went to court again to testify. She sat in court waiting for the case to be called and finally in mid-afternoon her boss said that if she didn't come to work that her job was at risk. The case was called at 4:00 P.M. The judge chewed the officer out for letting the witness leave and dismissed the charges. "I'll never forget how that kid and his mother stood there and laughed, laughed at me," recalls the officer. The jeering by the accused, the verbal humiliation by the judge, the release of a budding criminal, guilty in fact but exonerated by the system, "certainly were stressful experiences for the law enforcement officers."[44] There were other defendants, lawyers, clerks, and street cops in the room. They too had feelings about the case, feelings about the cop. Was he to be trusted with other cases, other witnesses? What about the next time the officer arrests this defendant, would a sharp lawyer talk about harassment? It's one more occasion when a street cop loses face, feels bad about the job he did, and looks like the proverbial Sisyphus, forever rolling the stone uphill, only to have it forever roll backward over him and other officers who experience similar outcomes.

The officer says that he stored the experience somewhere inside himself even though he knew it would never end, even after the courtroom doors closed behind him. But tomorrow he would face the same judge and see many of the same faces who looked at him in wonder. The experience was layered with other similar experiences that "contributed to and perhaps maybe even caused drinking to become the biggest thing in my life."[45]

Injuries to other officers refers generally to an officer harmed as a result of an altercation with a suspect.[46] As you already know (from Chapter 2), 56,000 officers, or 261 per 1,000 officers, were assaulted, most often while delivering police services, especially while providing services during family and domestic calls.[47]

Lack of recognition refers to officers receiving honorable mention or a reward for excellent police performance. Many police commanders tend to ignore the good work of their officers.[48] One example comes from New York City after 9/11. Officers reported that their superiors, who had never come into their presence before, gathered rank-and-file officers together and said a few laudatory and consoling words, then disappeared.[49] Some of the strongest feelings of frustration that are expressed by law enforcement officers seem to relate to inequities in the system associated with recognition particularly linked to promotion.[50] Officers tend to describe this problem as "politics," revealing that there are a variety of ways in which the process of promotion, task assignment, and unit assignment is tainted. For instance, Officer Kenisha Stewart, a Boston police officer, says that assignment to special units within the department is difficult unless you know somebody who will support you. "Doesn't matter how hard I work, I just can't get the preverbal nod."[51] Also, an officer in Dunstable, Massachusetts, reports that a substantial stressor for him is within the administration.[52] That is, the promotion process lacks integrity because politics play a tremendous role in deciding who gets promoted and who doesn't rather than promotion decided on performance.

Poor supervisor support appears to be a constant theme among officers. They report that their supervisors have little regard for the well-being of the officers on the streets.[53] One distinctive characteristic of law enforcement organizations is that virtually everyone in the organization "from station house broom to chief, shares the common experience of having worked the street as a patrol officer."[54] Moving down the hierarchical ladder, lateral entry is unknown because supervisor positions are filled only from the pool of candidates directly below the vacant slot. One result of this system is that most supervisors had experienced street action (yet that does not mean they were compatible with it). However, the competition in most police organizations for sergeant is keen and the results are generally uncertain, suggesting that becoming a sergeant is anything but an orderly, well-defined passage.[55] Sergeants learn their job by doing it and often that means taking risks, but it is a solitary process. Nonetheless, sergeants are probably one of the most powerful individuals in the station house.[56] First-line supervisors can be sources of stress because they are faced daily and their authority is hard to avoid.[57] For instance, one officer says that her sergeant assigned her to the worst part of Boston, and checked on her every move every 20 minutes through her graveyard shift. The officer adds that "there was little question in my head who was the boss. I hated that kind of intimation but had to take it if I wanted to keep my job."[58]

Another account explains that police executives have forgotten what policing is about. An officer explains, "The people in this building [headquarters] are not policemen. Most wouldn't know how to be a policeman, and I don't say that bitterly. It's just how it is. Some are good book guys, you know, studied and quickly moved up the ladder if they were liked by the brass, but because they didn't like what they were doing they wanted to be big bosses, and so they are."[59] Many rank-and-file officers have similar feelings for their supervisors.

Disrespect of the courts refers to the perception held by officers about how the court views them as a group. Because court rulings tend to be too lenient on violators and too restrictive on procedural issues such as evidence admission, officers view the courts as an adversary.[60] One officer says that "a judge told me off for doing my job in front of the suspects and his criminal friends. What is going to happen if I have to re-arrest this guy?"[61]

Findings concerning public disrespect can be linked with Carl Rogers[62] and his notion about a "fully functioning person." Rogers implies that human beings have within themselves "vast resources for self-understanding, for altering" self-concept, attitudes, and self-directed behavior—and "these resources can be tapped if only a definable climate" can objectively guide, without judgment, individuals toward becoming fully functional.[63] With so much (perceived) disrespect from the public, courts, and their supervisors, it is a wonder how officers continue to strive to become fully functional.

Shift work refers to the various assignment periods for officers to work. Since policing is never closed, officers are required to assist in the 24 hour a day, 7 day a week schedule. Because humans are biologically equipped with the circadian system, there is a propensity toward day-oriented routines.[64] The circadian system's job is to prepare the body for restful sleep at night and active wakefulness during the day. Work patterns that tend to change are met with resistance that an individual often has few initiatives to control because the body's circadian rhythm is negatively affected and results in desynchronization (the relation that exists when things occur at unrelated times; for instance, deviation from the night-sleep, day-wake pattern).[65]

Shift work is related to the hazards of fatigue that tend to impair decision making, increase irritability, cause greater impulsiveness and aggression, slow reflexes, and decrease attentiveness.[66] Tired officers manage people, make observations, and communicate with less effectiveness than when not tired. The complex interactions between thinking, feeling, and acting are affected.[67] Obviously, reduced skill levels as a result of fatigued officers and shift work affects the quality of law enforcement services provided by officers.[68]

Some experts say that people, in general, are less able to cope with fatigue and sleep disruption as they age.[69] The way most departments assign officers to their shifts tends to affect older and experienced officers more. When departmental needs take priority over shift work assignment, a substantial amount of the fatigue is reported by night shift officers, who are older officers. The reverse was true in departments where preference in shift assignment was based on seniority. In brief, older officers who could select their own shift tend to be less fatigued.[70] Or do older cops complain more than younger cops? True, they aren't as worried about keeping their jobs as younger officers.

Death notification refers to officers advising family members or friends of an individual who died, for instance, in an auto accident or in a violence crime. Injuries to children also create a great deal of stress among police officers.[71] Further evidence comes from an officer who said, "I investigated a double fatality recently in Peabody, Massachusetts. What a tough, tough thing, seeing needless death caused be speeding. And how do you tell a mother and father the pride of their life, their beautiful 16-year-old daughter, is dead? You might as well be going to their home to cut their legs out from under them."[72]

Then, too, victim notification among robbery and aggravated assault victims, especially to families residing in disadvantaged neighborhoods, is not a pleasant event for many officers.[73] There exists in many sectors of the American population groups of individuals who feel alienated from mainstream society and its institutions. Furthermore, they hold a profound lack of faith in the police and the judicial system.[74] The level of stress officers making notification calls encounter tends to be far greater than expected. "I had to notify this family that their son was in the hospital in serious condition for a hit-and-run after school. His parents had no phone so off I go. They threw a pot of hot water on me as I climbed the steps to their fifth floor walk-up. I yelled that I was there to help about Jesse, their son. 'He doesn't live here no more,' the mother shouted back."[75]

Poor fringe benefits refers to a form of remuneration for the performance of services provided to a recipient.[76] Another way to say it might be an incidental benefit awarded for certain kinds of services. One source suggests that fringe benefits are rigidly structured by civil service procedures and union contracts. However, both pay and fringe benefits are tied to rank.[77]

Fringe benefits can consist of health insurance, life insurance, dental insurance, workmen's compensation, unemployment compensation, retirement, Social Security, and funeral benefits. Fringes can also include vehicles, tuition reimbursement, travel expenses for professional development, free inservice training, legal guidance, counseling, and financial advisers and lawyers for the employee and his or her family members. One source suggests that relative to budget categories in police departments that typically 20–25% is allocated toward fringe benefits.[78] Typical of many occupations in the private sector, 30–35% of payroll budgets tend to be allocated to fringe benefits.[79] Some of those fringes that exceed those in policing might be vacation pay, paid leave of absence, stock options, retail discounts, educational opportunities for family members, new cars (for personal use), housing, environmental amenities, parking spots, large severance pay and retirement agreements, extensive travel funds, flexible work schedules, and assistance in conducting a task or job.

Also, when an officer dies while on duty, the amount of red tape concerning wills, insurance policies, funeral schedules, and plans for the distribution of possessions overwhelm grieving survivors. "Both the department and the families cope with the mind-numbing bureaucratic superstructure of death in contemporary American society. Departments must deal with confidential emergency notification forms"[80] and so on. This process overwhelms all other discussion of inadequate fringe benefits among police officers.

Accidents in patrol cars refer to officers involved in auto accidents with police vehicles while involved, most often, in police business.[81] Researchers have shown that there is a link between tired officers and accidents but there exists too few studies in the literature to say with certainty that fatigue and vehicle accidents are highly related variables.[82] However, the literature does provide data about the results of officers engaged in pursuit of criminals on the highways. For instance[83]:

- A collision of some type can be expected in 32% of police pursuits.
- When severity of these collisions are analyzed, 20% result in property damage, and 13% result in personal injury.
- A fatality will occur in 1.2% of police pursuits.
- Approximately 70% of all pursuit-related injuries and fatalities will involve the occupants of the pursued vehicle.

- 14% of those pursuit-related injuries will involve law enforcement, and 15% will involve innocent uninvolved parties.
- Police were successful in apprehending suspects in more than 72.2% of the pursuits.

Two studies tested the general work stressors described above using a similar survey.[84] One study consisted of 415 officers before 9/11 and the other surveyed 310 officers after 9/11. The officers were from various law enforcement agencies from Boston to Miami, primarily in the eastern part of the country.

RESULTS OF GENERAL WORK STRESSOR STUDY

The question in the survey read: "Following is a list of experiences that law enforcement officers like yourself experience some time in your careers. How often do these experiences create major stress for officers? What's your guess? If 5 = always, 4 = very often, 3 = often, 2 = seldom, and 1 = never."

The responses are shown in Table 6.1 based on the 5–1 rating described in the survey question.

The sample surveyed after 9/11 reports a 4.75 (almost an always response) as their average numerical response to the question about conflict with regulations and

Table 6.1   RESULTS OF THE GENERAL WORK STRESSOR STUDY

General Work	Sample A: After 9/11 (N=310)	Sample B: Before 9/11 (N=415)
	Mean Score	Mean Score
Conflict with regulations	4.75	3.90
Domestic violence	4.46	3.89
Losing control	4.29	2.89
Child beaten/abused	4.18	4.39
Excessive paperwork	3.46	2.86
Public disrespect	3.18	3.41
Another officer hurt	3.15	3.08
Lack of recognition	3.03	2.80
Poor supervisor support	2.62	3.64
Disrespect of courts	2.34	2.86
Shift work	2.25	3.08
Death notification	1.92	2.45
Poor fringe benefits	1.84	2.25
Accidents in patrol cars	1.37	2.30

Missing cases and "other" and lesser reported categories are not shown.

ranks this issue as their largest general work stressor. The before group ranked this item second and with a significant difference in their scoring than the after group. This finding promotes the question (assuming all things relative to the study were equal): Did 9/11 change the perspectives of local officers so much that they question the rules and regulations of the law enforcement organization that employs them?

The sample polled before 9/11 reports a 4.39 median score for child beaten or abused and ranks that issue as their largest general work stressor. It is easy to discover the similarities in the responses of both groups as you peruse through the items listed in Table 6.1 and use it as a guide to better understand what some officers are reporting as general work stressors because as you already know, most surveys have methodological errors or limitations of some type or another and data can be manipulated.

It can appear as though there are differences between the responses of the two groups. However, other than their top three answers, the responses are statistically similar.[85] As we study the findings of both samples, it seems that general work stressors can give rise to inappropriate if not disastrous levels of behavior among law enforcement officers. That is, the conflict with regulations and losing control variables seem to give rise to street justice or greater interpretation of the goals and objectives of the department and while those variables are compounded with other general work stressors, critical incident stressors, and organizational inconsistencies, the gap between street cops, their supervisors, and the public widens. One implication of this thought is that officer performance would become more subjective than objective, which subsequently might compliment corrupt and inappropriate behavior on the streets and at home among family members if an officer chose that form of behavior as an option. At the risk of sounding like an educator, recall the comments in Chapter 1 about how many countries would have less anarchy and government corruption if the human rights of their populations were safeguarded through professional police initiatives.[86] It could be speculated (without an attempt at taking the results as gospel) that an effect 9/11 had upon American law enforcement was that many officers individually question human rights as a priority.

FAMILY STRESSORS

Most law enforcement officers have frequent interactions with their own family members such as parents or siblings, intimates such as a spouse or live-in partner, and extended family members such as grandparents and nieces and nephews. In one study, it was revealed that the impact of job on family ranked 15th (past) and 19th (current) among 21 sources of stress.[87] In a separate question, 7 out of 10 officers reported that work-related stress had sometimes or very often affected their family lives. Also almost one-half of the participants reported that family stress affected their job. And it was revealed that 37% of the officers said they were currently experiencing family-related problems.

When the 538 officers in the study conducted for this book were asked how often they experienced stress as a result of their own family relationships, seldom or never were the most popular answers for over 64% of the respondents. This answer appears to be consistent with the results from the above study but close enough to imply that a consistency exists.

However, when another study asked spouses of law enforcement officers about their experiences with stress, a large percentage said they had experienced unusually high levels of stress because of their spouse's job.[88] Stress felt by a spouse is of concern because a stressful home environment can adversely affect the officer's job performance and family relationships, even if an officer reports his or her family may not be seen as a stressor. This finding is consistent with Detective William H. Martin (retired) of the Los Angeles Police Department who says that police officers do not always recognize the signs of how the job adversely affects their daily routines.[89] The detective adds that the response of most officers to violence on the job is so subtle and long term that officers ignore it until one day their family is gone, as are friends, health, spirituality, honor, commitment, and sense of self-worth.

Conditions, situations, or incidents that may not trouble officers themselves—or that they may even enjoy, such as shift work or undercover work—can mean severe problems for their families. Sources of stress commonly cited by the spouses of officers include[90]:

- Shift work and overtime
- Concern over the spouse's cynicism
- The need to feel in control in the home
- An inability or unwillingness to express feelings

Regardless of what an officer says about stress and his or her family members, the relationship between job and family is more intricate than those officers imply. For one, problems at home can affect job performance because in the real world, there are few guaranteed methods of entirely neutralizing one's feelings.[91] Somehow, one way or another, frustrations will influence the performance of an officer, yet that is not to say that all the behavior acted out as a result of frustration would be negative or even inappropriate. Sometimes frustrated people involve themselves in sports, volunteering, working out, going to school, and numerous other activities. Often, those frustrations motivate an officer to deliver higher quality police services. A Miami-Dade deputy explains how her job demands influenced her family relationships[92]:

A typical shift for me? Try this. One day last week I was good to go home after my shift. My sergeant comes to me in the locker room and says he needs me to fill in for Sanchez who took sick because of some raw fish. I worked two shifts and eventually went home. It was around 11 when I pulled into the drive. The house was dark, kids were asleep. I could hear Jay Leno on the tube coming from my bedroom. When I peeked into the room, my husband was asleep too. I tiptoed in and clicked it off. Another night alone. I had several cups of coffee to stay alert while I worked, and there was no way I was tired. I think I was wired. About an hour later, I couldn't stand the silence any more and ran over to Harry's, a cop hangout near the station, for some conversation and a beer. Some of the guys were there talking about a guy I hooked-up last week. The conversation was comforting but I knew it was time to roll home when the sun was beaming through the windows. Got home, slept for about an hour, got the kids off to school, and told my husband that I'd be home for dinner. That was a joke! Didn't get home till 10 and he was already in bed watching the tube. I didn't wanna sneak out for a beer, but I did as soon as he dozed off. It didn't take long after that. We're separated and he's got the kids and the house. I gotta little place of my own. I go to Harry's probably more than I should but so do a lot of the guys I work with. We have much to share. I miss my kids but never really saw them.[93]

The truth about stress is that many officers, regardless of their rank,[94] let the job control their daily routines. Officers tend to surround themselves with police-related matters and each other, isolating themselves from family members and their daily routines. As the officer conveyed her experiences above, she began a deeper descent into the police subculture[95] (as discussed in Chapter 4).

It might be appropriate to characterize a police subculture as a product of the "working personality" of police officers (and other occupational groups).[96] Although police subculture is discussed in future chapters, its relevance in this chapter is demonstrated above in the Miami-Dade officer's narrative. The "big curtain of secrecy" surrounding officers shields knowledge of the nature of the police personality from outsiders, which includes family members.[97] Finally in this regard, police subculture promotes solidarity among officers and seems to justify dysfunctional relationships and unlawful performance, as evidenced in the CRASH example discussed previously.

Some officers have difficulty with the pressures of the job and this affects their sexual ability with their intimate other. Sexual dysfunctions range from impotence to promiscuity, which is an added burden on their loved ones who might wonder if their partner is involved with someone else because their intimate moments are few and far between. Additionally, some officers isolate themselves from family members and friends, especially those who are not police officers.[98] Then, too, evidence has shown that police officers have a significantly increased risk of certain diseases when compared to other occupational groups.[99] When those diseases place an officer's family at risk, it might be clear that police families share in many problems not necessarily experienced by other families or at least not to the same level of intensity. Finally, many officers with difficulties in coping with their situation drink, and drink often. Police officer alcoholism is more related to divorce rates than all other problems experienced by officers and their families.

REASONS WHY DIVORCE RATES ARE HIGH

A police therapist explains that one of the best predictors of success in a troubled, or merely a troubling, marriage (police or civilian) is whether both husband and wife are willing to own up to their responsibility for needing to change.[100] Colleagues of the therapist share a consensus about many of their clients. They agree that one of the primary causes for divorce among police officers relates to the amount of chauvinism held by the officer, especially if the officer is an alcoholic and the spouse isn't one (yet). Also, among therapists who have an anti-police bias, they add that male police officers tend to have an authoritarian personality and that one reason for divorce is that they will not change. A retired chief of police cites four primary reasons why police officers' divorce rates are high[101]:

1. The psychological makeup of a great many officers drives them to experiment and seekout adventure. Which means officers are fundamentally driven toward infidelities of various kinds.

2. Vast numbers of women start out by being attracted to cops. The symbolism of the weapon and badge are believed to be strong attractions. That magnetism is readily communicated to the members of the opposite sex who, all too frequently, either cannot or don't even try to resist.

3. With many men, the number of conquests about which they can brag is of great importance to ego-building. (This is sometimes true of women as well, although they are usually less braggadocio about it.) It is extremely hard for anyone to avoid "adventures" when attractive members of the opposite sex are openly, persistently inviting.

4. The hours put in by law enforcement and the neighborhoods in which they work, which are commonly a distance from home (where they may not be recognized by family and friends), provide opportunities to "get away with it" with little chance of being caught.

In other words, according to the chief's perspective (which certainly applies to other individuals in other occupations), the average police officer is exposed to temptation with only limited likelihood of getting caught.

There is another truth. Divorce rates of police officers have been unfavorably compared with divorce rates of individuals in other occupations.[102] Evidence shows that the rate is indeed high, however, is it high because they are habitually unfaithful to their spouses or because some officers tend to treat family members like suspects? Studies are indecisive as to the cause of divorce among officers but "suspect" treatment of family members and infidelity are important causes. The "best available evidence supports the argument that police divorce rates are lower than the popular depiction of police life would lead one to anticipate."[103]

POLICE OFFICER MORTALITY AND SUICIDE

As young cadets, police officer recruits are generally part of a healthy work population. As they experience police work, their health as a group tends to deteriorate physically and psychologically.[104] Since officers are exposed to many stressors, which include traumatic events, diseases, and fatigue from the job, an increased rate of mortality because of their occupation is both expected and documented by the literature.[105] One study found that officers have a high rate of premature death, suicide, and admissions to the hospital.[106] Police officers tend to have greater rates of cancer of the colon and liver, diabetes mellitus, heart disease, pulmonary embolism, and homicide.[107] Age-specific mortality ratios for atherosclerotic heart disease are actually highest for younger law enforcement officers. Poor health would clearly have an effect upon family relationships.

Studies show that police officers, as compared to other occupations and the general public, are more likely to kill themselves. Also officers are more than twice as likely to die by their own hand than to be killed by others.[108] A wide suicide rate disparity exists between various cities. For instance, the New York City Police Department shows 15.5 per 100,000 (1990–1998) to 35.7 per 100,000 in San Diego over the same time period, and 45.6 per 100,000 for U.S. Customs Service in 1998–1999.[109] The general rate of the U.S. public was 11.8 per 100,000 from 1995–1996. The reasons officers commit suicide are varied and are often difficult to determine. The "typical" officer who does tends to be white, 36.9 years old, married, 12.2 years of law enforcement experience, was committed off duty (86.3%), with a gun (90.7%), and at home (54.8%).[110]

However, one finding suggests that police suicide rates as recorded are less sensitive than the rates of other workers in detecting actual suicides and have less predictive value in determining actual nonsuicides.[111] Said another way, police suicide rates could be suspect because other officers often are the ones to discover the bodies of their dead colleagues. They could easily cover up the cause of death, including the destruction of evidence, for the benefit of the family. Under provisions of life insurance and police benefits, suicide is one reason policies do not pay survivors. Yet in an autopsy/investigation, it should be obvious if gunshot residue is very narrow, indicating a contact wound, versus wide residue, indicating a distant shot from several feet away. There are cases, for instance, labeled "undetermined," which involved gunshot wounds to the head.[112] Arriving officers could have brought out the dead officer's gun cleaning kit to make the suicide look like an accident. One estimate puts that number at a 20% undercount of suicide for officers.[113] Without adding the 20% increase to the numbers, police officers have a threefold rate of suicide compared to municipal workers.[114] However, police suicides rank third behind laborers and pressmen, and another study puts officers behind dentists, doctors, and entrepreneurs.[115] The individuals who take their own lives as an occupational group do not carry weapons as part of their job descriptions, yet they all serve the public.

FEMALE POLICE OFFICERS

Male and female street cops share similar experiences, and as demonstrated in the Miami-Dade deputy's previous narrative, emerging into a police subculture might be an easy process. However, female officers experience more stress than male officers simply because of their gender. For some, this thought rings with patronizing remarks from officers and offenders alike but it is as simple a truth as realizing that female officers must unbelt while visiting a restroom. The hurdles female cops jump over every day are the same ones male officers jump over, but then they have an entire set of hurdles designed for them. The more we know about those hurdles, the more stress can be controlled.

The male officers in one study reported more family-related problems than the female officers.[116] For instance, one out of five male officers reported that work-related stress had often spilled over into their home lives, but only 1 out of 20 female officers said that that had been their experience. However, one-half of the males and 46% of the female officers reported difficulties in balancing job and family responsibilities. One implication of this finding is that stress results in their personal lives are similar for both female officers and male officers.

In the study of 558 officers for this study, 133 of the participants were female officers. Their responses were similar to questions about job stress and work stressors as males. But significant differences emerged in their answers about stress from other police officers, their supervisors, the courts, and the public. For instance, a comment by one female street cop is typical of the way many females officers responded in the study: "Those of us who really like being out there can do the job as effectively as a guy. But we want to be respected as an equal. We're still women and I expect that when it comes to the badge, that that respect is there and other times, I am a woman and I expect others to be mindful of that. Mostly, when guys find out that I'm a cop, they're intimidated by me. Other times, other cops including my supervisor just deal with me because they don't want a lawsuit down their ass," Officer Maria Gonzalez says.[117] "I just want to do my job," she adds. "And I expect to be respected as a cop, a woman, and a Puerto Rican woman at that. I don't disrespect other people even when I hook'em up." Women cops experience other pressures, too.

Another female officer explains it this way: "We have pressures the men never thought of. There was the expectation by the men, as soon as I came on the job that I would automatically screw up. And then there's also the other problem, the expectation because you wear the uniform, you are somehow no longer a woman. You cannot win. I keep telling people that by putting on the uniform, I didn't have a sex change operation. But few seem to believe [me]."[118]

The director of the Massachusetts state trooper stress unit says, "There has been more difficulty with the assimilation of female police officers than other groups."[119] He thinks that some of their problems are because of the perception that women receive preferred treatment, that their attributes of courage and strength are not similar to that of males, and that they are not able to meet the physical standards of males. Another stress practitioner from the Boston police adds, "When a woman takes on a macho male job, she takes on the macho male disease. Also she feels she has to prove herself even better than the men, many of whom feel castrated by a woman on the job. And a woman has been raised to show her emotions, been taught that it is okay to cry, and now she comes on the job and feels she has to start covering up those feelings."[120]

A female Massachusetts state trooper says the stress practitioner above offers "typical macho crap. In my generation, guys grew up knowing that women are equal. It's those good ole boys that keep playing their macho shit. Since they're in charge, from the stress units to the training to duty assignments, they keep thinking I'm like their little daughter. Let me give you an example. Sometime after 9/11, we had machine gun practice. They handed me this outdated canon and said 'take your point' at the range. If I said no to the instructor he'd tell my boss and the next thing ya know, he'd cut me out of overtime at Logan [Boston's airport]. These good ole boys wanna control their turf and that's their little freggen way of controlling me. For young guys they have another approach. We're still early in the evolution of that process."[121]

Upon investigating a neighborhood dispute in the country, one female officer was told by the caller that he would not speak with her—that she should "go home and send a real cop."[122] When the officer refused, the man dialed 9-1-1 but was told to deal with the officer, but he ignored her. Another female officer experienced constant harassment from a male officer who kept telling her she was not up to the job. On the advice of another male officer, she finally dropped her belt at the station house and told him, "OK! Let's go at it." They engaged in a tussle before the sergeant separated them. Later, the hostile officer changed his attitude toward the female officer, becoming her friend.

Female officers are often frustrated by some of the actions taken by their supervisors who think of them as incapable of responding to at-risk encounters. For example, in my own experiences while riding with an Aiken, South Carolina, police officer (one of my students) in the late afternoon, the dispatcher advised the officer of an armed robbery in progress at a convenience store. The officer advised that her ETA was 3 minutes. As her police cruiser made the corner and she had the location in sight, her sergeant advised her to "back off." "But sir, I am almost in the parking lot." "Break it off now, that's an order," he said over the radio.

The following day I asked why she was pulled from the call. Maybe the sergeant realized that she had nonsworn personnel in the cruiser. "Nah, that wouldn't of mattered. I often get bumped from those calls," the former U.S. Army MP says.

One researcher has suggested that despite the extra sources of stress women officers face, many women do not report it because they are willing to talk about their feelings and the related stress, rejected competitiveness with others, and made a conscious effort to reduce stress through actions such as taking time off from work and seeking legal support.[123] Then, too, many studies emphasize conformity to male stereotypes by female officers. But those studies fail to provide a representative sampling of police tasks and situations, while overemphasizing the violent and dangerous aspects of policing.[124] Many female officers take less aggressive—yet what they feel are no less effective—approaches to stressful work situations than male officers typically adopt. However, women officers can be great warriors, as evidenced by a Fayetteville, North Carolina, officer who took a call about a family fistfight in the park. Upon arriving, the five-foot-tall, slender officer asked the men to tell her what was going on while still sitting in her cruiser.[125] She was waiting for backup. One of the men told her that since he was a ranger (Fort Bragg is adjacent to "Fayettnam," as it is called) he didn't need her help. She told him that he was right and that things would go better if they could wait a bit, but talk. With that he moved toward the officer's vehicle in a highly aggressive manner. The officer exited (advising her passenger to remain in the vehicle and lock the doors) the police cruiser. In a quick motion, she slammed her aggressor to the ground, the officer's boot pushed down on his esophagus, holding him steady on the ground while she advised him of his rights to remain silent.

Other Sources of Stress Impacting Female Officers

Depending on individual personality and experience, some female officers can be offended and intimidated by degrading language more than others. However, some female officers may find exchanges of insults to be a way to use humor to relieve stress. Female officers say that some other stress is a result of[126]:

- Lack of acceptance by the predominantly white, male force and subsequent denial of needed information, alliances, protection, and sponsorship from supervisors and colleagues.
- Lack of role models and mentors.
- Pressure to prove oneself to colleagues and the public.
- Exclusion from informal channels of support.
- Lack of influence on decision making.

Many female officers imply that there is a "good ole boy" system in place. However, it should be mentioned that that system is invisible to male officers who are not part of the good ole club.

Female Police Mobility

Chief Nan Hegerty of Milwaukee, Wisconsin, says that males do not respect women who try to be one of the guys.[127] "They understand that women officers are essential, but they really want you to be a woman," the chief suggests. "On the other hand, they don't want you to be afraid to mix it up [fight] when the situation calls for it."

However, organizational structures are changing (discussed in Chapter 13) and part of that change has to do with women promoted to top-command positions across the nation. For instance, Chief Beverly Harvard of the Atlanta Police Department and Commissioner Kathleen O'Toole of the Boston Police Department joins Detroit Chief Ella Bully-Cummings, Milwaukee Chief Nan Hegerty, San Francisco Chief Heather Fong, and acting chief Suzanne Devlin of Fairfax County, Virginia, belong to a unique sorority: women top executives of urban police departments.

An average of 13% of America's police officers are female, according to the National Center for Women and Policing, a division of the Feminist Majority Foundation in Arlington, Virginia. Of the approximate 18,000 police departments across the United States, some 200 have women chiefs.

"We're not talking a lot of progress here, just to put it in some perspective. But we are talking high visibility, and all eyes will be on them," said Margaret Moore, director of the national center who retired as the highest-ranking woman in the Federal Bureau of Alcohol, Tobacco and Firearms.

The vice president of the National Association of Chiefs of Police says he was not surprised to see women reaching the top position in increasing numbers, since women have been working their way up for several decades.[128, 129] He also notes that academy training is different now than it was 30 years ago. He advises that training is not necessarily softer, but less paramilitary.

Female Street Cops

It might be informative to share the findings from data of female officers in this study. There were 133 female officers in the study that consisted of 559 officers, which made up 24% of the sample. Of that number, most were patrol officers, two were captains with command responsibility, and five were sergeants. Most worked in New England and the Midwest, one worked in Florida. Most of the females were white and many of the New England female officers were Latino (see Appendix III for details). The average age of the female officers was younger than that of the males (37 years of age), but the female officers were better educated and had less years of experience than their male counterparts. The answers to the question of how often do you experience job-related stress contained similar responses as their male counterparts. Yet, responses about stress coming from their own family members were significantly higher than male officers.

Three other questions produced significant differences between the female and male responses: immediate supervisor, disrespect of the courts, and use of intimidation by brass or commanders. Most of the female officers report that they trusted their immediate supervisors and that they were the source of less stress than the male officers, however, females overwhelmingly felt that the courts' level of disrespect and the brass' use of intimidation was significantly higher as compared to male officer response. In a write-in answer: if you could change anything in policing, what would it be, the typical female response was the way the courts and police commanders disrespectfully relate to female law enforcement officers.

Female street cops had greater difficulties in getting their job because they had more standards placed on them than males, they said. From the perspective of male officers, one commonly held perspective was that females got the job because of "quotas." Nonetheless, one female officer explains it this way: "I'm a cop not because I can't find another job or because this one was easy to get, but because this is what I wanted to do since I was in high school. I'm here to stay." Another female officer writes, "After the military where I was an MP, I came home and applied to the Boston PD. They offered me a dispatcher's job. I turned it down and signed on with the city of X who lost three court cases against women cops. I knew they had to hire me, but I didn't know they were going to treat me like a child."

WHY FEMALE OFFICERS RESIGN

Every year about 5% of all police officers leave their jobs. This "attrition rate appears" to have been steady since the 1960s.[130] Reasons they leave include retirement, death, dismissal, voluntary resignation, and layoffs resulting from financial constraints. When female officer attrition rates were studied, findings showed that female officers left the department at higher rates (6.3% annually versus 4.6%

annually) than male officers.[131] Female officers are more likely to resign voluntarily (4.3% annually versus 3.0% annually) than males and are terminated involuntarily more often (1.2% annually versus .6% annually) too. "Women officers experience a more hostile work environment" than males.[132] Female officers who are single parents are often confronted with different problems than males in the workplace, and as evidenced by the comments from the female officers above, they are treated differently than male officers by their commanders.

Little research has been done on the reasons officers resign their jobs voluntarily. However, what we know is that women officers and minorities resign at higher rates than "mainstream" officers. One reason for this finding is that much is done in the recruitment process to hire women and minorities, yet little is done to maintain those individuals once they are trained and working in the department.[133] Another study suggests that female police turnover may be due to their having a higher educational level than traditional male officers, since college-educated personnel are more likely to grow disenchanted with routine beat duties. However, that study assumes that education is the primary concern while at the same time ignoring the notion that gender is an issue in itself. The researchers assume that all educated officers grow disenchanted with the profession of policing and yet that conclusion remains only a tentative thought.[134] A Memphis study shows that dissatisfaction is a necessary but not a sufficient condition to cause resignation.[135] There are turning points leading to voluntary resignation among female police officers that, in the order of importance, consist of:

1. A perception of a stagnated career ("I just can't see any future in being a police officer.").[136]
2. A particularly intense experience that brought accumulated frustration to a head (e.g., a gunfight or the mangled, bloody remains of a child).
3. Lack of a sense of fulfillment on the job ("That job just doesn't fit me anymore.").
4. Family considerations ("I wanna be there for my kids in first grade and third grade. I'm missing too much. No job is worth not watching them grow up.").
5. The conduct of coworkers: ("It's so degrading how the male officers treat me, especially the older ones who treat me like I'm their little daughter.").
6. Particular department policy or policies ("The regs [regulations] say cap our speed during felony pursuit at 65, get approval for increased speed, and by the time we do, the creep's gone.").
7. New employment opportunities ("Wachenhut [private police] offered me a stable shift, more pay, automated report writing, uniform allowance, take-home vehicle privileges, and day care.").

SUMMARY

General work stressors can be characterized as stressors that arise during the daily work routine of a police officer. Fourteen general work stressors were described, which include conflict with regulations, domestic violence stops, losing control, child abuse calls, excessive paperwork, public disrespect, injuries to other officers, lack of recognition, poor supervisor support, disrespect of the courts, shift work, death notification, poor fringe benefits, and accidents in the patrol vehicle.

In several studies it was revealed that many officers see their family as less a stressor than expected, but families see the job of the officer as creating a great deal of stress for them in their daily routines. Spouses of officers say that shift work and overtime, concern over the spouse's cynicism, the need to feel in control in the home, and an inability or unwillingness to express feelings are among the biggest problems they face. Marriage therapists explain that whether both the husband and wife are willing to own up to their responsibility for needing to change is usually the best predictor of success. A chief of police adds that high divorce rate among officers is because of (1) the psychological makeup of many cops drives them to experiment, search, and seek adventures, which includes infidelity; (2) vast numbers of women start out by being attracted to cops and their uniforms; (3) men brag about conquests with women since it adds to their ego; (4) because of the hours officers work, the neighborhoods in which they work are commonly distant from home, and therefore can "get away with it" with little chance of being caught.

Police mortality and suicide issues relate to the health concerns of officers and stressful experiences. However, it was shown that other occupational groups commit suicide more often than police officers and yet those groups are not engaged in violence or even carry weapons.

Female police officers share similar general work stressors as male officers, as evidenced by their responses in one study. But significant differences emerged in their answers about stressors associated with the treatment they experience from male officers, supervisors, the courts, and the public. Most female officers want to be treated with respect but also want the respect of fellow police officers. Stress, in association with their gender, comes from a lack of acceptance by the predominantly white, male force and subsequent denial of needed information, alliances, protection, and sponsorship from supervisors and colleagues; a lack of role models and mentors; pressure to prove oneself to colleagues and the public; exclusion from informal channels of support; and a lack of influence on decision making. There are turning points leading to voluntary resignation among female police officers that consist of perceptions of a stagnated police career, an intense experience that brought accumulated frustration to a head, a lack of a sense of fulfillment on the job, family considerations, the conduct of coworkers toward them, particular department policy or policies, and new employment opportunities. Despite the extra sources of stress women officers experience, which includes high-ranking female professionals, they tend to respond to serious stress more often than male officers because they are willing to talk about their feelings and the related stress, they rejected competitiveness with others, and they make a conscious effort to reduce stress through actions such as taking time off from work and seeking legal support.

WHAT WOULD YOU DO IF YOU WERE IN CHARGE?

A 12-year-old child told state prosecutors how the first Philadelphia police officer that responded to her victimization refused to believe her.[137] The child implied that the initial investigator from Philadelphia's sex crimes unit also botched the case. Five years after her first report, this child again insisted that she knew the name of the rapist—and eventually a DNA test proved she was right. Finally, a Philadelphia jury convicted Jasper Washington, the man who raped her. This child's fight is vivid evidence of a broken system in Philadelphia and perhaps in other cities where police ignore and dismiss rape complaints, fail to report rapes, miscategorize and disguise rape complaints and manipulate statistics in order to simplify their work or bolster their departments' or their cities' images. Often, police categorize rape complaints as "unfounded" or say that the victims were lying.

OFFICER KILLED IN NEW ORLEANS, LOUISIANA

Officer Latoya Johnson, age 27, of the New Orleans Police Department was killed while responding to a call of protective custody with her 26-year-old female partner on a 38-year-old male, who was reported by his family to be mentally unstable. When the officers arrived at 934 North Broad Street in New Orleans shortly before 11:00 P.M., they confronted the man inside of the home. The man produced a gun and fired, striking Officer Johnson. Officer Johnson stumbled to the kitchen area where the suspect approached, stood over her, and fired several more times. There was also an exchange of gunfire between Officer Johnson's partner and the suspect. Moments later, a backup officer arrived and he too exchanged gunfire with the suspect, who ran into a bedroom. Two other officers arrived on the scene and confronted the armed suspect in the bedroom. Those officers fired at the suspect, wounding him.

The wounded officer and the suspect were transported to Charity Hospital where both were pronounced dead. The suspect, 38-year-old Chester Solomon and another individual, a 55-year-old male, were also dead. Officers also found a 55-year-old male lying in the hallway of the residence, suffering from multiple gunshot wounds. At this time the investigation is undetermined if the 55-year-old man was shot by the suspect.

The 26-year-old female officer was not wounded in the attack but did have bullet holes in her clothing. Officer Latoya Johnson, a 3-year member of the department, was assigned to the First District.[138]

DISCUSSION QUESTIONS

1. Characterize general work stressors among police officers.
2. Identify the 14 general stressors described in the chapter. Which general work stressors are absent from this list and why?
3. Describe each of the 14 general stressors. In what way are several of these stressors associated with the organizational police structure?
4. Characterize family problems concerning officer stress. Which family problems should be added to the list.
5. Explain the reasons why the divorce rate is high among officers. In what way might you agree and disagree with this list?
6. Discuss police mortality and suicide issues. In what way do you agree or disagree with the ideas presented?
7. Characterize female officer stress. Some commanders have said that most women knew prior to entering police service that policing is a man's world. What way might that be a fair and unfair statement and how would that impact female officers?
8. Explain the pressures female officers often face on the job. Describe some similar pressures females experience in other jobs. Describe pressures that might be unique to law enforcement.
9. Clarify the female officer advancements made by female officers. Why should more chiefs be females?
10. Explain why female officers resign their jobs as officers. In what way do you agree with these findings?

ENDNOTES

1. Bryan Vila and Dennis J. Kennedy (2002, March). Tired cops: The prevalence and potential consequences of police fatigue. NCJ 190634. Washington, DC: U.S. Department of Justice, Office of Justice Programs. Retrieved online May 20, 2005: http://www.ncjrs.org/pdffiles1/jr000248d.pdf
2. Mark Leccese (2005, September 1). Overtime elevates police pay. *Boston Globe*. Retrieved online March 26, 2006: http://www.boston.com/
3. National Commission on Sleep Disorders Research. Retrieved online June 7, 2005: http://www.helpguide.org/aging/sleep_disorders.htm
4. Bureau of Justice Statistics (2002). *Sourcebook of criminal justice statistics, 2002.* Full time officers assigned to calls in local police departments. Table 1.32. Retrieved online June 7, 2005: http://www.albany.edu/sourcebook/pdf/t132.pdf
5. Bureau of Justice Statistics (2006). Retrieved March 8, 2006: http://www.ojp.usdoj.gov/bjs/sandlle.htm#contact

6. R. M. Ayers (1990). *Preventing law enforcement stress. The organization's role.* Washington, DC: Bureau of Justice Assistance, U.S. Department of Justice. Office of Justice Programs. Also see Katherine W. Ellison (2004). *Stress and the police officer.* Springfield, IL: Charles C. Thomas. p. 67.

7. Gary W. Sykes (1999). Street justice: A moral defense of Order Maintenance Policing. In Victor E. Kappeler (Ed.), *The police and society*, 2nd ed. (pp. 134–149). Prospect Heights, IL: Waveland.

8. Gary W. Sykes (1999). p. 134.

9. Carl B. Klockars (1999). The Dirty Harry problem. In Victor E. Kappeler (Ed.), *The police and society*, 2nd ed. (pp. 368–387). Prospect Heights, IL: Waveland. Carl B. Klockars (1999). Street justice: Some micro-moral reservations. In In Victor E. Kappeler (Ed.), *The police and society*, 2nd ed. (pp. 150–153). Prospect Heights, IL: Waveland.

10. Thomas Barker and David L. Carter (2001). *Police deviance*, 2nd ed. Cincinnati OH: Anderson. p. 276.

11. The Rampart Scandal (2005). *PBS News.* Retrieved online March 26, 2006: http://www.pbs.org/wgbh/pages/frontline/shows/lapd/scandal/

12. Media reports connected to the Los Angeles Police Department Scandal (2000). Federal officials arrive in Los Angeles for corruption inquiry. Retrieved online March 26, 2006: http://www.streetgangs.com/topics/rampart/031300feds.html

13. The Rampart Scandal (2005).

14. Vivian B. Lord (2005). The stress of change: The impact of changing a traditional police department to a community oriented, problem solving department. In Heith Copes (Ed.), *Police stress* (pp. 55–77). Upper Saddle River, NJ: Prentice Hall.

15. Herbert Goldstein (1980). *Problem-oriented policing.* New York: McGraw-Hill. p. 183.

16. Judy Van Wyk (2005). Hidden hazards of responding to domestic disputes. In Heith Copes (Ed.), *Policing and stress* (pp. 41–54). Upper Saddle River, NJ: Prentice Hall.

17. Some believe that domestic violence calls are the most serious of police calls and that in 75% of the cases, evidence suggests that serious conflict had existed. See Denise K. Gosselin (2004). *Heavy hands: An introduction to the crimes of domestic violence*, 2nd ed. Upper Saddle River, NJ: Prentice Hall. Also see A. Roberts (1999). The police response. In L. Gerdes (Ed.), *Battered women* (pp. 32–40). San Diego, CA: Greenhaven.

18. J.M. Brown and E.A. Campbell (1990). Sources of occupational stress in the police. *Work and Stress*, 4, 305–318.

19. J.M. Brown and E.A. Campbell (1994). *Stress and policing: Sources and strategies.* New York: Wiley.

20. Personal communication with the author. A Hartford, Connecticut, police officer. June 5, 2005.

21. Judy Van Wyk (2005). Hidden hazards of responding to domestic disputes. In Heith Copes (Ed.), *Policing and stress* (pp. 41–54). Upper Saddle River, NJ: Prentice Hall.

22. Ruth Teichroeb (2003, October 21). Abused officers can fall victim to system. *Seattle Post.* Retrieved online March 27, 2006: http://seattlepi.nwsource.com/local/144939_cops22.html

23. Ruth Teichroeb (2003, October 21).

24. Dennis J. Stevens (2004). Battered women's syndrome revisited. In Dennis J. Stevens (Ed.), *Corrections perspective* (pp. 18–24). Madison, WI: Coursewise.

25. Dennis J. Stevens (2006). Sexual assault evidence, sexual offenders, and sexual assault convictions: Why sexual assault convictions are low in Boston. *Police Journal*, 74.

26. Judy Van Wyk (2005). Hidden hazards of responding to domestic disputes. In Heith Copes (Ed.), *Policing and stress* (pp. 41–54). Upper Saddle River, NJ: Prentice Hall.

27. Katherine W. Ellison (2004). *Stress and the police officer*, 2nd ed. Springfield, IL: Charles C. Thomas. p. 67.

28. Geoffrey P. Albert and Mark H. Moore (2001). Measuring police performance in the new paradigm of policing. In Roger Dunham and Geoffrey P. Albert (Eds.), *Critical issues in policing: Contemporary reading*, 4th ed. (pp. 238–254). Prospect Heights, IL: Waveland.

29. Thomas V. Brady (1996). Measuring what matters part one: Measures of crime, fear, and disorder. Washington, DC: U.S. Department of Justice, Office of Justice Programs. Retrieved online June 7, 2005: http://www.ncjrs.org/txtfiles/measure.txt

30. John Wiggins and Dennis J. Stevens (2000). The effects of police management. *The Journal: The Police Official Journal*, 6(2), 14–17.

31. Patricia A. Kelly (2002). Stress: The cop killer. In John M. Madonna, Jr. and Richard E. Kelly (Eds.), *Treating police stress* (pp. 33–54). Springfield, IL: Charles C. Thomas.

32. Patricia A. Kelly (2002). Stress: The cop killer. In John M. Madonna, Jr. and Richard E. Kelly (Eds.), *Treating police stress* (pp. 33–54). Springfield, IL: Charles C. Thomas.

33. Peter Manning. (1997). *Police work: The sociological organization of policing.* Prospect Heights, IL: Waveland.

34. Wayne W. Bennett and Karen M. Hess (2004). *Management and supervision in law enforcement*, 4th ed. Springfield, IL: Charles C. Thomas. p. 152.

35. Katherine W. Ellison (2004). *Stress and the police officer*, 2nd ed. Springfield, IL: Charles C. Thomas. p. 66.

36. Katherine W. Ellison (2004). p. 66.

37. W.C. Terry (1981). Police stress: The empirical evidence. *Journal of Police Science and Administration*, 9(1), 61–75. Also see H. Madanba. (1986). The relationship between stress and marital relationship of police officers. In J. Reese & H. Goldstein (Eds.), *Psychological services for law enforcement*. Washington DC: American Psychological Association

38. Michael D. Reisig, John D. McCluskey, Stephen D. Mastrofski, and William Terrill (2004). Citizen disrespect toward the police. *Justice Quarterly*, 21(2), 241–268.

39. FBI. Washington, DC: U.S. Department of Justice. Reported crime, 2003. Retrieved online June 7, 2005: http://www.fbi.gov/ucr/cius_03/pdf/03sec2.pdf

40. Vivian B. Lord (2005). The stress of change: The impact of changing a traditional police department to a community oriented problem solving department. In Heith Copes (Ed.), *Policing and stress* (pp. 55–72). Upper Saddle River, NJ: Prentice Hall.

41. Mike Seate (2003, January 24). Disrespect can turn violence. *Pittsburgh Tribune-Review*. p. 7.

42. Mike Seate (2003, January 24).

43. Patricia A. Kelly (2002). Stress: The cop killer. In John M. Madonna, Jr. and Richard E. Kelly (Eds.). *Treating police stress: The work and the words of peer counserlors* (pp. 33–54). Springfield, IL: Charles C. Thomas

44. Patricia A. Kelly (2002). p. 41.

45. Patricia A. Kelly (2002). p. 41.

46. Richard Kelly (2002). Psychological care of the police wounded. In John M. Madonna, Jr. and Richard E. Kelly (Eds.). (2002). *Treating police stress* (pp. 15–32). Springfield, IL: Charles C. Thomas.

47. FBI (2003). *Law enforcement officers killed and assaulted, 2003*. Table 36. Retrieved online May 5, 2005: http://www.fbi.gov/ucr/killed/leoka03.pdf

48. O. Finn and J. E. Tomz (1997). *Developing a law enforcement stress program for officers and their families*. Washington, DC: U.S. Department of Justice, Office of Justice Programs. National Institute of Justice.

49. Katherine W. Ellison (2004). p. 140.

50. Hans Toch (2001). *Stress in policing*. Washington, DC: APA. p. 49.

51. Officer Kenisha Stewart, Boston Police Department, in a conversation with the author. April, 2005.

52. Officer Ben Sargeant, Dunstable, Massachusetts, Police Department, as reported to assistant researcher Kathryn Tiezzi, April 26, 2005.

53. John P. Crank and Michael Caldero. (1991). The production of occupational stress among police officers: A survey of eight municipal police organizations in Illinois. *Journal of Criminal Justice*, 19–24, 339–350.

54. John Van Maanen (2001). Making rank: Becoming an American police sergeant. In Roger Dunham and Geoffrey P. Alpert (Eds.), *Critical issues in policing: Contemporary readings*, 4th ed. (pp. 132–148). Prospect Heights, IL: Waveland.

55. John Van Maanen (2001). p. 136.

56. Wesley G. Skogan, Susan M. Hartnett, Jill DuBois, Jennifer T. Comey, Marianne Kaiser, and Justice H. Lovig (1999). *On the beat*. Boulder, CO: Westview Press.

57. Hans Toch (2001). *Stress in policing*. Washington, DC: APA. p. 46.

58. Personal communication with a Boston police officer about her job, during the spring of 2005.

59. Hans Toch (2001). *Stress in policing*. Washington, DC: APA. p. 48.

60. Vivian B. Lord (2005). The stress of change: The impact of changing a traditional police department to a community oriented problem solving department. In Heith Copes (Ed.), *Policing and stress* (pp. 55–72). Upper Saddle River, NJ: Prentice Hall. p. 59.

61. Personal communication with Boston police officer. February 2005.

62. Carl R. Rogers (1980). *A way of being*. Boston: Houghton Mifflin. Rogers is the founder of the human potential movement in the United States and he expands his ideas on personal growth. Most counselors-in-training take numerous courses dedicated to Rogerian perspectives and working counselors apply Rogerian concepts to their daily profession.

63. Carl R. Rogers (1980). *A way of being*. Boston: Houghton Mifflin p. 49.

64. Wayne W. Bennett and Karen M. Hess (2004). *Management and supervision in law enforcement*. Springfield, IL: Charles C. Thomas. pp. 411–412.

65. Wayne W. Bennett and Karen M. Hess (2004). *Management and supervision in law enforcement*, 4th ed. Springfield, IL: Charles C. Thomas. p. 411.

66. Wayne W. Bennett and Karen M. Hess (2004). p. 411.

67. Bryan Vila (2002). Cops learn you're A, B, Zzzzzzs. *The Law Enforcement Trainer*, September/October, 44–47.

68. Also see, Peter Finn (1997). Reducing stress: An organization centered approach. *FBI Law Enforcement Bulletin*, August. Retrieved Online May 20, 2005: http://www.fbi.gov/publications/leb/1997/aug975.htm

69. Bryan Vila and Dennis Jay Kenney (2002). Tired cops: The prevalence and potential consequences of police fatigue. *NIJ Journal*, 248. NCJ 190634. Retrieved, March 26, 2004. http://www.ncjrs.org/pdffiles1/jr000248d.pdf

70. Peter Finn (1997). Reducing stress: An organization centered approach. *FBI Law Enforcement Bulletin*, August. Retrieved Online May 20, 2005: http://www.fbi.gov/publications/leb/1997/aug975.htm; Bryan Vila and Dennis J. Kennedy (2002, March);

71. Douglas Paton (2005). Critical incidents and police officer stress. In Heith Copes (Ed.) *Police stress* (pp. 25–40). Upper Saddle River, NJ: Prentice Hall.

72. Patricia A. Kelly (2002). p. 43.

73. Eric P. Baumer (2002). Neighborhood disadvantage and police notification by victims of violence. *Criminology*, 40(3), 579–616.

74. Elijah Anderson (1999). *Code of the street: Decency, violence, and the moral life of the inner city*. New York: W.W. Norton. p. 34.

75. Officer Thomas Holly, Oak Park Illinois Police Department.

76. Internal Revenue Services. Retrieved online June 6, 2005: http://www.irs.gov/businesses/small/article/0,,id=101065,00.html

77. Samuel Walker and Charles M. Katz (2005). *The police in America: An introduction*, 5th ed. New York: McGraw-Hill. p. 170.

78. Wayne W. Bennett and Karen M. Hess (2005). *Management and supervision in law enforcement*, 4th ed. Springfield, IL: Charles C. Thomson. p. 167.

79. Bureau of Labor Statistics (2004). Retrieved online June 6, 2005: http://www.bls.gov/ncs/ebs/sp/ebsm0002.pdf

80. John P. Crank (2004). *Understanding police culture*, 2nd ed. Cincinnati OH: Anderson. p. 346.

81. Bryan Vila and Dennis Jay Kenney (2002). Tired cops: The prevalence and potential consequences of police fatigue. *NIJ Journal*, 248. NCJ 190634. Retrieved, March 26, 2004. http://www.ncjrs.org/pdffiles1/jr000248d.pdf

82. Bryan Vila and Dennis J. Kennedy (2002, March).

83. Geoffrey P. Alpert (1997). *Police pursuit: Policies and training*. NCJ 164831. Washington, DC: U.S. Department of Justice. Office of Justice Programs. Retrieved online June 6, 2005: http://www.ncjrs.org/txtfiles/164831.txt

84. Dennis J. Stevens (2005). Police officer stress and occupational stressors: Before and after 9/11. In Heith Copes (Ed.), *Policing and stress* (pp. 1–24). Upper Saddle River, NJ: Prentice Hall.

85. Further calculation shows: Sample A and Sample B Critical incident scores reflect a Kendall's tau-b value of .612, asymp. Std.error of .80, T score of 7.588 producing significance at .000 level.

86. Chief Charles H. Ramsey (2002). Preparing the community for community policing: The next step in advancing community policing. In Dennis J. Stevens (Ed.), *Policing and community partnerships* (pp. 29–44). Upper Saddle River, NJ: Prentice Hall.

87. Hans Toch (2001). p. 105.

88. National Institute of Justice Journal (2000, January). *On the job stress in policing. Reducing it, preventing it.* Washington, DC: U.S. Department of Justice. Office of Justice Program. NCJ 180079. Retrieved online May 29, 2005: http://ncjrs .org/pdffiles1/jr000242d.pdf

89. Allen R. Kates (2001). *CopShock: Surviving posttraumatic stress disorder.* Tucson, AZ: Holbrook. Detective William H. Martin, p. xvii.

90. National Institute of Justice Journal (2000, January).

91. Hans Toch (2001). *Stress in policing.* Washington, DC: APA. p. 7.

92. Personal communication with Miami-Dade officer who wished to remain anonymous, July 2005.

93. Personal communication with Officer Denise Evertt of the Denver Police Department.

94. National Institute of Justice (2004, February). *National Institute of Justice 2001 Annual Report.* NIJ 195076. Washington, DC: U.S. Department of Justice. Office of Justice Programs. Retrieved online May 20, 2005: http://www.ncjrs.org/ txtfiles1/nij/195076.txt p.

95. John P. Crank (2004). *Understanding police culture,* 2nd ed. Cincinnati, OH: Anderson. p. 29.

96. Jerome Skolnick (1966). *Justice without trial: Law enforcement in a democratic society.* New York: Wiley.

97. Thomas Barker and David L. Carter (1994). *Police deviance,* 3rd ed. Cincinnati, OH: Anderson. p. 50.

98. Katherine W. Ellison (2004). p. 56.

99. John M. Violanti (2005). Dying for the job: Psychological stress, disease, and mortality in police work. In Heith Copes (Ed.), *Policing and stress* (pp. 87–102). Upper Saddle River, NJ: Prentice Hall.

100. Hal Brown (2000). The key to a happy police family is a happy police marriage: But what happens when your police husband needs to change? In Hal Brown (Ed.), *Police stress line.* Retrieved online June 10, 2005: http://divorcesupport .about.com

101. Chuck Pratt (2000). Why do police officers have such an outlandish rate of marital and domestic failure and calamity? In Hal Brown (Ed.), *Police stress line.* Retrieved online June 10, 2005: http://divorcesupport.about.com

102. Hans Toch (2001). pp. 6–7.

103. W. Terry (1981). Police stress: The empirical evidence. *Journal of Police Science and Administration,* 9, 61–75. p. 68.

104. John M. Violanti (2005). p. 93.

105. John M. Violanti (2005). p. 93.

106. John M. Violanti (2005). Law Enforcement Wellness Association. Retrieved online June 11: http://www.cophealth.com/articles/articles_dying_a.html. Also see W. Richard and R. Fell (1976). Health factors in police job stress. In W. Kroes and J.J. Hurell, Jr. (Eds.) *Job stress and the police officer* (DHEW Pub. 76-187). Washington, DC: U.S. Government Printing Office.

107. S. Milham (1983). Occupational mortality in Washington State (DHEW Pub. 83-116). Washington, DC: U.S. Government Printing Officer.

108. John M. Violanti (1996). *Police suicide: Epidemic in blue.* Springfield, IL: Charles C. Thomas.

109. Katherine W. Ellison (2004). p. 56.

110. Michael G. Aamodt and Nicole A. Stalnaker (2001). Police officer suicide: Frequency and officer profiles. In D.C. Shehan and J. I. Warren (Eds.), *Law enforcement and suicide*. Quantico, VA: Federal Bureau of Investigation.

111. A comparative evaluation of police suicide rates. Washington, DC: Occupational Safety and Health. Retrieved online June 11, 2005: http://infoventures .com/osh/abs/lawe0002.html

112. Katherine W. Ellison (2004). p. 57.

113. G.T. Bergen, A. Deutch, and S. Best (2001). Police suicide: Why are the rates in some places so low? In D.C. Sheehan and J. I. Warren (Eds.), *Suicide and law enforcement*. Washington, DC: U.S. Government Printing Office.

114. John M. Violanti (2005). p. 94.

115. A. Ivanoff (1994). *The New York City police suicide training project*. New York: Police Foundation.

116. Hans Toch (2001). p. 106.

117. Personal communication January 12, 2005, with a female Boston police officer.

118. Patricia A. Kelly (2002). Stress: The cop killer. In John M. Madonna and Richard E. Kelly (Eds.), *Treating police stress* (pp. 33–54). Springfield, IL: Charles C. Thomas. p. 40.

119. Richard E. Kelly (2002). Psychological care of the police wounded. In John M. Madonna and Richard E. Kelly (Eds.), *Treating police stress* (pp. 15–34). Springfield, IL: Charles C. Thomas. p. 40.

120. Richard E. Kelly (2002). Critical incident debriefing. In John M. Madonna and Richard E. Kelly (Eds.), *Treating police stress* (pp. 139–149). Springfield, IL: Charles C. Thomas.

121. Personal communication November 7, 2003, with Massachusetts State Trooper Lisa Cesso, and a former student and research assistant.

122. Merry Morash and Robin N. Haarr (1995). Gender, workplace problems, and stress in policing. *Justice Quarterly*, 12, 113–140. Also see Robin Haarr and Merry Morash. (2005). Police coping with stress: The importance of emotions, gender, and minority status. In Heith Copes (Ed.). *Policing and stress* (pp. 158–177). Upper Saddle River, NJ: Prentice Hall.

123. Merry Morash and Robin N. Haarr (1995). Gender, workplace problems, and stress in policing. *Justice Quarterly*, 12, 113–140. This paper focuses on the connection of workplace problems with stress for women and men working in police departments. Field research was used to identify the problems that women experience in police departments, and quantitative measures were developed to measure these problems in a survey of women and men in 25 departments. Although women and men experience many of the same work-related problems, and although such problems account for a high proportion of workplace stress in both groups, the gendered nature of police organizations causes unique stressors for women. Overall, however, women do not report higher levels of stress than men.

124. Merry Morash and Jack R. Greene. (1986). Women on patrol: A critique of contemporary wisdom. *Evaluation Review*, 10, 230–255.

125. Officer Marie Durrant, Fayetteville Police Department. The author was riding with this officer. She was a student of the author.

126. See P. Morrison (1991, July 12). Female officers unwelcome—But doing well. *Los Angeles Times*. Additional stress for female, gay, and ethnic literature pro-

vided by the National Center on Women and Policing, 8105 West Third St., Suite 1, Los Angeles, California 90048, (213) 651-0495.

C. Fletcher (1995). *Breaking and entering: Women cops talk about life in the ultimate men's club.* New York: HarperCollins.

127. Karen Testa. (2004, May 24). Women rise to top of police ranks in several major U.S. cities. The Associated Press. *Boston Globe.* Retrieved Online July 4, 2004: http://www.policeone.com/policeone/frontend/parser.cfm?object=NewDivision s&rel=46210&operation=full_article&id=87594

128. Karen Testa. (2004, May 24). Women rise to top of police ranks in several major U.S. cities. The Associated Press. *Boston Globe.* Retrieved Online July 4, 2004: http://www.policeone.com/policeone/frontend/parser.cfm?object=NewDivision s&rel=46210&operation=full_article&id=87594

129. Jim Kouri, vice president of the National Association of Chiefs of Police. Retrieved online June 12, 2005: http://mensnewsdaily.com/blog/kouri/2005/04/ minuteman-project-in-eyes-of-us-border.html

130. Samuel Walker (2001). *Sense and nonsense about crime and drugs.* Belmont, CA: Wadsworth. p. 348.

131. Susan E. Martin. (1994). Outside within the station house: The impact of race and gender on black women police. *Social Problems,* 41, 398.

132. Samuel Walker (2001). p. 348.

133. Jerry Sparger and David Giacopassi. (1987). Swearing in and swearing off: A comparison of cops and ex-cops' attitudes toward the workplace. In Daniel B. Kennedy and Robert J. Homat (Eds.), *Police and law enforcement* (pp. 35–54). New York: Ams.

134. Michael Buerger (2004). Educating and training the future police officer. Federal Law Enforcement Bulletin, 73(1). Retrieved online March 11, 2006: http://www.fbi.gov/publications/leb/2004/jan2004/jan04leb.htm#page_27

135. William G. Doerner. (1995). Officer retention patterns: An affirmative action concern for police agencies. *American Journal of Police,* 14(3/4), 197–210.

136. Each of these statements was articulated by female officers in written (questionnaire) or verbal (derived from interviews) forms conducted during the study for this work, or the comments were derived from classroom participation among police officers.

137. Mark Fazlollah (2005). City, national rape statistics highly suspect. RAINN Hotline Retrieved online June 24, 2005: http://www.rainn.org/fazwenews.html

138. Policeone.com (2005, May 23). Officer down in Montreal. Retrieved March 26, 2006: http://www.policeone.com/policeone/frontend/parser.cfm?object=News& operation=officer_down_full&id=98992

7

War on Crime and Paramilitary Model of Policing

In my youth, I stressed freedom, and in my old age, I stress order. I have made the great discovery that liberty is a product of order. —Will Durant

Learning Objectives

After reading this chapter, you will be able to:

- Define and describe the effectiveness of the paramilitary model of policing.

- Articulate how the "war on crime" is linked to a paramilitary model of policing.

- Characterize the development and components of the Posse Comitatus Act of 1878.

- Provide the rationale for a paramilitary model of policing.

- Explain what the federal government does to encourage local tactical units.

- Provide a comparison between the police and the military.

- Identify the characteristics of a paramilitary police organization.

- Explain the public response to tactical units.

- Articulate the primary criticism of paramilitary models of policing.

- Describe the ways the paramilitary model of policing acts as a stressor.

- Describe what is meant by police-blind and provide some examples of behavioral patterns produced by this pneumonia.

- Explain the dynamics of the paradoxical quandary that influences officer stress.

- Identify other stressors of the paramilitary model of policing.

KEY TERMS

Crime prophylactic model

Community cooperation model

Paramilitary model of policing

Police-blind

Police knowledge model

Posse Comitatus Act of 1878

Social work model

SWAT

Tactical policing

INTRODUCTION

Traditional police strategies are prioritizing their initiatives towards a war on crime through a *paramilitary model of policing* or what can be called *a command and control model* which can be defined as law enforcement using the equipment, training, rhetoric, and group tactics of war, which includes the hierarchal chain of command[1] to deliver police services.[2] At first glance, a paramilitary model of policing gives rise to a police renaissance, of sorts. One writer refers to this priority of paramilitary models or (Militarized Swat Units) as a postmodernization affect that undermines the traditional identities and practices associated especially among law enforcement organizations.[3] Nothing wrong with a paramilitary tactical model of policing if it protects the due process guarantees and provides public safety to constituents. Nonetheless, it will be argued that the war on crime conducted through a paramilitary police tactical unit enormously contributes to the stress levels of typical law enforcement officers across the country and it serves law enforcement command as opposed to serving the public.

The focus of this chapter is fitting because it is an examination of two compatible concepts: the "war on crime" and the police tactical units designed to fight that war. To determine the merits of tact units, it is helpful to compare a military model with the traditional police model to better understand how these two American institutions work. Many agree with Will Durant who clarifies how his maturity and experience taught him that freedom is the prize of social order. Yet, like many police policymakers, Durant might have inadvertently neglected to examine the appropriateness of the vehicle or the means that can provide order maintenance. This chapter will accomplish just that – an examination of the appropriateness of the paramilitary model of policing or tact unit as the best initiative during a time of an alleged "war."

PARAMILITARY MODELS

Paramilitary models of policing refer to one of two different, yet related activities in response to the war on crime, drugs, and terrorism (Chapter 8): (1) American military engaged in local police capacities and (2) local police employing American military strategies, which includes the use of military weapons to conduct routine policing.

Using American military in a police capacity can be illustrated in this example: The Pentagon was under increasing pressure from Congress to militarize America's borders with Canada and Mexico. That pressure led to a 6-month deployment of some 1,600 federalized (answered to U.S. military authority) National Guardsmen that ended in August 2002, a deployment carried out in violation of the Posse Comitatus Act of 1878 (discussed later in this chapter). Although most of those soldiers were unarmed, the tasks they undertook involved regulation and compulsion of civilians and was constituted as active police work.[4]

A U.S. Immigration and Customs Enforcement (ICE) press release announced that guardsmen were assigned to the border and performed "cargo inspections, traffic management, and pedestrian control."[5] Because the soldiers were operating under federal command and performing typical policing tasks, the deployment was illegal according to the provisions of the Posse Comitatus Act of 1878.[6] This chapter looks primarily at the second strategy; paramilitary models of policing of local departments, but this examination includes the use of federal government aid to further local law enforcement efforts.

It is not hard to accept the suitability of a paramilitary model of policing in a democratic nation, especially as terrorists engage in horrendous crimes against civilians, such as criminal acts on the subways in London in July 2005,[7] on the trains in Madrid in March 2004, and at the World Trade Center in New York City in September 2001. Trying to keep focus, a war on crime, especially when fueled by terrorism, should be examined as two distinctive occurrences.

The war on crime is "fought" on the streets of vast megacities such as Chicago and Los Angeles and in towns such as Gulfport, Mississippi, and Alamogordo, New Mexico, between dangerously armed thugs and police. Despite the paramilitary advantage during hostage situations, at-risk warrant encounters, and other hazardous police–criminal altercations, human rights and due process are ignored when tact units take precedence over a traditional model of policing. Some police candidates consider the tact unit accolades as a giant motive to pursue a law enforcement career and some police veterans look forward to the excitement of a violent altercation with criminals, especially if a tactical approach is deployed.[8]

That said, what is known about wars on crime is that the Constitution of the United States prohibits declaring war on domestic social problems.[9] Yet, federal and local policymakers may ignore those perspectives in their "war campaigns," but sometimes, could it meet with approval? For example, concluding a 1-year "war on gangs," or what was called "Operation Community Shield" in March 2006, agents from the Department of Homeland Security's U.S. Immigration and Customs Enforcement (ICE) teamed up with local police agencies and arrested over 2,400 gang members in 239 gangs residing in 23 states.[10] Those arrested included members of MS-13, Surenos, 18th Street Gang, Latin Kings, Bloods, Crips, Armenian Power, Street Thug Criminals, Brown Pride, Asian Dragon Family, Avenue Assassins, Spanish Gangster Disciples, Big Time Killers, and Hermanos Pistoleros Latinos. Roughly 922 of those arrested were from the seriously violent street gang Mara Salvatrucha (MS-13). Those arrested under Operation Community Shield were prosecuted criminally or removed from the United States through immigration proceedings. For federal and local law enforcement agencies to find a legal yet appropriate balance between enforcement and rights is probably one of the largest challenges in this century.

WAR ON CRIME: OPERATION GHETTO STORM[11]

War can be defined as a form of international relations where organized violence is used as an instrument of power by sovereign nation-states.[12] The term has been used so loosely by well-intentioned U.S. Presidents such as Nixon, Reagan, and the Bushes. Crime has always been on the agenda of state and local politicians, and since 1964 it has been on every President's domestic agenda.[13] Karl von Clausewitz (1780–1831), best known for his book *On War*, defined war as "an act of violence intended to compel opponents to fulfill our will." America's founders such as Thomas Jefferson regarded war as the largest single threat to democracy because war clouds the nation's populace with an anti-intellectual climate, and it is impossible to remain ignorant and free at the same time.[14]

The downside of a proposal such as the war on crime is that similar training, expectations, and mandates that help breed young men and women into soldiers and outstanding warriors produce a dangerous street cop and a dangerous environment. What we thought were our local police have become a federally funded, militarily trained, asset-forfeiture-empowered, multijurisdictional narcotics task force that specializes in home invasions and forceful actions against American citizens suspected of smoking marijuana or being a suspect as a sports bookee.[15] For instance, Fairfax police declared that the killing of Salvatore J. Culosi, age 37, was an accident and that the SWAT officer who fired had done so unintentionally.[16] Fairfax Commonwealth's Attorney Robert F. Horan, Jr., said that when a person fires a gun without malice and unintentionally kills someone, "they do not commit a crime." Had the shooter not been a police officer, he would have been charged criminally. Police spokeswoman Mary Ann Jennings of the Fairfax police said they are continuing to review their policies on the use of force and also on the use of SWAT teams in serving search warrants.[17] She said that the use of SWAT teams by Fairfax police was appropriate for apprehending bookees.

Then, too, Florida authorities deployed a tank outside Miami International Airport over the Thanksgiving holiday in 2001, as if the next terror attack would come in the form of an Al Qaeda mechanized column, rather than a shoe bomb or a smuggled boxcutter.[18] In what way could American public safety be satisfied through this attempt to demonstrate paramilitary police power? Another example relates to the Amadou Diallo verdict, which sought to legalize an expanded "rules of engagement" to justify "excess force" and to cover these murders in a defense based on the notion that the officers "did what they were trained to do."[19] In this sense, the defense strategy goes beyond the acquittal of the four officers. The entire affair could be considered another link in an evolving (counter) revolution of police power but now linked to an "increasing reliance upon and acquisition of technology developed by the military for use in domestic law enforcement."[20] Rather than using technology and training to murder citizens, what if the police were routinely equipped with handheld weapon detectors that could alert officers from a distance whether a suspect is armed?

For over 40 years, the United States has waged a "war on crime," and many police departments have adopted a *crime fighter model* in response to President Lyndon B, Johnson's declaration on crime in 1965. President Richard N. Nixon announced his own war in 1969, followed by President George H. W. Bush, who modified it as a "war on drugs" in 1989.[21] Even today political hopefuls rely on a war on crime, a war on drugs, and the *criminalization of poverty* ("status" laws punish individuals for their economic condition, rather than their behavior),[22] which seems to justify tactical police control over the lower classes, and one way to describe this un-American conduct is to refer to it as Operation Ghetto Storm.[23] For example, the world's self-professed leading democracy lacks a national health care policy, a universal right to health care, and a comprehensive family policy. Welfare applicants are subjected to personal intrusions, arcane regulations, and constant surveillance, all designed to humiliate recipients and deter potential applicants.[24] The War on Poverty (1964–1968) was a campaign of legislation and social services aimed at reducing or eliminating poverty in the United States. The term was first introduced by President Lyndon B. Johnson during his State of the Union address on January 8, 1964. The legislation was designed in response to the poverty affecting over 35 million Americans as of 1964. The poverty line was on a sharp decline and not a rise nor fluctuation at the time Johnson was campaigning. Johnson said in his address, "This administration today, here and now, declares unconditional war on poverty in America." That war was lost. Poverty is pervasive in America. Criminal justice response has been to criminalize poverty by intruding, apprehending, prosecuting, and incarcerating members of the lower class (or what can be referred to as the criminalization of poverty) more often than members of other social classes.[25]

According to *Criminalization of Poverty*, there are two kinds of laws that discriminate against the poor and homeless. "Homeless" laws specifically target homeless individuals and their activities. "Status" laws punish individuals for their economic condition, rather than their behavior. That is, many cities across the country have homeless laws, falling into a few general categories. Panhandling is restricted or banned altogether (Massachusetts passed a law of this kind several years ago but it was struck down by the state courts as unconstitutional). Anti-camping ordinances, such as in Austin, Texas, prohibit sleeping on streets or in parks after curfew or at all. In many cities, the homeless are excluded from downtown areas and places where they congregate. Austin and Los Angeles, for instance, have no-standing zones and no-sitting areas where people cannot linger. A question that arises asks who actually has ownership rights over open spaces. There are also such arcane laws as the prohibition of public parking lot crossing in Atlanta.

In Tucson, a special zone was created in which it is a crime simply to be homeless. Police were arresting homeless people without cause and releasing them only when they agreed to stay out of the area for a certain period of time. Alan Mason, arrested under this law, was banned from an area that covered just about all of downtown, including his lawyer's office, all the courthouses, the voter registration office, and several places of worship.

The line between homeless laws and status laws blurs. Most disorderly conduct laws are considered status laws because many homeless are mentally ill, or predisposed to erratic behavior, caused by (or causing) their homelessness.

Whether this idea sits well with readers or not, the fact remains that the Presidential campaigns of 2004 showcased the continual war on crime platform and the 2008 campaigns will heat up the old dialogue. In part, there were several outcomes that emerged from all this war talk:

1. Winning the war and incarceration
2. Posse Comitatus Act of 1878: Revisited
3. Paramilitary interchangeable terms
4. Rationale of paramilitary policing

5. Increase in tact unit outs
6. Police units altered to resemble military units
7. Weapons and training provided by the federal government
8. A comparison between the police and the military
9. Characteristics of the paramilitary police organization
10. Results of tact units
11. Public response
12. Police tact units engage the "enemy"
13. Occupational army
14. Targeted neighborhoods

Winning the War and Incarceration

One purpose of the "war" is to control crime, and America is winning that war since trends of reported crime across the country show a decline from 1993 to 2003.[26] However, since police strategies and technology have improved since 2003, it is expected that crime would plummet but the crime trend is picking back up, suggesting the police war-tactics might not have been responsible for the reduction of crime after all. Nonetheless, the incarceration rate rose from 96 per 100,000 of the American population in 1970 to 496 per 100,000 in 2002 and appears to rise all the more in 2006.[27] This compares with an incarceration rate of 111 per 100,000 in Canada, 79 in Australia, and 42 in Japan. As part of this equation, you can imagine that the courts have been breaking at the seams, so much so that in Philadelphia, for example, the police commissioner described the criminal courts as being "on the verge of collapse."[28] One product from a war on crime is associated with the huge incarceration rates across the country and some of the criminal justice communities seem like they are on the verge of collapse. Added to criminal justice personnel being overworked and probably underpaid, federal legislation such as "Posse Comitatus" requires attention because it prohibits the U.S. military and their commanders from engaging in local police activities.

Posse Comitatus Act of 1878: Revisited

The *Posse Comitatus Act* is a statute (18 USC 1385, passed in 1878) that prohibits the use of the military or armed forces from conducting law enforcement activities in the United States.[29] Originally, Posse Comitatus was introduced after the end of Reconstruction in 1878, and was intended to prohibit federal troops from supervising elections in former Confederate states. It generally prohibits federal military personnel and units of the National Guard under federal authority except where expressly authorized by the Constitution or Congress. This law is mentioned whenever it appears that the

Department of Defense (DOD) is interfering in domestic disturbances. There are exceptions to the act, which include:

- National Guard units while under the authority of the governor of a state such as during recovery efforts from Hurricane Katrina in coastal Mississippi and New Orleans.
- Troops when used pursuant to the federal authority to quell domestic violence such as during the Rodney King riots.
- The President of the United States can waive this law in a military emergency.
- In December 1981 additional laws were enacted (codified 10 USC 371-78) clarifying permissible military assistance to civilian law enforcement agencies—including the Coast Guard, which is a division of the Department of Homeland Security (DHS), as opposed to the military, especially in combating drug smuggling into the United States.

Posse Comitatus clarifications emphasize supportive and technical assistance (e.g., use of facilities, vessels, aircraft, intelligence, tech aid, surveillance, etc.) while generally prohibiting direct participation of DOD personnel in law enforcement (e.g., search, seizure, and arrests). For example, Coast Guard Law Enforcement Detachments (LEDETS) serve aboard Navy vessels and perform the actual boardings of interdicted suspect drug smuggling vessels and, if needed, arrest their crews. Positive results have been realized, especially from Navy ship/aircraft involvement. But that fine line is always in the minds of the personnel who engage in these activities and crossing over the line is considered a serious breach of job descriptions, which can include disciplinary action. Whatever the term used, of which there are many, paramilitary models of policing are easy to find within a police organization.

Then, too, Schwarzenegger-esque domestic shootouts between U.S. military forces and dirty-bomb-toting terrorists in an Amtrak tunnel is entertaining but the truth is much more sobering.[30] The federal government has yet to prove that it can properly interpret the intelligence that leads them to deploy the antiterrorist commandos in the right place at the right time. The evidence of local intervention associated with terrorists (World Trade Center), border protection (U.S. and Mexico), and national calamities (Hurricane Katrina) suggest it is unlikely that federal agencies or troops, regardless of their authority or affiliation, are capable of providing homeland security as well as locals.

While a modification of Posse Comitatus makes Americans practically no safer, it would open the door to old abuses. Had the initiative to repeal the Posse Comitatus Act passed in 1995, Bill Clinton would have been free to deploy troops to Florida to ensure the validity of the Presidential election recount.

Paramilitary Interchangeable Terms

Paramilitary or tactical policing (sometimes called tact units are law enforcement units that employ the equipment, training, rhetoric, and tactics of warfare) is on the rise nationwide.[31] America has more than 30,000 paramilitary teams. However, like much of the information available about what cops do or are, most of it comes from liberal academics who often fail to apply common sense in their assessments. For instance, 30,000 teams would suggest 600 per state, and many states are very small. Since the average police department, depending on how we evaluate it, employs an estimated 40 sworn officers in each department. It is hard to imagine that a state like Vermont or Rhode Island, to name two, have 600 SWAT teams. Also, since most SWAT or technical units service more than one jurisdiction, it is probably more likely that an estimated 2,000 exist across America.[32]

Nonetheless, the terms for paramilitary policing are interchangeable, although paramilitary policing can refer to the organizational philosophy or style of tactical units, tact units, SWAT, first-response units, anti-gang units, and so on. There are many titles given to police units that fit the definition of military tactical policing efforts, but the rationale of early tactical units basely had one source.

Rationale of Paramilitary Policing

Tact units were originally developed by a young LAPD commander named Daryl Gates in 1966 and called *SWAT* (special weapons and tactics) units. They were conceived as an urban counterinsurgency bulwark. The idea behind SWAT is their officers are trained to be super warriors because typical patrol officers might have difficulty in controlling radicals, revolutionaries, and cop haters. They might also have difficulty in confronting competent suspects who are excellent marksmen, bomb builders, and ambushers of law enforcement officers. For these reasons, and others, there has been an increase in tactical callouts.

Increase in Tact Callouts

Nationwide, tactical units have metastasized from emergency response teams into a standard part of everyday policing.[33] Raids are no longer confined to big cities or limited to critical incidents. In 1982, 59% of police departments that responded to a study had an active paramilitary police unit.[34] Fifteen years later, nearly 90% of those same agencies had an active paramilitary unit.

A commander of a paramilitary unit in a midwestern town of 75,000 describes how his team cruises the streets in an armored personnel carrier. "We stop anything that moves. We'll sometimes even surround suspicious homes and bring out the MP5s [an automatic weapon manufactured by Heckler and Koch and favored by military special forces teams]. We usually don't have any problems with crackheads cooperating."[35] SWAT teams that used to be called to handle the occasional barricaded or hostage-taker suspects now conduct routine drug raids and as illustrated above, SWAT teams are used to apprehend unarmed sports bookees.

More troubling are results of another study revealing that tact units are called out to perform relatively mundane police work such as patrolling city streets and serving warrants.[36] Indeed, with the mainstreaming of police tact units, cities including Fresno, Indianapolis, and Boston send police to maintain order during nonemergency situations in full battle dress—giving some communities all the ambience of the West Bank. In the final analysis, the truth that remains is that law enforcement officers are sworn to guard human rights and due process despite tact teams that have been altered in appearance to resemble a military unit.

Police Units Altered to Resemble Military Units

A colleague says, "The Posse Comitatus Act serves as a guide to tell us exactly what Congress does not want in our streets, a military structure and operation."[37] Yet, we look around, and it will be clear that the police intentionally try to resemble the military in many respects:[38]

- Training: often the federal government and military engage in training exercises for local officers
- Weapons: military weapons are supplied to local organizations
- Uniforms resembling those worn by SS Storm Troopers of Nazi Germany
- Hierarchy: top down, chain of command
- Discipline: to follow orders without question
- Deployment: assignments[39]
- Resembling an "occupying force": weapons, air support, and communication
- Treating civilians like the enemy: officers are trained to deface suspects and distance self from altercations[40]

These characteristics among others have been encouraged and supported by federal government intervention in local police agencies.

Federal Government Provides Weapons and Training

There are many heavily armed, militarily trained police units in the United States, and the number of paramilitary police "callouts" quadrupled between 1980 and 1995.[41] The tactical buildup has been fueled by fattened drug-war budgets and a wave of federal generosity in the form of equipment, training, and funds. Between 1995 and 1997 the Department of Defense gave local police 1.2 million pieces of military hardware, including more than 3,800 M16 automatic assault rifles, 2,185 Rugar M14 semiautomatic rifles, 73 M79 grenade launchers, and 112 armored personnel carriers (APCs). One tactical outfit calls its APC "mother"; another, in east Texas, has named its APCs "Bubba One" and "Bubba Two." Since 9/11, one confidential source indicates that almost 60% of every police agency in the United States has been supplied weapons of war by the U.S. military with the approval of the President of the United States and selected members of those departments have been trained by active members of the U.S. military to aggressively respond to any altercation with the "same technical know-how and weapons systems employed in military battles."

Military gear given to the San Francisco Police Department (SFPD) alone includes two helicopters, several electrical generators, vehicles, and office furniture, according to tactical officer Dino Zografos of the SFPD. Several years ago the department acquired two APCs from the United Kingdom. The department's 45-officer tact squad bought its own AR 15 and MP53 assault rifles. Most of the SFPD's tactical training is done in-house, though SWAT officers have received special instruction from FBI, U.S. military, and private instructors. Bottom line, not only are paramilitary models of policing equipped and trained by military units and those units are employed more often than ever before, but tactical units have increased in number, too. However, in a comparison between police and military characteristics, finding the gap and the similarities between the two institutions is an easy task.

A Comparison between the Police and the Military

There are many similarities and differences between the American police and the American military, as evidenced in Table 7.1. Both the police and the military are institutions of force and the occasion to use force among both are unpredictably distributed.[42] Members of both institutions must always be prepared to use force. Yet the question that arises from paramilitary police is whether peacekeepers can perform like soldiers, or the other way around.[43]

A key difference between police and military are the populations under their jurisdiction. Police further public safety in a free society. Military is deployed to destroy and control targeted populations. Police are designed to help people and provide due process, and are constrained by laws protecting the rights of individuals. Military's first mission is its mission (see Soldier's Creed). Street cops routinely exercise individual discretion to serve the mission of pubic safety. Military personnel are trained and expected to operate as members of a military unit.[44] Since police provide public safety, their weapons, equipment, training, and tactics are very different from the military, which is expected to control a population.[45] The military is trained to defeat the enemy and is not generally concerned with collateral damage. Police and paramilitary units generally function very poorly as military units and are usually destroyed when they attempt to fight a military force. Conversely, the military considers police activities to be a distraction from their primary goal,

Table 7.1 COMPARISON BETWEEN POLICE AND MILITARY

General Characteristics	Police	Military
Institutions of force	Yes	Yes
Use of deadly force	Last response	First response
Prepared to use violence	Yes	Yes
Priority of assignment	Public safety first	First
Individual discretion	Yes	No
Purpose of strategies	Public safety and human rights	Destroy enemies of the U.S.
Collaterial damage	Priority	Not priority
Military act as police		Alienate population
Police act as military	Alienate population	
Promotion and awards	Internal discipline	Internal discipline
Bureaucratic discipline	Redefine action to comply	Follows mandates

Note: The above are generalizations and there are always exceptions to everything. Take this table as a guide.[50]

and when the military attempts to operate as civil police forces, they usually alienate the population that they attempt to serve, as America has experienced in Iraq in 2003–2005. Military jailers just don't make it in a free society. Conversely, police tact units provide alienation among lawful populations, even during critical incidents.[46] Promotion and rewards are centered on a system of internal discipline mandates and events including justifiable homicide. Due to the military bureaucratic discipline, an officer must go great lengths to remain free from indiscretions.[47] If an infraction of a specific regulation is accomplished, law enforcement officers can redefine the situation into an instance of police work that is not regulated. On the other hand, soldiers are seldom trained in riot control, are expected to deliver deadly force (police can deliver deadly force as a last response,[48] more on the use of force later in this chapter), and seldom redefine incidents to fit work that is not regulated. Lawrence Korb, former assistant secretary of defense in the Reagan administration, put it succinctly: the military "is trained to vaporize, not Mirandize."[49] Democracy cannot thrive under marshal law or military control because the centerpiece of democracy is freedom.

Comparing the LAPD's mission statement with a Soldier's Creed might aid in a better understanding of the similarities and differences between local police efforts and military action.

The Los Angeles Police Department's (LAPD) mission statement centers itself in a reverence for the law.[51] For instance, the main thrust of a peace officer's job description consists of an attempt to enforce the law. LAPD officers are expected to perform their job within the legal spirit of the law as set forth by the framers of the Bill of Rights. That Bill of Rights' centerpiece elevates the rights of each citizen to a position equal with the state and with each other to further justice and equity. The LAPD supports the Bill of Rights theme that the dignity of the individual is placed in a sacred position of importance.

The mission statement of the LAPD adds that an officer's enforcement effort should not be done in grudging adherence to the legal rights of the accused, but in a sincere spirit of seeking that every accused person is given all of his or her rights as far as it is within the powers of the officer. The statement includes the idea that a peace officer must scrupulously avoid any conduct that would make the officer a violator of the law. Peace officers should do their utmost to foster a reverence for the law and at all times display a reverence for the legal rights of constituents.

The Soldier's Creed

I am an American Soldier.
I am a Warrior and a member of a team. I serve the people of the United States and live the Army Values.

I will always place the mission first.
I will never accept defeat.
I will never quit.
I will never leave a fallen comrade.

I am disciplined, physically and mentally tough, trained and proficient in my warrior tasks and drills. I always maintain my arms, my equipment and myself.

I am an expert and I am a professional.
I stand ready to deploy, engage, and destroy the enemies of the United States of America in close combat.
I am a guardian of freedom and the American way of life.
I am an American Soldier.

Source: U.S. Army. Retrieved Online July 4, 2004: http://www.army.mil/thewayahead/creed.html

The Soldier's Creed implies that "teamwork" is a part of the military model. While teamwork is an excellent strategy, one problem with a "military mind" is that "everyone" thinks like a team member and as a result there is less focus on morale reasoning, independent judgment, courage outside combat, and critical thinking. It would be impractical for an individual soldier to critically decide on a situation or assess the ethics of an order whether in combat or peacetime. Police officers, on the other hand, have discretion built into their jobs. Should they wish to become soldiers instead of cops, let's remove their discretion. However, the concept of military mind in the military and police has been degraded and demeaned the way soldiers and police officers interpret it—"helping my brother no matter what."[52] Police and military training have not helped personnel distinguish when to act as a team member and when to act as a morale individual who should be exercising good judgment independent of the team concept (which to one expert's way of thinking is really acting like an ultimate team player—the team is "society," not a police force or a branch of the military).[53] Few would argue that crime control is a priority, but controlling crime through storm trooper initiatives is counter to the democratic foundations of this nation.

Characteristics of the Paramilitary Police Organization

There are 19 characteristics of the paramilitary police organization listed below in no particular order[54]:

1. A centralized command structure with a highly adhered-to chain of command.
2. A rigid superior–subordinate relationship defined by prerogatives of rank.
3. Control exerted through the issuance of commands, directives, or general orders.
4. Clearly delineated lines of communication and authority.
5. The communications process primarily vertical from top to bottom.
6. Employees who are encouraged to work primarily through threats or coercion.
7. Initiative at the supervisory and operational levels neither sought, encouraged, nor expected.
8. An authoritarian style of leadership.
9. Emphasis on the maintenance of the status quo.
10. Highly structured system of sanctions and discipline procedures to deal with nonconformists within the organization.
11. Usually a highly centralized system of operations.
12. Strict adherence to organizational guidelines in the form of commands, directives, general orders, or policy and procedures.
13. Lack of flexibility when confronted with problems or situations not covered by existing directives, general orders, or policy and procedures.
14. Promotional opportunities that are available only to organizational members.
15. An impersonal relationship between members of the organization.
16. Feelings of demoralization and powerlessness in the lower levels of the organization.
17. Concept of the administration and top command as being arbitrary.
18. Growing level of cynicism among supervisory and operational-level personnel.

19. Development of a "we–they" attitude among supervisory and operational personnel toward top management and between police personnel and citizens.

A word of caution: A paramilitary police unit refers to the organizational structure. Certainly, commanders and some parts of the public become frustrated with what they perceive to be lawlessness and calling out SWAT makes them feel better. Factually, it doesn't change the face of crime nor does it go to the roots of crime. No one said that managing a democratic society was easy. In fact, a few hundred years ago, one prominent visitor, Alexis de Tocqueville, wrote that in a democratic nation, it is extremely natural but dangerous that certain strategies will lead to "despise and undervalue the rights of private persons."[55] He said that the rights of private persons is of little importance, yet rights must be sacrificed without regret. Is de Tocqueville correct, or must human rights prevail? On the other hand, are there times when a paramilitary unit should be deployed for the greater good and what results might be expected when tact units are called out?

Results of Tact Units

Of 186 critical incidents across the country in a 1-year period, 96% of those incidents were resolved without shots fired after a tact unit's arrival.[56] Fifty-seven of those involved firearms and only five resulted in the death of the suspect by SWAT. Overall, safe arrests without serious injury were reported by hostage-barricade units in New York, Chicago, and elsewhere. Those reports serve as a lesson that traditional police responses can be supplanted by a more aggressive but less violent means of public safety. Police tact units can provide safe resolutions to dangerous encounters more so than alternative methods and it makes sense to be prepared for high-volatile situations. With that said, one question might be, What does the public think about tact units?

Public Response

Many individuals have an awareness of police tactical strategies as fostered through the popular media. Some experts and civil leaders argue that law enforcement can be better prepared to deal with critical incidents by developing police tact units. They encourage tact units and provide resources including funding for such initiatives.

Nonetheless, one study consisting of 282 residents who lived in three cities where police tact units were active reported that they lacked confidence in the success of police tactical units.[57] An implication from those results is that the public is more afraid of police violence or a police-led revolution than criminal violence. One reason for this fear could be that the police represent an organized force as opposed to criminals who tend to operate independently of other criminals. Then, too, perhaps Americans are responding to the "loose cannon" officers on patrol, suggesting that a greater likelihood exists that individual street cops might be considered the problem. The realities of the LAPD's CRASH units and other corrupt performance among officers across the United States is well documented.

Overwhelmingly, Americans view international terrorism and the possible spread of weapons of mass destruction as the two most critical threats facing this country, reports a recent Gallup survey.[58] Yet, as of early 2004, Americans see the economic sector as their real battleground as opposed to crime and the spread of mass destruction.[59] This data reveals that the attention of the public is on economic issues as opposed to terrorism and therefore it should come as no surprise that most Americans are uncertain about police tactical units unless those units operated in their neighborhood.

Police Tact Units Engage the "Enemy"

As both the public and the criminal justice system adapt a strong punitive attitude toward criminals, and tact units become a common strategy, the notion of a war on crime can be described as an example of a "metaphor that fits police work in many ways."[60] Criminals become an "enemy combatant" and crime control becomes a "military battle." War carries the full force of a vibrant, polyvalent metaphor, with auxiliary meanings about combatants, training, policing urban areas, weaponry, and crime control.[61]

As part of the military battle, special police units across the country engage in military deployments armed with U.S. military know-how and U.S. state-of-the-art weapons to accomplish their mission in local neighborhoods (see below for specifics). SWAT teams of selected police personnel are trained to utilize specialized equipment and tactics (both stealth and dynamic entries) to resolve critical incidents. The goal of stealth was to reduce casualties and was used in preference to an explosive, dynamic entry unless the stealth entry was compromised. Critical incident refers to any high-risk encounter with police–civilian contracts when officers reasonably believed they are legally justified in using deadly force, regardless of whether they use such force or avert its use.[62] Examples of such incidents are in Chapter 5.

A flip of the coin can show the results of soldiers performing as police officers. Confusing the police function with the military function can lead to dangerous, unintended consequences—such as unnecessary shootings and killings of innocent Americans.[63] For instance, in 1997 a Marine antidrug patrol shot and killed 18-year-old Esequiel Hernandez as he was tending his family's herd of goats on private property in Texas. The Justice Department settled a wrongful death lawsuit with the Hernandez family for $1.9 million. Efficient strategies to deal with the war on crime has produced passionate adversaries on both sides of the question. The downside implies that paramilitary units treat constituents as though they were the "enemy." Of interest, tact units are often trained, equipped, and guided by the federal government including the U.S. military. One implication is that paramilitary models of policing can appear to represent an occupational army when deployed.

Occupational Army

When the police are outfitted in military uniforms carrying military weapons and accompanied by armored personnel carriers, the idea that the police are an *"occupational army"* is reinforced as opposed to the police representing partners in the community.[64] Yet this perspective tends to be held by residents in communities where tact units are active and for that reason when educators in universities attempt to instruct students from privileged backgrounds about an occupational army, it is difficult for students to relate to its significance because they have never experienced it.[65] Living in a targeted neighborhood produces other perspectives about paramilitary units.

Targeted Neighborhoods

One reason those who hold police purse-strings do not oppose tact raids is because most SWAT raids are operationalized in poor and slum neighborhoods. For example, Fresno, California (near San Francisco Bay), is a poorly planned city of 400,000, which includes a sprawling ghetto in the southwest side of the city.[66] There, on the pocked streets, among the stucco bungalows and dying rail yards, massive paramilitary tactical operations are underway almost every night of the week, not so long ago.

Can you imagine waking up to clatters from a low-flying helicopter, sweeping its lights across shabby trees and flat homes where you live? Nearby in the shadows, three squads of 10 police officers in combat boots, black fatigues, and body armor lock and load Heckler and Koch (H&K) MP-54 submachine guns (the same weapons used by the elite Navy SEALs), and fan out through the community.[67] Can you see the terror in a child's eyes wondering if this is the last time he'll see his big brother? These officers were part of Fresno's Violent Crime Suppression Unit (VCSU), the local law enforcement's version of "special forces." Their adrenalin is masked by black war paint to keep the shine of the moon off their faces as they secure an outer perimeter (composed of a middle-class population), and with the precision of army rangers, they close in on some unsuspecting dealer who specializes in pharmaceuticals to out-of-towners. Since 1994 these soldier-cops have been conducting the criminal justice equivalent of search and destroy missions in Fresno's "gang-ridden" badlands. One attorney representing Tom Neville, a former professional football player who was killed by the VCSU, referred to them as a band of rogue cops who were out of control when they shot Neville and other community members down on their luck.[68]

"People often feel these raids do not take place in white, middle-class neighborhoods and, by and large, that is accurate," one police chief says.[69] Based on the above events, it might be uncomfortable to discuss the other side of the coin. For instance, nowhere has alienation associated with the police use of tactical units been more profound than in the minority and lower class neighborhoods of America, especially neighborhoods comprised of people without hope. But make no mistake, communities without resources are subject to police brutality and other forms of corruption conducted by law enforcement officers.[70]

Two experts substantiated that urban communities in the United States experience the brunt of tact unit activity.[71] Another expert outlines some examples[72]:

- At 4:30 A.M., the first wave of SWAT teams clothed in battle dress uniforms (BDUs) with black hoods and wielding submachine guns swarmed into nine homes in a rural community in Washington state. Some 150 officers executed search warrants in 1994, alleging that the residents were running a massive international drug cooperative and harvesting marijuana in underground farms. The multijurisdictional SWAT team members came from 13 separate police agencies including the federal Drug Enforcement Administration, the Bureau of Tobacco, Alcohol and Firearms, the Washington Air National Guard, the Washington State Patrol, three county sheriffs SWAT teams, and four small city police departments. A massive, essentially military operation, the raid netted a few arrests for possession and 54 marijuana plants. It also terrorized eight children asleep in their beds when hooded figures burst in, guns ready. One officer put a gun to the head of a 3-year-old, according to witnesses, and ordered him down on the floor. Because the police were masked, had no badge numbers, and represented so many different agencies, the victims decided to settle out of court.

- In "Operation Readi-Rock" an entire block of an African-American neighborhood was raided and nearly 100 people were detained and searched. As Cleave Atwater tended his customers at his club and pool room in Chapel Hill, North Carolina, the door suddenly splintered open and a mob of men in ninja-hoods and fatigues waving automatic rifles rushed in and shouted for people to get down on the floor. Terrified, Atwater slipped out while his bar assistant sprawled face down in a pool of his own terror-provoked urine. On reaching the street, Atwater entered a surreal landscape in which paramilitary-style police taking part in "Operation Readi-Rock" were selectively stopping and searching black people. Atwater, proprietor of the Village Connection, had called the police months before to complain about drug trafficking near his Graham Street business. But when the North Carolina State Bureau of Investigation's Special Response Team (SRT) and the local police that held the warrant for the blockwide raid finally arrived in full battle dress, they brought little comfort or remedy.

After Operation Readi-Rock, plaintiffs in a successful lawsuit claimed that all those arrested were black since whites were allowed to leave the area. No prosecutions resulted from the raid.[73]

- The victims of North Carolina's Operation Readi-Rock raids survived their ordeals. In another incident, in Oak City, about 70 miles north of Chapel Hill, Jean Wiggins, a cleaning woman, was less fortunate. The same SRT team that went into Graham Street put seven rounds through her body as she ran from a bank where she had been held hostage for 15 hours after a robbery attempt. In less than 2 years, a single paramilitary police team destroyed a lot of public trust and claimed the life of a woman who should have had every reason to expect she would be safer with the police than with her captors.[74]

Fresno Revisited

Before moving on to the next section, the question arose: Is the Fresno Police Department still engaged in utilizing tact units? The police website reports that the mission of the Fresno police is to provide a professional, effective, and timely response to crime and disorder, and to enhance traffic safety in our community.[75] Their vision is that the Fresno Police Department is a model law enforcement agency, nationally accredited, and viewed internally and externally as professional, enthusiastic, and trustworthy. The police website is devoid of any mention of SWAT or VCSU because the unit was disbanded by April 2001. Many citizens complained about the unit's activities and there were a number of lawsuits.[76] The city added 57 patrol officers, 25 investigators, and tripled the number of officers in the downtown district. And the courts found that six officers were absolved of any wrongdoing in the shooting death of former pro football player Tom Neville in 1998. When crime, especially homicides, increased, citizens asked the chief to reinstate the VCSU unit.[77] Another group of a SWAT-type unit was developed through the department called the Multi-Agency Gang Enforcement Consortium (MAGEC).

In addition, Fresno was chosen as one of five communities nationwide in 2005 to receive targeted help in reducing gang crime, the U.S. Department of Justice said.[78] As part of the relatively new Violent Crime Impact Team program, the Justice Department plans to target armed career criminals with a combination of state, federal, and local forces. Federal officers will coordinate with police, sheriff's deputies, probation officers, and state prosecutors. The team will be led by a supervisory special agent with the Federal Bureau of Alcohol, Tobacco, Firearms and Explosives, and use intelligence specialists from the agency. In addition to placing federal agents on Fresno's streets, the federal government intends to assist in paying some overtime costs for officers. One officer confidentially explained, "Same shit, different flies."[79] What appears to be happening in Fresno might well be what's happening in many other jurisdictions. Tact units are similarly redefined and their commando tactics continue. The public's view, at least the part of the public that controls the purse-strings, and their philosophy of crime control apparently encourage or allow tact units to exist in one form or another as long as their neighborhood is not targeted. Many community members and officers must see some of these injustices, after all they can't be blind.

CRITICISM OF PARAMILITARY MODELS

Criticism of paramilitary models can include an examination of the philosophy or belief systems held by constituents and police offices about tact units, a review of the evidence implying that law enforcement officers are not necessarily warriors, a discussion on what officers like best and least about their jobs, and finally, an examination about tact models as stressors.

Philosophy

America has arrived at a threshold of paramilitary tact units through its own militarism, its pathological Puritanism, and its unshakable racism, some say.[80] After a decades-long national addiction to waging war on drugs—framed largely as a war against "unruly minority ethnics"—the deployment of cops dressed like extras in a *First Blood* Stallone movie waving automatic weapons around poor neighborhoods seems inevitable. After 50 years of living as a nation in a peacetime state of emergency managed by the military, the sight of cops cruising the streets in war-surplus-armored personnel carriers to remedy social, cultural, and economic problems is not as much as a shock as Muslims, but that is another story (see Chapter 8). Sometimes the impression that America needs an enemy is a compelling thought, yet the cost to operate, equip, and train Ninja cops does not get to the root of the problem—the root of crime. Rather, violence is glorified and honored. Some even talk about a *triumphalism over crime*. Elliott Currie, for instance, suggests that there has been a "new kind of *triumphalism* about crime, and the capacity of the criminal justice system to control it."[81] By triumphalism, the American model of crime control promoted by the war on crime resulted in harsh criminal justice action by the police, courts, and corrections, which says that plans, strategies, and tact units are working—a feeling that "we've got it fixed here in the United States," Currie explains. The secret of American success is associated with zero tolerance and tact units such as SWAT, advocates of paramilitary tact units argue.[82]

The lesson we are supposed to ingest from this "success" on the crime front is that it's *OK* now: after years and years of doing it wrong, we're finally doing it *right*, Currie says.[83] And a deeper implication is that we've now proven that we *can* indeed control crime through the criminal justice system alone, despite the preponderance of evidence and the thousands of years of history revealing that criminals will commit crime regardless of his or her situation, which includes incarceration as best portrayed by Pee Wee Gaskins who, while on death row, took an assassins' contract and killed the death row inmate in the cell next to his.[84]

The flip-side of this is that there is no need to address contributors to causal factors of crime such as poverty or social exclusion or other "root causes" of violent crime.

Clearly, because of media, the generosity of the federal government, and punishment advocates or strong conservatives, more tact units exist, producing a militarized police organization and culture. Considering what has happened around the country, those charges do not seem far-fetched. According to a CBS News survey of tact unit encounters, police use of deadly force has increased 34% between 1995 and 1998.[85]

Ideologically, the government's war on drugs with its rhetoric and actions associated with war dovetails with a thesis on the growth of paramilitary culture:[86]

> The 1980's saw the emergence of a highly energized culture of war and warrior. For all its varied manifestations, a few common features stood out. The New War culture was not so much military as paramilitary. The new warrior hero was only occasionally portrayed as a member of a conventional military or law enforcement unit; typically, he fought alone or with a small elite group of fellow warriors. Moreover, by separating the warrior from his traditional state-sanction occupation—policeman or soldier—the New War culture presented the warrior role as the ideal identity for all men. . . . To many people this new fascination with warriors and weapons seemed a terribly bad joke. The major newspapers and magazines that arbitrate what is to be taken seriously in American society scoffed at the attempts to resurrect the warrior hero. . . . But in dismissing Rambo so quickly and contemptuously, commentators failed to notice the true significance of the emerging paramilitary culture. They missed the fact that quite a few people were not writing Rambo off as a complete joke; behind the Indian bandanna, necklace, and bulging muscles, a new culture hero affirmed such traditional American values as self-reliance, honesty, courage, and concern for fellow citizens. Rambo was a worker and a former enlisted man, not a smooth-talking professional.[87]

In part, this notion of a paramilitary culture is tied to America's defeat in Vietnam and America's inability to resolve the wars in the Mideast, some argue.[88] In present thinking among segments of the population, America won its earlier wars because America was morally right—we deserved to win. But others say that the result of those wars produced a massive disjunction in American culture, a crisis of self-image. If Americans were no longer winners, then are they losers? It can be argued that a "regeneration through violence" associated with tactical units linked to the war on crime and the war on drugs, America can rebuild its self-respect.[89] As one tact officer says, "We gotta win the war on drugs or face total defeat at everything." The drug war has affected every component of the criminal system community, including the police, who turn to tact units to do the job street cops used to do.[90] It is fashionable for departments to win financial and moral support from various organizations including city hall. It is no coincidence that the police crackdown on drugs in economically deprived neighborhoods, with an increase in investigatory, no-knock drug raids, is conducted largely by tact units.[91] "Politically it works. Scare the people with bucks into believing that ghetto savages are about to invade their side of town, and those people will produce the legislation, funding, and hell, they'll even make the freggin uniforms for SWAT," says a divisional commander.[92]

"When taking on drugs, anything goes," one tact officer says. Does that include shooting to kill? "Only special ops (tact) units have that privilege," is heard. One primary difference between traditional law enforcement and tact units is that tact units can justify "shoot to kill" mandates. If you as a reader are frustrated at this point, imagine what typical police officers think every day on the job making decisions within tactical support or low-flying helicopter. Only a few are selected and there are two sides to the sword. The problem is that law enforcement officers just aren't warriors, just as warriors have a difficult time at performing police duties as evidenced by American troops in Iraq who do the best they can as police officers.

Cops are Not Warriors

The literature is consistent with the perspective that the primary activity of most law enforcement officers is from the social work model, which represents over 90% of an officer's daily work routine.[930] Evidence supporting this perceptive comes from many sources, however, the following may provide a reasonable guide:

- Noncrime routines
- Longitudinal analyses about domestic violence
- Traffic violators
- Police used or threatened force
- Columbine High School attack

Noncrime routines. New York City officers were asked about their experiences in handling noncrime incidents, and typically most of those officers were consistent in their descriptions[94]: 31% said they questioned individuals to elicit the nature of a crime, and the other three activities that took a great deal of their time included seeking the identity of relationships, asking citizens to explain themselves, and verbally trying to defuse potential altercations.

Longitudinal analyses about domestic violence. Researchers did not see this result as significant, but what they found in their longitudinal analyses suggests that police involvement has a strong deterrent effect upon domestic violence intrusions while the effect of arrest is small and statistically insignificant.[95] The implication of this finding is that social work is the centerpiece of officers who interact with domestic violence service calls and persuade aggressors to refrain from inappropriate behavior.

Traffic violators. In almost 17 million stopped drivers, police issued a ticket to 59%, conducted a search of some kind (a physical search of the driver and/or a search of the vehicle) of 5%, handcuffed almost 3%, arrested another 3%, used or threatened force against 1%, and used or threatened force that the driver deemed excessive against 1%.[96] Yet 84% of the drivers stopped by police reported that they had been stopped for a legitimate reason, and 88% of them felt police had behaved properly during the traffic stop.

Police used or threatened force. Of the 45.3 million residents age 16 or older who had contact with police in 2002, about 2% (664,500 persons) had contact whereby the officer used or threatened force against them, which generally amounted to a push or a grab. Also 19% (126,255) of the 664,500 (or less than .0027% of the total) reported force incidents involving police pointing a gun at the driver. Finally, about 87% of the 664,500 persons (or less than .012 of the total) who experienced the threat or use of force reported that the police acted improperly. One implication of these findings is that the performance of most police officers during face-to-face interaction with the public is meritorious, and equally important, their first option is to engage in conversation with an individual as opposed to any other option.

Columbine High School attack. One final piece of evidence that can help an understanding of tact units relates to the Columbine High School attack in 1999. Schools across the nation adopted violence prevention and response programs after the Columbine attack.[97] During the crisis at Columbine, after officers arrived, they waited for appropriately 40 minutes before entering the facility. Critics said that that decision might have contributed to the death of teacher Dave Sanders, who bled to death from gunshot wounds. Nonetheless, "Police were trained under a doctrine that had patrol officers wait until SWAT teams could be assembled to enter shooting scenes."[98]

During an officer's shift, it appears that a social work model takes precedence in police performance whether that performance includes noncrime routines, domestic violence altercations, traffic violations, face-to-face encounters, or protecting a school.

Talking through altercations is obviously an officer's first option when confronted with public intervention. As a matter of information, 90% of 45 million persons who had contact with a law enforcement officer felt the officer(s) acted properly.[99] One question that arises after reviewing the above evidence is why police trainers instruct law enforcement officers in the "art of war" when 90% of police work is social service work.[100] One answer comes from a Boston cop who says, "We're at war. Cops must be trained to deal with the freggen element."[101] It is doubtful that Boston is one of the few cities where officers think of their jobs as being at war. The above statistics take issue with the perspective that most cops think that we're at war.

Some observers see the militarization of law enforcement in America as a disturbing development. "Police officers are not supposed to be warriors. The job of a police officer is to keep the peace while adhering to constitutional procedures."[102] The point of this chapter should not have passed you by. That is, law enforcement personnel know exactly what their job is and how they are supposed to go about it. Knowing what your job is and not doing it is a major stressor for most employees regardless of their occupation. In this regard, for example, it is an easy progression to realize that police stress levels are affected by these military strategies largely because many officers have other ideals about their jobs. Most cops know that violence leads to more violence and their first choice is never the use of force.

What Officers Like about Their Job and Police Models. What many officers like about their job is that most of their experiences can be characterized as associated with social work perspectives, as revealed in the above section. Most officers would never use the term "social work," but when they describe what they like best about their job, it sounds like a social worker model. After reviewing many responses among police officers, a typical description resembles Boston officer Mila De Pina's conversation. When Officer De Pina was asked what she liked best and least about her job, she reported she liked "walking" her beat.[103] The merchants all waved at her and she enjoyed speaking with them. What does Officer De Pina like least? When she saw her first homicide victim while on patrol. She found a gunshot victim sitting in his car with his family at his side. She attended to the victim, called EMS, and called her supervisor. Officer De Pina made sure that the victim's children had a safe environment while waiting for their father's results. Officer De Pina drove them to the hospital. One impression is that De Pina could be a great warrior if she wanted, but she sounds like most officers who go out of their way to help others.

This thought is congruent with the 63% of the 558 officers surveyed for this work who reported that even "fresh and continued pursuit" of suspects is not the most important part of their job and that SWAT training is less important than health issues including stress training, community policing training, and advanced traffic crash investigation.

Also, a review of the above evidence implies that law enforcement officers are not necessarily warriors in the military sense of the word. It certainly is apparent that many police officers see a *crimefighter model* as related to the paramilitary model as the most appropriate model of police response, and order maintenance calls are seen as "bullshit calls."[104] Crime prophylactic, police knowledge, social work, and community cooperation models were also described.

Of course, one practical way to perform when policy demands a *crime prophylactic model* (police intervention can defuse potentially violent situations and prevent them from escalating) might relate better to a military police response.[105] The *police knowledge model* holds that noncrime calls give officers broader exposure to the community with the results that they have more knowledge that will help them solve crimes. The *social work model* holds that the latent coercive power of the police can help to steer potential lawbreakers into law-abiding behavior. And the *community cooperation model* holds that effective response to noncrime calls can help the police establish greater credibility with the public.[106] Officers like the social worker model in parts of their job more than the tactical perspectives, but they don't like to call it that. And finally, we are ready to examine paramilitary model stressors.

PARAMILITARY MODEL STRESSORS

To better understand the nature of paramilitary models as stressors, what officers think about tact units might prove helpful in a final analysis. Paramilitary model stressors seem to further a *police-blind* about law enforcement officer conduct, which produces a paradoxical quandary for many street cops. Part of that quandary includes the selection process into tact units, the rejection of tact unit participation, and violence as the first option; team use of violence reduces discretion and diminishes self-respect, and tact units produce overreactions to violence and loss of public trust.

What Some Officers Think about Tact Units. Law enforcement officers realize far too well that the war on crime is a "scam," politically powered and reinforced by the media because after all, they are the "troops" engaged in the "war" and although their shifts can be challenging, their experiences are for the most part routine and devoid of "action-packed drama."

The criticism of tact models showed that the philosophy or belief systems held by constituents and policymakers toward tact units is positive despite reservations of its use (that is, if those units are used as ghetto blasters, then it's okay). This thought is confirmed when Fresno's tact unit was revisited. It was disbanded because of the complaints against its activities only to be redeployed under a new regime with federal support donning a new label, supported through federal funds, training, weapons, and personnel to help it work better.

Police-Blind

The average law enforcement officer is caught in an impasse between demands by the powerless for a more equal share of the wealth and power and the powerful who want to keep what they have.[107] To resolve this obvious inequity, many law enforcement officers employ police-officers who are blind to the many horrors of their jobs, which includes injustices through tact unit abuse and from abuses of people to themselves and to their loved ones. Sgt. Stephanie Redding of the New Haven Police Department describes some observations about this police blindness: "It would be ridiculous to try to act like you don't have any feelings, especially when you see horrible things."[108]

If an officer is proficient at being police-blind, the officer can practice crime control and bust heads when deployed in tact units when dealing with the poor, but observe due process when dealing with the privileged.[109] The literature implies that many officers practice their craft in exactly that manner, or what this chapter is calling police-blind behavior. Officers know what they are doing, they just don't see it.

There are other behavioral patterns that characterize police-blind behavior. For instance, it could be that the differences between political perspectives and police experiences represent a major stressor for most street cops; in fact, it could be such a dividing point between top command (for implementing policy mandates) and police officers that one way to cope with this contradiction is "in a cop bar slamming down brews chased with several shots of JD," responds one Chicago officer.[110] "Is there another way to deal with this situation?" the interviewer asked. "Yeah, Early Times instead of Jack Daniels will do it," the officer added.

One explanation is that an individual's impression or misrepresentation of reality is rarely a concern, but when that impression shapes policy and ultimately police practice, compliance to an impression can be an excruciating experience. Think of it this way: apprehending and processing criminals who do not really exist can have its downside. For instance, if a supervisor during a compstat meeting lays out the profile of "an armed boogie man who trades in bodies and drugs" appeared in front of a specific apartment building at a specific time. A "suspect" fitting the profile stands at the exact time while an officer drives past the exact apartment building: does the officer make an arrest, call for backup, ignore it, or call the supervisor who will assuredly will call out SWAT? This police blindness does not mean police performance is invisible to the officers all the time because it helps foster a paradoxical quandary or a catch-22.

Paradoxical Quandary. It seems that a paradox or contradiction exists since police (like all members of the criminal justice community) hold a public safety obligation toward constituents but often employ police blindness to shield them from their actions (as described above). Factually, it is more than an obligation, it is the law and it is the same law that provides law enforcement with their enforcement powers—in a sense, law enforcement is a privilege. Nonetheless, one of the greatest obligations of those who provide public safety is as guardians of the U.S. Constitution—defenders of human rights associated with due process. Despite the recent rhetorical turn toward democratic police reforms and practice, the paramilitary model takes exception to human rights.[111] It promotes the rights of "legalized violence," and coupled with the war on terrorism, it now has an enormous partnership that allows local agencies to associate with other local and federal agencies. Some officers accept the contradiction and believe that federal training and weapons mean they were "knighted," while others see community relations strategies as ploys to lure citizens into meetings so that they can be better controlled.

Akin to this contradiction, it justifies and validates paramilitary performance regardless of outcomes. One assumption police high command holds is that most officers agree with the paramilitary model to control crime. The question should be do law enforcement officers actually agree with high command? One answer comes from the results of the study conducted for this book. Of the 558 officers surveyed, over 71% of them reported that top command always or very often are a source of stress for them. Sixty percent said the integrity of most commanders was nonexistent. It might be easy to understand why commanders get the idea that their subordinates agree with them because most officers, at least the ones in this study, provide lip service and go about their business but practice their profession through police blindness. It might follow that locking officers into a cogent battle-ready force is not what most officers had in mind about their jobs. Setting aside your thoughts about tact units and the fear and pain some individuals encounter when confronted by tact units, another question arises about the fear and pain of some officers. Of course, many officers are faced with the realities of the contradiction between high command and integrity and their own police-blind, yet there are other factors that push the buttons of their stress such as in the officer selection process associated with tact units.

Selection Process into Tact Units

A rotation by street cops onto paramilitary units is often seen as a reward.[112] Not all cops are chosen and not all officers want to participate. Not being chosen might have to do with the experiences of the officer, the terms of a union contract, prejudice, networking, or because of some rivalry. On the other hand, some law enforcement officers have little interest in participating in tact units because that might removed the mask of their police blindness. Officers who wanted to be invited into the tact unit but were not asked might develop feelings of frustration and alienation. Of course, what do members of the tact unit think when a qualified person is past over on the selection process or the members do not trust the newest candidates?

Rejection of Tact Unit Participation. From the officers' viewpoint, both no invitation or their own rejection to become a member of a tact unit have implications. Tact unit participation would mean more training, more periods away from home, and trading in your current partner or duty backups even though an officer might continue to be on regular assignment. There are feelings of camaraderie before, during, and after work but joining a tact unit could mean an enhanced camaraderie, and provide a feeling of belonging. For other officers, working whenever called could be problematic—birthdays, children's birthdays, and hanging on to those season tickets would be out of the question. Then, too, most often, officers given an opportunity to partici-pant in these paramilitary units are current army and marine national guard participants and veterans, especially those with recent combat experiences.[113]

Whether an officer was ignored during the selection process or rejected an invitation, there are consequences from the other officers. For instance, an officer says, "I remember when the commander told my sergeant that he wanted me to participate with the first response team [tact unit].[114] I told him no. The whole shift, the guys were down my throat about it. As if that wasn't bad enough, that shit lasted the month. They called me everything from candy ass to yellow shit chicken." Another law enforcement officer who also turned down a tact unit says, "When I went up for sergeant [promotion], the captain from the training squad reminded me that I made a bad choice a few years back [by turning down a tact unit] and that he wasn't giving me a rec-ommendation because the troops would see me as weak. They ain't going to follow you into battle, son."[115]

Violence as the First Option. Individual members of a tact unit require a great deal of training and "privilege," which typical street cops do not neces-sarily receive. Police tact units can be distinguished from what one observer calls "cop-on-the-beat policing,"[116] simply by their appearance, heavy weaponry, training, and status. It could be argued that since the use of force is validated, legal, and expected among street cops in general, often this "legiti-mate" specialized status of tact officers might be seen as an "elite" unit sup-ported by high command and policymakers.[117] How much stress might this put on street cops who are not involved in this elite unit can only be guessed, but a good guess is that it is a source of stress even among those officers who rejected the invitation. Promotions are tied to elite service as might extra duty (street cops are not generally at the top of the salary pyramid) within the de-partment and security work outside the department. Also, one count shows approximately 18 paramilitary officers for every 100 regular patrol officers and this count includes small departments as well as others.[118]

Continuing along this line of reasoning, a tact unit must have at the forefront of their function to threaten or use force collectively, and most offi-cers disagree with the mandate that violence is their last option.[119]

Team Use of Violence Reduces Discretion. Tact units are deployed to deal with altercations that require team use of force. That is, they operate as a re-active unit. One implication from these findings is that officers cannot engage in discretion or independent process to reduce danger, they are obligated to force issued upon command. One problem that individuals are unlikely to learn from their tact experiences is that they underestimate the central values of the initiative.[120] Officers who engage in a tact unit for career considera-tions but see the tact initiative as inappropriate might not learn that protect-ing human rights is the primary objective of policing and as those officers enhance their careers through promotions and become top commanders who see the frequency and intensity of tact units as beneficial and necessary to maintain social order.

Also, what action can be experienced by officers who disagree with a "silent" shoot to kill order (since police officers do not hold that mandate)? One divisional commander says that those officers would be "weeded out" early in the training process.[121] Yet the question suppose the particular altercation has other dynamics unseen by the commanding officer was asked. The reply was, "The officer who hesitates can be up on negligence charges and even dismissal from the department." It would seem that not every office is going to agree with command at any level especially if a field commander has an agenda other than public safety. Should an officer follow orders under conditions that clearly a reasonable officer would not perform, it could seem that a great amount of stress will be experienced by that officer, his family members, and his friends. The point is that tact unit response to serve and protect sees their goals met through combat, but in a community protected by a Constitution, in what way can combat resolve the issues of law and order? In what way has crime been reduced or neutralized through the use of a tact unit (or any police strategy for that matter)?

Tact Units Diminish Self-Respect. The more an officer is caught up in the police-blind, the more the officer attempts to cope with paradoxical quandaries of tact units, the more some officers get drunk. In one sense, we are "round robin" here. That is, alcoholics tend to demonstrate characteristics representative of individuals with low self-respect, and the more experiences they have as a drunk, the more salient or observable become the other behavioral patterns of alcoholics such as habitually lying, incoordination, impairment in attention or memory, and a loathing for the welfare of others.[122]

Tact Units Produce Overreactions. Tact units can cause tact officers to overreact and treat ordinary policing situations as military operations.[123] "The fundamental problem with the SWAT model is that if police become soldiers, the community becomes the enemy," says Tony Platt, one of the first scholars to analyze the rise of tactical policing.[124] Paramilitary policing erodes the idea of police as pubic servants subordinate to community needs. For example, Los Angeles SWAT was called out to deal with a single weapons incident.[125] There were three exchanges of gunfire between SWAT and Jose Lemos. In the final exchange, Lemos held his 17-month-old daughter as though she were a shield as he fired on the SWAT unit who returned fire, killing both the toddler and her father. The return fire consisted of an estimated 300 rounds from SWAT officers. Could there have been another procedure for those SWAT officers to follow?[126] What does the public think about tact units?

Tact Units Create a Loss of Public Trust. One of the greatest costs of militarization of local law enforcement, implies Joseph McNamara, a research fellow in the Hoover Institution at Stanford University and a former chief of police in San Jose and Kansas City, has been in the loss of public trust in police institutions, the increase of stress among patrol officers, and the alienation of communities from police resources.[127] This idea of a loss of public trust is already a known quality among officers, especially the officers surveyed for this book. That is, of the 558 officers polled, 7 out of every 10 reported that public distrust among officers is a constant source of stress for them. Feelings of distrust would work on an officer's self-image and there is little question that for some cops, this low opinion of themselves would affect their performance in the field. In what way can tact units enhance public trust? One answer comes from the nature of tact units themselves. That is, tact units treat policing as war, and that is what makes them fundamentally dangerous. If police are soldiers instead of civil servants, and their task is destruction and conquest, then it follows that the civilian community will be the enemy. Therefore, it could be said that a tact unit might have a difficult time in winning public trust even if one community sees the advantage in a tact attack. In part, that attack is not necessarily on their community but another community and usually one that is lower in social status than theirs.

All in all, it appears that tact model stressors promote police blindness about their conduct, which produces a paradoxical quandary for many officers and part of that quandary includes the selection process into tact units, the rejection of tact unit participation, shows that violence is the first option of tact units, that team use of violence reduces discretion and diminishes self-respect among officers, and finally, tact units produce overreactions to violence and loss of public trust. Upon reading this chapter it becomes clear that despite the gains for tact units, their role should be minimized in the scheme of police performance and called out as a last resort because they are giant stressors among most officers and have less to do with crime control than other initiatives.

In the final analysis, the vast majority of law enforcement agencies continue to be coerced into waging war against crime and drugs by politicians who ignore history and mislead the public into believing such wars are definitive and winnable through police initiatives such as zero tolerance especially operated by tactical units.[128] Consequently, hundreds of thousands of illegal police searches take place and are lied about in court while drug war hawks pontificate about the immorality of people filling their bloodstream with various types of evil chemicals.

SUMMARY

Paramilitary models of policing relates to two perspectives: one deals with the American military performing police duties, and the other relates to local police utilizing paramilitary strategies to conduct police duties. This chapter is about the latter. Traditional police strategies are prioritizing initiatives toward a "war on crime" through a *paramilitary command and control model*, which was described as law enforcement using the equipment, training, rhetoric, and group tactics of war, which includes a hierarchal chain of command to deliver police services. It was reported that America is winning that war through punitive actions, which includes incarceration for many violators. The Posse Comitatus Act of 1878 was offered as one reason why the American military is prohibited from local police efforts. Some of the interchangeable terms of paramilitary models are tactical units, tact units, SWAT, and first-responders. Tactical units were originally developed by an LAPD commander named Daryl Gates in 1966 and called *SWAT* (special weapons and tactics) units, which were conceived as an urban counterinsurgency bulwark.

The idea behind tact units is their officers are trained to be super warriors and those units were called upon to handle the occasional barricaded or hostage-taker suspects. Now tact units conduct routine drug raids and incidents involving a weapon. Police units have been altered to resemble military units, which includes training, uniforms, weapons, hierarchy of command, deployment, treating civilians as the enemy, and discipline to follow orders without question. The federal government encourages tact units and provides weapons, training, personnel, and funding to local police organizations.

Some of the key differences between the police and military are the populations under their jurisdiction. Police further public safety in a free society. The military is deployed to destroy and control targeted populations. Police are designed to help people, and are constrained by laws protecting the rights of individuals first. The military's first mission is the mission itself. Use of deadly force tends to be their first response and for cops, use of deadly force is their last response. Street cops routinely exercise individual discretion to serve the mission of pubic safety. Military personnel are trained and expected to operate as members of a military unit.

The characteristics of the paramilitary police organization include, among others, a centralized command structure with a highly adhered-to chain of command; a rigid superior–subordinate relationship defined by prerogatives of rank; and a control exerted through the issuance of commands, directives, or general orders.

Police tact units can provide safe resolutions to dangerous encounters more so than alternative methods and it makes sense to be prepared for high-volatile situations. However, residents who lived in cities where tact units were active reported that they lacked confidence in the success of tact units. Maybe it depends on who you ask because tact units treat civilians as though they were the enemy, so any targeted neighborhood member might see tact units as an occupational army.

Criticism of paramilitary models relates to its philosophy, the notion that tact officers are warriors despite the evidence that most of what officers do relates to a social work model, a perspective described by many officers as their performance preference. It was noted that many see a crimefighter model as the most appropriate model of police response, and order maintenance calls were seen as "bullshit calls." Crime prophylactic, police knowledge, social work, and community cooperation models were also described.

Because many officers see tact units as scams and politically positioned, many see paramilitary models as stressors. Officers employ a police-blind to manage the horrors of their jobs, which includes injustices through tact unit abuse and from abuses of people to themselves and to their loved ones. One practical way to describe police-blind behavior is for an officer to practice crime control and to fight hard when on tact unit deployment when dealing with the poor, but to observe due process when dealing with the privileged. Officers are faced with the destructive nature of their jobs, which was described as a paradoxical quandary since the greatest obligation of those who provide public safety is as guardians of the U.S. Constitution—defenders of human rights associated with due process. Despite the recent rhetorical turn toward democratic police reforms and practice, the paramilitary model takes exception to human rights. Then, too, other stressors of tact units included the selection process into tact units, rejection of tact unit participation, violence as first options, team use of violence reduces discretion, tact units diminish self-respect, tact units produce overreactions, and tact units create a loss of public trust.

WHAT WOULD YOU DO IF YOU WERE IN CHARGE?

The Houston Police Department has a crime laboratory whereby rulings in cases still working their way through the courts suggest that the death sentences of at least three Texas inmates could have been based on faulty work by HPD's ballistics division in the fall of 2005.[129] The latest decision granted a new trial for one inmate citing "serious questions" about the accuracy of HPD analysts' work. Other judicial rulings also have prompted concerns about other cases. The police department is expected to hire a special investigator to review the work of all divisions of its crime lab. However, one Houston lawyer representing inmates says ballistics cases should also receive special scrutiny—like the DNA lab, where the discovery of poor working conditions and shoddy science forced the retesting of evidence in almost 400 cases. What would you do to aid the officers who processed the investigations of these cases and made the arrests?

OFFICER KILLED IN WASHINGTON, DC

At approximately 3:37 P.M. on Saturday, May 14, 2005, 59-year-old Reserve Officer Joseph Pozell was directing traffic at Wisconsin Avenue and M Street, in Washington, DC. A Honda CR-V, operated by 19-year-old Julia R. Matthews, of McLean, Virginia, was starting out from a green light going north on Wisconsin Avenue and turning left onto M Street headed west. It was at this time that the SUV collided with Reserve Officer Pozell.[130] Reserve Officer Pozell, a 9-year veteran volunteer of the Metropolitan Police Department, 6 years with the Police Auxiliary Service, and 3 years as a Reserve Officer, was taken to the George Washington University Hospital and admitted in critical condition. At approximately 9:47 P.M. on Tuesday, May 17, 2005, Reserve Officer Pozell succumbed to his injuries and was pronounced dead. The investigation conducted by members of the department's Major Crash Investigations Unit indicates that Pozell, while directing traffic, apparently stepped back into the path of the oncoming vehicle. The facts of the case were presented to the Office of the United States Attorney, and no charges will be placed against the driver of the Honda.

DISCUSSION QUESTIONS

1. Define and describe the effectiveness of the paramilitary model of policing.
2. Articulate how the war on crime is linked to the paramilitary model of policing.
3. Characterize the development and components of the Posse Comitatus Act of 1878.
4. Describe the contemporary debate surrounding the Posse Comitatus Act and the role it plays in contemporary policing issues linked to the war on crime.
5. Provide the rationale for the paramilitary model of policing.
6. Explain what the federal government does to encourage tact units and comment on why the federal government engages in this type of encouragement. What do they gain?
7. Provide a detailed comparison between the police and the military and highlight the primary difference between the two.
8. Identify the characteristics of a paramilitary police organization. Which factor plays the leading role in this type of an organization? The less role?
9. Explain the public response to tact units. In what way are those responses justified?
10. Articulate the primary criticism of paramilitary models. Provide examples.
11. Describe the ways the paramilitary model of policing acts as a stressor.
12. Describe what is meant by police-blind and provide some behavioral examples produced by this pneumonia. What other professions include personnel who might use a "blind" to perform an undesired policy?
13. Explain the dynamics of the paradoxical quandary that influences officer stress levels. Use an example.
14. Identify some of the other stressors of paramilitary policing models. Provide examples when appropriate.

ENDNOTES

1. Christian Parenti (1999). *Lockdown America: Police and prison in the age of crisis*. NY: Verso. p. 111. Parts of his book available on line retrieved online June 7, 2004: http//www.thirdworldtraveler.com/Prison_System/War_All_Seasons_LA.html

2. The actual definition of *paramilitary* is "a group of civilians organized in a military fashion (especially to operate in place of or to assist regular army troops)." Dictionary.com. Since the police are civilians as opposed to being military, I refer to this model as a paramilitary model.

3. Jonathan Simon (1999). Paramilitary features of contemporary penalty. *Journal of Political and Military Sociology*. Retrieved online July 5, 2005: http//www.findarticles.com/p/articles/mi_qa3719/is_199901/ai_n8834565

4. See *Bissonette v. Haig*, 800 F.2d 812 (8th Cir. 1986) (furnishing equipment and advice did not violate PCA, but roadblocks and armed patrols do, because they are regulatory, proscriptive, and compulsory).

5. "INS Signs Memorandum of Agreement with Department of Defense, National Guard Troops to Assist INS at Northern and Southern Borders," U.S. Department of Justice, Immigration and Naturalization Service, press release, February 25, 2002, www.immigration.gov/graphics/publicaffairs/newsrels/nguard.htm

6. Although the troops were removed after 6 months, the pressure for militarization has not abated. Politicians like Rep. Tom Tancredo (R-CO) and Sen. Trent Lott (R-MS) and conservative pundits like Bill O'Reilly and Michelle Malkin have called for armed soldiers to enforce U.S. immigration law. In her new book, *Invasion*, Malkin writes that "at the northern border with Canada . . . every rubber orange cone and measly 'No Entry' sign should immediately be replaced with an armed National Guardsman." Malkin suggests that something in the neighborhood of 100,000 troops would be appropriate. See Michelle Malkin (2002). *Invasion: How America still welcomes terrorists, criminals, and other foreign menaces to our shores*. Washington: Regnery. p. 233. See also Bill O'Reilly (2003, February 7). Porous U.S. borders. *FoxNews.com*. www.foxnews.com/story/0,2993,77898,00.ht

7. Caroline Alexander (2005, July 7). Al-Qaeda claims responsibility for London attacks on internet. Bloomberg.com Retrieved online July 7, 2005: http://www.bloomberg.com/apps/news?pid=10000085&sid=aTmt3j5vkwHw&refer=europe

8. Dennis J. Stevens (1999). American police resolutions and community response. *The Police Journal*, 140–151. Also see Dennis J. Stevens (1999). Police tactical units and community response. *Law and Order*, 48–52.

9. Thomas O'Connor (2003). *War on crime*. Retrieved online July 6, 2005: http://faculty.ncwc.edu/toconnor/111/111lect15.htm

10. Department of Homeland Security Press Release (2006, March). ICE Arrests 375 Gang Members and Associates in Two-Week Enforcement Action. Retrieved online March 11, 2006: http://www.dhs.gov/dhspublic/interapp/press_release/press_release_0878.xml

11. Peter Cassidy (1997). Operation Ghetto Storm: The rise in paramilitary policing. *Covert Action Quarterly*, 62.

12. E. Luttwak and S. Koehl (1991). *The Dictionary of Modern War*. New York: Gramercy Books.

13. Willard M. Oliver (2003). *The Law & Order Presidency*. Upper Saddle River, NJ: Prentice Hall.

14. Thomas O'Connor (2003).

15. Loretta Nall (2005). Thugs, assassins and zealots. Retrieved online March 27, 2006: http://www.americandrugwar.com/

16. Tom Jackman (2006, March 24). No charges in shooting of unarmed man. *Washington Post.* Retrieved online March 27, 2006: http://www.washingtonpost.com

17. Tom Jackman (2006, March 24).

18. Gene Healy (2003). Deployed in the U.S.A.: Creeping militarization of the home front. *Policy Analysis,* 503. Retrieved Online July 15, 2004: http://www.cato.org/pubs/pas/pa503.pdf

19. Frank Morales (2000, May). City financing a "School of the Americas" in the Bronx. Retrieved online March 27, 2006: http://www.covertaction.org/content/view/60/75/

20. Frank Morales (2000, May).

21. On the history of "war" on crime, see Samuel Walker (1989). *Popular Justice: A History of American Criminal Justice,* 2nd ed. New York: Oxford University Press.

22. Tony Platt (2003, October). The state of welfare: U.S. 2003. *Monthly Review.* Retrieved online July 8, 2005: http://www.monthlyreview.org/1003platt.htm

23. Randall G. Shelden (2001). *Controlling the dangerous classes: A critical introduction to the history of criminal justice.* Boston: Allyn & Bacon. pp. 16–20.

24. Tony Platt (2003, October).

25. Dave Oehl (2000, February). The American criminalization of poverty. *Peace Work.* Retrieved online July 8, 2005: http://www.afsc.org/pwork/0200/0208.htm

26. Bureau of Justice Statistics (2005). *Crime characteristics.* Washington, DC: U.S. Department of Justice. Office of Justice Programs. Retrieved online July 12, 2005: http://www.ojp.usdoj.gov/bjs/cvict_c.htm

27. Bureau of Justice Statistics (2004). *Sourcebook of criminal statistics 2003.* Table 6.22. Albany, NY: U.S. Department of Justice. Office of Justice Programs. Retrieved online July 12, 2005: http://www.albany.edu/sourcebook/pdf/t622.pdf

28. In 1990. See Samuel Walker. (2001). *Sense and nonsense about crime and drugs.* Belmont, CA: Wadsworth. p. 11.

29. Police compared to military. Wikipedia, the free encyclopedia. Retrieved online February 19, 2005: http://en.wikipedia.org/wiki/Police#Police_compared_to_military

30. Gene Stephens (1995). Rethinking the war on crime. Retrieved online March 18, 2006: http://www.scpronet.com/point/9508/s07.html

31. Christian Parenti (1999). *Lockdown America: Police and prisons in the age of crisis.* New York: Verso.

32. Jim Casey (2006, March). SWAT. Retrieved online March 11, 2006: http://www.policeguide.com/Contact_Policeguide_com/contact_policeguide_com.html

33. Samuel Walker (2001). *Sense and Nonsense about crime and drugs.* Belmont, CA: Wadsworth. p. 8. Elliott Currie (1999). Reflections on crime and criminology at the millenium. *Western Criminology Review* 2(1). Retrieved Online June 6, 2004: http://wcr.sonoma.edu/v2n1/currie.html

34. Peter Kraska and Victor Kappeler (1997). Militarizing American police: The rise and normalization of paramilitary units. *Social Problems,* 44(1), 101–117.

35. Peter Cassidy (1997). Operation Ghetto Storm: The rise in paramilitary policing. *Covert Action Quarterly,* 62.

36. Peter Kraska and Victor Kappeler (1997). Militarizing American police: The rise and normalization of paramilitary units. *Social Problems,* 44(1).

37. Professor Tim Bakken. Westpoint. US Army. Personal communication with author. July 15, 2004.

38. Peter Cassidy (1997).

39. Peter Kraska and Victor Kappeler (1997).

40. Gene Healy (2003). Deployed in the U.S.A.: Creeping militarization of the home front. *Policy Analysis,* 503. Retrieved Online July 15, 2004: http://www.cato.org/pubs/pas/pa503.pdf

41. Peter Kraska and Victor Kappeler (1997). Also see Peter B. Kraska (1996). Enjoying militarism: Political/personal dilemmas in studying U.S. paramilitary units. *Justice Quarterly,* 13(3), 405–429.

42. Egon Bittner (1999). The quasi-military organization of the police. In Victor E. Kappeler (Ed.), *The police and society,* 2nd *ed.* (pp. 170–180). Prospect Heights, IL: Waveland Press.

43. David B. Kopel and Paul M. Blackman (1997). Can soldiers be peace officers? The Waco disaster and the Militarization of American law enforcement. *Akron Law Review,* 30, *619–659.* Retrieved Online July 14, 2004: http://www.davekopel.com/Waco/LawRev/CanSoldiersBePeaceOfficers.htm#h6

44. See Samuel Walker (1999) for more details. *The police in America: An introduction.* Boston: McGraw-Hill College. pp. 355–361. Also it could be argued that local police agencies were originally formed, due in part to counter the possibility of military intervention at local levels.

45. Police compared to military. Wikipedia, the free encyclopedia. Retrieved Online June 18, 2004: http://en.wikipedia.org/wiki/Police#Police_compared_to_military

46. Dennis J. Stevens (1999). Police tactical units and community response. *Law and Order,* 48–52. Also see Dennis J. Stevens. (1999). American police resolutions and community response. *The Police Journal,* 140–151.

47. Egon Bittner (1999). The quasi-military organization of the police. In Victor E. Kappeler (Ed.), *The police and society,* 2nd *ed.* (pp. 170–180). Prospect Heights, IL: Waveland Press.

48. Bureau of Justice Statistics (2005). Use of deadly force. Data for 1999, the last year for which complete data from participating agencies is available, shows that police used force at a rate of 3.61 times per 10,000 calls-for-service. This translates to a rate of use of force of 0.0361%. Expressed another way, police did not use force 99.9639% of the time.

49. Quoted in Douglas Holt (1997, June 4). DA questions military account of border slaying; drug unit. Spokeswoman calls remarks surprising. *Dallas Morning News.* p. 1A.

50. Dennis J. Stevens (2007). *Police officer stress and organizational strategies that cause stress.* Upper Saddle River, NJ: Prentice Hall.

51. Los Angeles Police Department. Retrieved Online July 4, 2004: http://www.lapdonline.org/

52. John P. Crank (2004). *Understanding police culture.* Cincinnati, OH: Anderson. p. 27.

53. Professor Tim Bakken (2004).

54. James H. Auten (1985). The paramilitary model of police and police professionalism. In A. Blumberg and E. Niederhoffer (Eds.) *The Ambivalent Force,* 3rd ed. (pp. 122–132). New York: Holt, Rinehart and Winston.

55. Richard D. Heffner (1956). *Democracy in America: Alexis de Tocqueville.* New York: Mentor Books. p. 310.

56. Dennis J. Stevens (1999a, March). Police tactical units and community response. *Law and Order,* 47(3), 48–52.

57. Dennis J. Stevens (1999a, March). Also see Dennis J. Stevens (1999b). American police resolutions. *Police Journal,* LXXII(2), 140–150.

58. Gallup Survey Online. Threats. Retrieved June 8, 2004: http://www.gallup .com/content/login.aspx?ci=10894

59. Gallup Survey Online. Retrieved June 8, 2004: http://www.gallup.com/

60. John P. Crank (2004). *Understanding police culture.* Cincinnati, OH: Anderson. p. 113.

61. John Anglell. (1971). Toward an alternative to the classic police organizational arrangements: a democratic model. *Criminology,* 9, 185–206.

62. Dennis J. Stevens (1999a, March). Dennis J. Stevens (1999b).

63. There exists evidence that this is already the case. Sam Howe Verhovek (1997, June 29). In Marine's killing of teen-ager, town mourns and wonders why. *New York Times.* p. A1. Retrieved online February 21, 2005: http://www.dpft.org/ hernandez/nyt_062997.html Also see William Branigin. (1997, June 22). Questions on military role fighting drugs ricochet from a deadly shot. *Washington Post,* p. A3.

64. Peter Cassidy (1997). The rise in paramilitary policing. *Covert Action Quarterly,* 62. Retrieved online February 19, 2005: http://www.copi.com/articles/gstorm.html

65. Personal experience of the writer and most of my colleagues will easily confirm the notion that privileged students have difficulty in understanding the concept of a police occupational army. When those students begin to understand it, my experience suggests that those students see it as if it were a game or something "ghettoized" and therefore, cool. Yet, students who have experienced an occupational army understand the consequences of such inappropriate and illegal police action.

66. Christian Parenti (1999). *Lockdown America: Police and prison in the age of crisis.* New York: Verso. p. 111. Parts of his book available online retrieved June 7, 2004: http://www.thirdworldtraveler.com/Prison_System/War_All_Seasons_LA .html

67. William Booth (1997). Exploding number of SWAT teams sets off alarms. *Washington Post.* Retrieved online July 9, 2005: http://www.duke.edu/~bub/ booth.htm

68. Doug Hoagland (2001, March 25). Shattered lives. *The Fresno Bee.* Retrieved online July 9, 2005: http://www.lawandpsychiatry.com/html/shattered%20lives.htm

69. Joseph McNamara (1995). Cops against the drug war. Retrieved online July 9, 2005: http://www.drcnet.org/cops/responses.html

70. Mark Blumberg (1994). Police use of deadly force: Exploring some key issues. In Thomas Barker and David L. Carter (Eds.), *Police deviance,* 3rd ed. (pp. 201–223). Cincinnati, OH: Anderson.

71. Peter Kraska and Victor Kappeler (1997).

72. Peter Cassidy (1997). The rise in paramilitary policing. *Covert Action Quarterly,* 62. Retrieved online February 19, 2005: http://www.copi.com/articles/gstorm.html

73. Gene Healy (2003). Deployed in the U.S.A.: Creeping militarization of the home front. *Policy Analysis,* 503. Retrieved Online July 15, 2004: http://www .cato.org/pubs/pas/pa503.pdf

74. Associated Press. "NAACP President Calls for Civilian Review in Hostage Shooting," October 16, 1992.

75. Fresno Police Department. Retrieved online July 9, 2005: http://www.fresno .gov/fpd/fpd_vision_mission.asp

76. George Hostetter (2001, April). Fresno disbands cop unit. *The Fresno Bee.* Retrieved online July 9, 2005: http://www.fresnobee.com/local/story/ 1276280p-1344823c.html

77. *The Fresno Bee* (2002, August 22). Time to bring back Fresno's violent crime unit. Archives of the Fresno Bee.

78. Know gangs (2005, March). *Fresno gets aid in battle with gangs.* Retrieved July 9, 2005: http://knowgangs.com/gangs_news/extra/March/march_2005_007.htm

79. Personal confidential communication with Fresno police officer, July 15, 2005.

80. Gene Healy (2003). Deployed in the U.S.A.: Creeping militarization of the home front. *Policy Analysis,* 503. Retrieved online July 15, 2004: http://www.cato .org/pubs/pas/pa503.pdf

81. Elliott Currie (1998). *Crime and punishment in America.* New York: Metropolitan Books. p. 1.

82. William J. Bratton (1998). *Turnaround: How America's Top Cop Reversed the Crime Epidemic.* New York: Random House. George L. Kelling (1995). How to run a police department. *City Journal,* 5(4). Retrieved online July 12, 2005:http:// www.city-journal.org/html/5_4_how_to_run.html. George L. Kelling and William H. Sousa, Jr., (2001). *Do police matter? An analysis of the impact of New York City's police reforms,* civic report. New York: Manhattan Institute. p. 9. And James Q. Wilson (1975). *Thinking about crime.* New York: Basic Books. p. 209.

83. Elliott Currie (1998).

84. Seamus McGraw (2004). *Donald Gaskins and Wilton Earle. The autobiography of a serial killer: The final truth.* Retrieved online July 10, 2005: http://www .crimelibrary.com/about/authors/mcgraw/

85. ITVS News (NA). *Paramilitary policing.* Retrieved online July 10, 2005: ihttp://www.itvs.org/NewCopOnTheBeat/paramilitary.html

86. J. W. Gibson (1994). *Warrior dreams: Manhood in post-Vietnam America.* New York: Hill & Wang.

87. J. W. Gibson (1994). pp. 6–10.

88. Richard Slotkin (2000). *Regeneration through violence: The mythology of the American frontier 1600-1860.* OK: University of Oklahoma Press. Also see Endthewar (2006, March). EPIC. Retrieved online March 12, 2006: http://www.epic-usa .org/Default.aspx?tabid=1257

89. Richard Slotkin (2000). *Regeneration through violence: The mythology of the American frontier 1600–1860.* Norman: University of Oklahoma Press.

90. John Irwin and James Austin (1997). *It's about time: America's imprisonment binge.* Belmont, CA: Wadsworth.

91. Peter B. Kraska and Louis J. Cubellis (2004). Militarizing Mayberry and beyond: Making sense of American paramilitary policing. In Steven G. Brandal and David S. Barlow (Eds.), *The police in America* (pp. 387–406). Belmont, CA: Wadsworth.

92. Personal confidential communication between the writer and divisional commander in New Orleans.

93. Carl L. Klockars (1988). The rhetoric of community policing. In J.R. Greene and S.D. Mastrofski (Eds.), *Community policing: Rhetoric or reality* (pp. 239–258). New York: Praeger.

94. David H. Bayley and James Garofalo (1989). The management of violence by police patrol officers. *Criminology,* 27, 1–25.

95. Richard B. Felson, Jeffery M. Ackerman and Catherine Gallagher (2005, June). *Police intervention and the repeat of domestic assault*. NCJRS 210301. Washington, DC: U.S. Department of Justice. Office of Justice Programs. Retrieved online July 7, 2005: http://www.ncjrs.org/pdffiles1/nij/grants/210301.pdf

96. Matthew R. Durose, Erica L. Schmitt, and Patrick A. Langan (2005 April). Contacts between police and the public. Findings from the 2002 national survey. Bureau of Justice Statistics. NCJ 207845. Washington, DC: U.S. Department of Justice. Office of Justice Programs. Retrieved online July 7, 2005: http://www.ojp.usdoj.gov/bjs/pub/ascii/cpp02.txt

97. CBS News (2004, April 10). *Columbine Legacy: Schools Safer?* Retrieved online July 10, 2005: http://www.cbsnews.com/stories/2004/04/19/national/main612556.shtml

98. CBS News (2004, April 10). *Columbine Legacy: Schools Safer?* Retrieved online July 10, 2005: http://www.cbsnews.com/stories/2004/04/19/national/main612556.shtml

99. Matthew R. Durose, Erica L. Schmitt, and Patrick A. Langan (2005 April). Contacts between police and the public. Findings from the 2002 national survey. Bureau of Justice Statistics. NCJ 207845. Washington, DC: U.S. Department of Justice. Office of Justice Programs. Retrieved online July 7, 2005: http://www.ojp.usdoj.gov/bjs/pub/ascii/cpp02.txt

100. Samuel Walker and Charles M. Katz (2005). *The police in America*. Boston: McGraw-Hill. p. 233.

101. Personal communication with Boston police officer February 19, 2005.

102. Diane Cecilia Weber (1999, August 26). Warrior cops: The ominous growth of paramilitarism in American police. *The Architecture of Modern Political Power*, 50. Retrieved Online July 18, 2004: http://www.mega.nu:8080/ampp/weber_swat.html

103. Michael McDonald (2004, October 17). Police officer Mila De Pina. *Boston Globe*, p. D 18.

104. Samuel Walker and Charles M. Katz (2005). p. 233.

105. Samuel Walker and Charles M. Katz (2005). p. 233.

106. Samuel Walker and Charles M. Katz (2005). p. 233.

107. Randall G. Shelden (2001). *Controlling the dangerous classes: A critical introduction to the history of criminal justice*. Boston: Allyn & Bacon. p. 98.

108. ITVS News (2004). *The new cop on the beat*. Retrieved online July 10, 2005: http://www.itvs.org/NewCopOnTheBeat/story.html

109. Randal G. Shelden (2001). Also see Jeffrey Reiman (2003). *The rich get richer and the poor get prison*, 7th ed. Boston: Allyn & Bacon. pp. 107–108.

110. Personal communication between the writer and a Chicago police officer who wishes to remain anonymous. Note that this response is a similar response articulated by many officers interviewed concerning this contradiction between policy mandates, top command implementation of those policies, and practitioner experience.

111. Jerome Skolnick and James Fyfe (1993). *Above the law: Police and the excessive use of force*. New York: Free Press.

112. Peter Cassidy (1997). Also see Joseph McNamara (1995). *Cops against drug wars*. Retrieved online July 9, 2005: http://www.drcnet.org/cops/responses.html

113. A former student and participant in a recent police study conducted by this author volunteered information about his military training at Fort Bragg in North Carolina. "As I looked around at the other guys in my training unit, most of us are Marines and a few of us served together in Operation Desert Storm. So this

was like old home week. I finally felt like I could put my experience in special ops to good use." One impression the author received was that younger patrol officers with military training now have an edge on experienced street cops with a lot of experience. The new cop mentality is "simplify."

114. Personal confidential communication between the writer and a Boston officer.

115. Personal confidential communication between the writer and a New Orleans police officer.

116. C. Enloe (1980). *Police, military, and ethnicity: Foundations of state power.* New Brunswick, NJ: Transaction.

117. Peter B. Kraska and Louis J. Cubellis (2004).

118. Peter B. Kraska and Louis J. Cubellis (2004).

119. Peter B. Kraska and Louis J. Cubellis (2004). p. 390.

120. Hans Toch (2001). *Stress in policing.* Washington, DC: APA. p. 193.

121. Personal communication between the writer and a divisional commander in Boston who wishes to remain anonymous.

122. Mayo Clinic (2005). *Alcoholism.* Retrieved online July 10, 2005: http://www.mayoclinic.com/invoke.cfm?id=DS00340. Also see Diagnostic criteria for 303.00 alcohol intoxication (1994). *Diagnostic and statistical manual of mental disorders,* 4th ed., Washington, DC: APA. p. 197.

123. Tony Platt (1982). *Iron fist and the velvet glove: An analysis of the U.S. Police,* 3rd ed. New York: Social Justice. Also see Gene Healy (2003). Deployed in the U.S.A.: Creeping militarization of the home front. *Policy Analysis,* 503. Retrieved Online July 15, 2004: http://www.cato.org/pubs/pas/pa503.pdf

124. Tony Platt and Cecilia O'Leary (2003). Patriot acts. *Social Justice,* 30(1), 5–17.

125. Andrew Dalton (2005, July 11). *L.A. police kill gunman, child in shootout.* Associated Press. YAHOO News. Retrieved online July 11, 2005: http://news.yahoo.com/s/nm/20050711/ts_nm/usa_court_bush_dc

126. Easy for me to ask since I am on the other side of the country and not being fired upon.

127. Joseph McNamara (1995). *Cops against the drug war.* Retrieved online July 9, 2005: http://www.drcnet.org/cops/responses.html

128. Mike Madigan (2001, March). Law enforcement's dirty little secret. Retrieved online June 27, 2005: http://twistedbadge.com/feature_profiling_1.htm

129. Steve McVicker (2005, March 14). Ballistics lab results questioned in 3 cases. *Houston Chronicle.* Retrieved online July 11, 2005: http://www.chron.com/cs/CDA/ssistory.mpl/topstory/3083288

130. Police One (2005, July). Officer killed directing traffic. Retrieved online July 3, 2005: http://www.policeone.com/news_internal.asp?view=100765

8

Policing of Terrorism and Stress

None are so hopelessly enslaved as those who falsely believe they are free.
—*Johann Wolfgang von Goethe*

Learning Objectives

Once you've read this chapter, you will be able to:

- Characterize the primary focus of this chapter.

- Define terrorism.

- Describe the differences between war and acts of terrorism.

- Provide some data about America that makes it a difficult country to guard.

- Describe the primary components of the Bush Doctrine.

- Describe the importance of the U.S. Immigration and Nationality Act.

- Articulate some of the primary components of the USA Patriot Act I and II.

- Describe some of the criticism of the USA Patriot Act.

- Identify some general responses developed by the FBI to terrorism.

- Describe the speculation about federal intention linked to terrorism strategies.

- Identify the DOJ's accomplishments in the War on Terrorism.

- Explain some of the changes among police jobs after 9/11.

- Discuss local police concerns about immigration control.

- Identify some of the local police strategies to control terrorism.

- Describe terrorism strategies that add to officer stress.

KEY TERMS

Bush Doctrine
Collateral casualties
Department of
   Homeland Security

Maritime Transportation
   Security Act of 2002
Terrorism
U.S.A. Patriot Act I & II

U.S. Immigration and
   Nationality Act

INTRODUCTION

September 11th changed everyone's lives and their job descriptions from the office of the President to the patrol officer cruising down a desolate county road. It has effected policy, expectations, and outreach among every criminal justice institution and their personnel. Different opinions about what terrorism is and what should be done about it are plentiful, but when it comes right down to it, many answers regardless of the source are couched in political agendas and anger. Consensus has been elusive even now that other terrorist attacks have taken lives in other countries and in the names of cities many Americans could hardly pronounce. Some Americans are anxious to close national borders,[1] others demand retribution[2] while still others lobby to restrict Constitutional guarantees in the name of public safety.[3] Johann Wolfgang von Goethe's implies that restriction upon freedom would tend to enslave a free society, and maybe he is right. America's justice community, which includes federal and local law enforcement organizations, must find ways to respond to both foreign and local terrorist aggression without altering the freedoms enjoyed by their constituents.

Examined in this chapter are the criminal justice community's responses or the policing of foreign terrorism (as opposed to the terrorist event itself and domestic terrorism) and how those responses can act as a stressor to law enforcement officers whether those officers are employed by the Palm Beach County Sheriff's office, the San Diego Police Department, or Boston's Mass Transit Police Authority. As you already know, terrorism and its protocols seem to take center stage among federal law enforcement agencies, or so they say.[4] This chapter will provide a definition of terrorism, descriptions of war and acts of terrorism, and provide data that influence federal terrorism policy and practice. It will also examine local efforts to respond to terrorism, and finally it will focus on the stressors of federal and local terrorism policy that effect street cops.

TERRORISM DEFINED

Terrorism has many definitions, for instance, the Central Intelligence Agency says that they are guided by the definition of terrorism contained in Title 22 of the U.S. Code, Section 2656f(d):[5]

> *Terrorism* means premeditated, politically motivated violence perpetrated against noncombatant targets by subnational groups or clandestine agents, usually intended to influence an audience.
> - The term "international terrorism" means terrorism involving the territory or the citizens of more than one country.
> - The term "terrorist group" means any group that practices, or has significant subgroups that practice, international terrorism.

> *Terrorism* is the unlawful use of force or violence against persons or property to intimidate or coerce a government, the civilian population, or any segment thereof, in furtherance of political or social objectives.[6]

Another useful attempt at a definition is from Paul Pillar, the former deputy chief of the CIA's Counterterrorist Center. He says that there are four key elements of terrorism that includes:

1. Premeditated—planned in advance, rather than an impulsive act of rage.
2. Political—not criminal, like the violence that groups such as the mafia use to get money, but designed to change the existing political order.
3. Aimed at civilians—not at military targets or combat-ready troops.
4. Conducted by subnational groups—not by the army of a country.

An objective of terrorist aggression is to force a government and its people to respond to their violence in a harsh manner, hoping that such repression will lead to discontent among the people and ultimately to revolution. In this sense, terrorism is used to destabilize colonial governments and occupation forces.[7]

WAR AND ACTS OF TERRORISM

War can involve acts of terror, but every act of extreme violence is not terrorism. The Nazi's "Final Solution," the London Blitz, the atomic bombs on Hiroshima and Nagasaki fall in the categories of genocide, war crimes, or simply elements of brutal, total war, but are not necessarily terrorism. Do *collateral casualties* (the death of innocent populations) constitute the acts of terrorism if not the product of deliberate strategy? Probably not. But to say that an act fits better in the category of war crimes than terrorism does not lessen our need to condemn it.

> What sets terrorism apart from other forms of mass destruction is that terrorism consists of acts carried out in a dramatic way to attract publicity and create an atmosphere of alarm that goes beyond the actual victims.[8]

Identification of victims is secondary or irrelevant to the terrorists who aim their violence at the people watching.

> The distinction between terrorism and other modes of armed conflict is in the difference between actual victims and the target audience.

That would make terrorism—theater.

World leaders struggle to define terrorism, but at least by identifying and outlawing specific tactics and targets, countries can cooperate to limit the tools terrorists use.[9]

DATA ABOUT AMERICA

Data about America will help in understanding the problems faced daily by law enforcement to guard its borders. The DEA[10] provides the following data about the U.S. in 2003:

- 60 million visitors arrived on 675,000 commercial and private flights
- 6 million more visitors came by sea
- 370 million more came by land
- 116 million vehicles crossed Canadian and Mexican borders
- 90,000 merchant and passenger ships docked at U.S. ports
- 9 million shipping containers came into the U.S.
- 400 million tons of cargo arrived for distribution
- 157,000 smaller vessels visited coastal towns

As you can imagine, guarding this country might be a bigger job than expected. How do the authorities prevent terrorists from entering the country in a post-9/11 world?[11] The assistant director of the FBI provides one answer:

"With a shield made up of agents, police, and sheriffs standing shoulder-to-shoulder."[12] When asked how do we create such a shield? His response was, "By shaping national strategies and approaches in tandem; by working seamlessly at the ground level to investigate potential threats and suspicious activities in local communities; and by fully sharing terrorist-related information including details on everything from wanted suspects to potential targets, from threats on communities to terrorists." In part, the comments of the FBI assistant director are guided by the Bush Doctrine.

THE BUSH DOCTRINE

President George W. Bush in January 2004 directed the FBI to make prevention of terrorist attacks its number one priority.[13] This is part of the President's strategy to defeat, deny, diminish, and defend against terrorism. When the President spoke at FBI Headquarters, he reemphasized to FBI personnel that "the FBI has no greater priority than preventing terrorist acts against America." Implicit in this directive, the President referred to both foreign terrorism and domestic terrorism.

The *Bush Doctrine* calls on American forces to aggressively target terrorist groups, and, if necessary, the countries that harbor them. That is, the United States is officially at war with terrorism. Some of the President's strategies include the development of the Department of Homeland Security, the Maritime Transportation Security Act of 2002, the U.S. Immigration and Nationality Act, and the U.S.A. Patriot Act.

The *Department of Homeland Security* is a new cabinet approved by Congress in November 2002. It is designed to consolidate U.S. defenses against terrorist attacks and better coordinate counterterrorism intelligence.[14] Incorporating parts of eight other cabinet departments, it is the first new department since the Veterans Affairs Department in 1989. Under the terms of its legislation, the department had 1 year to consolidate 22 agencies it adopted—but given the scale of the reorganization, experts warn that it may be much longer before the department has fully assumed all of its new functions.

The responsibility of Homeland Security is to develop and implement preparedness strategies in the event of a terrorist attack. To:

1. Develop procedures and policies to guide actions of first-responders
2. Conduct training and exercises to first-responders
3. Enhance partnerships with state and local governments and private-sector agencies
4. Fund the purchase of much-needed equipment for first-responders in states, cities, and towns.

These activities, along with an active American community, contribute to a level of national preparedness that is critical to achieving the goal of a better prepared America. The department is designed to absorb several federal agencies dealing with domestic defense, including the Coast Guard, the Border Patrol, the Customs Service, the Immigration and Naturalization Service, the Secret Service, and the Transportation Security Administration (which was created after September 11 to oversee airline security). It will explore ways to respond to terror attacks involving chemical, biological, or nuclear weapons, and work to better coordinate intelligence about terrorist threats. The department is also expected to implement much of the National Strategy for Homeland Security, the domestic security plan unveiled by President Bush.

The *Maritime Transportation Security Act of 2002* is consistent with the President's objectives is a landmark legislation designed to protect the nation's ports and waterways from a terrorist attack.

The *U.S. Immigration and Nationality Act*[15] sees terrorist activity as any activity that is unlawful under the laws of the place where it is committed. It broadens the definition of terrorism to include highjackings and sabotage of any conveyance (including aircraft, vessel, or vehicle). Also it includes the seizing or detaining, or an attempt to kill, injure, or continue to detain, another individual in order to compel a third person to do or abstain from doing any act as an explicit or implicit condition for the release of the individual seized or detained. Foreign terrorists in particular are often immigrates or in America illegally, or have ties with individuals in the United States. Professionally managing immigration both at American borders and internally is an excellent strategy toward controlling terrorism. (Note: Most immigrants are not terrorists and many are fleeing from terrorists to what they believe is a safe haven.)

The *U.S.A. Patriot Act* (both I and II) was designed to provide the appropriate tools required to intercept and obstruct terrorism.[16] One of its objectives is to prevent future terrorist attacks. Some examples of the Act are:

1. The Patriot Act allows investigators to use investigative tools that were already available to investigate organized crime and drug trafficking such as wiretaps and electric surveillance without obtaining warrants the same way local law enforcement obtains their warrants.

- Many of the tools the Act provides to law enforcement to fight terrorism have been used for decades to fight organized crime and drug dealers, and have been reviewed and approved by the courts. As Senator Joe Biden (D-DE) explained during the floor debate about the Act, "The FBI could get a wiretap to investigate the mafia, but they could not get one to investigate terrorists. To put it bluntly, that was crazy! What's good for the mob should be good for terrorists."[17]

- Allows law enforcement to use surveillance against more crimes of terror. Before the Patriot Act, courts could permit law enforcement to conduct electronic surveillance to investigate many ordinary, nonterrorism crimes, such as drug crimes, mail fraud, and passport fraud. Agents also could obtain wiretaps to investigate some, but not all, of the crimes that terrorists often commit.

- Allows federal agents to follow sophisticated terrorists trained to evade detection. For years, law enforcement has been able to use "roving wiretaps" to investigate ordinary crimes, including drug offenses and racketeering. A roving wiretap can be authorized by a federal judge to apply to a particular suspect, rather than a particular phone or communications device.

- Allows law enforcement to conduct investigations without tipping off terrorists. In some cases if criminals are tipped off too early to an investigation, they might flee, destroy evidence, intimidate or kill witnesses, cut off contact with associates, or take other action to evade arrest.

2. The Patriot Act facilitated information sharing and cooperation among government agencies so that they can better "connect the dots."

- The rationale is offered by Senator John Edwards (D-NC). The Senator said, "We simply cannot prevail in the battle against terrorism if the right hand of our government has no idea what the left hand is doing."[18]

3. The Patriot Act updated the law to reflect new technologies and new threats.

- The Act brought the law up to date with current technology, so we no longer have to fight a digital-age battle with antique weapons—legal authorities leftover from the era of rotary telephones.

4. The Patriot Act increased the penalties for those who commit terrorist crimes.

- Americans are threatened as much by the terrorist who pays for a bomb as by the one who pushes the button. That's why the Patriot Act imposed tough new penalties on those who commit and support terrorist operations, both at home and abroad.

CRITICISM OF THE U.S.A. PATRIOT ACT

The *American Civil Liberties Union*[19] (ACLU) argues that the Patriot Act grants sweeping powers to the government, eliminates or weakens the checks and balances that remained on government surveillance, wiretapping, detention, and criminal prosecution. Among its most severe problems, the bill:

- Diminishes personal privacy by removing checks on government power, specifically by making it easier for the government to initiate surveillance and wiretapping of U.S. citizens under the authority of the shadowy, top-secret Foreign Intelligence Surveillance Court. (Sections 101, 102, and 107)

- Permits the government to bypass the Foreign Intelligence Surveillance Court altogether and conduct warrantless wiretaps and searches. (Sections 103 and 104)
- Shelters federal agents engaged in illegal surveillance without a court order from criminal prosecution if they are following orders of high Executive Branch officials. (Section 106)
- Provides for general surveillance orders covering multiple functions of high-tech devices, and by further expanding pen register and trap and trace authority for intelligence surveillance of United States citizens and lawful permanent residents. (Sections 107 and 124)

There were pages and pages of criticism from the ACLU, yet while their perspective is relevant it is beyond the scope of this chapter. Should you have an interest in reviewing the ACLU's entire criticism, go to their website (http://www.aclu.org/). In the meantime, in sum, the ACLU reports that the U.S.A. Patriot Act:

- Undercuts the traditional checks and balances on governmental power
- Alters constitutional protections of freedom.
- Diminishes personal privacy by removing important checks on government surveillance authority.
- Reduces governmental accountability by the public.
- Increases government secrecy.
- Erodes the right of all persons to due process of law.

TERRORISM AND HUMAN RIGHTS

Since local law enforcement officers are the primary protectors of Constitutional rights, policing as an American institution must continue to rise to the challenge of terrorism, especially in this day of federal intervention. That is, street cops must uphold the rule of law while federal officers practice a different rule as indicated by the U.S.A. Patriot Act discussed above. At an extreme, there could be an impropriety of due process conducted by federal officers, which for some, has a resemblance of the police in pre-Nazi Berlin in the late 1930s. As Metro (Washington, DC) Chief Charles Ramsey argues, had the officers of Berlin defended German citizen rights, how different would Nazi Germany history be? "If history tells us anything, it tells us that if calls for these types of actions should occur in the future, we the police must be the first and the loudest to speak out."[20] The chief referred to orders directed to the German police during the Nazi regime.

Can conditions under which governments and people will commit large-scale murder, torture, and arbitrary imprisonment be identified? One observer thinks so and says that authoritarianism, war, and poverty can lead to large-scale human rights violations.[21] For instance, decades of civil war prior to the attacks of September 11 in Afghanistan will make it difficult for any post-Taliban regime to protect human rights and establish the rule of law. Certain kinds of ideals or actions can lead to human rights violations too. For instance, dehumanizing others can exclude them, individually and as a group, from the realm of human obligation and law as Americans had witnessed through the eyes of the slave, the forced backwoods and railroad laborer, and the interment and confiscation of property (and dignity) of an Asian American during World War II. In the early 21st century, American street cops continue to defend democracy through due process guarantees. Should a democracy allow human rights to be suspended in cases of public emergency that can threaten the life of a nation or is the suspension of those rights more deadly than the threat? As the activity of federal agencies is reviewed, it might be helpful to consider the question: Is there a time when federal law enforcement takes precedence over local law enforcement jurisdiction and human right guarantees? "Or is federal law enforcement another name of the U.S. Army?", an officer in Gulfport, Mississippi, asked.

FBI's Response to Terrorists

Before September 11, the FBI collected information to solve crimes.[22] For the most part, the FBI says they shared information and collaborated with other officials and agencies on a case-specific basis. Now, the FBI shares information, a FBI spokesperson says, for the purpose of preventing future terrorist acts.[23] The FBI tries to develop innovative ways to use technology as a device in sharing information, collaborating with international law enforcement and intelligence agencies, and developing global benefits that would aid in a reduction of terrorist activities. The FBI uses technology to share up-to-the-minute information with local law enforcement officers and intelligence agencies around the world, the spokesperson advises.[24]

The FBI and the Joint Terrorism Task Force

The FBI developed the FBI's Joint Terrorism Task Force, which is comprised of small cells of highly trained, locally based, passionately committed investigators, analysts, linguists, SWAT experts, and other specialists from dozens of U.S. law enforcement and intelligence agencies.[25] The task force chases down leads, gathers evidence, makes arrests, provides security for special events, conducts training, collects and shares intelligence, and responds to threats and incidents at a moment's notice. They are in 100 cities nationwide, including at least one in each of the FBI's field offices, most of which were organized after 9/11.

Federal Intention

Some observers imply that the federal government is using the threat of terrorism to reduce local control and power in law enforcement.[26] While this thought seems doubtful, Chapter 7 revealed that the generous support consisting of training, personnel, weapons, equipment, and funding to local police by the federal government can be a reflection of "Big Brother's" intent. Others see federal support as an exercise in duty within a check and balance system to aid local government in moving toward their objectives. The assistant director of the counterterrorism division of the FBI explains that the "FBI is part of a vast national and international campaign dedicated to defeating terrorism. Working hand-in-hand with partners in law enforcement, intelligence, the military, and diplomatic circles, our job is to neutralize terrorist cooperative here in the U.S. and to help dismantle terrorist networks worldwide."[27] Striking a balance these days is a challenge for every law enforcement agency, yet we have learned in Chapter 5 that nothing seems to be what it appears to be and before making decisions, an evaluation would aid toward an informed decision.[28] That is, before you decide on how well the federal government has accomplished its objectives, there are other issues worth noting especially in how those efforts may eventually impact the stress levels of local law enforcement officers.

FBI ACCOMPLISHMENTS AND THE BUSH DOCTRINE

Depending on whose version of the truth you're looking at, you might see something different than expected. Local agencies are saying that a lack of cooperation exists among federal personnel and federal agencies toward local law enforcement organizations. For instance, during the early operations of the U.S.A. Patriot Act, Baltimore's Police Commissioner Edward T. Norris told a panel of the House Committee on Government Reform that while the FBI has shared names, descriptions, and addresses of suspected terrorists, the agency has not provided photographs. "While the FBI has done nothing to prevent us from doing this work on our own, they have not given us anything but a watch list to read," Norris says.[29] The head of the Philadelphia Police Department, Commissioner John F. Timoney, has also criticized the FBI for not being forthcoming with information. He says that the information supplied to the FBI is "worthless."[30] The former commissioner of the Boston police and the former Charlotte police chief both agree with Commissioner Timoney and add that this federal strategy is employed for the purpose of keeping local people "out of the loop" so that "fed agencies hold control over local agencies."

Also, the FBI attempted to resolve some of those problems through the Department of Homeland Security, which has reached some moderate success. In part, Homeland Security and the FBI have utilized new communicative methods and in the process have bolstered the paramilitary model of policing. In a recent visit to the Federal Law Enforcement Training Center, it was emphasized that pre-9/11 federal law enforcement agencies were criticized for their inability to communicate with each and therefore, even though a lot of "intel" (knowledge) was known by several federal agencies about 9/11 potentials, the challenge for every federal law enforcement agency was to share information. One result was that the huge federal law enforcement apparatus (the tentacles of an octopus) were restructured:

- Antitrust Division
- Asset Forfeiture Program
- Attorney General
- Bureau of Alcohol, Tobacco, Firearms, and Explosives
- Bureau of Justice Assistance (OJP)
- Bureau of Justice Statistics (OJP)
- Civil Division
- Civil Rights Division
- Community Capacity Development Office (OJP) (includes Weed and Seed and American Indian and Alaska Native Affairs Desk)
- Community Oriented Policing Services (COPS)
- Community Relations Service
- Criminal Division
- Diversion Control Program (DEA)
- Drug Enforcement Administration
- Environment and Natural Resources Division
- Executive Office for Immigration Review
- Executive Office for U.S. Attorneys
- Executive Office for U.S. Trustees
- Federal Bureau of Investigation
- Federal Bureau of Prisons
- Foreign Claims Settlement Commission of the United States
- Immigration and Naturalization Service—now part of the Department of Homeland Security
  U.S. Citizenship and Immigration Services (USCIS)
  Bureau of Customs and Border Protection (BCBP)
  Bureau of Immigration and Customs Enforcement (ICE)
  Office of Immigration Statistics

- INTERPOL—U.S. National Central Bureau
- Justice Management Division
- National Criminal Justice Reference Service (OJP)
- National Drug Intelligence Center
- National Institute of Corrections (FBOP)
- National Institute of Justice (OJP)
- Office of the Associate Attorney General
- Office of the Attorney General
- Office of Attorney Recruitment and Management
- Office of the Chief Information Officer
- Office of the Deputy Attorney General
- Office of Dispute Resolution
- Office for Domestic Preparedness—now part of the Department of Homeland Security
- Office of the Federal Detention Trustee
- Office of Information and Privacy
- Office of the Inspector General
- Office of Intelligence Policy and Review
- Office of Intergovernmental and Public Liaison
- Office of Justice Programs
- Office of Juvenile Justice and Delinquency Prevention (OJP)
- Office of Legal Counsel
- Office of Legal Policy
- Office of Legislative Affairs
- Office of the Pardon Attorney
- Office of the Police Corps (OJP)
- Office of Professional Responsibility
- Office of Public Affairs
- Office of the Solicitor General
- Office of Tribal Justice
- Office for Victims of Crime (OJP)
- Office on Violence Against Women
- Professional Responsibility Advisory Office
- Task Force for Faith-Based and Community Initiatives
- Tax Division
- U.S. Attorneys
- U.S. Marshals Service
- U.S. Parole Commission
- U.S. Trustee Program

The Department of Homeland Security is now responsible for the following federal agencies:

- **Federal Emergency Management Agency (FEMA)** prepares the nation for hazards, manages Federal response and recovery efforts following any national incident, and administers the National Flood Insurance Program.
- **Transportation Security Administration (TSA)** protects the nation's transportation systems to ensure freedom of movement for people and commerce.
- **Customs and Border Protection** is responsible for protecting our nation's borders in order to prevent terrorists and terrorist weapons from entering the United States, while facilitating the flow of legitimate trade and travel.
- **Immigration and Customs Enforcement (ICE),** the largest investigative arm of the Department of Homeland Security, is responsible for identifying and shutting down vulnerabilities in the nation's border, economic, transportation, and infrastructure security.
- **Federal Law Enforcement Training Center** provides career-long training to law enforcement professionals to help them fulfill their responsibilities safely and proficiently.
- **Citizenship and Immigration Services** is responsible for the administration of immigration and naturalization adjudication functions and establishing immigration services policies and priorities.
- The **U.S. Coast Guard** protects the public, the environment, and U.S. economic interests—in the nation's ports and waterways, along the coast, on international waters, or in any maritime region as required to support national security.
- The **U.S. Secret Service** protects the President and other high-level officials and investigates counterfeiting and other financial crimes, including financial institution fraud, identity theft, computer fraud; and computer-based attacks on our nation's financial, banking, and telecommunications infrastructure.

Yet, with all the complexity of the federal government and their serious budget requirements (not to mention their alleged requirement of secretive operations) there is little evidence to support a federal claim that cooperation in communicative methods has been successful (or the claim that they are capable of protecting the American public). Additionally, it could be said that the rise of the paramilitary police model of control is attributed to federal intrusion, which includes military resources and training of local cops promoted by the attacks of 9/11 as discussed in the proceeding chapter, but little evidence is available that demonstrates local law enforcement agencies play pri-

Department of Homeland Security
Organization Chart

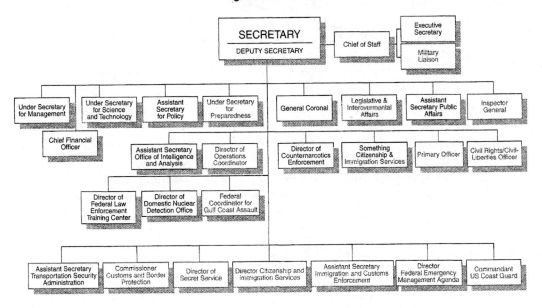

FIGURE 8.1
Organizational chart of the DHS.
Source: Department of Homeland Security, 2006.[31]

mary roles in foreign terrorist investigation, apprehension, and processing unless those agencies pursue those objectives themselves. For instance, Foreign
Intelligence Surveillance Court of Review sharply criticized the DOJ and FBI
for providing the tribunal with "misleading information in 75 cases."[32]

Also, "locals front the federal investigations because cops are deployed
as the street fighters protecting the federal investigation," says a divisional
commander in Boston.[33]

Corruption and misinformation from the FBI is well documented. The
corruption of FBI agents before 9/11 had been confirmed by a Congressional
Report: federal officials in Washington and Boston inflicted "incalculable
damage of the public by protecting murderous government informants over
30 years."[34] Federal law enforcement thwarted major homicide and criminal
investigations in numerous states (including states where the original study
on officer stress was conducted such as Boston) and the report highlights that
"it appears that federal law enforcement actively worked to prevent homicide
cases from being resolved." The street cops represented in this study and
homicide investigators are a different people, yet, over time, the knowledge
of federal law enforcement corruption becomes common knowledge and locals close ranks to protect their ongoing investigations, which far outweigh
those at a federal level in their minds.

Furthermore, local officers must stand aside while those same federal
agents "serve and protect" local constituents; however, those federal officers

are not exposed to civil lawsuits, which plague locals even when locals are right in their assessments. Federal agents, on the other hand, who knowingly abridge the rights of residents, whether those residents, are linked to a terrorism investigation or just got in the way of a federal investigation, possess few rights.[35] When a police expert claimed that local police officers were the possessors of "ultimate power," he should have been characterizing federal agents as opposed to local officers.[36] Maybe the U.S. Commission on Civil Rights should focus their attention on federal officers rather than exclusively on local officers. Nonetheless, it should come as no surprise that DOJ says that America is winning the war on terrorism at home "until another incident occurs and then the feds will come up with another reason why it was out of their grasp," advises a chief in a New England metropolitan jurisdiction. "In the meantime, it's a turf war," says the chief. "And often the feds have the media and television shows supporting their heroism and knowledge."

ACCOMPLISHMENTS IN THE WAR ON TERRORISM

Specifically, DOJ says that they are winning the war on terrorism in the spring of 2006 in six ways[37]:

1. By disrupting terrorist threats, and capturing the terrorists that would carry them out. Since 9/11, Department of Justice (DOJ), U.S. intelligence, law enforcement communities, and DOJ's local and abroad partners have:
   - Identified and disrupted over 150 terrorist threats and cells.
   - Worldwide, nearly two-thirds of al Qaida's known senior leadership has been captured or killed—including a mastermind of the September 11th attacks.
   - Worldwide, more than 3,000 operatives have been incapacitated.
   - Four terrorist cells in Buffalo, Detroit, Seattle, and Portland (Oregon) have been broken up.
   - 305 individuals have been criminally charged in terrorism investigations in the United States.
   - Already, 176 individuals have been convicted or have pled guilty in the United States, including shoe-bomber Richard Reid and "American Taliban" John Walker Lindh.
   - Over 515 individuals linked to the September 11th investigation have been removed from the United States.
2. Gathered and cultivated detailed knowledge on terrorism in the United States:
   - Hundreds of suspected terrorists have been identified and tracked throughout the United States.

- Our human sources of intelligence have increased 40% since 9/11, and the quality of this human intelligence has improved significantly.
- Our counterterrorism investigations have more than doubled since 9/11.

3. Gathered information by leveraging criminal charges and long prison sentences. When individuals realize that they face a long prison term, they often try to lessen their prison time by pleading guilty and cooperating with the government.
   - These individuals have provided critical intelligence about al-Qaida and other terrorist groups, safe houses, training camps, recruitment, and tactics in the United States, and the operations of those terrorists who mean to do Americans harm.
   - One individual has given us intelligence on weapons stored here in the United States.
   - Another individual has identified locations in the United States being scouted or cased for potential attacks by al-Qaida.

4. Dismantling terrorist financial networks. For instance:
   - Designated 36 terrorist organizations
   - Frozen $133 million in assets around the world
   - Launched 70 investigations into terrorist financing
   - Won convictions or guilty pleas in 23 terrorist cases
   - Established an FBI Terrorist Financing Operations Section (TFOS)
   - Utilized the Joint Terrorism Task Forces to identify, investigate, prosecute, disrupt, and dismantle terrorist-related financial and fundraising activities.

5. Using legal tools to detect, disrupt, and prevent potential terrorist plots. Congress has provided tools such as the Patriot Act, which passed with overwhelming bipartisan majorities in the Senate by 98–1 and in the House of Representatives by 357–66. The Patriot Act:
   - Allows investigators to use the tools that were already available to investigate organized crime and drug trafficking.
   - Facilitates information sharing and cooperation among government agencies so that they can better "connect the dots."
   - Updates laws to reflect new technologies and new threats (i.e., digital rather than rotary age).
   - Increased penalties for those who commit terrorist crimes and those who support it.

6. The Department of Justice is building its long-term counterterrorism capacity since September 11th:
   - A nearly three-fold increase in counterterrorism funds.

- Approximately 1,000 new and redirected FBI agents dedicated to counterterrorism and counterintelligence.
- 250 new assistant U.S. attorneys.
- 66 Joint Terrorism Task Forces.
- 337% increase in Joint Terrorism Task Force staffing.
- FBI Flying Squads developed for rapid deployment to hot spots worldwide.

DOJ claims that its success in preventing another catastrophic attack on the American homeland since September 11, 2001, would be more difficult, if not impossible, without the U.S.A. Patriot Act II. Although the activity after 9/11 by the federal government is meritorious, there are concerns that federal agencies had accomplished less than expected prior to 9/11 despite all the known information that other attacks were likely. This thought (whether accurate or not) provokes the anger of many local officers concerning local federal priorities toward controlling the threat of terrorism. In essence, federal performance is a huge stressor for most local officers.

KNOWN TERRORIST ISSUES BEFORE 9/11

Terrorist issues and potential objectives were common knowledge among the public, the federal government, and local police prior to 9/11. This perspective is largely avoided by most federal agency informational sources. Yet, evidence exists that many police agencies were active in determining jurisdictional threats centered on both domestic and foreign terrorist attack long before 9/11, the media sensationalized terrorism, and justice academies were aware of the potential of terrorist attacks.

For instance, materials and training for Boston street cops linked to domestic terrorists with a lesser focus on foreign terrorists was underway in the early 1990s, Boston Police reports show. Other jurisdictions such as Chicago, Columbus, Miami, and Los Angeles had "hate crime" investigation departments as far back as the early 1980s, official records show. In most cases, hate crime investigators were trained to deal with domestic terrorists, and individual crimes imposed upon individuals of color. Moreover, police department personnel including street cops were under the impression that the threat of foreign terrorism was only within the jurisdiction of the FBI, the lead U.S. counterterrorism agency, and the CIA, the lead U.S. intelligence agency. The belief was that those agencies were "taking care of business" in order for local police agencies to do their part, which is to provide public safety at home. Some feel that the needless destruction of innocent lives with the attack on the World Trade Center evidenced federal failure to protect the America public and signaled to police policymakers that the police are the primary local defense against all terrorist attacks—both domestic and foreign. Federal personnel say they were caught off guard and never saw attacks coming.

1998: Reporter John Miller of ABC News interviewed bin Laden who said, "Our battle against the Americans is far greater than our battle was against the Russians. We anticipate a black future for America. Instead of remaining the United States, it shall end up separated states and shall have to carry the bodies of its sons back to America."

1/16/99: DOJ indicted bin Laden and 11 other members of al Qaida for killing and conspiring to kill U.S. citizens. FBI placed bin Laden in its Most Wanted list, with a reward of $5 million.

2/1/00: An al Qaida defector, Jamal Ahmed al-Fadl, revealed many secrets about the al Qaida network and with that information, it was expected that the appropriate federal agency would step and end the treat.

10/12/00: Suicide bombing of the *U.S.S. Cole.* The ship was refueling at the port city of Aden in Yemen when attacked. A boat filled with explosives got near the *Cole* and exploded, killing 17 and injuring 37 American sailors. bin Laden released a videotape claiming responsibility for attack.

After all, the media, especially the motion picture industry, was active in uncovering sources of domestic terrorism and implied that foreign terrorism on a large scale was both possible and likely to happen in American cities. For instance, the movie *Die Hard* (1988), although alleged terrorists were portrayed as Germans, the plot was about a New York cop, John McClane, who gave terrorists a dose of their own medicine as they held hostages in a huge Los Angeles office building. Recall *Die Hard II: Die Harder* (1990) where Dulles Airport in Arlington, Virginia, which services Washington, DC, was under siege and *Die Hard with a Vengeance* (1995) where a bomber destroyed a New York City department store. There were many other motion pictures prior to 9/11 that characterized large-scale destruction by terrorists, many of whom were Muslim and movie goers were already sensitized to collateral damage and weapons of mass destruction. The American public by and large knew the potential of foreign terrorism and an assumption is that federal personnel and elected officials also go to the movies and read the *Wall Street Journal* and the *New York Times*, which are a few among many publications that reported terrorist attack potentials upon American soil.

Then, too, Ed Bolte, former deputy director of the North Carolina Justice Academy commented in a speech in the fall of 1997 that following attacks of the 1993 bombing of the World Trade Center, the 1995 bombing of Oklahoma City's Murrah Federal Building, and the 1995 sarin gas attack in the Tokyo subway system that many police agencies including justice academy personnel and instructors were paying more attention to security in certain buildings and transportation systems around the nation. His indicator was that terrorism would take center stage among many police department investigations. Deputy Director Bolte talked about collateral damage and weapons of mass destruction and particularly the need for well-trained street cops to deal with "expected terrorist attacks upon major American targets." Street cops were provided with data that implied more attention should be directed toward the safety of key properties in all jurisdictions. Those of us in the audience were amassed with the insight and planning in process among police academies at the grassroots level.

"It is likely that if NYPD had technology the federal government had at that time, 9/11 would never have happened," says a district NYPD commander.[38] Yet, for the most part, terrorist attacks to American property were considered a remote possibility by key federal agencies, even in urban areas. This thought is consistent with Ronald Kessler[39] who writes that Andrew J. Duffin, head of Houston's FBI office and chairman of the SAC advisory board to FBI's top brass, says, "We have a history of recording facts. That's what we do for a living. . . . But by the time we communicate to (our) employees issues that affect them, they've already been on the news or front page of the *Wall Street Journal*."[40] The implication is that the FBI and other federal agencies gather data and have a difficult time disseminating the data even to their own personnel. The question raised is not how accurate this information is, but how much of this information is known by street cops and in what way might that information affect their performance. One indicator might be that in the survey conducted for this book among 558 cops, over one-half of them report that homeland security was not part of their job description, 73% report that they disagreed or strongly disagreed with federal enforcement strategies at the local levels, and only 14% thought is was okay. One implication from this recent poll is that the locals have little confidence in federal strategies or their personnel.

LOCAL POLICE RESPONSE TO TERRORISM

Changes in Police Jobs

Although ensuring public safety is still the first priority of local law enforcement agencies, terrorism has triggered a shift in police issues around the country. For instance:

1. Many agencies devote increased resources to prepare for terrorist attacks and gather intelligence to head off possible threats.
2. Street cops are being trained as first-responders at a terrorist scene (on 9/11, thousands of NYPD rushed to the World Trade Center, and 23 were killed when the towers collapsed).
3. Street cops are being trained to respond, investigate, and communicate civilian reports of terrorism-related activity.

However, recall that police agencies were already changing to meet the threat of terrorism in many ways prior to the events that lead to 9/11. However, it is unlikely that many local agencies will accept federal intervention in local terrorist investigations in the future because of "federal screw-ups linked to 9/11, but we will take their money with a smile," says a commissioner of police.[42]

For instance: Anniston, Alabama at the federal Center for Domestic Preparedness, smoke fills the cafeteria as a piercing alarm sounds. Panicked voices scream. Help them.

A few doors away, there's a bomb hidden in an office. Find it. And down the hall, injured bodies litter a room. Who gets treated, and who gets left for dead? Figure it out.

These are a few of the challenges that firefighters, police, and other emergency workers face when they come to this former Army base for a different kind of boot camp. The goal, set well before Sept. 11, is to prepare first-responders to handle a terrorist attack. It opened in June 1998 with a $2 million budget that had reached $18 million before 9/11. A post-9/11 emergency appropriation doubled the center's budget to $35.2 million, and officials there expect it to continue to grow.[41]

Police Departments and ICE Enforcement

Many police agencies want to join the federal government in apprehending visa violators. But, the federal Department of Justice (DOJ) takes the position that before they would essentially deputize local officers to enforce immigration laws, it must be ensured that police will not engage in racial profiling, especially of Latinos, officials say.[43] "Sounds a little on the redundant side," argues one cop, who adds, "I really think that that's one way the feds can keep control over their turf." The mistrust and suspicion of federal agencies among local officers appears to be a common perspective no matter which federal agencies are examined. For instance, of the 558 officers surveyed for this book, over 47% strongly disagreed that U.S. Department of Homeland Security practices are necessary, revealing that federal intervention in local terrorist investigations (and the way I am reading it) is not vital or preferred in controlling foreign terrorism at home or at least in their jurisdiction. "The feds are quick to believe their own super cop propaganda, but when it comes down to it, they pick the cases, the time, and the jurisdiction to work a case and they have unlimited cash and manpower to do whatever. Ain't like a patrol officer at 2:00 in the morning whose mak'en a stop on the highway knowing backup is 15 to 30 minutes away and the yahoos in a stopped vehicle are drunk and have no regard for the law. The cops don't get to pick and choose their cases, they take whatever comes their way," said a chief of police of a municipality in the Midwest who wishes to remain anonymous.

However, street officers might not push the issue since some tend to hold a close relationship with immigrant communities and are on the receiving end of federal grants. "The feds have long memories when it comes to giving bucks," responded a commander in Boston. The ties local officers have with immigrants help solve other, often serious crimes. If officers figuratively wear a federal badge and have the ability to detain illegal migrants or make arrests, they may not receive as much (and at that, the "much" is too little) cooperation.

Then, too, a chief of a large municipal department says that there is always "a power play over who controls what, and the FBI in particular like ICE wants more control over local law enforcement—not less. Giving officers the authority to take immigrants into custody is not a 'privilege' my cops want or need, but it would help them keep peace on the streets."[44] Another chief adds, "The feds are basterds. All of 'em [agencies]. They want it all and nothing comes back. They keep info and cooperation from us in the name of national security, but to be honest with ya, the real issue is control. Without us [cops], there ain't no national defense. It's like DEA, they provide a dual authority for my officers and when there's a drug bust and property confiscated, the feds want it all but they ain't paying my guys. When my officers are do'en federal tasks, they ain't serving and protecting the citizens they're accountable to."[45] Police see the hesitation of federal agencies to authorize street cops in immigration enforcement as issues linked to "turfs" and the feds see racial profiling as police weakness to lawfully serve the public. Finally in this regard, most police agencies are struggling with small budgets, shortages of sworn officers, and restricted police power to accomplish their mission, added to federal intervention, "talk about stress," a commander added.

Police Strategies to Control Immigration

Local and state police currently cannot arrest illegal immigrants on immigration laws based on a 1996 legal opinion by DOJ that prohibits local authority over immigration regulations. On March 1, 2003, service and benefit functions of the U.S. Immigration and Naturalization Service (INS) transitioned into the Department of Homeland Security (DHS) as the U.S. Citizenship and Immigration Services (USCIS) and their enforcement—U.S. Immigration and Customs Enforcement (ICE). The job of apprehending an estimated 8 million illegal immigrants (some of whom are expected of terrorist links) has been left to an estimated 15,000 federal (less than one-half of law enforcement authority) employees and contractors working in approximately 250 headquarters and field offices around the world comprise the USCIS. The USCIS is responsible for the administration of immigration and naturalization adjudication functions and establishing immigration services policies and priorities. These functions include:

- Adjudication of immigrant visa petitions
- Adjudication of naturalization petitions
- Adjudication of asylum and refugee applications
- Adjudications performed at the service centers
- All other adjudications performed by the INS

After 9/11, Attorney General John Ashcroft recognized an urgent need to improve screening of visa violators and other illegal visitors. The federal government recognized that local police are their best chance to deal with immigrants primarily because street cops are on the streets and generally knows who lives there and who does not. On many fronts, the war on terrorism needs better coordination among all levels of government including local police agencies that are already hard at work developing and maintaining their own strategies.

For instance, shortly after 9/11, the chiefs of police for nine cities in southwest Los Angeles County (known locally as the South Bay) created a committee to study and make recommendations related to the proper local law enforcement response to terrorism.[46] They recognized that a proper response would require more resources than local budgets could handle. For example, one local city was unable to obtain the use of an explosive detection canine shortly after 9/11 because the L.A. Sheriff's Department, which normally responds to such requests, did not own enough dogs to be able to respond to the many calls for assistance coming in at that time. The committee decided to build its own capacity to respond to immigrants' suspected or confirmed terrorist activity, but of course the question remained as to how individual departments would pay for that capacity since budget cuts already left little room for anything extra.

Furthermore, local police already can, and frequently do, make arrests for other federal offenses and work in tandem with many federal agencies: with the Bureau of Alcohol, Tobacco, and Firearms on gun-smuggling; with the Drug Enforcement Agency on interdiction efforts; and with the FBI on bank robberies. Most police managers agree, however, that federal agencies do not work with locals yet those federal agencies expect cooperation and will often try to undermine commanders to obtain their missions. Then, too, the FBI is considering to drop the latter task of bank robbery investigations—a long-time staple of G-man work—and provide authority to street cops, who effectively do the bulk of the investigation anyway. About 96% of all law enforcement personnel in America are state and local. So the likelihood that a local is a first-responder at most altercations is a reality. Indeed, it was a state trooper who caught Oklahoma City bomber Timothy McVeigh.

Officers Require ICE Training

Street cops require appropriate training in the basics of immigration law. Who will pay for that? Without such training, civil rights violations will dramatically increase. For instance, when 400 people suspected of being illegal immigrants were arrested by local authorities in Chandler, Arizona, in 1997, those suspects sued the city and won after a court found local police were wrongly asking for proof of citizenship. The city (not DOJ) had to pay out $400,000.

Another example is linked to Detroit police officers after an arrest in 2003; the suspects said they were falsely accused of being terrorists based on ethnic profiling.[47] The lawsuit said the suspects were accused of videotaping the Ambassador Bridge, the busiest U.S.–Canada border crossing, though the men claim they never filmed there. A video camera was seized during the arrest last April of Mohamed Elmathil and Hazaa Shahit, both of Dearborn, Michigan. Police said the arrests were justified because the officers thought they had witnessed suspicious activity. Police found fireworks in Elmathil's car, and initially thought they were sticks of dynamite. The suspects said they were questioned for hours about whether they were members of al-Qaida.

Pushing visa enforcement down to the state and local level may be a necessary step; after all, that's where the first-responders are. Also, in a nation with such diverse migrant populations and laws against discrimination, the federal government would need to do far more than just rewrite a legal opinion. Expanding the number of ICE agents and improving their coordination with local police would be a safer first step.

AMERICAN POLICE STRATEGIES TO CONTROL TERRORISM

The American government's response to terror is inconsistent with many of America's allies. For instance, after July 7, 2005's bombing on London's subways, killing 52 and wounding over 300 persons, four suspects were apprehended by the police. And *The Times of London*, quoting unidentified police sources, said detectives were interested in locating Magdy el-Nashar, 33, an Egyptian-born academic who recently taught chemistry at Leeds University.[48] Yet the British officers were not placed on high alert. Also, after 190 people were killed and 1,900 were injured during the bombings of a Madrid train by terrorists, Spaniards remained calm since they were hardened by decades of struggle against terrorism; the police investigated the bombings and brought a number of the suspects to justice.[49] Both countries moved on from the attacks, which like many other European nations that were also attacked, was a vastly different response than the United States.[50] For example, in response to 9/11 (although tragic and creating many causalities), the U.S. launched a "war on terrorism." European countries have expressed a more quiet but collective resolve to work within an international consensus to fight terrorism. "In the eyes of many European counterterrorism specialists and officials,"[51] the Bush administration's reliance on conventional military as opposed to local law enforcement can serve to provoke more terrorism and to increase stress levels of many local officers, some believe.

The reality of public safety regardless of the source of a threat should rest with local cops. And with the added burden of a sagging economy, many local governments face budget deficits and focus on trimming costs. Nonetheless, there is little "wiggle room" at the local levels of law enforcement to do the job of protecting the public as compared to federal agencies.[52] As the federal government saga unravels into the fall of 2005, their efforts to team up with local law enforcement agencies to create a centralized "terror watch list" has shortcomings. The goal is to ensure that al-Qaeda members and other terrorist group members could not slip into the United States undetected as they did before 9/11. Yet, as recently as June 2004, a top Homeland Security official told Congress the list was still a "work in progress."

With that realization, police agencies across the country have moved to shore up their terrorism strategies, which vary according to their respective community's resources and perceived vulnerability. These include some or all of the following[53]:

- Strengthened liaisons with federal, state, and local agencies, including fire departments and other police departments.
- Refined training and emergency response plans to address terrorist threats, including attacks with weapons of mass destruction.
- Increased patrols and shored-up barriers around landmarks, places of worship, ports of entry, transit systems, and nuclear power plants.
- More heavily guarded public speeches, parades, and other public events.
- Created new counterterrorism divisions and reassigned officers to counterterrorism from other divisions such as drug enforcement;
- Employed new technologies, such as X-ray-like devices to scan containers at ports of entry and sophisticated sensors to detect a chemical, biological, or radiation attack.
- Inspection of bags and identification of public transportation passengers[54]

Also, it should be noted that many police agencies for the most part disagree with the philosophy of hiring more cops, one of President Clinton and James Q. Wilson's favorite remedies to deal with the threat of terrorism (and crime). "Many experts have suggested better-quality training," reports a commander from Columbus, Ohio. "But at the local level," he adds, "sending locals to the Federal Law Enforcement Training Center is just another way of the feds to control local law enforcement."

NYPD Strategies to Control Terrorism

Counterterrorism measures put into place by the New York City Police Department (NYPD), which has firsthand experience in handling terrorist attacks and continues to respond to a flurry of threats, have made it a national and world model for police preparedness and training. The measures taken by the NYPD include[55]:

- Creating a counterterrorism division and hiring a deputy police commissioner for counterterrorism to oversee related training, prevention, and investigations and to work with state and federal agencies.

- Hiring a deputy commissioner for intelligence and an in-house intelligence officer for each of the NYPD's 76 precincts.
- Training the department's 39,000 officers in counterterrorism, including how to respond to a biological, chemical, or radiation attack.
- Assigning detectives to train abroad with police departments in Israel, Canada, and potentially other countries in the Middle East and in Southeast Asia.
- Assigning one detective to Interpol, the France-based international police agency, and two detectives to FBI headquarters in Washington.
- Placing command centers throughout the city to back up headquarters in the event of a large-scale terrorist attack.
- Acquiring equipment such as protective suits, gas masks, and portable radiation detectors.
- Cards giving possible indicators of terrorists were issued, which include phone numbers of counterterrorism investigators. Suspicions over anyone who is, among other things, carrying driver's licenses from different states, videotaping utilities and tunnels, or wearing fake uniforms.[56]

In the latter initiative, NYPD officers were advised to take note of "overtly hostile" people who "express hatred for America and advocate violence against America and/or Americans," or who "support terrorists and their goals."[57]

Also, state and local police in New York and Vermont can tap into federal counterterrorism data under an FBI-run pilot program, which started in the summer of 2004.[58] FBI Director Robert Mueller says this initiative will enable street cops to check watch lists of suspected terrorists and other information stored in databases maintained by the FBI, CIA, State Department, Customs, and other agencies. A former FBI assistant director in charge of the New York office and now a senior adviser to Pataki on counterterrorism says the system is the prototype for other states. "If we have our cops deaf, dumb, and blind as to what the federal government knows in databases in Washington, how are we going to protect our society?"[59]

"The chances of a terrorist hitting a trip wire in state and local police is much higher. I think this is the single most important thing we can do to protect our people from the next attack," he added.[60]

The federal authorities might have missed an opportunity to detain hijacker Ziad Jarrah 36 hours before the attacks of September 11, 2001, when a Maryland state trooper stopped Jarrah driving 90 mph on Interstate 95. Then, too, White House Counterterrorism czar Richard Clarke acknowledges that the CIA knew there were al Qaeda terrorists in the United States, and the FBI knew there were Arabic people taking lessons at flight schools, including some asking strange questions about crashing planes. Clarke says,

"Red lights and bells should have been going off. They had specific information about individual terrorists from which one could have deduced what was about to happen." What else was known prior to 9/11 that federal agencies are pressed to accept responsibility for? (This is no attempt to indict or vindicate federal performance, you'll have to do that.) Yet, the following are only a few of a very long list at Matthew Robinson's website.[61]

- September 2000–September 2001—NORAD conducts regional war games exercises simulating hijacked airliners used as weapons to crash into targets; one target is the World Trade Center. In another exercise, jets conduct a mock shootdown of airliners over the Atlantic Ocean. In another, the Pentagon is the target (but this one was called off). Exercises are called Vigilant Guardian and Northern Vigilance, and another is being held at the National Reconnaissance Office, which included an airplane being used as a flying weapon.

- February–July 2001—Trial of embassy bombers in New York features testimony of two UBL associates that received flight training in Texas and Oklahoma. One UBL aide gives evidence to government about pilot training.

- March 2001—Fox's show *The Lone Gunmen* depicts an attack by terrorists using a remote-controlled 727 aircraft against the World Trade Center (the real attackers turn out to be U.S. government agents who want to justify continued, large military budgets by creating fear of terrorism).

- April 2001—FBI translators Sibel Edmonds and Behrooz Sarshar learn of a warning given to the FBI by an FBI informant that al Qaeda is planning to attack the U.S. and Europe with airplanes and that al Qaeda agents are being trained in the United States as pilots. Edmonds says: "President Bush said they had no specific information about September 11, and that's accurate. However, there was specific information about use of airplanes, that an attack was on the way two or three months beforehand, and that several people were already in the country by May of 2001." Says U.S. claims about not knowing of 9/11 plan were outrageous lies: "That's an outrageous lie and documents can prove it's a lie."

- June 2001—German intelligence warns CIA, M16, and Mossad that Middle Eastern terrorists are planning to hijack commercial aircraft to use as weapons to attack "American and Israeli symbols, which stand out."

- July 2001—FBI agent Ken Williams sends a message warning of suspicious activities involving a group of Middle Eastern men taking flight training lessons in Arizona: subtitle of memo is "Osama bin Laden and

Al-Muhrjiroun supporters attending civil aviation universities/colleges in Arizona."

- August 2001—Zacarias Moussaoui is arrested in Minneapolis with letters that connect him to Malaysia (where a meeting of al Qaeda operatives occurred under the watch of the CIA in 2000) and some of the hijackers. He also has an unexplained $32,000 bank balance, two knives, fighting gloves, shin guards, and has prepared for violence through physical training. He paid $8,300 for flight training, mostly in cash, to use a 747 aircraft simulator. He asked, "How much fuel is on board a 747 and how much damage could it cause if it hit anything?" He has no aviation background, little previous training, and no pilot's license; he wants to fly only as an ego-boosting thing, he is extremely interested in the operation of the plane's doors and control panel, and wants to know how to communicate with the flight tower. He is evasive and belligerent when asked about his background. He mostly practices flying in the air rather than taking off or landing. The flight school sends information to the FBI and receives little interest, so it contacts them again, saying. "Do you realize how serious is this? This man wants training on a 747. A 747 fully loaded with fuel could be used as a weapon." Moussaoui is arrested but not connected to the 9/11 attackers until after 9/11.

- August 23–27, 2001—FBI agents in Minneapolis are convinced Zacarias Moussaoui is planning to do something with a plane. One agent writes that he might "fly something into the World Trade Center." They decide to pursue a Foreign Intelligence Surveillance Act (FISA) warrant—in more than 10,000 requests over 20 years, every single warrant has been granted—yet FBI headquarters decides against it due to a mistaken understanding by its legal experts of the FISA rules.

- August 24, 2001—A Minneapolis FBI agent contacts CIA's Counter Terrorism Center and calls Moussaoui a "suspect 747 airline attacker" and a "suspect airline suicide attacker." FBI headquarters chastises the Minneapolis office for contacting headquarters without permission.

- Bob Graham explained the Moussaoui failure by the FBI, and in doing so, discussed in depth the warnings that should have been clear. From June to July 2001, the National Security Agency (NSA) noted an increase in threat activity (the third such rise since the winter). The U.S. military declared ThreatCon Delta and all ships in the Persian Gulf were sent to sea. And Attorney General John Ashcroft began traveling only on government jet. Graham says this was "opposed to the commercial aircraft Attorneys General normally take, despite the fact that senior FBI and CIA officials knew of no specific threat against the Attorney General" (p. 72). In July 2001, when the FBI's Phoenix office sent a memo voicing concern that UBL might be using U.S. flight schools to infiltrate America's civil aviation system, it was ignored by superiors and never reached the FBI's Minneapolis office (which arrested Zacarias Moussaoui 1 month later for suspicious activities at a flight school). This is called stove-piping [when information did not move across FBI field offices].

One way to sum up the above is that "The whole discussion for two and half years was that federal agencies couldn't connect the dots," James Kallstrom says, and adds that "none of these databases talked to each other."[62] Today, more than 70,000 local officers in New York and Vermont will have direct access to FBI counterterrorism information through a new intelligence center near Albany.

Local Police Terrorism Strategies and Officer Stress

In earlier studies, compelling evidence surfaced revealing that most street cops do not think they control the "mean" streets in their jurisdictions.[63] If in part not controlling the streets in their jurisdiction includes federal intrusion of local matters producing "perceived" ineffective terrorist strategy coupled with a local cop's poor management practices within a hieratical organizational structure, it might be easy to see why local law enforcement officers experience federal initiatives (and police organizations) in response to terrorism as a stressor. It could also be speculated that officers would deliver quality police services less often while under the thumb of federal terrorist investigation intrusion on their "turf" and inappropriate police management from an incompatible police structure in a free society. Street cops require the authority and training to investigate, apprehend, and detain terrorist groups that the federal agencies are inadequately prepared to control.

As more and more departments initiate terrorism strategies in the realization of their responsibilities of public safety, it is the street cop who carries out the orders from a paramilitary hierarchical organizational leader. From the perspective of the street cop, the idea that the bottom line for local public safety lays with law enforcement officers and not necessarily high command or federal agencies, a typical response among officers, sounds like this: "That ain't new news," says a frustrated street cop in Boston. "The problem is that while I know what every cop with a brain knows that, the level of respect from the public is downright nasty." This thought is consistent with the 73% of the 558 cops surveyed for this book who report that the public largely disrespects police officers. Equally important are the reported low levels of respect held by the courts, prosecutors, and police supervisors for police officers. Begging inquiry then might be the question of stress within this role of public defender against terror and other forms of crimes and low levels of respect or what can be called a lack of confidence. The failure to enact that modest reform in a timely fashion is one example of the security gaps that persist months after this book is published after the most devastating intelligence failure in U.S. history.

Justice Response to Terrorists and Street Cop Stress

Experts agree that street cop stress can be found in external stressors, creating frustration with what appears to be a lenient criminal justice system, internal stressors created by the police organization itself, and role conflicts that include fears about the job and in this case, feelings of inadequacy and frustration about the limitations of their job as produced by continual federal intrusion in local matters.[64]

To the street cop, his or her "mean" streets belong to the officer at least until federal agents arrived. Federal agencies continue to control the investigations against terrorists including immigrants, despite the fact that those investigations are local targets involving local constituents that impact local public safety issues. During an investigation, federal personnel can set aside basic due-process guarantees under the U.S.A. Patriot Act, but street cops cannot set aside those guarantees, nor should they.[65] The responsibility and expectations of street cops has changed since 9/11, yet street cop exposure to civil litigation is unchanged. In this regard, federal agents can make more arrests than street cops who are prohibited from utilizing U.S.A. Patriot guidelines and lack the authority of federal agents. Unless of course if local officers receive a dual jurisdiction as a federal agent. Then the questions about authority, command, payroll, and so on come into play and local chiefs are going to be hard pressed to explain how some officers work for the federal government as opposed to managing traffic and answering service calls in the community.

Furthermore, street cops are subject to federal prosecution under federal laws such as 42 U.S.C. Section 1983 (a statute that imposes civil liability on any person acting under state laws who deprives another person of Constitutional rights). Apparently, this lack of authority and control or even participation in one of America's most televised criminal elements affects the self-respect levels of the officers surveyed in the study conducted for this book.

How much does the activity of the federal government linked to 9/11 frustrate the typical officer? Apparently, when street cops see themselves as cops carrying the weight of the world on their shoulders and little ability to cope with their problems, their first response is alcohol abuse, which helps overcome their "perceived" inadequacies of serving and protecting the public.[66] This pathway (self-respect) has been reduced in part due to the strategy used by federal law enforcement agencies and local police agency exclusion in defending "local turf." It could be argued that federal strategies have reduced the self-worth or self-respect of the typical street cop in Boston and the other city cops surveyed for this study. Since these officers have similar characteristics of street cops at large, it is likely that most city cops resent federal intrusion in local matters. Officers around the country are generally aware of the role officers in other countries play in the investigation, control, and custody of terrorists. Worse, street cops feel inadequate in fulfilling their personal obligations of helping to serve the public against terrorists. Most street cops want to aid individuals in distress and put away a few bad guys in the process.

SUMMARY

Since 9/11, some Americans are anxious to close national borders, others demand retribution, while still some lobby to restrict Constitutional guarantees to further public safety measures. Yet you might ask, "Isn't that the purpose of constitutional guarantees?" Nonetheless, the focus of this chapter is associated with federal and local law enforcement response to foreign terrorism as opposed to the terrorist event itself and domestic terrorism, and how those responses act as a stressor to street cops. One way to define terrorism is the unlawful use of force or violence against persons or property to intimidate or coerce a government, the civilian population, or any segment thereof, in furtherance of political or social objectives. What sets terrorism apart from other acts of violence is that it consists of acts carried out in a dramatic way to attract publicity and create an atmosphere of alarm that goes beyond the actual victims. That is, the distinction between terrorism and other modes of armed conflict is in the difference between actual victims and the target audience.

Data about America can help in understanding the problems faced daily by law enforcement to guard its borders, which includes among other findings that 60 million visitors arrived on 675,000 commercial and private flights, 6 million more visitors came by sea, and 370 million more came by land in 2003 alone.

The *Bush Doctrine* promotes a war on terrorism and calls upon American forces to aggressively target terrorist groups and the countries that harbor them. The President's strategy is designed to prevent future terrorists' acts and includes the development of the Department of Homeland Security, the Maritime Transportation Security Act of 2002, the U.S. Immigration and Nationality Act, and the U.S.A. Patriot Act.

The importance of the U.S. Immigration and Nationality Act is that it widens the definition of terrorism because foreign terrorists can be immigrants or have immigrant connections in this country. The U.S.A. Patriot Act was designed to provide the appropriate tools required to intercept and obstruct terrorism. The Patriot Act allows federal investigators to use investigative tools that were already available to investigate organized crime and drug trafficking such as wiretaps and electric surveillance without obtaining warrants the same way local law enforcement obtains their warrants. Conversely, criticism of the U.S.A. Patriot Act is that it diminishes personal privacy by removing checks on government power, specifically by making it easier for the government to initiate surveillance and wiretapping of U.S. citizens under the authority of the shadowy, top-secret Foreign Intelligence Surveillance Court.

Today, the FBI tries to develop innovative ways to use technology as a device in sharing information, collaborating with international law enforcement and intelligence agencies, and developing global benefits that would aid in a reduction of terrorist activities. The FBI uses technology to share up-to-the-minute information with local law enforcement officers and intelligence agencies around the world. Also, the FBI developed the Joint Terrorism Task Force comprised of small cells of highly trained, locally based, passionately committed investigators, analysts, linguists, SWAT experts, and other specialists from dozens of U.S. law enforcement and intelligence agencies. Some observers imply that the federal government is using the threat of terrorism to reduce local control and power in law enforcement. While this thought might seem suspect, Chapter 7 implies that the generous support consisting of training, personnel, weapons, equipment, and funding to local police by the federal government is a reflection of "Big Brother's" intent. Others see federal support as an exercise in duty within a check and balance system to aid local government in moving toward their objectives. However, local police agencies are saying that a lack of cooperation exists among federal personnel and federal agencies associated with terrorist activities. DOJ cites several war on terrorism accomplishments since 9/11, which include identifying and disrupting over 150 terrorist threats and cells, capturing or killing nearly two-thirds of al Qaida's known senior leadership including a mastermind of the September 11th attacks, and worldwide, incapacitating more than 3,000 terrorist operatives.

Some of the changes in police jobs are that agencies are increasing resources to prepare for terrorist attacks and gathering intelligence, training street cops as first-responders at the terrorist scene, and training patrol officers to respond and investigate civilian reports of terrorism-related activity. Some of the local police concerns about immigration is that they suspect ICE of wanting to control their "turf" rather than aid local cops in apprehension and investigation of aliens. It comes down to the job of apprehending an estimated 8 million illegal immigrants.

Some local police strategies to control terrorism since 9/11 include strengthening liaisons with federal, state, and local agencies, including fire departments and other police departments; refining training and emergency response plans to address terrorist threats, including attacks with weapons of mass destruction; increasing patrols and shored-up barriers around landmarks, places of worship, ports of entry, transit systems, and nuclear power plants; more heavily guarded public speeches, parades, and other public events; creating new counterterrorism divisions and reassigned officers to counterterrorism from other divisions such as drug enforcement; employing new technologies, such as x-ray-like devices to scan containers at ports of entry and sophisticated sensors to detect a chemical, biological, or radiation attack; and inspecting bags and identifying public transportation passengers.

Centered in the evidence in this chapter, it appears that policing of terrorism (not the event) is a stressor among officers. The stressor that contributes the most stress and frustration among local law enforcement officers and apparently police management from sergeants to chiefs to commissioners is the suspect federal intrusion of local terrorist matters producing a "perceived" ineffective strategy that apparently is linked to "turf" control as opposed to terrorist control. Yet, local officers engaged in the policing of terrorism are also confronted with a hierarchal paramilitary police structure that adds to the frustration and uncertainty of federal intrusion despite the uncertainty of top command about federal intentions. Often feelings of inadequacy of street cops when it comes to both policing terrorism and as first-responders at terrorist attacks and police strategies such as zero tolerance in subways, for example, lead to reduce self-esteem among officers. Federal officers do not concern themselves with collateral casualties mainly because the law protects them from their indiscretions differently than local cops, adding to an officer's significance and public respect. Finally, officers are aware of the investigative priority practices of the police in other countries, which further demonstrates to American cops their inadequacies. The present initiatives to manage terrorism produce incredible stressors for local law enforcement officers and their commanders, and eventually must impact their ability to provide quality law enforcement services.

▨▨▨▨ WHAT WOULD YOU DO IF YOU WERE IN CHARGE? ▨▨▨▨

The cruisers were destroyed, but an Anderson County, TN, deputy survived two crashes in 8 hours.[67] Deputy Mike Nations, 47, lost control of his patrol car around midnight Saturday while responding to a domestic call.

A tire apparently blew out, causing the vehicle to roll several times.

His wife, Robin, who was participating in the sheriff's ride-along program, was a passenger. Both were taken to the University of Tennessee Medical Center for injuries. She was treated and released. He was kept a little longer.

Deputy Nathan Brown picked up Nations around 7:00 A.M. Sunday. While driving him home, Brown, 27, apparently went into a diabetic shock, lost control of his cruiser, and crashed.

"We are thankful that no one was seriously injured or killed in either accident. We expect both officers to return to full duty soon," Sheriff Bill White said.

Brown was listed Tuesday in stable condition at UT Medical Center, recovering from surgery Sunday for his minor injuries. He had to be cut out of the wreckage.

While the cars were lost, White said, "Our primary concern is with our deputies."

OFFICERS KILLED IN CALIFORNIA

Wednesday, July 13, 2005, Sacramento County Sheriff's Department Deputy Blount and Deputy Joseph Kievernagel were killed in a helicopter accident while on aerial patrol.[68] During their flight Deputy Kievernagel, who was the pilot, called in a mayday as the result of a mechanical failure and on-board fire.

Deputy Kievernagel made an emergency landing on a hilly area near Lake Natoma. When the Eurcopter-EC120 landed the tail end broke off, causing the fuselage of the helicopter to roll down a hill. It is believed that Deputy Kievernagel and Deputy Blount survived the initial landing with minor injuries, but were killed as the result of the helicopter rolling down the hill. A third deputy, who was first on the list to become a co-pilot, was also in the helicopter and received life-threatening injuries.

Deputy Blount had served with the Sacramento County Sheriff's Department for 7 years. He is survived by his parents, brother, and sister. Deputy Kievernagel had served with the Sacramento County Sheriff's Department for 17 years. He is survived by his wife, parents, and seven siblings.

DISCUSSION QUESTIONS

1. Characterize the primary focus of this chapter and its importance to public safety.
2. Provide at least one definition of terrorism and explain why you selected this definition versus the few others in the chapter.
3. Describe the differences between war and acts of terrorism. Use examples.
4. Provide some data about America that makes it a difficult country to guard against immigration, drug traders, and terrorists. Of the data offered, what surprised you the most and why?
5. Describe the primary components of the Bush Doctrine and its significance.
6. Describe the importance of the U.S. Immigration and Nationality Act and its significance to terrorists.
7. Articulate some of the primary components of the U.S.A. Patriot Act I and II. Explain the rationale behind its primary perspective. It what way might you agree with this rationale? Disagree?
8. Characterize the criticism of the U.S.A. Patriot Act.
9. Identify some general responses developed by the FBI to terrorism before and after 9/11.
10. Describe the speculation about federal intention linked to terrorism strategies. In what way might you agree and disagree with this speculation?
11. Identify the DOJ's accomplishments in the War on Terrorism. Of the accomplishments listed, which one surprised you the most and why?
12. Explain some of the changes among police jobs after 9/11.

13. Discuss local police concerns about immigration control. In what way is immigration control disadvantageous for local police?

14. Identify some of the local police strategies to control terrorism.

15. Outline the city of New York's initiatives to police terrorism and explain in what way it might deter terrorist attacks.

16. Characterize the primary stressors associated with policing terrorism among local police officers. In what way do you agree with these descriptive outcomes? Disagree?

17. Characterize the concern of local command relative to federal policing of terrorism. In what ways do you agree and disagree with this perspective?

END NOTES

1. Although there are many groups that want to close American borders, this group is the most vocal about the American-Mexican border and might be worth your review. Arizona Minute Man Project to patrol border (2005, January 26). Retrieved online July 16, 2005: http://www.securityarms.com/cgi-local/sa.cgi?noframes;read=1521

2. Lance Morrow (2001, September 12). The case for rage and retribution. *Time.com.* Retrieved online July 16, 2005: http://www.time.com/time/nation/article/0,8599,174641,00.html

3. David Koppel (2001, October 22). Will the war kill the Bill of Rights. *Cato Institute.* Retrieved online July 16, 2005: http://www.cato.org/dailys/10-22-01.html

4. FBI (2005). *Joint Terrorism Task Force.* Retrieved online July 13, 2005: http://www.fbi.gov/page2/dec04/jttf120114.htm

5. Central Intelligence Agency (2005). *The war on terrorism.* Retrieved online July 13, 2005: http://www.cia.gov/terrorism/faqs.html

6. FBI (1997). *Terrorism.* Retrieved online July 13, 2005: http://www.fbi.gov

7. Erica Fairchild and Harry R. Dammer (2001). *Comparative criminal justice system,* 2nd ed. Belmont, CA: Wadsworth. p. 281.

8. Erica Fairchild and Harry R. Dammer (2001). pp. 281–283.

9. Christian Science Monitor. *Terrorism.* Retrieved June 15, 2004. http://www.csmonitor.com/specials/terrorism/start.htm

10. DEA website retrieved June 18, 2004: http://www.usdoj.gov/dea/

11. Partnerships Protecting America. Assistant Director Louis Quijas Discusses the Importance of Federal, State, and Local Law Enforcement Partnerships. January 30, 2004. Retrieved June 10, 2004: http://www.fbi.gov/page2/jan04/partnership013004.htm

12. FBI (2005). *Fact and figures 2003.* Retrieved online July 16, 2005: http://www.fbi.gov/priorities/priorities.htm Also see FBI. Testimony of Gary M. Bald, Acting Assistant Director, Counterterrorism Division, Before the Senate Judiciary Committee, Subcommittee on Terrorism, Technology, and Homeland Security. January 27, 2004. "Covering the Waterfront—A Review of Seaport Security Since September 11, 2001" Retrieved June 10, 2004: http://www.fbi.gov/congress/congress04/bald012704.htm

13. FBI. Testimony of Gary M. Bald, Acting Assistant Director, Counterterrorism Division, Before the Senate Judiciary Committee, Subcommittee on Terrorism,

Technology, and Homeland Security. January 27, 2004. "Covering the Waterfront—A Review of Seaport Security Since September 11, 2001" Retrieved June 10, 2004: http://www.fbi.gov/congress/congress04/bald012704.htm

14. Homeland Security Website. Retrieved June 14, 2004: http://www.whitehouse.gov/homeland/

15. U.S. Immigration and Nationality Act. Chapter 12. Retrieved June 11, 2004: http://www.fourmilab.ch/uscode/8usc/www/t8-12-II-II-1182.html#(a)(3)(B)(iii)

16. Department of Justice. USA Patriot Act Website. Retrieved June 14, 2004. http://www.lifeandliberty.gov/

17. Senator Joe Biden (2001, October 25). Congress Record (2001, October 25). Washington, DC.

18. Senator John Edwards (2001, October 26). The Patriot Act. Retrieved online July 16, 2005: http://forums5.aclu.org/messageview.cfm?catid=118&threadid=7066

19. American Civil Liberties Union. Retrieved online June 15, 2004. http://www.aclu.org/SafeandFree/SafeandFree.cfm?ID=11835&c=206

20. Dennis J. Stevens (2003). *Applied community policing in the 21st century.* Boston: Allyn & Bacon. p. 36.

21. Kathryn Sikkink (2004). Understanding the September 11 terror attacks: A human rights approach. In John J. Macionis and Nijole V. Benokraitis (Eds.), *Seeking ourselves: Classic, contemporary and cross-cultural readings in sociology* (pp. 309–313). Upper Saddle River, NJ: Prentice Hall.

22. John E. Lewis (2005, March 14). Deputy Assistant Director, Counterterrorism Division Federal Bureau of Investigation. 4th Annual International Conference on Public Safety: Technology and Counterterrorism. Counterterrorism Initiatives and Partnerships San Francisco, California.

23. John E. Lewis (2005, March 14).

24. John E. Lewis (2005, March 14).

25. FBI (2005). *Joint Terrorism Task Force.* Retrieved online July 13, 2005: http://www.fbi.gov/page2/dec04/jttf120114.htm

26. Sam Walker and Charles M. Katz (2005). *The police in America: An introduction,* 5th ed. Boston: McGraw-Hill. pp. 527–529. Also see Terrorism and personal liberty (2005). *Constitution Party.* Retrieved online July 16, 2005: http://www.constitutionparty.com/party_platform.php#Terrorism%20and%20Personal%20Liberty

27. Willie Hulon, Assistant Director, Counterterrorism Division (2005). Counterterrorism. Retrieved online July 13, 2005: http://www.fbi.gov/terrorinfo/counterrorism/waronterrorhome.htm

28. Peter L. Berger (1963). *Invitation to sociology: A humanistic perspective.* New York: Anchor Books. pp. 23–25.

29. Judy Holland. (2001, October 6-7). FBI frustrates police chiefs. *The Patriot Ledger* (Boston), p. 9.

30. Dennis J. Stevens (2003). *Applied community policing in the 21st century.* Boston: Allyn & Bacon. p. 270.

31. Department of Homeland Security. Retrieved online March 13, 2006: http://www.dhs.gov/interweb/assetlibrary/DHS_OrgChart.pdf

32. Foreign Intelligence Surveillance Court of Review (2002, August). Retrieved online March 13, 2006: http://www.epic.org/privacy/terrorism/fisa/

33. Personal confidential communication between the writer and a divisional commander employed by the Boston Police Department.

34. Maggie Mulvihill, Jonathan Wells and Jack Meyers (2001, January 1). The White House connection: Saudi 'agents' close Bush friends. *Boston Herald*. Retrieved online July 17, 2005: http://www.bostonherald.com/news/americas_new_war/akin1112001.htm Also see Rob's Blog (2004, November 1). Latest chance for a slow dance. Retrieved online July 17, 2005: http://www.chromedecay.org/rob/archives/000480.html

35. American Civil Liberties Union. Retrieved June 15, 2004. http://www.aclu.org/SafeandFree/SafeandFree.cfm?ID=11835&c=206 Also see, David Koppel (2001, October 22).

36. Stephen J. Vicchio (2001). Police corruption. Retrieved online July 16, 2005: http://www.enotes.com/police-corruption/39279

37. Department of Justice Website on preserving life and liberty. Retrieved June 15, 2004: http://www.lifeandliberty.gov/subs/a_terr.htm

38. Personal confidential communication between the writer and a NYPD divisional commander.

39. Ronald Kessler (1993). *The FBI: Inside the world's most powerful law enforcement agency*. New York: Pocket Books.

40. Ronald Kessler (1993). p. 371.

41. Laura Meckler (2002) Federal center trains for terrorists threats. Retrieved online March 13, 2006: http://www.firehouse.com/frontlines/news/02/0813.html

42. Personal confidential communication between the writer and a commissioner of police of a large city.

43. Local Cops and Visa-Violators. *Problems in deputizing police in war on terrorism*. Retrieved June 14, 2004: http://www.csmonitor.com/2002/0430/p10s02-comv.html

44. Personal confidential communication between a chief of police and the author.

45. Personal confidential communication between a chief of police and the author. It is interesting that a similar comment was offered by six other police commanders and chiefs but of the eight, these comments represent the case. There were 10 chiefs and commanders of large metropolitan departments who provided and insight into sharing of federal authority. This information was gathered between January and May 2004. The author met individually with the chiefs.

46. Lt. John Skipper (2004). *Foundation Seeks to Aid Local Law Enforcement in the War on Terrorism*. Retrieved June 14, 2004: http://www.adl.org/learn/columns/John_Skipper.asp

47. Men sue Detroit cops who arrested them as terror suspects on U.S.-Canada bridge. (2004, March 26). *CNNEWS*. Retrieved Online June 16, 2004: http://cnews.canoe.ca/CNEWS/World/WarOnTerrorism/2004/03/26/397246-ap.html

48. Beth Gardiner (2005, July 14). London identifies four suicide bombers. *Mercury Online News*. Retrieved online July 14, 2005: http://www.mercurynews.com/mld/mercurynews/news/world/12131530.htm

49. BBC News (2004, April 9). Madrid train attack. *BBC News*. Retrieved online July 14, 2005: http://news.bbc.co.uk/1/hi/in_depth/europe/2004/madrid_train_attacks/default.stm

50. Charles M. Sennott (2004, September 26). Europe's terror fight quiet, unrelenting. *Boston Globe*, pp. A1, A19.

51. Charles M. Sennott (2002, June 21). Bombs on trains kill. *Boston Globe*. Also see Charles M. Sennott (2004, April 21). Wide dragnet splinters Al Qaeda: Global crackdown slows a network aiming to regroup. *Boston Globe*, p. A20.

52. Post-9/11 reforms haven't fixed intelligence failings. (2004, April 15). *USA Today*. Retrieved online June 16, 2004: http://www.usatoday.com/news/opinion/editorials/2004-04-15-our-view_x.htm

53. Police Departments. Council on Foreign Relations. In cooperation with the Markle Foundation. Retrieved online June 16, 2004: http://cfrterrorism.org/security/police_print.html

54. For instance, the city of Boston in the summer of 2004 began security precautions in their subways. Dogs will sniff packages and trained cops will ask for identification. "The desire for a higher standard of security on city trans is reasonable," say experts. For the rest of the story, see Security precaution hits subways: Is it too much? (2004, June 10). *The Christian Science Monitor*. Retrieved Online June 16, 2004: http://www.csmonitor.com/2004/0610/p03s01-usju.htm

55. Police Departments. Council on Foreign Relations. In cooperation with the Markle Foundation. Retrieved online June 16, 2004: http://cfrterrorism.org/security/police_print.html

56. New York City police officials have issued terror prevention tips to patrol cops—including suspecting people who "express hatred for America" (2004, May 18). *US/Eastern* (1010 WINS): Retrieved online June 16, 2004: http://1010wins.com/topstories/winstopstories_story_139070556.html

57. Donna Lieberman, executive director of the New York Civil Liberties Union, called the directive so broad that it invites civil rights abuses. Lieberman noted that criticism of our country is protected by the First Amendment (2004, June 16).

58. Phil Hirschkorn and Deborah Feyerick (2004, May 26). CNNEWS New York Bureau. Retrieved online June 16, 2004: http://www.cnn.com/2004/LAW/05/25/fbi.sharing.data/

59. Phil Hirschkom and Deborah Feyerick (2004, May 26). Feds to start sharing terrorist information. *CNN.com*. Retrieved online July 16, 2005: http://www.cnn.com/2004/LAW/05/25/fbi.sharing.data/

60. Phil Hirschkom and Deborah Feyerick (2004, May 26).

61. Matthew Robinson (2004). Threat about airplanes and 9/11. Retrieved online March 13, 2006: http://www.justiceblind.com/airplanes.html

62. Phil Hirschkom and Deborah Feyerick (2004, May 26).

63. Dennis J. Stevens (2005). Police officer stress and occupational stressors.

64. Katherine W. Ellison (2004). *Stress and the police officer*. Springfield, IL: Charles C. Thomas. p. 62. Hans Toch (2001). *Stress in policing*. Washington, DC: APA. pp. 24–26.

65. American Civil Liberties Union. Retrieved June 15, 2004. http://www.aclu.org/SafeandFree/SafeandFree.cfm?ID=11835&c=206

66. Dennis J. Stevens (2005). Police officer stress and occupational stressors. In Heith Copes (Ed.), *Policing and stress* (pp. 1–24). Upper Saddle River, NJ: Prentice Hall.

67. Deputy involved in two wrecks in 8 hours (2005, June 29). Retrieved online July 15, 2005: http://www.lefande.com/weblog/

68. The Officer Down Memorial Page. Retrieved online March 13, 2006: http://www.odmp.org/officer.php?oid=17814

9

Stress in Small-Town and Rural Policing

"Stress in small-town and rural law enforcement? Hell, yes we have stress. Nothing to do, I'm bored off my a**, and my only friends are the drunks and cows. This job's killin' me!" —West Virginia law enforcement officer

Learning Objectives

Once reading this chapter, you will be able to:

- Define what is meant by small-town and rural.

- Understand how stress can impact small-town and rural police similar to their urban counterparts

- Identify the unique stressors that impact small-town and rural police.

- Define the four types of stress in policing and explain how they impact small-town and rural police.

- Define the four types of stress unique to small-town and rural police, specifically security, social, working conditions, and inactivity.

- Describe the findings from recent research on small-town and rural police stress.

- Explain the four constraints faced by small-town and rural police, specifically knowledge, resources, politics, and the nature of small communities.

KEY TERMS

Inactivity	Security	Social
Rural	Small-town	Working conditions

INTRODUCTION

In our study of policing and thinking about police officers, we have a tendency to think that "a cop is a cop is a cop." Often it is true that police officers from the east coast resemble officers from the west coast and throughout middle-America. However, there are often subtle differences amongst police officers that should not be lost in our generalizations. For instance, sheriff's deputies often perform the very same roles as police officers, but there are differences in the way they are organized and managed which can impact these two bodies of law enforcement very differently. However, in some jurisdictions sheriff deputies are primarily jailers (such as the sheriffs and their deputies in Massachusetts), sometimes they provide court and specific buildings with public safety, sometimes they are fire fighter personnel (such as Palm Beach County Florida), other times they are airport public safety officers (Miami Dude County Florida), and sometimes there are investigators such as Harrison Country Mississippi. Officers too have many different roles including some who deliver police services one-half of their duty time and become fire fighters the other one-half of their duty time (Aiken, South Carolina). It is the same variety of tasks for small-town and rural police in America as well. While they do perform many of the same roles and functions as their counterparts, there are some unique differences between these two levels of policing. And, when it comes to the more specific topic of stress in policing, again there are many similarities, but many differences as well. Police officers in these environments face many of the same stressors as their urban counterpart. The perceived level of danger regarding their job, the stress of placing someone under arrest, and the difficulties that result from the stress of shift work are no different. However, there are some stress factors that are unique to small-town and rural police. These unique factors have not been given adequate attention in either police training or research conducted on the police.

The purpose of this chapter, then, is to explore more fully the types of stress that small-town and rural police officers and sheriff's deputies face in the performance of their duties that are unique to their situation. In order to achieve this end, this chapter will first define what is meant by small-town and rural. It will then detail how the four areas of police stress research still apply to small-town and rural policing, but in its own unique way. The chapter will then turn to detailing four stress factors that are unique to small-town and rural policing. Next it will discuss the limited research in this area and provide an overview of some of the recent research conducted by the chapter's authors. Finally, it will detail the constraints faced by small-town and rural law enforcement agencies when it comes to the important issue of police stress.

SMALL-TOWN AND RURAL DEFINED

Defining what is small town and rural is no easy matter. The Census Bureau of the United States provides its own definitive definition of what is considered small town and rural.[1] They place any city or town that is under 50,000 in population as being a *small town* or *rural* environment. Although this can be a somewhat arbitrary figure, it does provide for an operational definition to defining the concepts at hand. As a result, this chapter is concerned about police departments and sheriff's departments that service populations under 50,000 in their respective jurisdictions (which includes the surrounding area as opposed to a single city), regardless of the size of the police department.

Police departments that serve populations under 50,000, however, tend to be small. In fact, most police departments in the United States are small in number. Of the approximately 18,000 police departments in the United States, 90% of all local agencies have fewer than 50 officers in their employment.[2] Nearly one-half of all local departments employ less than 10 police officers and a small percentage (approximately 5%) employ no full-time officers, but rather depend on paid part-timers and volunteers. It should also be pointed out that there are many small towns and rural areas that do not have their own police department due to the expenditures and must rely on the county sheriff or the state police for police assistance. When it comes to policing in small-town and rural areas, these two entities become much more important than in their urban counterparts.

Although many small towns, villages, and small cities do have their own police departments, they still rely on the county sheriff's office. Although the sheriff's office generally provides many of the same services as a local police department, it is organized very differently. Sheriffs are mostly elected officials and thus they have to run for their positions. They usually serve a 4-year term before coming up for reelection and they typically run on a party platform as either a Democrat or a Republican. The only two exceptions are Rhode Island and Hawaii where sheriffs are appointed much like a chief of police. The employees of a sheriff's department are deputy sheriffs who serve at the "will and pleasure" of the elected official. Although approximately half of the sheriffs in the United States are law enforcement officers prior to their election as sheriff, having police experience is not a requirement, which makes the stability of their job come into question every 4 years. Perhaps what is most interesting is the diversity of responsibilities that a sheriff has in the execution of his or her office. The sheriff is often responsible, depending on jurisdiction, for the following[3]:

1. Criminal law enforcement and other general police services
2. Executing arrest warrants (99.7%)[4]
3. Custodial and correctional services, involving the transportation of prisoners and the management of the county jail
4. The processing of judicial writs and court orders, both criminal and civil
5. Security of the court via bailiffs (97%)
6. Miscellaneous services, such as the transportation and commitment of the mentally ill
7. Seizure of property claimed by the county
8. Collection of county fees and taxes
9. Sale of licenses and permits, plus other services that do not fall neatly under the statutory responsibilities of other law enforcement or social service agencies
10. Firefighting responsibilities
11. Operation of local jails

This multitude of services creates a very different dynamic regarding policing, one that brings a very administrative and political element not seen in most local police departments.

In addition to county sheriff's departments, many rural jurisdictions are also covered by the state police agency. Although nearly every state has a state police agency (the exception being Hawaii), not all function in the same way. For many states, however, the state police serve as an additional means of police services for many rural jurisdictions. Some small-towns and rural areas are limited in their staffing and the state police will often supplement their police coverage. In other cases, the police or sheriffs only work during the day and state police must take over during the evening and overnight hours. In other cases, where local police and sheriffs do provide 24-hour coverage, the state police tend to the highways and accidents and only provide a means of backup for police and sheriffs when necessary. Regardless, the state police provide a far more limited presence in any small-town and rural community and they are limited in the services they are able to provide.

One final consideration for defining small-town and rural is the environment in which these officers serve. Geography tends to be a key factor in our understanding of what is small-town and rural. Cities, towns, and villages that are often categorized as "small-town" tend to be found in isolated areas of the United States. They are not necessarily located along interstates or main state highways, but rather off the so-called "beaten path." In addition, when it comes to rural living, the areas tend not to be populated areas with any concentration, but rather spread across the geographical terrain. Neighbors can be miles apart from one another and tens of miles from the nearest small-town. Municipal police departments tend to police an area that is on average about

25 square miles in size. Sheriff's departments, on the other hand, police areas that are on average 920 square miles (Los Angeles County is 4,061 square miles, Aiken County, South Carolina, is 325 square miles).[5] In addition, this is often done with the same number of police officers/deputies, making the sheriff's duties more difficult due to the size of the counties they patrol.

STRESS IN POLICING AS APPLIED TO SMALL-TOWN AND RURAL POLICING

The research in the area of police stress has been plentiful over the past 30 years and has yielded an extensive literature on the subject. Most of the research, particularly stress studies, have been relegated to urban and metropolitan police and most of the research has been conducted in cities with populations over 250,000. As a result, most of the research is very adequate for understanding the stress factors faced by large metropolitan police officers. The question is whether or not that research can apply to police and sheriff's departments that service populations under 50,000. There is a strong argument that large-city research on police-related stress can be applied to small-town and rural police, because many of the factors remain the same regardless of size. However, what this research fails to take into account is some of the factors that are very unique to small-town and rural policing that are clearly missing when looking at studies regarding metropolitan police.

One example might serve to make this very clear. In urban policing, due to the rather confined space geographically (remember, on average 25 square miles), the high number of police officers and resources, police officers will generally have a backup on any call that is within a 5-minute response. In rural policing, due to the large geography (remember, on average 920 square miles), a low number of officers and a lack of resources, sheriff's deputies may have no backup readily available and if they do the response time can sometimes be as long as an hour.[6] The stress that can be invoked from this type of scenario is not revealed or discussed in the studies on urban policing and stress. This is simply because it is not a situation faced by urban police. Thus, when applying urban police studies on stress to small-town and rural police, the studies are often missing the situations these police officers face.

This is still not to say that the studies on large metropolitan police are not applicable to small-town and rural police. In fact, they are. However, it must be noted that sometimes the way these factors stress urban police is very different for rural police. Yet, regardless of size, they still are factors that cause stress. These factors are generally broken down into four categories: organizational stress, external stress, task-related stress, and personal stress.[7] Each of these factors are briefly reviewed for a definition, how they have been found to stress urban police, and how they apply to small-town and rural police as well.

Organizational Stress

Organizational stress refers to the types of stress placed upon officers that come through the police department itself.[8] These often take form in the policies and procedures that the department dictates, as well as the administrative methods for supervising police officers on the street. It should be mentioned that many rural law enforcement organizations have either inadequate or no policies at all, which adds to stress levels because an officer never knows what the policy is until the task is completed.[9] They also include a host of other factors that elevate the stress of the job such as "poor pay, excessive paperwork, insufficient training, inadequate equipment, weekend duty, shift work, limited promotional opportunities, poor supervision and administrative support, and poor relationships with supervisors or colleagues."[10] These types of stressors are very evident in medium- and large-size police departments and have been found by previous research to be the most significant causes of stress in police work.[11]

While organizational stress causes high levels of stress for urban police officers, some research suggests that this is also the case of small-town and rural agencies.[12] Intuitively this would make sense to at least argue that organizational stress is just as prevalent in small-town and rural police as it is in their urban counterpart. These officers face the problem of poor pay, insufficient training, inadequate equipment, weekend duty, shift work, limited promotional opportunities, and poor supervision. However, these organizational stressors may possibly be even more exacerbated by the very fact that small-town and rural police are small-town and rural. These types of organizations tend to have a weaker economic base and thus poorer pay, limited training, and fewer opportunities for purchasing new equipment. In addition, the nature of small-town and rural policing, with its limited number of officers and deputies, often means that these police officers and sheriff's deputies not only have to work weekends and shift work, but they also have to be on call during some of their days off in order to back up the limited workforce actually on patrol. Finally, if there is a problem with poor management or relationships with administration or colleagues in a small department, it is far more difficult to "escape" these stressors than it is in a larger department. So, while organizational stressors are the key stressor for urban police, it is not too difficult to understand why this would be the same for small-town and rural police.

External Stress

External stress comes from those sources that impact the police, but lie outside of their realm of control.[13] Police officers spend an inordinate amount of their time dealing with external agencies and organizations that impact their job and these include "the courts, the prosecutor's office, the criminal process, the correctional system, the media, and public attitudes."[14] All of these greatly impact the police officer in the performance of his or her job, he or she often must deal with these other actors and institutions through negotiations or through their own policies and procedures. Because these influences are beyond the control of the officers, they can often induce stress, but they can do little to alleviate or control the stress. These external stressors have been found to cause high levels of stress in urban police officers.[15]

As small-town and rural police must also face these same external actors and institutions, there is no reason to suspect that these do not cause stress in these officers as well. Small-town and rural police officers and sheriff's deputies have to deal with the courts and prosecutor's office as well as the correctional and juvenile systems. These institutions can place demands on these officers that can elevate their levels of stress. In addition, the local media and public attitudes toward the police can also affect the stress levels of small-town and rural police just like their urban counterpart. What is perhaps most notably different between the small-town and rural environments with the larger metropolitan police, however, is the nature of these external actors and institutions. The local courts and prosecutor's office is just as small as the police and sheriff's departments in these rural environments. Whereas police in large cities often have to deal with large bureaucracies within their local courts and prosecutor's office, small-town and rural police will often deal with the same judge and the same prosecutor day-in and day-out. So, while external stress is just as prevalent for small-town and rural police and sheriff's deputies, the forms that it takes are often different. The same can be said for the local media and public attitudes. Small-town and rural environments tend to have a more personable quality to their news that borders on gossip and this gossip is often spread from person to person in a tightly knit, small-town atmosphere. As a result, rumors about the police and sheriff's deputies can often spread throughout a community and wind up in the local newspapers. This is very different from the large media conglomerates that often serve to shape public attitudes in the large cities, but the end result is the same—these external stressors increase the level of stress in a police officer's life.

Task-Related Stress

Task-related stress has to do with the types of situations that police officers encounter in their work and how they can increase the level of stress in an officer.[16] A simple example is when a police officer has to make an arrest. The process of getting the suspect to comply, placing the handcuffs on the individual, and then conducting a search on the street can be highly stressful as it is often a point of danger for the officer. The officer must stay on alert and be ready for any potential harm that may come to him or her, thus with this elevated state of readiness comes an elevated state of stress. Task-related stress thus refers to a whole host of tasks that police officers face in their daily routine and include "inactivity and boredom, situations requiring the use of force, responsibility of protecting others, the use of discretion, the fear that accompanies danger to oneself and colleagues, dealing with violent or aggressive individuals, making critical decisions, frequent exposure to death, continual exposure to people in pain or distress, and constant need to keep one's emotions under close control."[17] All of these are clearly stressors for police officers working in large metropolitan areas, but they can also be stressors for police officers in small-town and rural environments as well. The essential difference is the frequency. Small-town and rural police have less calls-for-service and hence they experience fewer encounters like the ones listed above. The two stressors listed above that they are most likely to experience are inactivity and boredom, which can create their own high levels of stress.

Personal Stress

The last category of stress is personal stress.[18] Personal stress is essentially those things that come from outside work as a police officer, as well as those personal feelings and beliefs that may be derived from their police work, but affect the officer in both a physiological and psychological way. These stressors can include "marital relationships, health problems, addictions, peer group pressures, feelings of helplessness and depression, and lack of achievement."[19] These types of stressors have been found repeatedly in the research to be sources of stress for police officers and often include such factors as gender, ethnicity, education, years of service, shift assignment, supervisory duty, and various psychological traits exhibited by these officers.[20] It is clear that personal factors such as divorce, alcohol addiction, and depression not only affect the personal life of the officer, but their career as well. And often, it is the career that leads to such personal problems as divorce, alcoholism, and depression. These factors are just as prevalent in small-town and rural police as they are in urban police and there is no reason to believe that this would not be the case.

STRESS IN SMALL-TOWN AND RURAL POLICING

As should be fairly clear at this point, the four categories of stressors found in police stress research—organizational, external, task-related, and personal stress[21]—are found not only in urban police officers, but small-town and rural police officers as well. While the form of the stress may appear differently in small-town and rural environments, these stressors are still prevalent and still impact the stress levels of the police. Therefore, there is some application of large-city police officer stress research findings to small-town and rural police officers. There are, however, additional stressors that are unique to small-town and rural policing and not experienced by their urban counterpart.

Two researchers from Maine suggested that there are four categories of stress that are unique to small-town and rural police[22]: security, social factors, working conditions, and inactivity. Each of these factors are reviewed to show

how they are unique sources of stress for small-town and rural police officers and sheriff's deputies.

Security

The first factor unique to small-town and rural police officers and sheriff's deputies falls in the category of security. Although urban police must worry about their security, there are very unique circumstances that urban police officers do not face in their job. Small-town and rural police officers generally "experience an extreme sense of isolation in their attempts to confront both domestic and criminal situations"[23] and this is highlighted by the fact that these officers often do not have readily available backup. Almost invariably, when small-town and rural police officers respond to a domestic call, pull someone over for a traffic violation, or respond to a crime in progress, they are the only officers to respond. If they find themselves in a situation where they need backup, that backup is often miles away and it can take a long time to respond. One of the authors was a police officer in an urban setting whose backup was never less than a mile away.[24] That means, from a simple request on the radio, a backup could arrive on-scene within a minute or two. In such rural environments as Greenbrier County Sheriff's Department in West Virginia, one sheriff's deputy may be the only police official on duty in a hundred-mile radius and due to the nature of the geography and limited roads, his or her backup could potentially take as long as an hour to arrive. This means for all intents and purposes the officer or deputy is on his own when responding to a call and this knowledge can be stressful, as can the actual encounter.

One police officer described his experience in the following way:

> Not having backup nearby is always on my mind. I think about it more when I am going into a bar fight or a domestic disturbance. But even when you make a routine traffic stop and something just doesn't seem right, you look for cues about whether or not backup is required—like how many there are, if you know them, whether you need to search the vehicle. You always have to make the decision about whether or not to call backup. When it's late at night, then someone is going to have to get out of bed to come and back you up. If you call for help a lot, then some of the guys start to give you shit for being a wimp. Some of the guys pride themselves on never having to call backup.[25]

In addition to the isolation and lack of backup experience by these small-town and rural officers, some researchers also suggested that one of the factors that exacerbates the problem of security is the fact that small-town and rural citizens tend to be a more highly armed citizenry.[26] Whether this is in fact the case or whether it is only perception on the part of small-town and rural officers, in either case this fact or perception can serve to elevate the level of stress for small-town and rural police as this is constantly on their mind when they are the only officer responding to a call and backup is an hour away. As a result, security is an important factor that contributes to the level of stress in small-town and rural officers that is far different from those experienced by their urban counterparts.

Social

The second stress factor related to small-town and rural police are social factors.[27] The most unique of these social factors is the lack of anonymity amongst small-town and rural police officers. For anyone who has lived in a small-town or rural environment, this concept is easy to grasp. For those who live in an urban setting, this concept is very difficult to understand. In a small-town and rural setting, everyone knows who you are and they know everything about you, regardless of whether you communicate with these individuals or not. Some people give the apt analogy that it is like "living in a fishbowl," everyone sees you all the time. Police officers experience this in a small-town and rural setting when they go "off-duty" and are no longer wearing their uniform. Despite the fact they are no longer acting in their capacity as a police officer, everyone associates them with the police department because everyone knows they are a police officer. When one of the authors used to go off duty from working as a police officer, no one knew who he was because the urban setting provides an environment of anonymity. In the small-town and rural setting this cannot be obtained and, hence, this contributes to the stress of these officers.

In addition, this anonymity becomes further exacerbated by the problem of not having a peer support group. In the urban setting, police officers tend to spend their off-duty time with fellow police officers. These officers become a peer support group that allows the officer to communicate about life as a police officer with someone who understands the nature of police work. This is why most rookie police officers tend to gravitate toward spending their personal time with fellow police officers and less and less time with friends outside of policing. In the small-town and rural setting, because there are so few police officers there is a deficient support group with which to socialize. When one officer is off duty the others are on duty. A police department of only five police officers simply does not provide the officer with a peer group. Hence, if an officer wants to socialize it must be with non-police friends and these friends do not provide the same outlet for allowing the officer to discuss his or her job.

Finally, because the nature of small-town and rural environments is based on relationships, most of the officers hired to become members of the police department or sheriff's department are "local boys" who were born and raised in the same locale they come to police. This can create problems for the officer as most of the people he or she will encounter in calls-for-service, traffic stops, and criminal cases are going to be people he or she knows. There is almost always the possibility that the person they encounter as a victim or suspect is known to the officer, but there is also the chance they may be a friend as well. And, there is also an increased chance that one of the victims or suspects may in fact be one of the officer's very own family members. This can create difficulties for the officer who in his role as a police officer must remain objective and maintain their distance from the victims and suspects they encounter. Some experts relay an especially poignant story in this regard[28]:

> One officer graphically illustrated this dilemma in his description of some of the difficulties he had in responding to a domestic disturbance call at the home of the principal of the high school that he graduated from only a few years previous. This officer's inability to be perceived as an authority figure, a necessary prerequisite to establishing order in this domestic disturbance, was greatly diminished by the ex-principal's perception of this officer as a student rather than a law enforcement official.[29]

These preexisting relationships can create problems in other ways as well. Police officers may be forced to change their decisions regarding arrest or a traffic citation due to *who* the person is they are arresting or citing. Some experts provide the examples of "one officer . . . was ordered by the chief to drop charges against the owner of a large business because of the business owner's political influence in the small community" and "another officer described a case in which a relative of another officer was involved [and] charges were not filed because the arresting officer was afraid of the dissent it would cause within the department."[30]

These examples also raise another and highly related issue and that is the political dynamics of a small-town and rural environment. While large urban cities also must deal with political factors, small-town and rural environments tend to play politics at a social level. In other words, political power is gained and played out because of who one knows. This can create some difficult situations for small-town and rural police officers. An example of "one officer . . . reported that his chief of police ordered officers to *not* investigate further a burglary of one of the local businesses when a city council member's son became the prime suspect," and in another case a "supervisor called a friend to warn him that his daughter was under an investigation for selling drugs."[31]

Working Conditions

The third unique stressor among small-town and rural police officers consists of their working conditions.[32] While large metropolitan police officers also face stress in their working conditions, small-town and rural police have a unique set of circumstances due to the environment in which they work. The primary problem that faces small-town and rural police is a lack of resources due to the restricted financial environment in which they work. While urban police tend to be well outfitted in terms of uniforms, weapons, and police vehicles, small-town and rural police tend to lack the more modern and up-to-date equipment and often pay for their own uniforms and equipment including their service weapons (making deputies more financially stressed than urban officers). Some experts provide a particular case of these types of constraints when they discussed how one "small community would not allocate funds for a new squad car (there was only one) even though the current cruiser had over 200,000 miles on it" and "the car would quit running, not start, and had a top speed of 70 miles per hour."[33] The city simply decided it did not have the funds to purchase a new police cruiser and the agency had to make do with the vehicle it had.

Perhaps where the economic constraints are most noted by police officers and sheriff's deputies is in terms of their salary. Many large police departments have a starting pay of $30,000–$50,000 per year, whereas some small-town and rural agencies start their officers in the $12,000–$21,000 salary range. For example, Harrison County, Mississippi, deputies say their starting annual income is less than $18,000 per year and Wayne County, North Carolina, fares better at $19,000. Both say they max out around the low 30s.

Although the cost of living is less in small-town and rural America, it is still difficult to maintain a decent standard of living on only $12,000 a year. Small-town and rural agencies are often so strapped for funds that they are limited in the number of officers or deputies they can employ and are greatly restricted by the city when it comes to cost of living raises for its officers. One agency in West Virginia was so strapped for funds it essentially had to rely on a federal grant aimed at enhancing its community policing program, simply to provide basic police services.[34] The agency was essentially misusing the funds from the federal grant, but the realities behind their grossly limited budget demonstrated that they had little choice.

Added to this lack of funding for equipment and salaries is the inability to provide officers with adequate training. Urban police often receive 2–3 weeks of training each year, whereas many small-town and rural departments can only afford (and are only required) 8 hours of training each year. Even allowing for this one-day training session can be costly to the department due to the long distances at which most of the training sessions take place and for the fact that it places the agency short-handed and limits its ability to allow other officers to take vacation leave. In fact, taking this problem even further is the stress that is caused by being limited to the taking of vacation leave, sick leave, meeting with the local prosecutor regarding a case, or even appearing in court. Any one of these can severely handicap the staffing level of the agency and put other officers at risk when they have little or no backup available when needed.

There is an added stress to all of this for the common police officer as well. While large-city police also face resource limitations, they are not as aware of the politics involved regarding the relationship between the chief, mayor, and city council or the budgetary process. In small-town and rural agencies, every officer is fully aware of the political relationship and the budget implications that these relationships have. Hence, if the political relationship is strained, officers are aware of this strain, which can create an added level of stress to the officer's position.

Finally, some writers note that the organizational structure of small-town and rural police and sheriff's departments can create additional stress for officers and deputies.[35] Because there are so few layers of management and a limited number of positions, vertical movement within the police departments' rank structure is severely limited. Officers must often resign themselves to remaining in their positions as a street officer with little hope for an increase in authority, responsibility, or salary. A department that only has five sworn officers, a chief, a lieutenant, a sergeant, and three line officers provides little room for advancement. And, while officers in larger departments, faced with similar limitations for advancement, can't move vertically, they are often able to move into horizontal positions to obtain a different position with different types of authority and responsibility such as traffic, special weapons and tactic teams, follow-up units, or detective positions. In small-town and rural agencies these types of positions often do not exist, hence there is little room for horizontal movement.

Inactivity

The fourth and final unique stressor experienced by small-town and rural police is inactivity or, simply put, boredom.[36] All police officers often face the problem of boredom and inactivity on the job, but in the urban setting this boredom will generally only go for hours, days, or perhaps at the most, weeks. In small-town and rural agencies, police officers and deputy sheriffs will often go weeks without a call, sometimes months. Much of this has to do with the low amount of crime in small-town and rural neighborhoods, but it has been pointed out that this also has to do with a cultural phenomenon with the people that live in these environments. Most small-town and rural citizens have a very individualistic sense of responsibility and they prefer to keep things private, hence even if something does occur, they often are reluctant to call the police or report the crime. In some cases, they prefer to "handle it themselves."

This inactivity culminates to impact the small-town and rural officer in two ways. The first is that the lack of activity fails to provide the officer or deputy with an adequate amount of stimuli in their job and this inactivity can create stress. A good example is the opening quote to this chapter from a West Virginia law enforcement officer when questioned about his stress. His colorful response demonstrates how the isolation and limited activity elevated his level of stress.

The second way in which inactivity elevates an officer's stress is more psychological in nature. Officers become police officers to engage in police activity, to help other people, and because they have a perception of what it means to be a police officer. This last aspect, their perception, is often falsely created by friends, family, fellow police officers, and, more significantly, the media. As most citizens tend to form their image of what a police officer is through television shows and movies, so too do the individuals who become police officers. The problem lies in the vast differences between these perceptions and the reality. While large metropolitan police do not fully resemble the police officers found on television, many of the encounters they have are more similar in nature. When it comes to small-town and rural police officers, if they do not receive a call for weeks at a time and then it is only for some minor petty crime, their expectations of their role as a police officer does not conform to their reality. This can then generate feelings of uselessness or incompetency, resulting in low self-esteem, which can serve to elevate their level of stress on the job. This can also be further exacerbated by the officer becoming dissatisfied with the job and even hating the job, thus further elevating their level of stress. And, out of this frustration some officers will often resort to overinflating simple calls to make them appear more violent or serious than they actually were and, in the worst-case scenario, actually make up a call, as one rural officer who alleged to had been shot at, pursued the suspect, and lost him was found to have done. He had simply shot his own police cruiser and chased the phantom suspect out of boredom. Therefore, boredom in rural police terms could produce police corruption. One evening while riding with a deputy in a small county in the south, this author listened to deputies (on cell phones) who decided to meet and raid a hotspot in the woods because they wanted some excitement instead of checking the school yards, checking the business districts (four stores at an intersection and two others), or checking the interstate (from a bridge). Sometimes deputies would sit on the interstate in the wee hours for motorists and sometimes motorists would drive by. Other times, bored deputies would engage in non-crime or non-police-related calls.

RECENT RESEARCH ON STRESS IN SMALL-TOWN AND RURAL POLICING

There exists a very extensive and quite impressive body of research regarding police and stress that has built up over the past 40 years. There is, however, a paucity of research dealing with stress in the small-town and rural setting. The majority of stress studies have largely dealt with large urban police departments serving populations over 250,000 and with police departments numbering over 1,000 officers. There have been some studies that have dealt with smaller police departments, but these tend to be more medium-size police departments serving populations of over 50,000 and with over 100 police officers. When it comes to studies serving the under-50,000 population, the Census Bureau's threshold for qualifying as small-town and rural, there is a clear deficiency in the literature. The research that does exist, however, does shed some light on this particular area.

Scholarly Research on Stress in Small-Town and Rural Policing

The first article that truly directed its attention to this topic came in the previously cited article.[37] Four stress factors have often been cited in the sparse literature dealing with small-town and rural police stress and are often taken as being validated hypotheses.[38] Other writers did not test their hypotheses and no other researchers have tested these hypotheses until the authors conducted their most recent study (see below). So, despite the acceptance of conventional wisdom that the four categories—security, social, working conditions, and inactivity—are unique stressors in small-town and rural policing, no one really knew if this was accurate or not.[39]

The first researcher to really begin taking a critical look at small-town and rural police stress was Bartol who, over the past 20 years, has followed a cohort of small-town and rural police officers and has conducted a number of tests on these individuals.[40] Bartol has, since the early 1980s, followed the careers of nearly 900 small-town law enforcement officers and, as a psychologist, has conducted a number of psychological tests on these officers. In one of his early studies, Bartol found that small-town and rural officers who managed to deal more effectively with their stress tended to have higher performance evaluations and less problems on the job.[41] In a later study, Bartol examined the relationship between job performance and stress, especially as it related to women police officers in small-town and rural agencies. Bartol and his fellow researchers found that of the four categories of overall police stress, the external stressors emerged as the category that generated the most stress amongst small-town police officers. This was followed closely by both organizational and task-related stress factors. In terms of the four stressors unique to small-town and rural law enforcement, it appeared to be the social factors and working conditions that caused the highest stress. These included such responses as "politics within the departments," "insufficient personnel to help," and "inadequate equipment to do the job."[42] When it came to this study's findings regarding the differences between men and women and stress in small-town and rural settings, both tended to experience stress very much the same with the exception of the task-related stressors. However, in terms of job performance between men and women, as it related to stress, there were no differences.

A few studies in the late 1980s and early 1990s have also shed some light on stress among small-town and rural police. One such study compared the use of coping mechanisms to reduce stress amongst small-town police officers and rural sheriff's deputies in northern Louisiana.[43] Their research essentially found no differences between police officers and sheriff's deputies in these settings, suggesting, at least when it comes to coping with stress, there is little difference between the two types of law enforcement officials. Another study looked at eight medium-sized police departments in Illinois that ranged from 40–100 officers.[44] They were then asked what were the most significant stressors related to their job and organizational stress was given the highest response, with 68.3% stating this to be their largest source of stress. The second and third were task-related issues (16.2%) and external stressors, namely the judicial system (7.2%).

In the 1990s, one line of questioning has risen regarding stress in policing and that is whether or not the size of the police department matters. Two researchers conducted a study that looked across 10 police departments consisting of small, medium, and larger departments.[45] When looking across a series of nine stress scales, their findings suggested that size does matter when it comes to stress, but that the variance was not adequately explained by their research. The number one stressor cited by departments in all three sizes was organizational stress, suggesting that it did not matter the size of the department, as it was the key source of all officer stress. When it came to other types of stress, however, larger departments tended to have higher levels of stress, but the reasons why could not be adequately explained. One of the problems, statistically speaking, is that it is difficult to compare a large department with a small department. If you were to obtain a 50% response rate of a large police department that employed 1,000 police officers, you would have 500 surveys. If you obtain a 100% response rate from a small-town police department, this may still only yield five surveys. It is difficult to compare 500 responses to only five. Thus, not only is size an issue for the subject of stress, it is an issue for researching the topic as well.

Finally, the most recent findings from a study of small-town police departments in Pennsylvania found continued support for the previous findings.[46] This researcher utilized five distinct stress scales to assess the stressors amongst 135 small-town and rural police officers across 11 police departments.[47] Her findings, like the previous studies, found that organizational stress was the most significant stressor amongst small-town and rural police officers. Once again, it would appear that when searching for the greatest source of stress among police officers, regardless of the size of the agency, size does not appear to matter. However, it should be noted that the way in which organizational stress is derived is clearly different, despite the outcome—high stress—being very similar.

Our Research on Stress in Small-Town and Rural Policing

In 1997, the authors applied for a Bureau of Justice Assistance Open Solicitation Grant in order to conduct research on stress in small-town and rural policing in West Virginia.[48] The State of West Virginia provided a good source of small-town and rural police departments. The two largest cities in the state, Charleston and Wheeling, barely exceed the 50,000 population mark. The rest of the cities and towns throughout the state fall under 50,000 in population. In addition, based on data made available from the State Division of Criminal Justice Services and a previous survey of law enforcement agencies in the state, it was determined that the average number of officers employed within each police agency in West Virginia was 22. If the West Virginia State Police, which employed approximately 640 state troopers, was removed from this figure, the actual average number of officers/deputies fell to 18. The median number of officers/deputies per department was actually only 14 and if one looked at the modal average (the most frequent) it was only four police officers/deputies. Clearly, the State of West Virginia provided a good study population for assessing stress in small-town and rural policing.

The research on stress was actually one aspect of a larger project and that was to provide stress education to small-town and rural law enforcement throughout the state. In a survey of police chiefs and sheriff's deputies throughout the state, it was discovered that all officers, prior to 1998, had received 4 hours of instruction in the police academy on stress, the effects of stress, and stress management. After 1998, the number of hours was reduced to only a 2-hour block of instruction. It should be noted that every law enforcement official in the State of West Virginia had to be certified through the West Virginia State Police Academy, thus every officer in the state received the same training. When asked if any of the department's officers had received training beyond the 2–4 hours of training, only 6% of the 267 agencies in West Virginia reported they had. Therefore, the primary emphasis of this project was to provide an 8-hour block of in-service training, free of charge, to small-town and rural police officers and sheriff's deputies in the State of West Virginia.

The system of training was conducted by first hosting a train-the-trainer seminar in the summer of 1998 in Summersville, West Virginia. The attending officers, social workers, and college professors were provided 2-days of instruction on stress, symptoms of stress, stress research, stress in small-town and rural environments, stress management, and critical incident stress debriefing. These individuals then became a support network for the training as well as some of the trainers for the 8-hour block of instruction that the officers/deputies would receive. From there, the 8-hour block of instruction was set up with over 100 agencies and was provided to them either at their department or within close proximity. In addition, the training was often repeated over a period of 2–3 days in order to allow all the officers from a small department to attend the training without depleting the number of officers available to work their shift. The response to this format was very high, but it did create logistical problems and difficulties and in several cases only one officer was able to attend a session.

The training commenced in December 1998, but by January 1999 it had to be halted. During each of the 12 sessions that were conducted during this time frame, an average of two to three police officers/deputies, upon learning about the symptoms of cumulative stress and critical incident stress, came forward to the instructors during the course of the training to state that they were experiencing these problems and they wanted to know where they could get help. As the project did not entail establishing a mechanism for counseling or critical incident stress debriefing and none existed, the project had to be temporarily halted until these individuals could receive assistance and future officers/deputies could be referred. Throughout 1999 both psychological counseling and critical incident stress debriefings was established and it was not until December 1999 that these classes resumed. The training then continued from December 1999 until the spring of 2002.

At the beginning of each block of training, the officers and deputies were provided a survey that included several psychological scales to assess their level of stress, questions related to the four unique stress factors of small-town and rural police, and basic demographic questions. By the end of the project, a total of 776 officers and deputies had received the training. Because there was interest in the training by some of the larger agencies, including the West Virginia State Police, Department of Natural Resources, and both the Charleston and Huntington Police Departments, this training was provided to them and surveys were collected. Removing these agencies from the survey still provided a total of 664 surveys from small-town and rural agencies, which made up 32% of all law enforcement officers in West Virginia.

In looking at the basic demographic variables, including such variables as age, gender, race, marital status, education, and police experience, the three factors that were associated with higher levels of stress were gender and police experience. In terms of gender, women in West Virginia law enforcement were found to have slightly higher stress levels than their male counterparts. This is most likely due to the fact that the number of women in West Virginia law enforcement is approximately 3% of all police officers and sheriff's deputies, hence they are women working in a predominantly male environment. In terms of police experience, the study found that as the numbers of years increased for these officers, so too did their level of stress. Since stress is cumulative and signs and symptoms may not show up until years into a career, this finding is not too surprising.

In looking at the four categories of stress in policing—organizational, external, task-related, and personal—once again, our findings amongst small-town and rural law enforcement found very similar findings to nearly all other studies regarding police stress. The number one and most significant source of officer stress came from the organizational factors, more so than any other stressors. Both the external and task-related stressors followed in significance and there was no significance related to personal factors. This supports previous findings related to stress in both urban and small-town police.[49]

Also tested were the assumptions of previous researchers regarding the four stress factors unique to small-town and rural law enforcement: security, social factors, working conditions, and inactivity. A number of variables were established in order to assess the validity of these assumptions. Their responses were collected and a database was created. Then, utilizing regression models on each of the variables, the authors were able to assess whether or not these four assumptions were valid.

Under the topic of security, officers were asked how far away their typical backup was, whether or not they have feelings of isolation, and whether or not they feel vulnerable responding to such calls as auto accidents, domestic violence, and issuing simple traffic tickets. In addition, since sheriff's departments face more rural conditions than police departments, whether or not sheriff's departments experience higher levels of stress. Finally, a variable was added consisting of jurisdiction size (square miles) of the city, town, or county where participants served. The results demonstrated that every variable, except jurisdiction size, was significantly related to higher levels of stress. It was very clear from these findings that Sandy and Devine's hypothesis that security is a serious and unique stressor for small-town and rural law enforcement was validated.

The second dimension was the social factors. Here Sandy and Devine had discussed the smaller department size impacting an officer's lack of a peer support group. Questions were asked about their ability to talk to fellow officers after a shift or a bad call and whether the officer perceived him- or herself to have higher stress than their friends outside of policing. In addition, questions were asked to assess the small-town environment to determine how often they responded to calls with family, friends, or acquaintances, and how often they knew the person when responding to a dead on arrival (DOA). The only variables that were associated with high levels of stress were department size, the inability to talk after a shift, and the perception that they had more stress than their friends outside of policing. In addition, department size was found to be more stressful as the size increased, not as it got smaller, as Sandy and Devine predicted. What is perhaps most unique here is that these officers realized that they had higher stress levels than their friends outside of law enforcement, but the fact that they dealt with family and friends when responding to calls didn't seem to impact their level of stress. The reason may simply be that when you grow up in a small-town and rural setting that is simply how life is.

The third dimension, working conditions, consisted of such factors as the officer's level of income, the amount of stress training they had received in the previous year, and the amount of stress training they had received over a lifetime. The only variable found to be significant was the last one, the amount of stress training over the lifetime. This was also an inverse relationship, so as the amount of stress training over a lifetime decreased, their stress levels actually increased. Or, in other words, those officers who received stress training beyond the 2–4 hours in the academy were much less likely to report higher levels of stress. Education appears to work. However, income did not seem to be an important issue to the officers as related to their levels of stress.

The final category, inactivity, was assessed with four psychological questions. These questions asked if the officers believed they lacked the necessary self-confidence, if the participants felt they battled with themselves, if the participants felt they had "done wrong" (based on self-reports), and if the participants had feelings of uselessness. The two variables that were significant were "battle with self" and "feelings of uselessness." These support Sandy and Devine's assumptions that the inactivity and boredom officers in small-town and rural settings face can create a feeling of being useless and can create conflict within the officer based on the perception of what they think they should be doing as a police officer and the realities of policing in a small-town.[50]

In sum, Sandy and Devine, through their study in West Virginia, were able to test the four stress factors unique to small-town and rural agencies since they first hypothesized them in 1978. It terms of the validity of these assumptions, the security variable was the most supported of the four. Based on this research, there can be little doubt that the issue of security amongst small-town and rural law enforcement contributes significantly to their levels of reported stress. The inactivity dimension also appears to be well supported, especially for the two variables that were found to be significant. The vast differences between officer perception of being a police officer in this environment, when compared to the realities, does appear to contribute to higher levels of stress among officers. The last two factors, social and working conditions, did not appear to be supported overall except for the lack of stress training received by the officers (a similar finding in big-city departments; see Chapters 2 and 4). Therefore, in terms of addressing officer stress in small-town and rural environments, it would be suggested that the key may lie in ensuring these officers receive additional stress training, that one aspect of it should focus on the perceptions these officers have versus the realities of the job, and that officer safety and security should be more adequately addressed.

CONSTRAINTS IN SMALL-TOWN AND RURAL POLICING

One of the most in-depth longitudinal studies on police stress in small-town and rural officers has highlighted four key constraints facing these agencies.[51] Each of these constraints have been found to be a primary source of small-town and rural police officer stress and perhaps the keys to addressing officer stress lie in these constraints.

Knowledge

One of the key arguments regarding stress and how best to deal with it falls in the area of education.[52] The argument is that the more knowledge people have regarding stress, its effects, and how to cope with it, the better they are able to control their personal level of stress. Knowledge, then, is seen as the tool to dealing with stress, but in small-town and rural environments this is often a significant constraint. Police officers in large urban settings often receive at a minimum a 4-hour block of instruction on stress in the academy and along the way, through roll-call or in-service training, they typically will receive an additional 8 hours of training. However, often that training in those big-city police departments is inadequate to accomplish its mission. For instance, it was revealed that the Boston police, in cooperation with the FBI and Massachusetts State Police, conducted inservice training to aid officers in processing sexual assault evidence, but at the conclusion of a weeklong, intense course, the veteran officers felt they had learned little about the topic, and consequently became distressed over their inability to deal with sexual assault cases.[53] More training isn't the answer—quality training might be more on the mark.

In West Virginia, all police officers generally receive 2 hours of stress instruction at the state law academy and only a few of those surveyed had received any additional training on stress or how to deal with stress. If education is the key, the lack of resources, funding, and training presents a constraint in achieving this end.

It is recommended that police officers in small-town and rural agencies receive training and education about stress, how to recognize stress, and the symptoms of stress. These officers should learn the types of stress that are common amongst all police officers, and should specifically be taught about those four unique stressors that are relegated to their specific situation as small-town and rural officers. In addition, officers should be taught that stress is not just triggered by a specific event, which is what is generally referred to as critical incident stress (as discussed in Chapter 4), but that stress is cumulative over a career. I believe that Chapter 2 emphasized that stress is cumulative—it works off of itself and snowballs. Officers should then be instructed on how best to cope with stress through both psychological (e.g., counseling, critical incident stress debriefings, etc.) and physiological (e.g., diet, exercise, etc.) methods. Finally, a network of peers should be established for assisting fellow officers from other small-town and rural agencies to create a peer support group where none exist or are very limited in scope (as discussed in Chapter 10).

Resources

The lack of resources is clearly one of the constraints of small-town and rural law enforcement and is an extension of the problem of knowledge.[54] The lack of knowledge is often due to the lack of resources, as officers receive limited training in the academy and receive very little in the way of yearly training. In fact, many agencies, like those in West Virginia, are only required to have 8 hours of training each year in order to maintain their police officer certification and most of these tend to look for the least expensive training available in order to satisfy the requirement, rather than looking for training that would greatly benefit the officers.

In addition to the aforementioned lack of a peer support group or peer support group network, small-town and rural officers also tend to lack the resources for the provision of psychological counseling and services to their officers. As the authors discovered in their study of small-town and rural police agencies in West Virginia, when we began offering the 8-hour block of training on small-town and rural stress, we had to stop the study temporarily because officers were coming up to the instructors after the sessions stating they needed help. Because there was no mechanism in place, the study had to be halted in order to put a system into place before it could continue. This highlights, however, the significant deficiency of support found in the small-town and rural environment.

Politics

Politics is one of the key constraints when it comes to effectively dealing with the problem of stress in small-town and rural environments.[55] Politics in the small-town and rural setting tends to be very different from their urban counterparts in that politics is more centrally controlled by the mayor, city council, and police chief. As an extension of the above two topics, in order to obtain the resource allocation to enhance the knowledge among police officers regarding stress, the issue of stress must be seen by these few politicians as being something worthy of its time and attention. If these administrators do not see the need for stress counseling, education, and training, then resources are not going to be funneled toward alleviating these types of problems. As was seen in the case of the author's research in West Virginia, stress amongst small-town and rural police officers was real and the lack of any mechanism to deal with the problems associated with cumulative and critical incident stress did not exist. And, until the politicians come to see the benefits of providing these mechanisms, small-town and rural police officers are not going to receive the type of help that they need.

The Nature of Small Communities

The simple nature of small communities, is the last constraint.[56] This nature or environment has been previously described as the "fishbowl effect." When officers live in small-town and rural environments they are also perceived for their role as a police officer and even when off duty, everyone knows the individual as being a cop. In a sense, they cannot escape their job and must always live in the "fishbowl," always on display. In addition, because small-town and rural communities tend to share information about other people through the grapevine by gossiping and through the local newspapers (often one step above gossiping), the lives of a police officer are an open book. As one female officer who had transferred from a larger police department to a small-town police department explained, "Probably the worst source of stress that I have had is that any male officer friend that I am seen having coffee with or talking with, I am all of a sudden on the 'rumor mill' as 'doing.' When I worked at a larger department, I did not find that I was constantly on the rumor mill the way it is in a smaller department."[57] Living and working in this type of environment can obviously create problems.

One problem lies in the fact that many residents expect the police officer to be emotionally strong and that any sign of a personal problem resulting from stress, and especially counseling, can be seen as a sign of weakness. If word were to get out that a specific police officer was being counseled for stress, the information would spread rapidly through the community and would serve to undermine the respect and authority of the officer, which is so critical in the performance of his or her duties. Previous research has found that officers who maintained a strong emotional presence and hid their emotions were significantly more likely to have better performance evaluations over their careers than those who were willing to admit to the problems associated with stress.[58] Clearly, being a small-town and rural police officer or deputy sheriff places serious constraints on these officers receiving adequate support when it comes to stress and the problems it can cause merely because they do work in a small-town and rural environment.

SUMMARY

Stress in small-town and rural policing is a very serious issue and one that has been inadequately addressed in both research and training. Police officers and sheriff's deputies in these settings face many of the same types of stressors as their urban counterpart, such as organizational, external, task-related, and personal. Research has consistently found that organizational stress is the most profound and is often followed by external and task-related stressors as well. The research also suggests that there is little difference in regard to size when it comes to the rankings of these four categories. However, while the end result is generally the same, increased levels of stress, the way in which these four categories of stress impact small-town and rural law enforcement is often very different from the large metropolitan police that are often studied. In addition to these general stressors found in police officers of all sizes, small-town and rural law enforcement face their own unique stressors, which consist of security, social factors, working conditions, and inactivity. First put forth in 1978 by Sandy and Devine, the authors tested these assumptions and found strong support for security and inactivity, but less support for the social factors and working condition categories. Nonetheless, the study did reveal that small-town and rural police officers know they have high levels of stress; where they need help would appear to be in the area of dealing with this stress. Education clearly appears to be the key to resolving some of the issues by providing officers with training on stress, signs and symptoms of stress, and how to effectively manage stress, as well as dealing with the differences between perceptions and the realities of small-town and rural policing. Finally, there is evidence to suggest that officer safety and security needs to be more adequately addressed not only for its own sake, but to help alleviate the high levels of stress experienced by many officers in small-town and rural environments.

WHAT WOULD YOU DO IF YOU WERE IN CHARGE?

In a church basement, officers of an elite undercover narcotics team of the Bronx Task Force slowly arrive and are identified to the undercover team vouching for the credentials and identity of each other. Because of the highly confidential nature of their job and of this meeting and the need for absolute safety and security of all participants, no service records or participant lists are prepared and no notes will be taken during the intense 3-hour meeting. It is agreed that participants may not reveal anything spoken by any participant other than themselves at the end of the meeting. The success of the team is noted as meritorious, and yet it is noted that federal funding for the team comes to an end in 30 days. Officers can not be reassigned to patrol or investigative teams as those teams are overstaffed at this time.

OFFICER KILLED IN NEWARK, NEW JERSEY

On Monday, July 18, 2005, Officer Dwayne Reeves was gunned down and killed at the Newark School District Police Services in New Jersey. His partner approached a car outside of Weequahic High School at approximately 1400 hours. The officers had just broken up a fight between two female students and were talking with the girls when two men, one of whom was the brother of one of the girls, pulled up in a car and opened fire, striking Officer Reeves in the head and his partner in the hand. Officer Reeves' partner was able to return fire and shot one of the suspects in the stomach.

Officer Reeves was taken to University Hospital where he died from his wounds. The suspect who was shot in the stomach was taken into custody shortly after the shooting, but wasn't arrested until the following day.

Officer Reeves had served with the Newark School District Police for 3 years and worked a second job with the Newark Housing Authority Police for a total of 4 years. He is survived by his wife and children.

DISCUSSION QUESTIONS

1. Define what is meant by small town and rural.
2. Understand how stress can impact small-town and rural police similar to their urban counterparts.
3. Identify the unique stressors that impact small-town and rural police.
4. Define the four types of stress in policing and explain how they impact small-town and rural police.

5. Define the four types of stress unique to small-town and rural police, specifically security, social, working conditions, and inactivity.

6. Describe the findings from recent research on small-town and rural police stress.

7. Explain the four constraints faced by small-town and rural police, specifically knowledge, resources, politics, and the nature of small communities.

ENDNOTES

1. U.S. Census Bureau (2004). Retrieved online July 18, 2005: http://www.census.gov/

2. R. A. Weisheit, D. N. Falcone, and L. E. Wells (1999). *Crime and policing in rural and small-town America*, 2nd ed. Prospect Heights: Waveland.

3. R. A. Weisheit, D. N. Falcone, and L. E. Wells (1999). p. 100.

4. Bureau of Justice Statistics (2003). Sheriffs' offices 2000. Retrieved online March 13, 2006: http://www.ojp.usdoj.gov/bjs/pub/pdf/so00.pdf

5. Bureau of Justice Statistics (2003).

6. For example, the author recalls riding with student-deputies in Aiken County, South Carolina, after midnight when there were three deputies servicing the county. Asking for backup from another deputy was impossible, although sometimes asking locals or the state for help was a consideration but it also exposed a deputy to problems, primarily because everyone listened to the police calls. Unless a deputy had the cell number of a specific officer, things were tense.

7. W. H. Kroes, B. L. Margolis, and J. J. Hurrell (1974). Job stress in policemen. *Journal of Police Science and Administration*, 2, 145–155.

8. W. H. Kroes, B. L. Margolis, and J. J. Hurrell (1974).

9. Provided by one of the practitioner reviewers of this book, and in checking with former students still in rural policing, they confirm (via email) this perspective.

10. C. R. Bartol, G. T. Bergen, J. S. Volckens, and K. M. Knoras (1992). Women in small-town policing: Job performance and stress. *Criminal Justice and Behavior*, 19, 240–259. p. 242.

11. S. Zhao, N. He, and N. Lovrich (2002). Predicting five dimensions of police officer stress: Looking more deeply into organizational settings for sources of police stress. *Police Quarterly*, 5(1), 43–62.

12. J. P. Crank and M. Caldero (1991). The production of occupational stress in medium-sized police agencies: A survey of line officers in eight municipal departments. *Journal of Criminal Justice*, 19, 339–349.

13. W. H. Kroes, B. L. Margolis, and J. J. Hurrell (1974). Job stress in policemen. *Journal of Police Science and Administration*, 2, 145–155.

14. C. R. Bartol, G. T. Bergen, J. S. Volckens, and K. M. Knoras (1992). p. 242.

15. W. H. Kroes, B. Margolis, and J. J. Hurrell (1974).

16. W. H. Kroes, B. Margolis, and J. J. Hurrell (1974).

17. C. R. Bartol, G. T. Bergen, J. S. Volckens, and K. M. Knoras (1992). p. 242.

18. W. H. Kroes, B. Margolis, and J. J. Hurrell (1974).

19. C. R. Bartol, G. T. Bergen, J. S. Volckens, and K. M. Knoras (1992). p. 242.

20. S. Zhao, N. He, and N. Lovrich (2002).

21. W. H. Kroes, B. Margolis, and J. J. Hurrell (1974).

22. J. P. Sandy and D. A. Devine (1978, September). Four stress factors unique to rural patrol. *The Police Chief*, 42–44.

23. J. P. Sandy and D. A. Devine (1978).

24. W. M. Oliver (2001). Community policing in small-town and rural communities: An organizational assessment of West Virginia agencies. *Police Practices*, 2(3), 243–271.

25. W. Anderson, D. Swenson, and D. Clay (1995). *Stress management for law enforcement officers*. Englewood Cliffs, NJ: Prentice Hall. p. 209.

26. J. P. Sandy and D. A. Devine (1978).

27. J. P. Sandy and D. A. Devine (1978).

28. J. P. Sandy and D. A. Devine (1978).

29. J. P. Sandy and D. A. Devine (1978).

30. W. Anderson, D. Swenson, and D. Clay (1995), pp. 211–212.

31. W. Anderson, D. Swenson, and D. Clay (1995), pp. 211–212.

32. J. P. Sandy and D. A. Devine (1978).

33. W. Anderson, D. Swenson, and D. Clay (1995). p. 210.

34. W. M. Oliver and C. A. Meier (2001). The siren's song: Federalism and the COPS Grants. *American Journal of Criminal Justice*, 25(2), 223–238.

35. J. P. Sandy and D. A. Devine (1978).

36. J. P. Sandy and D. A. Devine (1978).

37. J. P. Sandy and D. A. Devine (1978).

38. W. Anderson, D. Swenson, and D. Clay (1995).

39. J. P. Sandy and D. A. Devine (1978).

40. C. R. Bartol (1982). Psychological Characteristics of small-town police officers. *Journal of Police Science and Administration*, 16, 58–63.

41. C. R. Bartol, G. T. Bergen, J. S. Volckens, and K. M. Knoras (1992). p. 242.

42. C. R. Bartol, G. T. Bergen, J. S. Volckens, and K. M. Knoras (1992). p. 249.

43. D. B. Fain and G. M. McCormick III (1988). Use of coping mechanisms as a means of stress reduction in North Louisiana. *Journal of Police Science and Administration*, 16, 21–28.

44. J. P. Crank and M. Caldero (1991). The production of occupational stress in medium-sized police agencies: A survey of line officers in eight municipal departments. *Journal of Criminal Justice*, 19, 339–349.

45. L. W. Brooks, and N. L. Piquero (1998). Police stress: Does department size matter? *Policing: An International Journal of Police Strategies and Management*, 21, 600–617.

46. Y. M. Scott (2004). Stress among rural and small-town patrol officers: A survey of Pennsylvania municipal agencies. *Police Quarterly*, 7, 237–261.

47. Y. M. Scott (2004).

48. W. M. Oliver and C. A. Meier (1998). *Bureau of Justice Assistance Open Solicitation Grant—1997*. Washington, DC: Bureau of Justice Assistance.

49. L. W. Brooks, and N. L. Piquero (1998). Police stress: Does department size matter? *Policing: An International Journal of Police Strategies and Management*, 21, 600–617. Y. M. Scott (2004).

50. J. P. Sandy and D. A. Devine (1978).

51. C. R. Bartol (1996). Stress in small-town and rural law enforcement. In T. D. McDonald, R. A. Wood, and M. A. Pflug (Eds.), *Rural criminal justice: Conditions, constraints, and challenges* (pp. 55–75). Salem MA: Sheffield.

52. Curt Bartol (1996).

53. Dennis J. Stevens (2006). Sexual assault evidence, sexual offenders, and sexual assault convictions: Why sexual assault convictions are low in Boston. *Police Journal, 81.*

54. Curt Bartol (1996).

55. Curt Bartol (1996).

56. Curt Bartol (1982).

57. C. R. Bartol, G. T. Bergen, J. S. Volckens, and K. M. Knoras (1992). p. 257.

58. C. R. Bartol (1982). Also see C. R. Bartol (1991). Predictive validation of the MMPI for small-town police officers who fail. *Professional Psychology: Research and Practice, 22,* 127–132.

10

Individual and Person-Centered Initiatives

I have every sympathy with the American who was so horrified by what he has read of the effects of smoking that he gave up reading. —Lord Conesford

Learning Objectives

Once you have read this chapter, you will be able to:

- Describe individual and person-centered initiatives.
- Describe the goal of an early warning system to detect stressed officers.
- Characterize the three basic phases of an early warning system.
- Describe why it is difficult for officers to seek help to reduce and control stress.
- Describe some of the methods an officer can initiate to cope with stress.
- Explain the ABC model of analyzing experiences.
- Describe how irrational beliefs can hold an officer back from managing stress.
- Identify and explain the relevance of healthy lifestyles.
- Identify at least 15 steps to individually reduce stress.

- Identify and articulate why positive attitudes and lifestyle are relevant variables to stress control.

- Describe the relevance of self-esteem in stress management.

- Identify components that would lead to the development of a peer support program.

- Explain the IACP's philosophy that should guide a law enforcement agency toward an efficient peer support program.

- Explain why stress programs should include family participation.

- Define needs assessment and describe six compelling reasons it is performed.

- Identify the historical path of person-centered stress programs in policing.

KEY TERMS

ABC method of analyzing   Multimodal treatment   Person-centered
Coping   Needs assessment   initiatives
Early warning systems

INTRODUCTION

This chapter is about individual and person-centered initiatives some of which are encouraged and sponsored by the employer of an officer. Individual attempts to reduce and control stress might be one way to describe *individual initiatives*. Because officers respond differently to stressors as suggested in Chapter 2, it should be clear that many officers effectively manage stress at a personal level when confronted. However, it needs to be said again as it had in Chapters 1 and 2 that police officers when confronted with negative stress do not necessarily act-out their experiences through negative behavior. Then, too, officers who do seek assistance can and do deliver quality police services, provide quality family care, are responsible, and are positive contributors to the law enforcement mission and their communities. Sometimes, some of us need to know where the light switch has been relocated, to turn on the lights. Yet, ridding ourselves of irrational beliefs that hold us back from changing our behavior is a difficult task even when we've learned what wall the light switch in on.

That said *person-centered initiatives* are designed to accomplish a similar goal as individually initiated methods and include individual and group programs operated (or contracted to private and public providers) by an officer's employer whereby groups of officers participate unless the mental health of the officer requires an official private session (such as critical incident debriefing, specific mental disorder counseling, or even family dysfunction sessions).

EARLY WARNING SYSTEMS

Researchers argue that *early warning systems* to detect stressed officers followed by various methods of treatment are beneficial to the department, officers, and the public. The primary goal of early warning systems is to change the behavior of individual officers who have been identified as having problematic performance records. There are three basic phases of an early warning system: selection, intervention, and post-intervention monitoring.[1]

Selection

There are few national standards established in identifying stressed officers for an early warning program. There is general agreement, however, about the criteria that should influence officer selection. Performance indicators that can help identify officers with problematic behavior include citizen complaints, firearm-discharge and use-of-force reports, civil litigation, resisting-arrest incidents, and high-speed pursuits and vehicular damage.[2] Although a few departments rely only on citizen complaints to select officers for intervention, most use a combination of performance indicators. Among systems that factor in citizen complaints, most (67%) require three complaints in a given timeframe (76% specify a 12-month period) to identify an officer.

Intervention

The basic intervention strategy involves a combination of deterrence and education. The theory of simple deterrence assumes that officers who are subject to intervention will change their behavior in response to a perceived threat of punishment.[3] General deterrence assumes that officers not subject to the system will also change their behavior to avoid potential punishment. Early warning systems also operate on the assumption that training, as part of the intervention, can help officers improve their performance.

In many systems (62%) of those tested during the initial intervention period reviews by the officer's immediate supervisor generally identify problematic officers.[4] Almost half of the responding agencies (45%) tested involved other command officers who counseled stressed officers. Also these systems frequently include a training class for groups of officers identified by the system (45% of survey respondents).

Post-Intervention Monitoring of Subsequent Performance

Nearly all (90%) of the agencies that have an early warning system reported that they monitor an officer's performance after the initial intervention. Such monitoring is generally informal and conducted by the officer's immediate supervisor, but some departments have developed a formal process of observation, evaluation, and reporting. Almost one-half (47%) of the agencies monitored the officer's performance for 36 months after the initial intervention. One-half of the agencies indicate that the follow-up period is not specified and that officers are monitored either continuously or on a case-by-case basis.

The impact of early warning systems linked to officers' performance appears to have a dramatic effect on reducing citizen complaints and other indicators of problematic police performance among those officers subject to intervention. In Minneapolis, for example, the average number of citizen complaints received by officers subject to early intervention dropped by 67% 1 year after the intervention. In New Orleans, that number dropped by 62% 1 year after intervention. In Miami-Dade, only 4% of the early warning cohort had zero use-of-force reports prior to intervention; following intervention, 50% had zero use-of-force reports.

Data from New Orleans indicate that officers respond positively to early warning intervention. In anonymous evaluations, officers gave those programs an average rating of 7 on a scale of 1 to 10. All of the officers made at least one positive comment about the program, and some made specific comments about how it had helped them.

In general, some observers could not determine the most effective aspects of intervention (e.g., counseling regarding personal issues, training in specific law enforcement techniques, stern warnings about possible discipline in the future) for officers detected through an early warning system especially derived from surveys.[5]

Nonetheless, there are always limitations that emerge from responses on national surveys. Some law enforcement agencies may have claimed to have an early warning system when such a system was not actually functioning. Several police departments created systems in the 1970s, but none of those appear to have survived as a permanent program.[6] It becomes clear that techniques used to identify stressed officers are highly suspect. That is, in what way are complaint letters associated with stress? Could street cops, depending on their assignment and the community, in the performance of their duties "ruffle the feathers" of citizens and "bad guys" alike. Those officers might be aggressive, but in what way are aggressive behavior and stressed behavior strongly related variables? Fact is, some policing involves an aggressive and controlling but professional manner, especially since some officers confront bad guys. A unique thing about experienced cops as well as experienced researchers is that it is common knowledge that observed "normal" behavior could in fact be "a stressed-out dude—waiting for an accident to happen."[7] The most serious of violent offenders, for instance, can easily fit into a category of a high-functioning individual whereby the community reported that even the killer clown (John Wayne Gacy) was seen as a respected member of the community who was "laid back" and seemed never to create any problem for others.[8] Therefore, the criticism about early warning signals might be that signals of a stressed officer ready to pounce upon an unsuspecting victim might not be the entire answer associated with real-life experiences. Sometimes the indicators aren't present in an officer's conduct and it only takes one time to "snap" and people die.

SEEKING HELP IS NEVER EASY

Choosing to be healthy is the best weapon against the negative influences of stress and against living a life of discomfort regardless of the occupation of an individual.[9] Many officers and other professionals accept the message shared by Lord Conesford (above) about smoking and the action taken by a smoker so that he can continue to smoke. It is difficult to pursue a healthy lifestyle when an individual is unaware of poor lifestyle influences or just wishes to ignore healthy lifestyle commitments. Nonetheless, arriving at the realization that changes are necessary in one's life does not automatically mean that an officer will change. Recall Chapters 1 and 2 where because of police subculture influence, many officers do not identify or treat their stressful condition for fear of ridicule by other officers, fear of a lack of job stability, and others, supported by the literature and practitioners recommending to officers to avoid stress control initiatives should an officer wish to hold the respect of his or her colleagues and to eventually be promoted. However, reading this and other books might be steps toward a remedy. Some practical works include:

- Herbert Benson and Eileen M. Stuart (1992). *The wellness book.* New York: Carol Publishing.
- Stephen R. Covey (1990). *Seven habits of highly effective people.* New York: Simon & Schuster[10] Stephen R. Covey (1991). *Principle centered leadership.* New York: Summit Books; and Stephen R. Covey (1995). *First things first.* New York: Simon & Schuster.
- Edward A. Charlesworth and Ronald G. Nathan (1984). *Stress management: A comprehensive guide to wellness.* New York: Ballantine Books.
- Norman Vincent Peale (1996). *The power of positive thinking.* New York: Fawcett.

Once a commitment is made to fight back against the negative factors of stress, life becomes easier. Of course, street cops have to overcome the obstacle of believing that getting help or showing feelings is a sign of weakness. Fighting back includes the deliberate adoption and implementation of stress reduction techniques and the vigilance of the law enforcement community to protect its members from the effects of negative stress as vigorously as officers protect society from lawlessness.

PREVENTING AND TREATING STRESS INDIVIDUALLY

Officers can choose to initiate some action on their own to remove or reduce the negative influences of stress by employing various coping methods. *Coping* can be defined as an attempt to deal with and overcome problems and difficulties.[11] It is easier to think of coping as managing and in this case, managing stress. Some methods of managing stress include deep breathing, muscle relaxation, meditation/prayer, positive thinking, self-talk, and mental imagery.[12] Officers can choose one of these or use them in combination, whatever is the most productive toward recovery and control. But whatever method is selected, it must be consistently practiced in order to see results.[13] That is, everyday for 20 minutes or every second day for 40 minutes. Since each person is different (and many of us are impatient), what method or what time might work well for one officer might not work for another officer.

These various techniques can work, and when an officer finds a technique that works best for him or her, it has to be practiced often to increase its effectiveness. Most important, officers can refine these coping skills to the point that they can employ them as stressful situations occur.[14] Using these techniques provides hope in dealing with most stressful situations and even preventing them from becoming destructive to an officer's overall health.[15] Practicing stress management also must be used in the context of practicing a healthy lifestyle, including regular exercise, wholesome nutrition and diet, spiritual renewal, and enriching social interactions.[16] Officer choices determine the health of the body, mind, spirit, and social interactions. If any one of these four areas weakens, other areas can weaken too, leading to total collapse. Conversely, if officers choose to practice a healthy lifestyle in these areas in some way or another, then they choose to take care of their bodies.

The ABC Method of Analyzing Experiences

When street cops become stressed, they usually claim it is because of an event or experience.[17] The *ABC method of analyzing* experience shows it to be somewhat more complex:

"A" = Activating event
"B" = Belief system
"C" = Consequence (stress)

The activating event results in a consequence only after being filtered through a belief system. For instance, if a suspect is found not guilty, the verdict can become activating event "A." The defendant's release does not produce the stress, but rather the perception of what this release means to the arresting officer makes it stressful. "Why did I risk danger in arresting that person?" a street cop might think. Suppose the release was due in part to the arresting officer's method of arrest? Maybe the arrest was considered unlaw-fully performed. The consequences of stress take on an entirely different meaning to a street cop. It is for this reason that a realistic understanding of a cop's job be clear, otherwise stress multiplies and eventually those conse-quences can take an "involuntary" path of its own because of the organiza-tional influences and any irrational beliefs held by the officer.

Irrational Beliefs

Articles in newspapers and books such as this one make it sound easy to change our beliefs, attitudes, and ultimately our behavior. However, in reality, motivating an officer to take care of him- or herself is entirely another matter because of many reasons, which include the idea that "beliefs are designed to enhance our ability to survive, they are biologically designed to be strongly resistant to change."[18] To change behavior, assuming this thought is more right than wrong, the brain's "survival" issues need to be addressed. That is, our survival values must be reassessed. This thought implies that irrational or dysfunctional beliefs should be replaced with rationale beliefs but the concern is that the brain (and police subculture) has a mind of its own.[19] Some exam-ples of irrational beliefs are[20]:

- Messages about life we send to ourselves that prohibit us from grow-ing emotionally. For instance, some might ask: "What would John Wayne do in a situation like this?"
- Scripts we have in our head about how we believe life "should" be. For instance, new officers tend to believe that the public will respect them because they are a law enforcement officer.
- Unfounded attitudes, opinions, and values we hold to that are out of synch with the way the world really is. For example, recruit officers have expectations about their jobs that rarely fit the reality of the job.
- Negative sets of habitual responses we hold to when faced with stress-ful events or situations. For instance, cops tend to believe that asking for help shows a personal weakness, a thought reinforced by the police subculture.
- Stereotypic ways of problem solving we fall into in order to deal with life's pressures. Officers tend to believe that staying strong through stressful experiences is to suffer in silence.
- Ideas, feelings, beliefs, ways of thinking, attitudes, opinions, biases, prejudices, or values with which we were raised. We have become ac-customed to using them when faced with problems in our current life, even when they are not productive in helping us reach a positive,

growth-enhancing solution, relying on the old ways of dealing with stressful situations.

- Self-defeating ways of acting. On the surface they may look appropriate for the occasion, but actually they result in a neutral or negative consequence for us. For instance, police officers tend to isolate family members from their job experiences, losing a network of help and often the trust of family members who count the most in their lives. Recall the officer in an earlier chapter who waited for her husband to fall asleep and then went to meet other cops at the local pub for friendship. Family conflict or divorce is not an unlikely prediction in her life or the lives of other officers in similar scenarios.

- Habitual ways of thinking, feeling, or acting that we think are effective; however, in the long run they are ineffectual. For instance, referring to most suspects as scumbags and treating them that way.

- Counterproductive ways of thinking, which give comfort and security in the short run, but either do not resolve or actually exacerbate the problem in the long run: "The guys would like the way I beat the crap out of this guy I stopped for a traffic stop."

- Negative or pessimistic ways of looking at necessary life experiences such as loss, conflict, risk taking, rejection, or accepting change: thoughts that say, no matter what I do, the bad guys are going to win.

- Overly optimistic or idealistic ways of looking at necessary life experiences such as loss, conflict, risk taking, rejection, or accepting change. Officers who think that they can never be emotionally harmed by their work might be a good example of this irrational belief.

- Emotional arguments for taking or not taking action in the face of a challenge. When followed they result in no personal gain, but rather in greater personal hardship or loss. For instance, one officer volunteered that he was more prepared to deal with weight gains because of his compulsion to eat than being nervous while on the job. He smoked too and explained it the same way.

- Patterns of thinking and acting out that make us appear to others as stubborn, bullheaded, intemperate, or authoritarian as typified by one officer, "I know what's best for the shit-heads I stop (while on patrol) and if they don't listen to me, I'll lock'em up." The "to me" was the emphasis of his statement.

- Ways of thinking about ourselves that are out of context with the real facts, resulting in our either undervaluing or overvaluing ourselves and our importance to the world of law enforcement. The truth is officers are the same person who went through basic training years ago. Their experiences and age have changed. Some officers forget that their body is older and if they worked out that what used to be bodybuilding is now body maintenance. Exercise is a fact of life.

- Lifelong messages sent to us either formally or informally by society, culture, community, race, ethnic reference group, neighborhood, church, social networks, family, relatives, peer group, school, work, or parents. They are unproductive in solving our current problem or crisis, but we are either unwilling or unable to let go of them. These messages can be very clear to us or they can be hidden in our subconscious.

- Conclusions about life that we have developed over time, living in an irrational environment not identified as being irrational. For instance, beliefs developed as a member of a high-stress family.

There are more, but space limits their inclusion. Generally, data or information (such as this chapter) that recommends an officer make personal charges in his or her life is often looked upon with suspicion and the police subculture is less likely to endorse change (see Chapter 4 for more details). Nonetheless, in order to effectively change beliefs, doubters must attend to his or her survival value as mentioned above, in addition to information and data accuracy values. This involves several concerns[21]: First, individuals rarely change as the result of information. Knowing something and doing something about it are two different things. It should be mentioned that knowing and not changing does not imply that an individual is unintelligent. The fact is that information such as this book is often necessary, but it is rarely sufficient toward change. Second, individuals have to learn to discuss or think about both the specific issues or beliefs addressed by information and the implications of change. If every officer after a work shift ends up at Brian's Pub, then giving up drinking might mean to give up some of the camaraderie of coworkers. How would an officer fill the camaraderie gap in his or her life? Third, skeptics need to appreciate how hard it is for individuals to have their beliefs challenged. It is, quite literally, a threat to their brain's sense of survival. It is normal for individuals to be defensive. Working around defensive behavior (mentally or physically) is part of what professionals are all about.

In regard to the third aspect, professional educators learn early in their careers or face a downward battle in many classes about defensive behavior of their students. It is unfortunate that providing new information for the purpose of change can produce behavior that is provocative, hostile, and even vicious, but it is understandable as well. Students learning new beliefs can be mean, contrary, harsh, or they might even feel stupid when challenged. That is, they take the information personally. Old ways are easier and within an individual's comfort zone. If some of our coworkers or you are skeptical, it should be clarified that winning the war for rational beliefs by continuing, even in the face of defensive responses from others, to use behavior that is unfailingly dignified and tactful is a battle.

Skeptics' ability to alter their own beliefs in response to data or information is a true gift; a unique, powerful, and precious ability.[22] It is genuinely a "higher brain function" in that it goes against some of the most natural and fundamental biological urges. They possess a skill that can be frightening, life-changing, and capable of inducing pain.

Then, too, beliefs are tied to goals. Human beings are goal driven.[23] But are goals always rationale? Individuals such as Andrew Carnegie (founder of U.S. Steel and the great American philanthropist) made a valid observation that reveals that what people need, they usually ignore, but show people what they want, and they will move mountains.[24] Then there is all the irrational behavior that results in crime and accidents as a large piece of evidence that cannot be ignored when looking at human behavior. People need to be careful on the highways and in their lives, but obviously being rational about decisions they are making is highly questionable. What about the cigarette industry that reported to the public that there was no link between cigarette smoking and cancer, and yet people ignored the information and smoked. Finally in this regard, the alcohol and drug industries thrive in part because of their advertising. How rational are their decisions to drink and drive? And lest we forget all the bad relationships that end up in the emergency rooms of hospitals all over America only to be treated—until next weekend. Do these folks know better?

Irrational beliefs are present if we[25]:

- Find ourselves caught up in a vicious cycle in addressing our problems.
- Find a continuing series of "catch 22s" where every move we make to resolve a problem results in more or greater problems.
- Have been suffering silently (or not so silently) with a problem for a long time, yet have not taken steps to get help to address the problem.
- Have decided on a creative problem-solving solution, yet find ourselves incapable of implementing the solution.
- Have chosen a problem-solving course of action to pursue and find that we are unhappy with this course of action, yet we choose to avoid looking for alternatives.
- Are afraid of pursuing a certain course of action because of the guilt we will feel if we do it.
- Find we are constantly obsessed with a problem yet take no steps to resolve it.
- Find we are immobilized in the face of our problems.
- Find that the only way to deal with problems is to avoid them, deny them, procrastinate about them, ignore them, run away from them, or turn our back on them.

- Find that we can argue both sides of our problem, becoming unable to make a decision.
- Find we can't resolve family dysfunctions.
- Provide less than quality police services.

There are many benefits of refuting irrational beliefs. By refuting our irrational beliefs we are able to[26]:

- Unblock our emotions and feelings about ourselves and our problems.
- Become productive, realistic problem solvers.
- Gain greater credibility with ourselves and others.
- Gain clarity, purpose, and intention in addressing our current problems.
- Reduce the fear of guilt or of hurting others in solving problems.
- Identify the barriers and obstacles that must first be hurdled before our problems can be resolved.
- Come to greater honesty about ourselves and our problems.
- Put our problem into a realistic perspective as to its importance, magnitude, and probability of being solved.
- Separate our feelings from the content of the problem.
- Live richer, more authentic lives.
- View our lives in a healthier perspective, with greater meaning and direction.
- Gain our sense of humor in the presence of our problems and in their resolution.
- Recognize our self-worth and self-goodness and separate it from the errors and mistakes we have made in our lives.
- Forgive ourselves and others for mistakes made.
- Give ourselves and others kindness, tenderness, and understanding during times of great stress.
- Gain a sense of purpose and order in our lives as we solve problems.
- Feel productive as we labor through the muck and mire of our problems.
- Respect our rights and the rights of others as we solve problems.
- Clarify our feelings about the behavior of others without the barrier of self-censorship or fear of rejection.
- Gain a "win-win" solution to problems, which involves ourselves with others. It opens us up to compromise.
- Keep our family together.
- Provide quality police services.

Winning the war of irrational beliefs is not to engage in a fight to the death over any one particular battle with any one particular individual or any one particular belief. Yet equally important is that early identification, consistent intervention, and the understanding that succeeding can mean to fail or to relapse must be part of the change. Officers should learn to deal with failure or a relapse along the way to change, and when that happens, you just move on. Those of us who want change can change by altering irrational beliefs and by keeping our eye on the goal of a healthy lifestyle, which can produce optimal outcomes.

Healthy Lifestyles and Optimal Outcomes

Practicing individualized stress management can produce optimal results within the context of practicing a healthy lifestyle, which includes regular exercise, wholesome nutrition and diet, spiritual renewal, and enriching social interactions. Officer choices determine the health of the body, mind, spirit, and social interactions. If any one of these four areas sickens, other areas can become ill as well. Conversely, if officers choose to practice a healthy lifestyle in these four areas, then they choose to take care of their bodies, at least that is what experts say.[27]

Herbert Benson's relaxation response is worth considering.[28] Based on studies at Boston's Beth Israel Hospital and Harvard Medical School, Benson showed that relaxation techniques can be accomplished without medication and other techniques practiced by clinicians. Benson was approached by practitioners of the Mararishi Mahesh Yogi of Transcendental Meditation (TM) fame. The TM'ers believed that they could control the blood pressure by their meditative thoughts alone. In the midst of a very conservative Harvard medical community, Benson was remiss to study something as "far out there" as transcendental meditation. After repeated and persuasive meetings, Benson finally acquiesced to study the TM'ers. From his studies, Benson found that individuals could lower their blood pressure voluntarily. This may sound like a small issue, but at the time the cardiovascular system was felt to be completely autonomic (functioning automatically on its own). To realize that we could exert voluntary control over an autonomic bodily function was big news. The bad news for the TM'ers was that the ability to control the blood pressure seemed related only to certain key factors in the meditative process and did not require a specific mantra to work. From this information, Benson discovered what he calls the "Relaxation Response," which is the distilled essence of what works in the TM process. This response is a built-in physiological antidote to the stressful events of our daily lives. Street cops, like the rest of us, can learn to trigger this response by following four simple instructions:

- Sit down or lie down in a comfortable position.
- Close your eyes.
- Repeat a single word or phrase mentally over and over again.

- When distracting thoughts enter into your mind, let them pass through and refocus on your word or phrase.

By doing these four things every day for 15–20 minutes, we can refresh our bodies physically and emotionally. On the other hand, taking a little time to think clearly might be the best advice.

15 Steps to Reduce Stress

One of the best ways to lower stress is to invest 30 minutes three to five times per week, in vigorous physical exercise (assuming your doctor doesn't have a problem with that). Work up a sweat. Other successful initiatives include many of the following[29]:

- Learn relaxation techniques
- Cut caffeine intake
- Eat right (stay away from fast-food establishments, e.g., McDonalds)
- Meditate, get still, "center"
- Develop better time management habits
- Play, have fun, recharge
- Get plenty of sleep
- Smile more, laugh, use humor to lighten your emotional load
- Count your blessings daily, make thankfulness a habit
- Say nice things when you talk to yourself
- Simplify
- Set personal goals, give yourself a sense of purpose
- Forgive—grudges are too heavy to carry around
- Practice optimism and positive expectancy, hope is a muscle—develop it

It is hard to follow all of the above recommendations, but officers who try feel better and for longer periods of time than those who do not try. One point often forgotten is that your body today is not the same body of yesterday.

Positive Attitude and Lifestyle

Because stress is both an emotional and physical reaction to change, the better you feel, the better you'll be able to manage everyday stress. A positive attitude and lifestyle are key elements of stress management.[30] Coping with stressful events can save your life (don't laugh, remember the logic of the ABC's). At an extreme, many individuals who have heart attacks needlessly die because they panic. When you think positively, exercise, eat well, and rest regularly, you'll be taking care of the most important person you know—you!

Stress response is axiomatic, like blinking your eyes. When faced with a challenging situation, your muscles tense, your heart rate and blood pressure increase, you perspire more, and you may even notice a gripping sensation in your stomach. You also feel more mentally alert and focused. This stress response prepares your body to meet an immediate, recognizable challenge. It is an involuntary action, as suggested in Chapter 2, every action has a reaction.

When stress is positive, your body automatically relaxes after you've handled the situation that caused your stress response: muscles relax and the heart rate, blood pressure, and other physical functions return to their normal, prestressed state. This relaxation response is the most important aspect of positive stress because it allows time to gather the physical and emotional energy needed to meet the next challenge. Positive stress is a series of heightened alert and relaxation responses that help deal with the changes and challenges of daily life, especially among those individuals in high-stress jobs.

With negative stress, there is no true relaxation between one stress "crisis" and the next. If a street cop remains "geared up," the involuntary physical and emotional strain results. Left uncontrolled, negative stress can lead to high blood pressure, ulcers, migraines, heart attacks—and worse. Fortunately, you can stop the cycle of negative stress by becoming aware of your stress and how you react to it, by practicing relaxation techniques, and by developing a positive attitude and lifestyle.

Developing a positive attitude depends on self-talk, rehearsal, developing an action plan, and developing an alternative when all else fails.

- Self-talk means telling yourself about what you can and cannot do. Positive self-talk is saying "I can," and setting your mind to meet the challenge at hand. Know your limitations (as Dirty Harry once said).
- Rehearsal is a way to prepare for a potentially stressful situation before it occurs. Think over the situation, go over details, plan to take action, and visualize successful results.
- Develop an action plan that can help turn a stress disaster into a new opportunity.
- Develop an alternative, which is probably the most important technique for most of us. Prepare for failure as previously expressed. Devise a way to deal with situations when all else fails. One concern is that often there are so many other variables effecting outcomes that if we devise a plan, and it fails because of unforeseen situations, we need a backup plan.[31] Some call it "Plan B."

Developing a positive lifestyle includes exercise, nutrition, rest and relaxation, proper planning, and goal setting.

- *Exercise.* Physically fit people handle stress more easily than those who are not fit since they feel better about themselves in general and they have a routine. A regular exercise program should include some form of aerobic activity. Join a baseball or volleyball team or create a league at the department. Sworn officers versus nonsworn personnel or administration versus street cops. Link the league with other ball teams in the community so that regular athletic events can be planned. Plan practice sessions. Running, walking, swimming, and bicycling are all excellent aerobic activities. Stretching exercises are also helpful in relieving tense muscles and improving overall flexibility. Do not expect too much out of yourself too soon.

- Nutrition refers to planning meals: we are what we eat. Junk foods are easy when riding around but are low in nutritional value and generally high in calories. Plan meals around servings from the four basic food groups: meats, dairy products, grains, and fresh fruits and vegetables. Eating well and limiting use of salt, sugar, caffeine, and alcohol can promote health and help reduce stress. Most officers I know have a great deal of fun with the basic food groups and redefine them to pizza, ice cream, donuts, and beer.

- Rest and relaxation are activities that are worth your attention because they are the keys to balancing stress. In addition to specific techniques, "slow down" and enjoy leisure time. The best thing an officer can do is nothing at all. Do not jam days off with endless chores—make an effort to relax and enjoy free time. (This is not a license to tell your intimate other that you don't have to work around the house.) Also, sleeping a reasonable number of hours pays off, especially since the body needs sleep to refresh itself.

- Proper planning and goal setting provides a sense of stability during the workday. Delegation alleviates some of the responsibility an officer carries in regular routines but aids an officer when things change. Take time for personal pursuits with the family, at meetings, hobbies, sports, and church.

INDIVIDUAL COPING

Attitudes, moods, and feelings affect law enforcement officer performance in "rolling with the punches" or coping, a well-documented perspective. Healthy self-esteem provides a "hardiness" to greet stressful events as challenges to be met rather than threats to be feared, which in turn provides a negative stress cycle.[32] If self-esteem and sense of mastery are low, there are ways of coping that do not require informing others (behaviors that you use for protection against threat). When coping effectively, officers see situations and altercations as an opportunity to learn and enhance experience. Researchers say that coping mediates or neutralizes stressors that affect an individual's health.[33] One way to understand these recommendations is that stressors are present and that officer routines change all the time. There is little an officer can do about change except go work for Wal-Mart or deal effectively with stress levels and the best initiatives must include a healthy body and mind. They make the difference between looking like you are 50 years of age when you're actually 35. Now you know why homeless people look so much older! Your choice.

Individual Coping and Prevention Strategies

Usually the principal goal of stress management training in a person-centered program is to increase the officer's ability to prevent stress by using a wide range of initiatives. Which initiatives are the best depends on the officer and his or her commitment level[34]:

- Effective learning skills make a difference in negotiating already stressful situations: domestic violence, serious traffic accidents, shootings, death notification, and dealing with the suicidal and the mentally ill.
- Understanding human behavior and the psychological processes relevant to police work so that officers can recognize when their own reactions should be seen as normal—or as not normal.
- Maintaining physical health and well-being through diet and exercise (which can be facilitated through a department wellness program).
- Increasing body awareness and relaxation through biofeedback, meditation, or yoga.
- Managing anger (see below: "Anger Management Training at the Rochester Police Department").
- Learning to communicate effectively with family members, peers, supervisors, and citizens.
- Restructuring attitudes or thoughts that contribute to stress.
- Planning his or her career.

Rochester Police's Stress Management Unit has been providing anger management training since 1987 in an effort to reduce the use of excessive force on the job, but also the health problems and domestic difficulties that can result from failure to deal appropriately with anger. Three full days of training are offered to officers over a 3-week period several times throughout the year. The classes are interactive, using role playing, videos, and group discussions, and they focus on the connection between anger and stress, the physical and emotional effects of anger, and ways to acknowledge anger and express and control it appropriately. Line officers, investigators, sergeants, and lieutenants are trained in separate groups.

After learning about Rochester's stress unit you might feel that an organized approach to stress control could be advantageous. The fact is, it does not matter if stress reduction is entirely an individual attempt or an individual attempt in concert with his or her peers and agency supported or not. Regardless how changes in thinking come about, those changes can profoundly enhance self-esteem and the ability to cope with stressful experiences. This subtle shift in thinking affects an individual's attitude and can mean the difference between viewing yourself as stress-hardy versus helpless and vulnerable. Changes can be seen everyday in healthy persons, especially since these individuals will try new ways to cope with old problems. In part, taking time to think through problems can produce new methods of coping alone or in concert with others.

Developing Peer Support Programs

It can prove useful to develop peer support for officers involved in stress programs. Sometimes, peer support can be the primary vehicle in person-centered stress programs. There are several steps to develop a peer support program and these steps vary from department to department depending on many factors such as resources and policy[35]:

1. Check with legal counsel, commanders, unions, and policymakers to determine the legal barriers or limitations when establishing a peer component in the agency.
2. Consult with other police departments and professional associations for guidance.
3. Develop a philosophy (more on this later in the chapter).
4. Select a peer support coordinator, facilitator, or provider from the private sector.
5. Develop criterion (rank, duties, training) for candidates to recruit them and their family members (more on this idea later in the chapter).
6. Develop (based on the literature) and conduct a needs assessment (more on this later in the chapter).
7. Design a preliminary approach and monitoring plan.
8. Consult with management. Will peers be given on-duty time to attend training?
9. Will the department pay for the coordinator?
10. Find an appropriate place to meet (off police property, see above for more information).
11. Develop written procedures and selection criteria in collaboration with others.
12. Secure funding (may occur earlier) and support from appropriate civil leaders.

Also, program practitioners recommend that planners maintain a "holistic" focus in moving through these planning steps, making sure that the program addresses personal and organizational sources of stress, officers and family members, and prevention and treatment. The sequence and exact manner in which program planners follow these steps, and the time that each step takes, will depend on local opportunities and constraints. A closer look at peer philosophy, family participation, needs assessment, and types of needs assessment would prove helpful.

Role of Peer Supporters

The peer supporter provides support and assistance to personnel and their family members in times of stress and crisis. According to the Metropolitan Nashville Police Department, the role of a peer supporter consists of the following[36]:

- Convey trust, anonymity, and assure confidentiality within guidelines to employees who seek assistance from the Peer Support Program.
- Provide assistance and support on a voluntary basis.
- Assist the employee by referring him or her to the appropriate outside resource when necessary.
- Be available to the individual for additional follow-up support.
- Maintain contact with the Program Coordinator regarding program activities.
- Attend the Peer Support 5-Day Training.
- Attend annual quarterly 8 hours of updated Peer Support Program training provided by the Behavioral Health Services Division.

The peer supporter is not exempt from federal, state, or local laws, or the rules and regulations of the police department.

Peer Support Philosophy

The International Association of Chiefs of Police (IACP) developed a philosophy that guides law enforcement agencies toward an efficient peer support program.[37]

The IACP argues that the goal of peer support is to provide all public safety employees the opportunity to receive emotional and tangible peer support through times of personal or professional crises. Peer support should help to anticipate and address potential at-risk situations. A peer support program should have a procedure for mental health consultation and training. And it should be developed and implemented under the organizational structure of the parent law enforcement agency.

The IACP is concerned with the maximum utilization of a program and should support confidentiality. A steering committee should be comprised of sworn and nonsworn individuals from the police organization, mental health professionals, and police administrators even during its planning and operation.

A Peer Support Person (PSP), sworn or non-sworn, is a specifically trained colleague, not a counselor or a therapist. A peer support program can augment outreach programs (e.g., employee assistance programs and in-house treatment programs), but not replace them. PSPs should refer cases that require professional intervention to a mental health professional. A procedure should be in place for mental health consultations and training.

It is beneficial for PSPs to be involved in supporting individuals involved in a critical incident such as an officer-involved shooting. PSPs also make an invaluable addition to group debriefings in conjunction with a licensed mental health professional.

Key Points Linked to Peer Support Philosophy

- No program will survive unless (within the limits of the law) it maintains strict confidentiality—that is, keeps information about officers and family members private.
- Because legislation and case law vary from state to state, clinicians need to obtain legal counsel regarding their exposure to lawsuits and methods of reducing this exposure.
- Communication between clients and licensed mental health professionals is usually privileged communication under state statute. However, exceptions to this rule require counselors to report certain information clients may reveal to them, such as homicidal or suicidal intentions.
- Program staff and independent practitioners can take a number of steps to ensure confidentiality:
  - Develop written confidentiality guidelines and share them with everyone in the department.
  - Obtain informed consent to treatment from clients in writing.
  - Learn about the exceptions to confidentiality and make them known to department administrators, line officers, family members, and clients.
  - Maintain appropriate client records.
  - Try to send mandatory referrals, especially fitness-for-duty evaluations (which usually require disclosure of client information to administrators), to external counselors or at least clearly separate the treatment of voluntary and mandatory referrals within the program.

The International Association of Chiefs of Police is available to provide legal advice to stress program staff by calling (703) 836-6767, or writing IACP, 1110 North Glebe Road, Suite 200, Arlington, VA 22201. Professional associations and schools that have continuing education programs often offer risk management courses, and some malpractice insurance carriers distribute tapes on risk management.

While they may help, legal advice, courses, and special precautions are no guarantee against lawsuits. Rather, the best defense against a suit—although still not foolproof—is always providing good clinical care.

Individuals vary greatly in their capacity to endure stressful situations, and there is, undoubtedly, self-selection in the kinds of jobs and stressors that individuals choose. However, because sources of stress may vary from officer to officer, providing a solution for one officer might not be the best solution for another officer.[38] A partial solution to this problem may involve intervening with "shifts" of street cops that are formed based on person–environment relationships and that contribute to the generation or reduction of stress.[39]

Trooper Richard Kelly designed a treatment program for the Massachusetts State Troopers.[40] Kelly explains that the level of commitment should be the first priority of a department when designing a program. He says that "a quarter of a century after the first stress units began, there is still debate over the need and method of providing services to the department employees."[41] A peer of Kelly's says that the debate has changed from whether there is a need to how the need should be met. One implication of this thought is that the level of commitment is not always as thought out as expected.

Developing a Peer Program for Officers and Their Families

Police stress programs should include family members because they are often scrutinized and criticized by the media and the public and consequently experience anxiety, isolation, and a loss of morale.[42] Additionally, the job of policing is frankly more complex than 10 or even 20 years ago, because of the sophistication levels of criminals, the threat of terrorism both domestic and foreign, and civil liability issues and officers require as much help as available toward recovery and prevention.[43] Add to the explanation that in recent years there has been increased recognition of long-standing sources of stress, "including those that some police organizations themselves may inadvertently create for officers because of their rigid hierarchical structures, a culture of machismo, minimal opportunities for advancement, and paperwork requirements."[44]

Forward Thinking about Family Participation

In considering family members as equal participants in stress programs, one assumption is that often they, too, are impacted by the job (as discussed below), and equally important their participation in the recovery or prevention process can ensure that stressed officers can receive help when they need it even long after the conclusion of a program. Knowledgeable family members can become an important source of support for the officer. Conversely, untrained family members could easily become "enablers" of stressed officers, permitting those officers to continue their "stressed" behavior at home.

When counseling family members together, an officer's spouse, father, sister, or whatever can learn what behavior might be indicators of stress, and relationships with counselors can provide professional contacts to aid the officer without the thoughts of jeopardizing his or her police job.

This thought lends itself well to the idea of *multimodal* or family treatment. As one researcher says, "Police families do not wear the badge or carry the weapon but are very much affected by those who do. Their support-role clearly contributes to maintaining law enforcement services in the community."[45] This professional connection with the department could break down those barriers, and finally, it would add some camaraderie within family units and among other families of officers, thereby creating some unity with an eye toward retaining officers and their family's support.

In one study of 479 spouses and intimate partners of police officers, 77% reported experiencing unusually high amounts of stress from the officers' job.[46] Commonly cited sources include:

- Shift work and overtime (which disrupts family activities and reduces the amount of time family can spend together)
- An officer's cynicism, need to feel in control in the home, or inability or unwillingness to express feelings
- The fear that the officer will be hurt or killed
- Officers' and other people's excessively high expectations of their children
- Avoidance, teasing, or harassment of children because of their parent's job
- The presence of a gun in the home
- Friends' discomfort because of the officer's weapon and 24-hour role as a law enforcer
- An impression that the officer would prefer to spend time with fellow officers rather than with his or her family
- Either excessive or too little discussion about the job
- The officer's perceived paranoia or excessive vigilance and subsequent overprotection
- Helping the officer cope with work-related problems
- Critical incidents or the officer's injury or death

Family members interviewed for this report offered glimpses into the stressful nature of being related to a law enforcement officer:

- One officer's wife described the difficulty of coping with her husband's rotating shifts while she also worked a full-time job and they tried to raise three children. Friends stopped inviting her to social functions because (she felt) they were uncomfortable about the absence of her husband. She and her husband finally settled on the 11:00 P.M. to 7:00

A.M. shift as the best option because it gave him the most time with the family.

- Another wife spoke of being constantly worried about her husband's safety: "I would hear reports of officers being shot and just have to wait to see if it was him. I even listened to the police scanner at night until he came home."
- A female officer said that her marriage had suffered because her difficult shift hours required her husband to do much of the childrearing, which he resented and she regretted.
- Another officer said that his 8-year-old daughter had witnessed one of his flashbacks to a shooting incident and had been frightened by her father "talking in tongues," saying, "I never want to see my kids exposed to that again."

Officers married to other law enforcement personnel may be less affected by some of the stresses listed above because they may have a mutual understanding of the difficulties of each other's jobs and socially share the same friends. However, dual-officer couples may also suffer the added burdens of blurred personal and professional roles, gossip among colleagues about their relationship, and, with both working different rotating shifts and working overtime, even less time for each other at home. Certainly this idea of family participation has many considerations before it is put into practice; however, decision makers initiating individual person-centered programs, including those initiated privately, should consider developing a needs assessment in order to benefit from the experience.

What Is Needs Assessment and Why It Should be Done

Needs assessment is a tool for program planning.[47] A goal of needs assessment is the coordination of services and police work schedules in order to facilitate control and prevention of stress and an attempt not to impede police services. Program providers need to know where they are going, why they are going there, and the best route to take to reach their destination. A careful, thorough needs assessment is the road map for change and provides the basis for a strategic plan that addresses specific problems that contribute to police officer stress and family participation.

There are five compelling reasons to conduct needs assessments, which include:

1. To identify perceived sources of stress experienced by officers and other target clients. Although some sources of stress are commonplace among most officers and family members (e.g., shift work), a needs assessment can reveal how widespread and severe stress-related

problems are among the target groups and what specific problems are unique to the department or jurisdiction (e.g., a detested supervisor, a hostile local press, deficient equipment).

2. To identify the services already available to clients, how extensively they are being used, and gaps in efforts to reduce and treat stress-related problems. Even when program administrators or consulting mental health practitioners believe that existing services are sufficient, a needs assessment may reveal that officers seldom use these services or are dissatisfied with them. Information from such an assessment may also help program planners identify those services they can expand and avoid duplication of effort.

3. To identify types of services that target clients want. In addition to giving clients a sense of ownership, asking questions regarding desired services, staff characteristics, location, and other program features—and paying attention to the answers—will help ensure that the program will be both accepted and effective. Nearly all the respondents to the Erie County survey indicated, for example, that they would want to attend stress debriefings if they were involved in a critical incident.

4. To generate information for use in selling the program to administrators, labor representatives, officers, and other potential clients, and to funding sources. Assessments conducted in Erie County revealed that nearly two-thirds of officers reported feeling serious stress because of their work duties in the previous year, a statistic that surprised most law enforcement administrators in the county.

5. To familiarize officers, family members, and others with the program. When distributing a needs survey, program staff can take the opportunity to promote the program if it is currently or soon to be operational. If the needs assessment is conducted using face-to-face conversations (see below), staff can also begin to gain the trust of targeted clients.

6. To periodically evaluate the impact of stress program results among the participants during and after the last session has ended in order to determine the program's strengths and weaknesses. One implication of this is to alter the program to bring outcomes more in line with the needs assessment original proposal.[48]

Needs assessments should continue during and after program participation. It should be noted that in order to build trust among officers and family members and to aid providers with information about this particular group, programs should attempt to meet the needs of their participants and equally important, meet their expectations of confidentiality and professionalism.[49]

Needs Assessment Debate

Some person-centered stress program planners consider a needs assessment unnecessary because it is thought that the needs of street officers and their family members are obvious, and they feel that enough information about cop stress is available from other sources within the department.[50] However, experienced program practitioners (regardless of the type of program being developed) have a different opinion. Bluntly, those practitioners argue that not developing a needs assessment is a misguided practice that could lead to the demise of a program or an inadequate attempt to aid others.[51] Then, too, a needs assessment makes the project defensible, fundable, and measurable. These final thoughts can make the difference in the program or a series of programs becoming operationalized or being buried somewhere in a "maybe" strategy file.[52]

Types of Needs Assessments

A formal needs assessment involves developing a survey and distributing it or using it for phone or face-to-face interviews. An informal assessment can consist of unstructured telephone or face-to-face conversations, but it is advised that from development to execution of an assessment that a trained professional input a large part of the devices or methods used. Structured surveys are time-consuming to design and conduct and should be objective and impersonal, but usually yield comprehensive and credible results if administrated appropriately.

Informal conversations can provide an inexpensive in-depth look into the needs and desires of officers and their family members, but, unless many respondents are contacted, the results may not be as representative of the entire target population and therefore not as credible. Of course, in small departments informal group or individual conversations may be the most practical way to determine the needs of officers. Even in such settings, however, officers' concerns about keeping their comments confidential is advisable and it is suggested to use a written survey without officers identifying themselves to the principle researcher or investigator.

HISTORICAL LOOK AT PERSON-CENTERED PROGRAMS

A brief history of officer person-centered assistance programs is telling[53]:

> *Traditional Programs Era* (1950s): The supervisory attitude was to (1) ignore stress; (2) reassign the officer to a desk job; (3) refer the officer to Alcoholic's Anonymous; or (4) refer the employee to a chaplain.
>
> *Referral Era* (1960s): A staff person, usually the Public Information Officer, would be in charge of granting employees, who requested it, a sick

leave with no questions asked and no pay while on leave. Often the officer was also referred to an outside mental health agency or counselor.

In-House Stress Units Era (1970s): A staff person, usually in conjunction with a union or an association official, would meet with an officer in an attempt to resolve, mediate, or arbitrate the officer's stress. The idea was to turn stressed officers into change agents. Sometimes, an outside counselor would be brought in, but this was usually for debriefing purposes after some major incident. Sometimes, a stress counselor or an officer of rank who volunteered might conduct stress seminars, but most often this task was contracted to private purveyors.

Ministry Programs Era (1980s): Officers would be assigned/referred to a victim survivor group, a police officer support group, a chaplain or a chaplain's group, a church-sponsored retreat, or some other kind of religious or nonprofit group–based program. Rarely were these programs used exclusively, but the notion of pastoral counseling was something that caught on quickly during this time period.

Critical Incident Stress Debriefing, or CISD (1990s): Critical incidents include line-of-duty deaths, suicide of a coworker, death of a child, failed rescue attempts, mass casualty incidents, and where victim is known to responder. A critical incident is presumed to be a precursor for PTSS if not responded to within 24–48 hours by a debriefing team, usually consisting of one mental health professional or a member of the clergy and one to three peer support personnel (see Chapter 5 for specifics on CISD performance).

Many supported programs for law enforcement officers in the 1990s, and it seems are common among police departments in 2006, are programs tied to factors inherent in the profession of law enforcement, which included[54]:

- Suicide—Police officers kill themselves at a rate six times greater than in the general population, and police officers kill themselves at a rate 8.3 times greater than those who die at the hands of criminals.[55] Although there is usually little history of counseling prior to a police suicide, autopsies have revealed that those suicides are often linked to diagnosable mental disorders, and most often involve depression, alcohol, or drug abuse. This phenomenon seems to be restricted largely to urban police officers.

- Alcoholism—The rates are high possibly because of the stigma associated with illegal drugs. Older officers have the highest rates, and there is significant female and minority involvement. Several studies conducted in the 1970s looked at drinking on duty as an indicator of alcoholism, and produced some frightening figures, 25–67%. Other studies have looked at the "cop ulcer" rate, estimated at 30%, and fitness and dietary habits of officers. More recent studies have looked at drug abuse.

- Infidelity—Perhaps the only occupation to have its infidelity rates studied, police work lends itself to temptations and opportunities in this regard, but there are no rate estimates. There is data on police divorce (1:10 succeed), how it is related to shift work, and when in the police career it usually happens.

Prevention and Reduction Programs (2000s): The National Crime Prevention Institute (NCPI) in Louisville, Kentucky, recommends that crime prevention is the "anticipation, recognition, appraisal of a crime risk; and the initiation of some action to remove or reduce it."[56] To reduce the potential of a crime, they contacted the business owner. It is strongly recommended that police agencies apply a preventive concept to negative stress reduction by removing the opportunity of negative stressors that leaves the doors open for some high-risk officers.[57] It could be said that the 21st century is at least ideally trying to make a case for stress prevention and stress reduction programs among officers. Many argue that stress reduction programs should include the "anticipation, recognition, appraisal of distress, along with a remove or reduce it among officers."[58]

Police agency employee assistance programs (EAP) have started to move toward general assistance and presently, many agencies have mandatory sessions for officers engaged in critical incident activities (see Chapter 5). Some police agencies have operated programs staffed with full-time counselors since 1976 but those programs were never fully developed. The number of police agencies who employ full-time psychologists, EAPs, or other types of mental health services has grown significantly since 1979. For instance, in 1979 one survey of police agencies showed that only 20% of the sample agencies offered some kind of psychological services.[59] In a 1988 national survey of state and municipal police departments, more than half of those agencies provided some kind of psychological service to officers. Fifty-three percent offered counseling to police officers for job-related stress, 52% provided counseling to officers for personal and family problems, and 42% counseled officers' family members. Then, too, whereas psychological services once focused mainly on basic counseling services, testing of officers, and assistance with criminal investigations, often on a part-time consulting basis, many programs now offer around-the-clock services that include[60]:

- Critical incident debriefing (Chapter 5)
- Training on stress management
- Consultation regarding organizational change in the department

One trend seemingly entrenched in police organizations in 2006 is the development of stress programs for personnel and their families.

SUMMARY

The focus of this chapter is about individual and person-centered initiatives, which consist of an individual's effort, often supported by a police agency for the purpose of reducing, controlling, and preventing stress among police officers. Individual attempts to reduce and control stress might be one way to describe individual initiatives. Because officers respond differently to stressors, it is clarified that many of them manage stress at a personal level and not always acted out through negative behavior. Person-centered strategies include individual and group programs operated (or contracted to private and public providers) by an officer's employer whereby groups of officers participate unless the mental health of the officer requires an official private session.

The goal of early warning systems to detect stressed officers is to change the behavior of individual officers who have been identified as having problematic performance records. Three basic phases of an early warning system includes selection, intervention, and post-intervention monitoring. Choosing to be healthy is the best weapon against the negative influences of stress and against living a life of discomfort regardless of the occupation of an individual but many officers refuse to see a personal problem because of the influence of the police subculture fostering ridicule by other officers and fear of a lack of job stability.

Law enforcement officers can choose to initiate some action on their own to reduce the negative influences of stress by employing various coping methods, which includes deep breathing, muscle relaxation, meditation/prayer, positive thinking and self-talk, and mental imagery.

Activating event, belief system, and consequence, or the "ABC method" of stress, implies that when individuals know their ABC's of stress that managing it might be more efficient. That is, because activating event results in a consequence occurs only after being filtered through a belief system and if that belief system is irrational, change is less likely. The question really asks about why stressed cops hold a belief about their mental health where data is inconsistent with their thoughts. Clearly, practicing individualized stress management can produce optimal results only within the context of practicing a healthy lifestyle, which includes regular exercise, wholesome nutrition and diet, spiritual renewal, and enriching social interactions. Officer choices determine the health of the body, mind, spirit, and social interactions. There are many steps to reduce stress, some of which include investing 30 minutes in vigorous physical exercise, three to five times per week.

Because stress is both an emotional and physical reaction to change, the better you feel, the better you will be able to manage everyday stress. A positive attitude and lifestyle are key elements of stress management. Also healthy self-esteem provides a "hardiness" to greet stressful events as challenges to be met rather than threats to be feared, which could in turn provide a negative stress cycle. The principal goal of stress management training in a person-centered program is to increase the officer's ability to prevent or cope with stress by using a wide range of initiatives. Which initiatives are the best depends on the officer and his or her commit level, which can include effective learning skills and understanding human behavior and psychological perspectives.

Developing peer support programs takes several steps that might vary from police agency to agency, depending on factors such as resources, stress history (of agency members), and policy. Some recommendations include checking with legal counsel, commanders, and policymakers to determine whether there are any legal barriers or limitations to setting up a peer component. The International Association of Chiefs of Police (IACP) developed a philosophy that guides law enforcement toward an efficient peer support program. Their philosophy promotes the objective of providing all public safety employees the opportunity to receive emotional and tangible peer support through times of personal or professional crises and those programs should have a procedure for mental health consultation and training.

Police peer stress programs should include family members because they are often scrutinized and criticized by the media and the public, and consequently experience anxiety, isolation, and a loss of morale. That is, they are impacted by the job of the officer too. Equally important, family participation can ensure that street cops receive the help they need when they need it and could aid in the officer's recovery by not becoming an "enabler" of a stressed officer. When counseling family members together, an officer's spouse, father, sister, or whatever can learn what behavior might be indicators of stress, and relationships with counselors can provide professional contacts to aid the officer without the thoughts of jeopardizing his or her police job. Finally, this chapter presents a brief historical path of police person-centered programs beginning with the traditional programs in the 1950s to complex programs of the 2000s.

WHAT WOULD YOU DO IF YOU WERE IN CHARGE?

On Monday, July 25, 2005, there were two problems with the feast delivered to officers at the Devonshire Police Station in Northridge, California: pizza and barbecue aren't the best match—and nobody at the station had ordered food.[61] The station, the apparent butt of a practical joke, received the food after somebody identifying himself as "Officer O'Neil" ordered $400 worth of barbecue meat, salads, and bread from the Outdoor Grill and $150 in pizza from Pizza Pazza to be delivered to the station. Officer O'Neil doesn't exist, but there were plenty of hungry officers to take his place. And both restaurants donated the food to the station, creating an impromptu party, Devonshire Captain Joseph Curreri said.

David Sainoz, manager of the Outdoor Grill, said the restaurant usually requires a credit card number for such large orders, but figured that an order delivered to a police station wouldn't be a problem. "My boss took the order to the police station, and what a surprise. It was kind of strange."

"We wanted to thank both of those establishments for their generosity in donating the food, and we want to get the word out to other establishments in our area: It's probably a good thing to verify large orders like this."

OFFICER KILLED IN GEORGIA

Sergeant Howard (Howie) Stevenson of the Ceres, California, Police Department was shot and killed on Sunday, January 9, 2005.[62] Sergeant Stevenson was 39 years old, had been on the department for 20 years, and is survived by his wife, son, and two daughters. His badge number was 143.

Sergeant Stevenson succumbed to gunshot wounds sustained the previous night during a shootout with a suspect armed with a semiautomatic rifle. Sergeant Stevenson and other officers had responded to a liquor store on North Central Avenue to investigate reports of an armed male who was acting strangely. The first officer on the scene was shot and wounded by the suspect. This officer took cover behind a car and returned fire as Sergeant Stevenson arrived at the scene. Sergeant Stevenson exited his patrol car and immediately engaged the suspect, firing eight shots before being shot. He was struck three times in his torso and legs before the suspect shot him twice in the head as he lay on the ground. The suspect exchanged shots with responding officers before fleeing the scene. He was shot and killed approximately 3 hours later during a second shootout. The suspect was believed to be under the influence of cocaine at the time of the incident.

DISCUSSION QUESTIONS

1. Describe individual and person-centered initiatives among police officers.
2. Describe the goal of an early warning system to detect stressed officers.
3. Characterize the three basic phases of an early warning system.
4. Explain the negative potential outcomes of an early warning system.
5. Describe why it is difficult for officers to seek help to reduce and control stress. In what way might you disagree with this perspective?
6. Describe some of the methods an officer can initiate to cope with stress.
7. Explain the ABC model of analyzing experiences. In what way does this analysis make sense?
8. Describe how irrational beliefs can hold an officer back from managing stress.
9. Identify and explain the relevance of healthy lifestyles. In what way might an unhealthy lifestyle contribute to reducing stress recovery and prevention?
10. Identify at least 15 steps to individually reduce stress. What thoughts might you have to increase this list?
11. Identify and articulate why positive attitudes and lifestyle are relevant variables to stress control. Provide some examples from your own experiences.

12. Describe the relevance of self-esteem in stress management including stress prevention.

13. Identify components that would lead to the development of a peer support program.

14. Explain the IACP's philosophy that should guide a law enforcement agency toward an efficient peer support program.

15. Explain why stress programs should include family participation. In what way do you agree with this perspective? Disagree?

16. Define needs assessment and describe six compelling reasons it is performed.

17. Identify the historical path of person-centered programs among police personnel.

ENDNOTES

1. Samuel Walker, Geoffrey P. Alpert, and Dennis J. Kenney (2001). Early warning systems: Responding to the problem police officer. National Institute of Justice. Retrieved online June 18, 2004: http://www.ncjrs.org/txtfiles1/nij/188565.txt

2. For discussions of recommended performance categories, see International Association of Chiefs of Police (1989). *Building integrity and reducing drug corruption in police departments.* Washington, DC: U.S. Department of Justice, Bureau of Justice Assistance, 80. Lou Reiter (1998). *Law enforcement administrative investigations: A manual guide,* 2nd ed. Tallahassee, FL: Lou Reiter and Associates. p. 18.

3. John M. Violanti (2005). Dying for the job: Psychological stress, disease, and mortality in police work. In Heith Copes (Ed.), *Policing and stress* (pp. 87–102). Upper Saddle River, NJ: Prentice Hall p. 88. Also see John M. Violanti (1996). *Police suicide: Epidemic in blue.* Springfield, IL: Charles C. Thomas. Franklin Zimring and Gordon Hawkins (1973). *Deterrence.* Chicago: University of Chicago Press.

4. John M. Violanti (2005). p. 88. Franklin Zimring and Gordon Hawkins (1973).

5. Samuel Walker, Geoffrey P. Alpert, and Dennis J. Kenney (2001).

6. Catherine H. Milton, Jeanne Wahl Halleck, James Lardner, and Gary L. Albrecht (1977). *Police use of deadly force.* Washington, DC: The Police Foundation. pp. 94–110.

7. Personal confidential communication from a police stress program provider with the author at the University of Maryland, July 25, 2005.

8. Dennis J. Stevens (2004). John Wayne Gacy, Jr. *Famous American Crimes and Trials,* 4, 233–253.

9. Herbert Benson and Eileen M. Stuart (1992). *The Wellness Book.* New York: Carol Publishing.

10. Note: This particular book is used at the Federal Law Enforcement in Glencoe, Georgia, to aid law enforcement in dealing with many of the issues that confront them.

11. Dictionary.com (2005). Retrieved online July 25, 2005: http://dictionary.reference.com/search?q=cope

12. Edward A. Charlesworth and Ronald G. Nathan (1984). *Stress management: A comprehensive guide to wellness.* New York: Ballantine Books.

13. Herbert Benson and Eileen M. Stuart (1992). *The Wellness Book.* New York: Carol Publishing.

14. Patricia Carrington (1985). *How to relax.* New York: Warner Audio Publishing.

15. Joseph A. Harpold and Samuel L. Feemster (2002, September). The negative influences of police stress. *FBI Law Enforcement Bulletin.* Retrieved online June 22, 2004: http://articles.findarticles.com/p/articles/mi_m2194/is_9_71/ai_92285044

16. Joseph A. Harpold and Samuel L. Feemster (2002, September).

17. Dennis L. Conroy and Karen M. Hess (1992). p. 213.

18. Gregory W. Lester (2000). Why bad beliefs don't die. *Skeptical Inquirer.* Retrieved online April 3, 2006: http://articles.findarticles.com/p/articles/mi_m2843/is_6_24/ai_66496166

19. Psychological self help (2005). *Methods for changing behavior.* Retrieved online April 2, 2006: http://mentalhelp.net/psyhelp/chap11/

20. James J. Messina and Constance M. Messina (2006). *Tools for personal growth.* Retrieved online April 4, 2006: http://www.coping.org/growth/beliefs.htm#What

21. Gregory W. Lester (2000).

22. Gregory W. Lester (2000).

23. Abraham Maslow (1970). *Motivation and personality,* 2nd ed. New York: Harper & Row.

24. Andrew Carnegie (2005). Retrieved online March 13, 2006: http://en.wikipedia.org/wiki/Andrew_Carnegie For quote see, Andrew Carnegie retrieved online March 13, 2006: http://en.thinkexist.com/quotes/andrew_carnegie/

25. James J. Messina and Constance M. Messina (2006).

26. James J. Messina and Constance M. Messina (2006).

27. Robin Gershon (1999, March 23). U.S. Department of Justice, National Institute of Justice, Public Health Implication of Law Enforcement Stress, video presentation.

28. Herbert Benson (1975). *Relaxation response.* New York: Carol Publishing.

29. Price Pritchett and Ron Pound (1998). *A survival guide to the stress of organizational change.* Plano, TX: Pritchett Rummler-Brache. p. 35.

30. *Business management and management skills' workbook.* Mike Holt Enterprises. Reprinted in *Labor Management - Stress.* National Electrical Internet Connection. Retrieved online June 22, 2004: http://www.mikeholt.com/mojonewsarchive/BM-HTML/HTML/LABOR-MANAGEMENT-STRESS~20040401.php

31. This last plan was added to emphasize the original outline by the author because of its importance to stress management.

32. Carol L. Wells-Federman, Ann Webster, and Eileen M. Stuart (1992). Feelings, moods, and attitudes. In Herbert Benson (Ed.), *The wellness book* (pp. 209–228). New York: Carol Publishing.

33. M. Robin DiMatteo and Howard S. Friedman cited in Carol L. Wells-Federman, Ann Webster, and Eileen M. Stuart (1992). Feelings, moods, and attitudes. In Herbert Benson (Ed.), *The wellness book* (pp. 209–228). New York: Carol Publishing. p. 227.

34. Renee B. Meador (2004). Model policy and procedures for critical incident stress management /critical incident stress debriefing for law enforcement internal programs: Virginia critical incident stress management. Law enforcement

critical incident stress management. Retrieved online June 18, 2004: http://www.geocities.com/~halbrown/cism_cisd_procedures.html

Also see Julie Esselman Tomz and Peter Finn (1997). Developing a law enforcement stress program for officers and their families. *National Institute of Justice*. Retrieved online June 18, 2004: http://ncjrs.org/txtfiles/163175.txt

35. Richard Kelly (2002). Program building from the peer's eye view. In John M. Madonna, Jr. and Richard E. Kelly (Eds.). *Treating police stress: The work and the words of peer counselors* (pp. 225–231). Springfield, IL: Charles C. Thomas. Also see John Violanti (2004). *Law Enforcement Wellness*. Retrieved online March 13, 2006: http://www.cophealth.com/peer.html

36. Metropolitan Nashville Police Department (2006). Retrieved online March 13, 2006: http://www.police.nashville.org/bureaus/chief/peer_supporters.htm

37. International Association of Chiefs of Police. Retrieved online March 13, 2006: http://www.theiacp.org/documents/index.cfm?fuseaction=document&document_type_id=1&document_id=168

38. R. Lazarus (1991). Psychological stress in the workplace. *Journal of Social Behavior and Personality*, 6, 1–13. B. A. Israel, J. S. House, S. J. Schurman, C. Heaney, and R. P. Mero (1989). The relation of personal resources, participation, influence, interpersonal relationships and coping strategies to occupational stress, job strains and health: A multivariate analysis. *Work & Stress*, 3, 163–194. U. Wiersma and P. Berg (1991). Work-home role conflict, family climate, and domestic responsibilities among men and women. *Journal of Applied Social Psychology*, 21, 1207–1217. B. C. Long (1988). Stress management for school personnel: Stress inoculation training and exercise. *Psychology in the Schools*, 25, 314–324.

39. R. Lazarus (1991).

40. Richard Kelly (2002). Program building from the peer's eye view. In John M. Madonna, Jr. and Richard E. Kelly (Eds.), *Treating police stress: The work and the words of peer counselors* (pp. 225–231). Springfield, IL: Charles C. Thomas.

41. Richard Kelly (2002). p. 231.

42. Julie Esselman Tomz and Peter Finn (1997). Developing a law enforcement stress program for officers and their families. *National Institute of Justice*. Retrieved online June 18, 2004: http://ncjrs.org/txtfiles/163175.txt

43. As explained in an earlier chapter, 9/11 was traumatic but there were indicators and events of terrorism that many officers were well aware of prior to 9/11, especially domestic terrorism.

44. Judy Van Wyk (2005). Hidden hazards of responding to domestic disputes. In Heith Copes (Ed.), *Policing and stress* (pp. 41–54). Upper Saddle River, NJ: Prentice Hall. Also see Julie Esselman Tomz and Peter Finn (1997). p. 3.

45. The library of the International Conference of Police Chaplains in Livingston, Texas, has a number of publications available on loan to chaplain members, which provide guidance for how chaplains can counsel police officers and their families, provide critical incident counseling, and start a chaplaincy program. Also see, in particular, D. W. De Revere, W. A. Cunningham, T. Mobley, and J. A. Price. (1989). *Chaplaincy in law enforcement: What it is and how to do it*. Springfield, IL: Charles C. Thomas.

46. Testimony by A. W. Zavaras (1991, May 20). Hearing: On the front lines. Police stress and family well-being. Before the Select Committee on Children, Youth, and Families, House of Representatives, 102nd Congress, 1st Session. Washington, DC: U.S. Government Printing Office, p. 71.

47. World Health Organization (2000). Retrieved online July 25, 2005: http://whqlibdoc.who.int/hq/2000/WHO_MSD_MSB_00.2d.pdf

48. This sixth point is originated by the author as a recommendation because of his experience with various programs in police departments and elsewhere.

49. The author feels that these final points should be considered by all program leaders, policymakers, and participants.

50. E. Kirschman, E. Scrivner, K. Ellison, and C. Marcy (1992). Work and well-being: Lessons from law enforcement. In J. C. Quick, L. R. Murphy, and J. J. Hurrell (Eds.), *Stress and well-being at work: Assessments and interventions for occupational mental health*. Washington, DC: American Psychological Association. pp. 178–192.

51. Julie Esselman Tomz and Peter Finn (1997). Developing a law enforcement stress program for officers and their families. *National Institute of Justice*. Retrieved online June 18, 2004: http://ncjrs.org/txtfiles/163175.txt

52. Community guide on needs assessment and strategic planning (2000). Retrieved online July 25, 2005: http://www.nhtsa.dot.gov/people/injury/alcohol/Community%20Guides%20HTML/Book2_NeedsAssess.html#benefits

53. Tomas O'Connor. Police stress and employee assistance programs. Retrieved online June 22, 2004: http://faculty.ncwc.edu/toconnor/417/417lect09.htm

54. Thomas O'Connor. (2004). Police stress and employee assistance programs. Retrieved online June 23, 2004. http://faculty.ncwc.edu/toconnor/417/417lect09.htm

55. John M. Violanti (2005). John M. Violanti (1996).

56. National Crime Prevention Institute (1986). *Understanding crime prevention*. Stoneham, MA: Butterworth. p. 2.

57. Joseph A. Harpold and Samuel L. Feemster (2002, September). The negative influences of police stress. *FBI Law Enforcement Bulletin*. Retrieved online June 22, 2004: http://articles.findarticles.com/p/articles/mi_m2194/is_9_71/ai_92285044

58. Joseph A. Harpold and Samuel L. Feemster (2002, September).

59. R. P. Delprino and C. Bahn (1988). National survey of the extent and nature of psychological services in police departments. *Professional Psychology: Research and Practice*, 19, 421–425.

60. J. T. Reese (1987). *A history of police psychological services*. Washington, DC: U.S. Department of Justice, Federal Bureau of Investigation, 35, 11.
      See text and references in Ayres, *Preventing Law Enforcement Stress*, 1; and C. A. Gruber (1980, February). The relationship of stress to the practice of police work. *The Police Chief*, 67, 16–17.

61. Police officer over-issues (2005). Retrieved online July 25, 2005: http://www.lefande.com/weblog/

62. Officer killed memorial page (2005). Retrieved online July 25, 2005: http://www.odmp.org/

11

Options and Obstacles of Person-Centered Stress Providers

The state of your life is nothing more than a reflection of your state of mind. —
Dr. Wayne W. Dyer

Learning Objectives

Once you have read this chapter, you will be able to:

- Describe some of the selection process linked to a stress program provider.
- Characterize the specialized services available to conduct stress programs.
- Identify the three basic options of stress programs.
- Explain external program options.
- Describe in-house program options.
- Detail eight hybrid program options.
- Characterize medication issues linked to stress.
- Identify and explain the obstacles confronting program planners.

KEY TERMS

External program   In-house program   Operant perspective
Hybrid program   Multimodal   Shedding the uniform

INTRODUCTION

A traditional goal of stress control was offered over a hundred years ago by William James in 1893. James talked about breaking bad stressful habits, and gave this advice: Learn a new habit to replace the old one. To do this, he said (1) launch yourself with as much initiative as possible (e.g., change your work schedule, make a public pledge, and so on), (2) permit no exceptions until the new habit is established, and (3) seize the first opportunity to act on every resolution you make ("the road to hell is paved with good intentions" that never get acted on). Outsiders of law enforcement might say that things haven't changed in 100 years.[1] But the hard facts are that officers can't change their shift work as easily as expected, can't rearrange their assignments or responsibilities, nor can they seize the first opportunity to act on a resolution even if they had a good intention. Their task is not associated with the idea on how to win friends and influence people, or to deal with "warm and fuzzy" ideas and things, but rather to deal with the situations and people most Americans don't want to deal with: violators, thugs, angry and often ignorant people who have little respect for others or themselves and hate cops enough to kill them.

William James also gave another bit of advice, a self-help method called the "as if" technique. He said, "If you want a quality, act as if you already had it." When cops act as though they are respected because they engage in one of America's most important occupations, they are run over by motorists,[2] gunned down by children, and are even sued by survivors of law breakers.

Run Over by Motorists

A 38-year-old male police officer (the victim) was fatally injured when a motorist drove into a roadway work zone, striking him. The victim was standing at a four-way intersection directing traffic through a detour. The main flow of traffic followed the detour, making a right-hand turn at the four-way intersection. The motorist that struck the victim failed to turn right at the construction site detour, and her pickup truck skidded sideways through the detour, striking the victim, striking the victim's parked truck, and finally coming to a stop partially on top of a stone wall and against a tree. A call was placed for emergency assistance and the victim was transported to a local hospital where he was pronounced dead.

Gunned Down by Children

The chief of the Grant Police Department was shot and killed while attempting an arrest.[3] The chief was assisting other officers who were picking up from a residence a juvenile who had failed to appear in court. At the residence, the

48-year-old chief and three other officers spoke to the homeowner and proceeded to a back bedroom, calling out to the wanted juvenile. As the chief entered the center of the bedroom, the wanted youth opened fire from his hiding place in a closet with a .45-caliber semiautomatic handgun, fatally striking the 29-year veteran of law enforcement in the front of the head. The wanted juvenile and a second juvenile, who also shot from the closet with a .45-caliber semiautomatic handgun, fired three or four rounds. As a second officer entered the room, he returned fire, striking the juvenile who shot the chief. A third officer returned fire from the doorway, helping to suppress additional shots from the subjects. Both juveniles, who were known drug users and dealers, were under the influence of narcotics at the time of the incident. The wanted suspect, a 17-year-old on conditional release and pending criminal prosecution at the time of the incident, was hospitalized for two injuries. He was arrested after being released from the hospital. The other 17-year-old, who was found hiding in the closet and uninjured, was arrested at the scene. Both youths were charged with capital murder.

Sued by Survivors of Law Breakers

In *Tom v. Voida*,[4] an officer saw a young man fall from his bicycle and remain on the ground with his arms and legs in the air "like a bug."[5] The officer did not suspect him of any crime but stopped to see if medical assistance was needed. Without responding to the officer's inquiries, the young man got up and began rapidly walking away with the bicycle. When the officer asked him to "wait a minute," the young man looked over his shoulder at the officer, threw down the bike, and ran away.

Suspecting that the bicycle was stolen, the officer pursued the suspect on foot for several blocks until the suspect slipped on ice and fell down. The officer's efforts to handcuff the suspect led to a violent struggle in which the suspect repeatedly hit the officer's head against the concrete pavement. When the suspect broke free and continued to flee, the officer resumed pursuit. The officer overtook the suspect once more, initiating a second struggle in which the suspect again struck the officer repeatedly. The officer managed to pull away from the suspect and draw her sidearm even though her left arm had been disabled during the struggle. When the suspect ignored commands to stop and continued to act aggressively, the officer shot and killed him. A lawsuit against the officer and the police department alleged that the officer had used excessive force and had no legal justification to stop the suspect in the first place. The federal district judge granted summary judgment in favor of the officer and the department. The judgment was affirmed later by the appellate court.

The court concluded that from the moment the individual ignored the officer's inquiries and began running away, the officer had a reasonable suspicion that the suspect was engaged in criminal activity. Moreover, the suspect's continued flight from the officer "ripened [the officer's] reasonable suspicion into probable cause . . ." and justified the suspect's arrest for stealing the bicycle and resisting a law enforcement officer. Accordingly, the court considered that the officer was reasonable in trying to restrain the suspect with handcuffs and in using deadly force to protect herself against the suspect.

Although William James's thoughts are visionary and meritorious, and under some conditions can be applied by enforcement officers (I can hardly envision any of the above officers reflecting on old habits versus new habits while performing their jobs), let's provide other possibilities that might prove workable, which include an agency-sponsored program. It might become clear that when it comes to law enforcement occupations, stress control initiatives must be redefined to fit the profession as opposed to trying to make a stress control program fit all professions. One challenge for most law enforcement agencies is the process of selecting a stress provider: someone or some agency to aid officers in controling stress.

SELECTING A STRESS PROGRAM PROVIDER

By some estimates, most law enforcement organizations in the country employ fewer than 40 officers.[6] These departments and even larger departments probably find that choosing an external provider is the most economical way to provide professional stress services for their officers and the families of those officers. However, many options are available, which includes private psychologists or other mental health practitioners (individual or group practices), many employee assistance programs (EAP) are already in place in other agencies and program planners may be amenable to aiding another agency, or other similarly qualified practitioners are available, particularly in college towns where faculty members could also be qualified to operate programs. An administrator may choose a provider informally, based on personal knowledge or recommendations, or identify a provider more formally by requesting competitive proposals from multiple practitioners. Then, too, many departments decide to design their own stress program as discussed in Chapter 12, but there are many specialized services available for police officers across the country.

SPECIALIZED SERVICES FOR POLICE OFFICERS

A number of outside treatment organizations serve only law enforcement personnel.[7] For example, the On-Site Academy in Gardner, Massachusetts, is a nonprofit agency for training and treating emergency services personnel involved in traumatic incidents. Crossroads, in Delmar, New York, provides complete outpatient treatment services for police officers and their families, addressing alcoholism, critical incident stress, anger management, and relationship problems. These providers often feel that officers are more likely to use services that are sensitive to the job-related concerns of law enforcement personnel. Many of these types of agencies are contracted with departments across the United States and their personnel travel to and from various destinations.

BASIC OPTIONS: EXTERNAL, IN-HOUSE, AND HYBRID PROGRAMS

The basic options associated with person-centered stress programs can be referred to as an employee assistance program (EAP) and can be an *external program* outside of the department, an *in-house program* within a police department, or a *hybrid program* consisting of a combination of in-house and external programs.[8]

External Program Option: Five Variations

1. *Stanislaus County, California (11 police agencies)*
   A single psychologist serves police officers in 5 of the 11 police agencies within Stanislaus County, California, east of San Francisco. The Modesto Police Department is the largest agency served, with 215 sworn officers; other agencies have as few as 15 officers. The psychologist has contracted with the police departments to provide counseling services to sworn officers and their families since the early 1980s.

2. *The Counseling International Team, San Bernardino, California*
   The Counseling International Team, in San Bernardino, California, is a private psychology practice that has been providing counseling to police officers and firefighters in over 80 public safety agencies throughout the state of California since 1983.[9] The group employs seven full-time clinicians and five part-time counselors at the program's office, and refers some cases to five independent mental health professionals who live in jurisdictions some distance from the office. The Counseling International Team has a separate written contract with each agency and bills on a fee-for-service basis for individual counseling, critical incident debriefing, and peer supporter training.

3. *Palo Alto, California, Police Department*
   A police psychologist has been the health resources coordinator for the Palo Alto, California, Police Department for 13 years. She works as a contract employee and maintains an office at the police station for meeting with clients. She provides training and counseling 8 hours a week for the department's 100 sworn officers and is available for emergencies 24 hours a day. The department also hired an organizational consultant to respond to the department's organizational sources of stress.

4. *The U.S. Postal Inspection Service Self-Referred Counseling Program (12-state Western Region)*
   The U.S. Postal Inspection Service recently established a Self-Referred Counseling Program for postal inspectors in the 12 states that make up its Western Region. Contracts were established with police psychologists chosen from the region. The psychologists bill the Inspection

Service for treatment provided to inspectors. A police psychologist, not an employee of the Inspection Service, serves as coordinator of the program, putting inspectors who need services in touch with a contracted service provider.

5. *Psychological Services, Tulsa, Oklahoma*
Psychological Services was originally set up as a private, nonprofit corporation to provide counseling services for the Tulsa, Oklahoma, police and fire departments. The organization was not completely external, however, because its board of directors included four high-ranking city employees (the police and fire chiefs and the city budget and personnel directors). When the city attorney expressed concern about this arrangement, Psychological Services became an independent for-profit corporation, still with a contract with both the police and fire departments. A critical incident response team consisting of peer supporters trained by Psychological Services talks with, refers, and helps train other officers to deal with critical incidents.

In-House Program Options: Six Variations

1. *Philadelphia Police Department*
Negative publicity resulting from eight officer suicides in 5 years—three of them in 1994—prompted the department to create an in-house stress manager's position in 1995. Among other duties, the stress manager examines departmental policies and procedures and recommends ways to make them less stressful.

2. *The Michigan State Police Behavioral Science Section*
Trains both experienced and new sergeants every year in techniques to manage critical incident stress among officers. After a critical incident, support comes from the chief down through the command staff to the field officer. Command-level staff can also offer assurance and support to family members—including helping with paperwork, providing telephone numbers for follow-up assistance, and simply spending time with them. Word of the command staff's concern typically spreads through the department grapevine to every officer on the force, instantly improving morale and alleviating stress.

3. *Massachusetts State Police Stress Unit*
Like most in-house police agencies, the Massachusetts State Police Stress Unit started off in guiding state trooper and Boston officers who had an alcohol problem in the 1970s.[10] Psychology entered the world of law enforcement through the training centers and the hiring process in the 1980s, and eventually to stress units in the 1990s. However, stress units engaged psychology first through chaplains, then peers, to volunteers who eventually became paid personnel to aid

troopers and other officers toward mental health. Today sworn troopers with appropriate university credentials provide stress counseling to officers in Boston and the unit has it own facility, career paths, and chain of command. (In different departments across the country, they are following similar paths toward professionalized units and, as expected, are at different evolutionary peaks.)

4. *Adams County, Colorado, Sheriff's Department Stress Program*
   The Adams County, Colorado, Sheriff's Department's stress program consists of an in-house peer support program that was initially coordinated and now is also supervised by a contracted psychologist. The psychologist and a peer support team coordinator developed guidelines for and selected members of the peer support team. The contracted psychologist trains the peers as well as other officers, and he meets individually with each team member to review his or her support contacts.

5. *Rochester, New York, Police Department Stress Management Unit*
   The Rochester, New York, Police Department's Stress Management Unit is housed in the Professional Development Section. An in-house mental health professional provides counseling services, coordinates a small group of peer supporters, and conducts stress training for officers and their family members. The department also contracts with the University of Rochester Department of Psychiatry for additional mental health services as well as assistance with training program design and clinical reviews.

Hybrid Programs: Six Variations

Most program practitioners with hybrid programs claim to have the advantages of both the internal and external options, with few of their shortcomings. It is possible that some of the disadvantages will remain. Also, unless well-coordinated, hybrid programs may risk confusion among clients about how the program operates as well as conflicts between internal and external program staff.

1. *Eric County, New York, Law Enforcement Employee Assistance Program*
   The director of the Eric County Law Enforcement Employee Assistance Program in New York originally served as director of the EAP for all county employees. As her services for law enforcement employees grew, county administrators asked her to focus solely on the needs of law enforcement officers and hired another counselor to take over the general county EAP responsibilities. The director is still a county employee, thus serving the sheriff's department on an in-house basis, but to fund her new position as director of the separate law enforcement EAP, the county commissioner established subcontracts with other law enforcement agencies that continued to want

program services. Each agency pays $14 a year per officer and nonsworn personnel in the department (if the department includes nonsworn personnel as eligible clients).

2. *Rhode Island Centurion Program*
   The Rhode Island Centurion Program is operated by a licensed clinical social worker (who is also a sworn active-duty reserve officer with the Coventry Police Department), his wife (a licensed counselor and a sworn active reserve officer), and a network of peer supporters from various law enforcement and correctional agencies. The director of the program is the sole contracted provider of stress or EAP services to eight police agencies, many of them small, and he furnishes bimonthly stress training or EAP-related services to 10 other police agencies every other month to support these departments' own in-house stress prevention efforts. Contracts are usually with the department's management, union, or both. The Centurion Program acts as an "affiliate" for other departments that request services on certain occasions such as critical incidents. The director serves his own department (consisting of 65 sworn officers) as the in-house stress program director, providing direct counseling services to about six officers a year and training and oversight to the department's peer police officer.

3. *Drug Enforcement Administration*
   The Drug Enforcement Administration (DEA) has a 5-year contract with an outside provider to coordinate EAP services to DEA employees nationwide. However, the agency has a full-time in-house administrator who directs the program from DEA headquarters and supervises the contracted services, which are provided by a combination of contract support unit personnel and a subcontracted area clinician network consisting of practitioners across the country. The DEA also trains and certifies agents as trauma team members to respond to critical incidents.

4. *Bureau of Alcohol, Tobacco and Firearms*
   The Bureau of Alcohol, Tobacco, and Firearms employs a private contractor to coordinate professional stress-related counseling services and also operates three peer support programs (specializing in critical incidents, substance abuse, and sexual assault). The peer support programs are administered out of the ombudsman's office at the agency's headquarters in Washington, DC, while the contracted EAP services are supervised by the Office of Personnel.

5. *Pennsylvania Fraternal Order of Police (FOP) and the Officer Assistance Program (OAP)*
   The Fraternal Order of Police has established stress services in several of its lodges across the country. Through the Pennsylvania FOP Offi-

cer Assistance Program, different lodges throughout the state designate a lodge liaison officer who educates members about the program and calls in a critical incident debriefing team when necessary. The program also offers confidential access to professional counselors for members and their families. Active members pay $3 per month to receive program benefits, and retired members pay $2 per month.

6. *New Jersey State Police: Cop 2 Cop Program*
Many police officers can easily access the Fraternal Order of Police (FOP) website because this organization represents an estimated 310,000 police officers across the United States.[11] Many officers are familiar with the organization's legal representation during police officer litigation. Some chapters or lodges have stress management components such as the New Jersey State Lodge.[12] Cop 2 Cop is a new, free, and confidential 24-hour telephone helpline. It is available exclusively for law enforcement officers and their families to help deal with personal or job-related stress and behavioral health care issues. There is more that needs to be developed with services such as this, but it is a step in the right professional direction of cops helping cops.

A WORD ABOUT MEDICATION

Often some stress professionals prescribe antidepressants such as Prozac, Zoloft, Paxil, Celexa, Lexapro, and other medications or antidepressants, which work in a rather elegant fashion because they enhance rather than change brain chemistry to achieve positive mood changes.[13] Antidepressants tend to improve the way brain receptors (neurotransmitters) process crucial brain chemicals, most notably serotonin. Medication, when it works, essentially "readjusts" the way the brain functions back to its optimal condition. Wellbutrin works in a different way but is equally effective.[14] Other drugs such as serzone have been removed from the market. Bristol-Myers Squibb announced: "It has come to the attention of Health Canada that nefazodone (brand name serzone) has been associated with adverse hepatic events including liver failure requiring transplantation in Canada. Following discussions with Health Canada, Bristol-Myers Squibb Canada has decided to discontinue sales of nefazodone, effective November 27, 2003."[15]

The use of medication is not encouraged for street cops simply because it is too risky for an officer, his or her partners, and the individuals he or she serves. Too often officers have an opportunity to use a number of drugs to aid them as a sort of magic bullet, but the promise is rarely fulfilled. In some situations at one extreme, officers are randomly drug tested, and at the other extreme, a psychological, and in some cases a physiological, dependence is possible. Medication is an excellent "last resort" but only after more than one medical recommendation toward its use is advised. What is never advised is to purchase depression medication without a doctor's recommendation even if it is available online without a "real" medical doctor's prescription. Officers on medication should probably be reassigned another position in the police department other than active duty while utilizing a prescribed drug on a regular basis.

OBSTACLES ASSOCIATED WITH PERSON-CENTERED STRESS PROGRAMS

There are many obstacles associated with person-centered programs. The primary obstacles can be characterized in six categories:

1. Stress intervention must be multimodal
2. Treatment is not encouraged by the public, commanders, and the police culture
3. Seeking help or showing feelings is seen as a weakness among most cops
4. *Shedding the uniform*   .
5. Unrealistic view of the job
6. Organizational contributors

Obstacle 1: Stress intervention must be multimodal. Most studies about the functional aspects of person-centered stress are from a strict operant perspective[16] (voluntary action).[17] Gary Kaufman, manager of psychological services at the Michigan State Police, explains that stress intervention must be multimodal since controlling stress cannot be a zero-sum game. One way to define *multimodal* is utilizing various means to manage stress. A thorough process dealing with the multiple causes of behavior requires acknowledgment of street cops' behavior from multiple theoretical perspectives, as we have done throughout this book. And we learned that individual street cop stress is a result of multiple causes consistent with most behavioral conditions.[18] Multimodal refers to the consideration of multiple causes from multiple theoretical perspectives, and consideration should not only be given to multiple theories for the functions of behavior, but also to multiple theories for intervening or treating the problem. The functions of behavior are linked to multiple, simultaneous interventions (officer and the organization) designed to treat the "whole" cop.

Obstacle 2: Neither the public nor the police subculture encourage professional counseling and treatment among street cops and commanders think that officers involved with counselors, especially stress counselors, should be put on "desk duty." The public is fascinated by the police profession, but when it comes to law enforcement officer stress this is not part of the "glamorous" aspect of the job (or any job for that matter). Also, for every depiction in the media of police stress there are hundreds of complicated gunfights and police brutality stories that excite movie viewers. One concern is that street cop stress affects officers individually, but it is an issue for everyone around the officers too, including those close to them, and others "on the front line" professions, who need to fully understand and in a sense "inoculate" themselves against it as best they can. Police counseling, police peer counseling, even critical incident stress management, and critical incident stress debriefing[19] (CISM and CISD), while they have been known to be helpful for some time now, are still not encouraged or employed often enough among street cops.

Some administrators believe street cops involved in treatment regardless of the program are "hiding" from the responsibilities of their job and the realities of their obligations. Some commanders think street cops "hide" in treatment "when other actions should be taken against them or when they might be dangerous to themselves or others."[20] On the other side of the spectrum, counselors, unions, and the FOP don't want administrators using treatment as a source of information at any level that might bring harm to an officer getting treatment or that would, as other officers learn of the breach of confidentiality, destroy the integrity of the program.

This latter point is one source of much debate: administrators are reluctant to relinquish their right for access to information about those under their command, and counselors feel the need and mandate to maintain absolute confidentiality (discussed later). Imagine how many officers would seek out an in-house or even external service to aid them with their stress if their lives were an open book to their superiors? "It's better to bury your problems all together and go through the motions of being a cop," says one officer.

Then, too, it is too easy and entirely natural for people working in these professions to use humor and denial as ways to avoid the emotional impact of what they see and do as part of their jobs. For instance, a MedFlight nurse at a training exercise relates how she and her colleagues use humor to cope with the fact that they see only the most serious cases and have the most loss of life despite their valiant efforts.[21] At least she works in a team and can bounce thoughts off colleagues who are experiencing similar thoughts. Street cops usually return to solo patrol duty after an incident, which brings them together with other officers or members of the EMS team.

Street cops experience more stress when their assignment is such that they work cases or crime scenes alone, or when, because of the culture within their department, they keep their feelings to themselves because they don't want to take the time and energy to explain details to their colleagues, who, after all, may have problems of their own.[22] Police stress gets worse if in these circumstances the officer doesn't have a spouse or partner to open up to. A commander who wishes to remain anonymous, typical of many commanders, reports, "They should buy a dog and whine to that little creature instead of me."

Obstacle 3: Seeking professional help or even showing emotion when "debriefing" after handling a trauma is sometimes seen as a weakness by law enforcement personnel.[23] From the perspective of the street cop, stress in itself is ignored for several reasons[24]:

- Initial naiveté and high level of enthusiasm
- Difficulty in measuring performance
- Lack of organizational support
- Poor distribution of resources
- Necessity of dealing with the public and police administration as adversaries

Most officers began their careers with a great deal of optimism and high levels of enthusiasm.[25] The greater the initial naiveté when hired, the more disillusioned an officer becomes once in the field. Statistics about crime, response time, and arrest rates (the traditional measures of productive officers) have little to tell about the performance of an officer and reaching personal goals. Organizational support that leans toward statistics isolate personal feelings and resources of agencies are spent on high-profile "models" rather than traffic stops and domestic violence calls. Therefore, some officers can feel a lack of support from the public they serve and the police administration that supervises them.

The attitude of officers changes significantly during the first weeks and months on the job. One researcher found that the percentage of officers agreeing with the statement: "Patrolmen almost never receive the cooperation from the public that is needed to handle police work properly" rose from 35% at the beginning of their practical training to 50% after 2 years on the job.[26] Also, the thoughts of using force on the job rose too among those participants. In another study conducted in Detroit, officers who participated in a special victims service training program substantially changed their attitudes about "listening attentively when victims express feelings or emotions" after 4 months on the job.[27] As a side note: One source of stress clearly arises from the early thoughts of street cops polled in the study in this book who have great expectations of aiding others to coping with the hostility of the public who resent their very presence.

What to do about personal stress is usually buried in stereotypes: street cop chain smoking, a stakeout car filled with fast-food debris, late-night phone calls to former spouses, infamous doughnut runs, having affairs, contemplating "eating your gun," and the ultimate 'cop bars.' What is dangerous about these characterizations is that they all to some extent "glamorize avoiding coping head on with the underlying causes of the stress."[28] Furthermore, the public and the administration believe that most police stress is centered in actual stress of the job as opposed to organizational stressors and therefore, the public's perspective and the officer's perspective about the cures are different. The problem is that often, family members also believe that the source of stress is "duty related."

It is important to have good mental health that critical incident stress management, critical incident stress debriefing, and police counseling can provide.

Obstacle 4: *Shedding the uniform* is probably one of the most common problems among officers. Some officers have learned to hide or mask their personal experiences from their professional experiences in numerous ways even in the appearance (judgment is nonetheless impaired) of performing their job well. This pneumonia is not that unusual among high-functioning alcoholics, for instance, who appear to be sober. A personal communication helps convey this message: "I didn't know my T.O. was a drunk until one day I caught him sober. I worked with that guy 6 years. Been to his house a dozen times." Here's another example, a service call takes an officer into a home where the parents are having difficulty with their 16-year-old son who quit school and is abusing drugs.[29] The mother blames the teenager's problems on his father. She screams at the husband in the presence of the officer, "You and your damn job. All you care about is your work." If an officer had a fight with his spouse before work and heard similar words out of the mouth of his spouse, the question arises: How do you separate a personal life experience from what's going on in front of you? The service call consists of two people who probably have been involved in similar exchanges during most of their 20-year marriage, the officer suspects. And now this officer must bring some relief to the altercation in seconds, a situation that reminds him of his own relationship with his spouse and child.

Not being able to separate the professional from the personal can result in one of the most commonly shared and most critical stress-inducing syndromes—the figurative inability of the street cop to shed the uniform.[30] "Cops would like to be one of the guys, but they can't," says Richard Walsh, from the Massachusetts District Police in Boston. "They go to a party, and if they're introduced as a cop, the joint which would have normally got passed around does not, the talk about the 'good buy' on a CB radio that normally would have happened does not, and the cop is not able to surrender his job."[31] "I get paranoid about it sometimes," says an officer from Salem, Massachusetts. "I went into a bar to have a drink off duty, and I saw someone there I arrested for drunk driving. So I left being afraid to let him see me drink. Look, I also smoke pot sometimes and maybe that's bad, but I do it. I feel bad because I'm supposed to set an example and I feel there's a terrible double standard when I arrest someone on a pot charge."[32]

In another sense, this perspective might be easier to comprehend by considering the response of crime victims who have experienced a violation of their inner selves, too. Street cops easily can empathize with them because of the realization that this crime could have happened to anyone. Each time officers encounter this poisonous contact, the potential exists for their spirits to erode.[33] After a period of time, the mind builds a wall to protect itself from experiencing any more pain. When this occurs, some street cops can act out their feelings by being cold, unfeeling, or cynical in their attitudes, even though those patterns of behavior are far from their intention. To prevent this from occurring, officers need the skills to combat this exposure and avoid becoming depressed and dispirited. They need to learn how to cope. Anticipation through education and peer group discussions can aid in their understanding on how this distress may be contagious and will help to initiate action to guard against this phenomenon.[34] But many cops think the best way to deal with the problem of street action and personal life experiences is to keep quiet about their feelings and "put in your time at the job."[35]

Obstacle 5: Unrealistic view of the job. The most common method for preventing stress is to train officers to recognize its sources and signs, and to develop individual strategies for coping with stress.[36] Often it comes down to an officer saying "no." Street cops, like most of us, must redefine and take stock of their role as a street cop.[37] At the top of the list is the eventual reality that an officer is not going to change the world. Street cops provide assistance wherever, whenever, and to whomever they can—and they can change a little of the world for some people, but not all the people, all the time. Making an arrest, successfully prosecuting a suspect, convicting a defendant, and carrying out the sentence of a court are different jobs performed by different professionals—legally, morally, and realistically in a democratic society. The final thought linked to realistic views of a street cop is that since beliefs become reality, when you perceive an environment as stressful, it is stressful. Recall that each of us responds differently to different events and situations: one person's pressure is another person's motivation. But in reality, the view of changing the world is unlikely for any individual let alone an officer. At best, changing the world of a few individuals by providing a safe environment is probably the most that officers will accomplish in their entire careers. Everything else above that is gravy.

Obstacle 6: Organizational contributors to a law enforcement officer's stress. As we unravel street cop stress throughout each chapter thus far, the indicators are that the primary stressor is linked to organizational contributors as well as the individual officer. It occurs therefore that a "single vision" linked to a "cause" of street cop stress lays with factors outside the control of the officer and should an officer engage in treatment, almost regardless of the expertise or elegance of the strategy, it would be an insufficient or inappropriate intervention and ultimately would lead to poor police service and an officer's inability to cope with a host of personal and professional obligations and expectations. Why? After the "cure," the officer continues to work in an unchanged police organization.[38] That is not to say that some street cops have dealt well with stressful remedies but those remedies are never permanent and at best are remedies in "going with the flow," indicating that the stressor continues to be present, now that the cop is ignoring it—or at least he or she thinks so. In the final analysis, there are many causes for police stress and most of them are associated with the organizational structure as opposed to the street cop and his or her duty.

Equally important, person-centered interventions can produce more harm than good since the "treated" street cop once again experiences similar organizational or environmental stimuli, which continue to produce the stressor/s in the first place.[39] These researchers found among other things that "sleep hygiene raises the possibility that this problem reduces the effectiveness of patrol and presents some danger to troopers." Aiding North Carolina troopers through a stress buffer is helpful but altering the organizational structure to control the stress "object" in the first place might be more effective by eliminating future stress.

Obviously, if the organizational or environmental stressors remain unchanged, an officer can be set up for failure by believing that he or she is, indeed, the problem. They blame themselves for their predicament and see themselves operating in a vacuum. To feel alone and betrayed by the system could be a normal reaction at times (to act on those feelings, suddenly a cop's career will change). As mentioned in an earlier chapter, most officers see themselves and their performance as unique and independent of any influences. In reality, street cops are influenced by many institutional actions and often, what and how they perform is predicated upon the "larger picture" contributors. This thought is consistent with other occupational issues and perspectives.[40] Street cops need to see the link between their own personal problems or private troubles and the larger problems built in to the schools they attended, neighborhoods where they live, laws and regulations they must enforce, and the supervisors they report to. The big picture shapes the rules about the way a cop makes an arrest and whether or not he or she participants in a stress program or not.[41] For instance, consider the officer who enjoys neighborhood parties or music concerts. "Did you ever notice that whenever a policeman goes somewhere, even socially, he sits with his back to the wall—casing the joint?" asks Edward C. Donovan, a 25-year veteran of the Boston Police Department who once aspired to be a professional comedian but went into police work because he wanted to help people.[42] "His juices never stop flowing," Donovan adds. "I've ruined quite a few parties by my presence," he laughs. "Most often, people wander away from us into other rooms to do what they're going to do, to dabble in what they are going to dabble in, and I find myself alone with my wife and maybe a close friend, usually another officer."

Finally in this regard, Lance Franklin, a convicted felon and former sergeant on the Durham, North Carolina, Police Department, said something like this: "I wish there were folks out there who could have helped me when I got screwed up.[43] I got so deep in my own shit after killing a 15-year-old suspect during a shootout that the only thing that made me feel good was a touch off a [cocaine] pipe that I 'acquired' [confiscated from a drug bust].

I sold more drugs at Duke University than I took off the hard-ass punks in the slums [of Durham]. The campus babes were easy cause they didn't want to be lawed-up [arrested] and the guys were pussies, afraid of their own shadows. Shit man, I lost my wife and kids, I lost my job, and everything I worked for since I left my teens. I woke up here [Eastern Correctional Institution, Maury, NC]. I don't know how many people I destroyed, but I know I can't account for the 10 years of my life before I got here."

This lack of control of the stressors of a police organizational structure might be one reason why street cops have a high burnout rate, engage in brutality and corruption, lack an ability to cope with family problems and occupational expectations including low status and lack of public trust, and are likely to be involved in a civil liability suit more than any other occupation.[44]

Nonetheless, the focus of this chapter is on strategies toward individual stress among street cops. There is optimism that policymakers and commanders comprehend the foolishness of it all since many cops, no matter how successful individual treatment might be, are waiting for help just like Lance Franklin had but never received. Had Franklin's stress been controlled, would there have been a different outcome or would the organizational stressors had their way with him anyway?

SUMMARY

The chapter is about the various options available of person-centered stress providers and the obstacles program planners face concerning those options as they attempt to develop a program that would be available to street cops in a police organization. There are many choices available among providers, depending on the resources and objectives of a police agency. Providers can represent in-house units, external units of either private or public agencies contracted to perform services, or those providers can provide hybrid services. For instance, private psychologists or other mental health practitioners and employee assistance programs that already serve other agencies might accept additional clients, and sometimes agencies develop their own unit to deal with stress at various levels. There are specialized outside providers who deal specifically with officers and their families, which are contracted with many departments across the country. The basic options associated with person-centered stress programs can be referred to as an employee assistance program (EAP) and can be an external agency outside of the department, an in-home agency within a police department, or a hybrid-type strategy consisting of a combination of in-house and external programs.

External program options were characterized through departments, which included Stanislaus County and Palo Alto, California, the U.S. Postal Inspection Service, and Psychological Services, in Tulsa, Oklahoma. In-house program options were characterized through the behavioral sciences or psychological services of the Philadelphia Police Department, Michigan State

Police, Massachusetts State Police, Adams County, Colorado, Sheriff's Department, and Rochester, New York, Police.

Hybrid program options were typified through accounts of police agencies in Eric County, New York, Rhode Island State Police, Drug Enforcement Administration, Bureau of Alcohol, Tobacco and Firearms, and the Pennsylvania Fraternal Order of Police (FOP).

Some stress practitioners prescribe antidepressants such as Prozac, Zoloft, and other antidepressants, which do little to achieve positive mood changes. Those drugs improve the way brain receptors (neurotransmitters) process crucial brain chemicals, most notably serotonin. Medication, when it works, essentially "readjusts" the way the brain functions back to its optimal condition. Wellbutrin works in a different way but is equally effective. The use of medication is not encouraged for street cops simply because it is too risky for the officer, his or her partners, and the individuals he or she serves. In some situations, officers are drug tested, and in other situations a psychological dependence is possible. Medication is an excellent "last resort" but only after more than one medical recommendation toward its use. What is never advised is to purchase depression medication without a doctor's recommendation or purchase online without a medical doctor's prescription.

Obstacles associated with person-centered stress strategies included stress intervention performed through a multimodal process; treatment is not encouraged by the public, commanders, and police subculture; seeking help or showing feelings is seen as a weakness among cops; shedding the uniform; unrealistic view of the job; and organizational contributions.

WHAT WOULD YOU DO IF YOU WERE IN CHARGE?

The Right to Self-Defense: On June 27, 2005, in the case of *Castle Rock v. Gonzales*, the Supreme Court found that Jessica Gonzales did not have a constitutional right to police protection even in the presence of a restraining order.[45]

By a vote of 7-to-2, the Supreme Court ruled that Gonzales has no right to sue her local police department for failing to protect her and her children from her estranged husband.

The postmortem discussion on Gonzales has been fiery but it has missed an obvious point. If the government won't protect you, then you have to take responsibility for your own self-defense and that of your family. The court's ruling is a sad decision, but one that every victim and/or potential victim of violence must note: calling the police is not enough. You must also be ready to defend yourself.

In 1999, Gonzales obtained a restraining order against her estranged husband Simon, which limited his access to their children. On June 22, 1999, Simon abducted their three daughters. Though the Castle Rock Police Department disputes some of the details of what happened next, the two sides are in basic agreement: After her daughters' abduction, Gonzales repeatedly phoned the police for assistance. Officers visited the home. Believing Simon to be nonviolent and, arguably, in compliance with the limited access granted by the restraining order, the police did nothing.

The next morning, Simon committed "suicide by cop." He shot a gun repeatedly through a police station window and was killed by returned fire. The murdered bodies of Leslie, 7, Katheryn, 9, and Rebecca, 10, were found in Simon's pickup truck.

In her lawsuit, Gonzales claimed the police violated her 14th Amendment right to due process and sued them for $30 million. She won at the appeals level. What were the arguments that won and lost in the Supreme Court?

Local officials fell back upon a rich history of court decisions that found the police to have no constitutional obligation to protect individuals from private individuals. In 1856, the U.S. Supreme Court (*South v. Maryland*) found that law enforcement officers had no affirmative duty to provide such protection. In 1982 (*Bowers v. DeVito*), the Court of Appeals, Seventh Circuit held, ". . . there is no Constitutional right to be protected by the state against being murdered by criminals or madmen."

OFFICER KILLED IN MICHIGAN

Twenty-four-year old Owen Fisher (Badge Number 838) of the Flint, Michigan, Police Department was killed on Saturday, July 16, 2005, after only 4 months of police service.[46] Fisher was killed in an automobile accident when the patrol car he was riding in was involved in a collision with a second patrol car during a vehicle pursuit. The pursuit crossed through three jurisdictions. The collision caused the patrol cars also to collide into a house. Officers from the Flint Police Department and Michigan State Police continued the pursuit and apprehended the suspect a short time later. He is survived by his fiancée, parents, sister, and grandmother.

DISCUSSION QUESTIONS

1. Describe the selection process linked to a stress program provider. In what way might you argue that outside agencies and personnel would be more advantageous than developing an in-house unit.
2. Characterize the specialized services available to conduct stress programs. In what way could specialized contracted services have an advantage over local services?
3. Identify the three basic options of stress programs.
4. Explain external program options utilizing some of the examples provided.
5. Describe in-house program options utilizing some of the examples provided.

6. Detail hybrid program options utilizing some of the examples provided.

7. Characterize medication concerns linked to stress management. In what way might you agree and disagree with the textbook's perspective on this matter?

8. Identify and explain the obstacles confronting program planners. What other obstacles should be mentioned within this context?

ENDNOTES

1. Psychological self help (2005). *Methods for changing behavior.* Retrieved online April 2, 2006: http://mentalhelp.net/psyhelp/chap11/

2. National Institute of Safety and Health (2006). Retrieved online April 6, 2006: http://www.cdc.gov/niosh/face/stateface/ma/00ma054.html

3. FBI (2006). Law enforcement officers killed and assaulted in 2003. Retrieved online April 6, 2006: http://www.fbi.gov/ucr/killed/leoka03.pdf

4. *Tom v. Voida* 963 F. 2d 952 (7th Cir. 1992).

5. John Hall (2006). Police use of deadly force to arrest. *FBI Publications.* Retrieved online April 6, 2006: http://www.fbi.gov/publications/leb/1997/oct975.htm

6. Bureau of Justice Statistics (2004). *State and local law enforcement statistics.* Washington, DC: U.S. Department of Justice, Office of Justice Programs. Retrieved online July 25, 2005: http://www.ojp.usdoj.gov/bjs/sandlle.htm#personnel

7. Julie Esselman Tomz and Peter Finn (1997). Developing a law enforcement stress program for officers and their families. *National Institute of Justice.* Retrieved online June 18, 2004: http://ncjrs.org/txtfiles/163175.txt

8. Ellen M. Scrivner (1994). Controlling Police Use of Excessive Force. *National Institute Justice.* NCJ 150063/. Retrieved June 22, 2004: http://www.ncjrs.org/txtfiles/ppsyc.txt

9. Counseling International. Retrieved online March 13, 2006: http://www.thecounselingteam.com/agencies.html

10. John M. Madonna, Jr. and Richard E. Kelly (2002). *Treating police officers: The work and the words of peer counselors.* Springfield, IL: Charles C. Thomas. pp. 7–23.

11. Fraternal Order of Police. Retrieved online February 26, 2006: http://www.grandlodgefop.org/

12. New Jersey State Lodge. FOP. Retrieved online February 26, 2006: http://www.njfop.org/cop2cop.html

13. Adam R. Aron and Russell A. Poldrack (2004, December). The cognitive neuroscience of response inhibition: Relevance for genetic research in attention-deficit/hyperactivity disorder. *Society of Biological Psychiatry.* Retrieved online July 27, 2005: http://www.uclaisap.org/AddClinic/documents/JournalWatch/2005/January4/Tom/endophenotype-executive%20systems.htm

14. Important safety information about Wellbutrin XL: it is prescribed for the treatment of depression, but it is not for everyone nor should anyone order this drug or any other drug from online sources. Always allow a medical doctor to prescribe drugs. If you take Wellbutrin XL, there is a risk of seizure, which is increased in patients with certain medical problems or in patients taking certain medicines. Do not take if you have or had a seizure or eating disorder. Don't use if you take an MOAI, or any medicine that contains bupropion such as Wellbutrin SR or Zyban. You should not take Wellbutrin XL or most

depression-type drugs if you are abruptly stopping the use of alcohol or sedatives, as the risk of seizure may increase. When used with a nicotine patch or alone, there is a risk of increased blood pressure, sometimes severe. To reduce risk of serious side effects, tell your doctor if you have liver or kidney problems. Other side effects may include weight loss, dry mouth, nausea, difficulty sleeping, dizziness, and sore throat. Whether or not you are taking antidepressants, you or your family should call the doctor right away if your depression gets worse, or thoughts of suicide persists, or sudden or severe changes in your mood or behavior, especially at the beginning of treatment or after a change in dose.

15. Internet mental health (2005). Retrieved online July 27, 2005: http://www. mentalhealth.com/drug/p30-n05.html

16. In learning theory, an action or other unit of behavior that does not appear to have a stimulus.

17. G. Dunlop, L. Kern, M. dePerczel, S. C. Clarke, D. Wilson, K. E. Childs, R. White and G. D. Falk (1993). Functional analysis of classroom variables for students with emotional and behavioral disorders. *Behavioral Disorders, 18,* 275–291.

   V. M. Durand (1990). *Severe behavior problems: A functional communication training approach.* New York: Guilford Press. Also see B. A. Iwata, T. R. Vollmer, J. R. Zarcone, and T. A. Rodgers (1993). Treatment classification and selection based on behavioral function. In R. Van Houten and S. Axelrod (Eds.), *Behavior analysis and treatment* (pp. 101–125). New York: Plenum Press.

18. M. M. Bandura and C. Goldman (1995). Expanding the contextual analysis of clinical problems. *Cognitive and Behavioral Practice, 2,* 119–141.

   J. D. Cone (1997). Issues in functional analysis in behavioral assessment. *Behaviour Research and Therapy, 35,* 259–275.

   J. A. Miller, M. Tansy and T. L. Hughes (1998, November 18). Functional behavioral assessment: The link between problem behavior and effective intervention in schools. *Current Issues in Education, 1*(5). Retrieved online June 17, 2004: http://cie.ed.asu.edu/volume1/number5/

19. A closed confidential discussion of a critical incident relating to the feelings and perceptions of those directly involved prior to, during, and after a stressful event: intended to provide support, education, and an outlet for views and feelings associated with the event. Debriefings are not counseling nor an operational critique of the incident. This definition is provided by: Renee B. Meador (2004). Model Policy and Procedures for Critical Incident Stress Management/Critical Incident Stress Debriefing for Law Enforcement Internal Programs: Virginia Critical Incident Stress Management, Law Enforcement Critical Incident Stress Management. Retrieved Online June 18, 2004: http://www.geocities.com/~halbrown/cism_cisd_procedures.html

20. Richard Kelly (2002). What needs to be done. In John M. Madonna, Jr. and Richard E. Kelly (Eds.), *Treating police stress: The work and the words of peer counselors* (pp. 217–224). Springfield, IL: Charles C. Thomas.

21. For a number of great articles on the subject of cop stress and antidotes such as this, see: Hal Brown (2004). *Depression.* Retrieved online June 19, 2004: http://www.geocities.com/~halbrown/depression_041002.html

22. Gene Sanders (2004). Why police officers have so much trouble getting psychological support? Retrieved Online June 19, 2004: http://www.geocities.com/~halbrown/sanders_02.html

23. Hal Brown (2004). *Am I stressed out?* Retrieved online June 19, 2004: http://www.geocities.com/~halbrown/index1.html

24. Guided in part by Dennis L. Conroy and Karen M. Hess (1992). *Officers at risk: How to identify and cope with stress.* Custom Publishing. p. 210–211.

25. Katherine W. Ellison (2004). *Stress and the police officer,* 2nd ed. Springfield, IL: Charles C. Thomas. p. 6.

26. John H. McNamara (1967). Uncertainties in police work: The relevance of police recruits' backgrounds and training, In David J. Bordua (Ed.), *The police: Six sociological essays* (pp. 163–252). New York: Wiley.

27. Arthur J. Luirgio and Dennis P. Rosenbaum (1992). The travails of the Detroit Police—Victims experiment: Assumptions and Important Lessons. *American Journal of Police* 11(3), 24–37.

28. Hal Brown (2004). *Am I stressed out?* Retrieved online June 21, 2004: http://www.geocities.com/~halbrown/index1.html. Brown is a police clinician who has treated officers for stress for most of his professional life.

29. John Madonna (2002). Getting started. In John M. Madonna, Jr. and Richard E. Kelly (Eds.). *Treating police stress: The work and the words of peer counselors* (pp. 69–80). Springfield, IL: Charles C. Thomas.

30. Patricia A. Kelly (2002). Stress: The cop killer. In John M. Madonna, Jr. and Richard E. Kelly (Eds.). *Treating police stress: The work and the words of peer counselors* (p. 33–54). Springfield, IL: Charles C. Thomas.

31. Patricia A. Kelly (2002). p. 47.

32. Patricia A. Kelly (2002). p. 47.

33. Robin Gershon (1999, March 23). U.S. Department of Justice, National Institute of Justice, Public Health Implication of Law Enforcement Stress, video presentation.

34. Eugene R. D. Deisinger (2002). Executive summary of the law enforcement assistance & development (LEAD) program: Reduction of familial and organizational stress in law enforcement. NCJ 192276. Retrieved Online June 23, 2004: http://www.ncjrs.org/pdffiles1/nij/grants/192276.pdf

35. Personal confidential communication between police officer-student and the writer.

36. Renee B. Meador (2004). Model policy and procedures for critical incident stress management/critical incident stress debriefing for law enforcement internal programs: Virginia critical incident stress management. Law enforcement critical incident stress management. Retrieved online June 18, 2004: http://www.geocities.com/~halbrown/cism_cisd_procedures.html

37. Hal Brown (2004). *Depression.* Retrieved Online June 19, 2004: http://www.geocities.com/~halbrown/depression_041002.html

38. James J. Messina and Constance M. Messina (2006). Tools for personal growth. Retrieved online April 4, 2006: http://www.coping.org/growth/beliefs.htm#What

39. Thomas Griggs, Thomas Caves, and Edward S. Johnson (2001). Reaching out to North Carolina's law enforcement community. NCJ 188874. Retrieved online June 24, 2004: http://www.ncjrs.org/pdffiles1/nij/grants/188874.pdf

40. David R. Simon (1995). *Social problems & the sociological imagination: A paradigm for analysis.* New York: McGraw Hill. p. 9.

41. Victor Kappeler, Michael Blumberg, and Gary Potter (1996). The social construction of crime myths. In B. W. Hancock and P. M. Sharp (Eds.), *Criminal justice in America: Theory, practice, and policy.* Upper Saddle River, NJ: Prentice Hall.

42. Patricia A. Kelly (2002), p. 47.

43. Personal communication with the author while Lance Franklin took a university course at the prison.

44. Mark L. Danzker (1998). *The effect of education on police departments. The stress perspective.* Doctoral dissertation. University of Michigan. Ann Arbor, MI: UMI Dissertation Service. Vivian Lord (2005). The stress of change: The impact of changing a traditional police department to a community oriented, problem solving department. In Heith Copes (Ed.), *Policing and stress* (pp. 55–72). Upper Saddle River, NJ: Prentice Hall. Hans Touch (2001). *Stress in policing.* Washington, DC: APA.

45. Police over issues (2005). Retrieved online July 25, 2005: http://www.lefande.com/weblog/

46. Officer killed memorial page (2005). Retrieved online July 25, 2005: http://www.odmp.org/

12

Change, Professionalization, and Hiring Process

A candle loses nothing by lighting another candle. —Erin Majors

Once you have read this chapter, you will be able to:

- Characterize the importance of stress prevention.
- Describe how a public health model or disease prevention model could work as a stress initiative.
- Identify 12 issues toward stress control.
- Identify the compelling reasons why police organizations must change.
- Identify the real task of most police organizations linked to stress.
- Describe the components of a profession.
- Characterize the elements of any profession.
- Explain the efficiency versus effectiveness standard linked to officer professionalization.
- Explain the collaboration versus order standard linked to police professionalization.

- Characterize Chief Bowman's plan in Arlington, Texas.
- Describe the basic qualifications for employment as a law enforcement officer.
- Characterize the preemployment screening strategies recommended.
- Describe the five personality profiles related to law enforcement candidates.
- Describe the characteristics of good officers.
- Describe the recommended training for recruits and command staff linked to stress.

KEY TERMS

Amenability to treatment
Candidate profiles
Efficiency versus
effectiveness

Five personality profiles
Preemployment
psychological screening
Corporateness

Expertise
Responsibility

INTRODUCTION

Previous chapters revealed that law enforcement officers are blamed for their stressed condition and therefore person-centered programs are provided to restore officer mental health. While engaged in reviewing the literature for this chapter an analogous relationship between police organizational change and officer corruption was also uncovered. The argument appears to be similar—blame cops for both police corruption and stress.

Some scholars furthered this perspective by suggesting that as, "police organizations of the future must take steps to increase officer accountability, maintain positive morale, improve the quality of service to communities, and enhance police community relations."[1] That is, increase organizational control over officers. And others followed a similar path in their suggestion that "every new scandal and investigation" of the New York Police Department "reveals that corruption is flourishing despite layers of reform designed to prevent it."[2] In the final analysis, the significant contributors such as the organizational structure are rarely disturbed except to intensify control over rank and file personnel. Even though we have moved into the 21st century, policymakers and police executives continue their exploitation through the hierarchical chain of command in an antiquated bureaucratic organizational structure. Sometimes, colleagues get it right. For example, "The most important role that citizen oversight can play, particularly in terms of identifying management problems that are often the underlying causes of police officer misconduct."[3] One way to understand this thought is to say that just being a member of an organization and wanting to succeed can provide so much stress and corruption that unless appropriate organizational changes are made, personnel are more likely to fail than succeed. One question many writers ask is how many hard working and dedicated officers must take the edge off their frustrations with a bottle of Jack before appropriate action is taken to bring the police organization into our new age? Many officers are not great police leaders or want to be great leaders. They are individuals who want to help others and put away some bad guys. In a similar sense university professors are not all giants in their fields, but are content in helping students make better life decisions. Unfortunately, some of the organizational structures that employ professors place organizational success as a priority and student development is measured in how well students conform to the organizational standards as opposed to instructing those students how to engage the organization and contribute to the success of others. If you're a police officer does that sound familiar? Also, some students never heed the guideposts of their teachers, some just don't care, and the few who want to succeed quickly realize in the process that their professors have to spend a lot time with the ones who just don't get it and probably never will. How many professors end their careers as drunks or worst? Interesting analogy, don't you think?

The focus of this chapter is about compelling reasons the police organizational structure must change, it's about the professionalization of police officers, and it's about the hiring process which subsequently could help reduce officer stress and probably police corruption, too, while satisfying public safety concerns. To acquaint you with this chapter, fifteen issues that require attention are offered along with several recommendations. It should be mentioned that these recommendations should be considered starting points to help officers cope with stress and ultimately deliver quality police services.

TWELVE ISSUES THAT REQUIRE ATTENTION

To guide a reader through Chapter 12, it might help to review twelve issues that require attention toward stress control (although it is not expected that everyone will or should agree with each issue or the recommendations offered), which include:

1. There are many compelling reasons why police organizations must change the way they deliver police services and the way they manage their personnel in order to meet the challenges of the 21st century.

2. The support of policymakers and police executives should not be limited to treating individual officers of stress but preventive strategies should take priority in controlling stress.

3. Police organizations should utilize a public health or disease prevention model toward stress prevention.

4. Many departments attempt to develop and promote person-centered intervention as their primary remedy toward law enforcement officer stress, yet of concern is that organizations must be treated too because "cured" officers continue in their work environment that stressed them out in the first place.

5. Recovery and rehabilitation are not for everyone.

6. Police agencies need to be healthy before they can treat the community's illnesses and injuries.

7. The police organization must support and encourage police officers to practice the primary characteristics consistent among professional personnel.

8. Organizations that employ professionals encourage their personnel to behave in a socially responsible manner, and their personnel should enjoy considerable freedom and responsibility for their sacrifice.

9. Policing should have a legitimate claim to a professional status.

10. A reasonable control initiative for preventing stress and moving toward a professionalism in the department is to hire worthy candidates, to appropriately train candidates prior to their becoming an officer, and to train them after they become officers to recognize signs and sources of stress and to develop individual coping strategies.

11. It is recommended that a serious preemployment psychological screening process be in place to alert hiring committees as to the potential risk that could be generated by certain personalities.

12. The characteristics of "good" officers should become standardized and those characteristics should become the benchmark to identify candidates who have the potential to become a professional officer and leader.

Compelling Reasons Police Organizations Must Change

There are many compelling reasons why police organizations must change the way they deliver police services and the way they manage their personnel if they want to meet the challenges of the 21st century for a host of reasons offered below in no particular order[4]:

1. *Terrorism Changes:* Advancement of domestic and foreign terrorism.

2. *Criminal Changes:* The sophistication and tactical advancement of officers.

3. *Demographic Changes:* Needs of communities and constituencies have changed; racial, ethnic, and sexual diversity compounds community orientation and priorities. Police departments are faced with new challenges in those communities and in their hiring and disciplinary processes.

4. *Technological Changes:* Computers, cell phones, and forensic methods such as DNA and automated fingerprint identification systems (AFIS); residents have real-time information relating to crime, and many departments provide officers with their own computers. Also, Cyber crime is on the rise.

5. *Economic Changes:* The U.S. is in an era of unparalleled growth, and many local governments, especially those relying on property and sales taxes, have enhanced their tax base. Concurrently, revenues available for law enforcement agencies, including federal funding, have dramatically increased but only in certain areas such as military technology. On the other hand, with unemployment rates at one of the lowest levels in history, law enforcement finds itself competing with the higher pay and better benefits of the private sector and other departments in their quest to hire the best and brightest young people beginning their professional careers.

6. *Environmental Changes:* Environmental changes now pose a major concern to law enforcement. In such states as California, Texas, Florida, and Arizona the infrastructure cannot handle the population explosion. Dealing with the urban sprawl, traffic congestion, and water restrictions have become law enforcement matters. Disasters, from hurricanes to tornadoes to fires, increasingly occupy the attention of law enforcement agencies and their personnel.

7. *Political Change:* Finally, political change has tremendous impact on law enforcement agencies. Significantly, an increased focus on communitarianism and the emergence of strong grassroots involvement at the neighborhood level have increased in recent years. Now, more than before, citizens want to be involved in the governance of their communities. As a direct result, community-based criminal justice (policing, victim services, corrections, and prosecution) is increasingly the norm, and criminal justice agencies continue to remold their philosophy, structure, and tactics to meet community expectations and needs.

8. *Institutional Changes:* Most American social institutions are changing and those changes directly affect law enforcement policy and practice, which compounds the stress inherently associated with the police profession.

9. *Legal Changes:* The legal changes that have taken place in the last few decades specifically affect the way law enforcement provides its services and equally important the level of sophistication of the American people to utilize litigious methods to safeguard their human rights is noteworthy. For instance, Title 42 USC 1983 applies to all state and local officers acting under the color of law who subject any person to the deprivation of any rights, privileges, or immunities guaranteed by

the U.S. Constitution may be liable even if the person is conducting police business.[5] The legal do's and don'ts of street cops' performance is different than 10 or 20 years ago, and officers are more likely to be a litigant in a civil rights or police misconduct case today than at any other time in police history.[6]

10. *Profession Changes:* Changes within the police profession are observed and monitored by personnel, other institutions, family members, and researchers. Also, because of the numerous changes in the law associated with personnel, their performance, and human rights issues of criminals and suspects, police organizations must change in keeping with those changes or face litigation, state or federal intervention, or some other form of intervention from outside organizations.

11. *Future Police Strategies in Space:* Where humanity goes, so go lawyers who are busily writing laws that can ultimately govern the universe or space stations. Which waste and recycling laws should govern a city on the moon? Will custody rights and restraining orders pertain to families in space stations?[7]

12. *Preventive Measures:* The greatest change necessary is to develop preventive measures to control stress among their personnel who are sworn to serve and protect constituents who provide the resources making it possible for police organizations to operate.

Preventive Measures

Law enforcement "reacts" to crime and therefore, as we all know, policing is thought of as a reactive, incident-driven organization. However, what has been well documented in the past few decades is that when agencies develop and practice preventive or proactive strategies in response to public safety, crime has been more efficiently controlled, the number of victims has been reduced, the professional nature of officers has been enhanced, and compliance by the general population to police directives has been more likely.[8] Therefore, it is an obvious recommendation that policymakers and police executives support a similar strategy when attempting to control officer stress. That is, agencies should adapt a preventive strategy to control stress rather than waiting for a law enforcement officer to be victimized, and then responding. A preventive strategy should be in place to inoculate new law enforcement personnel against the poisonous effects of organizational stress. The following story illustrates the need for this action.

There were two doctors standing in the middle of a river.[9] Gradually, dead bodies began coming toward them. At first, there were only a few, and the doctors were successful in pulling those bodies out of the river. Later, more bodies were coming downstream, and it was impossible to get them all out of the river. At that point, one of the doctors got out of the water and went up on the bank. The other doctor, still in the river, asked "Hey, where are you going? I can't get all of these bodies out of the water by myself." With that, the doctor on the bank replied, "I am going upstream to find out who is throwing all of these bodies in the river."

Likewise, policymakers and police executives must go upstream to prevent the negative impact of stress because once a street cop is nailed, it is unlikely that that street cop will perform as well as expected. Prevention, or at least the reduction of the negative impact of stress, proves crucial to the health of law enforcement officers and subsequently the delivery of quality police services. Stress prevention should also meet with similar efforts employed in a public health or disease prevention model as a guide.

How A Public Health or Disease Prevention Model Works

The law enforcement community can borrow the three phases of disease prevention from a public health model to help prevent street cop stress. In the primary phase of disease prevention, medical doctors focus on educating individuals who live healthy lifestyles about unhealthy behaviors so that they will not choose to engage in those behaviors and become ill. For example, they teach individuals who do not drink or smoke about the dangers of drinking and smoking so those individuals will choose not to do either and reduce the chances of becoming ill. In the secondary phase of disease prevention, individuals engaged in behavior that place them at risk of disease but are still healthy are targeted for education that might prevent them from continuing their at-risk behavior before they contract such ailments as lung cancer, emphysema, or heart disease. The final prevention phase involves treating sick individuals and educating them to choose not to continue the behavior that resulted in their illness. This represents the most costly phase of the three, and the one that stands the least chance of being effective because treatment usually offers no guarantee of success once a serious illness has developed.

If the law enforcement community applies a public health model to a stress reduction model, then choosing the primary phase makes the most sense.[10] Why wait until the negative influences have broken into a healthy lifestyle and the individual officer is so sick with stress that the final phase is required to attempt to restore health?

Phase 1 Educate the healthy
Phase 2 Educate those at risk
Phase 3 Treat those infected

Prevention also means doing the right thing. Part of the right thing means to develop and promote person-centered intervention for their officers.

Police Organizations Largely Operationalize Person-Centered Intervention

Many departments attempt to develop and promote person-centered intervention as their primary remedy to respond to law enforcement officer stress. Even the American Psychological Association emphasizes individual officer care and person-centered programs supported by psychologists, police administrators, and the public, which have overshadowed the importance of addressing organizational stressors affecting officer stress. Once "cured," officers return to (or never left) the police organizational environment and are expected to comply with the same hierarchal orders, issued from the same paramilitary mouths, drowned by the same flood of disrespect from courts, federal agencies, and criminals. Cured officers will be promoted, be assigned more command responsibility, and be honored for deeds well done less often than officers who never went to person-centered programs (as documented in Chapters 3 and 5). Cured officers have an "X" branded upon their foreheads and are watched for any sign of faulting by peers, bosses, and psychologists. Also if a former stressed officer is a litigant in a civil action suit, his or her past participation in a stress program takes center stage and can be used against the cured cop. One concern is that not all officers are treatable and equally important; organizations must be treated too.

Recovery or Rehabilitation is Not for Everybody

It should be acknowledged that recovery or rehabilitation is not for everybody. One perspective that can aid in an understanding of this thought is an *amenability to treatment*, which for the purposes of this discussion can be defined as a documented willingness and capability toward treatment. Documentation refers to evidence obtained through interviews, records, and observations. The thinking goes that not every officer is amenable toward treatment, and that not every officer wants help. Yet, amenability-to-treatment determinations are usually associated with past history of an officer.[11] Then, too, many officers are able to stay under the "radar" and deal with his or her stress without calling attention to themselves or involving others.[12]

Many factors aid in ascertaining amenability levels of officers. Sometimes officers could be ordered to take treatment, however, some officers might do it but they have no intention of fulfilling a promise to stop drinking, for instance. Most often, the most important individual linked to any treatment is the participant. Nonetheless, how effective any treatment might be has much to do with the ability of the treatment specialist or clinician. The significance of any answer linked to amenability levels (other than the intention of the participant) depends on the ability, thoroughness, and expertise of the examiner.[13] However, when determining the amenability levels of officers, there are some indicators that could help:

1. *Officer's response to previous treatment:* This can be documented through discharge summaries of former providers and collateral contacts of the examiner.[14] How has the officer performed in previous stress interventions? Most often, we think about a first-time stressed officer and forget that many of them have had past experiences with stress and intervention methods or techniques.

2. *Officer's ability to formulate goals:* This is found in self-reported goals and demonstration of goal formulations by client.

3. *Accepting personal responsibility:* A statement of personal accountability.[15]

4. *Attendance to previous treatment:* Records.

5. *Gains in previous treatment:* Statement of gains, explanations of personal change.

6. *Participation (verbal) in treatment:* Case summaries, collaboration with providers.

7. *Insight (connecting behavior and cause):* Evidence during interview.

8. *Reality contact:* Oriented and responsive to reality with no delusions, thought disorder, or hallucinations that significantly distort reality.

9. *Emotional reactance to situation:* Self-statement, MMPI,[16] collateral contact with family members, former partners, and coworkers.

10. *Self-disclosure:* Personal history and ease of disclosing history.

11. *Problem-solving skills:* Records and self-reported indicators. Goals reached.

12. *Motivation:* Personal statement, energy during interviews, and data in records.[17]

13. *Medication cooperation:* Regularly takes prescribed medications.

This list seems complete, although one other item requires attention.[18] In this regard, a recommendation from William N. Elliott relates to what he calls the three Rs concerning officer resistance[19]: redirection (officers tend to distract or divert a clinician), reframing (officers distort the truth about their stress, addiction, or sobriety), and reversal of responsibility (because of the excuses and justifications verbalized by officers to explain their condition).[20] This last point reveals that many officers attribute their stressed condition, addiction, or alcoholic urges to the unfairness of the criminal justice system or societal injustices or they blame the individuals whom they have arrested.

On the other hand, some clinicians usually are under an assumption that they will change the behavior of all their clients. Unfortunately, providing a quality program by a dedicated and well-trained clinician or behaviorist does not mean that every participant will change. There are many reasons a participant successfully completes a program and some of those reasons have to do with being instructed to take the program or else. Also, many practitioners, including this one, know that a relapse can be part of the success of a participant who must be prepared with appropriate "new" behavior to deal with the relapse. Behavioral practitioners realize that sometimes a group participant or treatment participant might do well in-group or during a treatment session, yet gains can evaporate once desperation sets in and the individual is alone.[21]

Another side to this stress discussion relates to the concern that it seems officers are fighting to receive amenities from the department that can aid them in delivering quality public service and yet I am mindful that recovery methods are provided to convicted defendants on a daily basis. Often services are delivered by quality social staff personnel and outside providers and there are few questions about funding those programs. Frankly, from my years of experience in high custody penitentiaries, there is something unsettling about advice from popular writers, god-peddling entrepreneurs, and bleeding heart liberals who proclaim rehabilitation is a breath away from every serial murderer, chronic pedophile, and spouse basher.[22] Yet rehabilitation is provided as though it is a magic bullet when in fact the evidence suggests otherwise. The truth is that some people do not nor can they be rehabilitated, yet many convicted defendants are mandated to be in one or more recovery-type programs. We want convicted defendants to live healthy, law-abating lifestyles. But 99% of most cops are not criminals, so why are more rehabilitative programs provided 2 million prisoners and 4 million probationers than to 600,000 law enforcement officers, you might ask?[23] Don't we want cops to live healthy, law-abiding lifestyles, too?

In a study of the Baltimore City Police Department it was implied that as long as research and practice continued on reactive person-centered programs linked to officer family problems resulting from stressed officers, it was learned that domestic violence in police officer families is curbed less often and more lip service is provided to protect the job of the officer.[24] Therefore, the issues associated with the consequences of a limited police initiative to manage stress adversely alters the delivery of police services, as well as poses a threat to the safety of police officers, their coworkers, their family and friends, and the general public.

On the other hand, person-centered programs are required and encouraged because so many cops are ill prepared to interface with the organizational inconsistencies from the day he or she became a police candidate (the inference is that qualifications for police candidates require enhancement and this thought is discussed later in this chapter). While person-centered programs make sense toward a healthy lifestyle, it is only part of the cure primarily because cured officers return to the same tub of hot water they left. "That's like giving a recovering alcoholic a job as a bartender," a Washington, DC, street cop observed.[25] "Some former alcoholics would never touch a drop, but most would," the author responded.

Police Agencies Need to Be Healthy

It is advantageous for a police agency to aid street cops toward good health, yet police organizations must also change the organizational health of the department. "Police agencies need to be healthy before they can treat the community's illnesses and injuries. Signs of good health include pride, self-esteem, quality leadership, comprehensive training, and board certification."[26] Changes also have to do with a new philosophy aimed at organizational stress prevention through the hiring process, preemployment psychological evaluations, privatization of agencies, military models of policing, hierarchical leveling, curbing the fear of crime among constituents, and organizing for empowerment.

The potential of "professional policing" actually grew during the reform era of policing discussed in an earlier chapter but it was never fully realized.[27] It stands to reason that a lack of professional policing is associated with a focus on street cops as opposed to taking a hard look at the organizational structure that dictates policy.

In earlier chapters, it was argued that organizational stressors included police strategies developed as a product of a military model department as a response to the war on crime, drugs, and terrorism. Elements of those strategies, which include inadequate training, leadership, and philosophy within a hierarchical structure, produce greater stress to officers than the job or dealing with family members. Consistent with those thoughts, a strong recommendation to control stress, which will enhance the quality of police services and meet the challenges of the 21st century, is that policymakers must circumvent the organization's adversary relationship with their rank-and-file personnel and promote professionalism. That is, the police organization needs to provide leadership toward a professionalized department.

Thinking about Professionalism

The police organization must support and encourage police officers to practice the primary characteristics consistent of professional personnel. A profession is an occupation requiring extensive education or specialized training.[28] Samuel P. Huntington writes in his work *Soldier and the State* that a profession displays three primary characteristics to some degree or another: *responsibility, expertise,* and *corporateness.*[29]

Responsibility: The profession consists of practicing experts, who work in a social context, and perform a service, such as the promotion of health, education, or justice, which is essential to the functioning of society. The client of every profession is society, individually or collectively. The profession is a moral unit promoting specific values and ideals that guide its members in their interactions with others. This guide may be a set of unwritten norms transmitted through the professional educational system and it may be codified into written canons of professional ethics.[30]

Expertise: Professions consist of experts who possess specialized knowledge and skill in a significant field of human endeavor. This expertise is acquired only by a prolonged combination of education, training, and experience. It is the basis of objective standards of professional competence. Professionalism through objectivity (as opposed to subjectivity or a personal agenda) is a goal.

Corporateness: Professional experts who share a common sense of organic unity and consciousness of themselves as an individual and as a group apart from other occupations. The origin of this collective feeling or set of experiences can be found in the discipline and training necessary for professional competence, the common bond of work, and the sharing of a unique social responsibility.

What Is a Profession?

Organizations that employ professionals should encourage their personnel to behave in a socially responsible manner, and their personnel should enjoy considerable freedom and responsibility for their sacrifice. When we think of professionalism, we should also think about Allan Millett's[31] six elements of a profession:

1. Full-time stable occupation serving a continuum of societal needs. (Firefighters)
2. Lifelong occupation held by practitioners who identify themselves personally with their area of expertise and the subculture of other similar experts. (Trial lawyers)
3. Organized as a collaborative group that guides boundaries, performance, and recruitment and training. (The American Bar Association's decision-making process consists of lawyers, researchers, educators, and staff members engaged in a dialogue without huge concerns of social rank.)
4. Formal and informal education, training, and specialized training. (Teachers; education includes academic certification, internships and practice semesters at schools).
5. Service orientation in which primary loyalty is to standards of competence and needs of clients as opposed to profit and organizational efficiency. (Doctors treating illnesses among the poor)
6. Individual and collective autonomy since practitioners have proven their high ethical standards and trustworthiness. (College educators have within limits a degree of academic freedom)

Millett notes that a profession holds a monopoly and furthers human progress. Autonomy or discretion of the professional is conditional and ultimately depends on continuous social approval. Without constant self-policing

TABLE 12.1   LIST OF PROFESSIONAL ATTRIBUTES

- Full-time occupation
- Client-centered
- Service ideal
- Caters to human needs (not wants)
- Efficiency moving toward client-needs mission
- Collaboration between participants of all ranks to enhance profession
- Self-policing
- Ethics
- Pecuniary profit is not primary objective
- Esoteric language (job-specific words and phases)
- Professional associations, symbols, artifacts
- Autonomy/discretion/judgment

and task success, a profession can narrow its own freedom and destroy public trust as rapidly as it gained its relative autonomy. Therefore it is strongly recommended that authority within police organizations should be flattened, thereby empowering officers to make professional decisions concerning their authority and expectations.

Also, there are numerous other marks of a profession worth noting, detailed in Table 12.1.[32]

IS POLICING A PROFESSION?

Policing should have a legitimate claim to a professional status. Regarding *responsibility* the police are practitioners who hold an expertise along their line of work, and perform a social service essential to the individual and collective functioning of society. Policing is a moral, ethical unit that promotes and maintains specific formal and informal values and greater-good ideals to its members and the public. Concerning *expertise*, it has formal and informal norms and policy transmitted through a professional training and educational system. It is self-policing dealing with the indiscretions of its members usually through senior officers trained to specifically deal with those indiscretions. Officers are entrusted with greater authority than most occupations since they have both a professional and bureaucratic dictate to enforce those standards. Finally, *corporateness* is seen in the unity of street cops who are bound by a cooperative sense of union based on shared expectations, lifestyles, and obligations. Overall, a police department looks to ethics and integrity as touchstones for judgment and service and therefore inherently shares elements of a profession. Some might even talk about a police culture to help make this point.

We can see that a number of Huntington's ideals about responsibility, expertise, and corporateness are linked to Millett's thoughts, too. The list above can aid to connect these professional attributes with police practice. How many matches can you find that would suggest policing is a profession? Before applauding professionalism among police agencies there are two attributes to professionalism that require your attention: efficiency versus effectiveness and collaboration versus orders.

Efficiency versus Effectiveness

Efficiency generally means competence: the ability to do something well or achieve a desired result without wasted energy or effort. Effectiveness generally means producing a result, especially the intended result. In order for policing to meet the criterion of community efficiency, public safety issues take priority over other issues. Jerome H. Skolnick implies that obtaining better-equipped police vehicles or state-of-the-art computers does not necessarily translate to an efficient police department. "What is necessary is a significant alteration in the philosophy of police so that police 'professionalization' rests upon the values of a democratic legal polity, rather than merely on the notion of technical proficiency to serve the public order of the state."[33] Professionalism and policing are linked to efficient practice, but that practice is to be efficient toward the needs of their constituents. One expert reminds us that "In this turbulent period it is more important than ever that we have a police capacity that is sensitive, effective, and responsive to the country's unique needs, and that, above all else, is committed to protecting and extending democratic values. That is a high calling indeed."[34] Specifically, the most immediate objective of the police is to use a greater range of alternatives to improve their effectiveness. "Quite simply, mediating a dispute, abating a nuisance, or arranging to have some physical barrier removed—without resorting to arrest—may be the best way to solve a problem."[35] There should be little confusion between the terms in the sense that efficiency is doing the job right, providing "value for money" to the community. Effectiveness is doing the right job and includes rewarding street cops who help attain the goals of the department.[36] (It could be asked in what way military tactical training, mandates, and weapons would further effectiveness or efficiency toward public safety?)

Nonetheless, for policing to meet professional levels, it must be both efficient and effective but the needs of the community must be served first. That is, the ends never justify the means. One way to think about this idea is that public safety outweighs new equipment or a better-managed police department. Another way is to say that professionals generally possess the capability and serve the needs of their clients or constituents before serving themselves. How closely does this perspective represent the performance of most street cops? Finally, one observation Skolnick clarifies for us in this regard of meeting the needs of constituents enhancing the enterprise is that

"The law often, but not always, supports police deception."[37] Thus, there appears to be little question that the ends can justify the means, calling a number of issues into question about professionalism.

Collaboration versus Orders

Collaboration generally means working together with one or more people in order to achieve an objective. It refers to communication at a give-and-take level. Decisions are reached through a give-and-take process that could include articulation at both written and verbal levels. For instance, in an innovative program designed for troubled juveniles, the Commonwealth of Massachusetts developed the Trial Lawyers community centers. Personnel in those centers collaborate with each other and various juvenile departments throughout the Commonwealth such as the Department of Youth Services (DYS), the Office of the Commissioner of Probation (OCP), Boston Public Schools, and other human service agencies.[38] Most juveniles entering the program are referred by the court once adjudicated a delinquent and through DYS. Those referrals generally are youth in custody with the intent of "stepping them down" to the community but only after a lengthy process of counseling, drug tests, and educational courses such as life skills and anger management. Yet each juvenile in the system's performance is discussed at meetings consisting of drug counselors, supervision officers, teachers, and both middle and upper managers from several (county and state) agencies prior to disposition, treatment, release, or referral to service providers. That is, no one individual makes a decision without input from other individuals, some whom are linked to the case and some that are not. Often those meetings are heated and cases are disputed, yet everyone provides input toward disposition. How close does this description fit the activities of street cops and their chain of command? A strong recommendation is that police officers and command engage in a dialogue on a regular basis, which should include decision-making practices directly related to officer assignments. This recommendation would lay the groundwork toward prevention and prosocial measures as a department-wide philosophy.

That is, the police organizational structure must be sure they are employing the most appropriate candidates. A change in hiring practices is underway in many departments yet there is more to be done.

Law Enforcement Qualifications

Part of prevention is getting the right candidates for the job. Civil service regulations govern the appointment of police and detectives in practically all states, large municipalities, and special police agencies, as well as in many smaller ones, reports the U.S. Department of Labor.[40] Candidates must be U.S. citizens, usually at least 21 years of age, and must meet rigorous physical

See How Many Elements of Professionalism You Can Find in this Abbreviated Version of the Accounts of Chief Theron Bowman, Arlington, Texas, Police Department[39]

I head a police department that has evaded most of the public scandals, drama, historical antagonism, violent crime waves, and controversies so prevalent in the chronicles of police's greatest servant leaders. In Arlington, Texas, we have never had a major scandal involving on-duty behavior of more than one officer and have never experienced a mass civil disturbance.

[Our last chief] believed that police officers capable of adjusting to change would provide desirable short-term policing solutions. More importantly, he recognized that police officers and supervisors who were inclined to adjust and adapt to sociological changes were essential components of a culture of professional stability and publicly ordained successes. Simply stated, the Arlington Police Department was expected to consist of a competent, professional workforce responsive and accountable to, and reflective of, the community.

A competent, professional workforce, by Arlington police definitions, consists of knowledgeable, learning, thinking, and experimenting executives and supervisors who lead and manage. The line consists of intelligent agents who are representative of the service population. Achieving this mix of human resources has been the key to my organization's success.

We have learned over the years that the recipe for assembling and maintaining a competent and professional workforce contains three ingredients: total commitment to higher education, workforce diversity, and professional management. The three ingredients are distinct but interrelated. The linchpin, thus most significant of the three, is the minimum entry-level educational requirement of a bachelor's degree.

A Commitment to Higher Education

When I became an Arlington officer in 1983, police officers were expected to be militaristic, submissive to authority, and follow policy and supervisory directions. Policies attempted to address every conceivable situation so as to release officers from the necessity of thinking for themselves. Decisions were made at the top of the organization. Communication flowed mostly one way: from the top down. That authoritarian style of management stifled creativity and innovation, but was necessary when employees were expected to fail.

Today, we have greater respect for the autonomy of police officers. We recognize that police officers must be able to understand and apply the law, the nature of social problems, and the psychology of the persons whose attitude toward the law may differ from theirs.

The degree brings with it an air of self-respect and professional demeanor that builds organizational morale. It tends to enhance their research and analytical skills, preparing them for solving complex problems without the need for strict supervision. Educated officers tend to have a better grasp of organizational imperatives and are inclined to work toward altruistic goals.

Arlington officers have a great amount of autonomy. Officers are expected to be computer literate, conduct community meetings using PowerPoint for presentations, and to read, interpret, prepare, and analyze statistical data. Supervisors are expected to analyze trends and data using contemporary sociological research methods. Sergeants and lieutenants routinely employ survey research to determine citizen priorities for service delivery options.

Most requests for changes in police policy or protocols submitted to my office by line-level employees are accompanied by thorough research documentation. Officers are expected to recognize trends and develop cost–benefit analyses in weighing operational options. The results are very well-reasoned, high-quality, and dependable decisions, mostly attributable to a well-educated workforce.

A Commitment to Workforce Diversity

In Arlington, rapid population growth has resulted in major demographic changes in the city population. Many critics believed that raising educational standards would adversely affect department diversification efforts. To the contrary, our department has the highest entry-level standards in Texas, yet is the most racially and ethnically diverse among major cities. We are rated 16th nationally by the International Association of Women in Policing and are climbing in gender diversity.

Optimal police service in a democratic society cannot be provided to a community without police officers who are fluent in its language and culture. A culturally diverse workforce is difficult if not impossible to attain without support from the various constituent communities. Obtaining the requisite community support often hinges on building a trusting relationship. A trusting relationship is built over time as mutual respect accrues.

An educated and sophisticated workforce is better at understanding cultural differences even when they don't have experience with other cultures. During a recent visit to the department, for example, the Heritage Foundation's Eli Lehrer rode along with an officer who responded to a noise complaint caused by a practicing Samoan dance group. The group didn't have a church and practiced in backyards in the daytime so as to disturb as few people as possible. The officers understood this and negotiated with the neighbors to reach a solution that left everyone pretty happy and let the practice go on. The officers also stayed for a few minutes to watch the practice and see what was really going on. This is a good example of respect for diversity, but neither of the officers involved was Samoan.

Professional Management

The final ingredient of this three-pronged recipe for success is a professional approach to managing the organization. This professional management requires a culture of winning, leading by example, democratic governance, authority commensurate with responsibility, high standards, working with the rank and file instead of against them, selling ideas instead of generating mandates, and perseverance. This can be observed in our process of transitioning the APD from community-oriented policing to geographic problem solving. Geographic policing is a community-oriented policing strategy built on problem-solving methodology. Police administration started moving the workforce into geographic policing approximately 1 year prior to implementation.

(continued)

We knew the entire workforce would see enormous changes. Community policing asks officers to partner with community groups and to see arrest as only one of the tools at their disposal. It's an important and valuable idea, but it alone often lacks accountability measures necessary to produce the results we were looking for. Rather than decreeing the whole organization adopt a new philosophy and then diving in head first, we conducted internal focus groups with employees from various segments within the department and separate groups involving citizens in the community.

A final key element in professional management is a compressed hierarchy of command. At APD, sergeants are line-level supervisors. Lieutenant is the next higher level, and is the highest rank to which one can competitively promote. Deputy chiefs followed by assistant chiefs are the subsequent higher ranks. The police chief appoints all incumbents in both executive ranks. The ability to appoint executive staff grants the chief the ability to handpick professional managers with a track record of superior performance without the constraints of a rank-ordered system. This forces the police chief to be entirely accountable for the performance of his administration.

In Arlington, professional management is a continuous process. We subscribe to management journals, continually review management literature, and hold membership in professional associations. We recently reviewed a case study detailing why the Container Store was named as the "Best Employer to Work For" in America. Not satisfied with being a great police department, we continually seek to be the greatest organization of any kind.

Printed with Permission of Chief Theron Bowman, Arlington, Texas, Police Department.

and personal qualifications. Physical examinations for entrance into law enforcement often include tests of vision, hearing, strength, and agility. Eligibility for appointment usually depends on performance in competitive written examinations and previous education and experience. In larger departments, where the majority of law enforcement jobs are found, applicants usually must have at least a high school education. Federal and state agencies typically require a college degree. Because personal characteristics such as honesty, sound judgment, integrity, and a sense of responsibility are especially important in law enforcement, candidates are interviewed by senior officers, and their character traits and backgrounds are investigated. In some agencies, candidates are interviewed by a psychiatrist or a psychologist, or given a personality test. Many candidates take a lie detector examination and are tested for drugs. Some agencies put sworn personnel through random drug testing as a condition of continuing employment.

Should a police agency wish to follow a disease model of prevention, then their pool of candidates must, among other things, consist of individuals who possess the ability to learn. Often, this would suggest that departments would have to change the typical hiring criteria of age, a valid driver's license, and a high school diploma. For instance, Connecticut increased minimum qualifications, requiring that all state and municipal police officers hired after September 30, 1999, to obtain an associate's degree from an accredited college or university within 5 years after they become officers. It requires the Police Officer Standards and Training Council to monitor those accomplishments.

Getting a Police Job

When police officers are asked what it takes to get a job in the department, one answer stands out more than other answers—"Who you know." While that idea represents a reasonable policy, it is recommended that police candidates, once the education, training, and work standards are met, be exclusively selected on (*preemployment psychological screening*) for three reasons: (1) policing is moving away from lethal practices to nonlethal practices, (2) to identify violence-prone candidates, and (3) to predict future officer performance.

Only over the past few years has greater attention been given to these issues. For instance, the policing moving away from lethal practices was discussed earlier in the context of the Deputy Director of the North Carolina Justice Academy, Ed Bolte, who some years back discussed domestic and foreign terrorism as becoming a major factor in policing of the future. He also revealed that many justice academies were moving away from a priority of tactical training to nonlethal force training. Of interest, the Federal Law Enforcement Training Center in Georgia takes a more lethal approach to training federal officers, it was emphasized during a recent visit to the facility. Nonetheless, the wave of the future, Director Bolte says, would be based on using nonlethal tactics as opposed to violent tactics to take a suspect into custody. Another clue comes from the Commonwealth of Massachusetts where Governor Mitt Romney signed into law on July 15, 2004, the use of stun guns by Massachusetts police before unleashing other means of force.[41] The 50,000-volt tasers are considered the "modern billy club," Governor Romney says. Tasers are effective from a distance of 21 feet. Of course, tasers can kill, too.[42]

Research has identified multiple determinants of the use of excessive force, raising questions about organizational reliability. Two reports that followed the Rodney King incident—the 1991 report of the Independent Commission to Study the Los Angeles Police Department and the 1992 Los Angeles County Sheriff's Report by James G. Kolt and staff—questioned the effectiveness of existing psychological screening to predict propensity for violence.[43]

Psychologists were asked about the characteristics of officers who had been referred to them because of the use of excessive force. Their answers did not support the conventional view that a few "bad apples" are responsible for most excessive force complaints.[44] Rather, their answers were used to construct five distinct (described below) profiles of different types of officers, only one of which resembled the "bad apple" characterization. In particular, recent developments related to the Americans with Disabilities Act will change screening procedures. According to an EEOC enforcement guidance issued in May 1994, some tests administered before a position is offered are now allowable only after a conditional job offer has been made.

Preemployment Psychological Screening

One of the first steps in prevention logically entails not hiring officers who would present a problem. Therefore, it is recommended that a serious pre-employment screening process be in place to alert hiring committees as to the potential risk that could be generated by certain personalities. Such deselection is the aim of preemployment screening, a function in which the police psychologist has a role. Of the psychologists who perform preemployment screening, almost all rely on fairly traditional assessment tools—psychological tests and clinical interviews. By contrast, they make limited use of more innovative approaches.

Tests that might detect mental impairment or disorder are included in this category. There are other hurdles most police candidates experience such as civil service exams, oral interviews, polygraph exams, agility tests, written examinations such as general knowledge and psychological tests, (including the MMPI), aptitude tests, criminal records check, background investigations, driving record checks, and medical exams.

Scrivner placed her data into *five personality profiles*, which constitute human resource information that can be used to shape policy. These profiles support the idea that excessive force is not just a problem of individuals but may also reflect organizational deficiencies. These profiles are presented in the following sections in ascending order of frequency, along with possible interventions, but officers experiencing temporary personal problems such as going through a divorce would not necessarily make this list. The below five profiles refer to ongoing experiences, or what can be referred to as patterns of behavior.

1. Officers with personality disorders that place them at chronic risk.
2. Officers whose previous job-related experience places them at risk.
3. Officers who have problems at early stages in their police careers.
4. Officers who develop inappropriate patrol styles.
5. Officers with personal problems

1. **Officers with personality disorders that place them at chronic risk.** These officers have pervasive and enduring personality traits (in contrast to characteristics acquired on the job) that are manifested in antisocial, narcissistic, paranoid, or abusive tendencies. These conditions interfere with judgment and interactions with others, particularly when officers perceive challenges or threats to their authority. To provide a look into their behavior, antisocial behavior is consistent

with individuals who demonstrate a violation of the rights of others, deceitfulness, and impulsivity while narcissistic behavior is characterized by a pervasive pattern of grandiosity or fantasy, a sense of entitlement, and a need for admiration.[45] Both antisocial and narcissistic personality disorders share a tendency to be tough-minded, glib, superficial, exploitative, and unempathic. They have little regard for the feelings of others. The number of street cops who fit this profile is the smallest of all the high-risk groups.

These personality characteristics tend to persist through life but can be intensified by altercations with others, and because of their highly manipulative personalities, these traits might not be apparent at preemployment screening. Also, street cops who exhibit these personality disorders generally do not learn from their experiences or accept responsibility for their behavior. It is not uncommon for these individuals to be at a greater risk for repeated citizen complaints. Also, while they often appear to be brave in the face of conflict, in fact they do whatever necessary to escalate a situation into becoming more dangerous than it is in order to employ force including deadly force. As a consequence, they may appear to be the sole source of problems in police departments. If these individuals are commanders, the job of controlling them is less likely.

2. **Officers whose previous job-related experience places them at risk.** Traumatic situations such as justifiable police shootings put some officers at risk for abuse of force, but for reasons totally different from those of the first group. These officers are not unsocialized, egocentric, or violent. In fact, personality factors appear to have less to do with their vulnerability to excessive force than the emotional "baggage" they have accumulated from involvement in previous incidents. Typically, these officers verge on burnout and have become isolated from their squads. Because of their perceived need to conceal symptoms, some time elapses before their problems come to others' attention. When this happens, the event is often an excessive force situation in which the officer has lost control.

   In contrast to the chronic at-risk group, officers in this group are amenable to critical-incident debriefing, but to be fully effective, the interventions need to be applied soon after involvement in the incident. Studies recommend training and psychological debriefings, with follow-up, to minimize the development of symptoms.

3. **Officers who have problems at early stages in their police careers.** The third group profiled consists of young and inexperienced officers, frequently seen as "hotdogs," "badge happy," "macho," or generally immature. In contrast to other inexperienced officers, individuals in this group are characterized as highly impressionable and impulsive, with low tolerance for frustration. They nonetheless bring

positive attributes to their work and could outgrow these tendencies. Unfortunately, the positive qualities can deteriorate early in their careers if field training officers and first-line supervisors do not work to provide them with a full range of responses to patrol encounters.

These inexperienced officers were described as needing strong supervision and highly structured field training, preferably under a field training officer with a lot of street experience. Because they are strongly influenced by the police subculture, such new recruits are more apt to change their behavior if their mentors show them how to maintain a professional demeanor in their dealings with citizens. These individuals are more subject to assimilating into the normative behavior of cops. If those norms are violent, it is likely that they will be reinforced when they follow patterns of behavior that emulate unnecessary use of force.

4. **Officers who develop inappropriate patrol styles.** Individuals who fit this profile combine a dominant, commanding presence with a heavy-handed policing style; they are particularly sensitive to challenge and provocation. They use force to show they are in charge; as their beliefs about how police work is conducted become more rigid, this behavior becomes the norm. Their thoughts are rigid and ideals are centered in their "authority."

In contrast to the chronic risk group, the behavior of officers in this group is acquired on the job. It can be changed. The longer inappropriate patterns continue, the more difficult it is to change. As street cops become invested in police power and control, they see little reason to change. Officers in this group are often labeled "dinosaurs" in a changing police world marked by greater accountability to citizens and by adoption to community accountability. These officers must be supervised and trained by strong, ethical trainers early in their career or the likelihood of changing later is less likely and the likelihood of using unnecessary force is probable. Peer programs or situation-based interventions in contrast to traditional individual counseling is probably best for them. Making these officers part of the solution, rather than part of the problem, is the best way to change their behavior.

5. **Officers with personal problems.** The final risk profile was made up of street cops who have experienced serious personal problems, such as separation, divorce, or even perceived loss of status that destabilized their job functioning. In general, street cops with personal problems do not use excessive force, but those who do may have elected police work for all the wrong reasons. In contrast to their peers, they seem to have a more tenuous sense of self-worth and higher levels of anxiety that are well masked. Some may have functioned reasonably well until

changes occurred in their personal situation. These changes undermine confidence and make it more difficult to deal with fear, animosity, and emotionally charged patrol situations.

Before they resort to excessive force, these officers usually exhibit patrol behavior that is erratic and that signals the possibility they will lose control in a confrontation. This group, the most frequently seen by psychologists because of excessive-force problems, can be identified by supervisors who have been properly trained to observe and respond to precursors of problem behavior. Their greater numbers should encourage departments to develop early warning systems to help supervisors detect "marker behaviors" signifying that problems are brewing. These officers benefit from individual counseling, but earlier referrals to psychologists can enhance the benefit and prevent their personal situations from spilling over into their jobs.

Prevention of the Use of Excessive Force

Because the above profiles reveal different reasons for the use of excessive force, police departments should develop a system of interventions targeted to different groups of officers at different phases of their careers. Major changes need to take place within police organizational structures to identify, treat, and reassess patterns of behavior among these officers. If potentially problematic street cops go untreated, it is likely that he or she will engage in lethal force among less than dangerous conditions because among these personality characteristics risk behavior is intensified by other experiences. Most of those experiences implicate the organizational practices of the departments in which the officers work. To the extent this is true, it indicates the need for remedial intervention at the level of the department as well as the individual level. A word of caution: this might sound like traditional screening methods, which are valid, reliable, and often standardized measurements, yet traditional methods upon untraditional clients seems redundant. Also those methods focus on identifying the characteristics of "bad" officers, and as a result, less is known about the characteristics of "good" officers or about how career experiences mitigate or reinforce these characteristics. Therefore it is recommended that characteristics of "good" officers become standardized and those characteristics become the benchmark to identify candidates who have the potential to become a professional officer and leader.

Good Officers

There are negative qualities of police candidates that hiring committees want to stay away from, and there are ideal personality traits that might indicate a candidate can perform well as a police officer and cope with the stress of the job. Although a discussion about the personality traits that make a good cop are above the scope of this work, a guide of what constitutes a "good officer" can aid in the hiring process, and it can aid officers who want to enhance their professionalism by upgrading certain qualities about themselves. You might want to contrast these qualities with the leadership skills recommended of police executives in Chapter 3. Nonetheless, here's a list of 14 qualities that should guide a hiring committee's thoughts for entry-level police officers[46]:

- *Enthusiasm:* believing one is doing and going about even routine duties with a certain vigor that is almost contagious.
- *Good communication skills:* having highly developed speaking and listening skills and the ability to interact equally well with all people, regardless of their income. (Incidentally, this skill is the most important skill of police leaders.)
- *Good judgment:* having wisdom and the ability to make good analytic decisions based on an understanding of the problem.
- *Sense of humor:* being able to laugh and smile, to help oneself cope with regular exposure to human pain and suffering.
- *Creativity:* using creative techniques to place oneself in the mind of the criminal and accomplish legal arrests.
- *Self-motivation:* making things happen, proactively solving difficult cases, and creating one's own luck.
- *Knowing the job and the system:* understanding the role of a police officer, the intricacies of the justice system, and what the administration requires; using both formal and informal channels to be effective.
- *Ego:* believing one is a good officer, having self-confidence that enables one to solve difficult crimes.
- *Courage:* being able to meet physical and psychological challenges; thinking clearly during times of high stress; admitting when one is wrong; standing up for what is right.
- *Understanding discretion:* enforcing the spirit of the law, not the letter of the law; not being hard-nosed, hardheaded, or hard-hearted; giving people a break; showing empathy.
- *Tenacity:* staying focused; seeking challenges not obstacles; viewing failure not as a setback but as an experience.
- *A thirst for knowledge:* being aware of new laws and court decisions, learning from the classroom and informal discussions with others and from experiences.
- *Honorable:* wanting to perform in a professional manner to help others before yourself.
- *Knowing your limits:* understanding an individual's physical and mental limits.

It is more likely that these personality traits can help an officer cope more often with police stress than other candidates.[47] However, quality traits are only as good as the training.

Law Enforcement Training

Training is related to stress prevention. In fact, it is recommended that preventing stress relates to training officers prior to them becoming officers, and after they become officers to recognize its signs and sources and to develop individual coping strategies.[48]

Program administrators, mental health practitioners, and training officers say that the best time to teach officers about stress is when officers are at the academy at the beginning of their careers and during inservice training. Because new recruits are anxious to please and because they are a captured audience at that time, this would be an excellent opportunity for them to learn about stress. There are some concerns that stress training during recruit training is not the best approach because most recruits are not experienced enough to recognize that stress comes with the job.[49] The optimal time to reach them may be 6–8 months into the job after experiencing actual on-the-job stress. Yet, because the organizational structure in and of itself produces stress, recruits and police managers should be well informed. One source recommends[50]:

- Train command staff in effective supervision
- Instruct field training officers to constructively supervise rookies
- Eliminate rotating shift work
- Improve the match between officers' capabilities and the demands of specific assignments

SUMMARY

The focus of this chapter is on compelling reasons why the police organizational structure must change, professionalization of police officers, and the hiring process that subsequently could help prevent and control officer stress and probably police corruption, while satisfying public safety concerns. To help a reader better understand this chapter, twelve issues that require attention along with a few recommendations were offered as a starting point to aid police officers. It was suggested that stress treatment should not be limited to treating personnel, but that the organization requires attention, too; prevention should become departmental philosophy, policymakers must circumvent the organization's adversary relationship with their dedicated officers and promote professionalization, authority and expectations should be "flattened," and the characteristics of "good" officers become standardized and become the benchmark to identify candidates who have the potential to become a professional officer and leader.

If the law enforcement community applies the three phases of public health medicine's concept of prevention to developing a stress reduction model, then choosing the primary phase makes the most sense. Those phases are: educate the healthy, educate those at risk, and treat those infected. Among the 11 reasons police organizations must change, terrorism, criminal, and demographic changes lead the list. However, include technological, economic, and environmental changes along with political, institutional, legal, profession, and future changes. Person-centered programs are important because so many cops are ill prepared to interface with the organizational inconsistencies from the day he or she became police candidates. Also the real task of most police agencies is that they need to become healthy before they can treat the community's illnesses and injuries and prevent and control officer stress.

The three primary characteristics of a profession include to some degree or another: responsibility, expertise, and corporateness. The six components identified as important elements of any profession include full-time stable occupation serving a continuum of societal needs; lifelong occupation held by practitioners who identify themselves personally with their area of expertise and the subculture of other similar experts; organized as a collaborative group that guides boundaries, performance, and recruitment and training; formal and informal education, training, and specialized training; service orientation in which primary loyalty is to standards of competence and needs of clients as opposed to profit and organizational efficiency; individual and collective autonomy since practitioners have proven their high ethical standards and trustworthiness. A "professional" status encourages its participants to behave in a more socially responsible manner and they would enjoy considerable freedom and responsibility for their sacrifice.

However, before deciding if officers are indeed a profession, efficiency versus effectiveness standards suggest that generally efficiency means competence or the ability to do something well or achieve a desired result without wasted energy or effort. Effectiveness generally means producing a result, especially the intended result.

A second model relates to collaboration versus orders whereas collaboration means working together with one or more people in order to achieve an objective. It refers to communication at a give-and-take level. Decisions are reached through a give-and-take process that could include articulation at both written and verbal levels. It was implied that officers might not fit either model as well as expected.

Nationally, a GED, a valid driver's license, 21 years of age, and who you know are hardly relevant when the responsibility and expectations of an officer are so vast.

Because the organizational structure in and of itself produces stress, recruits and police managers should be well informed and trained in effective supervision, instructing field training officers to constructively supervise rookies, eliminate rotating shift work, and improving the match between officers' capabilities and the demands of specific assignments

Preemployment screening should search out officers with personality disorders that place them at chronic risk, officers whose previous job-related experience places them at risk, officers who have problems at early stages in their police career, officers who develop inappropriate patrol styles, and officers with personal problems. The various personality profiles discussed in preemployment evaluations each might have a different reason for the use of excessive force. Therefore, police departments should develop a system of interventions targeted to different groups of officers at different phases of their careers. Major changes need to take place within police organizational structures to identify, treat, and reassess patterns of behavior among these officers. If potentially problematic street cops go untreated, it is likely that he or she will engage in lethal force among less than dangerous conditions because among these personality characteristics risk behavior is intensified by other experiences. Good police characteristics are highlighted suggesting that if police candidates possessed these that it would be more likely that he or she would be able to cope with stress. Finally, quality personality traits can be enhanced when officers are trained prior to them becoming an officer and after they become officers to recognize signs and sources of stress and to develop individual coping strategies.

WHAT WOULD YOU DO IF YOU WERE IN CHARGE?

Buffalo, New York, could pay tens of thousands of dollars to a man who was driving with a suspended license when he was permanently injured in an alcohol-related crash.[51] Under a settlement approved by Buffalo's Common Council, Richard Adam of Buffalo would receive $75,000 for injuries he suffered in the October 2001 crash. Police say his alcohol level was double the legal limit at the time of the crash. Authorities say Adam was driving with a suspended license in connection with an earlier drunken driving incident.

Despite the nature of the 2001 crash, city officials say Buffalo could be hit with a $1 million liability if the case goes to trial. The city admitted it had not installed safety measures on the streets near the crash site until after the accident occurred.

OFFICER KILLED IN CALIFORNIA

On Monday, July 25, 2005, Police Officer Nels (Dan) Niemi of the San Leandro, California, Police Department was ambushed, gunned down, and killed while investigating a disturbance call.[52] Officer Niemi responded to a report of a disturbance on Doolittle Drive at 2300 hours. As Officer Niemi spoke to some of the residents, a man drove up to the scene and engaged Officer Niemi in conversation. Without warning, the man produced a handgun and shot Officer Niemi several times, killing him. The suspect fled the scene on foot and was apprehended the next day. Officer Niemi had served with the San Leandro Police Department for 3 years. The officer is survived by his wife, son, and daughter.

DISCUSSION QUESTIONS

1. Characterize the importance of stress prevention.
2. Describe how a public health model or disease prevention model could work as a stress initiative.
3. Identify 12 issues toward stress control.
4. Identify the compelling reasons why police organizations must change.
5. Identify the real task of most police organizations linked to stress.
6. Describe the components of a profession.
7. Characterize the elements of any profession.
8. Explain the efficiency versus effectiveness standard linked to officer professionalization.
9. Explain the collaboration versus order standard linked to police professionalization.
10. Characterize Chief Bowman's plan in Arlington, Texas. In what way do you agree and disagree with his organizational strategies toward professionalism?
11. Describe the basic qualifications for employment as a law enforcement officer.
12. Characterize the preemployment screening strategies recommended.
13. Describe the five personality profiles related to law enforcement candidates. In what way do you agree or disagree with the predictive values of these profiles?
14. Describe the characteristics of good officers.
15. Describe the recommended training for recruits and command staff linked to stress. In what way do you see this training as helpful?

ENDNOTES

1. Todd E. Bricker and Donna C. Hale (2005). Police organizational change: Strategies for effective police management in the twenty-first century. In Roslyn Muraskin and Albert R. Roberts (Eds.), *Visions for change: Crime and justice in the twenty-first century. 4h edition.* (pages 390–403). Upper Saddle River, NJ: Prentice Hall. p. 393.
2. Frank Anechiarico and James B. Jacobs (1996). *The pursuit of absolute integrity.* Chicago: University of Chicago Press. p. 317.
3. Samuel Walker (2001). *Police accountability: The role of citizen oversight.* USA: Wadsworth. p. 149.

4. Rolando V. del Carman (1991). *Civil liabilities in American policing.* Englewood Cliffs, NJ: Prentice Hall. Also see James D. Sewell (2002, March). Managing the stress of organizational change. *FBI Law Bulletin,* 71(3). Retrieved online July 14, 2004: http://www.fbi.gov/publications/leb/2002/mar02leb.htm#page_15

5. Dennis J. Stevens (2002). Civil liabilities and arrest decisions. In Jeffrey T. Walker (Ed.), *Policing and the law* (pp. 53–70). Uppers Saddle River, NJ: Prentice Hall. In particular, 42 USC Section 1983 creates no substantive rights: rather it is a vehicle for suing defendants acting under the color of state law for violating another person's federal rights. By its very terms, Section 1983 applies only to persons acting under the color of law. It is applicable only to state and local law enforcement officers who exert authority derived from state law.

6. Civil Laws Governing Law Enforcement Misconduct. The texts of the three principal statutes that authorize the Department of Justice to seek civil remedies for police misconduct are as follows:

Section 210401 of the Violent Crime Control and Law Enforcement Act of 1994, 42 U.S.C. § 14141 (Police Misconduct Provision):

Sec. 210401. Cause of Action. Unlawful Conduct—It shall be unlawful for any governmental authority, or any agent thereof, or any person acting on behalf of a governmental authority, to engage in a pattern or practice of conduct by law enforcement officers or by officials or employees of any governmental agency with responsibility for the administration of juvenile justice or the incarceration of juveniles that deprives persons of rights, privileges, or immunities secured or protected by the Constitution or laws of the United States.

Civil Action by Attorney General—Whenever the Attorney General has reasonable cause to believe that a violation of paragraph (1) (sic) has occurred, the Attorney General, for or in the name of the United States, may in a civil action obtain appropriate equitable and declaratory relief to eliminate the pattern or practice.

NOTE: The lack of commas in paragraph (a) is potentially confusing. One incorrect reading of that paragraph resulting from the lack of commas would restrict the scope of the Police Misconduct Provision to persons involved with the juvenile justice system. The clause relating to the juvenile justice system expands the scope of paragraph (a), and does not restrict it.

Title VI of the Civil Rights Act of 1964: "No person in the United States shall, on the ground of race, color, or national origin, be excluded from participation in, be denied the benefits of, or be subjected to discrimination under any program or activity receiving Federal financial assistance." 42 U.S.C. § 2000d.

NOTE: The Department's regulations for enforcing Title VI appear at 28 C.F.R. Part 42, Subpart C.

Section 809(c) of the Omnibus Crime Control and Safe Streets Act of 1968:

(1) No person in any State shall on the ground of race, color, religion, national origin, or sex be excluded from participation in, be denied the benefits of, or be subjected to discrimination under or denied employment in connection with any programs or activity funded in whole or in part with funds made available under this chapter.

(2) Whenever the Attorney General has reason to believe that a State government or unit of local government has engaged in or is engaging in a pattern or practice in violation of the provisions of this section, the Attorney General may bring a civil action in an appropriate United States district court. Such court may grant as relief any temporary restraining order, preliminary or permanent

injunction, or other order, as necessary or appropriate to insure the full enjoyment of the rights described in this section, including the suspension, termination, or repayment of such funds made available under this chapter as the court may deem appropriate, or placing any further such funds in escrow pending the outcome of the litigation.

42 U.S.C. 3789d(c)(1) and (3).

NOTE: The Department's regulations for enforcing this provision appear at 28 C.F.R. Part 42, Subpart D.

The Police Misconduct Provision is enforced through litigation. Title VI is enforced through an initial administrative review, which may lead to litigation if there is a violation and an administrative settlement is not reached. The Safe Streets Act may be enforced either through a similar administrative review/litigation approach or through a strictly litigation mode. U.S. Department of Justice. Washington, DC: Office of Justice Programs. Retrieved online July 15, 2004: http//www.usdoj.gov/usao/eousa/foia_reading_room/usam/title8/cvr00005.htm

7. Sheera Frenkel (2004, August 4). Writing the rules to govern the cosmos. *The Christian Science Monitor.* Retrieved online July 27, 2005: http://www.csmonitor.com/2004/0804/p15s02-stss.html

8. Vivian Lord (1996). An impact of community policing: Reported stressors, social support, and strain among police officers in a changing police department. *Journal of Criminal Justice,* 24, 503–522. Kenneth J. Peak (2006). *Policing in America.* Upper Saddle River, NJ: Prentice Hall. pp. 88–97. Stress Unit (2006). Central Florida Police. Retrieved online April 7, 2006: http://policestress.org/index.htm

9. Presentation given by Deborah ProthrowStith, M.D., FBI Academy, October 15, 1991.

10. Edward A. Charlesworth and Ronald G. Nathan (1984) *Stress management: A comprehensive guide to wellness.* New York: Ballantine Books.

11. C.C. Cottle, R.J. Lee, and K. Heilbrun (2001). The prediction of criminal recidivism in juveniles: A meta-analysis. *Criminal Justice and Behavior,* 28, 367–394. J. Monahan, H.J. Steadman, E. Silver, P.S. Appelbaum, P.C. Robbins, E. Mulvey, L.H. Roth, T. Grisso, and S. Banks (2001). *Rethinking risk assessment: The MacArthur study of mental disorder and violence.* New York: Oxford University Press.

12. John M. Violanti (2005). Dying for the job: Psychological stress, disease, and mortality in police work. In Heith Copes (Ed.), *Policing and stress* (pp. 87–102). Upper Saddle River, NJ: Prentice Hall. James Bonta (2002). Offender risk assessment: Guidelines for selection and use. *Criminal Justice and Behavior,* 29, 355–379.

13. David X. Swenson (1999, November). Adult certification evaluation: Adolescent certification to adult status for court. Retrieved online January 9, 2005: http://www.css.edu/users/dswenson/web/psyeval/adolcertification.html. The process developed by Swenson is consistent with another observer who provides a plan for probation agencies. See Jennifer L. Ferguson (2002). Putting the "What Works" Research Into Practice: An Organizational Perspective. *Criminal Justice and Behavior,* 29, 472–492.

14. This idea is congruent with Karl Hanson (2005, February). Twenty Years of Progress in Violence Risk Assessment. *Journal of Interpersonal Violence,* 20(2), 212–217.

15. This thought is also consistent with Paul Gendreau, Claire Goggin, and Paula Smith (2003, December). Erratum. *Criminal Justice and Behavior,* 30(6): 722–724.

16. Minnesota Multiphasic Personality Inventory. For history and further descriptions of MMPI, see Richard Niolon. A history of MMPI. Retrieved online January 9, 2005: http://www.psychpage.com/objective/mmpi2_overview.htm.

17. Other observers discuss a similar perspective concerning participant motivation specifically developed for employment in residential units. See Matthew L. Hiller, Kevin Knight, Carl Leukefeld, and D. Dwayne Simpson (2002). Motivation as a Predictor of Therapeutic Engagement in Mandated Residential Substance Abuse Treatment. *Criminal Justice and Behavior*, 29, 56–75.

18. This thought is congruent with William N. Elliott (2002, December). Managing officer resistance to counseling. *Federal Probation*, 66(3), 43–45. Retrieved online January 13, 2005: http://www.uscourts.gov/fedprob/2002decfp.pdf

19. William N. Elliott (2002, December). pp. 43–44.

20. William N. Elliott (2002, December). p. 45.

21. For that reason, a relapse process must be part of every program and every group encounter. Think of it as a way to process failure. What to do when things happen must be regularly clarified to participants whether it is treatment toward sobriety, a program such as vocational skills, or group encounters dealing with anger issues, a process must be in place to deal with failure. If lifelines are arbitrary or don't exist, continued failure is more likely.

22. Dennis J. Stevens (2003). *Applied community policing in the 21st century*. Boston: Allyn & Bacon. p. 36.

23. Bureau of Justice Statistics (2006). Retrieved online April 6, 2006: http://www.ojp.usdoj.gov/bjs/

24. Robyn Gershon (2000). Police stress and domestic violence in police families in Baltimore, Maryland, 1997–1999. NACJD. Retrieved online July 15, 2004: http://www.icpsr.umich.edu:8080/NACJD-STUDY/02976.xml

25. Personal confidential communication between a DC police officer and the author, July 27, 2005.

26. Joseph A. Harpold (2000, June). A medical model for community police. *FBI Law Enforcement Bulletin*, p. 26.

27. George L. Kelling and Mark H. Moore (2004). The evolving strategy of policing. In Steven G. Brandl and David E. Barlow (Eds.), *The police in America: Classical and contemporary readings* (pp. 5–26). Belmont, CA: Wadsworth.

28. MSN Encarta—Dictionary. Retrieved Online July 2, 2004: http://encarta.msn.com/encnet/features/dictionary/DictionaryResults.aspx?search=profession

29. Samuel P. Huntington (1981, September). *Soldier and the state: The theory and politics of civil-military relations*. New York: Belknap Press.

30. Samuel P. Huntington (1981) was used as a guide. The interpretation of his work is that of this author.

31. Allan R. Millett is a Professor of Military History at the Ohio State University and an author of many military books.

32. As a guide, David L. Carter and Louis A. Radelet (1999). *The police and the community*, 6th ed. Upper Saddle River, NJ: Prentice Hall. pp. 133–136.

33. Jerome H. Skolnick (1967). *Justice without trial: Law enforcement in a democratic society*. New York: Wiley. p. 83.

34. Herman Goldstein (2002). The new policing: Confronting complexity. In Wilson R. Palacios, Paul F. Cromwell, and Roger G. Dunham (Eds.), *Crime & justice in America: Present realities and future prospects* (pp. 102–110). Upper Saddle River, NJ: Prentice Hall.

35. Herman Goldstein (2002). p. 110.

36. David L. Carter and Louis A. Radelet (1999). p. 139.

37. Jerome Skolnick (1997). Retrieved online July 5, 2004: http://www.fact-index.com/j/je/jerome_skolnick.html

38. For a full account of the Trial Lawyers Community Corrections Program, see Dennis J. Stevens (2005). *Community Corrections for a New Millenium.* Upper Saddle River, NJ: Prentice Hall. Chapter 14.

39. Chief Theron Bowman, Arlington Texas Police Department. Heritage Foundation. (October 21, 2001). Diversity, education, and professionalism: Arlington's Path to Excellence in Policing. Retrieve online August 1, 2005: http://www.heritage.org/Research/Crime/hl719.cfm

40. Bureau of Justice Statistics (2004). *Occupation Outlook Handbook.* Washington, DC: U.S. Department of Labor. Retrieved Online June 29, 2004: http://stats.bls.gov/oco/ocos160.htm

41. Dave Wedge (2004, July 16). Stun done: New law lets cops use tasers. *Boston Herald,* p. 15.

42. Of interest, tasers can kill as evidenced by the death of a young woman by the Boston Police Department during a Red Sox celebration. See Ric Kahn (2005, February 20). Tased and confused: Lifesaver, lethal weapon, aid for crowd control, tool of torture? *Boston Globe.* Retrieved online April 10, 2006: http://www.boston.com/news/local/massachusetts/articles/2005/02/20/tased_and_confused?mode=PF

43. Ellen M. Scrivner (1994). *Controlling police use of excessive force.* Washington, DC: National Institute Justice. Office of Justice Programs. NIJ 150063/. Retrieved June 22, 2004: http://www.ncjrs.org/txtfiles/ppsyc.txt

44. Ellen M. Scrivner (1994).

45. DSM IV (1994). *Diagnostic and Statistical Manual of Mental Disorders, 4th Edition.* Washington, DC: APA. pp. 649, 661.

46. Kenneth J. Peak (2006). *Policing in America.* Upper Saddle River, NJ: Prentice Hall. pp. 88–89.

47. The author included some of these points based on experience, but acting as a guide was work conducted by Dennis Nowicki (1999). Twelve traits of highly effective police officers. In Broderick, *Police in a time of change* (44–46). Law and Order.

48. On-the-Job Stress in Policing—Reducing It, Preventing It (2000, January) Washington, DC: National Institute of Justice Journal. NCJ 180079. Retrieved June 24, 2004. http://www.ncjrs.org/pdffiles1/jr000242d.pdf

49. On-the-Job Stress in Policing—Reducing It, Preventing It (2000, January).

50. International Association of Chiefs of Police (2006). *Police department leadership.* Retrieved online March 15, 2006: http://www.hitechcj.com/chiefslist/index.html Several authors were included: Mark Sullivan, Lieutenant Darren Stewart, and Rick Michelson.

51. Police, public safety, and homeland security issues (2005, July 25). Buffalo gives cash to man hurt while driving illegally. Retrieved online July 27, 2005: http://www.lefande.com/weblog/

52. The Officer Down Memorial. Retrieved online July 27, 2005: http://www.odmp.org/officer.php?oid=17827

13

Organizational Issues

Once you have read this chapter, you will be able to:

- Articulate the central theme or focus of this chapter.
- Describe the rationale of police privatization.
- Characterize both positive and negative perspectives of privatizing law enforcement agencies.
- Describe governmental incentives to ensure accountability of private police agencies.
- Explain the issues related to a paramilitary model of policing and the recommendations to control stress.
- Characterize the reason command supports a paramilitary model of policing.
- Describe the advantages of decentralizing the lines of authority.
- Explain the rationale and outcomes of rank and the hierarchical of command.

- Describe how empowering police officers might advance professionalism.

- Discuss the issues linked to a downward–upward approach of communication.

- Articulate the advantages of horizontal communication.

- Describe advantages arising from a professionalized police agency.

- Identify and explain 10 steps toward police organizational change.

- Identify two examples that support the idea that a flattening of authority and elimination of the bureaucratic military model of policing can lead to quality decision-making responsibilities of police personnel.

- Describe the primary obstacle faced by a police agency in transition from a paramilitary model to a problem-solving agency.

- Define the neutral zone and explain its relevance toward department change.

KEY TERMS

Decentralized lines of authority

Horizontal communication

Neutral zone
Privatization

INTRODUCTION

Evidence continues to mount confirming the idea that just being a member of an organization can provide so much stress and opportunities toward corruption for an individual that unless appropriate organizational changes are made, personnel are more likely to fail than succeed.

This is the final chapter of a four part series about programs and change. The focus of Chapter 13 advances the idea that because officer stress originates and is reinforced by the police organization, officer stress is a symptom of an antiquated system that has performed well and now, must be redesigned to meet the challenges of a new people, a new time. To "cure" organizational ills such as police officer stress, several ideas (although most of them have been around for a while) are provided in this chapter and they may or may not be "best" answers, but are provided to foster additional dialogue towards change. The centerpiece of organizational change is to enhance professionalism associated with the occupation of law enforcement, and the issues raised in this chapter include privatization of police agencies and governmental incentives to guide privatization accountability, elimination of the paramilitary model of policing philosophy, redesigned deployment priorities of tactical units, decentralization and a flattening of the bureaucratic chain-of-command, and a redesigned communication and empowered relationship between between officers and superiors, encouraging a mentorship. An example around the experiences of New Orleans police officers after Hurricane Katrina destroyed that city is provided to demonstrate what can happen when central command remains steadfast to its authority rather than flattening that authority which would lead to the decision-making responsibilities of personnel who implement, operate, and evaluate specific initiatives and strategies—the street cop. Two examples are provided supporting a flattened authority and empowerment: the rise of females to command positions and an enhanced system to aid domestic violence victims. Ten steps to change a police organization are offered along with experiences of a police agency that attempted (and succeeded) in a transitition from a paramilitary reactive agency to a prosocial preventive one.

That said, it is unlikely that all of the suggestions and recommendations from this chapter and the other chapters in this series (Chapter 10-13) are appropriate for every organization and every individual police officer but they can be seen as a work in progress adding to the hundreds of writers cited throughout this work who have a single thought in mind—to guide police policymakers towards reducing stress among officers and their constituents. In a concluding paragraph of this chapter and this book, the question about organizational membership and behavior are answered.

PRIVATIZATION OF LOCAL POLICE DEPARTMENTS

A thought shared by some observers that would resolve police organizational problems including street cop stress is privatization among departments. *Privatization* consists of private enterprises as opposed to public operations. This is not necessarily a new idea, and has been around for some time. A global phenomenon was first widely noted by a 1972 Rand Corporation study commissioned by the National Institute of Justice.[1] In fact, a global privatization trend of police services is growing.[2] Others have observed a "quiet revolution" toward private policing in Canada, and in both Western and Eastern Europe.[3] In fact, private security companies are used extensively in England to perform the duties of sworn officers whom they presently outnumber, claims one source.[4] An update of the original Rand assessment in 1985 concludes that private security outspent public law enforcement by 73% and employed two and a half times as many people.[5]

Historically, recall that Pinkerton agents were hired by early American companies to keep railroads safe and helped develop the U.S. Secret Service.[6] Of particular concern, however, is that the earlier private concerns were unable to suppress riots, demonstrations, and strikes that became frighteningly frequent during the 1830s without the assistance of the militia.[7] The Coal Police, Railroad Police, and company town police agencies hired by industrials were used against Irish and German immigrants in the urban seacoast slums to break strikes and suppress hunger riots. More often, military personnel were deputized for guard duty or for the duration of a strike. Even today, private guards pop up everywhere, patrolling shopping malls, workplaces, apartment buildings, and neighborhoods. The phenomenal growth of massive private shopping malls, gated communities, and the steady loss of public police patrols means the public is more likely to encounter private security than public police on a daily basis.[8] The business and industrial communities already pay for security in malls, stores, offices, banks, manufacturing plants, and highly congested public places such as New York City's Grand Central Station. There is a small, privately owned police organization called the Cincinnati Private Police whose officers have the same powers as city police officers and enforce criminal laws and ordinances.[9] Their officers patrol certain sections of the city as well as special events. The Cincinnati Private Police was established in 1914 as the Private Police Association Company.

As federal funding recedes, many municipalities are looking to cut costs further by hiring "rent-a-cops" to work ambulance services and parking enforcement, as well as to watch over crime scenes and transport prisoners who increasingly face incarceration in corporate-run prisons. Privatization extends to the federal government, which is increasingly handing over security functions to corporations, particularly in airports. In 1971, there were 5,000 federal police providing security at government buildings. Today there are 409, with private contract guards making up the difference. Private cops have been part of the U.S. Department of Energy sites across America and overseas for the past 30 years.[10] Often, these officers hold similar law enforcement powers as sworn officers. Additionally, in a recent visit to the Federal Law Enforcement Training Center (FLETC) at Glynco, Georgia, the police department, which provides public safety for this federal facility, is a privately owned organization whose officers have detainment and use of excessive force mandates similar to public officers.[11] The FLETC instructs some 30,000 federal and local enforcement officers each year. In this regard, the Office of Personnel Management (OPM) has a private organization performing background investigations for federal jobs.

As rent-a-cops supplant functions once performed by police, the private security industry is creating a separate and unequal system under which the rich protect their privileges and guard their wealth from barbarians at the gate. These heavily armed private guards are accountable not to the public, but to the well-manicured hand that feeds them.[12] Meanwhile, it is left to public police forces to maintain a coercive order within deteriorating inner cities. If the present path were uninterrupted and policymakers rejected redesigned police organizational structures and initiatives, one guess is that public officers would eventually become ghetto fighters and private policing would police all the other jurisdictions.[13]

There is little question that policymakers, interest groups, and the American public know little about policing, yet there is a consensus that they want change. One issue is that they cannot agree on what to change, although police professional conduct is on the agenda, as discussed in Chapter 1.[14] The public and experts have concerns about police privatization, too.

Privatization Concerns

It would seem that public accountability of a private enterprise is the primary argument against privatization, in addition to the compliance of federal and local laws and regulations. Will private cops also be defenders of the Constitution or will they pay homage to their employers?

When Vera Institute of Justice (VIJ) researchers examined the privatization of police, they asked: How are private police actually held accountable for effectiveness and misconduct? What criteria are used to assess their effectiveness? Are there incentives for superior performance?

During a VIJ study, researchers explored the nature of internal monitoring and disciplinary structures, media coverage of the security service, civil and criminal actions filed against private police officers, the role of the public police in monitoring misconduct among private police, and the role of trade associations in setting and overseeing performance standards.[15]

Three case studies conducted by VIJ (Private Police Lessons from New York, Johannesburg, and Mexico City) show that private police can be made accountable. While governmental controls played a limited role, they can still be powerful incentives for private firms to develop internal controls. The firms examined felt strong incentives to avoid embarrassment to their clients, and displayed a clear aversion to civil lawsuits filed against their officers. Government oversight that threatened embarrassment to their clients when their private security firms misbehaved seemed to be potentially effective, as were laws that make clients and security firms liable in the civil courts for the misconduct of their officers. On the other hand, where public accountability does not result in strong internal accountability, it appears to be relatively ineffective. External accountability may have symbolic importance in its own right, but its functional importance appears to lie in its ability to provoke effective management and internal controls. This may turn out to be true of external accountability for public police as well.[16]

Privatization Studies

More than a decade ago, a comprehensive assessment of private policing in the United States concluded that it might prove more benign than some experts had feared.[17] The authors of that assessment saw the trend toward privatization as irreversible, but they concluded that private policing was appropriate for certain routine police activities such as surveillance, parking enforcement, and traffic control. They predicted that privatization of some services would allow public police to concentrate on activities requiring more education and training. Five years later, however, another report showed that private police had begun to perform all activities once thought to be the exclusive domain of the public police.[18] Nonetheless, while privatization studies might indicate that the trend toward privatization is irreversible, it might also represent a cyclical trend, from private to public to private, every 125–150 years.[19] Any conclusions at this point might be indecisive if that thought has any validity.

Government Incentives to Guide Accountability of Private Police

It is suggested that government can align incentives to private police agencies by ensuring that the employers of private police are:

- Periodically reviewed by an oversight agency that aggressively seeks public comment on the performance of the private firm.
- Subject to civil liability in the courts for the misconduct of their officers; required to provide training to their officers appropriate to the roles they will play.
- Required to document an annual review of each officer's performance against written standards.
- Required to maintain records of their officers' movement and activities for occasional external review.
- Encouraged to participate in professional associations that certify firms' compliance with industry standards.

These safeguards can protect against misconduct by private police. But the strongest incentive for high standards of behavior by private police is accountability of the organization to its clients. As long as clients have an interest in respectful conduct by private police, the behavior of the officers is likely to be held to a high standard. Yet, there are concerns about what a high standard really means and how to enforce those standards. Suppose a managing director of a private police agency says, "No, our board has changed our standards." Can a private police agency, duly sworn under state law with all the duties and authority of regular police officers, with jurisdiction over a large land and population mass within a municipality, operate independently and without public oversight or review?[20]

One answer arises from Mercer University in Georgia where a legal complaint sought a temporary restraining order against Mercer and its private police department. The plaintiff asked that either the court declare immediately that the Mercer University Police Department is, under Georgia definition, a public agency and therefore subject to the Open Records Act, or that it force the Mercer police to stop acting as a public agency. Similar lawsuits were pending across the country in the summer of 2004. In the other three cases, one school is being sued over its police records by a former student, one by the commercial newspaper in the city, and one by a former student, all of which illustrates the diverse and very public interests in what the campus police are doing. All the other schools—Harvard University, Cornell University, and Taylor University (in Indiana)—claim, as Mercer does, that they are private institutions and that their campus police records are not subject to their respective states' open records laws.

In the case of Mercer, their campus police have full arrest powers, carry guns, make arrests, and charge violators with crimes. But there is no way for any citizen to access their records. If campus police departments function solely as security guards who patrol and call in the city police for investigations and arrests, the universities might have a better case for claiming what they do is all a private matter.

The way the Mercer Police Department is designed seems similar to the analogy with a walking, talking, quacking duck. If you act like a police department, are equipped and have the powers of a police department, then you should abide by the same rules the others do. It might be well into the fall of 2006 that these cases will be resolved.

The private security industry's rapid growth challenges those seeking progressive solutions to problems of crime and violence. Calling for more authority for public police is not an appealing remedy in communities where police-inflicted beatings like that rained on Rodney King are the rule rather than the exception. Community organizations are emerging that recognize the dangers of placing too much trust in either public or private police, while acknowledging the need for action to combat crime, which strikes disproportionately at low-income neighborhoods. The Oakland-based Center for Third World Organizing has helped to bring some sponsors of locally focused initiatives together to share strategies and resources.

The nationwide Campaign for Community Safety and Police Accountability (CCSPA) addresses the need to make security forces accountable to the public while implementing programs designed to reduce crime by meeting social needs. The organization calls for programs geared toward ending police brutality, giving communities greater control over anti-crime resources, and generating alternatives to imprisonment. Such efforts pose a progressive alternative to vigilante-style neighborhood watch groups and the increased deployment of armed guards from the public and private sector.

Community initiatives to rein in police forces need to focus on the abusive potential of the private security industry as well. In a democracy, a public police force, with all their abuses, have at least a theoretical potential for accountability through citizen review boards and other community pressures. Private security firms, however, are inherently a law unto themselves, only accountable to the corporate bottom line.[21] In what way would private police reduce street cop stress? Frankly, it appears that it might escalate stress if the FBI's war on terror can be used as an guide. That is, private cops would hold more power than public cops and private cops are still rent-a-cops. Then, too, does anyone or any organization have the right to operate a private police force with full state powers, without public oversight?

PARAMILITARY MODEL OF POLICING

Chapter 7 examined the paramilitary model of policing and it was determined that a military philosophy within a police organization is counterproductive, especially among community relations or preventive initiatives. A product of the paramilitary philosophy is the common callouts of tactical units. Both the philosophy and the tactical units create more problems than they resolve among police officers and the public because the military is trained to defeat an enemy and is less concerned about collateral damage. Police activities of public safety are a distraction from the primary directive of a military unit. America has (sadly) learned that military units acting as peacekeepers alienate the population.

In America, paramilitary police units or tact units have metastasized from emergency response teams to a standard part of everyday policing and have moved from the hot spots in the ghetto to the suburbs. Under a guise of community and problem-oriented policing initiatives, tact unit intervention has become commonplace.[22] As this trend picks up speed, given the war on terrorism and the (suspect) generosity of the U.S. government to local departments, it appears to be the future of American police initiatives. For that reason it deserves further mention associated with street cop stress because many commanders and apparently some members of the public feel the best response to crime, drugs, and terrorism are paramilitary tact units staffed by young warriors equipped with military assault weapons trained by U.S. Army Special Ops commandos.[23] A reverse trend is required to prevent street cop stress (and ultimate government control over a free nation) because a paramiliatary police agency does not deal with issues of crime nor does it deal with democratic principles. The truth is that crime cannot and will not be eliminated. The best we can expect is to control it. As for democracy, that's another matter that is at risk as long as the philosophy of a paramilitary model of policing is a priority.

If tact units are a necessary (which they are on a limited basis) evil, then deploy them to aid community stability. For example, HomeSight, an affordable housing development corporation in southeast Seattle supported by the Community Safety Initiative (CSI), had always focused on increasing home ownership to stabilize poor, crime-ridden neighborhoods.[24] When gang members threatened community members, the organization contacted the Seattle Police Department's Weed and Seed commander, and a unique partnership was born—one that would earn HomeSight and its police partners one of seven national MetLife Foundation Community-Police Partnership Awards in 2003.

Three components of HomeSight's strategy were to more explicitly share information and resources with the police department, target its development efforts in high-crime areas and involve police in its planning, and build the capacity of business owners and residents to organize and address crime problems. HomeSight embraced its responsibility to improve public safety conditions and communicated and cooperated with the police department through Seattle's Weed and Seed. To create a stronghold in the neighborhood, HomeSight acquired several lots, and the police department complemented these efforts with increased patrols and enforcement on these blocks.

HomeSight began to use its primary funding stream, real estate development financing, to advance crime reduction efforts. But the multimillion-dollar project planners felt they could produce more than homeownership opportunities and asked the police department to participate in the planning stages of the project. The project produced a 75-unit residential development for first-time home buyers.

While the community development corporation finalized the financing and predevelopment process, their police partners asked to use the site for SWAT team training. HomeSight agreed and it appeared that as a training site it strengthened organizational ties with the police department, increased police presence where it had been lacking, and, with police department backing of the project, helped HomeSight acquire demolition permits for the existing structure. Furthermore, the heightened police presence kept crime down during the 2 years of project construction, thereby minimizing construction and cleanup costs.

This continued partnership between the police department and HomeSight has taught both parties the benefits that come from combining law enforcement and community development strategies to revitalize and empower low-income and crime-ridden neighborhoods.

One safeguard might be for civilian supervision and accountability measures to ensure the public that tact units are upholding the law and defending the U.S. Constitution.

This notion should not be understood as an antipolice message, quite the opposite. The military system with its paramilitary tact units, rigid organizational structure, and authoritarian management style is called into question. That is, associated with the paramilitary model of policing is a hierarchy chain of command operating in a bureaucratic impersonal structure, which from all standards lends less to public safety but more to government power, and has earned itself the distinction of being the centerpiece of law enforcement officer stress. The primary components of the paramilitary model of policing that require change (it should be noted that these components are in no particular order and both compliment and affect one another) include its hierarchy, decentralized lines of authority, organizing toward empowerment, hidden agendas among policymakers, rank and hierarchy, and communication standards.

Hierarchy

One way to describe most police organizations is to say that command represents a paramilitary pyramid—commands flow from the top of the organization to lower levels—and reports of progress flow from subordinates upward to supervisors.

Law enforcement officers have little if any influence over command decisions or policy in this agreement. Police structures have been hotly debated for that reason, as discussed in Chapter 7. Supporters argue that reinforcing the hierarchy, including the paramilitary structure, within police organizations and providing greater resources for aggressive strategies such as patrols, zero tolerance, and tact units are the most effective ways to guarantee crime reduction and public safety.[25] Others question the long-term utility of such an approach and seek redesign of police agencies consistent with decentralized structure.[26] Decentralization will help in controlling stress among street officers, enhance their professionalism, and improve their quality of performance when delivering police services. Then, too, decentralization shifts authority and responsibility to others further down the chain of command, aiding personnel who would have never had an opportunity toward top command jobs.

Decentralized lines of authority refers to a shift of authority from a central or upper place to another less central place (reduce the orders from the top of the organizational pyramid and the reports from the bottom, as described above). It has been done once with great success when division commanders were provided the authority to make specific divisional decisions as opposed to the chief making all the decisions. Now, decentralization should be flattened more within the division to other personnel. It could be argued that when the bureaucratic hierarchy maintains centralized control over police personnel, the quality of police services is at risk, and confusion and chaos rule the day.

Take Hurricane Katrina, for example. After Katrina left the Mississippi gulf coast and the city of New Orleans, crater-sized destruction jarred the population into desperation, which spared few homes, businesses, schools, or churches.[27] Buried alive in Katrina's jaws, life rafts of food, electricity, and public safety were unusually delayed, and protecting any thin possession including your life depended on how strongly an individual accepted man's primitive desire to survive through the use of the natural law of retribution better known as *lex talionis* (an eye for an eye).[28] Prescriptions went unfilled, toilets never flushed, and children hadn't sung, if you could find them or their pets (over 3,000 children were separated from parents/caretakers, and many continue to be missing).[29] Eight months later on the Mississippi gulf coast cell phones and public safety were finally back to normal aside from police command operating from trailers and abandoned warehouses.[30] How well did law enforcement fair since Katrina touched land in August 2005?

Examining New Orleans Police Department's (NOPD) experiences might serve to answer this question because what happened in New Orleans didn't stay in New Orleans, because those experiences were shared among law enforcement officers throughout every jurisdiction along Katrina's path to some degree or another. For instance, there were photographs of NOPD officers stealing items such as DVDs from Wal-Mart and cleaning out a variety of stores, ranging from grocery stores like the A&P in the French Quarter to pharmacies to hardware stores to gun shops to car dealerships.[31] Accusations flew about officers failing to halt looters, child molesters, and gangbangers.[32] Over 249 officers (15% of the NOPD force) allegedly deserted active duty during the storm.[33] The looting and lack of public service was eventually blamed on dedicated officers (see Chapter 1) the lack of response by the federal government, and a very angry God.[34]

Captain Kevin Anderson, NOPD commander of the 8th District based in the French Quarter, said he wasn't concerned about police staffing adding to the frustration of many officers who served the 8th District, noting that in addition to 4,000 national guards as many as 1,000 officers from federal and local agencies protected the city force.[35] A curfew was enforced everywhere including the Mississippi coast, which meant 8:00 P.M. to 5:00 A.M., and it was enforced by an armed national guard stationed along most roadways supported by concertina razor wire and ugly HMMWVs (high-mobility multi-purpose wheeled vehicles). In small communities such as Long Beach and Gulf Port, Mississippi, 200 state troopers from Virginia and 45 mounted horse patrols from Fort Lauderdale were bitterly engaged in public safety because of the looting and disrespect for life and property, particularly by outsiders.[36] But, like most local cops, Captain Marlon DeFillo, NOPD spokesman, said 1,450 New Orleans police officers were on duty, working 12-hour shifts, but the actual number of hours, according to the officers interviewed, was far more, resulting in their inability to tend to the needs of their own families, 7 days a week. Several months later, most officers were still trying to receive their overtime pay. And although many officers were eventually cleared of looting, many were suspended without pay for a period of time because the allegations were that they failed to stop others from looting, raping, and terrorizing the public.

One New Orleans officer says, "If officers were among some of the desperate survivors stranded throughout New Orleans, that didn't count with the boss. Many officers went to work in whatever district they lived in and since communications were nonexistent, it was useless to contact others.[37] Also, a few dedicated cops who I know had large families to take care of and had no help from any official so they took care of their families first."[38] Another officer adds, "Hell, even Chief Eddie Compass stepped down to take care of his family after Katrina."[39] An 8th distinct officer states, "Hell yeah, a few of our guys [cops] were cowards, and we'll take care of them when and if they return, but most of New Orleans' finest were out there going above and beyond. I watched my partner perform so bravely that I wanted to give her a medal myself."[40]

As for the investigations, because so many vehicles including police vehicles were destroyed, officers patrolled in their own private cars (if they weren't destroyed), and other officers commandeered vehicles from dealerships. More than 200 vehicles were taken from the Sewell Cadillac Chevrolet dealership in New Orleans, and in the most chaotic hours after Hurricane Katrina, some NOPD officers pulled up outside the mobile command center at Harrah's Casino in bright, shiny Cadillac SUVs.[41] The fancy rides appeared at a time when a desperate force, having already lost scores of its marked units to floodwaters, was siphoning gas from abandoned vehicles scattered throughout the city. But officers "thought they were operating under emergency orders that allowed them to commandeer necessary supplies," a brave officer says.[42]

As investigations later showed, the police were either obtaining critical supplies for their own efforts or removing potentially attractive targets for looters.[43] Looters used garbage cans and inflatable mattresses to float away with food, blue jeans, tennis shoes, TV sets—even guns. Outside one pharmacy, thieves commandeered a forklift and used it to push up the storm shutters and break through the glass. The driver of a nursing-home bus surrendered the vehicle to thugs rather than being murdered.

The centerpiece lies in the enormous sacrifices made by local and federal law enforcement officers who delivered police services to individuals affected by Katrina. Because of a bureaucratic hierarchy bound in a chain of command, a sensationalized press, and agenda-ridden interest groups, it is doubtful that the "real" stories of these gallant men and women will ever be told. Also because of law enforcement command inadequacies, it is doubtful that the "real" problems of law enforcement will be critically investigated. There are large lessons that can be learned as a result of Katrina that could aid law enforcement policymakers to prepare for the anticipated collateral damage that will arise from terrorism, national calamities, and epidemics in 21st-century America. Finally in this regard, much of this new knowledge will help to control stress among street cops because the problem-solving processes will move into the decision-making responsibilities of the personnel who implement, operate, and evaluate police initiatives and strategies.

One way to interpret the experiences of officers linked to Katrina is that citizens retaliated against authority in part because of a perceived unjust hurricane, which officials, civic leaders, and ministers across the United States promoted. Citizens were more likely to retaliate against the most visible form of authority, cops. The more an officer experienced citizen retaliation, the more likely an officer questioned his or her mission of public safety. This thought is consistent with writers who see vengeance and retaliation as a common response among (ancient and modern) populations that have fewer "perceived" alternatives than other populations.[44] For instance, looting and gang activity were so widespread in New Orleans that police officers were ordered to forget search-and-rescue missions, and return to the besieged streets to stop violence that had uncompromisingly placed the public at risk.[45] Officially, law enforcement command was unprepared for Katrina but when it tried to rally through its adequated chain of command, officers continued to make independent decisions, or what can be called street justice, as the righteous response to belligerent and defiant Katrina victims.[46] The more law enforcement practiced street justice, the more often the police organizational structure should have realized it was an inadequate method of command, both before and after Katrina.[47]

A flattened system of authority would be more efficient with the shifting paradigm in policing—from an emphasis on a paramilitary bureaucratic structure to one more reliant on communication, community relations, and empowerment.[48] When police agencies move toward a decentralized command model, they have contributed to enhancing dedicated officers by increasing the success of minorities including women in policing and victims.[49] There is a concern of developing a mini-hierarchy; however, the primary goal is an attempt to move problem-solving processes into the decision-making responsibilities of the personnel who must implement, operate, and evaluate specific initiatives and strategies. Had that been done in New Orleans, how better would the officers have faired in the performance and the impressions of the public?

Flattened authority enhances compliance to policy and regulations and opportunities for advancement, and aids in improving quality of life experiences among victims.[50] Compliance suggests that when officers have input into the decision-making process, they tend to comply with the final decisions more often than those who do not (this could have improved the performance of officers in New Orleans). Opportunities might include enhancing officer development and merited promotion and improving the quality of life experiences among victims. For instance, to help in a better understanding of the products of a flattened bureaucratic military model of policing, two examples might help: the slow rise of female executives to command positions and the success narratives associated with empowered domestic violence officers.

Slow rise of female executives to police command

The second issue is equally important but not as flamboyant as Katrina. The rise to top police positions in several major U.S. cities has been well documented as the lines of authority moved from hieratical structures to level structures, giving others a chance to advance themselves. The new top police executives at six large jurisdictions—Atlanta, Boston, Detroit, Fairfax County (Virginia), Milwaukee, and San Francisco—share similar credentials and they all boast over two decades of law enforcement experience.[51] All have worked their way up the ranks, and all are women (as discussed in Chapter 6).[52]

For most of these women, being named to the top-cop position was not the fulfillment of a lifelong dream. In fact, as girls they did not see these jobs as even a possibility because women simply did not hold those positions. "Not in my wildest dreams did I think I'd be in this position," says Boston's Commissioner Kathleen O'Toole.[53]

"When I first came on the police department, we were trained in a more paramilitary-type environment," says Commissioner O'Toole.[54] "We were trained as soldiers to go out and fight the war on crime, and it was the police versus the community. We came to realize in the mid- to late-80s that that model of policing was failing miserably," the Commissioner explains.[55]

Margaret Moore, formerly the highest-ranking woman in the Federal Bureau of Alcohol, Tobacco and Firearms, says that the literature indicates the support for community policing is stronger among women, who have traditionally shown better communication skills.[56] Still, the paramilitary structure—which works well for critical incidents—continues to "hang on by their nails," Moore says, despite the arrival of high-profile female chiefs. "Don't undervalue what women bring to policing," Moore adds. "I wouldn't call it the feminization of policing, but a little gender balancing and critical mass could certainly change the way we do policing in this country."

Empowered domestic violence officers

Another success story emerging from a decentralization and an empowered (discussed later in the chapter) unit to enhance public safety relates to the 83rd Precinct of the New York Police Department's domestic violence program.[57] The program is operated in cooperation with the Victims Service Agency, which provides professional counseling and social service follow-up in cases involving domestic violence calls to the precinct. The program is administered by one sergeant and five police officers assigned to the 83rd Precinct to track all domestic violence cases in the command. They advise and make referrals for victims of domestic violence. Each member of the team is empowered to make appropriate decisions from the bases of the original contact to follow-up reviews of the referrals. There were over 7,600 domestic violence reports prepared in 2002, and in 2003, domestic violence was down by 25% because of the efforts of the domestic violence unit. It is in the best interests of a police department to organize toward empowerment of their officers in order for officers to bring the department closer to its goals, aid victims, and enhance the professionalism of the personnel.

Organizing toward Empowerment

Some authors feel that changing titles and rank structure is not enough to elevate the professional standing of police officers.[58] The suggestion is to decrease the number of levels of authority, especially at the bottom of the hierarchy, in order to enhance officer professionalism and aid in victim outcomes, as discussed above. For instance, some police strategies associated with community relations require an officer's independent action to resolve a specific community problem through empowered participation with community members and in collaboration with other public personnel. As discussed earlier, strategies linked to community relations promotes stress for street cops in the first place since most officers involved with those strategies actually hold little authority to fulfill the expectations of the job. "I wanna help ya little brother, but I don't have the clout to do it," says a Chicago street cop when explaining his response to a victim.[59] By providing appropriate authority (and training) to accomplish community relation objectives, professionalism would be enhanced, officers involved in the problem-solving activities would be less stressed and more accomplished, community member respect for law enforcement would be improved, and issues such as fear of crime would be curbed.

Such a version of street cop responsibilities is a far cry from the realities of most experiences. Most officers spend a great deal of time riding in a patrol vehicle, filling out paperwork, and complying to the rigid structure of detailed rules that will keep the officer from being criticized or penalized by supervisors.[60]

One officer explains his work day, which includes a wide variety of duties. He says that he might spend the first part of his shift on neighborhood patrol, he could take a couple of hours directing traffic or cleaning up an accident, and then he might investigate an assault charge or a burglary. He adds: "A large part of any police officer's day is paperwork! We have to document everything we do, because the information may be critical later as trial evidence. These days we have computers to help us, and it's important to know how to use them because they save a lot of time that we can put to better use out on the street."[61]

A police expert notes:

> The dominant form of policing today continues to view police officers as automations. Despite an awareness that they exercise broad discretion, they are held to strict account in their daily work—for what they do and how they do it . . . especially in procedural matters, they are required to adhere to detailed regulations. In a large police agency, rank and file police officers are often treated impersonally and kept in the dark regarding policy matters. Officers quickly learn, under these conditions, that the rewards go to those who conform to expectations—that nonthinking compliance is valued.[62]

These two accounts of the daily activities of a street cop suggest that professionalism, especially associated with autonomy, is lacking. Some experts suggest that most of these controls are set in order for a supervisor to focus on promotions without interference from the "troops" under his or her command.[63] As many of the participants in the study conducted for this work made clear, most of their superiors used intimidation to keep subordinates under control. By organizing for empowerment, professionalism would be enhanced, and a new philosophy of control would be advanced: manage subordinates through their own shared values and personal commitment to professionalization rather than intimidation and orders from the "high command."[64]

Hidden Agendas among Policymakers

It appears that there is a hidden agenda among some policymakers and police superiors associated with a paramilitary model that can be traced to a priority of internal discipline of officers through a bureaucratic chain of command that provides strict discipline in the name of law enforcement.[65] Police management promotes the paramilitary model because management could not avail themselves of any other options to secure internal discipline.[66] That is, one way to get control over your "troops" (and keep a commander's job while curbing potential police discretion) is through a military model, the thinking goes. However, an intrinsic weakness of the communication process in a police bureaucracy can lead to a weakening of administrative power or to leakage of authority, producing stress, corruption, and compromise of street cop integrity.[67] That is, because of its nature, it inadvertently downgrades the position of the primary figure in police service—the street cop. Isn't it true that often we think of the street cop as the lowest-ranking army person, the private? We see the shirt collar of a chief of police jammed with silver stars, suggesting what? He's a four-star general similar to General George Patton?

It is time to end the paramilitary philosophy and its hierarchical method of control and hold tact units in reserve for a real crisis as opposed to routine "lock and load" raids in targeted communities.

In this regard the charting of realistic methods of peacekeeping and crime control are profoundly incompatible with regulations of internal discipline. Also, a paramilitary perspective maintains the chain of command strategy within the police hierarchy, which clearly reduces the changes of professionalism among police officers and the police enterprise as a whole.[68] As professionalism among police officers grows, the claw of the police subculture is more likely to weaken.

Rank and Hierarchy

One argument in favor of rank and hierarchy is associated with the discipline of police officers by their superiors. However, this notion is inconsistent with writers who argue that police policymakers, administrators, and supervisors have little control over the behavior of their officers or even that they know what their officers are doing when they are on patrol.[69] They need to know, but like the rest of us, they find out from the unwanted phone call or over the local news. So how do they maintain the illusion of control? One answer is sustained by changing the "organizational focus from goal-oriented measures of effectiveness, such as community levels of crime, to a detailed, ritualistic concern for intra-organizational images of orderliness."[70] Since a chief must provide the appearance of controlling street cops, the thinking might go, street cops learn about commander inadequacy early in their career and learn to protect themselves (CYA) from administrative or policy scrutiny. So much for the idea that hierarchy and rank are associated with discipline. Cutting into the chain of command would have a tendency to enhance discipline as there would be less need for CYA initiatives and probably less reliance on peer groups or the police subculture.

The quickest way to alter the hierarchy within a paramilitary organization is to revise the police rank system. That is, utilizing nonmilitary titles for some or all personnel grades.[71] Rank in itself seems to work against professionalism in that it determines the amount of authority one individual has over another regardless of his or her knowledge. When two individuals engage in a dialogue about police policy (or anything for that matter) and one holds a greater rank such as a captain and the other holds a lesser rank such as a patrol officer, "The patrol officer can't say no to the sergeant or captain. It's the old story of power, if the patrol officer wants his duty assignments to be sweet, ya agree with the boss, like his freggin' idea or not," one Chicago street cop says.[72] In what way does rank hamper professionalism? One way is because the admission of promotion-seeking by an officer in the patrol division is enough to invite ridicule from his colleagues. Part of this flows from the difficulties of obtaining promotion in the first place and consequently reflects the dead-end nature of many police careers, ("once a patrolman, always a patrolman") the perspective goes in bigger departments. "But another part of it reflects what patrol officers regard as the insensitivity, the aloofness, the detachment, the hyper-concern for appearances, and the blatant currying of favor by sergeants with those above them in the police hierarchy."[73]

Just as an example, several federal law enforcement agencies have moved away from military icons: both the FBI and the U.S. Secret Service classify their basic officers as special agents, a term used for all nonsupervisory positions from entry level through veteran members. There's still a hierarchy but not like it had been in the past. All agents are required to be college graduates; special agents are regarded as, and expected to perform like, professionals. Police professionalism and rank seem to contradict each other regardless of which is used to describe it in relationship to other ranks.

Communication between police professionals is vital for the success of the organization and the enhancement of the profession. The hierarchical method of communication as discussed above is the downward–upward approach.

Downward communication allows police commanders a clear path to send information down. It gives organizational members job-related information, job performance review, and indoctrination in recognizing and implementing department goals. Upward communication provides commanders with a primary source of feedback, allows lower-level staff to share information with managers, and can encourage personnel participation. Both types of paths have drawbacks. Downward communication is overused; "it is often unclear and can communicate superiors' lack of regard for subordinates."[74] Also, commanders sometimes distribute contrary and confusing messages to subordinates. Upward communication can be a risky affair for subordinates because commanders might not be receptive to criticism and how many others might review the information before it arrives on the desk of the commander is never sure. Suppose a street cop has confidential or personal information? Clearly, this system does not lend itself well to a professional environment for obvious reasons of which collaboration seems to be lacking. Then, too, there are gate-keepers who control the flow of information, producing individuals with a form of power or control. Does this method set up certain staff members in powerful positions at times? Can they use information as a form of barter?

Yet the question is how does a street cop dialogue with a commander about an arrest policy and disagree with that commander? Many commanders say they have an open door policy. They have just that—the door is open. However, recall what the sample reported in the survey for this book concerning commander or supervisor: the integrity of command is weak, commanders are subjective and unfair when dealing with street cop problems, and police leadership is highly suspect. How does a typical street cop walk into a divisional commander or chief's office and discuss strategy with someone he or she doesn't trust?

Horizontal communication (across the organization) can aid professionalism and can facilitate task coordination, provide a means of sharing information, provide a formal channel of communication for problem solving, and facilitate mutual support for personnel. Communication is the key to success. However, horizontal communication could isolate groups from the hierarchy with excessive reliance on horizontal communication even without the knowledge of a user.

Horizontal communication will aid officers in enhancing their professionalism in that they can collaborate to help shape policies that affect their jobs and obtain guidance from their superiors who would play a *mentoring role* (advising and guiding). A set of written organizational rules would be established and presented to each member of the organization, possibly at the initial training stages or if transferred, during new personnel initiation workshops. In addition to well-established and explicit communication procedures, rules can be subtle and based on the social system of the organization. For instance, rules when to meet face-to-face depending on the topic, rules who should be copied, and rules requesting specific information depending on the context (i.e., complaints require time, place, and the names of officers present). Additionally, officers should learn about communicational techniques in their early training periods so that they can participate early in their career.

ADVANTAGES OF PROFESSIONALIZED POLICE OFFICERS

The literature and police practice reveal that enhancing the professionalization of officers provides many advantages associated with achieving the mission of law enforcement and the mission of this textbook—to reduce and prevent officer stress. It stands to reason that the mission and obligation of policing and a reduction and prevention of stress can be achieved more often by a professionalized police organization. For instance, implicit in reducing the fear of crime among constituents, professional officers who work hard at talking and listening to constituents can reduce constituent fear of crime and, in some cases, reduce crime itself. Also, empowered officers can perform the task of reducing the fear of crime even while they engage in other police activities.[75] Here's how law enforcement professionalization can be achieved and the fear of crime reduced at the same time without departments increasing their budgets[76]:

- Every opportunity should be taken to increase the quantity and quality of police interaction with citizens.
- Police should initiate these interactions.
- Police should become good listeners.
- Police should develop strategies to solve problems identified by citizens.
- Citizens must be actively involved in these community crime-reduction strategies.
- Police officers and supervisors must be allowed to try new approaches and fail. (Without this support, officers will not innovate or take risks.)[77]

That is, professionalization of police officers reduces the fear of crime among community members and in turn aids street cops in enhancing their own feelings about themselves.

TEN STEPS TO MANAGE ORGANIZATIONAL CHANGE

All police agencies experience varying degrees of change due to such factors as a new administration, new policing methods, or new crime trends. However, the basic characteristics are very similar regardless of the nuances of the department. True integration of a new management philosophy requires a complete organizational transformation—the "new" relates to moving from reactive to proactive strategies associated with street cop stress.

To accomplish this, an agency must adapt its infrastructure to support the philosophies and ideologies being implemented; otherwise, the culture of the agency will not change.[78] The success of a police organization toward enhancing its professional personnel in dealing with change depends, in large measure, on the ability of the organization's leadership to recognize, understand, and actively manage change at the command level. Command can implement 10 interrelated steps.[79]

1. *Awareness.* To resolve a problem, it has to be admitted first. Command has three jobs:

a. Compellingly admit that the department is at fault not completely, yet it shares in a largest part of the blame for the stressful conditions.

b. Compellingly demonstrate to street cops that they are not at fault. Street cops, in concert with organizational stressors, were infected. One very large issue would be departmental liability. But this issue cannot be a deal breaker. It has to be worked out before the organization takes steps to admit its role in the stress of its personnel. However, being aware of a problem and really knowing the problem are two different things.

c. It is strongly advised that each department (outside providers) conduct empirical research to determine the attitudes of street cops and the attitudes of command prior to organizational change.[80]

Making informed decisions has merit over simply making "gut" decisions. Also, participants will feel as though they have contributed to whatever plans for change are announced. This is a recommendation that has produced a great deal of help to many departments across the country originally made in earlier works.[81] Many departments have acknowledged their support of this recommendation.

2. *Flatten Command Structure.* The organization must be flattened relative to its power structure, its operations must be streamlined, and improvements must be made toward efficiency and effectiveness (also see Chapter 15). Also, alter the hierarchical mandate, the traditional paramilitary model of management. Police agencies can no longer be immune to downsizing, dealing with unnecessary, or outdated, programs. Sometimes, the impact of such organizational change is so great and viewed so personally that individuals within an organization cannot handle it effectively without professional assistance. When employees believe something jeopardizes their jobs or their concept of themselves in the workplace, the perceived consequence of change can be tremendous. In such circumstances, access to a skilled employee assistance program (EAP), available either within the agency or through outside referrals, becomes vitally important. Employee assistance program providers should understand the law enforcement agency, the nature and process of the change, the organization's efforts during the change, and the potential impact on its personnel. When change results in the elimination of positions and departments lay off some of their employees, EAP providers, or other job placement experts, can make the transition a little easier, both for those who leave the organization and, equally important, for those who remain behind. In this approach, the chief executive identifies the need for change and decrees its forward motion *down* the organizational structure, with minimal involvement of personnel at the lowest levels

Chapter 13 Organizational Issues 411

and little demonstrated concern for the needs or fears of the agency's "people." Understanding and mitigating the stress resulting from major organizational change on both the organization and its individual members requires recognizing that it occurs. When executives take steps to change an organization, its personnel will have a number of reactions: fear, frustration, anger, resentment, inertia, active or passive resistance, depression, and, in many cases, a welcoming of necessary improvements. The success of the change will, in large measure, depend on the executive's ability to anticipate and effectively deal with these personnel and the source of their emotions. As one information technology executive has noted, "You have to be adaptable and flexible. If you take only a collaborative approach, the change will take 3 to 5 years, which is too long given the competitive urgency. Also, keep in mind that personnel in general have reservations about any change. Patience is emphasized."[82]

3. *Communication*. During a time of change, personnel search for meaning and an understanding of the actual impact of the change on each of them as individuals. The presence of accurate and, perhaps more important, timely information delivered by credible sources on a regular basis is critical. Executives should maintain an atmosphere that encourages employee questions without concern for the truthfulness of the response or fear of overt or subtle reproach for simply asking questions.[83]

4. *Leadership Presence*. Experts have identified the "high tech, high touch" nature of future change.[84] In times of major change in a law enforcement organization, the high touch component becomes particularly noteworthy. The visible presence of an agency's leadership, its highest command officers, is necessary and, in the eyes of the agency's personnel, absolutely expected. Throughout the course of major change, an aggressive policy of "management by walking around" and a leadership style that encourages interactive interpersonal communication best serve leaders and the organization. For example, in 2003, when Chief William Bratton took over the Los Angeles Police Department, he spent a great deal of time walking around meeting patrol officers, staff, and detectives. He accepted interviews with many influential individuals from various organizations such as Jack Newfield (award-winning journalist and documentary filmmaker), Mark Jacobson (a filmmaker), and Dr. Addie Mae Miller (a candidate for mayor of Los Angeles). Chief Bratton's conspicuous presence and visible leadership clearly shows his subordinates how important they are to him and the city of Los Angeles.

5. *Encouragement*. During changes surrounding major organizational strategies, encouragement by command and police policymakers takes

two forms. First, administrators should send a clear message that the change will make the agency stronger, serve the organization's members better, and eventually become fully implemented, which shows a real end in sight. At the same time, while stress accompanies change, each employee actively should adjust to it: "The organization is going to change—it must—if it is to survive and prosper. Rather than banging your head against the wall of hard reality and bruising your spirit, invest your energy in making quick adjustments. Turn when the organization turns. Practice instant alignment. Your own decisions may do more to determine your stress level than anything the organization decides to do."[85] Second, even though the pace of change may become demanding on all elements within a department, especially its managers and supervisors, all personnel should understand that major stress requires comprehensive stress mitigation practices. The need to maintain proper dietary and nutritional habits, an ongoing physical exercise and fitness program, and acceptable outlets outside the agency for pent-up emotions remain particularly crucial for personal stress resolution during such times.

6. *Stability.* During times of significant organizational change, even the most well-adjusted professionals will feel a loss of control over their environment. While emphasizing the importance of change throughout the organization, some organizational elements or activities should remain stable. The agency's leadership should allow their personnel to feel that there is still something over which they have control or which remains familiar. Organizational change requires adjustment, and well-thought-out plans can make that adjustment, and the success of the change, far more likely.

7. *Involvement.* Major organizational change within a law enforcement agency can come from a variety of sources: a natural evolution to better meet organizational or community needs; a revolution resulting from changes in the jurisdiction's or department's leadership or occurring amid allegations of criminal or professional misconduct; or a devolution of successful programs or ideas that the agency head viewed, heard of, or read about. Regardless of the source of the change, the change most frequently comes from the top down, with little input from or involvement of those personnel most directly impacted.

Increased education of America's police officers and the changing culture of the workforce have led line personnel to expect to be involved in decisions about their on-the-job fate. The most successful efforts at major organizational change involve the affected personnel in the tactical implementation of the program, under the strategic design of the agency's leadership. Their role can allow them to feel that they "own" part of the change, that they are responsible for its success, and that they can see the value of the change to them, their jobs, and their organization.

8. *Training.* At times, communication, no matter how effective, simply is not enough. Some types of organizational change, especially the kind built on enhanced or expanded technology, require formalized programs of education and training. Such training is important to enhance the technical skills needed to handle both the immediate impact of change, as well as its long-range effects. Educational efforts can produce a greater understanding of the need for and the anticipated results of such change. The key is an organized approach ensuring that personnel throughout the agency are prepared *now* for the future of their agency and their jobs.

9. *Timing.* One attorney responsible for implementing a number of major political and organizational changes in a large state investigative agency used to say, "Timing is not an important thing, it is the *only* thing." While this adage may cause some debate, its message remains: The most successful change agents, determined to ensure the results of their efforts are lasting, plan and time their change.

   This belief applies both to initial efforts at implementing change and to subsequent efforts to fine-tune that change or implement subsequent programs, projects, or efforts. As the organization changes, the organizational culture must absorb those changes for long-term effect. As this occurs, leaders of change must ensure that they do not foster an organizational counterreaction because those responsible for implementing or being affected by change are simply overwhelmed by too much over too short a period.

10. *Managerial Burnout.* Implicit in reducing fear of crime initiatives, officers who work hard at talking and listening to constituents can reduce constituent fear of crime and, in some cases, reduce crime itself. Empowered officers moving on a professional track can perform the task of reducing the fear of crime even while they engage in other police activities. A change-oriented leadership frequently expects that the agency's managers and supervisors will adapt readily to their changes. Because individuals charged with effecting change care deeply about their organization, they are just as susceptible, sometimes even more so, to the fears, frustrations, and anxiety of their subordinates.

   Too frequently, however, executives expect those managers to keep that "stiff upper lip," relegating their personal feelings to their unexpressed subconscious. Especially in agencies undergoing waves of change—no matter how needed or well-intentioned—managers are prone to stress overload and, as a consequence, can lose some of the sharpness and tenacity so necessary for them to ensure effective change. When that occurs, the chief executive risks burning out the very individuals necessary to ensure the success of his or her efforts.

Guarding against burnout of key staff requires the same awareness and aggressive tools that can protect the organization from its own burnout. Communication, stability, and support can help prevent this problem. Furthermore, agencies must recognize that managers in an organization, regardless of their rank, loyalty, skills, and zeal, are still human and, during times of stress associated with organizational change, need the same sensitivity and respect that agencies give their line troops.

TAKING TIPS FROM A POLICE AGENCY

In an earlier project, Commander Kent Shafer of the Columbus, Ohio, Division of Police (CPD) shared information as the department tried to accomplish a transition from a paramilitary crimefighting agency to a proactive, problem-solving one.[86] The CPD focused on four activities:

1. Taught problem-solving skills to officers
2. Collected, analyzed, and disseminated crime statistics
3. Group discussions with officers about "best solutions"
4. Officers results were monitored

Through skill development, application, and feedback, their officers learned to be proficient problem solvers.

Resistance to Change

However, even though a change was publicized and command thought they were poised to be an immediate success story, the first 2 years that followed the notoriety were riffed with struggles, frustrations, and unexpected circumstances. One expert described what he called the *"neutral zone,"* a "very difficult time" when police command becomes impatient and asks, "How long is it going to take you to implement those changes?" In retrospect, the "neutral zone" seemed to be one of the experiences of men and women of the CPD, too. Top command wanted quantifiable results and put pressure on Commander Shafer's division to demonstrate success. Meanwhile, members of the new operation felt the pressure to produce, yet found they were unable to follow their own plans of operation. The principal planners were unable to successfully implement the program. Many questioned the plan itself and the ability of those involved to conduct it. Little did they know that what they were experiencing was a normal part of a process of change. What the CPD was experiencing was the unpleasant period of transition known as the neutral zone. The expert lists six steps to take to survive the neutral zone. These include:

1. Protecting people from further changes
2. Reviewing policies and procedures
3. Examining relationships and organizational structure
4. Setting short-range goals
5. Promising obtainable goals
6. Helping supervisors and managers learn what they need to function successfully

The time in the neutral zone can actually be a creative period if proper actions are taken to make it so. Without the benefit of this expert's advice, Shafer eventually discovered these steps for himself. Policies and procedures were evaluated and changed with input of workers, supervisors, and community members. Unproductive reporting relationships were changed and the organizational structure modified to make communications easier and maximize the ability of the various components to accomplish their tasks and collaborate with other units. It should be noted that almost from the beginning of the new initiative at the CPD, outside, independent evaluation was conducted by the Ohio State University Criminal Justice Research Center, under the direction of Professor C. Ronald Huff.[87] The point is, change is a lot of hard work and like all things, if success were so easily attained, it wouldn't be worthy of obtaining.

SUMMARY

This chapter is about ways to redesign the law enforcement organization to enhance the professionalization of officers, which in turn will aid in curbing officer stress. The issues examined included privatization of policing, which reveals that public policing could be reduced to ghetto fighters and private cops would perform all other police services. Private police agencies have had reasonable success among federal government facilities, gated communities, and business and industry. Public accountability of a private enterprise is the primary argument against privatization in addition to concerns about officer and agency compliance of federal and local laws and regulations.

Case studies revealed that private police can be made accountable even when governmental controls play a limited role and can be powerful incentives for private firms to develop internal controls. Private concerns develop a strong incentive to avoid embarrassment to their clients and display a clear aversion to civil lawsuits filed against their officers. On the other hand, when public accountability does not result in strong internal accountability, it appears to be relatively ineffective. To control private agencies, their officers can become subject to civil liability in the courts, similar to public officers.

The chapter continued an examination of a paramilitary model of policing that originated in Chapter 7. It was shown that the primary directive of a military unit model of policing is employed far more often than necessary and that it takes issue with public safety perspectives. A reverse trend is required to prevent street cop stress (and ultimate government control over a free nation) because a paramiliatary perspective does not deal with issues of crime nor does it enhance democratic principles. Also, because of its nature, a paramilitary model of policing inadvertently demoralizes the primary figure in police service—the street cop.

The use of tact units must be redesigned to prevent stress among officers (and the public). An example was provided in how tact units helped a community build and maintain affordable housing. An explanation as to the acceptance of the paramilitary model of policing has less to do with controling crime and more to do with commanders ensuring control over their personnel and their own jobs. The charting of realistic methods of peacekeeping and crime control are profoundly incompatible with regulations of internal discipline promoted through a paramilitary perspective, which maintains the chain-of-command strategy within the police hierarchy that reduces the changes of professionalism among police officers and the police enterprise as a whole

Decentralized lines of authority, or the flattening of the system, would become more efficient with the shifting paradigm in policing—from an emphasis on a paramilitary structure to one more reliant on communication and community relations. Agencies moving toward a decentralized command model have contributed to the increasing success of minorities, persons of color, and women in policing. Changing titles and rank within a police structure is not enough to elevate the professional standing of police officers, until the basic qualifications of police candidates are enhanced to match the responsibility and expectation of the job.

Empowering officers to provide appropriate authority (and training) to officers accomplishes community relation objectives such as problem-solving activities, officers would be less stressed and more accomplished, and equally important, professionalism would be enhanced in many ways.

The communication of the dated paramilitary system allows command a clear path to send information and orders downward, and upward communication provides commanders with a primary source of feedback, allows lower-level staff to share information with managers, and can encourage personnel participation. However, downward communication is overused, commanders sometimes distribute contrary and confusing messages to subordinates, and upward communication can be a risky affair for subordinates because commanders might not be receptive to criticism and many others including gatekeepers can review the information before it arrives (or is diverted) on the desk of the commander.

Communication between police professionals is vital for the success of the organization and the enhancement of the profession. Horizontal communication can aid professionalism and can facilitate task coordination, provide a means of sharing information, provide a formal channel of communication for problem solving, and facilitate mutual support for personnel.

Enhancing the professionalization of officers provides many advantages associated with achieving the mission of law enforcement and the mission of this textbook—to reduce and prevent stress among officers. Ten steps were offered to aid policymakers and command in changing their organization, which includes awareness, flatten command structure, communication, leadership presence, encouragement, stability, involvement, training, timing, and managerial burnout.

Finally, the Columbus, Ohio, Division of Police shared information as they tried to accomplish a transition from a paramilitary model of policing to a proactive, problem agency. Resistance to change was probably the hardest obstacle for police managers during the transition period and many of the organizational struggles, frustrations, and unexpected circumstance related to the "neutral zone." The six steps linked to this perspective include protecting people from further changes, reviewing policies and procedures, examining relationships and organizational structure, setting short-range goals, promising obtainable goals, and helping supervisors and managers learn what they need to function successfully. It was suggested that the time in the neutral zone can actually be a creative period if proper actions are taken to make it so.

CONCLUSION

Maybe Chief Norm Stamper of Seattle is right in calling for a radical, top-down reform of the institution of policing because of its inherent nature, as discussed in Chapter 1.[88] The evidence of this book suggests that his remedy seems appropriate, but for different reasons. Because officer stress originates and is reinforced by the police organization, it has been said that officer stress is actually a symptom of an antiquated system that must be redesigned to meet the challenges of a new people, a new time. But equally important, it's been accentuated that the bottom line is how each officer perceives and reacts to his or her environment when it comes to reducing stress.

Officer stress is a symptom of the antiquated system that continues to infect the young men and women of law enforcement with its contradictions, imbalance, and outdated organizational structure. To "cure" or at least to ease the stressors generated and reinforced through police organizational initiatives designed to provide public safety, reduce the fear of crime, and enhance the quality of life for their constituents, this book has twisted through some pretty amusing worlds in an effort to tell our cops to take of themselves.

Nonetheless, the hypothesis of the work has been supported. That is, organizational membership guides and sometimes dictates the behavior of its membership. At an extreme, belonging to an organization can by its very nature turn nonviolent individuals into killers and violent men and women into passive beings. Although many observers want to deemphasize the police organization as the primary stressor and focus on the individual, let's understand two important conceptual elements:

1. Law enforcement is a complex profession because it and the populations policed by them are always changing. For example, technological advancements, initiatives, partnerships, laws, and regulations change often. Then, too, communities change in the sense of culture, language, customs, and expectations. It seems every change in the environment from the construction of new subdivisions, name changes of buildings, parks, and streets to new model vehicles and new criminal procedural mandates during an encounter with a citizen, requires a learning process for law enforcement officers regardless of the amount of knowledge they possessed yesterday.

2. There are indicators that law enforcement training tends to be inadequate in today's changing world, but what about tomorrow? One reason this question is asked goes beyond the changing conditions of both the police organization and the populations policed, but what is known about most individuals is that they tend not to "rise to the occasion," but rather they default to the level of their training. Generally, when police officers engage the public, especially with the employment of new technology or initiatives, they fall back on their learned responses. Most of those responses have been generated and reinforced by their police organization.

Therefore, even as stress training improves or an officer successfully copes with the ghosts of his or her stress, we're rearranging the chairs on the *Titanic*. Policymakers and the public must understand the big picture and provide the assistance to redesign one of the most important institutions in a free society. Consider the alternatives? In every previous society known to historians, when the welfare of its criminals took precedence over common good and morality, those civilizations eventually perished. We take great pride in administering due process guarantees among violators, even those who torture our children; we build technologically advanced facilities to house and feed those violators according to code; yet we ignore the humanness of the individuals who apprehend them as we indulge ourselves in the amenities of freedom, forgetting it has a price, which can be called responsibility. In the final chapter of this book, the examples of Hurricane Katrina experiences and the rise of females to top command positions supported the idea that an attempt to move problem-solving processes into the decision-making responsibilities of the personnel who must implement, operate, and evaluate specific initiatives and strategies would enhance the delivery of police services and probably reduce stress among street cops. Responsibility includes the thought that yes, we are responsible in accessing police conduct and changing police policy, but it also suggests that the police cannot and should not represent the only solution toward law and order in America.[89]

WHAT WOULD YOU DO IF YOU WERE IN CHARGE?

Dogged by scandal, the Los Angeles Police Department looked beyond human judgment to technology to identify bad cops.[90] July 25, 2005, is the day the agency began using a $35 million computer system that tracks complaints, lawsuits, uses of force, and other data about officers and alerts supervisors to possible signs of misconduct. The system is central to a federal oversight program ordered by the U.S. Justice Department after a wave of abuse allegations in the 1990s cast doubt on the LAPD's ability and willingness to police itself.

Community leaders hope the tracking system can restore public confidence shaken by high-profile shootings and scandals involving the LAPD. "I don't think any single thing will solve problems with the Police Department. But this could go a long way toward doing it," said the Rev. Cecil "Chip" Murray, an activist and former pastor of First African Methodist Episcopal Church. Although safeguards have been built into the system, any officer whose conduct differs sharply from their peers automatically gets flagged. That could mean a vice detective who fires significantly more shots than other investigators or antigang cops with a high number of excessive force complaints.

If the system pinpoints unusual conduct, it triggers an electronic message to direct supervisors, who must take a second look. The notices also travel up the command chain to a deputy chief as an extra level of oversight. Managers can access the system anywhere in the department through an internal Web site. Depending on their conduct, some officers could be ordered to undergo more training or counseling. Follow-up investigations could lead to firing or criminal charges. Some rank-and-file officers fear the tracking system could mistakenly tag hardworking personnel and hurt their careers.

"How many times do you have to get triggered before they slow you down, transfer you, and you get a bad reputation?" said Gary Ingemunson, independent counsel for the union that represents LAPD officers. "The subtle message is: stay in the middle of the pack. Don't stand out." Union lawyers also argue that bad cops could game the system by curbing their activities just enough to avoid being detected, while good cops might hesitate in life-and-death situations due to concerns about getting flagged.

"A lot of hesitation could get somebody killed," Ingemunson said. Police Chief William Bratton questions whether anything can end abuse and corruption by officers.

"Nothing will eliminate it," Bratton said as the city announced that payouts from a corruption scandal at the Rampart Division would cost taxpayers nearly $70 million.

"As long as you have police officers, you always have the potential for corruption," Bratton said. "As long as you have human beings, there is potential for crime."

Meanwhile, accusations of abuse persisted. Last year, the department fielded nearly 6,500 complaints ranging from excessive force to racial profiling. About 14% have been sustained, with 1,400 still under investigation. By comparison, there were 5,212 complaints in 1999, with 36% upheld after nearly all the investigations were completed.

OFFICER KILLED IN MICHIGAN

Police Officer Scot Beyerstedt of the Mattawan, Michigan, Police Department was killed in a vehicle pursuit on Tuesday, July 26, 2005.[91] Officer Beyerstedt succumbed to injuries sustained the previous night when his patrol car crashed during a vehicle pursuit at approximately 2100 hours. He and his training officer were pursuing a vehicle on 24th Street after trying to stop it for driving recklessly on I-94. The patrol car left the roadway and struck a tree as it rounded an S-curve.

Both officers were transported to Bronson Methodist Hospital where Officer Beyerstedt succumbed to his injuries the following day. Officer Beyerstedt was not wearing his seatbelt at the time of the accident. The vehicle they were pursuing fled the scene and the driver remains at large.

The 21-year-old officer had served as a part-time officer for the agency for only 2 weeks and had previously served with the Cassapolis Police Department.

DISCUSSION QUESTIONS

1. Explain the central focus or theme of this chapter and describe in your own words what you think is meant by this theme. In what way do you think this theme is supported in this chapter? Not supported?

2. Describe the rationale of police privatization. In what way would privatization overcome the problems faced by public law enforcement agencies?

3. Characterize both positive and negative perspectives of privatizing law enforcement agencies. How would the public respond to a rent-a-cop after being stopped for a traffic violation and after a 911 call for help?

4. Describe governmental incentives to ensure accountability of private police agencies. In what way do you see these incentives as working or failing?

5. Explain the issues related to a paramilitary model of policing and the recommendations to control stress. In what way is the paramilitary model compatible or incompatible with the mission and purpose of law enforcement?

6. Characterize the reason commanders support a paramilitary model of policing.

7. Describe advantages and disadvantages of decentralizing the lines of authority.

8. Explain the rationale and outcomes of rank and the hierarchy of command.

9. Describe how empowering police officers would advance their professionalism. Provide any examples from experiences on the job, from another job, or situations in the newspapers.

10. Describe two examples that support the idea that a flattening of authority and elimination of the bureaucratic military model of policing can lead to quality decision-making responsibilities of the police personnel who actually operationalize police initiatives. In what way do you agree or disagree with these examples?

11. Discuss the issues linked to a downward–upward approach of communication. Provide any examples from experiences on the job, from another job, or situations in the newspapers.

12. Articulate the advantages and disadvantages of horizontal communication.

13. Describe advantages arising from a professionalized police agency.

14. Identify and explain 10 steps toward police organizational change.

15. Describe the primary obstacle faced by a police agency in transition from a paramilitary model to a problem-solving agency. In what way do you agree or disagree with this finding?

16. Define the neutral zone and explain its relevance toward department change. If you were in charge of a transitional team to convert a reactive police agency to a prosocial one, how would you go about it?

17. Describe how the promise of a quality of mind ability or sociological imagination can aid police organizations and their personnel better to controlling and preventing stress.

ENDNOTES

1. J. Kakalik and S. Wildhorn (1971). *Private police in the United States*. Santa Monica, CA: Rand Corporation.

2. The public accountability of private police lessons from New York, Johannesburg, and Mexico City. (2000, August). *Vera Institute of Justice*. Retrieved online July 28, 2005: http://www.vera.org/publication_pdf/privatepolice.pdf

3. P. Stenning and C. Shearing (1980). The quiet revolution: The nature, development, and general legal implications of private security in Canada. *Criminal Law Quarterly*, 22, 220–248. N. South (1994). Privatizing policing in the European market: Some issues for theory, policy, and research. *European Sociological Review*, 10, 219–233.

4. Harry R. Dammer and Erick Fairchild (2007). *Comparative Criminal Justice Systems*, 3rd ed. Belmont, CA: Wadsworth/Thomson. p. 109.

5. The public accountability of private police lessons from New York, Johannesburg, and Mexico City. (2000, August). *Vera Institute of Justice*. Retrieved online July 28, 2005: http://www.vera.org/publication_pdf/privatepolice.pdf

6. *Detective History*. Retrieved online June 29, 2004: http://www.crimelibrary.com/gangsters2/pinkerton/

7. David E. Barlow and Melissa Hickman Barlow (2004). A political economy of community policing. In Steven G. Brandl and David S. Barlow (Eds.), *The police in America* (pp. 68–75). Belmont, CA: Wadsworth.

8. Mike Zielinski (2000). Private police: Armed and dangerous. *Covert Action Quarterly*. Retrieved online June 29, 2004: http://mediafilter.org/caq/CAQ54p.police.html

9. Cincinnati Private Police. Retrieved online June 29, 2004: http://www.micheo.com/lc/cppa/page1.htm

10. See Wachenhut Services, Inc. at Oak Ridge and other government facilities. Retrieved online June 29, 2004: http://www.oakridge.doe.gov/media_releases/1999/r-99-031.htm

11. The author visited FLECT March 9, 2006 to gather information for this and other publications.

12. Mike Zielinski (2000).

13. Dennis J. Stevens (2004). *Applied community policing in the 21st century*. Boston: Allyn & Bacon.

14. Robert C. Trojanowicz and S.I. Dixon (1974). *Criminal justice and the community*. Englewood Cliffs, NJ: Prentice Hall. Also see Dennis J. Stevens (2003), p. 20.

15. The public accountability of private police lessons from New York, Johannesburg, and Mexico City. (2000, August). *Vera Institute of Justice*. Retrieved online July 28, 2005: http://www.vera.org/publication_pdf/privatepolice.pdf

16. Private security services can be highly accountable, although not necessarily to all of the same governmental agencies that oversee the public police. Sometimes private agencies are accountable to elected officials, but they are also subject to criminal investigation and prosecution, civil liability, and various public reporting requirements. These external controls created incentives for the employers of the private security forces to establish their own strong internal accountability mechanisms.

17. M. Chaiken and J. Chaiken (1987). *Public Policing—Privately Provided*. Washington, DC: National Institute of Justice.

18. L. Johnston (1992). *The Rebirth of Private Policing*, London: Routledge.

19. The observer is a reviewer for this work who at the time of this entry is unknown to the writer.

20. Private police powers need public scrutiny. (2004, January 25). The Telegraph. Retrieved online July 1, 2004: http://www.macon.com/mld/telegraph/7783263.htm

21. Gary Marks (1987). The interweaving of public and private police undercover work. In C. Shearing and P. Stenning (Eds.). *Private policing*. Beverly Hills, CA: Sage. Retrieved online June 29, 2004: http://web.mit.edu/gtmarx/www/private.html

22. Steven G. Brandl and David S. Barlow (Eds) (2004). *The police in America*. Belmont, CA: Wadsworth. p. 236.

23. It might be well to review the U.S. Army's Soldier's Creed at their website. Retrieved July 4, 2004: http://www.army.mil/

24. Community Safety Initiative (2005, June). Affordable housing group and police band together. *Weed and seed in sites.* Community capacity development officer. Washington, DC: Office of Justice Programs. Retrieved online July 29, 2005: http://www.ncjrs.org/ccdo/in-sites/neighborhood_2.htmlghborhoods

25. For an excellent discussion on this matter see, Stan Stojkovic, David Kalinich, and John Klofas (2004). *Criminal justice organizations,* 3rd ed. Springfield, IL: Charles C. Thompson. pp. 243–255. Also see W. Bratton (1996, February 12). New York crime rate down forty-five percent. *New York Times.*

26. Herman Goldstein (2002). p. 110. Also see Stan Stojkovic, David Kalinich and John Klofas (2004). pp. 88.

27. Written by the author who moved to Pass Christian, Mississippi in August 2005 from Boston. A few days after the move, I was evacuated to Mobile, Alabama. In the months that followed, the author interviewed 14 New Orleans officers and 10 Mississippi officers to gain a better understanding of the stress among public officers after a national calamity such as Katrina.

28. Wikipedia: The Free Encyclopedia (2006).Retrieved online April 14, 2006: http://en.wikipedia.org/wiki/An_eye_for_an_eye

29. Mary Swerczek and Allen Powell II (2005, September). 2,000 kids still separated from parents. NOLA. Retrieved online April 14, 2006: http://www.nola.com/newslogs/tporleans/index.ssf?/mtlogs/nola_tporleans/archives/2005_09_17.html

30. In Louisiana, 658 bodies have been identified, and an additional 247 victims have not been identified. In Mississippi 250 bodies have been identified and another 200 continue to be missing. See Nathan Burchfiel (2005, December 14). Statistics suggest race not a factor in Katrina deaths. *CNSNews.* Retrieved online April 14, 2006: http://www.cnsnews.com/ViewNation.asp?Page=%5CNation%5Carchive%5C20 0512%5CNAT20051214b.html

31. *AP Associated Press* (2006, March 20). New Orleans police officers cleared of looting. Retrieved online April 14, 2006: http://www.msnbc.msn.com/id/11920811/

32. James Varney (2005). Deserters may have been working in other precincts. New Orleans News. Retrieved online April 13, 2006: http://www.nola.com/newslogs/tporleans/index.ssf?/mtlogs/nola_tporleans/archives/2005_09.html

33. Michael Perlstein and Frank Donze (2005). Missing officers were nearly 15% of force. Retrieved online April 13, 2006: http://www.nola.com/newslogs/tporleans/index.ssf?/mtlogs/nola_tporleans/archives/2005_09.html

34. N.O. Mayor Nagin said on national television. See America's View. Retrieved April 14, 2006: http://www.theamericanview.com/index.php?id=540. Also see, *The Spring Morning Harold* (2005, September 5). Hurricane is God's work: Christian extremists. Retrieved online April 14, 2006: http://www.smh.com.au/news/world/hurricane-is-gods-work-christian-extremists/2005/09/03/1125302770141 .html "God is responsible for this and in his own time he will reveal why," said Illinois Democratic congressman Jesse Jackson, Jr., at a news conference. p. 1.

35. By Coleman Warner and Doug MacCash (2005). N.O. police taking over for National Guardsmen

36. Personal communication with Lt. Billy Stone, Long Beach Police Department.

37. This fact has been confirmed by the NOPD. See James Varney (2005). New Orleans cops investigated. *New Orleans Times-Picayune.* Retrieved online April 13, 2006: http://www.pelicanfile.com/reporter.cfm?ReporterID=3486

38. Confidential personal communication between NOPD officer and the author, September 2005.

39. Confidential personal communication between NOPD officer and the author, September 2005.

40. Confidential personal communication between NOPD officer and the author, September 2005.

41. James Varney (2005). New Orleans cops investigated. *New Orleans Times-Picayune.* Retrieved online April 13, 2006: http://www.pelicanfile.com/reporter.cfm?ReporterID=3486

42. Confidential personal communication between NOPD officer and the author, September 2005.

43. AP Associated Press (2006, March 20).

44. Danielle S. Allen (2003). *Punishment in ancient Athens. Classical Athenian democracy.* Retrieved online September 19, 2005: http://www.stoa.org. Also see Peter Marongiu and Graeme Newman (1987). *Vengeance.* Totowa, NJ: Rowman & Littlefield. p. 1.

45. Associated Press (2005, September 1). New Orleans mayor orders looting crackdown. Retrieved online April 14, 2006: http://www.msnbc.msn.com/id/9063708/

46. John P. Crank (2004). *Understanding police culture.* Cincinnati, Ohio: Anderson. p. 107.

47. Lawsuits and the New Orleans Police (2005, September). *New York Times.*

48. Michael L. Birzer and Cliff Roberson (2007). *Policing: Today and tomorrow.* Upper Saddle River, NJ: Prentice Hall. pp. 334–335.

49. Michael L. Birzer and Cliff Roberson (2007). pp. 334–335.

50. Samuel Walker and Charles M. Katz (2005). pp. 319, 329–330.

51. Atlanta (Chief Beverly Harvard); Boston (Commissioner Kathleen O'Toole); Detroit (Chief Ella Bully-Cummings); Fairfax County, Virginia (Suzanne Devlin); Milwaukee (Chief Nan Hegerty); and San Francisco (Chief Heather Fong).

52. Karen Testa (2004, May 24). Women rise to top of police ranks in several major U.S. cities. The Associated Press. *Boston Globe.* Retrieved Online July 4, 2004: http://www.policeone.com/policeone/frontend/parser.cfm?object=NewDivisions&rel=46210&operation=full_article&id=87594

53. Karen Testa. (2004, May 24). Women rise to top of police ranks in several major U.S. cities. The Associated Press. *Boston Globe.* Retrieved Online July 4, 2004: http://www.policeone.com/policeone/frontend/parser.cfm?object=NewDivisions&rel=46210&operation=full_article&id=87594

54. Karen Testa (2004, May 24).

55. Karen Testa (2004, May 24).

56. Margaret Moore (2000). Opening remarks. Women in Federal Law Enforcement. Retrieved online July 26, 2005: http://www.wifle.org/conference2000/conf_speeches/opening_remarks.htm

57. New York City Police Department. Retrieved online July 29, 2005: apahttp://www.nyc.gov/html/nypd/html/pct/pgm083.html

58. Edwin Meese III (2000). Community policing and the police officer. In Willard M. Oliver (Ed.), *Community policing: Classical readings* (pp. 297–317). Upper Saddle River, NJ: Prentice Hall. p. 303.

59. Confidential communication with a Chicago police officer, September 2005.

60. Edwin Meese III (2000). p. 303.

61. Career Center. Retrieved online July 7, 2004: http://www.collegeview.com/career/careersearch/job_profiles/human/po03.html

62. Herman Goldstein (1990). *Problem-oriented policing.* NY: McGraw Hill. Page 27.

63. Edwin Meese III (2000). p. 303.

64. Edwin Meese III (2000). p. 304.

65. Egon Bittner (1999). The quasi-military organization of the police. In Victor E. Kappeler (Ed.). *The police and society,* 2nd ed. (pp. 170–180). Prospect Heights, IL: Waveland Press.

66. Edwin Meese III (2000). p. 300.

67. Stan Stojkovic, David Kalinich and John Klofas (2004). pp. 85–89. A. Downs (1967). *Inside bureaucracy.* Boston: Little, Brown. Carl B. Klockars, Sanja Kutnjak Ivkovich, Willliam E. Harver, and Maria R. Haberfeld (2000, May). The measurement of police integrity. National Institute of Justice. NCJ 181465. Retrieved Online July 6, 2004): http://www.ncjrs.org/txtfiles1/nij/181465.txt

68. Edwin Meese III (2000). Community policing and the police officer. In Willard M. Oliver (Ed.), *Community policing: Classical readings* (pp. 297–317). Upper Saddle River, NJ: Prentice Hall.

69. John P. Crank (2004). *Understanding police culture.* Cincinnati, OH: Anderson. Peter K. Manning (1997). *Police work: The social organization of policing.* Prospect Heights, IL: Waveland Press.

70. John P. Crank (2004). p. 316.

71. Edwin Meese III (2000).

72. Confidential personal communication between Chicago officer and the author, July 2005.

73. John Van Maanen. (2001). Making rank: Becoming an American police sergeant. In Roger G. Dunham and Geoffrey P. Alpert. *Critical issues in policing: Contemporary readings,* 3rd ed (pp. 132–148). Prospect Height, IL: Waveland Press.

74. Stan Stojkovic, David Kalinich and John Klofas (2004). p. 67.

75. Samuel Walker and Charles M. Katz (2005). *The police in America: An introduction.* Boston: McGraw-Hill. pp. 337–340. Also see Jack R. Green and Stephen D. Mastrofski (1988). *Community policing: Rhetoric or reality.* New York: Praeger.

76. Girmay Berhie and Alem Hailu (2000). A study of knowledge and attitudes of public housing residents: Toward community policing in the city of Charleston, South Carolina. *NIJ Research Review.* NCJ 182434. Retrieved online May 30, 2004: http://www.ncjrs.org/rr/vol1_3/27.html

    Research Brief. Police Foundation. Police strategies to reduce citizen fear of crime. Retrieved online July 6, 2004: http://www.policefoundation.org/docs/citizenfear.html Dennis J. Stevens (2003). *Community policing in the 21st century.* Boston: Allyn & Bacon.

77. One source suggests that failure in policing can demonstrate a "weakness." Frankly, that may be part of the problem. Officers require re-education to understand that weakness does not come from failure but from failure to understand that most success stories are filled with failing attempts to succeed. For instance, at the age of 7, a boy and his family were forced out of their home, and the boy was forced to go to work. When the boy was 9, his mother passed away. He had a job as a store clerk, but lost it when he was 20. The young man wanted to go to law school, but had no education. He went into debt when he was 23,

to become a partner in a small store. It was only 3 years later that his business partner died, and left him with a debt that took years for him to repay.

He dated a girl for 4 years and, at the age of 28, decided to ask her to marry him. She turned him down. Thirty-seven years into his life, he was elected to Congress . . . on his THIRD try. He then failed to be re-elected. This man's son died when he was only 4 years old. At age 45, he ran for the Senate . . . and failed to be elected. He persisted at politics and ran for the vice-presidency at age 47, and again lost. Finally, at the age of 51, this man was elected President of the United States. His name was Abraham Lincoln. Being strong opens the door for one of the primary perspectives of this work, which is being able to individually manage stress. Taking care of business, if you will. That means, getting the required help. That could mean merely to study our problems and reactions online to seeing a mental health professional.

78. Brian A. Ursino (2001). Systems approach to organizational transformation. *FBI Law Bulletin*, Retrieved online July 14, 2004: http://www.fbi.gov/publications/leb/2001/oct01leb.htm

79. James D. Sewell (2002, March). Managing the stress of organizational change. *FBI Law Bulletin*, 71(3). Retrieved online July 14, 2004: http://www.fbi.gov/publications/leb/2002/mar02leb.htm#page_15

80. Guidelines can also be found in Stuart A. Scheingold (2001). *Constituent expectations about the police and police expectations about constituents*. Retrieved online July 26, 2005: http://ncjrs.org/pdffiles1/170610-5.pdf

81. Dennis J. Stevens (2001). *Case studies in community policing*. Upper Saddle River, NJ: Prentice Hall. Also see Dennis J. Stevens (2003). *Applied community policing in the 21st century*. Boston: Allyn & Bacon.

82. Abbie Lundberg (1997, May 15). The people side of change. *CIO*, 105.

83. Abbie Lundberg (1997, May 15).

84. John Naisbitt (1988). *Megatrends*. New York: Warner Books.

85. Price Pritchett and Ron Pound (1998). *A survival guide to the stress of organizational change*. Plano, TX: Pritchett Rummler-Brache. p. 8. Also see Price Pritchett (2000). *Carpe manana: 10 critical leadership practices for managing toward the future*. Plano, TX: Pritchett Rummler-Brache.

86. For details, see Dennis J. Stevens (2003). *Applied community policing in the 21st century*. Boston: Allyn & Bacon. p. 163. And Dennis J. Stevens (2003). *Case studies in applied community policing*. Boston: Allyn & Bacon.

87. Professor Huff was president of the American Society of Criminologists in 2000–2001.

88. Norm Stamper (2005). *Breaking rank: A top cop's expose of the dark side of American policing*. New York: Nation Books.

89. Carl L. Klockars (1988). The rhetoric of community policing. In J.R. Greene and S.D. Mastrofski (Eds.), *Community policing: Rhetoric or reality* (pp. 239–258). New York: Praeger.

90. LAPD recruits computer to stop rouge cops. (2005, July 25). *USA Today*. Retrieved online July 28, 2005 http://www.usatoday.com/tech/news/surveillance/2005-07-25-lapd-cops_x.htm

91. The Officer Down Memorial. Retrieved online July 27, 2005: http://www.odmp.org/officer.php?oid=17827

Appendix I

DO YOU HAVE JOB STRAIN?

This test can give you a rough indication of how much job strain you may have at work. For scoring, refer to the Endnotes.[1]

Answer yes or no.

Demand

I have to work very hard _____

I am asked to do an excessive amount of work _____

I do not have enough time to get my work done _____

I do have difficulties in meeting deadlines _____

There are not enough hours in the day to do my job expertly _____

Control

I do not have to do a lot of repetitive work _____

I have (a job which allows me) to be creative _____

I have (a job which allows me) to learn new things _____

I have a lot of say about what happens _____

I have a lot of freedom to decide how I do my work _____

I make many contributions that ultimately develop into policy _____

Social Support

I work with helpful people _____

I work with people who take a personal interest in me _____

My supervisor is helpful _____

My boss' boss is fair _____

My supervisor is concerned with my welfare _____

My supervisor is fair _____

Acquired Skills

I use the skills that I have been trained to use on this job _____

I am encouraged to enhance my skill levels _____

I am encouraged to share my skills with other personnel _____

My supervisor is competent at my job and his or her job _____

My supervisor's boss is competent at my job, my supervisor's job, and his or her job _____

My supervisor (or the company or agency) rewards me for enhancing my skills through training _____

Interpretation: Because job strain is defined by the combination of high demands, low control, low social support, and is a catalyst reducing acquired skills (the dumbing-down effect), the more of each of these factors that personnel face, the more extreme their scores would be on each factor, the greater the job strain. Jobs where you experience all four features are generally high job strain, while jobs with three such features generate moderately high job strain. Those with only one factor may be moderate or moderately low in job strain, depending on how much the other three scores offset that factor. The jobs with the least job strain combine high control, high social support, and utilization of acquired skills with moderate demands.

Appendix II

RESEARCH DESIGN OF THIS STUDY

In the spring of 2003, a survey was developed as part of a university course conducted by the author. Most of the students were criminal justice or psychology majors interested in criminology. Many of the students were full-time students, yet many were also sworn officers employed by various jurisdictions including the city of Boston, neighboring communities, and a few were state troopers. Other occupations included employment with the juvenile and criminal courts in the Commonwealth of Massachusetts and the Massachusetts Department of Corrections. Additionally, seven students were on the frontline of this study since they conducted their own tests among police agencies along Massachusetts' North Shore and New Hampshire. Also, they presented their research findings at the 41st annual conference of the Academy of Criminal Justice Sciences in Las Vegas in a student panel.

CONFIDENTIAL POLICE SURVEY

Don't write your name on this survey. It's confidential. Your survey will only be seen by Dr. Dennis J. Stevens who will report on the experiences of police officers in many law enforcement agencies. Your input will be compared with other police officers to better understand your experiences, needs, and risks. Feel free to mail this survey or if you have any questions, I can be reached at: dennis.stevens@usm.edu Thanks.

1. Which of the following best describes your job most of the time? Please check one
   Patrol Officer _____ Investigator _____ Tactical _____ Narcotics _____
   Sexual Abuse _____ Admin _____
2. How often do you experience discomfort, uncertainty, or stress on the job?
   Always _____ Very Often _____ Sometimes _____ Seldom _____ Never _____

How often do you experience uncertainty or stress in any of the following areas? Circle your choice.

Item	Always	Very Often	Some-times	Seldom	Never/ NA
3. Hiring process	5	4	3	2	1
4. When policy is compromised	5	4	3	2	1
5. In dealing with FOP/union	5	4	3	2	1
6. During routine police patrol	5	4	3	2	1
7. Priority of service calls	5	4	3	2	1
8. When supporting prosecutors	5	4	3	2	1
9. Undercover in other jurisdictions	5	4	3	2	1
10. Arrest mandates	5	4	3	2	1
11. Use of necessary force	5	4	3	2	1
12. Department equipment	5	4	3	2	1
13. Officer disciplinary actions	5	4	3	2	1
14. DUI/OUI stops	5	4	3	2	1
15. Informants and witnesses	5	4	3	2	1
16. Paperwork requirements	5	4	3	2	1
17. Police leadership	5	4	3	2	1
18. Your immediate supervisor	5	4	3	2	1
19. B & E calls	5	4	3	2	1

20. How often do you experience stress from your own family that affects your job?

    Always _____ Very Often _____ Sometimes _____ Seldom _____
    Once _____ Never _____

21. How often would you say that you experience stress from working the streets?

    Always_____ Very Often _____ Sometimes _____ Seldom _____
    Once _____ Never _____

22. How often would you say officers are disrespected by the public?

    Always_____ Very Often _____ Sometimes _____ Seldom _____
    Never _____

23. In your opinion, how often are officers disrespected by the courts?

    Always _____ Very Often _____ Sometimes _____ Seldom _____
    Never _____

24. How much of what you learned as a young cadet do you apply to your job as an officer?

    90–100% _____ 80–89% _____ 70–79% _____ 60–69% _____
    Less than half _____

25. In your opinion, how much inservice training do you apply toward your job as an officer?
    90–100% _____ 80–89% _____ 70–79% _____ 60–69% _____
    Less than half _____

26. Who protects your back more?
    Supervisor _____ Brass _____ Politicians _____ FOP/Union _____

27. If testing were cut from the promotional process, what would you say is the best way to promote officers? _____

How strongly do you agree with the following issues? Circle the number that best fits your opinion.

	Strongly Agree	Agree	Don't Know	Disagree	Strongly Disagree
28. Fresh and continued pursuit is part of the job	5	4	3	2	1
29. Federal enforcement in local affairs is okay	5	4	3	2	1
30. Top Brass are objective in disciplinary action	5	4	3	2	1
31. Top Brass have their "favorites"	5	4	3	2	1
32. My family supports my position as a cop	5	4	3	2	1
33. I'm uneasy at domestic violent calls	5	4	3	2	1
34. The officer grievance process is fair	5	4	3	2	1
35. Residents are provided quality police services	5	4	3	2	1
36. I'm uneasy at child sexual abuse calls	5	4	3	2	1
37. I'm uneasy with mentally challenged stops	5	4	3	2	1
38. Brass uses intimidation to control officers	5	4	3	2	1
39. I'm uneasy when serving high-risk warrants	5	4	3	2	1
40. Police morale is higher today than before	5	4	3	2	1
41. Homeland security practices are necessary	5	4	3	2	1
42. Criminals have more rights than cops	5	4	3	2	1
43. Better to be tried by 12 than carried by 6	5	4	3	2	1

44. In your career as an officer, how often have you participated in a critical incident?

    Always _____ Very Often _____ Sometimes _____ Once _____
    Never _____ Name it _____

45. How often have you thought that inadequate information endangered your safety?

    Always _____ Very Often _____ Sometimes _____ Once _____
    No Answer _____

46. In your opinion, how high would you rate the integrity of most cops?
    Very High _____ High _____ Somewhat High _____
    Somewhat Low _____ No Answer _____

47. In your opinion, how high would you rate the integrity of most commanders?
    Very High _____ High _____ Somewhat High _____
    Somewhat Low _____ NA _____

48. Why did you want to become a police officer? _____

49. What do you usually do when you feel tense or stressed? Circle three only.

Exercise	Attend church or pray	Read
Listen to music	Get involved in a hobby	Shop
Sleep	Talk to my spouse/family	Drive/bike
See a professional	Talk to my supervisor	Search the Net
Party	Eat	Watch sports
Play with kids	Take extra duty	Sex
Be alone _____	Other _____ (what?) _____	Take a class

In your opinion, how valuable are the courses below to officers? How expertly do you think they are taught by academies across the country? Write only: 1, 2, or 3 in each box. Thank you.	How Valuable? 3 = very valuable 2 = kind of valuable 1 = not valuable	Taught Expertly? 3 = taught expertly 2 = kind of expertly 1 = taught poorly
50. Advanced Traffic Crash Investigation		
51. Basic Juvenile Officer Training		
52. Community Policing		
53. Crime Prevention		
54. Hate Crime Reporting		
55. Basic Investigation		
56. Sexual Assault Investigation: Victims		
57. Sexual Assault Investigation: Suspects		
58. Legal Issues of Searches		

59. First-Line Supervision
60. Ethics
61. Basic SWAT
62. Basic Ground Defense for Police Officers
63. Health Issues and Stress

64. How long have you been a sworn officer? _____
65. Are you male _____ female _____
66. How old are you? _____
67. How would you describe your race? _____
68. What police agency employs you? _____
69. Amount of education you have? _____
70. Your current rank as an officer? _____
71. If you could change anything in policing, what would it be? _____

DISTRIBUTION OF QUESTIONNAIRES

For this study, 580 questionnaires were distributed to six former university students of the author for distribution among their respective colleagues. In New England, three patrol officers who participated in an earlier study distributed 341 questionnaires at morning and afternoon roll-call at similar big city centers in New England. Officers who volunteered to complete the survey completed those surveys at that time and returned them to the research-officer assistant who later returned them to the principle researcher. Twenty-one of those questionnaires were less than one-forth completed and therefore rejected and one was illegible, leaving a total of 319 usable surveys.

At a state academy geographically situated somewhere in the middle between New England and southern Florida, 112 surveys were completed by officers employed by three large seaboard police agencies who were attending academy inservice training. Surveys were distributed and collected by two research-assistant-instructors who mailed (U.S. Mail, although about 20% were mailed by the participants) completed surveys to the principle researcher.

And, in a large southern Florida jurisdiction, another former student employed by a large police agency distributed and returned (U.S. Mail, although 31, or 24% were mailed by the participants) 127 completed questionnaires.

LIMITATIONS OF THIS STUDY

In the event you are asking why the police agencies utilized in this study are not identified, it would be unethical and inappropriate for any researcher to divulge specific groups tested (unless the study was designed for a specific group and the researcher had the consent of the agency and participants). In this case, the participants who volunteered information did so in confidence. Also, it is unlikely that most police officers would answer as truthfully as they had if they knew that their names or agencies would be identified. Also, agencies would tend to restrict tests if potential "dirty laundry" would be scattered everywhere on researcher pages. Between you and me, too many people take "cheap shots" at America's most valuable institution other than education—cops—and as you recall, the hard-working men and women who safeguard democracy want to do their best for their departments, their communities, and their country. But, remember what's being argued: the risks of the streets are less traumatic than the organizational factors police officers face, which includes policy developed by non-police professionals, top-down bureaucratic practices, and policy initiatives linked to strategies developed as a law enforcement response to the war on crime, drugs, and terrorism. That is, organizational mandates produce more strain upon patrol officers than police routine. This perspective was not known by any of the participants or contributors of this study.

Another limitation is that there is an estimated 18,000 police agencies in the United States comprised of 700,000 officers. Are the findings representative of all police agencies and all police officers in the country? Similar to most studies, unless we can evaluate 100% of the population involved in the study, we need to look to a sample of the designated population under study in hopes that there are enough similarities between the sample and the population at-large whereby we can generalize the findings over the entire group. In this case, most officers are trained and retrained in a similar fashion whether they are employed in New York or Los Angeles. There are similar ultimate and immediate goals of their agencies as there are similar strategies used to bring their agency closer to their mission. They interact with a similar "client," and operate under similar state, local, and, above all, federal laws and regulations in the efforts to deliver quality police services.

Also, typical of most research instruments utilized in studies, regardless of the elegance of the instrument, prominence of the researcher, or prestige of the institution conducting the test, the attitudes of its participants are recorded at a specific time in their individual history and are subject to change. As a research professor at Loyola University of Chicago lectured, "The data on a survey are a snapshot of the thoughts of your participants and nothing more. Don't take it too seriously because often they (your participants) are reacting to more than the questions asked." That is, how they feel, what they think the researcher wants to know, the content of the survey and the paper its written on, what they think the researcher will think about what answers they provide, what their peers think of their answers, and even the time and condition of the room where participants complete the survey will, in some way, come out in their answers. That said, let's talk about the sample of this test, which appears to have more similarities than differences than officers at-large.

In total, 558 questionnaires were used for this test. To guard validity, the results were compared with the seven student-researchers who conducted a similar test utilizing a similar questionnaire at police agencies (their data was not used in the calculations of the findings).

Appendix III
Sample

The sample consisted of 558 full-time sworn officers employed on the Eastern Seaboard from New England to southern Florida, as shown in the table. In the sample, 76% were male, who averaged 37 years of age, 63% were white, and they averaged 10 years' experience as an officer with the department where they were employed. The officers had an average of 14 years' formal education, and 73% were patrol officers. Also, 57% of the sample worked in New England, 20% worked in North Carolina, and 23% worked for southern Florida law enforcement agencies.

DEMOGRAPHICS OF POLICE SAMPLE

Characteristics	Number/Average	Percent/Range N = 558
Gender		
Male	425	76%
Female	133	24%
Age	37	20–60
Race		
White	352	63%
Black	143	26%
Latino	44	08%
Other/missing	19	03%
Experience	10 years	1–35 years
Education	14 years	12–19 years
Rank		
Patrol officer*	406	73%
Detective	26	04%
Sergeant	58	11%
Brass–missing	68	12%
Agency Location**		
New England	319	57%
North Carolina	112	20%
Southern Florida	127	23%

*All percents rounded; Patrol officer includes deputies whose primary assignments were general patrol duties, which includes 9-1-1 service and traffic control. **"New England" officers worked for a large municipal department and several adjacent cities. North Carolina officers worked for several police agencies in North Carolina; southern Florida officers worked at two large jurisdictions. This grouping was designed to make location discussions clear.

As completed surveys were received by the principle researcher, they were coded and data were placed into computer grids by a few consciencious students at a Boston university. All the data were evaluated by the principle researcher and discussed during various university courses to work out the wrinkles. Preliminary results were presented at the 41st annual conference of the Academy of Criminal Justice in Las Vegas in March 2004.

Appendix IV

FINDINGS

When the participants were asked how often they experienced discomfort, uncertainty, or stress on the job, 23% (129) reported that they were always experienced, 48% (269) reported that they were very often experienced, 22% (124) said sometimes, and 3% (16) said seldom or didn't respond to the question (see the table). This finding implies that almost three-fourths of the sample experience discomfort, uncertainty, or stress while working as a police officer. This finding is consistent with research that found an average of 64% of the participants (combining city and suburban courts) had reported that they experienced "a great deal" or "some" discomfort or stress on the job.[3]

When the participants were asked about stress from their own family, 28% (156) said that sometimes they do while 48% (267) said seldom or never. When their responses are compared to stress they experienced working the streets, over one-half (275) of the participants chose seldom as their first answer, and 28% (159) said never. That is, while over one-half of the sample experienced discomfort, uncertainty, or stress on the job, neither their home life nor their duties on the street as a police officer produced high levels of discomfort, uncertainty, or stress. Where did all that discomfort, uncertainty, or stress come from? Could it have come from the delivery of police services?

PERCENT OF STRESS EXPERIENCED BY OFFICERS*

Question	Always	Very Often	Some-Times	Seldom	Never N = 558
How often do you experience discomfort, uncertainty, or stress on the job?	23%	48%	22%	03%	04%
How often do you experience stress from your own family that affects your job?	06%	02%	28%	48%	16%
How often would you say that you experience stress working the streets?	03%	05%	13%	49%	30%

*All percents rounded. Missing data not shown.

Index